WORLD POPULATION

1984

WORLD POPULATION
AN INTRODUCTION TO DEMOGRAPHY

Edward G. Stockwell
Bowling Green State University

H. Theodore Groat
Bowling Green State University

A GROLIER COMPANY
Franklin Watts
New York
London
Toronto
Sydney

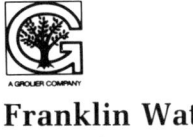

Photo research by Laurie Platt Winfrey

Franklin Watts
387 Park Avenue South
New York, New York 10016

Library of Congress Cataloging in Publication Data

Stockwell, Edward G.
    World population.

Includes bibliographies and indexes.
1. Population.   2. Demography.   I. Groat, H. Theodore.
II. Title.
HB871.S74   1984   304.6   83-26102
ISBN 0-531-05426-8

Copyright © 1984 Edward G. Stockwell and H. Theodore Groat
All rights reserved
Printed in the United States of America
5 4 3 2 1

CONTENTS

Preface	xvii

CHAPTER 1
INTRODUCTION TO THE STUDY OF POPULATION — 3

The Importance of Studying Population	4
The Framework of Demography	12
Scope and Organization of the Book	20
References and Suggested Reading	22

CHAPTER 2
WORLD POPULATION SIZE AND GROWTH — 24

Population Growth in Pre-Modern Times	29
Population Growth in the Modern Era	30
The Mechanics of Population Growth	33
The Third World Population Explosion	38
Regional Growth Trends	41
Summary	54
References and Suggested Reading	56

CHAPTER 3
MORTALITY LEVELS AND TRENDS — 57

Definitions and Concepts	58

Mortality Conditions throughout History	61
Mortality Decline in the Modern World	65
Mortality Trends in Developing Countries	73
Mortality Trends in the United States	76
Summary	85
References and Suggested Reading	86

CHAPTER 4
DIFFERENTIAL MORTALITY 92

Why Study Mortality Differentials?	93
Biological Determinants of Differential Mortality	94
Social Determinants of Differential Mortality	107
Morbidity	120
Mortality and Population Policy	121
Future Outlook	123
Summary	125
References and Suggested Reading	127

CHAPTER 5
HUMAN FERTILITY 129

Definitions and Concepts	130
Factors Affecting Fertility	132
Exposure to Intercourse	136
Family Size Norms	143
Fertility Trends in the Third World	144
Fertility Decline in the Modern World	148
Fertility Trends in the United States	155
Fertility Differentials	161
Summary	166
References and Suggested Reading	167

CHAPTER 6
FERTILITY CONTROL 175

Deficit Fertility	176
Unintentional Fertility	178
Birth Control Through History	184
Contraception Today	190

Methods of Fertility Regulation	192
Summary	208
References and Suggested Reading	209

CHAPTER 7
FERTILITY AND PUBLIC POLICY — 216

The United States	217
Controlling Societal Fertility	219
Pronatalist Policies	220
Antinatalist Policies	223
Providing the Means: National Family Planning Programs	225
Changing the Motivations: Beyond Family Planning	232
Summary	240
References and Suggested Reading	241

CHAPTER 8
PROBLEMS OF THIRD WORLD POPULATION GROWTH — 248

Population Growth and Economic Development	250
Population and Food	263
Population Growth and Nonfood Resources	273
Prospects for Slowing Population Growth	275
Summary	278
References and Suggested Reading	279

CHAPTER 9
HUMAN MIGRATION — 286

Social Significance of Migration	287
Definitions and Concepts	289
Migration in History	293
Immigration to the United States	295
Consequences of Migration	308
Some Consequences of American Immigration	310
International Migration in the World Today	317
Population Policy and the Future of International Migration	320
Summary	323
References and Suggested Reading	324

CHAPTER 10
POPULATION GROWTH IN THE UNITED STATES 327

Historical Growth Trends 328
Future Growth Outlook 335
Problems of Population Size and Growth 337
Summary 355
References and Suggested Reading 356

CHAPTER 11
INTERNAL MIGRATION AND POPULATION REDISTRIBUTION 362

Population Mobility in the United States 363
Problems Relating to Population Mobility 371
Migration and Population Redistribution 374
Internal Migration in Other Countries 388
Internal Migration Policies 394
Summary 396
References and Suggested Reading 397

CHAPTER 12
POPULATION COMPOSITION 404

Demographic Characteristics 405
Socioeconomic Characteristics 423
International Differences in Population Composition 444
Summary 446
References and Suggested Reading 447

POSTSCRIPT 449

APPENDIX A
NATURE AND SOURCES OF POPULATION DATA 453

Population Censuses 453
Vital Statistics 460
Sample Surveys 464
Continuous Population Registers 466
Sources of Population Data 467
Limitations of Official Statistics 469
References and Suggested Reading 471

APPENDIX B
MEASURING THE DEMOGRAPHIC PROCESSES — 473

- Measures of Mortality — 474
- Measures of Morbidity — 480
- Measures of Fertility — 482
- Measures of Migration — 488
- References and Suggested Reading — 493

APPENDIX C
THE LIFE TABLE — 494

- Description of the Life Table — 494
- The Stationary Population — 502
- Uses of the Life Table — 504
- References and Suggested Reading — 508

Picture Credits — 509
Index — 511

LIST OF TABLES

2.1	Estimated Size and Growth of World Population	25
2.2	Number of Years in Which Population Will Double at Specified Growth Rates	28
2.3	Population Size and Growth Trends, 1980	33
2.4	Population Growth Outlook for Africa, Early 1980s	42
2.5	Population Growth Outlook for Asia, Early 1980s	48
2.6	Population Growth Outlook for Latin America, Early 1980s	50
2.7	Population Growth Outlook for the Developed Countries, Early 1980s	52
3.1	Estimated Average Life Expectancy in the Past	61
3.2	Crude Death Rates and Infant Mortality Rates, c. 1980	74
3.3	Crude Death Rates in the United States, 1900–1982	79
3.4	Deaths per 100,000 Population from Selected Causes in the United States, 1900–1980	83
4.1	Age-Specific Death Rates for the United States	94
4.2	Infant Mortality Rates in the United States, Selected Years, 1915–80	98
4.3	Infant Mortality Rates for Selected Countries, Late 1970s	101
4.4	Deaths per 1,000 Population by Age and Sex: United States, 1980	102
4.5	Crude Death Rates for Selected Countries and Years	104
4.6	Crude Death Rates and Infant Mortality Rates: South Africa, 1974	108
4.7	Age-Specific Death Rates for Whites and Nonwhites: United States, 1978	108

4.8 Mortality Ratios by Occupational Class: England and Wales, 1910–63	111
4.9 Age-Standardized Average Annual Death Rates per 1,000 Population for Five Social Rank Areas, White Population: Chicago, 1930–60	112
4.10 Infant Mortality Rates in the Income Areas of Metropolitan Ohio, 1970	114
4.11 Deaths per 1,000 Population by Age, Sex, and Marital Status: Canada, 1976	117
5.1 Percent Single (Never Married), by Sex, among Persons 15 to 24 Years Old: United States	141
5.2 Preferred Family Size among Younger and Older Women in Various Third World Countries, Mid- to Late 1970s	146
5.3 Estimated Number of Children per Woman: United States, 1800–1980	155
5.4 Crude Birth Rates in the United States, 1910–82	156
5.5 Average Number of Births per Woman Age 35–44 by Selected Socioeconomic Characteristics: United States, 1980	162
5.6 Average Number of Live Births, Standardized by Duration of Marriage, by Selected Socioeconomic Characteristics in Various Industrialized Countries, Late 1970s	164
6.1 Percentage Distribution of Births to Married Women in the United States, by Planning Status	179
6.2 Contraceptive Use by Sexually Active Unmarried Women in Metropolitan Areas of the United States, 1976 and 1979	184
6.3 Legal Abortions per 1,000 Women Age 15–44, 1978	207
7.1 Crude Birth Rates in Selected East European Countries, 1950–80	221
7.2 Estimated Reduction in Birth Rates if All Unwanted Births Were Prevented	226
7.3 Recent Fertility Declines in Selected Developing Countries	227
7.4 Population Size and Crude Birth Rate Trends in the Sixteen Largest Developing Countries	229
7.5 Vital Rate Trends in the People's Republic of China	239
8.1 Per Capita GNP, 1980: Physical Quality of Life, Late 1970s	249
8.2 Average Annual Growth Rates in Per Capita Real GNP in Countries Grouped According to Annual Rates of Population Growth, Late 1970s	253
8.3 Population and Food	267
9.1 Number of Immigrants to the United States in Each Decade since 1820	298
9.2 Percent of American Immigrants Coming from Specified Areas of Origin since 1820	300
9.3 United States Immigration Data, 1981	305
9.4 Selected Migration Streams in Europe and the Middle East, 1975–76	319

Table	Page
9.5 National Views and Policies on Immigration and Emigration, 1978	321
10.1 Population Growth Trends in the United States, 1790–1980	329
10.2 Vital Statistics: United States, 1900–1980	333
10.3 Projections of the U.S. Population, 1980–2050	338
10.4 Estimated Life Expectancy of Selected Metal Resources at Two Different Rates of Consumption	341
11.1 Percent Distribution of the American Population in the Spring of 1960, 1970, and 1980 by Residence Five Years Earlier	364
11.2 Interregional Migration and Metropolitan-Nonmetropolitan Migration in the United States	366
11.3 Mobility Status of U.S. Population by Sex and Color	367
11.4 Regional Distribution of the Population of the United States, 1790–1980	375
11.5 Distribution of the Black Population: United States, 1860–1980	381
11.6 Urbanization Trends in the United States, 1790–1980	382
11.7 Population of the United States by Metropolitan and Nonmetropolitan Residence, 1950–80	385
11.8 Population of Standard Metropolitan Statistical Areas in the United States, 1950–80	387
11.9 Population of the United States in Metropolitan and Nonmetropolitan Areas, by Race, 1970 and 1980	388
11.10 General Mobility Rates in Seven Countries, c. 1970	389
11.11 Percent Increase in Urban and Rural Areas, 1970–1978/9	391
11.12 Percentage of the Urban Population Living in the Largest City, 1980	393
12.1 Selected Age-Sex Characteristics of the United States, 1900–1980	407
12.2 Distribution of the Population by Marital Status: United States, 1920–80	417
12.3 Selected Household Characteristics of the United States, 1970 and 1980	419
12.4 Percent of the Population in Specified Ethnic Groups: United States, 1900–1980	421
12.5 Selected School Enrollment Data: United States, 1950–80	425
12.6 Educational Attainment of the U.S. Population Age 25 and Over	427
12.7 Educational Attainment Differentials for Specific Sex, Ethnic, and Residence Groups: United States, 1979	429
12.8 Distribution of Families by Level of Income: United States, 1960, 1970, and 1980	431
12.9 Selected Family Income Characteristics of Specified Subgroups in the Population: United States, 1980	434
12.10 Median Income of Households by Age and Education of Householder: United States, 1980	435
12.11 Labor Force Status of the Adult Population: United States, 1940, 1960, and 1980	438

12.12 Occupational Distribution of Employed Persons: United States, 1940, 1960, and 1980	441
12.13 Labor Force Participation and Employment Status of the Population 16 Years Old and Over, by Age, Sex, and Color: United States, April 1980	442
12.14 Occupational Distribution of Employed Persons Age 16 and Over, by Sex and Color: United States, April 1980	444
12.15 Selected Characteristics of More Developed and Less Developed Countries, Late 1970s	445
A.1 Major Topics Covered by the 1980 Census of the United States	457
B.1 Age-Specific Death Rates for Guatemala and the United Kingdom, 1977	475
B.2 Death Rates by Age and Race: United States, 1978	477
B.3 Illustration of Period versus Cohort Fertility Rates	486
B.4 Native-born Population of Ohio by State of Birth and State of Residence, with Net Gain or Loss Through Interstate Movement, 1960 and 1970	492
C.1 Abridged Life Table for the Female Population of the United States, 1978	497
C.2 Computation of Reproduction Rates for the United States, 1978	505
C.3 Illustrative Use of Survival Rates in Estimating Migration and Projecting a Base Population	507

LIST OF FIGURES

2.1	World Population Growth, 1656–2000	26
2.2	Major Population Growth Periods	27
2.3	The Classical Demographic Transition Model	37
2.4	The Demographic Gap in the Less Developed Countries	39
2.5	Comparative Vital Rate Trends for Sweden and Sri Lanka	40
2.6	Growth Rate Trends since 1950	44
2.7	Crude Birth and Death Rates in Major World Subregions, 1980	45
3.1	Crude Death Rate Trends in Sweden, 1750–1980	62
3.2	Infant Mortality Rates in Selected Countries, Early 1980s	75
3.3	Crude Death Rate Trend in the United States, 1900–1980	80
4.1	Age-Specific Death Rates for Guatemala and the United States	95
4.2	Neonatal and Postneonatal Mortality Trends in the United States	99
4.3	Excess Life Expectancy at Birth of Women over Men: United States, 1920–78	103
4.4	Excess Life Expectancy at Birth of Whites over Nonwhites: United States, 1920–78	109
4.5	Average Infant Mortality Rates in Countries Grouped According to Annual Per Capita Gross National Product (GNP), c. 1980	115
5.1	Intermediate Variables Affecting Fertility	133
5.2	Social Factors Affecting Fertility	135
5.3	Median Age at First Marriage, by Sex, United States, 1890–1980	139
5.4	Crude Birth Rate Trends in Sweden: 1750–1980	149
5.5	Starting Dates of the Downward Fertility Transition in 700 European Provinces, 1780–1969	151

Figure	Page
6.1 Age Patterns of Contraceptive Use among Currently Married, Fecund Women, Late 1970s	194
6.2 Percent of Currently Married Women 15 to 44 Years of Age, by Contraceptive Status and Education: United States, 1976	196
6.3 Percent of Married Women 15 to 44 Years of Age Who Experienced Contraceptive Failure during the First Year of Use, by Contraceptive Intent and Method: United States, 1970–73	197
7.1 Crude Birth and Death Rate Trends: Singapore, 1950–80	228
7.2 Annual Number of Sterilizations: India, 1965/66—1980/81	231
7.3 Organization of Administrative, Political, and Birth Planning Units in Rural China	237
8.1 Percent of Population under Age 15 and under Age 5, c. 1980	260
8.2 Age-Sex Structure of Sweden and Mexico, 1978	262
9.1 Percent of American Immigrants Coming from North Central and Southeast Europe since 1820	299
9.2 Changing Origin of American Immigrants since 1960	307
10.1 Percent of U.S. Population Increase Due to Immigration, 1820–1976	331
10.2 Crude Birth and Death Rates: United States, 1900–1980	334
11.1 General Mobility Rate by Age: United States, 1980	368
11.2 General Mobility Rate by Level of Educational Attainment: United States, 1980	370
11.3 Percent Distribution of the Population of the United States by Region, 1790–1980	376
11.4 Geographic Regions of the United States	377
11.5 Urban and Rural Population of the United States, 1790–1980	383
12.1 Sex Ratios by Age: United States, 1980	409
12.2 Population Pyramids: United States, 1940, 1960, and 1980	411
12.3 Population Pyramids of Kenya and Sweden, c. 1970	414
12.4 Population Pyramids (Five-year age groups) of Three American Cities, 1980	415
12.5 Percent High School Graduates, by Age: United States, 1979	428
12.6 Percent of the Population Living in Families with Income below the Poverty Level: United States, 1960–80	432
12.7 Percent of Adult Population in the Labor Force, by Sex: United States, 1940, 1960, and 1980	439

PREFACE

This is a book about population trends in the world in general and in the United States in particular. It is designed as a basic introductory textbook for students as well as for the general reader who wishes to acquire a better understanding of demographic events. We have therefore kept the writing style as nontechnical and jargon free as possible without sacrificing scientific or technical accuracy. Because the book is concise yet comprehensive, instructors will find it sufficiently flexible for use within a variety of academic calendars. The twelve chapters and three appendixes are organized around the basic topics that virtually all demography instructors include in their introductory course. Moreover, we have made a special effort to draw our materials, including the numerous tables and figures, from the most recent research literature. The subject matter, therefore, is contemporary and reflective of current demographic research. Wherever appropriate to do so, we also have presented the different sides of conflicting theoretical or research perspectives. While we have strong personal feelings about several demographic controversies, an introductory textbook does not seem an appropriate place for the elaboration of our own biases.

Above all, we have tried to communicate to the beginning student our intense enthusiasm for the study of population. Of course, we do not pretend that studying population will provide all the answers toward an understanding of contemporary events. We firmly believe, however, that a basic knowledge of the demographics of any population—local, national, or global—is a prerequisite to understanding many of the issues and problems confronting that population.

In our attempt to be concise as well as comprehensive, we have had to make some compromises. Limitations of space, for example, have precluded the inclusion of all relevant topics, and in some instances it was not possible to give more than a brief consideration to a topic of potentially great interest to the student. We hope, however, that we have set the stage for additional classroom material by accomplishing two basic objectives: (1) to acquaint the reader with the nature of the major demographic developments taking place in various parts of the world today, and (2) to give him or her a better appreciation of the very close relationship, as both cause and effect, between population trends on the one hand and a wide variety of social, economic, and political issues and problems on the other.

As with any undertaking of this sort, the ultimate product reflects the contributions of many persons besides those whose names appear on the title page. To begin with, since some sections were taken from the senior author's earlier book, *Population and People* (Chicago: Quadrangle Books, 1968), all acknowledgments made there are equally applicable here. Beyond that, we both owe and hereby acknowledge a broad intellectual debt to our past teachers, to past and present colleagues, and to the many authors of the massive body of literature we have consumed over the years. Scholars and works specifically referred to have been cited in the bibliographies at the end of each chapter, but these specific citations by no means represent all the material we have relied on, and we do want to express our appreciation to all those unnamed scholars, past and present, for the indirect assistance they have given us.

Several of our colleagues have rendered more direct assistance by reading and commenting on all or parts of earlier drafts of the manuscript. Although we did not always follow their suggestions, we do want to extend our thanks to Craig R. Humphrey, Mostafa H. Nagi, Mary G. Powers, James A. Sweet, and Jerry W. Wicks. While they deserve a share of the credit for what we have done, we hasten to add that we alone accept full responsibility for any errors or inadequacies that may appear in the text.

Last of all, but certainly not least, we owe a very special debt of gratitude to Patricia Kane who bore the largest burden of typing and retyping the many drafts of the manuscript.

Edward G. Stockwell
H. Theodore Groat

Bowling Green, Ohio

WORLD POPULATION

INTRODUCTION TO THE STUDY OF POPULATION

1

One of the most serious challenges to human destiny in the last third of this century will be the growth of the population. Whether man's response to that challenge will be a cause for pride or for despair in the year 2000 will depend very much on what we do today. If we now begin our work in an appropriate manner, and if we continue to devote a considerable amount of attention and energy to this problem, then mankind will be able to surmount this challenge as it has surmounted so many during the long march of civilization—U.S. President Richard M. Nixon, in proposing the establishment of the Commission on Population Growth and the American Future, July 1969.

The population problem is one of universal concern. In mapping out our program, we should plan the size of our population as well as the growth of material production, so that the two can fit in with each other. For a long period in the past, chiefly in the 1960s, we slackened our efforts with regard to family planning. As a result, our population has grown too rapidly and will continue to grow substantially in the coming years. . . . If population growth is not controlled, there will be a dizzy peak, making it virtually impossible for the economy and all our social institutions to cope—Hua Guofeng, Chairman of the Chinese Communist party, in an address before the Third Session of the Fifth National People's Congress, September 7, 1980.

These two quotations from leaders of countries having such vast differences in history, culture, and political ideology clearly indicate that the so-called world population crisis has finally come of age. This common recognition of the existence of a problem was, however, a long time in coming. Although numerous scholars in antiquity concerned themselves with various issues relating to their populations, and although scholarly interest in the potential problems of population growth in the modern era dates back nearly two hundred years, it is only since the end of World War II that population has emerged as the subject of public debate and discussion. The reason for this new and growing concern lies primarily in the sharp rise in the rate of population growth and a concomitant tremendous increase in the number of people living in the world. In 1980 there were approximately 4½ billion inhabitants on this small planet of ours, more than twice as many as there had been thirty-five years earlier, at the end of the Second World War, and this number was increasing at an annual rate of 1.7 percent (U.S. Bureau of the Census, 1981). Should this rate of growth continue, there will be more than 6 billion people on the earth by the time we enter the twenty-first century, and a generation later the world population will number about 8 billion.

THE IMPORTANCE OF STUDYING POPULATION

At the outset it can be stated that we are interested in studying population because the overall population situation has had and will continue to have a profound impact on the nature of the world we live in, on the nature of our American society, and on the nature of our individual lives.

The World Population Crisis

The present size of world population, along with its projected growth, is regarded by many as the most critical problem facing the human race during the remaining years of the twentieth century. More people will suffer because of population-related problems than because of any other world development (excluding a nuclear holocaust); many will even die prematurely. The longer the population continues to increase the greater will be the suffering and misery. This is a very pessimistic statement to make; however, we feel that such a position is fully justified and that any other position would not only be intellectually dishonest but could also have disastrous consequences for the well-being of the human population. The very substantial improvements of recent decades notwithstanding, the sad fact of the matter is that in the developing countries of Asia, Africa, and Latin America millions of people, especially children, still suffer and die prematurely each year, many because of malnutrition or hunger-related diseases. As one recent analysis of the situation has noted, approximately a quarter of all the deaths in the world occur among children under five, and undernutrition is a contributing cause in most of them (Eckholm and Record, 1976).

Poverty and low levels of consumption among the less developed countries represent only one dimension of the world population problem. On another level, in the wealthier industrialized nations of Europe and those with populations of European origin (such as the United States), millions of people are today consuming the earth's nonrenewable resources at such a rapid rate that one can already pinpoint the time in the not too distant future when these resources will be exhausted (Council on Environmental Quality, 1980). The very high and increasing rates of consumption in these more highly developed nations are also accompanied by a high and increasing level of environmental pollution and even destruction. These two trends, if allowed to continue, will ultimately necessitate a marked change in the life-styles of the peoples of the industrialized world, and will perhaps even lead to a reversal in the long-term movement toward an ever higher standard of living for an increasing number of people.

Few who have studied the problem would be naive enough to suggest that this situation is directly attributable to population growth. Nevertheless, it is a fact that the explosively rapid growth in numbers since the end of World War II has indirectly contributed to the problem; and it is equally true that continued rapid growth in the years ahead will be a major factor behind the increasing severity of the present situation.

Just as we cannot blame world poverty, overuse of resources, and environmental degradation on population growth alone, we should not be naive enough to believe that an end to population growth will signal an end to all the ills of the world. We can assert, however, that continued population growth will not only lead to a continued postponement of solutions to many of the world's problems but will also mean that any solutions that are found will be reached with much more difficulty and will be much more costly than would be the case if population were not growing so rapidly.

The causes of the world population explosion are not difficult to comprehend. Until fairly recently, human survival was a touch-and-go affair in many parts of the world. Hunger and disease were widespread throughout most of Asia, Africa, and Latin America, and death rates were very high. In many places, the average life expectancy for a man was only thirty-five or forty years—in some places even less. It was not at all uncommon in some of these areas of the world for 20 to 30 percent of all infants to die before they were a year old. In the face of such high death rates, and especially because of the low probability of surviving infancy, it was necessary to maintain a very high birth rate. If the high death rate had not been balanced by a high birth rate, the population in question would quickly have passed out of existence. As a consequence, many societies in Asia, Africa, and Latin America have traditionally been structured so as to reward fertility. Women were accorded status only by virtue of their being mothers, for example; a man's prestige among his peers was often determined by the number of sons he had sired; in primitive family-centered societies, a person's economic and political strength was determined by the size of his family; religious doctrines extolled the virtues of childbearing and condemned any form of birth control; and economic security in one's old age could be ensured only by having children to provide support. But the worldwide war on poverty, hunger, and disease during the postwar years has done much to alter this situation. Efforts of the Food and Agricultural Organization and the World Health Organization of the United Nations—not to mention the variety of programs sponsored by individual national governments and a myriad of private organizations—have been most successful in curbing famine and disease throughout the world. By so doing, they have helped to bring about drastic reductions in the death rate.

In most areas of the Third World, the widespread reductions in the death rate since the end of World War II have not yet been matched by any substantial decline in birth rates. Although people have generally been receptive to health improvement programs and have been eager to adopt practices that would enable them to postpone dying, they have been much more reluctant to alter the many structural features of the society that might encourage a reduction in the birth rate. In contrast to death, which has always been regarded as a necessary evil, birth has been fairly universally regarded as a good. Whereas people are anxious to avoid evil, they will go out of their way to achieve what society regards as good. Thus birth rates have tended to remain at or very near the same high levels that were necessary in the past to ensure the survival of the species. This means that where once there were three or four deaths for every four or five births, there are now only one or two deaths for every four or five births. As a result, world population is today experiencing a very rapid rate of increase.

Regardless of whether or not the "population bomb" represents a greater threat to the peace and security of humankind than does the hydrogen bomb (as many writers and scholars would assert), the inescapable fact is that the rapid rate of population growth in recent decades has created an extremely dangerous situation in many parts of the world. Ironic as it may seem, the greatest numerical growth in the world today is taking place in those poverty-stricken underdeveloped countries that can least afford it. These nations have only recently emerged from an economically primitive stage and begun the long, hard road to modernization. To the extent that population growth has been rapid, it has acted as a major obstacle to economic development. Where population has been growing rapidly, a larger share of the national income has had to be diverted away from productive investment and directed toward the support of the added numbers; and in this way, too rapid population growth has retarded efforts to improve the lot of the underprivileged millions now living in Asia, Africa, and Latin America. In other words, we face a situation in which the poorer nations of the world are struggling valiantly to raise their standards of living, but in many cases their efforts have been and continue to be frustrated by rapid population growth, which offsets potential economic gains.

We must now face this question: What will happen in the years to come if the millions of people living in the developing nations of the world continue to encounter such frustrations in their efforts to improve their lot? It is hard to visualize continued failure in this struggle leading to anything but even greater international tensions than those that already exist in the world. The growing awareness of the seriousness of this population problem lies behind the now heightened public discussion of the causes and consequences of, and the possible solutions to, the world population crisis. Whether or not this discussion will produce workable and acceptable solutions to the many problems associated with world population growth trends, however, remains to be seen. In the meantime, we can only hope—and we can draw some encouragement from the fact that more and more people (and nations) are at last becoming aware of the problems that exist and are working toward finding solutions.

Population as a Problem in the United States

While the magnitude of the current world population crisis cannot be overemphasized, it should not obscure the fact that the growth of our own population has been extremely dramatic. When the first federal census was taken in 1790, the population of the United States numbered less than 4 million. We surpassed the 100 million mark during the First World War; we reached 150 million shortly after the Second World War; and the 1980 census enumerated nearly 227 million people living in this country. In the relatively short time since its formation as a nation, the United States has grown in population from a few million to more than 200 million, and has come to be the fourth most populous nation in the world, exceeded only by China, India, and the Soviet Union. The entire history of the human race records no other population having grown to such a size and at such a rate over such a relatively short period of time. Moreover, as we entered the 1980s the combined effects of natural increase (the annual excess of births over deaths) and foreign immigration, illegal as well as legal, were adding well over 2 million persons each year, and even the most modest projections called for a population in excess of 250 million by the time we enter the twenty-first century.

In discussing the extent to which population is or is not a problem in an affluent nation such as the United States, one needs to adopt a somewhat different perspective than one takes when considering the situation on a world level. Population is seldom stationary but is in a continuous state of change. The extent and direction of population change are in large part determined by other social, economic, or political aspects of society. In primitive agrarian societies, for example, a poor crop year will lead to population decline either because some people will move away to seek greener pastures or because the resulting food shortage will cause a rise in the death rate. Conversely, a good crop year will lead to a population increase both because people are more likely to marry and have children and because the children who are born will be less likely to succumb to an early death because of malnutrition or some related disease. The social, economic, and political determinants of population trends and changes can be illustrated by examples from history: (1) the vast numbers of people who left Europe and came to the United States in search of freedom of thought and expression; (2) the rapid populating of the American West after the discovery of gold in the middle of the nineteenth century; (3) the decline of the birth rate in the Western world as cultural values shifted from an emphasis on the group to an emphasis on the welfare and development of the individual; and (4) the particularly sharp reduction of the birth rate in the United States (and in many countries of Western Europe as well) during the depression years immediately preceding the Second World War. More recently, one can see in the United States such things as (5) the tendency for migration to flow from areas of low employment opportunities (for example, farm areas) to areas where jobs are more plentiful (such as urban industrial centers); (6) the existence of an inverse relationship between economic status and death rates; and (7) the sharp decline of the birth rate as a result of postponed marriage, increased female labor force participation, alternative life-styles, and social movements such as those relating to the environment crisis, zero population growth, and women's liberation.

Of equal importance is the fact that population trends are often a major factor influencing changes in other aspects of society. For example, it has long been a recognized sociological fact that the need for laws and other formal mechanisms of social control increases in direct proportion to population size. Similarly, it has long been a recognized economic fact that, in a given environment with a given level of technology, population increase will result in an increase in per capita productivity until an optimum point is reached, after which the "law of diminishing returns" begins to operate. Finally, a good example of the extent to which population trends may have a political influence is provided by developments in Japan following its defeat in World War II: high birth rates, rapid population growth, and an intensification of the pressure of numbers on a limited land space all combined to bring about the legalization of abortion as a method of birth control in this traditionally family-centered society. Still other illustrations of how population trends may influence national policy are provided by such post–World War II developments as (1) the erection of the Berlin Wall in an effort to stem the tide of refugees fleeing from East to West Germany; (2) the conclusion of an agreement between the governments of the overpopulated Netherlands and underpopulated Canada to effect an exchange of population between the two countries; (3) the growth and expansion of federal programs for the elderly in the United States as a response to a growing number and proportion of older persons in the population; and (4) the appointment of a presidential commission to study the long-run implications of population growth for the future of our country (Commission on Population Growth and the American Future, 1972).

The implication of the preceding examples is that as long as the changes being influenced by population trends are compatible with the basic values, organization, and goals of a society, then population will not be viewed as a problem. Population becomes a problem only when it is regarded as a threat to the established order of society or to the overall well-being of a people. In this regard, then, it may strike some people as absurd to talk about population problems in the United States. After all, didn't the rapid growth of the population during the nineteenth century greatly facilitate our industrial development and lead to the emergence of the United States as one of the richest and most powerful nations in the world? Moreover, aren't the people of the United States today living at a level of comfort and well-being unknown anywhere else in the world, in spite of continued population growth? Yes, but such questions fail to consider that America today is vastly different from the America of the nineteenth century. Moreover, the standard of living does not and should not represent the only criterion in evaluating the well-being of a population. There are also such concerns as the adequacy of school and college facilities, housing, public utilities, employment opportunities, hospitals, and a myriad of other services; and the continued growth of our population is daily putting more and more pressure on such services to meet the needs of the people.

Those who question the existence of a population problem in the United States also ignore the question of aesthetics. Given that the land area of our country is finite, long-range prognosticators point out that the increase in leisure time resulting from technological progress creates a greater need and demand for parks, wilderness areas, beaches, and other open spaces for recreational purposes. Then they ask how such open spaces can be provided where the amount of land remains constant but where population continues to increase? Instead of city parks they foresee city parking lots; instead of acres of meadow and rolling hills, acres of high-rise apartments; and instead of quiet stretches of sandy beach, bustling desalinization and seaweed conversion plants. Considerations such as these justify looking at population growth in the United States with a somewhat more critical eye.

Maybe it does not represent as serious a problem as some people think, but it is certainly not necessarily such a "good thing" as the traditional view would hold.

While the rate of growth and the increase in numbers generally represent the most dramatic aspects of the population problem, they do not encompass all of them. On the contrary, many problems of population are entirely unrelated to size or rate of growth. Populations consist of much more than specified numbers of people. Rather, they consist of numbers of people who are dispersed over a varied land area, who possess very different characteristics, and who must contend with a variety of different problems, many of which are determined by the nature of the area in which they live or the particular characteristics that they possess. People who live in large urban centers along the eastern seaboard face vastly different problems than do the farmers of the plains states; black Americans face certain problems simply because they are black, regardless of where they live; problems of youth differ from problems of old age, and so on. It follows that as the proportion of the population living in particular areas or possessing particular characteristics changes, then their unique problems become recognized as more general problems of the society as a whole. To take a specific illustration, the postwar rapid increase in the number and proportion of the United States population living in cities intensified national awareness of the problems of urban life to such an extent that the mid-1960s saw the creation of a cabinet position in the executive branch of the government (Housing and Urban Development) to concentrate on solving the problems of contemporary urban society. Other fairly recent developments that illustrate this phenomenon include the creation of Medicare legislation as a response to the increase in the number and proportion of older persons in the population; the establishment of the Job Corps and other programs to retrain persons who have been displaced from their traditional occupation through increased automation; the passage of more and stronger civil rights legislation as a growing black population has let it be known that a substantial segment of the society does not have an equal share in the general affluence characterizing midcentury America; and the tightening up of the labor market in the late 1970s as the baby boom cohorts graduated from college and entered the labor force.

But even adding distribution and composition to the major variable of size will not indicate all of the dimensions of the population problem. Population size, distribution, and composition are not constant. On the contrary, they are in a continuous state of change; and the processes through which population change is brought about (fertility, mortality, and migration) are another side of the population issue. For example, although the United States as a whole has one of the lowest death rates in the world today, several groups within the population have death rates substantially higher than those of other groups. Similarly, although modern techniques of contraception today make it possible for married couples to determine with reasonable success how many children they will have and when they will have them, many groups in the society either do not have access to these techniques or for one reason or another do not avail themselves of their use; and year after year these people continue to have many more children than they want to have or are capable of supporting at a decent level of living.

On the basis of the preceding discussion, there are at least two ways in which population can be viewed as a problem in the United States today. First, many of the major social issues and problems that we face today (or will face tomorrow) have been directly influenced by trends in the size, composition, and distribution of the population. Second, although the United States as a whole may be one of the healthiest, wealthiest, and wisest nations in the world, there are marked differences throughout our population in the extent to which the good things of our society are shared equally by all members. Such inequalities within a nation that has for so long stood as a champion of freedom, justice, and equality for all people certainly indicate the existence of a problem.

Population and the Individual

All of us, along with all persons in every corner of the world, are an integral part of the overall population situation: we contribute to it by our presence and by our behavior, and it in turn will influence much of what happens to us during our lifetime. In other words, we became a part of the population situation when we were born, and we will not cease to be part of it until we die. During the intervening years the population environment in which we live will exert important influences on our lives: the birth rate and the number and proportion of young children requiring formal education will determine the amount of taxes we will have to pay in order to provide these needs; the rate at which the population is growing will be a major factor influencing the rate of resource consumption and our overall life-styles; a change in the composition of population, such as might be occasioned by the influx of large numbers of culturally different immigrants, will have a significant impact on the entire institutional structure of the society; the size of our age cohort in relation to that of other age groups will have a profound influence on the opportunities that are available to us as well as the problems we will have to face at all stages of the life cycle; and so forth.

During the interval between the time when our birth adds one more person to the population and the moment when our death takes one person away from it, we will make numerous decisions and behave in ways that will in turn exert an influence on population trends. The decisions we make—to get married, to change our place of residence, to have a certain number of children—all of these individual acts that we commit will, when combined with the acts of myriad other individuals, exert a profound collective influence on the overall size, composition, and distribution of the population; and this in turn will have a further impact on the nature and magnitude of a variety of societal trends and problems.

Because of the very close association between population trends and other societal trends and problems, it is desirable if not essential that all students of human society have an understanding and appreciation of what the nature of the population situation is, how the present situation evolved, and what its future outlook is. Providing such an understanding and appreciation of the determinants and consequences of population trends, and of the important role of population in all our lives, is the central aim of this book. This knowledge can best be imparted within the general framework of the science of *demography*. As a first step, then, it is necessary to provide the reader with a broader understanding of the nature of demography and the general demographic frame of reference.

THE FRAMEWORK OF DEMOGRAPHY

The word "demography" comes from the Greek words *demos*, meaning "people" or "populace," and *graphy*, a combining form meaning "the writing of" and used to denote either the act of writing and describing, or a branch of learning descriptively treated. In the broadest sense, then, demography may be defined as the science that deals with the description of human populations. More specifically, when demographers (those who study population) look at the population of any given area, their objectives consist initially of finding answers to three basic questions:

1. How many people are there in the area? (population size)
2. What traits and characteristics do the people in the area possess? (population composition)
3. Where are the people located within the area? (population distribution)

These three aspects of population—size, composition, and distribution—are the *major demographic variables*, and they constitute the fundamental subject matter of the science of demography. On this basis, then, one can formulate an initial definition of demography as the science that is concerned with ascertaining the size, composition, and distribution of the population in any given area of human habitation.

Population Statics and Dynamics

Although the preceding definition indicates in rough outline the basic dimensions of the science of demography, it is far from complete and adequate. The interests of the demographer go far beyond the mere description of specific facts about a population at one point in time *(population statics)*. Demographers are also interested in seeing whether or not these three basic demographic variables are changing, and if so, the nature and extent of the changes taking place *(population dynamics)*. Is the number of people in the population increasing, remaining relatively stable, or decreasing? If the population is increasing or decreasing in size, how rapidly is this change taking place? Is the population becoming younger, or is the average age of the inhabitants rising? Is the number of men relative to the number of women at the marriageable ages changing, and if so, in what direction is it changing? What is the trend with regard to the proportion of the population that resides in large urban centers as opposed to the proportion living on scattered farms, and how rapidly is this trend progressing? These and many other similar questions are in the back of the demographer's mind when he or she undertakes a study of the population in any given area.

Sources of Population Change

In addition to observing and measuring the nature and extent of any changes that may be taking place in the major demographic variables of population size, composition, and distribution, the demographer is also interested in the means by which such changes are being achieved. When he or she observes, for example, that a population is increasing in size or that the pattern of its distribution in space is changing, he or she is interested in knowing what factors are operating to produce these changes.

Demographically speaking, there are only three ways in which any population can change: (1) people can be born into it (fertility); (2) people can leave it by dying (mortality); and (3) people can move into or out of the area of habitation (migration). These three variables—fertility, mortality, and migration—are known as the *basic demographic processes,* and it is through the operation of these processes that changes in population size, composition, and distribution take place. Thus, when demographers observe, for example, that the size of the population in a given area is increasing, they are interested in knowing if this increase is due to an excess of births over deaths, to a greater number of people moving into than out of the area, or to some combination of these two processes. Similarly, if they see that the population is becoming younger, they are interested in knowing if this is happening because there has been an increase in the number of births or because large numbers of young people have moved into the area (or older people have moved out). Finally, if demographers note that the spatial arrangement of the population within the area is shifting, the demographer seeks to determine whether this is being caused by people moving into or out of different regions within the area, or if it is due to significant differences among the various parts of the area with respect to levels of fertility and mortality.

We can now elaborate on the initial definition of demography as the science that is concerned with describing the size, composition, and distribution of human populations. Based on the preceding paragraphs, demography may now be defined more completely as the science that is concerned with ascertaining (1) the size, composition, and distribution of the population in any given area of human habitation; (2) changes that have occurred or are occurring in these three major demographic variables; and (3) the processes—or the trends with regard to fertility, mortality, and migration—by means of which such changes have been or are being achieved.

Formal Demography versus Social Demography

In its narrowest sense, demography is concerned largely with the statistical measurement and description of population phenomena. In the broader sense, however, it also involves the explanation and analysis of observed population facts. In this respect, it is convenient to distinguish between the narrow realm of pure or *formal demography* and the broader area of general population study or *social demography*. In general, the term "formal demography" is reserved for the purely mathematical aspects of population study and is used primarily to refer to the statistical description of the demographic variables and processes and the interrelations among them. Social demography, on the other hand, is largely interpretive and is concerned with enhancing our knowledge and understanding of the underlying determinants and consequences of observed population phenomena.

Formal demography concerns itself solely with population facts and the cause–effect relations among them. Social demography is interested in the effects of nondemographic factors (e.g., social, economic, and political variables) on demographic behavior, and vice versa. Formal demography entails such activities as computing birth and death rates, estimating the volume and direction of migration, and statistically describing how these processes, and changes in these processes over time, affect and are affected by the major demographic variables of population size, composition, and distribution. The formal demographer tries to answer questions such as these: What are the current trends in the levels of fertility and mortality? What influences will these trends have (or have they had) on the rate of population growth? What are the characteristics of the people moving into or out of an area? How is this pattern of migration affecting the composition of the population in that area? What differences are there among various parts of an area in the balance between births and deaths (or in the balance between in-migration and out-migration)? To what extent are such differences bringing about a redistribution of the population within the area? Answering such questions requires the statistical manipulation of population data, and such statistical analysis is the core of formal demography.

As noted earlier, however, demographers are not interested only in statistical description. They are not interested, for example, in noting merely that a sudden rise in the birth rate has caused an increase of such-and-such magnitude in the population of an area, or that migration out of an area has resulted in a decline in numbers in that area. Rather, demographers are also interested in the various underlying social, psychological, and economic forces that have influenced such changes; and they are interested in the possible implications of such changes for the established order of the society. For example, if fertility should increase while mortality remains fairly stable, as it did in the United States during the late 1940s, demographers are not only interested in how much fertility has risen or in how much the population has increased as a result. They are also interested in what forces in the larger society prompted births to increase in the first place. Have new attitudes and values emerged about the "ideal" number of children or desirable family size? Have there been any changes in marriage customs or in the structure of the family that could explain the increase in births (such as a younger age at marriage or a decline in the importance of economic self-sufficiency as a prerequisite to marriage and childbearing)? Or has the general economic and political climate altered in such a way as to create an atmosphere conducive to a higher level of fertility?

As well as asking the reasons for the increase in births, demographers are also interested in the consequences for society of the fertility increase and the resulting rise in the rate of population growth. What are its implications for the adequacy of the available school facilities? Will the increased number of consumers have any effect on the rate of saving and investment and thereby on the rate of economic growth? What effect will the growing number and proportion of young people in the population have on juvenile delinquency, the demand for housing and recreation areas, styles of dress, tastes in entertainment, and the general attitudes and values of the society as a whole?

To take another example, consider the process of urbanization. Urbanization is a demographic phenomenon that consists essentially of a change in the pattern of population distribution, a change characterized by a decline in the size of the rural population, an increase in the number and size of urban places, and an ever-increasing concentration of the population in these urban places. Taking the formal demographic point of view, a more or less complete explanation of urbanization can be arrived at through the observation, measurement, and description of such things as streams of migration from rural to urban areas, differences between rural and urban areas with respect to levels of fertility and mortality, and the settlement of a disproportionate number of immigrants in urban areas. But such an explanation does not really tell us much about the phenomenon of urbanization. It does not tell us why a population that had been predominantly rural should suddenly start undergoing a transformation to an urban society. It does not tell us what conditions had to be met in order for the process of urbanization to take place, nor does it tell us what changes urbanization implies for social life.

A more complete explanation of urbanization would have to go beyond the mere statistical description and analysis of the phenomenon and note such things as the creation of an agricultural surplus that freed part of the labor force from the necessity of engaging in food-producing activities. It would note the development of alternative employment opportunities through the emergence and growth of urban industries. It should also have to consider some of the consequences of urbanization—a need to increase housing facilities, to enlarge and expand local governments and administrative agencies to handle the growing urban population, to develop more efficient transportation and communication networks, to increase the number and size of schools, to expand the amount and kind of public services offered (for example, police and fire departments, hospitals, welfare programs), and so forth. What is more, attention should be given to the possible consequences of urbanization for the basic demographic processes, particularly to how it is likely to affect levels of fertility and mortality, and through them the rate of growth and the composition of the population.

In short, given a specific population fact or trend, the demographer is not content with a mere quantitative analysis of this fact or trend and how it came into being. Although such "what?" and "how?" analyses form an integral part of all demographic research, they do not lead to a complete knowledge and understanding of the population fact or trend in question. To gain a fully adequate knowledge and understanding of a specific population phenomenon, the demographer pushes a step further and asks "Why?" and "What does it mean?"

One particularly useful way to clarify further the distinction between formal demography and social demography is to describe them in terms of the role that demographic and nondemographic factors play as either *independent* (causal) or *dependent* (effect) variables (Kammeyer, 1971, pp. 2–4). In formal demographic studies some population facts are used to explain other population facts. That is, the independent and dependent variables are both strictly demographic facts (as when trends in birth and/or death rates are used to explain changes in the age structure of a population, or, conversely, when changing age composition is used to explain changes in levels of fertility or mortality).

In broader social demographic analyses, various nondemographic factors play a major role as either independent or dependent variables. On the one hand, there are studies in which nondemographic factors are used as *independent* variables to explain some demographic fact. Religion, for example, is used to explain differences in birth rates; income is used to explain differences in mortality; and the differential distribution of job opportunities is used to explain the volume and direction of migration streams. On the other hand, there are studies in which nondemographic factors are the *dependent* variables to be explained by means of certain demographic facts. For instance, variations in political ideology or voting behavior are explained in terms of differences in age composition; an increase in crime, mental illness, unemployment, or some other manifestation of social disorganization is attributed to a rise in the number of immigrants; and differences in the rate of economic growth are explained in terms of differences in the rate of population growth. In both types of social demographic studies the key factor is that nondemographic phenomena play a major role as either independent variables (causes or determinants of population trends) or dependent variables (effects or consequences of population trends).

Summary

The science of demography may be said to have four basic objectives:

1. To observe, measure, and describe the size, composition, and distribution of the population in any given area of habitation.
2. To observe, measure, and describe the changes that may be taking place in the size, composition, and/or distribution of the population over time.
3. To observe, measure, and describe the processes (the levels of fertility, mortality, and migration) through which such changes are effected.
4. To explain the underlying determinants and consequences of the observed trends and changes.

The first three objectives involve the measurement and description of the demographic variables and processes of change, and of the interrelations among them, and they constitute the core of pure or formal demography. The fourth objective constitutes the subject matter of the more general social demography. At this point, where the underlying determinants and the consequences of population trends and changes are sought, demographers leave the narrow confines of their own specialty and enter the broad area of interdisciplinary study.

Demography and Other Sciences

When demographers move beyond the realm of simple observation and description, when they seek to interpret and explain their data in nondemographic terms, they turn to a variety of theoretical sciences for help. They turn to *geography* for aid in explaining the spatial distribution of population over the world's land surface. They look to *medicine* and *public health* for help in analyzing mortality trends and differentials and in explaining the changing importance of specific causes of death. *Economics* provides an understanding of the effects of population change on such things as the size and the productive capacity of the labor force, the adequacy of available resources, and the rate of economic development. The demographer looks to *biology* for knowledge and understanding of the workings of the human reproductive system and the aging process; to *political science* for help in understanding the effects of population change on the balance of world power and on trends in international relations; to *social psychology* for an understanding of family size preferences and motives for the use or nonuse of different methods of contraception; and to *sociology* and *anthropology* for help in understanding and analyzing the intricate relationships between demographic phenomena and the sociocultural environment. In short, the study of population makes use of a wide variety of scientific disciplines, all of which aid demographers in broadening their knowledge and gaining a better understanding of the causes and implications of changes in human populations.

Just as demographers rely on a number of other disciplines for assistance in understanding and interpreting their data, scholars and practitioners in a variety of areas need and use population data to further their own endeavors. Economists, for example, use population data to help interpret temporal and spatial variations in employment opportunities and productivity. Political scientists use demographic variables (age, sex, marital status) to help explain trends and differentials in voting behavior. Businessmen use data on the size, composition, and distribution of local population groups in order to locate markets for particular consumer products, to determine the content of advertising campaigns, and to assess the qualifications of the labor force in potential market areas. And government officials on all levels need numerous kinds of population data on which to base their programs: educators have to know the present and projected number of young people in an area in order to assess the need for schools and faculties; public health workers use mortality statistics both to identify problems for which remedial programs are needed and to measure the effectiveness of such programs; state and federal legislators need to know the present and projected number of elderly people in order to budget adequately for retirement benefits; family planning workers need fertility data to identify and locate high risk groups in the population, and so forth.

Although demography is truly an interdisciplinary science that contributes to other areas of inquiry and draws on these other disciplines for help in explaining and interpreting population trends and phenomena, it must be emphasized that the main causes of population trends are social and that demography is essentially and basically a social science. To use the terminology of one well-known American sociologist: population trends are both *socially determined* and *socially determining* (Davis, 1948, p. 552). That is, the demographic processes take place within the man-made environment of human society, and they are influenced by and exert an influence on this environment.

The extent to which the social and cultural milieu of this human-made environment can influence population phenomena can easily be seen if we consider the reproductive capacity of the human female. During her reproductive span (roughly between the ages of fifteen and fifty) the average woman is biologically capable of bearing from fifteen to twenty or more children; yet very few women ever realize this potential. A whole complex of social factors prevents a woman from doing so and helps to keep human fertility on a level far below that which it is biologically capable of attaining. Among these factors, to name only a few, are laws governing the age of consent at marriage; the status of women relative to that of men in society; social attitudes concerning the age at which a person should marry (very few marriages actually take place immediately upon attainment of the legal age of consent); legal obligations to feed and clothe children; the economic handicap of supporting a large family; and moral obligations to provide one's children with more than the minimal requirements for survival (such as providing a college education if possible).

It is also easy to demonstrate the influence of population phenomena on the society. On the most fundamental level, population *size* determines the mechanisms of social control of a society: whereas informal normative sanctions may be sufficient to maintain order in small, face-to-face groups, growth in numbers necessitates a shift to more formal rules and laws. The size of a population is a rough indicator of a nation's military strength and may have a profound effect on national policy (as it did in Japan and Nazi Germany in the 1930s and 1940s). In our own society today, one can easily see how changes in population size will affect our needs with respect to schools and recreation areas, housing, transportation facilities, public and professional services, and welfare programs, to name just a few.

The *composition* of a population is closely related to many other differences that characterize various segments of the population. Furthermore, the specific needs of a given population are determined to a great extent by its composition (as well as its size). For example, a population with a higher proportion of older persons is likely to be more conservative than one composed predominantly of young people, and it is apt to be less productive economically. Similarly, the educational level of a population not only will determine the technical skills and productive capacity of the labor force, but will also affect such things as fertility levels, consumption habits, and tastes in entertainment. Also, levels of fertility and mortality will affect the age composition, and this in turn will have an influence on the burden of economic dependency, problems of aging, the adequacy of available school facilities, the general outlook or philosophy of life of the population, and so forth.

Finally, the influence of population *distribution* on society can be seen in such things as the increasing concentration of the population in large urban clusters (which was itself influenced by the transformation from an agrarian to an industrial society), leading to a greater freedom for the individual, the decline of community solidarity, the emergence of a more blasé outlook on life, and the development of a more liberal philosophy concerning people's relations to other people. This urbanization trend has also led to the emergence of a wide range of problems—housing shortages, the growth of slums and ethnic ghettos, daily traffic jams, air and water pollution, overcrowded schools, shortages of public health and welfare personnel, and so forth. More recently, the growing popularity of suburban living—encouraged by the emergence of the automobile and the development of a large, interconnected system of highways—has created a need for the expansion of local services, such as education, offered by the rapidly growing suburban communities. The suburbanization trend has also been influential in generating vast urban renewal programs in many of our larger cities in an attempt to make them more attractive places in which to live and thereby, it is hoped, slow down the exodus to suburbia.

SCOPE AND ORGANIZATION OF THE BOOK

The overall purpose of this book is to describe the major population trends in the world in general and in the United States in particular, and to outline the dimensions of some of the current problems that have been created by or are otherwise closely associated with these basic demographic trends. We hope that the background provided by this book will give readers a better understanding of the close and important relationship between demographic trends and broader societal changes and that this in turn will make them better prepared to comprehend the various population problems confronting our world as well as the specific society in which they live.

Operating within the general framework of demography, we shall try to accomplish our objective by describing and explaining the various determinants and consequences of trends in the three basic processes of population change (mortality, fertility, migration), and the determinants and consequences of changes in the three major demographic variables (size, composition, distribution). In each case we will focus not only on a description and analysis of a particular demographic trend but also on some of the broader problems associated with the trend in question. We will also devote some attention to the various things that need to be done to facilitate solutions to the many population problems confronting human society today. For the most part, our discussion of population trends and problems will focus on two separate and distinctive levels: (1) the level of the less developed countries of the Third World where the current problems of poverty, hunger, economic growth, and political stability are the most serious ones confronting us in the short run; and (2) the level of the industrialized countries, particularly the United States, where such problems as a high level of consumption, increasing use of nonrenewable resources, and environmental pollution are the most serious in the long run.

No book about population would be complete without some reference to the data that form the basis of demography, and especially to the various techniques used to measure and describe population phenomena. At the same time, however, we felt that it was highly desirable to confront readers with the more basic substantive issues without getting them too bogged down in the formal or mathematical aspects of our discipline. Accordingly, we have adopted a compromise approach whereby we present a minimal discussion of relevant methodological topics in those chapters where it is necessary for an adequate understanding of the topic in question. Those who want more than such a minimal discussion will find a somewhat more detailed consideration of the data and methods of demography in three appendixes at the end of this volume. Appendix A introduces the reader to the nature, major sources, and some of the limitations of the statistical data that form the basis for the study of human populations; Appendix B discusses some of the more common techniques used to measure and describe the basic demographic processes of mortality, fertility, and migration; and Appendix C describes the life table and briefly illustrates a few of the more simple applications of this very versatile tool of demographic analysis.

The rest of the book is divided into eleven chapters covering more substantive aspects of the world population situation. In order to provide readers with general background knowledge of this situation and to introduce them to some basic demographic concepts, we begin in Chapter 2 with a general discussion of past and present population growth trends in various parts of the world. In Chapter 3 through Chapter 7 we turn our attention to the fundamental processes of fertility and mortality. Chapter 3 presents a discussion of basic mortality concepts, the determinants of past and present world mortality trends, and the nature and causes of mortality trends in the United States. Then, Chapter 4 considers some of the major mortality differentials that exist today, the role of morbidity as a precursor to death, population policy as it relates to mortality, and likely future mortality trends in both the developed and the less developed areas of the world.

Chapter 5 introduces basic fertility concepts, discusses the various factors that affect fertility behavior, and describes some of the major fertility trends and differentials in the modern world. Chapter 6 presents a more detailed discussion of the broad issue of fertility control, the growth of the family planning movement, and the various techniques that people use in order to regulate their fertility. Chapter 7 focuses on fertility control and public policy, with special emphasis on what governments have done, are doing, and need to do to reduce national birth rates. Building on this background, Chapter 8 then zeros in on some of the major dimensions of the population problem confronting the less developed countries of the Third World, particularly the relationship of population growth to problems of poverty and economic development, the food supply, and nonfood resources.

In Chapter 9 a discussion of basic migration concepts is followed by a general overview of major historical migration trends, a more detailed discussion of immigration to the United States, and a brief consideration of other major international migration streams, current policies, and the outlook for international migration in the future. Chapter 10 then presents a brief history of population growth in the United States, considers the outlook for future growth, and discusses some of the problems we face today that are related to the growth of our population. In Chapter 11 we focus on internal migration as a component of population change, with particular emphasis on the relation between internal migration and the changing distribution of the American population. This chapter also considers some of the internal migration patterns and problems that today characterize many of the lesser developed countries in the Third World. Finally, Chapter 12 deals with the broad topic of population composition, again with special emphasis on the determinants and consequences of trends and differentials with respect to the demographic and socioeconomic characteristics of the population of the United States.

REFERENCES AND SUGGESTED READING

Commission on Population Growth and the American Future. *Population and the American Future.* Washington, D.C.: U.S. Government Printing Office, 1972.
Council on Environmental Quality. *The Global Report to the President: En-*

tering the Twenty-first Century, Vol. I. Washington, D.C.: U.S. Government Printing Office, 1980.

Davis, Kingsley. *Human Society*. New York: Macmillan, 1948.

———. "The Sociology of Demographic Behavior." In R. K. Merton et al., eds., *Sociology Today*. New York: Basic Books, 1959, pp. 309–33.

Eckholm, Erik, and Frank Record. *The Two Faces of Malnutrition*. Worldwatch Paper 9. Washington, D.C.: Worldwatch Institute, December 1976.

Hauser, Philip M., and Otis Dudley Duncan, eds. *The Study of Population*. Chicago: University of Chicago Press, 1959.

Hodgson, Dennis. "Demography as Social Science and Policy Science." *Population and Development Review*, 9 (March 1983): 1–34.

Kammeyer, Kenneth C. W. *An Introduction to Population*. Corte Madeira, Calif.: Chandler, 1971.

U. S. Bureau of the Census. *Demographic Estimates for Countries with a Population of 10 Million or More: 1981*. Washington, D.C.: U.S. Government Printing Office, 1981.

Weeks, John R. *Population: An Introduction to Concepts and Issues*, 2nd ed. Belmont, Calif.: Wadsworth, 1981, Chapter 1.

Weller, Robert H., and Leon F. Bouvier. *Population: Demography and Policy*. New York: St. Martin's, 1981, Chapter 1.

WORLD POPULATION SIZE AND GROWTH

2

There were no real statistics on the size and growth rate of the population in any part of the world until about two hundred years ago, and for many parts of the world reliable statistics are still not available. Thus, most of what we say about population in historical times and much of what we say about it today is based largely on conjecture, or on educated guesses. Nevertheless, while it is not possible to specify exactly how many people were living in the world at any precise time, it is eminently clear that our numbers have increased substantially over the years and are continuing to increase today at a rate that is much higher than those that prevailed throughout most of human history.

Estimates prepared by the United Nations indicate that the number of people living on earth at mid-twentieth century was slightly more than 2½ billion (see Table 2-1). By 1980 this number was approaching 4½ billion. This is a far cry from the half billion or so persons who were living on earth at the beginning of the modern era (generally taken to be about 1650), and it represents roughly a ninefold increase in numbers since that time.

We can readily appreciate the magnitude of the increase in population in the modern era if we imagine a compression of the time dimension. If the length of time that human beings have existed on earth is compressed into a single day, then this modern era represents less than one minute. Yet this briefest period of human existence has witnessed the greatest increase in numbers. It took hundreds of thousands of years for the population of the world to reach a half-billion at the start of the modern era. It took less

Table 2-1
Estimated Size and Growth of World Population

Year	Population in millions	Average annual rate of increase (percent) since previous date
7000 B.C.	5–10	—
A.D. 1	200–400	0.0
1650	470–545	0.0
1750	629–961	0.4
1800	813–1,125	0.4
1850	1,128–1,402	0.5
1900	1,550–1,762	0.5
1950	2,513	1.0
1960	3,027	2.0
1970	3,678	2.2
1980	4,415	2.0
1990	5,275	1.9
2000	6,199	1.7

SOURCES: United Nations, *The Determinants and Consequences of Population Trends,* Volume I (New York, 1973), and *Concise Report on the World Population Situation in 1979* (New York, 1980).

than two hundred years to reach the next half-billion. At the present rate of growth, however, it will take less than seven years for the world's population to increase by another half-billion persons.

Viewed in the long run, the growth of world population has been likened to a long, thin powder fuse that burned slowly and haltingly through centuries of human existence until it reached the charge and exploded in the modern era (Davis, 1945). Before the modern era, the number of people on earth increased with infinitesimal slowness—at rates substantially below one-tenth of 1 percent each year. But since that time the rate of increase has risen steadily; the annual average rate of increase exceeded half of 1 percent throughout the nineteenth century and has been greater than 1 percent ever since 1920. In the most recent period, the growth of world population has reached and even exceeded the unprecedented rate of 2 percent a year. At the annual rate of 1.7 percent that prevailed during the early 1980s, world population will pass the 6 billion mark before the end of the century; and it can be expected to double in size, to 9 billion, in just about forty years, which will be well within the lifetime of today's college student.

The radical change that has occurred in the size and rate of increase in world population can perhaps be better appreciated by a glance at Figure

Figure 2-1
World Population Growth, 1650–2000

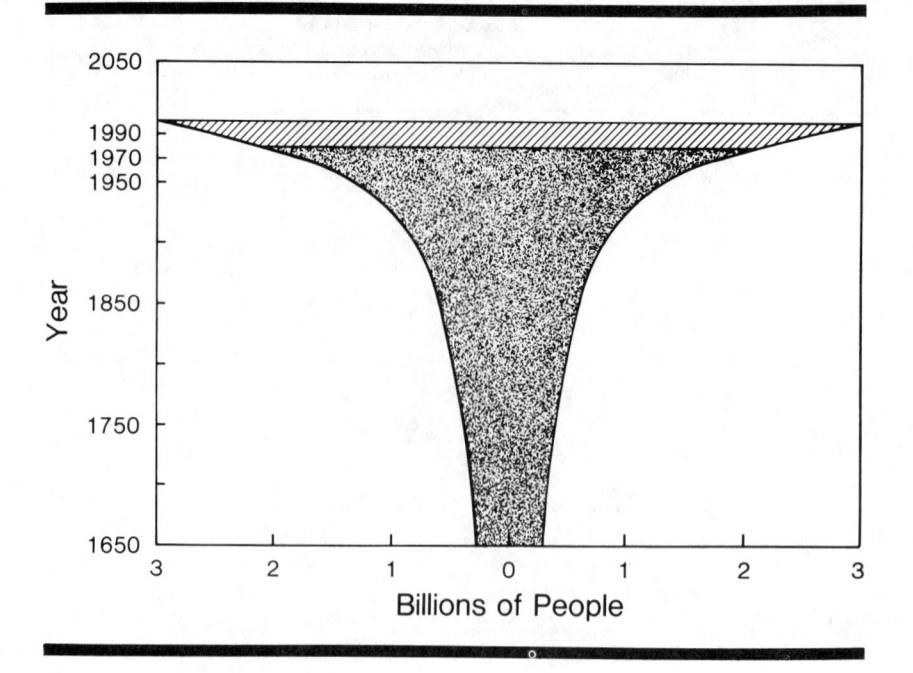

2-1. In this figure we have used the data presented in Table 2-1 and, for each of the dates since 1650, we have placed half of the estimated population on each side of the zero point. Thus, the total width of the shaded area at any date represents the number of people living in the world at that time. A glance at this figure makes it easy to understand why such terms as "population bomb" and "population explosion" have today become part of our vocabulary.

The remainder of this chapter takes a closer look at the determinants of past and present population growth trends in order to provide the background necessary to appreciate more fully the nature of the current world population growth situation. To begin with, one can identify four major periods of world population growth. In a narrower sense, one could identify hundreds if not thousands of periods of population growth interspersed with periods of stability, and even periods of population decline. On a broader level, however, one can distinguish at least four major cultural epochs during which the general pattern of population growth was significantly different than it was during preceding and succeeding epochs (Population Reference Bureau, 1962). Two of these epochs were part of the modern era;

two were earlier in history. These four growth periods, some of the major characteristics of which are summarized in Figure 2-2, are described more fully in the following sections.

In the remainder of this chapter (and indeed throughout the rest of the book) frequent reference will be made to three basic demographic measures with which the reader needs to be familiar. These are (1) the *crude birth rate*—the number of live births that occur in a population during a given year per 1,000 members of that population; (2) the *crude death rate*—the number of deaths that take place during a given year per 1,000 inhabitants; and (3) the *crude rate of natural increase*—the difference between the birth and death rates. The crude rate of natural increase indicates the net gain to a population during a given year per 1,000 members of the population. Thus, if in a population of 10,000 there are 400 births and 300 deaths in a year, we say that it has a birth rate of 40.0, a death rate of 30.0, and a crude rate of natural increase of $40.0 - 30.0 = 10.0$ per 1,000 people. With respect to the latter, it is common practice to shift the decimal one place to the left and refer to an annual population growth rate of 1.0 percent. These and other common demographic measures are described and illustrated more fully in Appendix B.

Figure 2-2
Major Population Growth Periods

Growth period	Approximate time span	Average number added per year	World population at end of period
PRE-MODERN			
I Pre-neolithic	Emergence–8000 B.C. (2 million years)	2–3	Approximately 5 million
II Neolithic	8000 B.C.–A.D. 1650 (10,000 years)	50,000	Approximately 500 million
MODERN			
III European population explosion	1650–1950 (300 years)	7 million	2½ billion
IV Third World population explosion	1950–	75–80 million in 1980	. . .

Table 2-2
Number of Years in Which Population Will Double at Specified Growth Rates

Annual rate of population growth (percent)	Population doubling time* (years)	Selected countries growing at or near rates specified (c. 1980)
0.1%	700	Belgium, Sweden
0.5	140	Czechoslovakia, France, Netherlands
1.0	70	New Zealand, Poland, Romania
1.5	47	Argentina, Chile, Iceland, People's Republic of China
2.0	35	Colombia, Lebanon, Surinam, India
2.5	28	Angola, Burma, Ethiopia, Mexico, Tunisia
3.0	23	Ecuador, Liberia, Nigeria, Sudan, Venezuela
3.5	20	Honduras, Iraq, Libya, Nicaragua
4.0	18	Kenya, Syria

* Population doubling time is an exponential function that can be calculated simply as 70 (the natural log of 2) divided by the annual rate of growth.

In the following discussion of population growth trends and differentials, many of the rates cited may seem very small by most standards: for example, one would not think much of a bank that paid 2 or 3 percent interest on savings accounts. It is important to realize, however, that such rates are very high when applied to human populations and they are capable of generating huge numbers of people in a very short time. This is because population growth rates, like compound interest rates, generate an exponential growth situation in which the number of people doubles and redoubles continuously with the passage of some specified unit of time (See Table 2-2). At an annual rate of 1 percent, for example, population will double itself every 70 years; at an annual growth of 2 percent it will double every 35 years; and with an annual rate of 3 percent the number of people will double every 23 years, or within the space of a single generation! Even the relatively modest rate of 0.5 percent will double population size in 140 years. Keeping these doubling times in mind during the following discussion will help one to appreciate the magnitude of the current world population growth situation.

POPULATION GROWTH IN PRE-MODERN TIMES

The first pre-modern phase of population growth, the Old Stone Age or pre-neolithic period, lasted about two million years—from the time homo sapiens first emerged as a separate identifiable species until the neolithic cultural achievements of agriculture and the domestication of animals roughly eight to ten thousand years ago. In fact, evidence has recently been uncovered that indicates some agriculture was practiced in Egypt as long ago as 15,000 B.C. (see Wendorf et al., 1982). Prior to the neolithic revolution, the brutally harsh conditions of life made human survival an extremely precarious affair. Although precise data are lacking, the evidence that can be gleaned from various anthropological and archaeological sources indicates that the death rate of our early ancestors was extremely high. A newborn infant had only about a fifty-fifty chance of surviving to adulthood, and the average length of life could not have been much more than twenty to twenty-five years. During this period, which saw the human species disperse from its origins in Africa throughout the habitable areas of the earth, population grew extremely slowly and erratically. Population probably increased during times of plenty and in the absence of any natural disasters (e.g., floods, earthquakes, drought), but declined when the always harsh living conditions deteriorated even further. This cyclical pattern was slightly weighted on the side of growth so that population did increase over the long run; however, the margin was so very narrow that by the end of this initial period of population growth, after approximately two million years of existence, it is not likely that the entire population of the earth numbered much more than five million. In other words, the average increment to the world's population during this pre-neolithic growth period amounted to no more than two or three persons a year!

The situation was markedly different during the second, or neolithic, period of population growth. During this period, which lasted approximately ten thousand years—from about 8000 B.C. to the beginning of the modern era in A.D. 1650—world population increased a hundredfold. It grew from an estimated five million to approximately a half-billion, representing an average annual increment of some fifty thousand people (compared to two or three a year during the pre-neolithic era).

As we have noted, this second growth period began with the practice of agriculture and the domestication of animals. These two achievements provided a more stable food supply and laid the base for the maintenance of a substantially larger population, for once a given area is put under cultivation it can support a far greater number of people than when left in its natural state. The neolithic achievements were significant for another reason. The greater abundance of food freed people from the necessity of spending virtually all of their time hunting and gathering. People now had time to devote to other pursuits: constructing permanent settlements, developing crafts and metallurgy, establishing religious and political institutions, and so forth. Thus they laid the groundwork for the beginning not only of population growth but also of the growth of modern civilization.

The more efficient use of the environment and the more nourishing diet it provided led to improvements in health and a lower death rate, thus bringing about an increase in the rate of population growth. Although numbers grew much faster than they had during the earlier period, growth was still very slow by modern standards. People were still at the mercy of the weather and natural disasters, and numbers were further held in check by the food-producing capacity of the environment. As in the pre-neolithic era, population growth continued to be cyclical, increasing during times of plenty and declining when food became scarce and when disease decimated large segments of the population. In the fourteenth century, for example, an estimated 20 percent of the population of Europe died during an outbreak of bubonic plague.

To summarize, the human population evolved and grew during the pre-modern era, but the rate of growth was extremely slow. It increased slightly faster during the later neolithic phase, but growth continued to be so slow as to appear almost stationary by modern standards; and at the dawning of the modern era, after more than two million years of development, the human species numbered only about 500 million persons.

POPULATION GROWTH IN THE MODERN ERA

World population growth did not really assume significant proportions until after the advent of the modern era in the middle of the seventeenth century. As in pre-modern times, population trends during this modern era can also be divided into two distinctive growth periods. The first of these, the period of the European population explosion, lasted about three centuries, roughly from 1650 to 1950. This period was characterized by the settlement of North America by European colonists, the rise of the Western capitalist economic system, the Industrial Revolution with its tremendous increases in human productivity, the increasing concentration of population in urban areas, and the spread of European civilization and influence to the far corners of the globe. Demographically this period was characterized by a gradual but steady decline in the European death rate and an asssociated acceleration in the rate of population growth. At first the declines in mortality were due to improvements in the quantity and quality of the food supply as a variety of new food crops (e.g., potatoes) were transplanted from the

New World to the Old World. Later, as the Industrial Revolution progressed and as scientific knowledge increased, the declines were due to preventive measures reflected in improvements in public health and sanitation (e.g., immunization, sewer construction, chlorination of drinking water) and to advances in the curative power of medical science (e.g., the widespread use of penicillin after 1940, the more recent mycin drugs).

Compared with earlier eras, this period of the European population explosion witnessed a tremendous increase in the rate of world population growth. This increase was generated by the mortality decline in the developing countries of Europe and by a steady rise in their rates of population growth; and the gradually accelerating rates of growth in Europe produced a corresponding gradual increase in the rate of world population growth.

During the first 100 years of this period, from 1650 to 1750, the growth rate for the world as a whole was 0.4 percent, a rate that would lead to a doubling of population in approximately 175 years. Throughout the next century, growth rates in the expanding European countries increased gradually, in some cases reaching as high as 1.0 percent or more; and by 1850 the world growth rate had risen to 0.5 percent a year (a doubling time of about 140 years). The annual rate of world population growth passed the 1 percent mark for the first time during the 1920s; and during the decade from 1940 to 1950, world population grew at an average rate of 1.3 percent a year, and the doubling time was down to only 45 years. All in all, this three-hundred-year period saw world population increase from 500 million to over 2½ billion, which represents an average annual increment of almost 7 million persons.

Beginning about 1950, world population embarked on its latest and most explosive growth phase, the Third World population explosion. Although falling birth rates had drastically slowed down the rate of population growth in Europe and North America by the 1930s, the years following the end of the Second World War witnessed the diffusion of modern methods of death control throughout the developing countries of Asia, Africa, and Latin America. As the death rates in these areas have declined dramatically, the rate of world population growth has soared. From an average annual rate of 1.0 percent during the first half of the twentieth century, the rate of population increase jumped to 2 percent a year or more during the succeeding three decades. By 1980 there were roughly 4½ billion people in the world, representing an average annual increment between 1950 and 1980 of more than 60 million people (compared with 2 or 3 persons a year during the earliest pre-neolithic growth period).

The rate of world population growth, which appears to have peaked during the 1960s, has been declining gradually in the most recent period. There are many reasons for this decline, including a slowing down of the rate of mortality decline among many of the less developed countries, fairly substantial drops in the birth rate in a number of the more highly developed countries, and the emergence of some significant fertility declines in a few of the less developed countries. It may well be that the explosive growth trend of the post–World War II era is coming to an end. The crucial questions still remain, however: Will the downward trend in the growth rate continue? If it does continue, how long will it take to decline to a point where world population is no longer growing? Only time can answer these questions. Meanwhile, as of 1980, world population was increasing by between 75 and 80 million persons per year; and it was expected to exceed the 6 billion mark well before the end of the present century.

In summary, over the long span of human history the rate of population growth has tended to accelerate—imperceptibly at first, and then faster and faster with the advancement and diffusion of material culture. It took more than 2 million years for the world to reach its 1980 level of about 4½ billion inhabitants, but at the current growth rate it will take only 40 years to add the next 4½ billion. Such a development would have a profound impact on our planet and on the lives of all of its inhabitants; and the prospect of its occurrence should be a matter of very serious concern to all people.

Current Growth Differentials

Of particular relevance to the world population situation today and for the foreseeable future is the marked difference in growth rates prevailing among the major regions. As the data presented in Table 2-3 clearly reveal, population is growing fastest in the most populous of the less developed regions of the Third World, areas that can least afford it. The less developed regions contain approximately three-fourths of the world's people, and this population has recently been growing at an annual rate of 2.2 percent (doubling time = 31 years). If the People's Republic of China is excluded, this annual growth rate would be about 2.5 percent, and numbers would double in only 28 years (U.S. Bureau of the Census, 1980).

Among the major geographic regions of the world, rates of population growth are lowest in the highly industrialized countries of Europe and North America. They are intermediate (roughly between 1 and 2 percent a year) in the USSR, Oceania, and East Asia (which includes the People's Republic of China). They are highest in South Asia, Latin America, and Africa. In Africa, the least developed region of the world, moderate declines in mortality since the 1950s in conjunction with persistently high birth rates have led to a steady rise in the rate of population growth (U.S. Bureau of the Census, 1980). The recent overall growth rate of 2.9 percent a year would double population in just twenty-four years, and in some countries (e.g., Botswana, Libya, Kenya, and Zimbabwe), growth rates are on the order of 3½ percent a year or more, and numbers can be expected to double in twenty

Table 2-3
Population Size and Growth Trends, 1980

Region	Estimated population, 1980 (in millions)	Average annual rate of growth (percent), 1975–80
World	4,415	1.8
More developed countries	1,131	0.7
Less developed countries	3,284	2.2
Africa	469	2.9
Latin America	368	2.7
North America	246	0.6
East Asia	1,136	1.3
South Asia	1,422	2.5
Europe	484	0.4
Oceania	23	1.3
USSR	267	0.9

SOURCE: United Nations, *Concise Report on the World Population Situation in 1979* (New York, 1980).

years or less. This situation, wherein the fastest population growth is taking place in the most populous and poorest areas of the world, represents the major population problem confronting the human species in the short run. Later in this chapter we will examine more closely the varying patterns of population growth and projected changes in the major regions of the world. First, however, let us consider a major model that has been developed to facilitate the description and understanding of past and present patterns of population growth.

THE MECHANICS OF POPULATION GROWTH

What has caused this tremendous spurt of population growth in the modern era? And how can we explain the pronounced differences in growth rates among the various regions of the world? To answer these questions, and also to appreciate better the magnitude of the present population growth problems and the likelihood that they can and will be solved in the years to come, one needs to be familiar with the concept and mechanics of the *demographic transition*. Demographically speaking, world population growth is determined by only two factors—fertility and mortality; population grows according to the extent to which the number of people born each year exceeds the number of people who die. Thus, the first step in attempting to explain the unprecedented growth trends of modern times is to ascertain the relative importance of these two variables.

Demographic Balance

The whole process of the demographic transition can perhaps best be understood as a change in the nature of a population's *demographic balance*. When we say that a particular population is in a state of demographic balance, we mean that birth and death rates are at relatively similar levels (i.e., they more or less balance each other), so that the rate of population growth is near zero or is at least very slow. Now, there are two basic kinds of demographic balance: (1) the pre-modern or *primitive demographic balance*, where birth and death rates are fairly stable and in relative balance with each other at *high* levels; and (2) the *modern demographic balance*, where birth and death rates are fairly stable and in relative balance with each other at a *low* level. Both of these two types of demographic balance, the primitive and the modern, are characterized by slow rates of population growth, but the dynamic growth component is different. In primitive demographic balance, the high birth rate remains relatively constant, and it is primarily fluctuations in the *death rate* that effect changes in the rate of growth. In modern demographic balance, however, it is the low death rate that is fairly constant, and the rates of population growth and change are determined largely by the level and trend of the *birth rate*.

The Demographic Transition

Stated most simply, the *demographic transition* is the transformation of a population from a state wherein it is characterized by a primitive demographic balance to one in which it is characterized by a modern demographic balance. This transformation begins when the old primitive balance is upset by the emergence of a sustained downward trend in the death rate, and it ends when a subsequent decline in the birth rate restores a balance at the low modern level. The intervening period is marked by fairly rapid and substantial increases in the size of the population.

    The demographic transition is a phenomenon of the modern era, and so far only a small number of countries have completed it. With a few exceptions (e.g., Japan, Singapore), those that have made the transition are the industrialized, developed nations of Europe and those with populations of European origin (e.g., Australia, Canada, New Zealand, and the United States).

Furthermore, those industrialized nations that have completed the transition and have achieved a modern demographic balance between relatively low birth and death rates have done so only fairly recently. As noted earlier in this chapter, the brutally harsh living conditions that prevailed throughout most of human history made survival an extremely precarious affair, and death rates were extremely high. In the face of such high death rates, a high level of fertility was necessary for the survival of the species, and birth rates often approached their biological maximum. As human culture developed over the ages, however, the chances of survival slowly began to improve. The first significant breakthroughs were the earlier noted neolithic cultural achievements, the development of agriculture and the domestication of animals, roughly ten thousand years ago. A more stable food supply meant a slight improvement in living conditions, and this in turn meant a slight decline in mortality and a corresponding increase in the rate of population growth. However, the widespread prevalence of disease resulting from poor nutrition and extremely unsanitary conditions continued to keep death rates high, and although population began to increase it did so very slowly.

It was not until well after the start of the modern era that any substantial reductions in mortality occurred (see Chapter 3). These declines in mortality occurred first in the modernizing nations of the European world, and their onset marks the beginning of the third historical epoch of population growth—the European population explosion. Although it was at one time popular to ascribe this mortality decline to the development of modern medicine and public health programs, it is now clear that the initial declines in the death rate were associated with an increase in the quantity and quality of the food supply. More and better food significantly improved the nutritional status of the population and increased people's ability to resist many of the microorganisms that cause disease and death (McKeown, 1976). As the food supply started to improve in the late seventeenth and early eighteenth century, death rates began to decline.

The initial mortality reductions that followed the improvements in diet were substantially enhanced by the tremendous cultural advances that accompanied the Industrial Revolution. In addition to the marked increases in human productivity, the Industrial Revolution brought with it the emergence and advancement of modern science. With this development, the mortality pattern that had prevailed for some two million years was finally broken. The discovery of vaccination for smallpox in 1796 was the first in a long line of discoveries and inventions that substantially improved the chances of human survival, particularly among infants and young children. This and other applications of the scientific method to biology and medicine—coupled with the continued improvements in agricultural technology, the development of better means of transportation and communication, improvements in sanitation, and all the social, economic, and psychological changes that accompanied the emergence of an urban-industrial civilization—combined to set in motion forces that dramatically lowered death rates and substantially increased human reproductive efficiency.

Although death rates began to fall during the eighteenth century, the birth rate continued to remain at fairly high levels. In fact, in many areas the initial response to the profound societal changes taking place was an increase in fertility (Tabbarah, 1971). The same improvements in nutrition and health status that led to mortality decline also contributed to such things as a reduction in involuntary sterility and greater fetal survival (i.e., fewer miscarriages). These general health improvements were enhanced by a number of societal changes (e.g., the breakdown of the old apprentice system, increased agricultural productivity) that made it possible for more people to marry, and to marry at a younger age. As a consequence, the initial response to the rising levels of living associated with the early stages of modernization in many European countries was an increase in the birth rate, and this contributed to an even greater difference between levels of fertility and mortality.

The widening spread between levels of fertility and mortality developed because more babies were being born and especially because an increasingly larger proportion of infants survived and lived through adulthood. This spread is commonly referred to as the *demographic gap*. The opening of this gap marks the beginning of rapid population growth. In Europe this gap began to open in the eighteenth century and continued to widen during several decades of declining mortality, thus producing steadily increasing rates of population growth. Eventually, however, the birth rate began to decline as social and cultural values shifted from an emphasis on the welfare and development of the group to an emphasis on the welfare and development of the individual, as the economic base of the society shifted from rural agrarian to urban industrial, and as continued technological progress provided the means for the more effective control of fertility. A new demographic balance between low birth and death rates was ultimately achieved, and the rate of population growth in the industrial nations of the Western world slowed down considerably, thus bringing an end to the European population explosion.

Transition Stages

In order to illustrate more clearly the nature of this classical demographic transition model, a graphic representation of a hypothetical set of birth and death rates over time is depicted in Figure 2–3. It may be helpful in understanding this transition process to look at this model in terms of three readily identifiable growth stages.

Stage 1. During the early primitive or pre-industrial stage, birth and

Figure 2-3
The Classical Demographic Transition Model

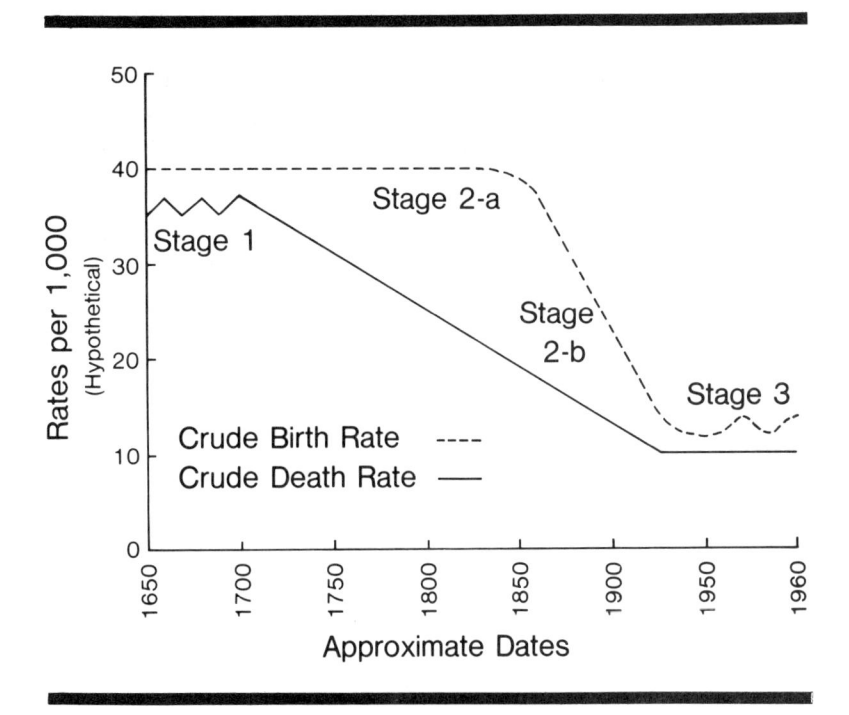

death rates remain fairly stable at relatively high levels, and fluctuations in the generally low rate of population growth result mainly from fluctuations in the death rate, which declines in times of plenty and rises in times of disaster as a result of crop failure and related food shortages, war, disease, or other misfortunes. This is the stage that characterized all human populations until the late seventeenth and early eighteenth century, at which time the rapidly modernizing nations of Western Europe began to enter the second or *transitional growth* stage.

Stage 2. The second transitional phase of rapid population growth, which often lasted a century or more, can be subdivided into two separate phases in terms of whether the rate of population growth is accelerating or slowing down.

Stage 2-A. The early or *expanding growth phase* is characterized by a persistent high birth rate, but the death rate is declining so that the demographic gap becomes wider and the rate of population growth increases. In general, the countries of Western Europe began to enter this accelerating growth phase sometime during the period from 1650 to 1750.

Stage 2-B. The late or *contracting growth phase* of this transitional period begins when the birth rate also starts to decline (generally several generations after the start of mortality decline). The onset of fertility decline was traditionally regarded as a natural accompaniment to the broad socioeconomic transition from a rural-agrarian to a modern urban-industrial society; and as the declining birth rate narrowed the gap created by the earlier decline in the death rate, it brought about a slowing down in the overall rate of population growth. Although the precise timing of the onset of fertility decline and the subsequent slowing down in the rate of population growth varied among the several European nations, this contracting phase generally began around the middle of the nineteenth century and lasted until the second or third decade of the twentieth century.

Stage 3. The final modern stage is one in which birth and death rates are in relative balance at a fairly low level, and where fluctuations in the generally low rate of population growth are due to fluctuations in the birth rate. This stage, which marks the completion of the transition and the end of uncontrolled rapid population growth, has characterized the industrialized advanced nations of the Western world since the 1930s, and its attainment signaled the end of the European population explosion.

THE THIRD WORLD POPULATION EXPLOSION

The population problem today derives from the fact that with few exceptions (most notably Japan and Singapore) only the European countries and those of European settlement in North America and Oceania have completed this demographic transition. The majority of the developing countries of the Third World have only recently entered the early accelerating-growth phase of Stage 2, thus signaling the start of the most recent population growth phase—the Third World population explosion. An especially critical aspect of this current situation should be stressed: *the gap that has opened between levels of fertility and mortality in these Third World countries has opened faster and is much wider than the gap that characterized the European countries during their transition.* Thus, most of these poorer countries are growing at rates that are substantially faster than those experienced by the modern European countries during their periods of transitional growth.

The explanation of the present situation in the developing regions lies primarily in the trend with respect to the death rate. In contrast to the European experience, where the decline of the death rate took place gradually over several generations, the ability to make immediate use of modern techniques for postponing death (techniques that took years to develop and per-

Figure 2-4
The Demographic Gap in the Less Developed Countries

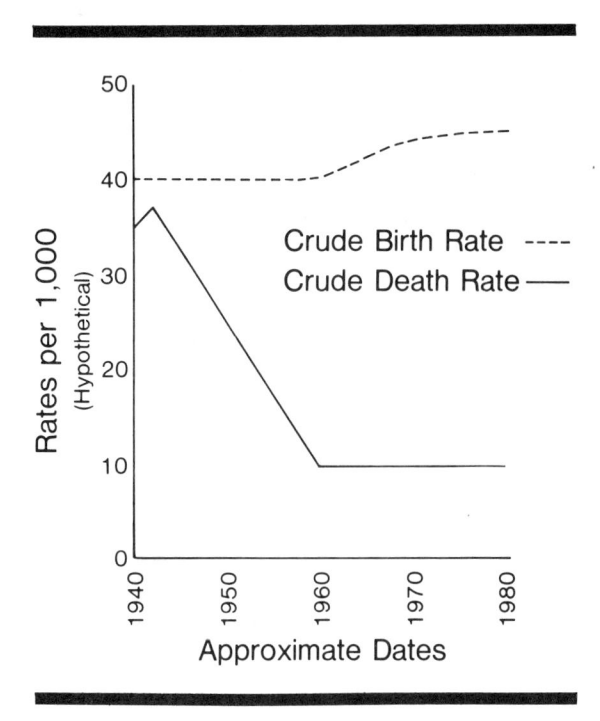

fect) means that the decline of mortality in the less developed areas of the world today has been more pronounced and has taken place much more rapidly than it did in the demographic history of the highly developed countries. Instead of the hundred or more years it took for the death rate of most European nations to decline from 30 or 35 to around 10 per 1,000 population, the years since the end of World War II have witnessed comparable reductions in many underdeveloped areas in the space of 20 to 25 years, sometimes even less. Fertility, on the other hand, has generally remained at fairly high levels. In many countries, in fact, as was the case in Europe historically, birth rates have risen; and the very rapid and substantial mortality decline in conjunction with a high, perhaps slightly increasing birth rate has produced unprecedented rates of population growth in many of the world's developing countries in recent years.

The general nature of the fertility-mortality gap that has recently emerged in many of the less developed countries is graphically illustrated in Figure 2-4. The significance of this recent gap can best be appreciated by comparing it with the gap that characterized the classical transition pattern depicted in Figure 2-3. In the demographic history of the European nations,

Figure 2-5
Comparative Vital Rate Trends for Sweden and Sri Lanka

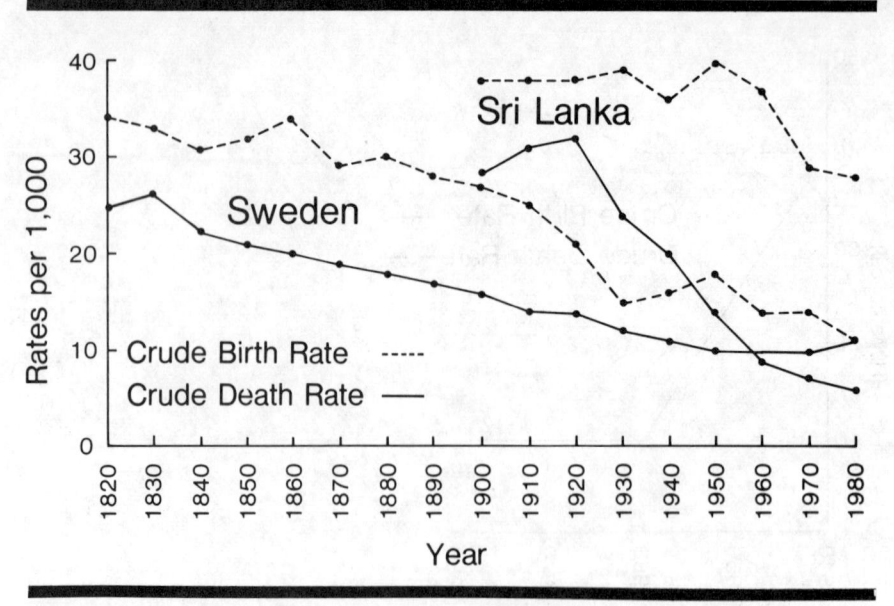

SOURCE: Based on data in E. G. Stockwell and K. A. Laidlaw, *Third World Development* (Chicago: Nelson-Hall, 1981), p. 80.

the gradual decline in the death rate meant that fertility decline was able to get under way *before* mortality reached its lowest levels, and this in turn meant that the rate of natural increase seldom exceeded 1½ percent a year. (A notable exception to this is the United States, whose very substantial transitional growth period is described in Chapter 10.) Today, however, the rapid and precipitous mortality declines that are possible frequently result in growth rates on the order of 3 to 3½ percent a year—rates that would lead to a doubling of population in about twenty years. So far, fertility in most of these areas has shown very little inclination to decline, and until it does they will continue to experience extremely rapid rates of population growth and all the problems that such rapid growth rates entail.

Let us take a more specific illustration. The contrast between the classical demographic transition that characterized the European population explosion and the growth pattern that has so far characterized the Third World population explosion is revealed dramatically in Figure 2-5, which compares birth and death rate trends for Sweden and Sri Lanka (formerly Ceylon). Here it can be seen that it took well over a hundred years for Sweden's death rate to decline from an annual level of 25 to 10 per 1,000. Most significantly, the slow pace of mortality decline meant that by the time the death rate had fallen below 20 per 1,000, the birth rate had also begun to decline. Thus, at no time during its transition did Sweden's annual rate of natural increase exceed 15 per 1,000 (or 1½ percent a year). In Sri Lanka, however, the death rate fell from about 25 to below 10 per 1,000 in less than thirty years, reaching this low level far in advance of any downward trend in fertility. Consequently, the rate of natural increase in Sri Lanka was between 25 and 30 a year until the most recent period when a slight fall in the birth rate reduced the annual growth rate to nearly 2 percent.

Further consideration of Figure 2-5 indicates that the traditional transition pattern may be undergoing still another modification. The fact that the birth rate in Sri Lanka has also started to decline in recent years (down 25 percent between 1960 and 1980) suggests that, as with mortality, the fertility transition *may* also take place more rapidly than it did in Sweden. A number of countries have in fact gone through the transition faster than was generally true for the industrial nations of Europe. That is, some countries have gone through an accelerated transition in which fairly rapid declines in mortality were followed shortly by equally rapid declines in the birth rate, facilitated by widespread reliance on induced abortion (Omran, 1977). Singapore, for example, was able to go through the fertility transition and close its demographic gap in a single generation. In 1955 Singapore had a birth rate of 45 per 1,000, and its population was increasing at an alarming rate of 3.7 percent a year. By 1978, however, the birth rate was down to 17 per 1,000 and the rate of population growth was only 1.2 percent.

The fact that some countries have been able to reduce their birth rates to a modern level in a fairly short period, thus avoiding an extended transitional growth phase such as that which characterized most Western European nations during the nineteenth century, may be taken as an encouraging sign with respect to the current demographic situation in other less developed nations. If all the poorer countries can undergo similar rapid fertility transitions, the future world population situation would look much less problematic. The possibility of such an accelerated transition in other Third World nations will be discussed more fully in Chapter 8. In the remainder of this chapter we will take a closer look at the present and projected growth situation in the major regions of the world.

REGIONAL GROWTH TRENDS

As we have noted, there are substantial differences in the nature and magnitude of the population growth patterns that characterize the major regions of the world. We will now examine these different growth patterns in more detail, paying particular attention to the current demographic situation and its implications for population growth during the remainder of this century.

Table 2-4
Population Growth Outlook for Africa, Early 1980s

Subregion and country	Population (in millions)	Crude birth rate	Crude death rate	Annual rate of growth (percent)	Projected population in 2000 (in millions)
AFRICA	498	46	17	2.9	847
Northern Africa	117	44	13	3.1	190
Algeria	20.1	46	14	3.2	36.3
Egypt	44.8	43	12	3.1	66.7
Libya	3.2	47	13	3.5	6.1
Morocco	22.3	45	14	3.2	37.5
Sudan	19.9	47	17	3.0	33.1
Tunisia	6.7	35	11	2.4	9.6
Western Africa	150	49	19	3.0	265
Benin	3.7	49	19	3.0	6.6
Cape Verde	0.3	29	8	2.1	0.4
Gambia	0.6	49	28	2.1	1.0
Ghana	12.4	48	17	3.1	21.5
Guinea	5.3	46	21	2.5	8.8
Guinea-Bissau	0.8	40	21	1.9	1.2
Ivory Coast	8.8	48	18	2.9	15.1
Liberia	2.0	50	20	3.0	3.8
Mali	7.1	52	24	2.8	12.2
Mauritania	1.7	50	22	2.8	3.0
Niger	5.8	51	22	2.9	10.4
Nigeria	82.3	50	18	3.2	149.7
Senegal	5.9	48	22	2.6	9.7
Sierra Leone	3.7	46	19	2.6	6.1
Togo	2.8	48	19	2.9	4.8
Upper Volta	6.7	48	22	2.6	10.9
Eastern Africa	141	48	18	3.0	246
Burundi	4.4	45	23	2.2	7.0
Comoros	0.4	44	14	3.0	0.6
Djibouti	0.5	49	22	2.6	0.7
Ethiopia	30.5	50	25	2.5	50.6
Kenya	17.9	53	14	3.9	35.4
Madagascar	9.2	45	18	2.7	15.2
Malawi	6.6	51	19	3.2	12.0
Mauritius	1.0	27	7	2.0	1.2
Mozambique	12.7	45	19	2.6	20.7
Réunion	0.5	25	7	1.8	0.7
Rwanda	5.4	50	19	3.0	9.5
Seychelles	0.1	28	7	2.1	0.1
Somalia	4.6	46	20	2.6	7.2
Tanzania	19.9	46	14	3.2	35.3
Uganda	13.7	48	16	3.2	23.9
Zambia	6.0	49	17	3.2	11.0
Zimbabwe	8.0	47	14	3.4	14.7

Table 2-4 (cont.)
Population Growth Outlook for Africa, Early 1980s

Subregion and country	Population (in millions)	Crude birth rate	Crude death rate	Annual rate of growth (percent)	Projected population in 2000 (in millions)
Middle Africa	56	46	20	2.6	90
Angola	6.8	48	23	2.4	11.3
Cameroon	8.9	45	20	2.5	13.8
Central African Republic	2.4	44	22	2.2	3.9
Chad	4.6	44	24	2.0	6.7
Congo	1.6	45	19	2.6	2.7
Equatorial Guinea	0.3	42	19	2.3	0.4
Gabon	0.7	34	22	1.2	0.9
Sao Tome and Principe	0.1	42	10	3.2	0.1
Zaire	30.3	46	19	2.8	50.5
Southern Africa	34	37	12	2.5	55
Botswana	0.9	51	18	3.3	1.6
Lesotho	1.4	40	16	2.4	2.2
Namibia	1.1	44	15	2.8	1.8
South Africa	30.0	36	12	2.4	48.9
Swaziland	0.6	48	19	2.8	1.0

SOURCE: Population Reference Bureau, *World Population Data Sheet, 1982* (Washington, D.C., 1982).

Africa

Considered overall, the African continent has been characterized by extremely high birth rates and moderately high but declining levels of mortality. This combination has produced a very high rate of population growth, and one that has steadily increased since the 1950s. At the beginning of the 1980s Africa, with a population of nearly 500 million, was the fastest growing region in the world. For the continent as a whole, numbers were increasing at an annual rate of 2.9 percent, a rate that would lead to a doubling of the population in a single generation. Morever, with only a few exceptions, growth rates of this magnitude were fairly commonplace. Of the fifty-three countries listed in Table 2-4, for example, nineteen were growing at rates of 3 percent or more, and another eighteen had growth rates between 2½ and 3 percent a year. Only three countries (Guinea-Bissau, Réunion, and Gabon), constituting a very small fraction of the African population, had growth rates of less than 2 percent a year, and of these only Gabon was increasing at a rate below 1½ percent.

Closer examination of the data in Table 2-4 reveals that these large rates of population growth are due to the widespread prevalence of extraordinar-

Figure 2-6
Growth Rate Trends since 1950

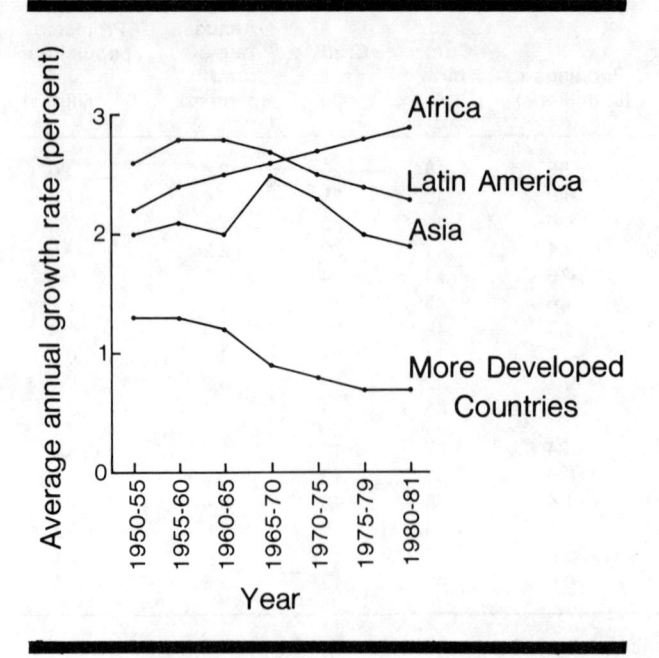

[Figure: Line graph showing average annual growth rate (percent) by year (1950-55 through 1980-81) for Africa, Latin America, Asia, and More Developed Countries]

SOURCE: Based on data in U.S. Bureau of the Census, *World Population—1979: Recent Demographic Estimates for the Countries and Regions of the World* (Washington, D.C., 1980). Data for 1980–81 taken from *1981 World Population Data Sheet* (Washington, D.C.: Population Reference Bureau, 1981).

ily high birth rates. All but seven of the fifty-three countries listed had preindustrial level birth rates in excess of 40 per 1,000; and in ten countries—including two of the most populous nations, Ethiopia and Nigeria—crude birth rates were as high as 50 per 1,000. The highest birth rate in Africa, or anywhere in the world for that matter, was found in Kenya (53 per 1,000). This very high birth rate was combined with a relatively low death rate so that in the early 1980s the 18 million or so inhabitants of Kenya were increasing at the unprecedented rate of 3.9 percent a year.

Although African population growth rates are the highest in the world, there is a very real possibility that they could go even higher. Although mortality has been declining slowly, many of the countries in this region are still experiencing fairly high death rates, along with their unusually high birth rates; and concerted efforts are generally well under way in most areas to bring mortality levels under still greater control. By contrast, official concern over high birth rates has been very slow to develop. In part this is because many of the countries are "new nations," having just emerged from colonial status within the past decade or two. The governments of such countries may be more concerned with the enhancement of their national identity than with problems of population growth, and in fact they may even look on high fertility and rapid population growth as a positive sign of national development. The apparent lack of concern over high birth rates is also in part a reflection of a belief that is prevalent in many less developed countries: the belief that only rapid social and economic development financed in large measure by massive foreign aid can create the conditions needed to bring about a decline in fertility.

For whatever reason, relatively little attention has so far been devoted to fertility control in Africa. On the contrary, as we entered the 1980s the

Figure 2-7
Crude Birth and Death Rates in Major World Subregions, 1980

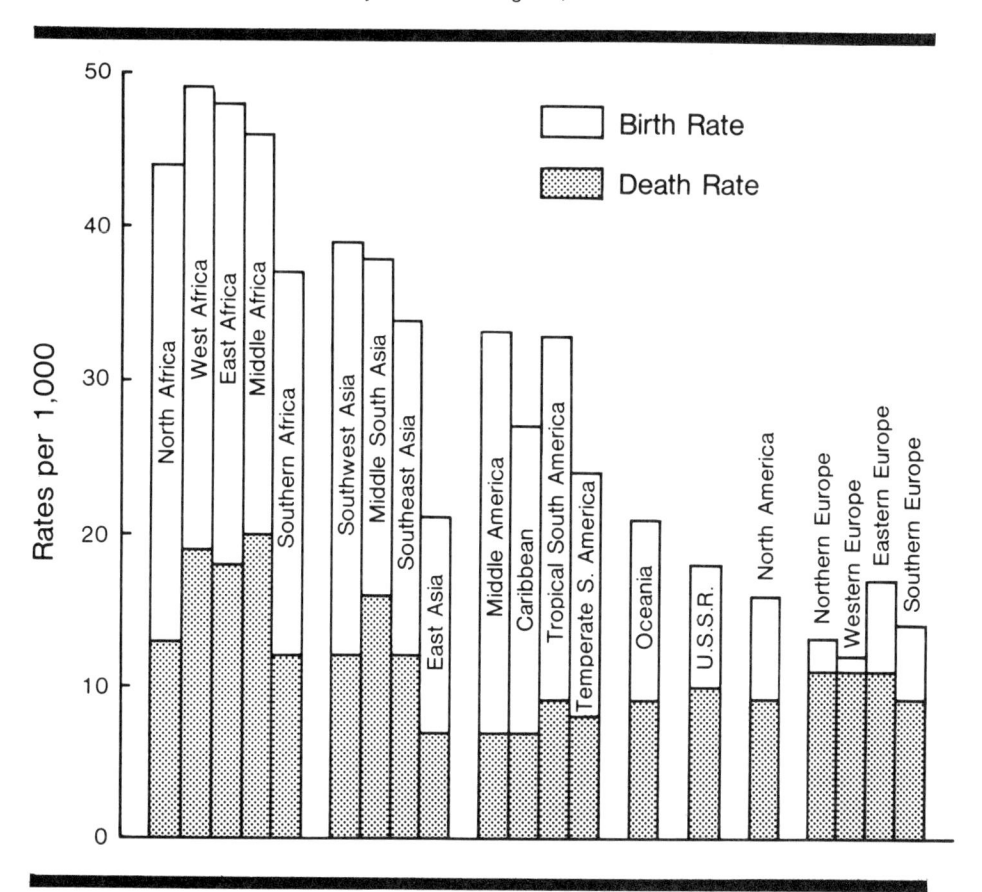

SOURCE: See Figure 2-6.

vast majority of African countries perceived the prevailing birth rates as either satisfactory or too low; and only a small minority of countries (fewer than one-fourth) had adopted policy measures designed to encourage a reduction in fertility (United Nations, 1980a). If this lack of concerted action persists, and if ongoing efforts to reduce mortality further succeed in the face of continuing high birth rates, then population growth rates cannot help but go up. Thus, it is well within the realm of possibility that many African countries will, like Kenya, experience growth rates approaching the unprecedented level of 4 percent a year during the 1980s.

Whether or not such extraordinarily high growth rates do emerge remains to be seen. What is certain, however, is that the population of Africa and of the vast majority of the African nations will continue to experience substantial increases throughout the remainder of this century. By the year 2000, for example, projections prepared by the United Nations indicate there could be as many as 847 million people living on the continent, representing a 70 percent increase over the number estimated in the early 1980s. Projected growth trends will be somewhat less for Northern, Middle and South Africa where an increase of 61 to 62 percent is forecast. In East and West Africa, however, the projected gains are 74 and 77 percent. The West African nation of Nigeria, which has the largest population of any country in Africa, and the East African nation of Kenya, which has the fastest growing population, have projected population gains by the year 2000 amounting to 82 and 98 percent. Clearly, the issue of population growth and related problems will dominate much of the African experience during the remaining years of the twentieth century.

Asia

Asia is the slowest growing region of the less developed world. Its annual rate of population growth appears to have peaked at about 2½ percent in the middle to late 1960s, after which it underwent a moderate decline. In the early 1980s the Asian population was increasing at a rate of only 1.9 percent a year, compared with annual growth rates of 2.3 and 2.9 percent respectively in Latin America and Africa. However, Asia contains over half of the world's population—2.7 billion in 1982; hence, even its relatively moderate rate of increase ensures the addition of substantial numbers to the world's total. For the region as a whole the population is increasing by roughly 50 million persons each year, and it is expected to surpass 3½ billion before the end of the twentieth century.

Population growth rates are lower in Asia than in either Africa or Latin America largely because government efforts have brought fertility under better control (Population Reference Bureau, 1976). Numerous national development programs were initiated throughout Asia during the 1960s, and many of them have been very successful. However, rapid rates of population growth often prevented the realization of any increases in average levels of living that should have accompanied these development programs, and the leaders of many countries became increasingly concerned with the problem of population growth. Reflecting this concern, national family planning programs, public and privately sponsored, were established throughout the region, and several countries (e.g., Singapore, Indonesia, Thailand, Taiwan, South Korea, and the People's Republic of China) have made substantial progress in reducing fertility and closing the demographic gap between birth and death rates that had opened so rapidly in the decade following the end of World War II. For the area as a whole, the years since 1960 have seen the crude birth rate drop from nearly 40 per 1,000 down to 30 per 1,000. The rate of population growth has also fallen, from 2½ percent a year during the 1960s to its most recent level of 1.9 percent.

It is important to note that not all Asian countries have made progress in reducing their fertility, and many of them are still characterized by annual rates of population growth of 3 percent or more (see Table 2-5). With few exceptions, major fertility declines have been limited to East Asia where the overall growth rate for the area as a whole is only 1.4 percent a year, and where only two countries—North Korea and Mongolia—still have birth rates in excess of 30 per 1,000. Since the countries in this region contain 45 percent of the population of Asia (the People's Republic of China accounts for 37 percent), they have a disproportionate impact on the total population situation and make it look less problematic than it really is. Outside this part of Asia, for example, only five major countries have crude birth rates of less than 30 per 1,000 (Cyprus, Israel, Sri Lanka, Singapore, and Thailand); and only three of these—Cyprus, Israel, and Singapore—have fertility under sufficient control so that population is growing at rates of less than 2 percent a year. Two other countries have annual population growth rates below 2 percent (Democratic Kampuchea and Indonesia), but in both of these nations the lower growth rate results from above average birth rates being partially offset by the persistence of fairly high death rates.

At the other extreme, levels of fertility and population growth rates are highest in Southwest Asia, especially among Islamic countries where crude birth rates are generally in the high 40s and where growth rates continue to remain at levels of 3 to 3½ percent a year. Population growth in this part of the world is of concern not only for economic reasons but also because of the political climate of recent years. While population by itself is certainly not the cause of this very complex situation, the persistence of rapid growth rates is not likely to contribute to any easing of the international tensions and political instability that exist in this part of the world.

Somewhat more moderate growth rates characterize the countries of Southeast Asia and Middle South Asia, but even these moderate rates (2.2 percent a year) are much higher than the overall rate of 1.4 percent in East

Table 2-5
Population Growth Outlook for Asia, Early 1980s

Subregion and country	Population (in millions)	Crude birth rate	Crude death rate	Annual rate of growth (percent)	Projected population in 2000 (in millions)
ASIA	2,671	30	11	1.9	3,528
Southwest Asia	**106**	**39**	**12**	**2.7**	**171**
Bahrain	0.4	37	8	2.8	0.7
Cyprus	0.6	22	9	1.2	0.7
Gaza	0.5	51	14	3.7	0.7
Iraq	14.0	47	13	3.4	24.2
Israel	4.1	24	7	1.7	5.6
Jordan	3.5	47	10	3.6	6.5
Kuwait	1.5	42	5	3.7	2.9
Lebanon	2.7	30	9	2.1	4.0
Oman	0.9	49	19	3.0	1.7
Qatar	0.3	37	10	2.8	0.4
Saudi Arabia	11.1	46	14	3.2	20.5
Syria	9.7	46	9	3.8	18.7
Turkey	47.7	33	10	2.2	70.7
United Arab Emirates	1.2	30	7	2.3	1.9
Yemen, North	5.5	49	24	2.4	8.8
Yemen, South	2.0	48	21	2.7	3.4
Middle South Asia	**988**	**38**	**16**	**2.2**	**1,396**
Afghanistan	15.1	48	23	2.5	26.5
Bangladesh	93.3	47	19	2.8	149.2
Bhutan	1.4	43	21	2.2	2.0
India	713.8	35	15	2.0	967.6
Iran	41.2	44	14	3.1	66.5
Maldives	0.2	47	14	3.1	0.3
Nepal	14.5	44	21	2.3	20.7
Pakistan	93.0	44	16	2.8	142.7
Sri Lanka	15.2	29	7	2.2	20.9
Southeast Asia	**374**	**34**	**12**	**2.2**	**519**
Brunei	0.2	28	4	2.4	0.4
Burma	37.1	39	14	2.4	55.1
Democratic Kampuchea	6.1	38	19	1.9	9.2
East Timor	0.5	44	21	2.3	0.7
Indonesia	151.3	34	16	1.7	197.1
Laos	3.7	44	20	2.4	5.5
Malaysia	14.7	30	7	2.4	21.3
Philippines	51.6	34	8	2.6	77.3
Singapore	2.5	17	5	1.2	3.0
Thailand	49.8	28	7	2.1	69.9
Vietnam	56.6	37	9	2.8	80.0

Table 2-5 (cont.)
Population Growth Outlook for Asia, Early 1980s

Subregion and country	Population (in millions)	Crude birth rate	Crude death rate	Annual rate of growth (percent)	Projected population in 2000 (in millions)
East Asia	**1,204**	**21**	**7**	**1.4**	**1,441**
China (PRC)	1,000	22	7	1.4	1,200
Hong Kong	5.0	17	5	1.2	6.6
Japan	118.6	14	6	0.8	126.4
Korea, North	18.7	32	8	2.4	27.3
Korea, South	41.1	19	5	1.4	52.8
Macao	0.3	28	8	2.0	0.4
Mongolia	1.8	38	9	2.9	2.7
Taiwan	18.5	23	5	1.8	24.6

SOURCE: See Table 2-4.

Asia. Moreover, some of the largest and poorest populations of the world are found in these regions. India, Bangladesh, and Pakistan, for example, all have massive populations living in poverty, and all are increasing at an annual rate of 2 percent or more.

The Asian population growth situation can be summed up as follows: (1) relatively slow growth rates characteize East Asia, but a very large base population will yield substantial numerical gains in the years immediately ahead; (2) moderate growth rates prevail in Southeast and Middle South Asia, but some of the largest and poorest populations of the world are found in these subregions; and (3) fairly rapid growth rates characterize the Islamic societies of Southwest Asia where they are likely to be a major force aggravating both the economic poverty and political instability of the area. Thus, despite the overall slower growth rate in Asia, as compared with Latin America and Africa, it is clear that population will continue to pose significant problems in this part of the world in the foreseeable future.

Latin America

In the two decades following the end of the Second World War, Latin America was the fastest growing region of the world. In more recent years, however, fertility reductions in a number of the larger countries—notably Brazil, Colombia, and Mexico—have led to a decline in the overall growth rate; as we entered the final two decades of the century, the region as a whole

Table 2-6
Population Growth Outlook for Latin America, Early 1980s

Subregion and country	Population (in millions)	Crude birth rate	Crude death rate	Annual rate of growth (percent)	Projected population in 2000 (in millions)
LATIN AMERICA	378	32	8	2.3	549
Central America	95	33	7	2.6	142
Belize	0.2	40	12	2.8	0.3
Costa Rica	2.3	29	4	2.5	3.4
El Salvador	5.0	35	8	2.7	8.6
Guatemala	7.7	42	10	3.2	12.7
Honduras	4.0	47	12	3.5	7.0
Mexico	71.3	32	6	2.5	102.3
Nicaragua	2.6	47	12	3.4	4.6
Panama	1.9	27	6	2.1	2.7
Caribbean	30	27	7	1.8	41
Antigua and Barbuda	0.1	16	6	1.1	0.1
Bahamas	0.2	22	5	1.7	0.3
Barbados	0.3	17	8	0.8	0.3
Cuba	9.8	14	6	0.8	12.3
Dominica	0.1	21	5	1.6	0.1
Dominican Republic	5.7	37	9	2.8	8.6
Grenada	0.1	24	7	1.8	0.1
Guadeloupe	0.3	19	6	1.3	0.3
Haiti	6.1	42	16	2.6	9.4
Jamaica	2.2	27	6	2.1	2.9
Martinique	0.3	23	7	1.6	0.3

was characterized by a moderately high fertility and low mortality, and an annual rate of population growth that fell between those of Asia and Africa.

As in Asia, there is a great deal of variation in the pattern of population growth throughout the region (see Table 2-6). At one extreme a relatively modern demographic situation exists in the three countries of Temperate South America, where the subregion as a whole is growing at a fairly moderate rate of 1.5 percent a year. The annual growth rate is somewhat higher in the Caribbean area (1.8 percent), but the countries in this subregion contain less than 10 percent of the Latin American population and the projected increases for the remainder of the century amount to less than 12 million persons. Moreover, with few exceptions—most notably Haiti and the Dominican Republic—the several island nations in this area are characterized by a relatively modern demographic balance between relatively low birth and death rates; and in a few nations (Antigua and Barbuda, Barbados, Cuba, and Guadeloupe) the birth rates are at levels comparable to

Table 2-6 (cont.)
Population Growth Outlook for Latin America, Early 1980s

Subregion and country	Population (in millions)	Crude birth rate	Crude death rate	Annual rate of growth (percent)	Projected population in 2000 (in millions)
Netherlands Antilles	0.2	29	7	2.2	0.3
Puerto Rico	3.3	23	6	1.7	4.1
St. Lucia	0.1	32	7	2.4	0.2
St. Vincent and the Grenadines	0.1	35	7	2.8	0.2
Trinidad and Tobago	1.1	25	6	1.9	1.4
Tropical South America	**209**	**33**	**9**	**2.4**	**313**
Bolivia	5.6	45	18	2.7	9.3
Brazil	127.7	32	9	2.4	186.7
Colombia	25.6	28	8	2.0	36.3
Ecuador	8.5	42	10	3.1	14.6
Guyana	0.9	28	7	2.1	1.2
Paraguay	3.3	34	7	2.6	5.4
Peru	18.6	38	11	2.8	30.7
Surinam	0.4	28	8	2.0	0.6
Venezuela	18.4	34	5	2.9	28.3
Temperate South America	**43**	**24**	**8**	**1.5**	**53**
Argentina	28.6	25	9	1.6	34.3
Chile	11.5	22	7	1.5	14.9
Uruguay	3.0	19	11	0.8	3.4

SOURCE: See Table 2-4.

those commonly found throughout the more developed countries. The moderately high growth rates that still prevail in many of the Caribbean nations are mainly due to the very low death rates that have recently emerged. In part, these crude death rates are artificially low because of the relatively young age composition of the population, but if the current low birth rates persist, one can expect an increase in the overall age composition. This aging process will in turn lead to an increase in crude death rates and corresponding declines in the rates of population growth.

At the other extreme, fairly high fertility levels and rapid rates of population growth characterize most of the countries in Tropical South America and especially in Central America. These two subregions together comprise 80 percent of the population of Latin America, and if present trends continue, they will contribute another 150 million people to the region by the end of the century.

Central America has consistently had the highest rates of population

Table 2-7
Population Growth Outlook for the Developed Countries, Early 1980s

Subregion and country	Population (in millions)	Crude birth rate	Crude death rate	Annual rate of growth (percent)	Projected population in 2000 (in millions)
NORTH AMERICA	**256**	**16**	**9**	**0.7**	**286**
Canada	24.4	16	7	0.8	26.9
United States	232.0	16	9	0.7	259.0
EUROPE	**488**	**14**	**10**	**0.4**	**511**
Northern Europe	**82**	**13**	**11**	**0.2**	**84**
Denmark	5.1	11	11	0.0	5.1
Finland	4.8	13	9	0.4	4.9
Iceland	0.2	20	7	1.4	0.3
Ireland	3.5	22	10	1.2	4.1
Norway	4.1	12	10	0.2	4.1
Sweden	8.3	12	11	0.1	8.0
United Kingdom	56.1	14	12	0.2	57.1
Western Europe	**154**	**12**	**11**	**0.2**	**155**
Austria	7.6	12	12	0.0	7.3
Belgium	9.9	13	12	0.1	9.9
France	54.2	15	10	0.5	56.4
Germany, West	61.7	10	12	−0.2	59.9
Luxembourg	0.4	12	12	0.0	0.3
Netherlands	14.3	13	8	0.5	14.9
Switzerland	6.3	12	9	0.2	6.2
Eastern Europe	**111**	**17**	**11**	**0.6**	**120**
Bulgaria	8.9	14	11	0.4	9.5
Czechoslovakia	15.4	16	12	0.4	16.6
Germany, East	16.7	15	14	0.0	16.8

growth in Latin America, and despite some notable fertility declines in recent years (in Costa Rica, Mexico, and Panama) it is still the fastest growing subregion. With the exception of Panama, all the countries in this area are increasing at annual rates of 2.5 percent or more, and Guatemala, Honduras, and Nicaragua are all growing at rates in excess of 3 percent a year. The subregion as a whole is growing at an annual rate of 2.6 percent, and its population is expected to increase by 45 percent by the year 2000. In this part of the world, much as in the Islamic societies of the Middle East, the rapid rates of population growth projected for the remainder of this century could exacerbate the widespread poverty and increasing political instability that characterized this subregion in the early 1980s.

Table 2-7 (cont.)
Population Growth Outlook for the Developed Countries, Early 1980s

Subregion and country	Population (in millions)	Crude birth rate	Crude death rate	Annual rate of growth (percent)	Projected population in 2000 (in millions)
Hungary	10.7	14	14	0.0	10.9
Poland	36.3	20	10	1.0	40.9
Romania	22.6	19	10	0.9	25.6
Southern Europe	**141**	**14**	**9**	**0.5**	**152**
Albania	2.8	29	7	2.2	3.9
Greece	9.3	16	9	0.7	10.6
Italy	57.4	11	10	0.2	57.4
Malta	0.4	15	9	0.6	0.4
Portugal	9.9	16	9	0.7	11.2
Spain	37.9	15	8	0.7	43.3
Yugoslavia	22.6	17	9	0.8	25.1
USSR	**270**	**18**	**10**	**0.8**	**302**
OCEANIA	**24**	**21**	**9**	**1.3**	**30**
Australia	15.0	15	7	0.8	18.0
Fiji	0.7	30	4	2.6	0.8
French Polynesia	0.2	30	7	2.3	0.2
New Zealand	3.1	17	8	0.9	3.8
Papua-New Guinea	3.3	44	16	2.8	5.2
Samoa, Western	0.2	37	7	3.0	0.2
Solomon Islands	0.2	44	9	3.5	0.4
Vanuatu	0.1	45	17	2.8	0.2

SOURCE: See Table 2-4.

The Developed Countries

The more developed countries of the Western world, most of which completed their demographic transition early in the present century, have consistently had the slowest rates of population growth throughout the postwar period. Moreover, the general trend since the late 1950s has been for population growth rates to decline even further. For all these countries taken together the overall average growth rate has declined from 1.3 percent a year between 1950 and 1955 to only 0.6 percent at the most recent date. The explanation for this latest decline is twofold. First, there has been a resumption of the long-term downward trend in fertility that was halted temporarily by the postwar baby boom; and crude birth rates throughout the developed regions are at an unprecedented low level. Indeed, in many countries current fertility rates are well below the replacement level. Second, the aging of the population that has accompanied the further declines in fertility has led to a slight increase in the crude death rate. As a consequence of these two trends, several countries are fast approaching a state of perfect demographic balance and a zero growth rate.

Among the several more developed subregions, population is growing most slowly in Europe, especially in Northern and Western Europe where overall annual growth rates are only 0.2 percent (see Table 2-7). All but two of the fourteen countries in these subregions are growing at annual rates of half of 1 percent or less; and in four countries—Austria, Denmark, Luxembourg, and West Germany—the population is either at or slightly below the zero growth point. The two remaining countries, Ireland and Iceland, have growth rates of 1.2 and 1.4 percent a year.

Overall annual growth rates are somewhat higher in Southern and Eastern Europe, but even here annual growth rates are less than half of 1 percent in five out of thirteen countries, and 1.0 percent or less in all but one of the remaining countries. Albania, which is the least developed of all the European countries, is still characterized by a relatively high level of fertility and a population growth rate of 2.2 percent a year.

The other more developed subregions include Canada, the United States, and the USSR, all of which are growing at rates of 0.7 to 0.8 percent a year, and Oceania, which has an overall annual growth rate of 1.3 percent. Except for Australia and New Zealand, which have population growth rates of 0.8 and 0.9 percent a year, the countries of this subregion do not really belong in the more developed category; they are included here because they represent less than 25 percent of the subregion's population.

SUMMARY

The human population increased extremely slowly throughout most of its existence, but ever since the beginnings of the modern era in the seventeenth century the growth rate has been accelerating. For the world as a whole, the rate of population growth rose gradually from the nearly stationary level that had prevailed prior to 1650 to an all-time high of 2 percent a year during the late 1950s and 1960s. During the years since then, however, it has declined slightly to a level of 1.7 percent in the early 1980s. Even at this rate, however, world population is increasing by nearly 80 million people each year, and the number of people living on this planet is expected to exceed 6 billion by the end of the twentieth century and be more than 8 billion a generation later.

Population growth in the past did not occur at the same pace throughout all areas of the world, nor will future growth be evenly distributed. Growth rates began to accelerate during the eighteenth century in the now developed countries of Europe and in the overseas European settlements. The increase in the growth rate of these countries was due to the onset of mortality decline and a gradual widening of the gap between the annual number of births and deaths. During the nineteenth century, fertility also started to decline, closing the gap between birth and death rates; and by the second or third decade of the present century this demographic transition had been completed throughout the European world, and population growth rates had been sharply curtailed. However, while growth rates reached modern low levels in the more developed regions, they were increasing throughout the rest of the world, and they have been increasing at especially rapid rates since the end of the Second World War. On the one hand, death control came much later to the less developed countries of the Third World, but once death rates started to fall they fell very rapidly. Fertility, on the other hand, has remained at traditional high levels throughout much of Asia, Africa, and Latin America; and this very wide gap between birth and death rates has generated unprecedented rates of population growth throughout these regions.

Today the more developed countries as a whole are increasing at a relatively modest rate of 0.6 percent a year, and many countries in this group are moving close to zero population growth. Among the less developed regions, however, population is growing at an annual rate of 2.1 percent, and in many countries, particularly in Africa and Southwest Asia, population growth rates are in excess of 3 percent a year. Such rates will lead to a doubling of population within a single generation.

These different growth rates have substantially altered the distribution of world population, and they will continue to do so in the years to come. In the late 1950s, when increasing attention began to be focused on problems of population and development in the Third World, it was commonly said that two-thirds of the world lived in the less developed countries. Today we can speak of three-fourths of the world; and, given the present and projected growth trends, by the end of the century we will be able to speak about four-fifths of the world's people living in the less developed areas of Asia, Africa, and Latin America. In Chapter 8 we will examine some problems likely to be associated with population growth throughout the Third World. First, however, we will turn our attention to a discussion of the basic demographic processes of birth and death.

REFERENCES AND SUGGESTED READING

Davis, Kingsley. "The World Demographic Transition." *Annals of the American Academy of Political and Social Science*, 237 (January 1945): 1–11.

Finkle, Jason L., and Barbara B. Crane. "The Politics of Bucharest: Population, Development, and the New International Economic Order." *Population and Development Review*, 1 (September 1975). A copy of the World Population Plan of Action adopted at the 1974 World Population Conference is reprinted on pp. 163–81 of this issue.

McKeown, Thomas. *The Modern Rise of Population*. New York: Academic Press, 1976.

Omran, Abdel R. "Epidemiologic Transition in the U.S." *Population Bulletin*, 32 (May 1977).

Population Reference Bureau. "How Many People Have Ever Lived on Earth?" *Population Bulletin*, 28 (February 1962): 1–19.

Population Reference Bureau. *World Population Growth and Response: 1965–1975, A Decade of Global Action*. Washington, D.C., 1976.

Stockwell, Edward G. "Population Growth and Fertility Control in the Third World: A Critical Appraisal." *International Review of Modern Sociology*, 10 (July–December 1980): 177–86.

Stockwell, Edward G., and Karen A. Laidlaw. *Third World Development: Problems and Prospects*. Chicago: Nelson-Hall, 1981, Chapter 3.

Tabbarah, Riad B. "Toward a Theory of Demographic Development." *Economic Development and Cultural Change*, 19 (January 1971): 257–76.

United Nations. *The Determinants and Consequences of Population Trends*, Vol. I. New York, 1973.

United Nations. *World Population Trends and Policies: 1979 Monitoring Report*, Vol. II. *Population Policies*. New York, 1980a.

United Nations. *Concise Report on the World Population Situation in 1979*. New York, 1980b.

U.S. Bureau of the Census. *World Population 1979, Summary—Recent Demographic Estimates for the Countries and Regions of the World*. Washington, D.C., 1980.

U.S. Bureau of the Census. *Demographic Estimates for Countries with a Population of 10 Million or More: 1981*. Washington, D.C., 1981.

Weeks, John R. *Population: An Introduction to Concepts and Issues*, 2nd ed. Belmont, Calif.: Wadsworth, 1981, Chapter 3.

Weller, Robert H., and Leon F. Bouvier. *Population: Demography and Policy*. New York: St. Martin's, 1981, Chapter 2.

Wendorf, Fred, Romuald Schild, and Angela E. Close. "An Ancient Harvest on the Nile." *Science '82* (November 1982): 68–73.

MORTALITY LEVELS AND TRENDS

3

We shall begin our discussion of the basic demographic processes with a consideration of mortality, or death. There are several reasons for choosing to focus on death first. First, mortality is a much simpler concept than either fertility or migration. Although death is not an entirely unambiguous state, there are relatively few problems of definition associated with it, whereas there may be numerous difficulties in defining birth or migration. Second, the problem of individual motivation hardly needs to be considered in analyzing the question of why people die. Questions of motivation may well be an issue when someone commits suicide or when one person takes the life of another (e.g., infanticide, homicide, human sacrifice, capital punishment), but death is generally an inevitable biological event that all of us will have to experience at some point, whether we like it or not. Fertility and migration are not necessarily inevitable, however, and motivation becomes a crucial factor in regard to the question of why people move and, albeit to a lesser extent the question of why women have babies. The latter question is simple enough on one level of analysis: women have babies because fertility is necessary for the continued survival of any species. Nevertheless, motivation is an important variable in that, assuming no physiological limitations, whether or not a given human couple produces offspring and the number they produce can largely be a matter of their own choice.

The third and by far the most important reason for starting with mortality is that the changes in this vital process have had the most profound impact on the demographic history of the human population. By far the most significant demographic development experienced by our species is the tremendous increase in numbers over the past two or three centuries; and, as we have seen, it was not a rise in fertility but a decline in the death rate that played the major role in bringing about the unprecedented numerical increase that is popularly referred to as the population explosion. Moreover, in contrast to the more highly developed industrial nations, many areas in the world today are still characterized by fairly high death rates. In the years ahead, as present worldwide development efforts continue, mortality declines in these high-death-rate countries can be expected to produce increases in rates of population growth that will contribute even more to the overall size of the human population.

DEFINITIONS AND CONCEPTS

Adequate study of mortality, or of any demographic process, requires the collection and compilation of statistical data pertaining to the basic variables and concepts. As a first step, then, it is necessary to provide formal definitions for some of the basic concepts. In general, death is easy to define, although recent developments in medical technology have sometimes led to situations wherein the distinction between life and death is unclear (as when it is possible to keep the heart and respiratory organs functioning with the aid of a life support system long after brain death has occurred). According to the World Health Organization of the United Nations, death is simply the permanent disappearance of life at any time after birth (Shryock et al., 1976, p. 221). Any problems in this definition of death are likely to be associated with the definition of a live birth. Again the World Health Organization suggests that a live birth be defined as "the complete expulsion or extraction from its mother of a product of conception, irrespective of the duration of pregnancy, which, after such separation, breathes or shows any other evidence of life, such as beating of the heart, pulsation of the umbilical cord, or definite movement of voluntary muscles" (Shryock et al., 1976, p. 273). Fetal deaths (e.g., stillbirths, miscarriages, abortions) are excluded from the above definition of death because they represent the disappearance of life *prior* to the expulsion or extraction from its mother of a product of conception.

Length of Life

In discussing the length of life, or longevity, of human populations, it is necessary to distinguish between two important terms: *life span* and *life expectancy*. The life span is the maximum age to which human beings are capable of surviving, whereas life expectancy is the number of years that the members of a given population will live, *on the average*. Looked at from a slightly different perspective, life expectancy can be defined as the average age at death in a population. As such it is a useful measure of the comparative health and mortality levels of different societies.

Life span is basically a biological variable, the limits to which are set by the physical durability of the human organism. Although one occasionally hears of persons who claim to be 120 or 130 years old, there is pretty good evidence to suggest that most such claims are greatly exaggerated (Meyers, 1978), and that the life span today, as measured by the oldest authenticated age to which a person has survived, would be no more than 115 years. Even this figure is somewhat unrealistic. Very few people today survive beyond the age of 100; thus, for all practical purposes, the normal human life span can be placed at 95 to 100 years.

There is no hard evidence to indicate that the life span has changed very much in the modern era or that it varies significantly from one level of societal development to another. Life expectancy, on the other hand, is in many respects a social variable. The age to which any individual survives will of course be partly influenced by the genetic characteristics with which he or she is born, but it will also be very much influenced by the general socioeconomic conditions under which a person is born and lives. This is clearly revealed both by the dramatic increases in life expectancy that have accompanied the economic growth and development of any society (e.g., in the United States the average length of life has risen from 47 in 1900 to more than 73 by 1980), and by the marked differences that characterize populations living at different stages of development in the world today. To illustrate, recent estimates show that in many of the poorer countries of Africa average life expectancy is still as low as or even lower than that which prevailed in the United States at the beginning of the century.

Cause of Death

In order to describe adequately as well as understand fully the mortality situation characterizing any population it is necessary to consider the causes from which people die. Generally speaking, the various causes that ultimately lead to death can be grouped into two broad categories: (1) *endogenous causes*—those that reflect some sort of degeneration or physiological deterioration of the body (e.g., heart disease, cancer, and diabetes), and (2) *exogeneous causes*—those that arise from purely environmental or external causes and that may result either from viral or bacterial infection (influenza, pneumonia, tuberculosis, diphtheria, typhoid fever, etc.) or from physical trauma (e.g., accidents, suicides, and homicides). The significance of including cause of death in any discussion of mortality lies in the fact that group differences in overall levels of mortality, both past and present, reflect the differential incidence of particular causes of death, and that different control measures are required to modify the killing force of the different causes.

Measuring Mortality

Before moving on to a more substantive discussion of mortality trends and differentials it is necessary to define more specifically two of the technical terms that we will use.

First, unless otherwise specified the term "death rate" will refer to the *crude death rate*, which is the number of deaths occurring in a given population during a calendar year per 1,000 people in the population. For example, in 1980 the crude death rate of the American population was about 9: this means that in 1980 there were 9 deaths for every 1,000 people in the United States. Compared with death rates of 20 or more per 1,000 population in some African countries, this clearly illustrates the relatively low mortality level that is characteristic of the United States and other modern Western nations.

The second common measure of the mortality level characterizing any population is the *infant mortality rate*—the number of deaths of infants under one year of age in a calendar year per 1,000 live births in that year. In the world as a whole, the estimated infant mortality rate in the early 1980s was around 95, which means that 95 out of every 1,000 babies died before reaching one year of age. The infant mortality rate is an especially useful measure for comparing the relative mortality levels of different populations both because it is especially sensitive to differences in social and economic well-being, and because it is not affected by other variables (e.g., age composition) that could have a major influence on the crude death rate.

Readers who wish to learn more about basic demographic measuring techniques should consult Appendix B. For the most part, however, a general familiarity with the simple measures just described as well as the concept of average life expectancy discussed earlier will be sufficient to enable the reader to understand fully the more substantive discussion of mortality in this and Chapter 4. We shall begin the discussion in this chapter with a general description and analysis of the level of mortality that has historically characterized human populations. Then we will examine the general trends in mortality during the modern era, in both the industrialized Western nations, particularly the United States, and in the less developed countries. In the following chapter, attention will focus on a discussion of some of the more important differences in mortality that can be found in most human populations.

MORTALITY CONDITIONS THROUGHOUT HISTORY

Although precise statistical evidence is lacking, the little that scientists have been able to compile from various anthropological and archaeological sources indicates that throughout most of its existence the human population has had to contend with an extremely high death rate. The brutally harsh conditions of life in the pre-industrial world made survival very much a touch-and-go affair. A newborn infant had no more than a fifty-fifty chance of surviving to adulthood; and the large proportion of deaths in infancy and childhood resulted in very low life expectancy. Although some of our primitive ancestors may have attained extreme old age, the *average* life expectancy was probably not much in excess of twenty-five or thirty years, and in some places it was substantially lower (see Table 3-1). The survival situation was not a great deal better even as recently as the middle of the eighteenth century. Early records for the state of Massachusetts, for example, indicate that average life expectancy in colonial America was still somewhat less than forty years.

The mortality situation in the Western world has changed markedly since then. Sweden, which is often cited because it was one of the earliest countries to establish birth and death registration, is illustrative of the gen-

Table 3-1
Estimated Average Life Expectancy in the Past

Population	Average life expectancy at birth (in years)
Ancient Rome	15–16
Gaul	21–23
Ancient Egypt	29
Medieval England	
Before 1276	35
1426–1450	33
France, mid-1600s	27–37
Massachusetts and New Hampshire, late 1900s	36

SOURCES: J. C. Russell, *Late Ancient and Medieval Population* (Philadelphia: American Philosophical Society, 1958); and Louis I. Dublin et. al., *Length of Life* (New York: Ronald Press, 1949).

Figure 3-1
Crude Death Rate Trends in Sweden, 1750–1980

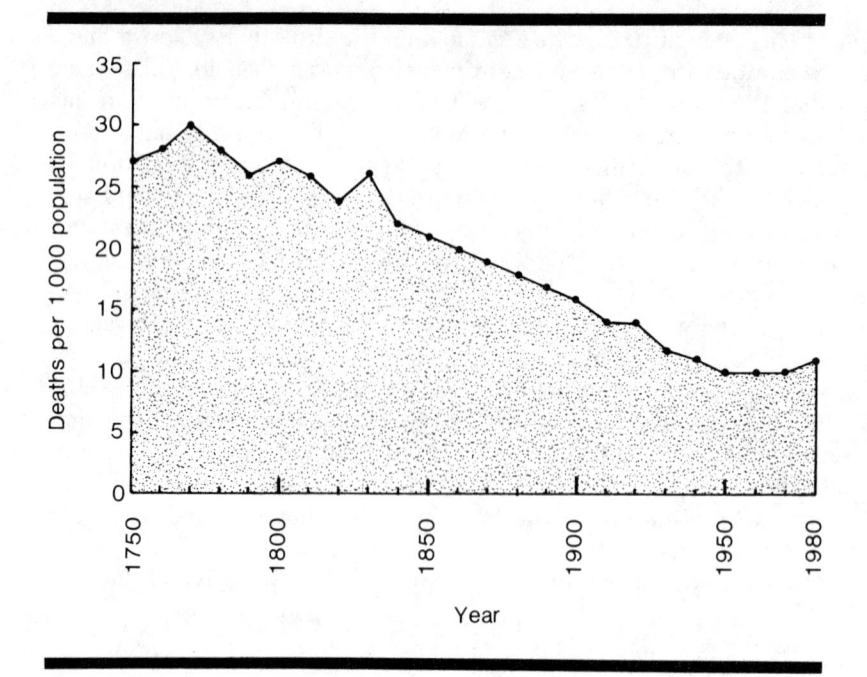

SOURCE: Based on data in Thomas McKeown, *The Modern Rise of Population* (New York: Academic Press, 1976), p. 28; E. G. Stockwell and K. A. Laidlaw, *Third World Development* (Chicago: Nelson Hall, 1981), p. 80; and Population Reference Bureau, *1983 World Population Data Sheet* (April 1983).

eral trend. Death rates in Sweden fluctuated at a fairly high level until the early decades of the nineteenth century, declined slowly but consistently over the next hundred years or so, and then gradually stabilized at their present low levels (see Figure 3-1). Today, the modern urban-industrial nations of the world are characterized by average life expectancies of anywhere from seventy to seventy-five years or more. This pronounced increase in life expectancy represents a radical departure from the situation that has prevailed throughout most of human history, and it is obvious that some very startling changes in the social and physical world must have occurred in order to bring it about. These changes and the impact they have had on the chances for human survival can best be appreciated by considering first some of the factors that combined to promote the much higher death rates of the past. Broadly speaking, the high levels of mortality in antiquity were primarily due to the high incidence of death from infectious diseases. Moreover, it is generally agreed that the high incidence of infectious disease can be traced to two factors: (1) the overall poor health of the population resulting from an unstable and nutritionally inadequate food supply, and (2) the extremely unsanitary environment in which people lived. The latter was the source of disease whereas the former accounted for its virulence.

Food Supplies and Nutrition

One of the causes of the high death rates in the past (and in some parts of the world even today) was the inadequate food supply. The impact of famine, or an acute food shortage, on the death rate is obvious and does not require much elaboration: if people do not have any food to eat, they will very soon starve to death. Famines were recorded in Europe as late as the middle of the nineteenth century (the most notable being the great Irish potato famine of the 1840s, during which the death rate rose to three times its normal level); and even today severe famines occur periodically in various parts of the Third World.

The more important aspect of the relationship between mortality and the food supply, however, is that chronic food shortages and a generally poor diet, especially among the less privileged classes in society, tend to cause fairly widespread undernourishment and malnutrition. While less spectacular than outright famine and starvation, malnutrition, which lowers one's resistance to even the mildest diseases, was a major factor leading to the high death rates of the past. Moreover, it is a major factor behind the high death rates that still exist in many parts of the world. In fact, hundreds of millions of people in the less developed countries of the Third World today do not get enough food to maintain a fully active and healthy existence (Eckholm and Record, 1976). Not only do they get too little food, but what they do get is often seriously deficient in basic nutrients. Their diets consist mainly of cereals and starchy foods and are lacking in fresh fruits and vegetables, meat, eggs, and milk. The lack of good-quality protein in the diet is an especially serious deficiency, and it has been estimated that protein malnutrition is the greatest single source of death in children between the ages of one and five. Large numbers of adults also die prematurely each year from various deficiency diseases such as beriberi, and those who do not die often show the results of undernutrition in irreversibly stunted minds and bodies, lack of energy, and low resistance to disease. Thus, even when malnutrition is not lethal it increases the probability of an early death from other causes. In these parts of the Third World the average life expectancy even today is only forty to forty-five years.

Sanitation

Although an unstable and nutritionally inadequate food supply has always been a major cause of high mortality, by far the most important factor has been extremely poor sanitation. Throughout most of our existence, human beings have somehow managed to keep themselves and their environment unbelievably filthy. Until well into the nineteenth century, sewage and refuse disposal were virtually nonexistent, and the street was the accepted place in which to dispose of garbage and other household refuse. Housing conditions were deplorable, especially in the cities. People lived crowded together in grimy, unlighted, rat-infested tenements where bathing and toilet facilities were, if they existed at all, extremely inadequate. It has been reported, for example, that in mid-nineteenth-century America from 3 to 5 percent of the population in larger cities such as New York and Boston lived in damp, vermin-ridden underground rooms:

> Narrow crooked streets, lack of proper sewage and ventilation, absence of open spaces for recreation, inadequate and unprotected water supplies, intramural burials, and fetid nuisances (such as slaughterhouses and manufactories of offensive stuffs) made pestilential enclosures of some cities both in North America and in Europe (United Nations, 1953, p. 53).

And if sordid living conditions were not enough, personal cleanliness was virtually unheard of: people seldom bothered to bathe (perspiration was looked on as nature's way of cleansing the body), and more often than not, cleaning one's clothes consisted of little more than an occasional shaking out to get rid of a few clinging lice.

The unspeakable filth served as an ideal breeding ground for a wide variety of infectious disease germs, and when people were not fighting hunger they were likely to be fighting one of the periodic epidemics of plague, cholera, smallpox, and typhus that were commonplace throughout the preindustrial world. The most infamous of these virulent killers was plague, or the Black Death as it was more popularly called. Outbreaks of this dread disease periodically decimated—or more than decimated—the population. It is estimated that plague in one form or another killed from 20 to 25 percent of the population in Europe between 1348 and 1350, and that outbreaks of bubonic plague killed one-fifth of the population of London in 1603 and another sixth in 1625. Epidemics of plague with accompanying tremendous increases in mortality were reported in Europe as late as the middle of the eighteenth century.

Although perhaps the most dramatic, the Black Death was not the only disease to assume epidemic proportions and contribute to excessively high mortality. Cholera also frequently caused heavy mortality, as did periodic outbreaks of typhus; and smallpox was a particularly deadly scourge before Jenner's discovery of a vaccine in 1798. During the seventeenth and eighteenth centuries, smallpox accounted for nearly one-tenth of all deaths in Europe. Between 1780 and 1800, for instance, as many as one-fifth of all deaths in the city of Glasgow were probably caused by smallpox; and roughly one-fourth of the people of France during the eighteenth century were killed, crippled, or severely disfigured by this dread disease. Epidemics have not been entirely unknown in the present century; the influenza epidemic of 1918, for example, resulted in a 50 percent increase in the U.S. death rate for that year.

Throughout most of human history, then, the general conditions of life were not only poor but also erratic and unpredictable. Crude death rates of 30 to 35 per 1,000 were fairly common, and when conditions were especially bad (as when there was a crop failure or an outbreak of one of the virulent epidemic diseases) they rose to levels of 40 to 50 per 1,000, or even higher. These erratic high death rates of the past contrast sharply with the relatively stable rates of 8 to 10 deaths per 1,000 in many countries of the Western world today. The decline in the death rate and its stabilization at these relatively low levels were due to better health resulting from general improvements in the everyday conditions of life: the creation of a more regular and varied food supply, and increasing control over epidemic diseases through advances in medical science and environmental sanitation.

MORTALITY DECLINE IN THE MODERN WORLD

To cite a more abundant, better quality food supply and improvements in the environment as the factors responsible for the decline of the death rate in the modern world is an oversimplification that does not take into account the many specific changes in human society during the past two or three hundred years. On the other hand, a list of all the significant developments of the past three centuries would be far beyond the scope of this book. It is possible, however, to cite a few of the more important changes that have contributed substantially to a reduction of the death rate in the Western world. To facilitate this discussion, the various developments may be considered in terms of whether they represent (1) a change in the material aspects of culture, (2) a change in the nonmaterial aspects of culture, or (3) advances in the broad areas of medicine, public health, and sanitation.

Changes in Material Culture

A substantial part of the mortality reduction during the modern era is the result of changes in the material aspects of culture, such as the many technological developments and advances in agriculture and industry that have done so much to make our lives easier.

Agriculture

Prior to the hygienic advances in the Western nations during the nineteenth century, by far the most significant development contributing to the reduction in mortality was the improvement in nutrition due to more and better food supplies (McKeown, 1976). Broadly speaking, this agricultural revolution can be divided into two periods. The first, which covers the eighteenth and early nineteenth centuries, witnessed some major changes in the organization of agriculture. During this period the enclosure of the common lands was completed. Enclosure enhanced productivity by encouraging more efficient farming, and, more significantly, it set the stage for and facilitated the exploitation of the mechanized farming advances that led to the tremendous productivity gains of the nineteenth century. This period also saw productivity increases as a result of better soil management (e.g., crop rotation and the increasing use of urban waste products as fertilizer). Another advance was the development of mixed farming and the adoption of a variety of new food crops such as maize and especially the potato, which was first introduced to Europe around 1600 and which quickly became a major food staple. These developments contributed to an increase in total food production and to an improvement in the quality of the diet, and these in turn led to the general improvements in the overall health status of the population that presaged the onset of mortality decline. The potato played such an important role in these developments that at least one historian has singled it out as the primary "cause" of the modern European population explosion (Langer, 1975).

The second phase of the agricultural contribution to mortality decline came during the second half of the nineteenth century with the introduction of mechanized farming and the growing use of chemical fertilizers and, later, pesticides. The greater abundance of food of higher quality generated by these agricultural developments reduced the incidence of famine, raised caloric intake, improved people's nutritional level, and raised their general health level so that they were less susceptible to infection.

Industry

The development and growth of industry had both positive and negative effects on the level of mortality in modern Western society. On the negative side, the Industrial Revolution intensified the overcrowded, unsanitary living conditions in urban areas. The factories that sprang up generally had inadequate ventilation, the temperatures were often much too high or too low, the lighting was bad, the hours were long and exhausting, and the risk of accidents was great. But in the long run these negative effects were offset by other developments that led to a safer and more healthful environment and that were conducive to a decline in the death rate. For one thing, the greater productive efficiency of machine factory industry over the old home handicraft industries greatly increased the amount and variety of products available for public consumption; at the same time, it substantially reduced the cost of such products. The growth of the textile industry, for example, and the availability of cheap cotton clothing made it possible for the masses of people to afford to own more than one or two garments: now people could change their clothes more often, put on something dry when it rained, keep warmer in the winter, and so forth.

The advent of the factory system also helped make many agricultural improvements possible through the mass production of needed farm tools such as the iron plowshare. The invention of the steam engine permitted many improvements in transportation and facilitated a wider distribution of the new agricultural and industrial products, thus reducing people's dependence on their immediate environment. Soap, once a scarce luxury enjoyed only by the rich, now became available to everybody; iron bedsteads replaced makeshift wooden frames and floor mats; more adequate housing was constructed; temperature and humidity control in the house as well as in the place of work not only made for greater comfort in living but also may have contributed to a decline in respiratory infections during winter months; and more recently the development of pesticides such as DDT has contributed substantially to a reduction in mortality from particular diseases such as malaria.

Changes in Nonmaterial Culture

The reduction of mortality in the Western world has also been greatly facilitated by changes in the nonmaterial culture—attitudes, beliefs, values, normative patterns of behavior, and the like. Although the elements of material culture can be seen and touched, while the elements of nonmaterial culture exist largely in people's minds, material and nonmaterial culture are dynamically interrelated so that a change in one is generally accompanied by a change in the other. For example, once people came to accept the belief that sewage disposal systems would be beneficial to their health and well-being (a nonmaterial change), a lot of time, effort, and money were put into the construction of such systems. Similarly, the material change represented by the growth of the textile industry and the provision of cheaper cotton clothing led to the emergence of an entirely new set of values about how often people ought to change their clothes. Because of this dynamic interrelationship, it is not always feasible to consider particular material or nonmaterial changes apart from one another.

Perhaps one of the most significant nonmaterial changes was the liberalization of philosophy during the nineteenth and twentieth centuries, as people moved away from the everyone-for-himself attitude and toward a point of view that was conducive to the acceptance of responsibility for the well-being of others. This new philosophy resulted in a number of significant social reforms, and its influence is clearly visible in the gradual adoption of measures directed toward the eradication of slums and the improvement of housing conditions; the establishment of minimum wage laws; the fixing of maximum working hours for men and women; the establishment of minimum working age laws for children; and a general improvement of the working environment as a result of widespread use of factory safety devices and the adoption of lighting, heating, and ventilation codes.

Evidence that this liberal social philosophy is still very much in force in the United States is clearly illustrated by the declaration of a "war on poverty" by a Democratic administration in the 1960s, and the establishment of a number of federal programs aimed at enhancing economic opportunities and levels of living of the American poor. The success of these programs is revealed by the fact that the percentage of Americans living in poverty households was reduced from 22 percent in 1960 to less than 12 percent by the end of the decade.

Still another illustration that this philosophy is still with us is provided by the fairly recent emergence of a belief that access to good medical care is a basic human right for all, rather than a privilege for those who can afford it, and by the associated reevaluation of the adequacy and limitations of the American health care delivery system (Julian, 1980, pp. 24–47). Improvements in the availability of health care to the less advantaged segments of the population could contribute to a narrowing of many of the mortality differentials that presently exist (see Chapter 4), and this in turn could lead to further reductions in the overall death rate. In noting such a possibility, however, one must also note evidence that this more liberal philosophy has not yet fully permeated the society. In fact, many health-promoting programs were eliminated or substantially reduced by a more conservative Republican administration in the early 1980s.

Public Health and Medical Science

Without a doubt, a very significant factor behind the decline of the death rate in the Western world can be found in the tremendous development and acceptance of disease prevention programs and, to a lesser extent, improvements in medical knowledge and practices. Although many of the specific developments in these areas can be included under either material or nonmaterial cultural changes, they have exercised such a profound impact on the death rate that they merit separate treatment. Moreover, the specific developments are so frequently tied to both material and nonmaterial changes that it would be exceedingly difficult to try to classify them as belonging more to one group than to the other.

Public health and medical science as we know them today are of relatively recent origin. Only since the late eighteenth and early nineteenth century have we freed ourselves from many of the traditional beliefs and practices with regard to the protection and care of the human body and its external environment. Any declines in mortality that occurred before the nineteenth century, therefore, must have resulted primarily from developments that were not directly concerned with physical health, for little was known at the time about the causes of and cures for disease. Since that time, however, a number of important discoveries and inventions have led to a substantial increase in our ability to control mortality. No longer are "evil spirits of the night" cited as a chief cause of illness and death, and no longer do medical practitioners apply leeches to their patients to draw off such evil spirits through the letting of blood. Rather, today programs and practices are specifically aimed at preventing disease (e.g., water purification programs and the practice of bathing regularly), and physicians use a wide variety of serums and "wonder drugs" to contain, if not cure, infections and those strains of virus that science has been able to isolate.

Immunization

If we were asked to single out the particular development that has exerted the most significant influence on a decline in the death rate, we would most likely cite immunology. The possibility of developing preventive serums for infectious diseases was first indicated in 1798 when Edward Jenner reported his discovery of a vaccine for preventing smallpox. Not until a full century later, however, did Louis Pasteur and Robert Koch clarify the basic principle of immunization: that inoculation with a mild strain of a particular virus will produce a minor case of the disease but will render the patient relatively immune to the disease later on. Following this breakthrough, preventive vaccines were soon developed for cholera, anthrax and hydrophobia, diphtheria, tetanus, typhoid, whooping cough, and scarlet fever. These diseases, which were once major killers, particularly among young children, are now virtually nonexistent in the United States and other industrialized nations. The fight to conquer infection continues even today. More recent years have seen the development of prophylactic serums for influenza, poliomyelitis, and measles, and the years ahead will likely see the development of still others, such as a chicken pox vaccine, perhaps.

The acceptance of Pasteur's germ theory, which preceded the full development of immunology, also led to the acceptance of the practice of asepsis, the adoption of prophylactic measures that have as their aim the exclusion from the body of bacterial organisms that may carry disease. In the area of cure rather than prevention, it also led to the development of antisepsis, the application of antibiotics and other chemicals for the purpose of destroying or otherwise inhibiting the growth of microorganisms already present. On the one hand, Joseph Lister revolutionized the entire practice of medicine and surgery and contributed substantially to disease prevention by introducing such simple practices as the wearing of masks by physicians, the washing of hands before operating, and the sterilization of surgical instruments. On the other hand, the curative power of medical science has been greatly enhanced by the emergence of chemotherapy and the discovery of a wide variety of antibiotic wonder drugs, beginning with Alexander Fleming's discovery of penicillin in 1928. Today when illnesses such as influenza and pneumonia do occur they are much less lethal than they were in earlier times.

Environmental Sanitation

The theory and methods of medical practice were not all that changed with the acceptance of the germ theory of disease and the concept of preventive health. On the contrary, these developments were in many instances preceded by a number of significant developments in public sanitation, particularly in urban areas. Early in the nineteenth century, for example, cities began to install sewage disposal systems; provisions were made for the collection of garbage and other refuse; drinking water supplies were separated from sewage depositories; water filtration and purification were introduced; and quarantine measures were adopted and enforced in order to prevent the spread of communicable diseases. Today, in the modern countries of the Western world, sanitation measures such as these have practically wiped out infectious, filth-caused diseases such as cholera, typhoid fever, and diphtheria.

Other sanitary improvements, although not directly related to the environment, also contributed significantly to mortality reduction. One of the more important of these, perhaps, relates to improvements in food hygiene, especially with respect to milk. The adoption of a wide variety of pure food and drug laws and policies helped enhance the health status of the population in general, but the increased regulation of the quality of milk through pasteurization contributed markedly to a reduction in the incidence and severity of the gastroenteric diseases that once took such a heavy toll among infants and young children.

All has not been progress in this area, however, and in recent years we have unfortunately witnessed the emergence of several new environment-related health problems associated with such things as industrial air pollution, the use of pesticides and herbicides, such as DDT, and the especially dramatic problems created by toxic chemical waste products (see Chapter 10). A poignant illustration of the latter occurred in 1983 when hundreds of residents of Times Beach, Missouri, were forced to abandon their homes because intolerably high concentrations of the chemical dioxin were found in the soil. Despite such setbacks, which identify areas where continued efforts are needed, in the long run, improvements in sanitation have contributed substantially to better health and lower death rates.

Medical Technology

The years since the early nineteenth century have also seen the invention of a number of important medical tools. Among them, to name just a few, have been the stethoscope, the microscope, the basal thermometer, the ophthalmoscope, and the X-ray. These inventions, which represent material culture changes, contributed to medical progress by greatly enhancing the doctor's ability to examine patients rather than merely observe them. This, in turn, facilitated the physician's ability to go beyond superficial symptoms and discover the underlying causes of particular ailments. These developments, which made it possible to study the human organism in more detail, also served to encourage such study. They helped to create an intellectual spirit in medicine that endorsed and encouraged research for its own sake (a nonmaterial culture change), and today research has become an inseparable component of medical science.

It is worth stressing at this point that many of these developments (e.g., immunology, asepsis and antisepsis, and public sanitation control measures) were possible only after scientists had abandoned the old "evil spirits" explanation of disease causation and had accepted the theory of Pasteur that "life is a germ and a germ is life." As we discussed earlier, the acceptance of this germ theory represented a major change in nonmaterial culture that had significant ramifications for the material aspects of culture. Another illustration of the interrelationship between material and nonmaterial culture can be seen in the decline in the attitude that the human body is a sacred temple that should not be tampered with. Not until this attitude had lessened were the taboos against autopsy removed, thereby making it possible for physicians vastly to increase their knowledge of the structure and functioning of the human body. A decline in opposition to cutting the body permitted the development and spread of therapeutic surgery. Similarly, a change in attitudes regarding hygiene and personal cleanliness encouraged regular bathing with soap, more frequent changing and washing of clothing, and so forth. All of these developments indicate the extent to which changes in nonmaterial cultural attitudes and changes in material culture techniques and practices are closely intertwined, especially when it comes to progress in the broad areas of medical science and public health.

Overview of Mortality Decline

In summarizing the many factors responsible for the decline of mortality in the Western world, it is important to note the relative timing and impact of the forces involved. Although the development of medical science and sanitation control have probably exercised the greatest effect on the death rate, an emphasis on these factors should not lead to a neglect of the more basic social and economic changes that underlie them. To give credit where credit is due, it must be stressed that the initial decline in the death rate came about as a result of rudimentary economic development as reflected in increases in the quantity and variety of agricultural products, and in simple improvements in transportation and communication, which made famine control easier. Only much later did medical progress begin to exert its influence on mortality levels.

To be more specific, it is possible to conceive of mortality reduction in the Western world as having occurred in three stages. For the sake of illustration, let us go back to the time when the death rate was on the order of 40 deaths per 1,000 population per year. The first 10-point drop in the death rate occurred during the seventeenth and eighteenth centuries and was due essentially to a reduction in the number of deaths from infectious diseases. This was in turn due to improvements in the overall health status of the population brought about by the improvements in nutrition that followed the increases in the amount, availability, and quality of the food supply. The second 10-point decline in the death rate (from 30 to 35 per 1,000 down to 20 to 25 per 1,000) took place during the late eighteenth and early nineteenth centuries and was primarily the result of public health measures, which led to a decline in the incidence of infections and facilitated the control of epidemic diseases (e.g., sewer construction, garbage and refuse disposal systems, purification of public drinking water supplies, and so forth). Finally, in the third stage death rates fell to levels of 10 to 15 per 1,000, and even lower in some areas, as a result of the development of medical science and the spread of improved individual medical care (e.g., immunization, better personal hygiene practices, the use of antibiotics, and so on).

This third stage of mortality decline, wherein crude death rates fall to levels well below 15 per 1,000, was reached in the United States and the more developed countries of the Western world early in the present century, but only recently have such low death rates emerged in other regions. Moreover, the more recent declines in mortality differ significantly from the historical pattern just described in terms of both cause and speed; and, as we saw in the preceding chapter, these differences have had a profound impact on the pattern of world population growth.

MORTALITY TRENDS IN DEVELOPING COUNTRIES

Although Western mortality decline dates back several centuries, it is only since about 1920 that the less developed countries of Africa, Asia, and Latin America have experienced any significant reductions in death rates. Moreover, the declines that have taken place in these areas during the past sixty or so years have not been uniform but have varied notably from one region to another. Generally speaking, the earliest and most pronounced mortality declines took place in those Latin American countries that were most heavily influenced by exposure to the expansion of European culture and society. Death rates in that part of the world started to fall shortly after the end of the First World War. In the ensuing decades mortality declines spread first throughout Asia and then to Africa, but they have continued to exhibit a considerable degree of unevenness (see Table 3-2). A number of countries in East Asia, for example, today have death rates as low as or even lower than those in most modern European countries, whereas countries in the central regions of Africa, which have been least affected by modernization, still have crude death rates well in excess of 20 per 1,000.

Part of the explanation for the very low death rates in some developing countries today is found in their fairly young age composition, a phenomenon that has resulted from the persistence of fairly high levels of fertility in the face of steadily declining death rates. The generally poor mortality conditions that still prevail throughout the Third World, even in those countries that are characterized by low crude death rates, is clearly revealed by their infant mortality rates. The infant mortality rate (i.e., the number of deaths of infants under one year of age in a year per 1,000 live births) is not influenced by population differences in age composition; hence it is generally regarded as a very sensitive index of the overall level of health and well-being of a given population. Thus, despite the existence of a few very low crude death rates, the data in the accompanying table and in Figure 3-2 clearly point to the relatively adverse mortality conditions found throughout the less developed world.

Perhaps the most significant difference between the less developed nations and the industrialized nations is not that the less developed nations continue to have higher levels of mortality but rather that their overall pattern of mortality decline has been different from that of the Western nations. Specifically, when mortality declines have occurred in the less de-

Table 3-2
Crude Death Rates and Infant Mortality Rates, c. 1980

Region	Crude death rate*	Infant mortality rate**
World	11	85
More Developed Regions	10	20
North America	9	12
Northern Europe	11	11
Western Europe	11	11
Eastern Europe	11	21
Southern Europe	9	19
USSR	10	36
Australia, New Zealand	7	12
Less Developed Regions	14	96
Northern Africa	13	110
Western Africa	19	140
Eastern Africa	18	112
Middle Africa	20	122
Southern Africa	12	98
Southwest Asia	12	102
Middle South Asia	16	125
Southeast Asia	12	86
East Asia	7	41
Central America	7	60
Caribbean	7	62
Tropical South America	9	74
Temperate South America	8	40

SOURCE: Population Reference Bureau, *1982 World Population Data Sheet* (Washington, D.C., April 1982).
* Number of deaths in a calendar year per 1,000 population.
** Number of deaths to infants under one year of age in a calendar year per 1,000 live births.

veloped countries, they have resulted from different causes and they have generally taken place much more rapidly. As noted in the preceding section, mortality decline in the Western world was initiated by rudimentary economic development in the form of the production of more and better food. The less developed countries, however, have skipped this first stage and have jumped right to the second and third stages. In other words, mortality decline has come about largely in response to improvements in public health facilities and medical care, especially the former. Such things as the eradication of malaria-causing mosquitoes by draining swamp land and dusting with DDT, the chlorination of drinking water, and the implementation of vaccination programs have brought about a marked reduction in

Figure 3-2
Infant Mortality Rates in Selected Countries, Early 1980s

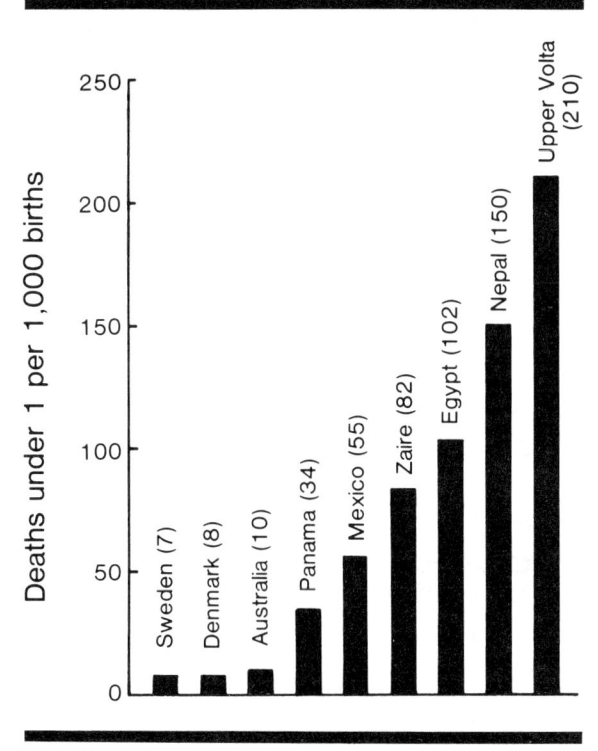

[Bar chart showing Deaths under 1 per 1,000 births: Sweden (7), Denmark (8), Australia (10), Panama (34), Mexico (55), Zaire (82), Egypt (102), Nepal (150), Upper Volta (210)]

SOURCE: Population Reference Bureau, *1983 World Population Data Sheet* (April 1983).

mortality levels, often in the face of an actual deterioration in the overall economic situation.

The much greater speed with which death rates have come down in the less developed countries is a function of the primary causes of the decline. That is, rather than having to go through long years of trial and error in order to discover and develop modern techniques of death control as we in the Western world did, the less developed countries were able to adopt, apply, and realize significant gains from our techniques in a relatively short period of time. In Sweden, for example, it took well over one hundred years for the crude death rate to decline from an annual level of 25 to 10 per 1,000, whereas a similar decline was achieved in Sri Lanka in less than thirty years (see Figure 2-5 in Chapter 2). Other Third World countries have experienced comparable reductions in mortality during the past forty to fifty years; and, as we saw in Chapter 2, these rapid and pronounced mortality declines in the less developed countries are largely responsible for the current crisis in world population.

Although the mortality declines that have occurred in most of the less developed countries during recent years have resulted largely from public health programs and improvements in environmental sanitation, it is important to stress that these short-term gains are not likely to be maintained, nor are additional gains likely to be achieved unless they are accompanied by overall improvements in the social and economic conditions of these societies. That is, while economic development may not have been necessary to initiate mortality declines, it will be necessary if the downward trends are to be continued, or even if the present relatively low levels are to be maintained. Already, in fact, there is evidence that the rapid and substantial increases in population generated by the earlier mortality declines have placed an ever-increasing burden on health care facilities and programs. As a consequence, the mortality situation in many countries has become extremely fragile and tenuous, and the pace of decline has slowed notably and may soon cease altogether (Gwatkin, 1980).

MORTALITY TRENDS IN THE UNITED STATES

One of the measures of a nation's accomplishments in raising the general level of living of the population has traditionally been a lowering of the crude death rate. It has in fact been demonstrated that the level of a nation's death rate (especially the level of mortality in infancy) has been a rough but usable measure of that nation's level of living and the state of its social, economic, and technological development. As noted in the preceding section, however, fairly substantial mortality declines have been experienced in some parts of the world in recent years solely as the result of sanitary improvements (often in the complete absence of any change in the social and economic level of living), and such developments have modified this traditional relationship. Nevertheless, the conquest of disease and the reduction of mortality have been closely associated with the growth and development of American society, and the history of the United States can in part be viewed as a history of declining death rates.

Unfortunately, the lack of adequate vital statistics for the early years of American history makes it impossible to document this mortality reduction with complete precision. Some areas such as the state of Massachusetts have fairly reliable data going back to the early nineteenth century, but national mortality data are available only for fairly recent times. Although some efforts were made by the U.S. Bureau of the Census to collect national data on mortality (characteristics of decedents and causes of death) in conjunction with the decennial censuses from 1850 through 1900, the results of these inquiries were not very good and they gave an imperfect picture of the mortality situation in this country. Not until 1900 were death statistics compiled by the federal government from registration sources on an annual basis. At that time, a "death registration area" was identified, which consisted of ten states and the District of Columbia. Over the years other states were added to this registration area as their systems for recording deaths were established and perfected, but not until 1933 were all states included. Thus, dependable nationwide death statistics are not available in the United States for the years before 1933, and almost no official registration statistics are available for years before 1900. In view of this situation, then, it is best to consider mortality trends in the United States in terms of (1) trends before 1900, before the existence of official national registration data, and (2) trends during the twentieth century, after the establishment of official registration statistics.

Mortality Trends before 1900

Several states as well as many cities have maintained birth and death statistics since the early days of the nation's history, but very little is really known about their completeness or accuracy. Thus, what is known about mortality conditions in the United States before 1900 has largely been pieced together from scattered vital statistics reports that are of questionable validity and that cover only a small segment of the total population. The data available, however, are fairly conclusive in pointing to a pattern of mortality in the eighteenth and early nineteenth centuries that closely resembled the pattern which has prevailed throughout most of human history: death rates were fairly high in normal times and they fluctuated rather sharply from one period to another. Records for Boston and New York City, for example, indicate that average annual death rates were between 30 and 35 per 1,000 but often rose to as high as 50 per 1,000 in epidemic years. Other historical sources reveal that the average life expectancy at birth in colonial America varied from a low of twenty-five years (Philadelphia, 1782–1790) to a high of thirty-five years (Massachusetts and New Hampshire, 1793). These compare with an average life expectancy at birth in the United States in the early 1980s of seventy-four years.

The first clear indication that the mortality level was declining in the United States was provided by the vital statistics data of Massachusetts. In that state the systematic registration of births and deaths by civil authorities was introduced as early as 1639, and by the end of the nineteenth century this system was fairly well established. According to these data, death rates were close to 30 per 1,000 in colonial Massachusetts but had fallen to a level of about 20 per 1,000 by the middle of the nineteenth century, and by 1900 the death rate in that state was still on the order of 18 to 19 per 1,000.

The decline in mortality during the nineteenth century is also indicated by a series of death probability tables that have been constructed on the basis of these early Massachusetts statistics. According to these tables, the average life expectancy at birth in 1850 was about thirty-nine years. By 1880 it had risen to approximately forty-three years, and by the end of the nineteenth century the average number of years that a newborn baby in Massachusetts could expect to live had risen to roughly forty-seven or forty-eight years.

These data for Massachusetts should not necessarily be taken as representative of mortality conditions in the United States as a whole. Massachusetts in the nineteenth century was, after all, an industrial state with a relatively high percentage of the population living in urban areas and a high proportion of foreign born. In contrast, the nation as a whole at this time was still predominantly rural and largely native born. Hence, it is likely that the death rates prevailing in Massachusetts were slightly higher than the national average. Nevertheless, taken together with what is known about public health advances being made during these years, the Massachusetts data clearly support the conclusion that the overall level of mortality in the United States was definitely on the decline during the nineteenth century.

Mortality Trends in the Twentieth Century

American mortality declines during the late eighteenth and the nineteenth century, like those of the industrializing world in general, were primarily due to a steadily increasing degree of control over communicable diseases as a result of medical and public health advances that facilitated the *prevention* of infection (e.g., sewer construction, water purification, the establishment of immunization programs). By the time the nation entered the twentieth century, these measures were quite firmly established, and their continued development, along with the gradual improvement in the ability of medical science to *cure* infection through the use of penicillin and other therapeutic drugs, has resulted in a rapid and fairly steady decline in mortality in this country in the years since 1900 (see Table 3-3 and Figure 3-3). From a relatively high level of 17.2 per 1,000 in 1900, the crude death rate had fallen to 9.6 by midcentury—a decline of nearly 45 percent—and estimates for the early 1980s indicate a crude death rate of less than 9 per 1,000, roughly 50 percent below the prevailing rate in 1900.

Careful inspection of the data presented in Table 3-3 reveals that the rate of decline in the crude death rate has not been uniform throughout the twentieth century. On the contrary, it has been extremely erratic. Most of the noteworthy fluctuations in the death rate reflect periodic epidemics of

Table 3-3
Crude Death Rates in the United States, 1900–1982

Year	Crude death rate	Year	Crude death rate	Year	Crude death rate	Year	Crude death rate
1900	17.2	1920	13.0	1940	10.8	1960	9.5
1901	16.4	1921	11.5	1941	10.5	1961	9.3
1902	15.5	1922	11.7	1942	10.3	1962	9.5
1903	15.6	1923	12.1	1943	10.9	1963	9.6
1904	16.4	1924	11.6	1944	10.6	1964	9.4
1905	15.9	1925	11.7	1945	10.6	1965	9.4
1906	15.7	1926	12.1	1946	10.0	1966	9.5
1907	15.9	1927	11.3	1947	10.1	1967	9.4
1908	14.7	1928	12.0	1948	9.9	1968	9.7
1909	14.2	1929	11.9	1949	9.7	1969	9.5
1910	14.7	1930	11.3	1950	9.6	1970	9.5
1911	13.9	1931	11.1	1951	9.7	1971	9.3
1912	13.6	1932	10.9	1952	9.6	1972	9.4
1913	13.8	1933	10.7	1953	9.6	1973	9.4
1914	13.3	1934	11.1	1954	9.2	1974	9.2
1915	13.2	1935	10.9	1955	9.3	1975	8.9
1916	13.8	1936	11.6	1956	9.4	1976	8.9
1917	14.0	1937	11.3	1957	9.6	1977	8.8
1918	18.1	1938	10.6	1958	9.5	1978	8.8
1919	12.9	1939	10.6	1959	9.4	1979	8.7
						1980	8.7
						1981	8.7
						1982	8.6

SOURCE: *Historical Statistics of the United States, Colonial Times to 1970,* Part I (U.S. Bureau of the Census, 1975). Rates for post-1970 dates are from various issues of *Monthly Vital Statistics Reports* (National Center for Health Statistics).

influenza. The best known of these outbreaks was the influenza epidemic of 1918. During that year the crude death rate rose to 18.1 per 1,000. In other words, it was 5 percent higher than the crude death rate recorded at the beginning of the century and 30 percent higher than the crude death rate of the preceding year. It has been estimated that this epidemic resulted in nearly half a million deaths in excess of the number that would have occurred with a normal level of mortality. Other years when epidemics of one sort or another seem to have influenced temporary upward swings in an otherwise declining death rate were 1904, 1923, 1926, 1928, 1936–1937, 1943, and 1957. (In 1957 the nation experienced a mild epidemic of Asian flu.) In 1963 and in 1968 the crude death rate again rose as high as 9.6 per 1,000, sug-

Figure 3-3
Crude Death Rate Trend in the United States, 1900–1980

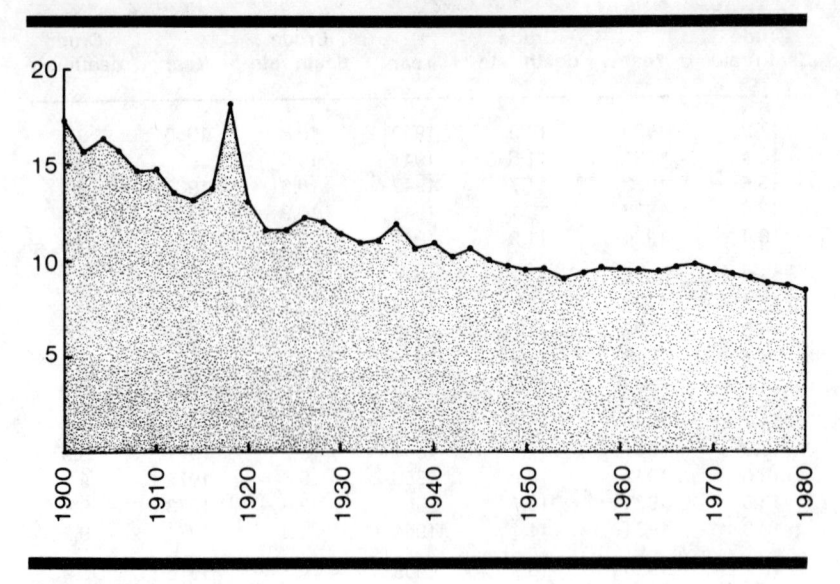

SOURCE: See Table 3-3.

gesting that there was an unusually high incidence of some form of flu during these years as well.

Although the general pattern is a fairly erratic one, it is nevertheless possible to identify at least five distinct phases in the trend of the U.S. crude death rate during the twentieth century. The first phase, and also the most dramatic, lasted from 1900 until just after the 1918 influenza epidemic (1900–1921). During this phase, the continued diffusion and establishment of the earlier public health measures led to a decline in the crude death rate from 17.2 to 11.5 per 1,000, a decline of approximately one-third. Although there were slight upturns in several of these years, the only major reversal of the pronounced downward trend during the first two decades of the twentieth century was the temporary rise occasioned by the 1918 influenza epidemic. All in all, this period of rapid and substantial decline in the crude death rate accounted for approximately two-thirds of all the mortality reduction that has occurred in the United States since 1900.

During the second phase, from 1921 to 1937, the crude death rate remained relatively stable. Although there were no major upswings during this period, neither were there any notable declines. Rather, the 1921 crude death rate of 11.5 appears to have reached a plateau, and during these years the crude death rate fluctuated between a low of 10.7 in 1933 and a high of 12.1 in 1923 and 1926. In 1936 it was 11.6 per 1,000, or one-tenth of a point higher than at the start of the period. In 1937, however, it dropped to a level of 11.3 per 1,000, and another period of declining mortality began. This third phase of the mortality experience of the United States, lasting from 1937 to 1954, saw sulfa, penicillin, and other wonder drugs come into fairly widespread use, and the crude death rate in this country declined by another 20 percent, falling from 11.3 in 1937 to a low of 9.2 per 1,000 in 1954, at which point the downward trend ceased and mortality levels once again stabilized.

The fourth phase in the trend of American mortality saw the crude death rate rise from 9.2 in 1954 to 9.6 in 1957, and for the next decade it hovered fairly consistently around 9.4 and 9.5 per 1,000. This cessation of the decline in the crude death rate in the 1950s was regarded as one of the major health problems confronting the nation, and a great deal of concern was expressed over what had caused it and what could be done to bring about a resumption of the downward trend. Some, in fact, reached the conclusion at this time that further substantial decreases in the death rate could not be anticipated (National Center for Health Statistics, 1964). Events since then, however, indicate that this pessimistic view was premature. Since 1968 another clear decline in mortality has been observed, and the 1982 death rate of 8.6 per 1,000 is the lowest ever experienced in this country. Moreover, this most recent downward trend, which reflects both an improvement in the overall socioeconomic status of the population (see Chapter 12) and an increase of certain practices that are conducive to better health (e.g., running), has resulted largely from a reduction in deaths due to cardiovascular disease (Crimmins, 1981). This is the first time in history that mortality decline has been dominated by decreases in degenerative rather than infectious diseases, and it may mark the beginning of a new era in American mortality decline. Past mortality declines, resulting from the prevention or cure of infectious diseases, had their greatest impact on infants and young children and contributed only slightly to the extension of adult life. However, if the declines in the incidence of degenerative diseases continue (or if breakthroughs are made in the prevention or cure of others, such as cancer), large increases in life expectancy at older ages could result, leading to corresponding increases in the number and proportion of elderly in our population.

In summary, then, the mortality experience of the United States population during the twentieth century can be divided into five distinct periods: (1) a period of fairly rapid and substantial mortality decline between 1900 and 1921, due primarily to preventive measures; (2) a period of relatively stable death rates between 1921 and 1937; (3) a second period of fairly marked mortality decline from 1937 to 1954, due largely to greatly enhanced curative powers; (4) a second period of relatively stable death rates following the cessation of the mortality decline in the mid-1950s and lasting until the late 1960s; and (5) the most recent period of a renewed decline since 1968 (due primarily to socioeconomic and life-style changes). As we have indicated, this most recent downward trend has resulted from a reduction of mortality due to cardiovascular diseases and its continuation will depend in large measure on further advances in the control of these and other degenerative diseases. In addition, further declines in the overall death rate of the American population could also come from a narrowing of some of the major mortality differentials that presently exist in this country. These differentials will be discussed more fully in Chapter 4. First, in order to appreciate more fully the various determinants of mortality trends and differentials it is desirable to consider more fully the changing importance of particular causes of death.

Cause-of-Death Trends

So far, the discussion of the mortality situation in the United States has been limited to the general trends in the overall crude death rate. However, the total mortality picture is not a single whole. Instead it is made up of many separate parts, each of which represents deaths from a particular cause. As noted earlier, two broad classes of causes ultimately lead to death: (1) endogenous causes, which reflect some sort of organic disintegration (e.g., heart disease and cancer), and (2) exogenous causes, which result from a virus or infection (e.g., influenza, tuberculosis, diphtheria) or from a trauma (e.g., accident or homicide). The data in Table 3-4 clearly reveal that the overall decline in mortality in the United States during the twentieth century has come about largely because of our growing ability to control infection. To illustrate, the *cause-specific death rate* (i.e., the number of deaths due to a particular cause per 100,000 population) for influenza and pneumonia, the leading causes of death in 1900, has been reduced by nearly 90 percent during this century. The decline in the tuberculosis death rate has been even more spectacular (down by 99.6 percent); and deaths from the major parasitic diseases (gastritis, diphtheria and typhoid fever) have been virtually eliminated in this country.

We are not immortal, however, and the elimination or reduction of certain causes of death has only meant that others have increased in importance. For example, although the death rates for infectious causes such as influenza and pneumonia have been substantially reduced since 1900, the rates for many chronic diseases have undergone marked increases. The death rate for cancer, for example, has nearly tripled since the beginning of the century, while the death rate from the major cardiovascular diseases (e.g., heart disease and stroke), although down significantly in recent years, is almost 30 percent higher than it was in 1900. In other words, the basic trend during this century has been a pronounced shift away from the predominance of exogenous causes to the predominance of endogenous diseases, as

Table 3-4
Deaths per 100,000 Population from Selected Causes in the United States, 1900-1980

Cause of death	1900	1910	1920	1930	1940	1950	1960	1970	1980
All causes	1,719.1	1,468.0	1,298.9	1,132.1	1,076.4	963.8	954.7	945.3	892.6
Influenza and pneumonia	202.2	155.9	207.3	102.5	70.3	31.3	37.3	30.9	23.7
Tuberculosis	194.4	153.8	113.1	71.1	45.9	22.5	6.1	2.6	0.8
Gastritis and related causes	142.7	115.4	53.7	26.0	10.3	5.1	4.4	0.6	*
Diphtheria	40.3	21.1	15.3	4.9	1.1	0.3	*	*	*
Typhoid fever	31.3	22.5	7.6	4.7	1.0	0.1	*	*	*
Major cardiovascular diseases	345.2	371.9	364.9	414.4	485.7	510.8	521.8	496.0	444.9
Malignant neoplasms (cancer)	64.0	76.2	83.4	97.4	120.3	139.8	149.2	162.8	186.3
Diabetes mellitus	11.0	15.3	16.1	19.1	26.6	16.2	16.7	18.9	15.4
Accidents	72.3	84.2	70.0	79.8	73.2	60.6	52.3	56.4	47.9
Motor vehicle accidents	*	1.8	10.3	26.7	26.2	23.1	21.3	26.9	24.2

SOURCE: *Historical Statistics of the United States, Colonial Times to 1970*, Part I (U.S. Bureau of the Census, 1975). The 1980 rates are from *Monthly Vital Statistics Reports*, 29:13 (NCHS, September 1981).

* No deaths, or not enough deaths to calculate a significant rate.

the killers of the old have replaced the killers of the young as the leading causes of death.

The increasing prominence of diseases characteristic of middle and older age has brought about a refocusing of medical research. As progress is made in uncovering the causes and improving the care and treatment of these chronic causes of death, we may look for further declines in the overall level of mortality. An encouraging illustration of what can happen is the trend in the death rate for diabetes mellitus. The diabetes death rate increased steadily up to 1940, at which time it was well over twice as high as it had been at the beginning of the century. It has declined since then, however, and in 1980 the death rate from this cause was 42 percent lower than it was in 1940 (although still substantially higher than it was in 1900). The death rate for the major cardiovascular diseases has also declined in recent years (down 15 percent since 1960), but the long-term upward trend in cancer mortality has not as yet shown any sign of abating.

One other point must be stressed in regard to possible future trends of mortality in the United States. Until recently it was generally believed that the major endogenous causes, which are associated with the genetic makeup of the individual, were more resistant to control than many of the exogenous causes. However, the evidence today is fairly conclusive in pointing out that many of these chronic conditions are indeed subject to a great deal of control, and that many lives could be saved by changing our life-style. The steady increase in cancer mortality, for example, especially lung cancer, is clearly associated with smoking and air pollution; and deaths from heart disease and stroke are known to be associated with smoking, a cholesterol-rich diet, obesity, and sedentary living. Most authorities today would concur that significant gains in longevity could be achieved at the middle and older ages through such things as not smoking, a diet that contains less animal fat and sugar and more fresh fruits and vegetables, and by following a moderate but regular exercise program.

Finally, it is interesting to note the trend in accident mortality in the United States. The accident death rate has declined from 72.3 per 100,000 population in 1900 to 47.9 per 1,000 in 1980, or by slightly more than one-third. But this decline would have been much greater—well over two-thirds—if it were not for motor vehicle fatalities. Automobile accidents, nonexistent at the beginning of this century, were responsible for 54,200 deaths in the United States in 1980. They account for slightly more than half of all accident fatalities in this country today and are in large part responsible for accidents now ranking as the fourth leading cause of death in the United States. For the age groups between five and thirty-four years, motor vehicle accidents are the number one cause of death, and for those between the ages of fifteen and twenty-four they account for roughly 40 percent of all fatalities. It is thus apparent that the overall mortality situation in this country could also be improved significantly through efforts entirely unrelated to biology, medicine, or life-style.

SUMMARY

Throughout most of human history mortality levels have been very high, with the average life expectancy at birth seldom exceeding thirty years. The high death rate in pre-industrial times was primarily the result of fairly widespread malnutrition and an absence of public sanitation facilities, both of which contributed to a substantially greater risk of mortality from infectious diseases, particularly among infants and young children. As the level of living has improved in the modern era, however, death rates have declined considerably, and their decline has been a major cause of the substantial increase in the size and growth of world population during the past couple of centuries.

Mortality declines began in the eighteenth century, first as a response to an improved diet and better health and later as one of the fruits of the increased productivity of the Industrial Revolution. In other words, mortality decline was initiated by the beginning of economic development and a rising standard of living. Declines accelerated during the nineteenth and twentieth centuries, with improvements in sanitation and advancements in medical science; and they continue today as we make further gains in our ability to prevent or cure various diseases and as our disease-control knowledge and technology are diffused throughout the world.

Until fairly recently mortality declines were pretty well confined to the more highly developed industrial nations, but during the last few decades they have begun to accelerate in the less developed countries of Asia, Africa, and Latin America. So far these more recent mortality declines have resulted primarily from the implementation of public health programs and medical technology borrowed from the more developed countries, and they have often occurred in the absence of any real improvements in the overall economic level. This fact has two implications for the future. On the one hand, it is unlikely that the lower death rates recently reached can be sustained for any length of time without some notable improvements in the level of living. On the other hand, if living levels do improve, mortality can be expected to decline even further; and this could generate rising rates of population growth and an intensification of many of the population-related problems they are presently confronted with.

The experience of the United States shows that the historical decline of mortality has taken place in stages, with periods of decline being interspersed with periods of relative stability. In the past, a period of decline in mortality was generally initiated by improvements in our ability to control infectious and parasitic diseases, either by preventing their occurrence (e.g., immunization) or by discovering a cure (e.g., penicillin). As we entered the 1980s, however, the new downward trend in mortality was due primarily to a reduction in deaths from the major cardiovascular diseases. This most recent trend reflects a refocusing of research efforts on the degenerative conditions as most infectious diseases have fallen to relatively insignificant levels; and future declines in the American death rate, if they come, will in large part result from continued progress in our ability to control the degenerative chronic diseases. Further declines may also come, as suggested earlier, from a narrowing of many of the subgroup mortality differentials that exist within our society. Group differences in mortality, their causes, and the prospects for their control are the subject of the next chapter.

REFERENCES AND SUGGESTED READING

Crimmins, Eileen M. "The Changing Pattern of American Mortality Decline, 1940–77, and Its Implications for the Future." *Population and Development Review*, 7 (June 1981): 229–54.

Eckholm, Erik, and Frank Record. *The Two Faces of Malnutrition*. Worldwatch Paper 9. Washington, D.C.: Worldwatch Institute, December 1976.

Gwatkin, Davidson R. "Indication of Change in Developing Country Mortality Trends: The End of an Era?" *Population and Development Review*, 6 (December 1980): 615–39.

Julian, Joseph. *Social Problems*, 3rd ed. Englewood Cliffs, N.J.: Prentice-Hall, 1980.

Langer, W. L. "American Foods and Europe's Population Growth, 1750–1850," *Journal of Social History* (Winter 1975): 51ff.

McKeown, Thomas. *The Modern Rise of Population*. New York: Academic Press, 1976.

Meyers, Robert J. "An Investigation of the Age of an Alleged Centenarian." *Demography* (May 1978): 235–37.

National Center for Health Statistics. *The Change in Mortality Trend in the United States*, Vital and Health Statistics, Series 3, No. 1. Washington, D.C., 1964.

Omran, Abdel R. "Epidemiologic Transition in the U.S." *Population Bulletin*, 32 (May 1977).

Shryock, Henry S., Jacob S. Siegel et al. *The Methods and Materials of Demography*. Condensed ed. by E. G. Stockwell. New York: Academic Press, 1976.

United Nations. *Determinants and Consequences of Population Trends* (ST/SOA/Series A/17). United Nations, 1953. A revised and considerably expanded edition of this excellent volume was published by the United Nations in 1973. See Chapter 5 especially for a discussion of mortality trends and differentials.

United Nations and World Health Organization. *Levels and Trends of Mortality Since 1950*. New York: United Nations, 1982.

Weeks, John R. *Population: An Introduction to Concepts and Issues*, 2nd ed. Belmont, Calif.: Wadsworth, 1981, Chapter 6.

Weller, Robert H., and Leon F. Bouvier. *Population: Demography and Policy*. New York: St. Martin's, 1981, Chapter 7.

Yang, Shu-O W., and Brian F. Pendleton. "Socioeconomic Development and Mortality Levels in Less Developed Countries." *Social Biology*, 27 (Fall 1980): 220–29.

Rush hour in Peking. In 1983 the People's Republic of China became the world's first "population billionaire."

A shopping scene in a village market in rural India

Egyptian wall painting dating from the 15th century B.C. depicts two farm workers preparing a threshing floor.

St. Sebastian interceding for the plague-stricken. Outbreaks of plague periodically killed large segments of the population in Medieval Europe.

WORLD POPULATION

Louis Pasteur. His germ theory revolutionized the field of preventive medicine.

Alexander Fleming (1881–1955), discoverer of penicillin

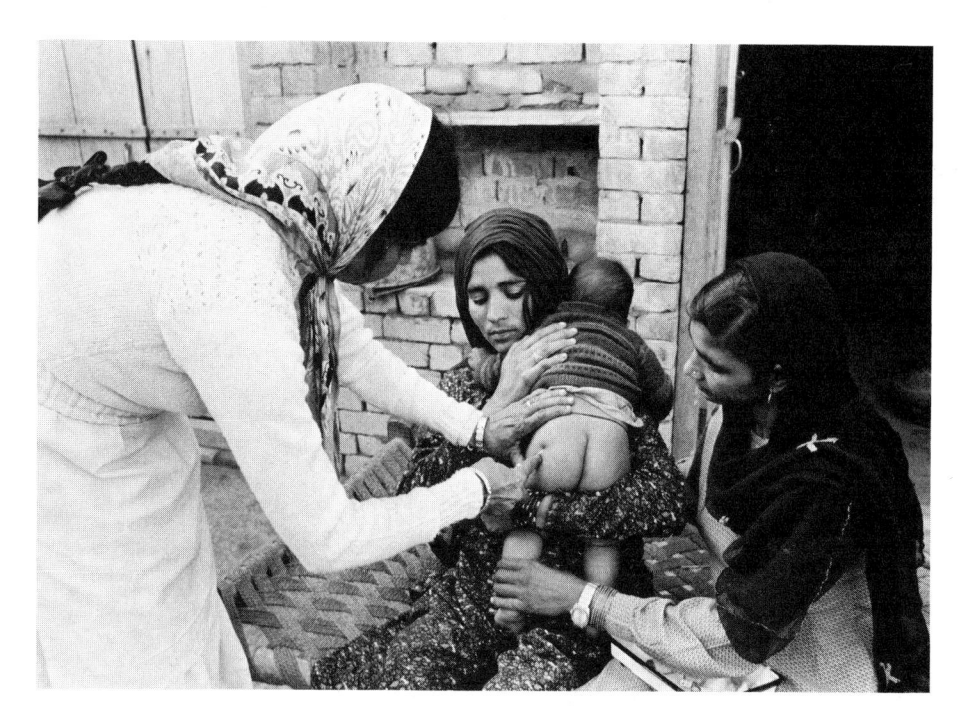

Since the end of World War II, vaccination programs have contributed to substantial mortality declines throughout the Third World, especially among infants and young children.

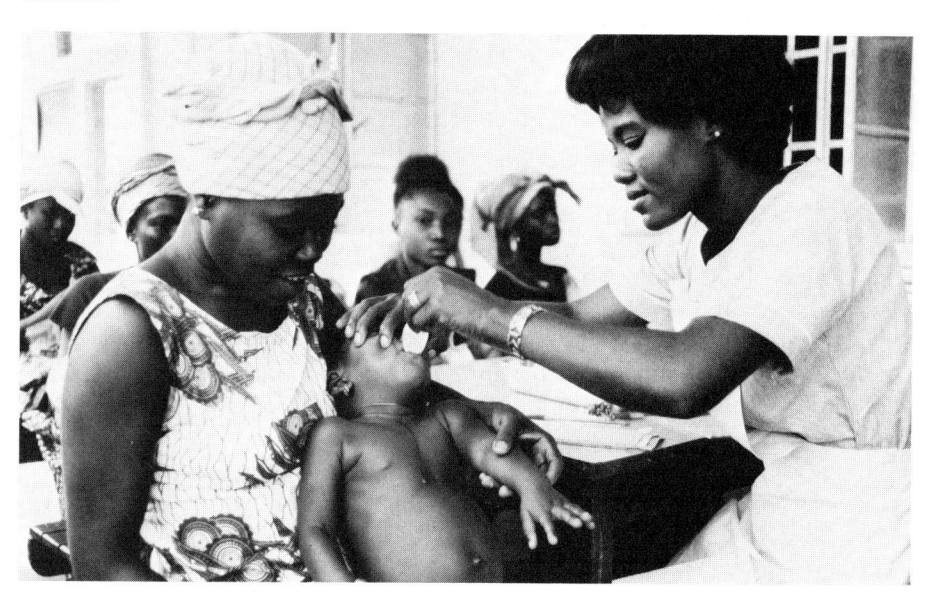

A nurse administering oral polio vaccine at a clinic in Sierra Leone

DIFFERENTIAL MORTALITY

4

We noted earlier that the general decline of mortality in the modern era has, until fairly recently, been largely confined to the urban-industrial nations of the Western world. In the less developed countries of the Third World, although downward trends in death rates are now well under way, overall mortality levels are still substantially higher than in the West. It is in these poor countries that the most serious health and mortality problems exist today, and this is where there is the greatest room for improvement in the years ahead.

However, this does not mean that higher death rates are no longer a problem in the Western countries. In the United States, for example, despite the impressive gains we have made overall in cutting the death rate in half since 1900, it must be acknowledged that some groups are still characterized by mortality levels considerably above the general average. For those groups that have already achieved a relatively low death rate, the prospects for any further appreciable reductions in the near future are minimal, but there is a definite possibility that fairly substantial reductions can be realized for some of those groups that are still characterized by comparatively high death rates.

Research on the mortality experience characterizing different segments of the population of the United States, and of other industrial societies, has established the existence of several differentials that are now widely recognized. It has even been suggested that some of these differences in mortality levels have so consistently distinguished various segments of the population throughout the years that they have become established laws. Such differences in mortality are associated with a variety of biological, social, and economic factors, and a knowledge of how these different factors are related to death rates is essential for an adequate understanding of the overall mortality situation.

WHY STUDY MORTALITY DIFFERENTIALS?

An understanding of the nature and cause of group variations in death rates is necessary for an adequate understanding of the overall mortality situation, as we have just noted. Beyond this general use, there are at least two basic reasons for being concerned with mortality differentials. First, there is the purely humanitarian reason. If some segments of the population have achieved very low death rates, other groups should be able to achieve the same low death rates, and we are all morally compelled to work toward this end. Mortality differentials are important in the first place, then, because they tell us which groups have a better or worse life expectancy; that is, mortality differentials allow us to identify the high-risk groups in a population on whom research and remedial action programs should be concentrated.

In the second place, there is a more practical reason: the elimination of the differences is one avenue toward the attainment of still further declines in low-mortality countries. Among groups whose death rate is already fairly low it does not seem likely that mortality levels will undergo any appreciable reductions in the very near future. As we have noted, however, the very fact that some groups have achieved a lower level of mortality than others may indicate that further reductions in mortality are possible for the high death rate groups; and as the mortality levels of high death rate groups are brought under control, an even further reduction in the overall death rate could be achieved. In fact, it might even be said that the elimination (or at least the narrowing) of some of the currently existing differentials will be a major factor in bringing about further declines in the overall level of mortality characterizing the population as a whole.

Finally, a knowledge of existing mortality differentials in any population is essential if we are to understand fully the overall level and trend of mortality in general. Some of the more significant mortality differentials are discussed below in terms of whether they reflect biological factors or whether they are largely due to social and economic forces.

BIOLOGICAL DETERMINANTS OF DIFFERENTIAL MORTALITY

The force of mortality will vary among the individual members of any population according to a number of biological factors—genetic makeup, nutritional well-being, susceptibility to different diseases, and so forth. From a demographic point of view the two most important biological determinants of the force of mortality are age and sex.

Age

One of the most obvious variables to which mortality levels are related is age. Death rates tend to be relatively high during the first year of life. After age one they drop off rapidly, reaching their lowest level in the early teens. They increase gradually from age fifteen to age forty-four, at which time they start to rise sharply with each advance in age. This general pattern, which is fairly uniform among all populations, past and present, is clearly revealed by the general series of age-specific death rates for the United States presented in Table 4-1. In 1980, for example, the death rate for the population under one year of age was nearly 13 per 1,000, but it dropped to well

Table 4-1
Age-Specific Death Rates for the United States

Age	Deaths per 1,000 population					Percent decline 1900–1980
	1900	1920	1940	1960	1980	
0–1	162.4	92.3	54.9	27.0	12.5	−92.3
1–4	19.8	9.9	2.9	1.1	0.7	96.5
5–14	3.9	2.6	1.0	0.5	0.3	92.3
15–24	5.9	4.9	2.0	1.1	1.1	81.4
25–34	8.2	6.8	3.1	1.5	1.4	82.9
35–44	10.2	8.1	5.2	3.0	2.3	77.5
45–54	15.0	12.2	10.3	7.6	5.9	60.7
55–64	27.2	23.6	22.2	17.4	13.8	49.3
65–74	56.4	52.5	48.4	38.2	29.7	47.3
75–84	123.3	118.9	112.0	87.5	71.8	41.8
85 and over	260.9	248.3	235.7	198.6	144.9	44.5

SOURCE: *Historical Statistics of the United States, Colonial Times to 1970,* Part I (Washington, D.C.: U.S. Bureau of the Census, 1975). Provisional data for 1980 from *Monthly Vital Statistics Reports,* 29:13, (NCHS, September 1981).

Figure 4-1
Age-Specific Death Rates for Guatemala and the United States

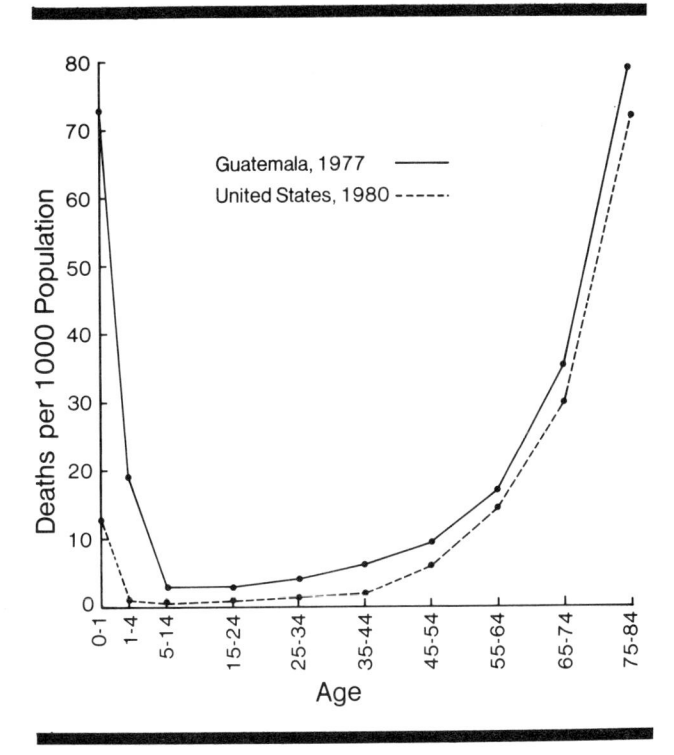

SOURCE: Based on data presented in Table 4-1 and Appendix Table B-1.

below 1 per 1,000 for ages one to four and five to fourteen. After age fourteen, however, it began to increase, slowly at first but then more rapidly in the older age groups: at ages forty-five to fifty-four, nearly 6 out of every 1,000 persons died during 1980; this figure rose to 30 per 1,000 for persons age sixty-five to seventy-four, and among persons eighty-five years of age and over there were roughly 145 deaths for every 1,000 people.

Although the general U-shape curve just described is characteristic of the age-specific death rates in all nations and for all time periods (see Figure 4-1), there can be great variations in the height of the curve at each age. The data in Table 4-1, for example, indicate that the height of the age-specific death rate curve in the United States for 1980 would be substantially lower at every age than the one for 1900. But a closer examination of these data reveals that the decline in mortality has not been evenly distributed among all of the various age groups. For ages under thirty-five, the death rate has declined by 80 percent or more, and for ages one to fourteen this decline has meant a near elimination of deaths (the rates for 1980 at these ages were all well below 1 per 1,000). The greatest decline has characterized the group one to four years of age: the 1980 death rate of this group (0.7 per 1,000) was 97 percent less than it was at the start of the century.

At the other end of the age spectrum, the decline in mortality has been much less pronounced. Among persons fifty-five years of age and over, death rates have declined by less than half since 1900; and at age seventy-five and over, mortality decline during the present century has amounted to less than 45 percent.

The fact that mortality declined at different rates for specific age groups is largely a reflection of the developments of medical science since the late nineteenth century. Following the pioneer work of Pasteur and Koch in the field of bacteriology, medical science has made tremendous progress in the cure and prevention of the acute and infectious diseases that formerly took such a heavy toll among the younger members of the population. Much less success has been achieved in preventing deaths from such chronic ailments as heart disease and cancer; and since these diseases are likely to attack older persons, the death rates at the advanced ages have until recently fallen at a much slower rate than the death rates in infancy, childhood, and young adulthood. Since the mid-1960s, however, significant progress has been made in reducing the death rate for the major cardiovascular diseases; and this has been reflected in an acceleration of mortality decline at the older ages. The group age eighty-five and over, for example, is the only one where the 1960–1980 decline (27 percent) exceeded that of the 1900–1960 period (24 percent). As suggested earlier, this emerging situation with respect to declines in chronic disease mortality could contribute to a marked lengthening of life at the older adult ages, thus producing a population in the years ahead with a much larger number and proportion of elderly people than has heretofore been forecast (National Center for Health Statistics, 1982). In the meantime, it is clear from the American experience depicted in Table 4-1 (an experience that is generally typical of other countries that have been through the modernization process) that by far the greatest mortality declines of the twentieth century have taken place at the youngest ages, and that these declines have contributed most to the overall drop in the death rate and to the corresponding increase in average life expectancy. Moreover, it is at the youngest ages that one finds the greatest differences between the mortality levels of the richer and poorer countries. In some of the very high death rate countries of Asia and Africa, for example, deaths of children under five years of age may account for as many as half of all the deaths in a year; and more than half of these childhood deaths will have occurred during the first year of life.

The general differences in the age patterns of mortality in more developed and less developed countries is illustrated in Figure 4-1. Here it can be clearly seen that the height of the mortality curve for Guatemala in 1977 is notably higher than that of the United States in 1980, but it is equally clear that the difference between the two curves is much more pronounced at ages one to four and especially in infancy. Since this youngest age group has historically experienced the most profound mortality changes and continues to contribute most to the major national and international differentials that still exist, it is desirable to look more closely at the pattern of mortality in infancy.

Infant Mortality

The infant mortality rate, or the number of deaths under age one per 1,000 live births in a year, measures the probability that a newborn baby will survive the hazards of infancy and live to celebrate its first birthday. It is important to note here, however, that the particular hazards of infancy vary significantly according to the age of infants and the overall level of societal development. In the more developed countries the risk of mortality is greatest just before and in the days immediately following birth, while in the poorer nations the risk of infant mortality increases with age. In order to take these factors into consideration, studies of infant mortality generally look at it in terms of two separate components: *neonatal mortality*, which refers to deaths during the first twenty-eight days after birth (or during the first month of life), and *postneonatal mortality*, which refers to deaths that occur between the ages of one month and one year. The significance of this division will become clear in the following discussion.

Infant mortality rates for the United States (total, neonatal, and postneonatal) going back to 1915 are presented in Table 4-2. It is clear from these data that the outstanding development with respect to the level of mortality in infancy in this country has been a steady and substantial decline. In colonial America it is estimated that roughly one out of every six babies failed to survive until its first birthday; and even in 1915, the first year for which official infant mortality data are available for the nation, as many as 10 percent of all live born infants still died before attaining one year of age. In marked contrast to this earlier situation, provisional data for 1980 reveal a national infant mortality rate of 12.5 per 1,000, indicating that the proportion of live born infants expected to die during the first year of life today is well below 1½ percent.

As with the death rate in general, the decline in the American infant mortality rate has not occurred at an even pace over the years. The decline was fairly rapid during the years preceding 1930; it slowed down somewhat during the depression period and then accelerated briefly from 1940 to 1950. Beginning in 1950, however, there was a pronounced change in the downward trend: the rate of decline slowed considerably between 1950 and 1955, at which time the infant mortality rate leveled off and remained fairly stable for the next decade. In the mid-1960s, however, another period

Table 4-2

Infant Mortality Rates in the United States, Selected Years, 1915–80

Year	Infant mortality rates		
	Total	Neonatal	Postneonatal
1915	99.9	44.4	55.5
1920	85.8	41.5	44.3
1925	71.7	37.8	33.9
1930	64.6	35.7	28.9
1935	55.7	32.4	23.3
1940	47.0	28.8	18.2
1945	38.3	24.3	14.0
1950	29.2	20.5	8.7
1955	26.4	19.1	7.3
1960	26.0	18.7	7.3
1965	24.7	17.7	7.0
1970	20.0	15.1	4.9
1975	16.1	11.6	4.5
1980	12.5	8.4	4.1

SOURCE: *Historical Statistics of the United States, Colonial Times to 1970*, Part I (Washington, D.C.: U.S. Bureau of the Census, 1975). Rates for 1975 and 1980 from *Monthly Vital Statistics Reports*, 29:13 (NCHS, September, 1981). Postneonatal rates calculated by authors as the difference between total infant and neonatal mortality rates.

of fairly rapid decline set in, and the fifteen years from 1965 to 1980 were characterized by nearly a 50 percent reduction in the level of infant mortality.

Although the overall downward trend has characterized both neonatal and postneonatal mortality, the pattern of decline has been considerably different (see Figure 4-2). During the earlier period the declines were much more pronounced for postneonatal mortality (down 84 percent from 1915 to 1950 as compared with a decline of only 54 percent in the neonatal death rate). In the most recent period, 1965–1980, however, the decline has been considerably more pronounced for neonatal mortality (down 53 percent) than for postneonatal mortality (down 41 percent).

In order to understand fully the historical trend as well as the most recent developments, it is necessary to examine the major causes of death in infancy and the ages at which the particular causes are most prevalent. As with mortality in general, the causes of infant deaths can be divided into two broad classes: *endogenous* causes, which are related to genetic characteristics and the physiological process of birth itself, and *exogenous* causes, which are external to the birth process and reflect conditions in the socioeconomic environment. The major endogenous causes of infant death are immaturity, birth injuries, postnatal asphyxia (suffocation due to failure of respiratory organs—e.g., collapsed lung), and congenital malformations (abnormalities of various organs—heart, spinal cord, lungs—acquired during fetal development and often related to maternal illness, especially rubella, or to various drugs taken during pregnancy). The major exogenous causes include pneumonia, influenza, diarrhea, and other infectious and parasitic diseases. Prior to the 1950s the major factors contributing to a falling infant mortality can be found in the gradual improvement in medical facilities and in the sanitary environment of the United States, the steadily improving economic condition of the masses of the population, and advances in medicine such as the discovery of penicillin and the development of other antibiotics. These developments had their greatest impact on the various in-

Figure 4-2
Neonatal and Postneonatal Mortality Trends in the United States

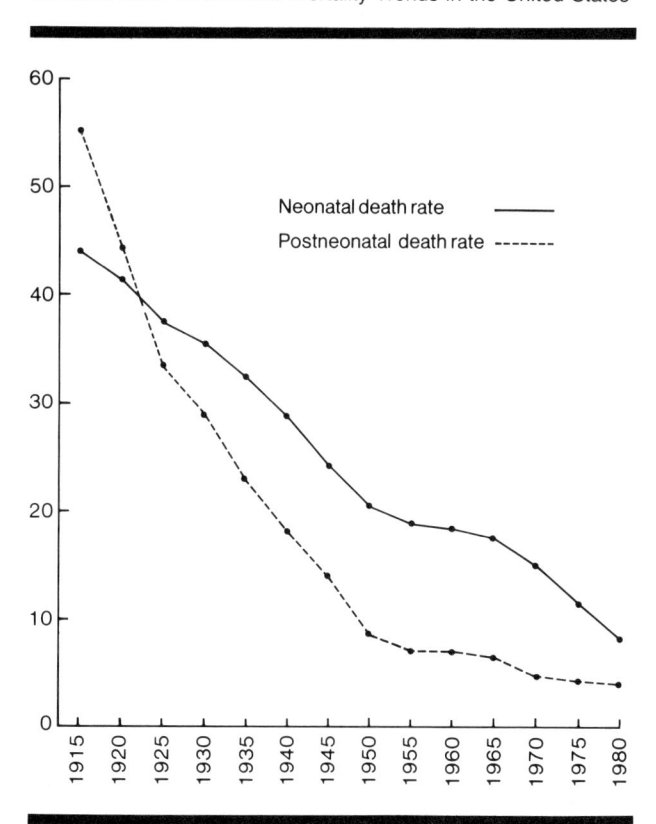

SOURCE: Based on data presented in Table 4-2.

fectious and parasitic diseases and on influenza and pneumonia, and it was the increasing control over these diseases, major killers of infants during the postneonatal period, that facilitated the marked reductions in infant mortality that occurred during the first half of this century. The decline in postneonatal mortality has in fact been so pronounced when compared to the neonatal declines that a significant shift has occurred with respect to the importance of the former. Specifically, the impact of postneonatal mortality on the overall infant death rate has changed from one of major importance to one of clearly secondary status. To illustrate, in 1915 some 55 percent of the infant mortality in the United States was accounted for by postneonatal mortality, but since 1950 this fraction has fluctuated generally between 25 and 30 percent.

Since the mid-1960s, continued advances in maternal and infant care and improvements in the general socioeconomic environment have combined with several important changes in the reproductive behavior of the American population to bring about this most recent downward movement of infant mortality. For example, declining birth rates since the mid-1960s, especially among younger women, and the liberalization of abortion laws have served to reduce the overall contribution to infant mortality of traditionally high-risk groups such as teenagers and unwed mothers. These more recent developments have influenced an infant mortality decline that has been more pronounced in the neonatal than in the postneonatal period.

Although the neonatal mortality rate has declined sharply in recent years, by far the heaviest loss of life among infants still occurs during the first month after birth. For the population as a whole, well over two-thirds of all infant deaths in the United States today occur during this neonatal period. Since neonatal deaths are predominantly due to endogenous causes that reflect certain physiological problems associated with gestation and birth, rather than socioeconomic or environmental conditions, they are likely to be much more difficult to bring under control. Thus, while we may anticipate continued declines in both neonatal and postneonatal mortality, it is not likely that we will soon see any substantial change in the current pattern wherein neonatal mortality accounts for the bulk of infant deaths.

Not all nations of the world have experienced infant mortality declines similar to those of the United States. In fact, infant death rates are still very high throughout the less developed countries of the Third World. To this observation can now be added the fact that the general pattern of mortality in infancy also varies according to the degree of development of particular countries, much as it did in the United States over time (see Table 4-3). That is, those countries that have been through the modernization process have infant mortality rates as low as or frequently lower than that of the United States; and in these more developed countries anywhere from 65 to 70 percent or more of all infant deaths take place during the first month of life. As the level of societal development declines, however, the overall

Table 4-3

Infant Mortality Rates for Selected Countries, Late 1970s

Country and year	Total	Neonatal	Postneonatal	Percent neonatal
Sweden, 1979	7.5	5.4	2.1	72.0
Switzerland, 1979	8.5	5.9	2.6	69.4
Australia, 1979	11.4	7.6	3.8	66.6
United Kingdom, 1979	12.8	8.2	4.6	64.0
Germany, Federal Republic, 1978	14.7	9.3	5.4	63.2
Austria, 1978	15.0	10.2	4.8	68.0
Czechoslovakia, 1977	19.7	13.2	6.5	67.0
Costa Rica, 1978	33.2	17.4	15.8	52.4
Yugoslavia, 1978	33.8	17.0	16.8	50.2
Portugal, 1975	38.9	22.1	16.8	56.8
Mexico, 1975	52.8	21.0	31.8	39.7
El Salvador, 1979	53.0	17.0	36.0	32.0
Ecuador, 1975	65.8	14.5	51.3	22.0
Guatemala, 1977	69.8	18.1	51.7	25.9
Egypt, 1977	85.3	14.2	71.1	16.6

SOURCE: *Demographic Yearbook, 1979* (New York: United Nations, 1980); and *Demographic Yearbook, 1980* (New York: United Nations, 1982).

infant mortality rate increases and there is a corresponding decline in the proportion of neonatal deaths. Among those poorer countries that still have infant mortality rates in excess of 60 per 1,000 for example, a situation the United States was in a half-century ago, less than 30 percent of the infant deaths occur during the neonatal period. We can optimistically assume that these poorer countries will continue to develop in the years to come and that future health progress will enable them to control more effectively the major infectious and parasitic killers of young children. If this does occur, then one can anticipate that they, too, will go through a mortality transition similar to that experienced by the United States and other Western nations, in which there is a steady shift in importance away from postneonatal to neonatal mortality.

One other international differential deserves mentioning before we conclude this discussion of infant mortality: although the persistence of a low level of infant mortality is a general characteristic of modern industrial states, there is at least one country in which this has not been the case. In the USSR there is evidence that there has been a substantial increase in the overall infant mortality rate during the 1970s—up from 23 per 1,000 in 1970–1971 to 31 in 1975–1976 (Davis and Feshbach, 1980). The reasons for this upward trend are highly complex and, because the Soviets stopped pub-

Table 4-4
Deaths per 1,000 Population by Age and Sex: United States, 1980

Age	Male	Female	Percent male excess
All ages	9.97	7.94	25.6
0–1	14.55	11.59	25.5
1–4	0.74	0.57	29.8
5–14	0.37	0.26	42.3
15–24	1.80	0.57	215.8
25–34	2.06	0.78	164.1
35–44	3.02	1.54	96.1
45–54	7.79	4.13	88.6
55–64	18.45	9.65	91.2
65–74	40.65	21.23	91.5
75–84	94.05	58.40	61.0
85 and over	169.02	134.27	25.9

SOURCE: *Monthly Vital Statistics Reports,* 29:13 (NCHS, September 1981). Male excess percentages calculated by authors.

lishing data on infant mortality in the late 1970s, any conclusions must be tentative. Nevertheless, it does appear that the major factors contributing to the higher infant mortality reflect institutional changes (e.g., increasing environmental pollution, rising divorce, inadequacies in public child care facilities, and poor quality of artificial infant formulas) rather than changes in individual behavior (such as increased smoking and alcohol consumption, and the increasing prevalence of induced abortion). A more adequate explanation of the situation, however, will have to wait until the Soviets release more information. Meanwhile, we are confronted with the fact that in recent years a modern, developed nation has experienced an unprecedented increase of nearly 35 percent in its overall infant mortality rate.

Sex

It has long been an established fact that women enjoy a pronounced mortality advantage over men. In the United States today, for example, the crude death rate of males is roughly 25 percent higher than that of females (see Table 4-4). The excess mortality of men is least marked among the very young and very old, but it is clearly evident at every age—most notably among young adults (ages fifteen to thirty-four) where male death rates are anywhere from two and one-half to three times as great as those of females.

Not only have women consistently managed to outlive men, but they have also been increasing their advantage. Between 1900 and 1978 the average life expectancy at birth of American women increased by 60 percent (from 48.3 to 77.2 years), whereas the mean life expectancy of 69.5 years estimated for men in this country in 1978 was only 50 percent higher than the 46.3 years recorded in 1900. The effect of these different rates of increase has been a steady widening of the mortality gap separating the sexes (see Figure 4-3). In 1920, for example, females could expect to live an average of one year longer than males. Ten years later the excess life expectancy of women was three and a half years; it was over six years by 1955, and by the 1970s the average American woman was living nearly eight years longer than the average man.

With rare exceptions (generally associated with unusually high maternal mortality, or where women are held in such low esteem as to encourage the systematic neglect of female infants and children) the sex mortality differential is found throughout all human societies, past and present. Its prevalence in the world today is clearly revealed by the male and female death rates of selected countries presented in Table 4-5. These rates, and the differences between them, generally reflect the trend and pattern just described for the United States. That is, for all countries it is clear that male

Figure 4-3
Excess Life Expectancy at Birth of Women over Men: United States, 1920–78

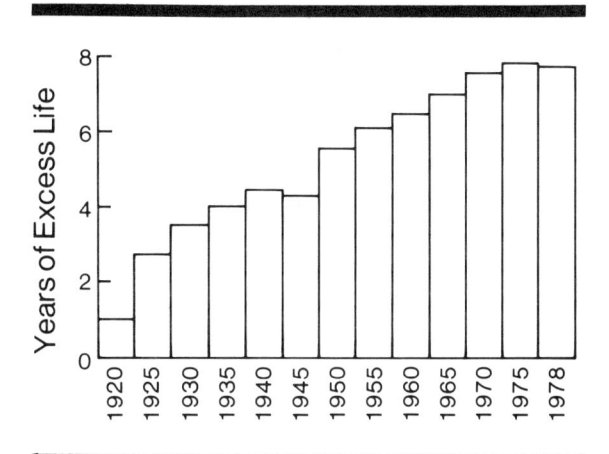

SOURCE: Based on data published in *Vital Statistics of the United States, 1978,* Vol. II, Section 5, *Life Tables* (NCHS, 1980).

Table 4-5
Crude Death Rates for Selected Countries and Years

Country	Year	Deaths per 1,000 population Male	Female	Percent male excess
Iceland	1973	7.7	6.1	26.2
Canada	1973	8.6	6.2	38.7
	1978	8.3	6.0	38.3
New Zealand	1978	8.7	7.1	22.5
Poland	1973	9.1	7.5	21.3
	1978	10.3	8.3	24.0
Denmark	1979	11.8	9.6	22.9
Portugal	1973	12.0	10.4	15.4
	1975	11.5	9.3	23.6
Egypt	1976	12.5	11.7	6.8
Hungary	1973	12.7	11.0	15.5
	1979	13.9	11.7	18.8
Guatemala	1970	15.5	14.3	8.4
	1977	11.7	10.6	10.3
Malawi	1977	27.3	22.9	19.2

SOURCE: *Demographic Yearbook, 1974* (New York: United Nations, 1975); and *Demographic Yearbook, 1980* (New York: United Nations, 1982).

death rates are significantly higher than those of females; moreover, the female advantage tends to increase with the level of societal development—in much the same way that the American sex differential became wider over time.

In the past (and perhaps even among some lay people today), higher male mortality was often explained in terms of the more strenuous role that men play in the life of society, or in terms of such things as occupational hazards affecting males, military deaths in wartime, and greater tensions among men because of the greater pressure to achieve that our society places on them. But there is ample evidence to suggest that differences in the life experiences of the two sexes cannot completely account for the higher mortality of men. The fact that the male death rate is higher in infancy as well as in old age, for example, and the fact that male stillbirths are more common than female stillbirths, would suggest that the lower mortality level of females stems at least in part from some unknown but inherent biological superiority. The possible significance of such a biological difference is further suggested by the fact that the female advantage has been increasing during a period when women have gradually been assuming a role and status in industry and business much more similar to that of men. Between 1940 and 1970, for example, the proportion of women age fourteen and over who were members of the labor force in the United States rose from 25 to 35 percent; and by the end of the 1970s well over half of the adult women in this country were working either full- or part-time. In short, the increasing participation of women in the labor force, as well as the movement of women into jobs traditionally regarded as male occupations, has not been accompanied by an equalization of the mortality experience of the two sexes. Moreover, although there may be insufficient evidence to justify citing the innate frailty of males as the sole cause of their higher mortality, at least one study, done under carefully controlled conditions, has provided strong evidence in support of the claim that biological factors are much more important than sociocultural pressures and strains in relation to the male–female mortality differential (Madigan, 1957). This study, which examined the life records of brothers and nuns living in religious communities from 1900 to 1954, found that despite similarities in life-styles nuns had higher life expectancies at all ages than brothers. Moreover, the magnitude of the mortality differential characterizing nuns and brothers generally paralleled the overall sex differential of the native-born white population in the United States. Thus, contrary to popular mythology, the female may not be the weaker sex after all—certainly not as far as the death rate is concerned.

It is important to point out that, while the biological superiority of the female may be a major factor explaining the apparent universality of the sex mortality differential, that differential is not without social determinants. For example, biological factors would not explain the marked differences in the size of the mortality gap between men and women in different countries, or in the same population at different points in time. In fact, such area and temporal variations in the magnitude of the sex mortality differential are largely due to sociocultural and medical factors associated with differences in the level of modernization (Omran, 1977). With respect to sociocultural factors, the smaller differential in less developed societies and in the past experience of modern nations is very likely a function of the different roles of women. In a time and place where women are expected to perform a variety of important roles (e.g., family nurse, cook, and maid; clothing maker; farm laborer), at the same time they are exposed to the hazards of frequent pregnancies and childbearing, they are more likely to become run down and more susceptible to a variety of infectious respiratory and deficiency diseases. With modernization come better nutrition, more effective treatment of infectious disease, and labor-saving devices that ease the lot of women—all of which enhance the life chances of women relative to those of men.

There is also evidence to suggest that the medical advances of the modern era have benefited women more than men, whereas some of the changes in life-style have had a more detrimental effect on men. In the first instance, for example, the major forms of cancer in women (breast, cervix, and uterus) are more easily recognized and diagnosed at early, treatable stages than the major forms of cancer among men (cancer of the lung and prostate). On the other hand, many of the labor-saving devices that eased the lot of all people encouraged a more sedentary life-style that may have increased the incidence of obesity among men and contributed to greater risk of mortality from the major cardiovascular disesases.

A specific illustration of the extent to which social factors can influence the mortality levels of males and females can be seen by considering the long-term widening differential in the United States. In an earlier analysis of this trend (Stockwell, 1968, p. 54) it was noted that the factors contributing to this widening gap included (1) a marked decline in maternal mortality (mortality due to complications of pregnancy and childbirth) as a result of improved medical knowledge and techniques; (2) a substantial increase in male deaths resulting from motor vehicle accidents; (3) a decrease in female mortality from cancer of the uterus, due to improvements in prenatal care and delivery practices and to improved diagnostic techniques and a greater awareness of the need for periodic pelvic examinations; and (4) a marked increase in male deaths from lung cancer and coronary heart disease, reflecting a greater prevalence of smoking and obesity among men than among women. A more recent analysis (Retherford, 1975) has in fact suggested that the widening sex mortality differential is primarily due to the effects of men's smoking patterns. Thus, while biological factors may be behind the sex mortality differential in general, the increase in the differential during the present century may be explained by material and nonmaterial cultural changes (or by reference to such things as the rise of the automobile, increased smoking, and a new attitude regarding the need for prenatal care).

Although the prominence of biological factors makes it difficult to visualize any immediate narrowing of the sex mortality differential, this is nonetheless a possibility. In fact, there is already clear evidence to suggest that the long-term widening trend has not only come to an end but may be in the process of reversing itself. Between 1970 and 1975, for example, the excess life expectancy of females increased by only two-tenths of a year, compared with average gains of half a year or more in preceding quinquennial periods; and between 1975 and 1978 it actually fell by one-tenth of a year (see Figure 4-3).

While this most recent drop is admittedly very small, it could mark the beginning of a new trend toward a narrowing of the sex mortality differential. And once again this new trend is likely to reflect the influence of various social factors that may have either an adverse effect on female mortality (e.g., the increase in smoking by women in recent decades) or an advantageous effect on the life chances of men (e.g., the growing awareness of the danger of too much animal fat in the diet and the benefit of regular moderate exercise). An examination of recent cause-of-death trends in the annual reports of *Vital Statistics in the United States* bears out these possibilities. Between 1970 and 1977, for example, the declines that took place in the death rate for the major cardiovascular diseases were nearly twice as great for men (−13 percent) as for women (−7 percent); and the continued increase in the respiratory cancer death rate has been more than three times greater for women (+64 percent) than for men (+20 percent).

SOCIAL DETERMINANTS OF DIFFERENTIAL MORTALITY

The influence of social factors on mortality was clearly illustrated by the international comparisons in Table 4-3, which showed that a country's infant death rate declined as the level of modernization increased. It also needs to be noted that similar mortality variations may be found within countries, regardless of their overall level of modernization. Two of these social differentials that deserve special mention are those pertaining to race and socioeconomic status.

Race

Although race is basically a biological variable, it is safe to say that most of the differences in mortality associated with race reflect social factors rather than biological differences. In most multiracial societies one group is clearly dominant over the others, and those racial mortality differentials that can be observed will largely reflect a variety of social and economic disadvantages that characterize the subordinate groups. This can be readily illustrated by some recent mortality data for South Africa, the most openly racist country in the world today. In that country the white population enjoys a clear and very pronounced mortality advantage over the "Asiatics" and especially over the oppressed "Coloureds" (see Table 4-6). This advantage is most readily apparent with respect to infant mortality, which is not influenced by the overall age composition of a population. In 1974, the Asiatic infant mortality rate was 73 percent greater than that of the white population, whereas "Coloured" infant mortality was more than three times greater than the Asiatic and more than six times greater than the white infant mortality rate.

In the United States, death rates have long been known to vary among ethnic groups. Historically, for example, immigrants from Europe and other

Table 4-6
Crude Death Rates and Infant Mortality Rates: South Africa, 1974

Age	White	Asiatic	Colored
All ages	8.4	6.8	12.9
Infant mortality rate	18.4	31.8	115.5

SOURCE: *Demographic Yearbook, 1980* (New York: United Nations, 1982).

parts of the world were characterized by much higher levels of mortality than the native-born American population. And in the Southwest today ample evidence indicates that Spanish Americans have a lower life expectancy than other white persons (Schoen and Nelson, 1981; Stockwell and Wicks, 1981). The most significant ethnic mortality differential in this country, however, has been and continues to be the difference between the white and black segments of the population. The death rates presented in Table 4-7, for example, show that nonwhites (the vast majority of whom are black Americans) are characterized by a much higher level of mortality than

Table 4-7
Age-Specific Death Rates for Whites and Nonwhites: United States, 1978

Age	White	Nonwhite	Ratio of nonwhite to white
All ages	8.96	8.05	.90
0–1	12.18	24.57	2.02
1–4	0.63	0.99	1.57
5–14	0.32	0.42	1.31
15–24	1.14	1.38	1.21
25–34	1.18	2.50	2.12
35–44	2.06	4.66	2.26
45–54	5.60	9.91	1.77
55–64	13.44	20.86	1.55
65–74	29.62	36.21	1.22
75–84	71.55	75.58	1.06
84 and over	153.16	92.29	.60
Age-adjusted death rate	5.80	7.98	1.38

SOURCE: *Monthly Vital Statistics Report,* 29:6 (NCHS, September 1980).

Figure 4-4
Excess Life Expectancy at Birth of Whites over Nonwhites: United States, 1920–78

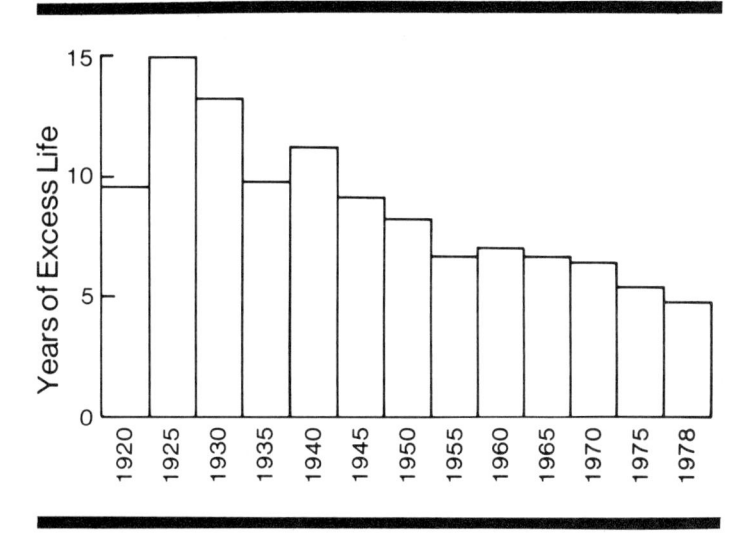

SOURCE: See Figure 4-3.

whites. Although the crude death rate is somewhat lower for nonwhites (a fact that reflects their higher birth rate and overall younger age composition), their specific death rates are higher than the corresponding white rates at every age except the oldest. Further, when the death rates are adjusted for differences in age composition (see Appendix B), the adverse status of the nonwhites is readily apparent: in 1978 the age-adjusted death rate of nonwhites was nearly 40 percent greater than that of the white population.

The gradual narrowing of the color differential at the older ages and the eventual reversal at age eighty-five and over (i.e., the so-called mortality crossover effect) is generally explained in socioeconomic terms. That is, the overall higher status of whites enables many who are physically and/or physiologically weak to survive to older ages whereas among the more disadvantaged nonwhite group, where death rates are higher at the younger ages, those who survive the longest are physically and/or physiologically stronger than their white counterparts (Nam et al., 1978). A somewhat similar effect has recently been observed in less developed countries where improvements in living levels that contribute to sharp reductions in mortality at young ages may be followed by increases in mortality at the older ages.

Although the nonwhite mortality level has consistently been notably higher than that of the white population, it is encouraging to note that this differential has been narrowing over the years (see Figure 4-4). During the first half of the twentieth century, for example, the average life expectancy at birth of nonwhites increased from 33.0 to 60.8 years, or by 84 percent. This compared to an increase of only 45 percent for whites (from 47.6 years in 1900 to 69.1 in 1950), and resulted in a substantial narrowing of the mortality differential characterizing these two racial groups (i.e., in 1900 the average life expectancy of whites exceeded that of nonwhites by 44 percent, but by 1950 this difference had been reduced to 14 percent). Between 1950 and 1978, the narrowing trend continued. During these years the rate of increase in life expectancy was twice as great for nonwhites (up 14 percent) as for whites (up by 7 percent), with the result that the differential was cut nearly in half: In 1950 the average white person had a life expectancy 8.3 years longer than the average nonwhite, but by 1978 this difference had been reduced to less than five years.

As noted earlier, such color, or racial, mortality differentials can largely be explained in terms of various social and economic differences between whites and nonwhites. In the United States, for example, data from the *Current Population Survey* (see Appendix A) reveal a 1980 median family income for the white population of $21,904 as compared with only $12,674 for black families. To cite another illustration, the median number of school years completed by whites in 1979 was 12.4 while that of blacks was 11.6 years. A major concomitant of these socioeconomic differences is likely to be a substantial difference between whites and nonwhites in general levels of living and particularly in levels of health and in the quantity and quality of medical care. The fact that the race mortality differential has narrowed over the years can, of course, be taken as evidence that there have been some very substantial improvements in the status of nonwhites in general. Should this trend continue—and we should do everything in our power to see that it does—Americans can look forward to the day when the difference between the death rates of whites and nonwhites may be reduced even further (perhaps even eliminated), or the day when the nonwhite segment of the population finally has equal access to all of the services and amenities available in our modern society. In the meantime, it is clear that the mortality experience of whites is still markedly lower than that of nonwhites, and that this mortality differential is a reflection of socioeconomic status differences that continue to exist between the two major color groups. The all-important significance of socioeconomic status as a determinant of mortality is discussed more fully in the following section.

Socioeconomic Status

By far the most significant social variable influencing group differences in mortality, on both national and international levels, is socioeconomic status. This differential is particularly significant for two reasons. First, many of the other mortality differentials that can be observed, such as the racial difference and the urban-rural differential, can be explained largely in terms of corresponding differences in socioeconomic status. Second, this differential is an indication of the extent to which all members of a society share equally in the various amenities, such as good health care, that the society has to offer. Put more directly, variations in mortality levels among different socioeconomic status groups are a measure of the failure of a society to provide equitable health care and treatment to its members.

Various methods have been used over the years to identify particular social class groups within a population (e.g., occupation, level of educational attainment, annual family income, housing characteristics of neighborhoods), and all of them have generally revealed the same basic relationship to mortality. There may be occasional discrepancies from one time period to another and from one population group to another, but for the most part it can be concluded that no matter how socioeconomic status is defined or measured, those groups that rank the highest will have the lowest mortality, and those groups that rank the lowest will have the highest

Table 4-8
Mortality Ratios by Occupational Class: England and Wales, 1910–63

Date and group	__	__	Occupational Class	__	__
	I	II	III	IV	V
1910–12					
Males age 25–64	88	94	96	93	142
1921–23					
Males age 20–64	82	94	95	101	125
1930–32					
Males age 20–64	90	94	97	102	111
Married women age 20–64	81	89	99	103	113
1949–53					
Males age 20–64	98	86	101	94	118
Married women age 20–64	96	88	101	104	110
1959–63					
Males age 15–64	76	81	100	103	143
Married women age 15–64	77	83	102	105	141

SOURCE: Presented in Aaron Antonovsky, "Social Class, Life Expectancy and Overall Mortality," *Milbank Memorial Fund Quarterly,* 45 (April 1967): 31–74. Data for 1959–63 from Metropolitan Life Insurance Company, *Statistical Bulletin,* 58 (January 1977). Class I, the highest socioeconomic level, is made up largely of professional workers; Class II covers technical, administrative, and managerial workers; in Class III are proprietors, clerical, sales, and skilled workers: Class IV consists of semiskilled workers; and Class V represents unskilled laborers.

mortality. Moreover, there is no evidence to suggest that the long-term decline of overall mortality in Western society has been accompanied by any significant narrowing of this differential.

The earliest and longest record of attempts to measure the relationship between socioeconomic status and mortality is found in England and Wales where studies of the association between occupational class and mortality have long been a major adjunct of the decennial population census. The overall findings of this research, as summarized by the mortality ratios presented in Table 4-8, are unequivocal in pointing to a pronounced inverse relationship between mortality and occupational class. These mortality ratios (MRs) measure the level of mortality of a particular population subgroup relative to the mortality level of all groups, which is set at 100. In this way they reveal at a glance both the direction and the magnitude of the deviations of subgroup mortality levels from the general average. For example, in the most recent period (1959–1963) one can easily note that the mortality level of adult males in the lowest occupational class (MR = 143) was 43 percent higher than the overall average, while mortality in the highest class (MR = 76) was 24 percent lower than that of all persons taken together. Closer examination of this table also reveals that a marked inverse relationship between occupational class and mortality is found at each time period, and that the magnitude of the differential is generally similar for both men and women.

The existence of social class mortality differences is also a long established fact in the United States. In the most detailed study of this topic car-

Table 4-9

Age-Standardized Average Annual Death Rates per 1,000 Population for Five Social Rank Areas, White Population: Chicago, 1930–60

Year and sex		I (highest)	II	III	IV	V (lowest)
1930	M	11.6	12.4	13.6	15.4	18.3
	F	6.6	7.2	8.4	9.9	13.2
1940	M	11.0	10.8	11.5	13.4	16.6
	F	5.8	5.6	6.3	7.8	10.4
1950	M	8.7	9.4	9.7	11.6	14.6
	F	4.2	4.9	5.1	6.4	8.6
1960	M	9.6	9.2	10.1	11.3	16.0
	F	4.7	4.5	5.2	6.0	8.6

SOURCE: E. M. Kitagawa and P. M. Hauser, *Differential Mortality in the United States: A Study in Socioeconomic Epidemiology* (Cambridge, Mass.: Harvard University Press, 1973), p. 53.

ried out to date in this country, Kitagawa and Hauser (1973) examined a variety of data for the nation as a whole as well as for certain local areas. On the basis of their analyses they concluded that "Socioeconomic differences in mortality were evident no matter which indexes of socioeconomic level were employed" (p. 152). Some of the findings from this study are presented in Table 4-9. These data, which are age-adjusted death rates for socioeconomic areas in Chicago that were defined on the basis of either the median rental value of neighborhood housing units (1930 and 1940) or median family income (1950 and 1960), clearly reveal the existence, and persistence, of a marked inverse relationship between socioeconomic status and mortality. Taken together, these data for England and Wales and Chicago readily support two generalizations: (1) no matter how the social class variable has been measured, one can observe a clear and pronounced inverse association between socioeconomic status and mortality; and (2) there is no evidence to indicate that this inverse relationship is being at all weakened as a concomitant of continued declines in the overall level of mortality.

Socioeconomic Status and Infant Mortality

It has been noted earlier that the level of mortality in infancy is especially sensitive to group differences in levels of social and economic well-being. Accordingly, it is not surprising that the socioeconomic mortality differential has been and continues to be extremely pronounced in infancy (Stockwell and Wicks, 1981). The extent to which the infant mortality rate (IMR) is influenced by socioeconomic status on an international level is clearly revealed by Figure 4-5, which shows an 87 percent drop in infant mortality as one moves from the poorest countries, those with a per capita gross national product of less than $500 a year (IMR=140), to the richest countries where the average GNP is in excess of $10,000 per capita (IMR=18). On a national level, the association between socioeconomic status and infant mortality has been a topic of concern and study since the early 1900s; and in spite of the dramatic declines in infant mortality during the present century, a recent review of several relevant research studies has concluded that there continues to be a marked inverse relationship between social class and all components of infant mortality in a number of modern Western nations, including the United States (Antonovsky and Bernstein, 1977). With respect to the United States, one recent study has found that the infant mortality rate of the lowest socioeconomic class was well over twice as high as that of the highest class (see Table 4-10). Moreover, this pronounced inverse differential was found for both the neonatal and postneonatal components of infant mortality, for all major causes of death, for both males and females, and for various ethnic subgroups at different dates and in different regions of the country. In short, the situation has changed little since Sir Arthur Newsholme (1910) wrote seventy years ago, "No fact is better

Table 4-10
Infant Mortality Rates in the Income Areas of Metropolitan Ohio, 1970

Income area	Infant mortality rates		
	Total	Neonatal	Postneonatal
All areas	19.3	14.4	4.9
I (highest income)	11.4	9.5	2.0
II	19.3	14.8	4.4
III	18.9	14.1	4.7
IV	21.4	15.6	5.9
V (lowest income)	28.7	20.2	8.6

SOURCE: E. G. Stockwell and J. W. Wicks, *Socioeconomic Differentials in Infant Mortality,* Maternal and Child Health and Crippled Children's Services, Bureau of Community Health Services, DHHS (Rockville, Md., 1981).

established than that the death rate, and especially the death rate among children, is high in inverse proportion to the social status of the population."

The reasons behind the existence and persistence of the inverse association between mortality and socioeconomic status, which can be observed for all major causes of death (Nagi and Stockwell, 1973), are not difficult to comprehend (Rainwater, 1974; Gortmaker, 1979). People in the lowest classes often cannot afford to eat an adequate diet and thus have a high prevalence of malnutrition, which makes them more susceptible to infection; they often live in less desirable neighborhoods, closer to concentrations of industrial air pollution and the concomitant greater risk of respiratory ailments; they live in older, run-down housing units that are poorly ventilated, inadequately heated, and often infested with insects and disease-carrying rodents; and the lack of discretionary income and the uncertainties that go along with low and intermittent incomes not only promote greater stress and associated chronic impairments but also impede people's ability to respond adequately to illness and to invest in preventive health care.

With respect to infant mortality specifically, a poor diet not only is harmful for the older infant but also is known to be associated with a higher risk of premature birth and low birth weight, both of which are major correlates of mortality in early infancy. Lower-class women also smoke more, which may affect weight gain during pregnancy and subsequent infant birth weight; certain aspects of their reproductive behavior (e.g., higher incidence of out-of-wedlock births, younger age at marriage and initial childbearing, more frequent pregnancies) contribute to a higher risk of infant mortality; and they are less likely to be cognizant of good health care prac-

Figure 4-5
Average Infant Mortality Rates in Countries Grouped According to Annual Per Capita Gross National Product (GNP), c. 1980

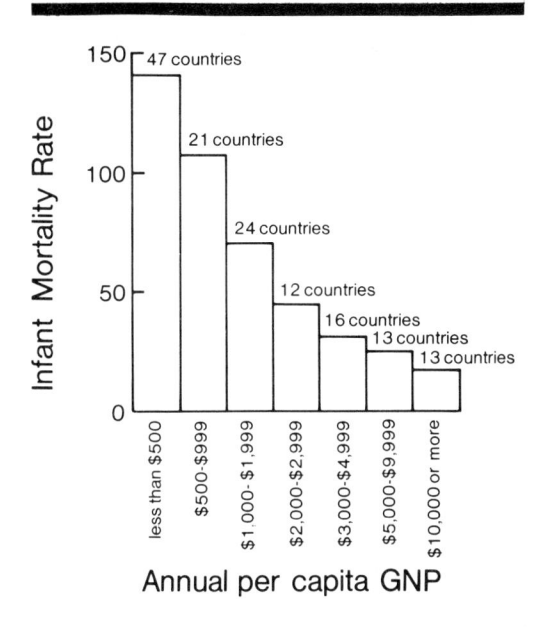

[Bar chart: Infant Mortality Rate vs. Annual per capita GNP]

- less than $500: 47 countries (~140)
- $500–$999: 21 countries (~108)
- $1,000–$1,999: 24 countries (~70)
- $2,000–$2,999: 12 countries (~45)
- $3,000–$4,999: 16 countries (~32)
- $5,000–$9,999: 13 countries (~22)
- $10,000 or more: 13 countries (~18)

SOURCE: Based on data from the *1981 World Population Data Sheet* of the Population Reference Bureau. Per capita GNP is an index of the average income level of a nation, and reflects the share of a nation's wealth that each member of the population would receive each year if the GNP were divided evenly among all the inhabitants of a nation.

tices (such as the need for various kinds of immunization shots) and, accordingly, less likely to avail themselves of many existing prenatal and postnatal health services and facilities. The influence of such factors is obviously not fixed, as the biological influence of age is more or less set. This means that they should be subject to modification, and that through such modification it should be possible to narrow substantially, if not eliminate, the social class mortality differential. Moreover, the narrowing of this differential should contribute to a further reduction in the overall death rate. In the meantime, however, the persistence of an inverse association between socioeconomic status and mortality in any society stands as a ringing indictment of the failure of that society to provide equally for all of its members.

Marital Status

Although race and especially socioeconomic status are the major social determinants of mortality levels, a number of other differentials have been documented and studied over the years. It has long been known, for example, that persons who are married have a lower death rate than persons in other marital status categories (single, widowed, or divorced). To illustrate, the Canadian data shown in Table 4-11 clearly show that overall marital status death rates are largely a function of age composition: singles (generally younger than persons in other categories) have the lowest crude death rate whereas widowed persons have the highest. However, for both males and females, the age-specific death rates are generally much lower for married persons than for any other category; and they tend to be highest for the divorced, or those who, for whatever reason, have been unable to remain in a stable marital relationship.

This marital status mortality differential, which has also been observed in a number of less developed countries as well as other industrialized nations (United Nations, 1982), and which characterizes both males and females in all age groups and for all major causes of death, is generally explained by reference to two sets of factors: (1) selective mating, and (2) home environment differences among married and unmarried persons. On the one hand, it is generally assumed that marriage selects the healthier people in the society. Men who are sickly or physically infirm are less likely to be married, not only because they may be hesitant about assuming the responsibilities of providing for a family but also because they are less likely to find a woman willing to accept them as a mate. Similarly, reasonably good health would seem to be an important factor in female marriageability, if only because most men would generally prefer to marry a healthy woman rather than a sickly one.

On the other hand, it is customary to explain the marital status differential partly in terms of differences in the home environment of married as opposed to unmarried persons. Married people generally adhere to a more orderly schedule in their daily living. A married man, for example, is likely to eat more regularly, eat a more nutritionally adequate diet, keep more regular hours, and get more sleep than his bachelor counterpart. Marriage also represents a better physical and mental adaptation to life than does celibacy (either self-imposed or involuntary); and there is likely to be a certain amount of comfort and satisfaction derived from the companionship of marriage and family living that contrasts quite sharply with the loneliness so often characteristic of the lives of the unmarried. The significance of lifestyle differences as they relate to female mortality has recently been studied by Verbrugge (1980), who found that the advantages of being married were enhanced if a woman also had a job outside the home. That is, the

Table 4-11
Deaths per 1,000 Population by Age, Sex, and Marital Status: Canada, 1976

Age and sex	Single	Married	Widowed	Divorced
Male				
All ages	3.4	10.7	84.5	19.5
15–19	1.5	0.6	2.2	4.0
20–24	2.2	0.8	8.8	4.2
25–34	2.8	1.0	10.9	4.0
35–44	6.5	2.0	9.3	8.2
45–54	14.5	6.1	16.2	16.6
55–64	28.5	15.9	30.4	36.1
65–74	54.6	37.3	54.3	63.8
75 and over	122.5	97.2	147.5	181.1
Female				
All ages	2.2	4.3	40.5	5.9
15–19	0.5	0.2	3.8	...
20–24	0.7	0.3	1.9	0.8
25–34	1.4	0.5	3.0	1.3
35–44	2.9	1.2	3.2	2.9
45–54	5.6	3.3	5.7	5.3
55–64	9.9	7.7	10.7	11.3
65–74	21.5	19.0	22.7	25.9
75 and over	76.8	60.6	86.2	68.6

SOURCE: *Demographic Yearbook, 1980* (New York: United Nations, 1982).

more social roles women had to perform, including the role of wife, the lower the death rate.

Persons who are widowed or divorced may have an added disadvantage over other single persons. Not only do such people not have the social, biological, and emotional advantages of a happy family life, but they also have frequently had to adjust to the sudden, often traumatic, loss of these advantages. This may further impair their chances for survival and may account for the fact that their death rates at all ages are higher than the rates of the comparable group of persons who never married. Widowed persons may have had their health adversely affected by the death of the spouse (perhaps being weakened as a result of caring for the spouse during a protracted period of illness prior to death) as well as by failing to overcome the hardships of widowhood. On the other hand, the divorced group obviously contains a disproportionate number of persons who have been unable to make a satisfactory adjustment to life, a fact that may be both a cause and an effect of physical weakness. Whatever the reasons, it is clear that a significant proportion of men and women who either do not marry or whose marriage becomes dissolved are relatively poor health risks and thus have higher death rates than married persons.

Place of Residence

Another mortality differential that should be discussed relates to place of residence, particularly to residence in rural as opposed to urban areas. Historically, cities have always had bad reputations as places where one's life chances were lower than in rural areas. This was not because the rural environment was such an auspicious place in which to live, but rather because the extremely unsanitary living conditions so widespread in the past (e.g., overcrowding in vermin-infested living quarters, open sewers, contaminated drinking water) were most pronounced in the larger cities. Not surprisingly, then, the level of mortality in cities was generally much higher than in the countryside. In the United States from 1900 to 1902, for example, the average life expectancy of white males in urban areas (forty-four years) was a full ten years less than that of rural white males (fifty-four years). For white females, corresponding figures were forty-eight years in urban and fifty-five years in rural areas (Dublin et al., 1949, p. 73).

What was true of the industrialized nations in the past is also found in many of the less developed countries today. That is, with a few exceptions where initial modernization programs may have had a very one-sided impact in urban areas to the neglect and detriment of the rural sector, generally in the less developed countries today the death rates in the larger cities are higher than those in rural areas. In the long run, however, as societies undergo modernization the various sanitary and medical improvements that accompany it improve drastically the life chances of urban dwellers. When this occurs, the traditional urban-rural mortality differential tends to narrow, and in many cases it has even reversed itself. In part such a reversal may occur because rural residents have less access to modern medical treatment facilities, which tend to be concentrated in the larger cities. It may also reflect differences in the age composition of urban and rural populations. The long-term movement of people away from farm areas to cities has generally been most selective of young people, leaving rural areas disproportionately populated by the elderly.

Although the modernization process generally leads to its narrowing, there is evidence to indicate that the traditional urban-rural mortality differential still persists in the United States. To illustrate, the annual report *Vital Statistics of the United States* for 1976 revealed an infant mortality rate in urban places (16.2) that was 14 percent higher than that of the balance of the country (14.2 infant deaths per 1,000 live births). The differential was even more pronounced in metropolitan counties where the urban place infant mortality rate of 16.0 exceeded the rural rate of 12.7 per 1,000 by 26 percent.

A number of reasons may be cited to explain this apparent persistence of the traditional urban-rural mortality differential in the United States. For one thing, it may reflect the same kind of differences in living conditions that accounted for the higher urban death rate of the past. That is, many of the environmental problems confronting our society today (e.g., industrial air pollution) are concentrated in urban areas where they contribute to excessively high death rates from respiratory ailments. Further, the greater tempo of life associated with urban living may lead to increased stress and tension, thereby enhancing cardiovascular mortality. However, the most significant factor contributing to the less favorable mortality experience of the American urban population is likely a decline in the overall socioeconomic status of the population in many of our large cities. A major population trend in this country since the end of World War II has been a movement of middle and upper socioeconomic groups out of the cities into the surrounding suburban and rural fringe areas, and an opposing movement of lower socioeconomic groups (especially blacks) away from rural areas into the core cities of the major metropolitan centers (see Chapter 11). In many parts of the country these trends have created a dual society characterized by cities that are inhabited disproportionately by poor blacks and other ethnic minorities and that are surrounded by affluent white suburbs. The higher urban death rate is largely the result of the fact that the high mortality subgroups in the population are disproportionately represented in the large cities.

Several mortality differentials can also be noted among the various geographic regions and individual states in the United States. For the most part, however, these geographic differentials can be explained in terms of differences in population composition (age, race, and socioeconomic status) or differences in the degree of urbanization. In 1980, for example, death rates were lowest in the northwestern part of the United States where urbanization is relatively low and where the number of nonwhites is negligible. At the other extreme, death rates were highest in the heavily urban Middle Atlantic states and in the Deep South. Among individual states, the 1980 death rates were lowest in Alaska (4.1 per 1,000), Hawaii (5.5), and Utah (6.1), and they were highest in Florida (11.6) and the District of Columbia (14.4).

Levels of mortality clearly vary substantially among different societies and among different subgroups within the same society. With the exception of such obvious factors as age, and to some extent sex, these mortality differentials are largely determined by a variety of social and economic factors. Since the influence of such factors is not fixed, it follows that the differentials themselves are not fixed but are subject to modification through an alleviation of their underlying determinants. As modernization trends continue in many parts of the Third World today, for example, one can expect a further narrowing of many of the international mortality differentials that presently exist; and further social progress in relatively low mortality countries such as the United States could also narrow some of their current differentials, thereby contributing to a further reduction in the overall level of mortality.

MORBIDITY

No discussion of mortality would be complete without some reference to *morbidity* (illness). In a general sense, morbidity is important because of its role as a precursor of death and because changes in the incidence and prevalence of particular diseases affect changes in the overall mortality picture. To illustrate, the decline of the death rate in the nineteenth and early twentieth centuries was due to an increasing ability to prevent various infectious and parasitic diseases. Likewise, the differences in levels of mortality between the more developed and less developed countries today reflect differences in the prevalence of acute infectious and parasitic diseases such as tuberculosis, dysentery, measles, whooping cough, influenza, and pneumonia. More recently, the slowdown of mortality decline in the United States and other Western nations during the 1950s occurred because the downward trend in the death rate for many of the infectious diseases halted at the same time that the incidence of the major degenerative diseases continued to increase, and the resumption of mortality decline in the 1970s reflects renewed declines in many infectious diseases as well as a reversal in the upward trend of the major cardiovascular diseases. First of all, then, a knowledge of trends in the incidence and prevalence of particular diseases is necessary for an adequate understanding of overall mortality trends and differentials.

A second reason for being interested in morbidity concerns its relationship to economic productivity and the general welfare of a society. Simply put, where the incidence of morbidity is high, worker productivity will be low, and this will be reflected in a lower level of living for the population as a whole. This relationship is equally as important on an individual level. Persons in any society who have a chronic illness or who suffer from poor health in general will have difficulty in finding a job, and if they do find a job, their illness may cause frequent absences from work and resulting loss of pay. In this sense, then, morbidity may act as an underlying cause in the circular chain of events leading to the higher death rates found among the lower socioeconomic status groups in society. That is, ill health leads to unemployment and/or high absenteeism from work; irregular and intermittent work leads to a low income; a low income means one is less able to maintain a level of living conducive to good health; and this generally lower level of living, of course, promotes ill health, a greater risk of mortality, and a higher death rate. In short, ill health may be both a cause and an effect of low socioeconomic status.

Although morbidity is an important topic, discussion of it must necessarily be limited by the subjective and relative nature of illness. One person's "ill health" may not be another's, and this makes it extremely difficult to obtain reliable morbidity data from all segments of the population. The information that we have been able to collect (through the U.S. National Health Surveys and other sources) suggests that although we cannot generalize from mortality to morbidity, there is a close similarity to their patterns. Thus, if we know that one population subgroup has a higher death rate than another subgroup, we will generally not be wrong if we assume that it also has a higher illness rate. For example, where poor housing and other adverse environmental conditions are associated with higher death rates from infectious respiratory diseases such as tuberculosis, it can generally be assumed that a higher incidence of the disease in question is associated with the same environmental conditions. The implication here is that a more equitable sharing of our current knowledge and techniques for preventing and treating illness among the less privileged members of the society would do more than lead to a reduction in their death rate; the resulting improvement in their overall level of physical well-being would also reduce the incidence of illness, and this in turn might affect such things as enhanced ability to find and hold a job. This, of course, would benefit not only the individual and his or her family but also the society at large, which would profit by the individual's increased productivity and by the reduction of unemployment and other welfare expenditures frequently associated with ill health.

MORTALITY AND POPULATION POLICY

A *population policy* may be defined as any official government program that has as its purpose the attainment of some stated demographic objective (a slower growth rate, a higher birth rate, a dispersal of population away from areas of urban concentration, etc.). There are two basic components to any population policy: a *goal* that the government seeks to accomplish, and the *program* it implements in an effort to attain the desired goal. The policy goal may be a very specific one (e.g., a zero population growth rate by the year 2000), or it may be a more general one (e.g., a slower growth rate and a more balanced distribution of population among urban and rural areas).

Either way, efforts to achieve the policy goal will entail programs that deliberately seek to manipulate one or more basic demographic processes. For example, if the general policy goal is to increase the size of a population, the government might adopt programs that restrict emigration and encourage immigration (e.g., refuse to issue exit visas, distribute free land for settlement, grant various concessions to immigrants such as tax breaks or exemption from military service), or it might adopt programs aimed at encouraging high fertility and large families (e.g., make contraception and abortion illegal, establish baby bonus schemes, impose special taxes on persons who remain single). Conversely, if the policy goal is to put an end to population growth, the government could adopt programs that restrict immigration and encourage emigration and that encourage a reduction in fertility (e.g., mount propaganda programs extolling the advantages of small families, provide free contraceptive services, impose marriage or fertility taxes).

Most population policy considerations in the world today pertain to fertility and migration, and they will be discussed more fully in the appropriate chapters. With respect to mortality, one's initial thoughts might understandably be that the only viable policy goal for a government to adopt is one of achieving as low a death rate as possible for all segments of its population. Unfortunately, history tells us that this has not always been the case. It was not at all uncommon in the past for societies to try to reduce population size or maintain it at a given level by resorting to such mortality practices as infanticide or abandonment of the aged and infirm. Stark evidence of the fact that such policies are not unheard of in modern times is provided by the purges carried out in the Soviet Union during the Stalinist era, the deliberate attempt by the government of Nazi Germany to exterminate the European Jewish population, and the more recent purging of intellectuals and the slaughter of thousands of its citizens by the government of Cambodia/Kampuchea.

In spite of the periodic occurrence of such grisly tragedies, and although persons who define abortion as the deliberate taking of a human life might disagree, there is no one today who explicitly advocates programs that would slow down population growth either by impeding mortality decline or by raising death rates up to former higher levels. However, there have certainly been discussions of such a mortality increase being imposed indirectly. On one level are those who argue that if population growth rates in some of the poorest countries are not soon brought down by reductions in fertility, then mortality could increase as a natural accompaniment to a steadily worsening economic situation. On a more callous level, some have even suggested that the imposition of higher death rates as a check to population growth in some of the poorest countries could originate externally through a policy of deliberate neglect. For example, there are those who subscribe to what is called the *lifeboat ethic*. They view the earth as already seriously overpopulated, much like a full lifeboat with limited provisions, tossing about aimlessly on the high seas (Hardin, 1974). It is so seriously overpopulated, in fact, that it cannot take on any more "passengers" unless they can clearly provide for themselves. Strict adherence to this ethic would require that the rich countries deliberately withhold food and medical aid from the poorest countries until they get their population situation under control.

A somewhat similar view would utilize the medical concept of *triage* as a basis for determining which poor countries are worth trying to save (Paddox and Paddox, 1967). Triage is used in times of medical emergencies to establish a priority order for treating casualties: the least seriously injured and the near dead are passed over in favor of those whose life may depend on immediate care. Those who advocate the triage approach to international aid would divide the poor countries of the world into three "medical" categories: (1) the *walking wounded,* or those that may be temporarily in a bad way but whose population/resource situation is such that they will ultimately be able to survive on their own; (2) the *basket cases,* or those countries whose population is already so large and growing so fast in relation to its resource base that a catastrophic disaster cannot be averted; and (3) the *chosen ones,* or those countries that have made a good start on achieving both economic development and fertility decline, but who desperately need external assistance in order to complete the process. This last group of countries, according to the triage orientation, would be selected to receive food surpluses and economic assistance from the more highly developed countries, whereas mortality would be left to run its course in the first two groups. No rational person is really advocating that the rich countries adopt such a Draconian policy, but triage has been discussed as an objective criterion for determining how to allocate scarce resources in a time of world crisis. What will countries like the United States do, for example, if a major worldwide food shortage leaves a billion people facing starvation, while the food-surplus countries have enough to feed only two or three hundred million? How would we decide which two or three hundred million should receive the limited surpluses? The numbers used in this illustration are irrelevant. The basic question is one of deciding which countries will receive food assistance when there is not enough surplus to aid all countries. Triage has been suggested as a method of resolving this very difficult moral dilemma.

FUTURE OUTLOOK

Although one must not ignore the existence of orientations such as triage and the lifeboat ethic, it is likely that any official policy adopted today will be concerned with reducing mortality. Furthermore, it is a fairly safe assumption that we can expect further declines in mortality in the years ahead—in the rich as well as in the poor countries. The anticipated mortality declines will be most pronounced in the less developed high mortality countries of the Third World. Although many of these countries have recently experienced notable declines in their crude death rates (partly in response to their changing age composition as persistent high levels of fertility have steadily increased the number and proportion of young people in the population), the fact that infant mortality rates in the Third World are still much higher than in the more developed nations clearly indicates that there is still room for substantial improvements. Moreover, the fact that the governments of many of the less developed countries are actively promoting vigorous programs for improving sanitation, public health, and medical care suggests that in the absence of some unforeseen catastrophe their mortality levels can be expected to fall even further. We can also anticipate that the rate and magnitude of mortality declines in the years ahead will likely be the reverse of what has occurred to date. That is, the declines will be least pronounced in those Latin American countries where the earlier European influence resulted in an earlier start on modernization, and most pronounced in the high death rate countries of Africa that have only recently emerged from colonial domination. Future mortality declines in Asia will likely fall somewhere between these two.

In making such optimistic projections about future mortality declines in the less developed countries it must be stressed that they are based on an assumption that general programs of economic development will continue to improve overall living conditions. In some countries this may not happen. Rather, as suggested earlier, some countries may experience population growth rates of such rapidity that they will wipe out potential economic gains and forestall further mortality declines, or perhaps even contribute to an increase in the death rate. While it is to be hoped that such cases will be either very rare or that it will be possible to modify them through some kind of international assistance program, it is a very real possibility that we cannot afford to ignore.

Many of the highly developed countries of the Western world can also anticipate further mortality declines in the years to come. However, since average life expectancy is already so high in these countries, future mortality declines will require greater effort to achieve and will be much less dramatic than those projected for the Third World. In this context it can be noted that there are two potential sources of future declines in the overall death rate in the more developed countries. First, substantial gains could come from a narrowing or perhaps even the elimination of some of the mortality differentials that presently exist, particularly those associated with socioeconomic status. Second, some mortality reduction may result from enhanced control over those degenerative diseases that are the major causes of death in the advanced societies today.

In speaking about the possible reduction of deaths from chronic diseases in the highly developed countries, we must stress that the greatest contributions medical science and public health have so far made in gaining control over mortality have been in the area of disease prevention rather than treatment. Naturally, curative powers have increased (witness the power of penicillin), but not nearly as much as preventive powers. It was not a miraculous cure that eliminated smallpox as a major cause of death; rather, it was the development of a serum that prevents the disease from occurring. Similarly, the preventive infant DPT shots have more or less done away with diphtheria, pertussis (whooping cough), and tetanus as major killers of young children. In other words, humanity's greatest progress in reducing deaths due to a particular disease has come through eliminating the disease in question. Future declines in chronic disease mortality are also likely to depend largely on finding ways to prevent the occurrence of those degenerative diseases that are the leading causes of death today.

Despite the importance of prevention as a means of reducing death rates from particular diseases, the bulk of the research being done in the medical profession today is focused on improving treatment techniques (e.g., the coronary bypass and transplant surgery) that will help postpone death from particular chronic conditions rather than preventing their occurrence altogether. Even so, a number of causal connections have already been definitely established (e.g., the relationship between cigarette smoking and lung cancer), and it is widely accepted that an individual's life chances can be considerably enhanced by such simple practices as following a regular regime of moderate exercise, avoiding excessive obesity, adhering to a diet that is low in animal fats, and not smoking. It must be stressed, however, that chronic diseases in the long run result from a disintegration of organic tissue as the body grows older, so we are not likely to witness any major breakthrough similar to those that have led to the conquest of many infectious diseases. Nevertheless, as medical science continues to learn more about the many factors that are causally related to the various chronic ailments, it is possible to anticipate minor breakthroughs. These could result in some reductions in the death rate at the older ages, which could in turn contribute to a further increase in average life expectancy.

SUMMARY

Mortality levels vary markedly from one country to another, and even within the modern low death rate nations there are pronounced differences in the risk of dying among the various subgroups of the population. A knowledge and understanding of these subgroup mortality differentials, and of their underlying causes, is essential for an adequate understanding of the overall mortality situation.

The determinants of mortality differentials can be divided into two broad groups: biological determinants such as age and sex, and social determinants such as marital status, race, and socioeconomic class. The influence of the biological determinants is relatively fixed, and the associated mortality differentials are not likely to change substantially unless there is some major technological breakthrough in either the prevention or the treatment of the chronic degenerative diseases. The influence of the social factors, however, is not necessarily fixed; hence, the mortality differentials that are associated with them are also not fixed but should be subject to considerable narrowing through the implementation or expansion of various health and welfare programs. During the 1980s, for example, it is anticipated that a more rapid decline in death rates for blacks than for whites will continue to narrow the traditional color mortality differential in the United States.

People die from a variety of causes, and there are substantial temporal as well as spatial and subgroup differences in the incidence, prevalence, and lethality of particular diseases. For example, where mortality has declined it has done so largely because of increasing control over communicable diseases, and many of the mortality differentials that currently prevail are due in large part to these infectious diseases. Thus, a knowledge of general morbidity patterns and variations is also necessary for a full understanding of trends and variations in the overall mortality situation.

Although induced mortality was sometimes used in the past as a means of population control, it is safe to say that all societies today seek to reach and maintain as low a death rate as possible. Efforts in this direction have in fact been very successful in recent years, and while some notable differentials still exist, death rates have been coming down all over the world. In many of the less developed countries, however, declining mortality and resulting increases in rates of population growth have led to a worsening of what was already a low socioeconomic level, and there is some concern over whether it will be possible to maintain the recent low death rates or whether mortality levels will rise again as an unintended but unavoidable response to a steadily worsening economic situation.

Barring such a development, and in the absence of a nuclear holocaust or a major world economic collapse, mortality is likely to continue to decline in both the developed and the developing countries. Future mortality declines will be most pronounced in the developing countries where death rates are still fairly high by modern standards, and they will come as a response to continued social and economic development. In the more highly developed countries some overall mortality reductions might be achieved as a result of increasing control over the major degenerative diseases and/or through a narrowing of some of the differentials that currently prevail, but they will be much less dramatic than the declines that are possible in the less developed areas.

REFERENCES AND SUGGESTED READING

Adamchak, Donald J. "Emerging Trends in the Relationship between Infant Mortality and Socioeconomic Status." *Social Biology*, 26 (Spring 1979): 16–29.
Antonovsky, Aaron, and Judith Bernstein. "Social Class and Infant Mortality." *Social Science and Medicine*, 11. Great Britain, 1977: 453–70.
Bouvier, Leon F., and Jean van der Tak. "Infant Mortality: Progress and Problems." *Population Bulletin*, 31 (April 1976).
Davis, Christopher, and Murray Feshbach. "Rising Infant Mortality in the U.S.S.R. in the 1970s." In U.S. Bureau of the Census, *International Population Reports*, Series P-95, No. 74. Washington, D.C.: U.S. Government Printing Office, 1980.
Dublin, Louis I., Alfred J. Lotka, and Mortimer Spiegelman. *Length of Life*. New York: Ronald Press, 1949.
Gortmaker, Steven L. "Poverty and Infant Mortality in the United States." *American Sociological Review*, 44 (April 1979): 280–97.
Hardin, Garrett. "Living on a Lifeboat." *Bio-Science*, 24 (October 1974): 561–68.
Kitagawa, Evelyn M., and Philip M. Hauser. *Differential Mortality in the United States: A Study in Socioeconomic Epidemiology*. Cambridge, Mass.: Harvard University Press, 1973.
Madigan, Francis C. "Are Sex Mortality Differentials Biologically Caused?" *Milbank Memorial Fund Quarterly*, 35 (April 1957): 202–23.
Markides, Kyriakos S., and Connie McFarland. "Recent Trends in the Infant Mortality–Socioeconomic Status Relationship." *Social Forces*, 61 (September 1982): 268–76.
Nagi, Mostafa H., and Edward G. Stockwell. "Socioeconomic Differentials in Mortality by Cause of Death." *Health Services Reports*, 85 (May 1973): 449–56.
Nam, Charles B., et al. "Causes of Death Which Contribute to the Mortality Crossover Effect." *Social Biology*, 25 (Winter 1978): 306–14.
National Center for Health Statistics. *Changes in Mortality among the Elderly: United States, 1940–78*, Vital and Health Statistics Series 3, No. 22. Washington, D.C., 1982.
Newland, Kathleen. *Infant Mortality and the Health of Societies*. World-

watch Paper 47. Washington, D.C.: Worldwatch Institute, December 1981.

Newsholme, Arthur. *Infant and Child Mortality,* 39th Annual Report of the Local Government Board, Report Cd 5312. London: Darling & Son, 1910.

Omran, Abdel R. "Epidemiologic Transition in the U.S." *Population Bulletin,* 32 (May 1977).

Paddock, William, and Paul Paddock. *Famine, 1975.* Boston: Little, Brown, 1967.

Preston, Samuel H. *Mortality Patterns in National Populations.* New York: Academic Press, 1976.

Rainwater, Lee. "The Lower Class: Health, Illness and Medical Institutions." In Lee Rainwater, ed., *Inequality and Justice.* Chicago: Aldine, 1974.

Retherford, Robert D. "Tobacco Smoking and the Sex Mortality Differential." *Demography,* 9 (May 1972): 203–16.

Retherford, Robert D. *The Changing Sex Differentials in Mortality.* Westport, Conn.: Greenwood Press, 1975.

Schoen, Robert, and Verne E. Nelson. "Mortality by Cause among Spanish Surnamed Californians, 1969–71." *Social Science Quarterly,* 62 (June 1981): 259–74.

Stockwell, Edward G. *Population and People.* Chicago: Quadrangle Books, 1968.

Stockwell, Edward G., and Jerry W. Wicks. *Socioeconomic Differentials in Infant Mortality.* Rockville, Md.: Maternal and Child Health and Crippled Children's Services, Bureau of Community Health Services, 1981.

United Nations. *Demographic Yearbook: 1980.* New York: United Nations, 1982.

Verbrugge, Lois M. "Recent Trends in Sex Mortality Differentials in the United States." *Women and Health,* 5 (Fall 1980): 17–38.

Weatherby, Norman L., et al. "Development, Inequality, Health Care, and Mortality at the Older Ages: A Cross-National Analysis." *Demography,* 20 (February 1983): 27–43.

Weeks, John R. *Population: An Introduction to Concepts and Issues,* 2nd ed. Belmont, Calif.: Wadsworth, 1981, Chapters 6 and 15.

Weller, Robert H., and Leon F. Bouvier. *Population: Demography and Policy.* New York: St. Martin's, 1981, Chapters 7 and 11.

HUMAN FERTILITY

5

The second basic demographic process is fertility, or the bearing of children. The birth of a child is of great individual and social significance in all societies. It marks the entry into the world of a new human being whose life chances are usually shaped by the circumstances into which he or she is born. A birth also affects the individual and social situations of the parents and any previously born children. Moreover, the birth of a child influences the wider circle of the family, extending to aunts, uncles, grandparents, and other relatives.

Like death, the other major demographic event, birth is enmeshed in social rituals and ceremonies. Where births are officially registered, as in the modern world, such registration also sets in motion a process by which the child is incorporated into the social order, and it establishes the child's access to such rights of citizenship as education and Social Security.

A birth may also be enhanced in significance by the sex of the child. Male children, and especially the first son, are considered especially important in most societies. The number and timing of births is also crucial to both parents and children. Depending on the nature of the society, and the circumstances of the parents, large families may be a cause for pride, a source of prestige, and a source of income, or alternatively, a cause of poverty and life-long disadvantage.

In societies with low rates of infant mortality, the size of families is determined largely by fertility. Moreover, since closed populations (those in which there is no migration in or out) are influenced solely by births and deaths, the level of fertility is a key variable affecting a society's future size and composition. Changes in birth patterns, for example, invariably are reflected in changes in the age structure of society. In fact, with mortality now fairly well under control in much of the world, it is fertility that is shaping the future of most populations.

No society has ever been indifferent to the birth of its children; individuals, therefore, always make their fertility decisions within a societal context. That is, human fertility is determined largely by such social factors as beliefs and attitudes, norms, and the structures of family and economic life. For this reason, behavior that at first seems irrational to us may take on a different meaning if we realize that reproductive choices are always made within a cultural context which includes, among other things, the realities of infant mortality, the economic value of children, and the social status of parenthood. At the same time we need to remain aware that fertility is not always, or even usually, the result of calculated decision-making (Neal and Groat, 1980). Couples in societies everywhere have children they did not plan and do not want. A major reason for this is that people seldom behave reproductively. Instead they behave sexually, and childbearing is a by-product, sometimes planned and sometimes unplanned, of their sexuality. Thus fertility is always determined partly by social rules, such as those related to courtship and marriage, which regulate sexual behavior. We will return to these and other determinants of fertility later. As in the discussion of mortality, however, we will first consider some of the basic concepts before moving on to a fuller discussion of the factors affecting fertility.

DEFINITIONS AND CONCEPTS

In order to discuss differences in fertility between various societies, or trends in childbearing throughout history, we must be able to denote levels of fertility by using accurate and meaningful terms. Several of these terms relate to the *measurement* of fertility. Such common measures of fertility as the *crude birth rate*, *total fertility rate*, and *age-specific rates* allow us to make different kinds of statements with different kinds of information about the fertility of various populations. These measures of fertility are defined and their usefulness explained in Appendix B. Here we will limit ourselves to a few of the most important fertility concepts, beginning with the distinction between fertility and fecundity.

Fertility refers to the births that occur in a population. Demographers measure fertility, or reproductive performance, on the basis of *live births*. Since a live birth can result only from sexual intercourse that has resulted in pregnancy, and from a *gestation* (carrying of the fetus in the uterus) that has resulted in successful *parturition* (the act of giving birth), our understanding of fertility involves a complex system of biological and social factors affecting each of these steps. Fertility as a biological process involves the capacity to conceive (or impregnate) and bear children. Biological variables affecting this capacity for reproduction include the woman's age, the general state of her health, and the age, health, and generative power of her sexual partner. This biological aspect of fertility is called *fecundity*. Fecund women and men, therefore, are those who are capable biologically of producing children; people who are *infecund* or *sterile* cannot produce children. Most lay people would think of "fertile" and "sterile" as being opposites, but for demographers the opposite of "sterile" is "fecund" and the opposite of "fertile" is "childless." A man or woman may be fecund, or capable of bearing children, but he or she does not become fertile until a live birth has actually occurred.

Two additional fertility concepts are *parity*, the number of live births experienced by an individual mother, and *family size*, the number of live births to a specific family (not the number of surviving children at a point in time). "Family size," to the demographer, therefore, means the number of live births ever experienced by a woman. Similarly, *completed family size* refers to the total number of live births to a woman who has finished her childbearing.

From a purely biological perspective, most women are capable of producing far more children in their lifetimes than they actually do. The major limiting variable of a physiological nature is age. The fecund years for women generally extend from the age of *menarche* (the onset of menstruation), typically in the early teens, to the age of *menopause* (the end of menstruation), around the late forties. Exactly how much fecundity declines with advancing age is still uncertain, although female fecundity is believed to peak in the early twenties and remain relatively high until at least the early thirties. The incidence of *involuntary fetal mortality* (i.e., miscarriage or spontaneous abortion) may also increase with age.

Although there are cases on record of individual women who have produced twenty or more children without ever experiencing a multiple birth, such feats are quite rare. Moreover, there are no known societies in which the average family size even approaches such a high level, because fertility, unlike mortality, is not inevitable. Rather, fertility is more a social process than a biological one, since the capacity for reproduction is only a starting point in explaining different levels of fertility. For instance, the number of children born to a couple will depend partly on the social norms prevailing in their society. Norms for family size, in turn, depend on such social and economic features of societies as the nature of family life and the participation of women in the labor force. Because couples make their reproductive choices within the constraints of societal norms, it is necessary in the study of fertility to take into consideration a wide range of attitudes and values regarding the bearing of children.

The extent to which social factors influence fertility behavior is clearly revealed by the wide range of childbearing patterns characterizing different populations, past and present, as well as different subgroups within the same population. In the world today, for example, the average number of children born per woman varies from two or fewer in most of the industrialized nations of Western Europe to seven or more in a number of the less developed countries in Africa, Asia, and Latin America. Even within low fertility countries like the United States some groups have markedly higher fertility levels than others. To illustrate, among the Hutterites, an Anabaptist religious group that migrated from Switzerland to the upper midwestern United States in the late nineteenth century and then to Canada, women were giving birth to an average of about eleven children each as recently as the 1950s (Eaton and Mayer, 1954).

The Hutterites, with their very high fertility, are a population in which *natural fertility* occurs—i.e., where births are not subject to any deliberate control. The Hutterites regard birth control as sinful, and their society is organized in such a way that large families are highly valued. All property is shared, for example, and children are cared for communally. Moreover, there is no individual pursuit of wealth, and divorce is unacceptable. Nevertheless, even among the Hutterites, fertility is well below the levels it could reach if only biological factors were operating. The major reason for this is that marriage is delayed until the Hutterite woman has been baptized, as a mature adult, around the age of twenty. The fact is that in every society the physiological maximum fertility is higher than the level of fertility actually achieved. Most women everywhere actually bear substantially fewer children than they are theoretically capable of bearing. A variety of social constraints and practices, only some of which involve the deliberate exercise of birth control, are responsible for this.

FACTORS AFFECTING FERTILITY

As we have said, a live birth is possible only if a couple has sexual intercourse that results in a pregnancy, and if that pregnancy is successfully carried to term. Every step in this process is affected by a combination of social and biological factors. To illustrate, a fecund woman who remains a virgin will never be exposed to the risk of conception. Similarly, a child will not result if a woman or her partner are infecund, or if they effectively practice contraception, or if any pregnancies that result are intentionally or unintentionally aborted. Therefore, when we find populations of women who are the same age but who have different levels of fertility, we might begin to understand the fertility differences by looking for variations in exposure to intercourse, or for differences in contraceptive practice, fecundity, or abortion. In any society, the factors that influence the fertility of the population must operate through one or more of the *intermediate variables* of reproduction: *intercourse, conception,* and *gestation* (Davis and Blake, 1956).

The Intermediate Variables

These variables are said to be intermediate in the reproduction process because they fall between fertility on the one hand and the normative and social structures of society on the other:

1. Factors affecting exposure to *intercourse*
   a. Those factors influencing the formation and dissolution of unions during the reproductive period, including age of entry into sexual unions, extent of permanent celibacy, and amount of reproductive period spent after or between unions as when unions are broken by divorce or death.
   b. Those influencing the exposure to intercourse within unions, such as voluntary or involuntary abstinence and the frequency of coitus.
2. Factors affecting exposure to *conception* such as fecundity or infecundity (either involuntary or voluntary), and the use or nonuse of contraception.

Figure 5-1
Intermediate Variables Affecting Fertility

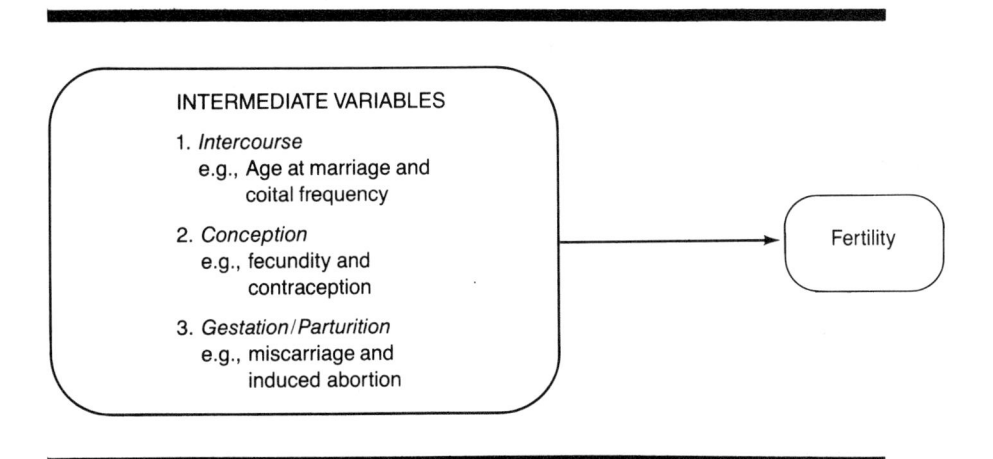

INTERMEDIATE VARIABLES

1. *Intercourse*
   e.g., Age at marriage and coital frequency

2. *Conception*
   e.g., fecundity and contraception

3. *Gestation/Parturition*
   e.g., miscarriage and induced abortion

→ Fertility

SOURCE: Adapted from Kingsley Davis and Judith Blake, "Social Structure and Fertility: An Analytical Framework." *Economic Development and Cultural Change,* 5 (April 1956): 211–35.

3. Factors affecting *gestation* and successful parturition, including fetal mortality from involuntary causes such as miscarriage or voluntary induced abortion.

The only direct causal influences on fertility, then, are necessarily through these three clusters of intermediate variables (see Figure 5-1). Kingsley Davis and Judith Blake (1956), the demographers who developed this classification, pointed out that different combinations of values for these variables can result in identical levels of fertility. For example, people who marry young and practice birth control could experience the same fertility level as people who marry at an older age but who do not use contraception. A society's level of fertility is dependent on the simultaneous balance of all the intermediate variables in combination. We should also note that the effect of these variables on fertility is often the unintended consequence of normative and structural conditions in a given society.

Before continuing our discussion of the intermediate variables in this and the following chapter, we must examine their relationship to the larger social and economic structures of society. Ronald Freedman (1975), a noted American demographer, has provided us with a model by which to examine some of the broader features of social life that affect fertility, and we use his work as the basis of discussion in this section. Freedman's model is summarized in Figure 5-2. Here we see that fertility can be affected directly only by the intermediate variables. Moving backward from fertility, however, we encounter broad classes of factors that help to determine fertility through their influence on the intermediate variables. To illustrate, every society has cultural norms regarding the number of children couples should have. As we noted at the beginning of this chapter, fertility is always regulated to a large extent by the nature of social life. The number of children couples have is always defined as consequential for the parents, children, relatives, and the larger society. For this reason, as Freedman points out, it would be a sociological anomaly if norms were not developed to deal with the issue of family size. Norms typically are expressed in terms of ranges of desirable numbers of children. A few decades ago in the United States, for example, couples were normatively encouraged to have three or four children. Today the normative range is lower, but cultural prescriptions still help to motivate couples toward having at least the one or two children considered necessary to have a "real" family (Blake, 1972).

Societies also have norms about each of the intermediate variables; however, we should recognize that the effects of these attitudes on fertility are often the unintended consequences of cultural patterns. For example, all societies regulate sexual behavior, including the age of entry into sexual unions, through the social institutions of marriage and family. Similarly, attitudes regarding a wide range of behaviors, such as premarital and extramarital sex, contraceptive use (when it is known), and abortion are found

Figure 5-2
Social Factors Affecting Fertility

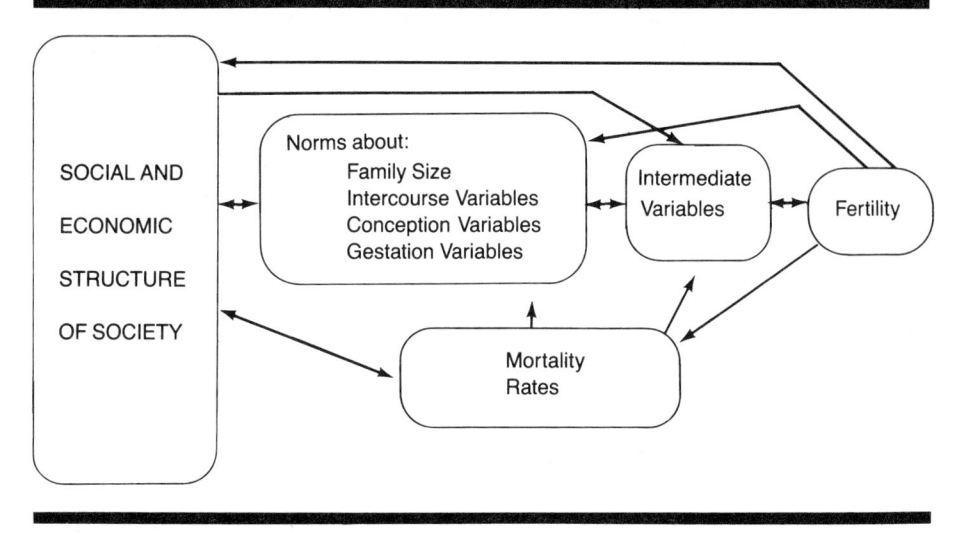

[Figure: Diagram showing relationships between SOCIAL AND ECONOMIC STRUCTURE OF SOCIETY, Norms about: Family Size, Intercourse Variables, Conception Variables, Gestation Variables, Intermediate Variables, Fertility, and Mortality Rates, with arrows indicating interactions.]

SOURCE: Adapted from Ronald Freedman, *The Sociology of Human Fertility* (New York: Irvington, 1975, Figure 1).

in all societies. While such norms may be grounded in moral or religious concerns, quite apart from an interest in fertility, they nevertheless exert an important influence on fertility.

Norms, the shared standards of desirable behavior, do not exist in a social vacuum. Rather, they are always anchored in the organization of social life—in other words, in the interacting patterns of statuses, roles, and institutions of society. These patterns, which shape the social and economic structure of society, support family size norms by providing social *rewards* and *punishments* that depend on the numbers of children couples have (as well as their timing and spacing). How can couples be rewarded or punished for having certain numbers of children? The answer is that family size can increase or decrease the probabilities of individuals and families attaining socially valued goals. Consider, for example, some basic social values in American culture at the present time. People in the United States are characterized by, and often even caricatured for, their life-style, which involves a heavy consumption of material goods (e.g., autos, stereos, and condos), along with an emphasis on "personal freedom" and individual status-striving. Americans seem to believe that in the pursuit of happiness one should strive to "get ahead" and personally "fulfill" oneself. These are socially valued goals.

What kind of fertility behavior is rewarded and what kind is punished by the social structure of American society? Given the contemporary organization of economic and family life, for example, individuals in the United States can get ahead faster and more certainly by postponing marriage and childbearing until they have completed their education, thereby maximizing their chances for advantageous placement in the occupational structure. Even after marriage, couples in which both wife and husband are employed full-time, unencumbered by childcare responsibilities, are in a more favorable position. In addition, as we will explain in more detail later on, children in modern societies are enormously expensive to care for and educate. For these and other reasons, small families are more compatible than large families with the attainment of many socially valued goals.

The final factor influencing fertility, shown in Figure 5-2, is the mortality level. In most societies throughout history, and in some even today, parents have needed to produce a surplus of offspring in order to produce the normatively desired number of children. Thus, where infant mortality is high, a norm of three or four surviving children would require a much larger average number of live births per woman (Chandrasekhar, 1975). Infant mortality can also affect fertility in another way. The death of an infant and the termination of breast-feeding will shorten the temporary period of reduced fecundity among nursing mothers and thereby expose them to a higher risk of conception.

To summarize, we have shown how the fertility of a population (or subgroup, stratum, etc.) tends to approximate a level prescribed by the prevailing social norms. The social norms, in turn, represent adjustments to the way in which having different numbers of children affects the achievement of socially valued goals. Other factors in the larger environment, not shown in Figure 5-2, also affect the intermediate fertility variables. Examples include migration patterns, famines, and venereal diseases. Also worth noting is that fertility interacts with the other variables shown in Figure 5-2 both as a cause and as an effect. For example, as we discuss more fully in Chapter 12, the high fertility levels of the postwar baby boom in the United States have had a dramatic impact on the social and economic structure of American society.

EXPOSURE TO INTERCOURSE

All societies recognize a special relationship between men and women whereby the children of such units are regarded as legitimate. This marriage relationship is based on the idea of the family, and functions to regulate sexual behavior as well as normatively to restrict reproduction to married couples. Historically, marriage has been virtually universal and, especially for females, has occurred at early ages. With the high mortality characteristic of most populations in the past, nearly universal marriage at an early age was of course essential to the very survival of populations. Beyond this, marriage has always been central to the kinship structure around which social behavior has been integrally organized in most societies.

Age at Marriage and Extent of Marriage

Age at marriage and the proportion of females who marry are important factors in determining the level of fertility within a society. Throughout the world, women who marry late tend to have fewer children than those who marry early. In Europe since the sixteenth century and Japan during the twentieth century, for example, delayed marriage has been an important factor in the decline of fertility. In the United States, both wanted and unwanted fertility are higher among women who marry at the earliest ages (Westoff and Ryder, 1977).

Of course, the actual extent of exposure to intercourse within a society depends on the age at which sexual activity begins and the proportion of women who remain permanently celibate. Age at marriage and age at entry into sexual unions are not the same thing, especially in the industrial societies of Europe and North America where premarital intercourse is now commonplace. Nonetheless, in most societies, including those in the Western world, fertility has been and remains closely linked to marriage. Moreover, on a worldwide basis age at marriage will continue to be an important determinant of fertility throughout the remainder of the twentieth century. Over the next two decades there will be more young adults in their prime marriage and reproductive years, ages fifteen to twenty-nine, than ever before in history. More than 40 percent of the population in Third World countries, for example, is currently under fifteen years of age. If this generation marries and reproduces at early ages, the prospects for lowering fertility and rates of population growth will be substantially reduced.

In many Asian, African, and Latin American countries the majority of women marry before they are twenty years old (Kendall, 1979). In both India and Bangladesh, in fact, many women are married before they even reach puberty. It goes without saying that such an early age at marriage constitutes a serious barrier to fertility decline in many Third World countries. The important relationship between age at marriage and levels of fertility has been noted for such low-income areas as the state of Kerala in India, which is famous among demographers for its success in lowering fertility. Among several reasons for this success (including widespread literacy and low infant mortality), Kerala's low fertility undoubtedly is explained partly by the relatively high average age at marriage for both women (twenty-one) and men (twenty-six)—the highest in all of India. Several countries, including India, have made later marriage a part of their national policies to reduce fertility (see Chapter 7). In India, however, raising the legal minimum age for marriage is little more than a gesture, given the widespread illiteracy, the ignorance of the law, and the lack of means for documenting age (Visaria and Visaria, 1981).

Where we find low mean ages at marriage we generally also find larger percentages of women who marry. In most developing countries with mean ages at marriage below twenty years, for instance, we also find nearly universal marriage. The high birth rates in these societies, needless to say, are partly the result of this high exposure to intercourse during a woman's early fecund years. Early, nearly universal marriage also has implications for the woman's status and role in society, and is especially common where extended families and joint households prevail. Because marriage under these circumstances does not involve splitting up an extended family, and since familial independence is not a prerequisite of marriage, the marriages are typically arranged by parents. Daughters are most attractive as prospective brides when they are young, fecund, and pliable enough to fit into a subordinate role in the households of their husbands.

Where societies are based on the nuclear family, as in the industrial world, marriage tends to be postponed to later ages, and the rates of nonmarriage are relatively high. The *European marriage pattern* has received considerable attention from demographers because it represents a major deviation from patterns of early and universal marriage observed elsewhere. In Western Europe beginning about the sixteenth century, and in countries settled by Western Europeans, marriages typically have been delayed to rather advanced ages and singlehood has been an accepted and more common status. John Hajnal (1965), a British demographer, has hypothesized that this unique European marriage pattern is closely linked to the economic independence of the European *stem family*. In the stem family only one son inherits the family land (the rule of primogeniture) and must postpone marriage until his father dies or makes some arrangement for the son to marry and earn a living on that land. Unlike most non-European societies, therefore, where young married couples could be incorporated into the larger economic unit of an *extended family* (i.e., fathers and sons, their wives and children, all in the same household), European men had to defer marriage until they could achieve an economic independence sufficient to support a family. From the perspective of the model in Figure 5-2, we might conclude that the European attitudes toward the intercourse variables had changed in response to changes in the social structure—specifically in regard to the family and economic institutions. In other words, as the costs of early marriage and parenthood increased, more and more people benefited from delayed entry into marital unions and postponed childbearing. Hajnal believes that this European pattern of marriage was an important factor in the economic transformation and modernization of Europe.

Figure 5-3
Median Age at First Marriage, by Sex, United States, 1890–1980

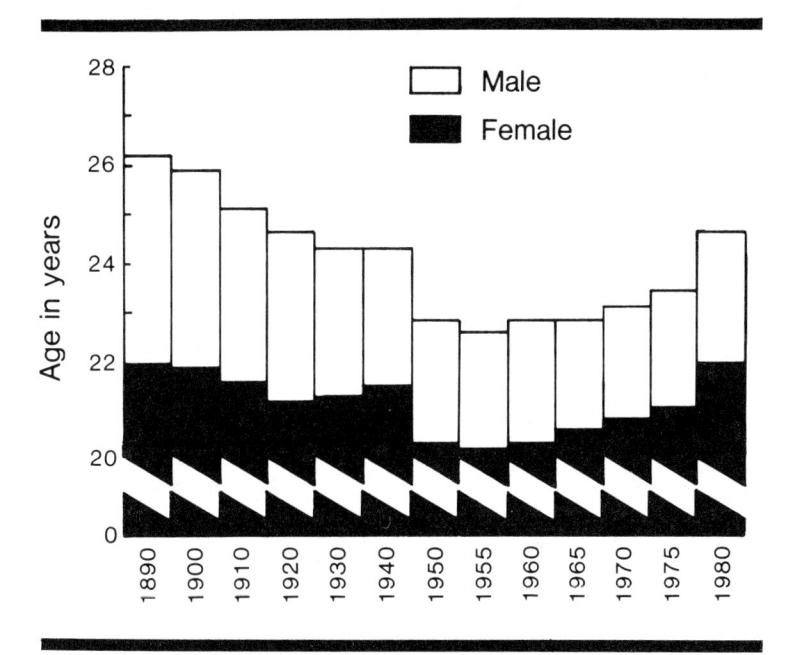

SOURCE: Drawn by authors from data in U.S. Bureau of the Census, "Marital Status and Living Arrangements: March, 1981." *Current Population Reports,* Series P-20, No. 372 (Washington, D.C., 1982).

Marriage in the United States

More than 90 percent of the people in the United States marry at some point in their lives. Indeed, the United States has one of the highest *marriage rates* (number of marriages per 1000 population) of any industrial country in the world. Nevertheless, there have been some substantial changes in the patterns of marriage through the decades (Glick and Norton, 1977). Two of the most noteworthy recent changes are closely interrelated: the increase in the median age at first marriage and the increased proportion of the adult population never married.

Turning first to changes in the median age at first marriage, as shown in Figure 5-3, we may note two major trends. The first trend, extending from 1890 to the mid-1950s, is a gradual decline in the age at marriage. After the 1950s the trend reversed, and the age at marriage gradually increased among both men and women during the 1960s and 1970s. What explains these trends?

We have already noted the European and Western pattern of rising age at marriage prior to the twentieth century. Marriage was postponed or avoided as a response to changed societal conditions. The pattern of postponed marriage did not last, however, as alternatives to it became feasible in the newly industrial and urban societies. New employment opportunities provided the potential for economic security at younger ages, and the availability of contraceptives meant that couples could bring both the number and timing of births under considerable control. The age at marriage in the United States was declining by the turn of the century, therefore, because the benefits of early marriage began to outweigh the costs. The rise in the divorce and remarriage rates over subsequent decades, along with increased female labor force participation and the government subsidy of home ownership, meant that couples could marry at younger ages without risking so much. Thus, changing conditions in the social and economic structure of modern society have made marriage less of a fateful decision, less of an economic and social commitment, and less of an irreversible step (Davis, 1972). As a partial consequence, couples in the United States married at progressively earlier ages until 1956 when age at first marriage fell to a median of 22.5 years for men and 20.1 years for women.

Since then, however, this trend has reversed, and by 1982 the median age at first marriage had risen to 25.2 for men and 22.5 for women. Why this reversal in the direction of change? Part of the explanation lies in the postponement of marriage traditionally associated with extending one's education. Higher proportions of young people are achieving more years of education than ever before. Meanwhile, increasing numbers of young women have participated in the paid labor force where they have been exposed to economic independence and attractive options to early marriage and parenthood. The so-called marriage squeeze (see Chapter 12) is also a partial explanation for the postponement of marriage. In the 1960s and 1970s the number of women reaching the usual ages at which women first marry (eighteen to twenty-four) exceeded by 5 to 10 percent the number of men who were reaching ages twenty to twenty-six, the usual ages at which men first marry.

Still, something more fundamental seems to be predisposing young people to remain single for longer periods of time. The data shown in Table 5-1 suggest that singlehood among young men and women has become quite fashionable. In 1980, nearly 69 percent of the men age twenty to twenty-four, and 50 percent of the women the same age, had never married. Each of these figures represents a significant departure from the comparable data shown for 1960.

Could it be that the reasons for getting married at an early age are simply less compelling today than they were in the past? Traditionally, young people have married in order to engage in socially sanctioned intercourse, to produce legitimate children, and to have a household division of labor

Table 5-1

Percent Single (Never Married), by Sex, among Persons 15 to 24 Years Old: United States

Sex and age	1960*	1980
Male		
15 to 24 years	79.5	83.2
15 to 17 years	99.0	99.4
18 years	94.6	97.4
19 years	87.1	90.7
20 to 24 years	53.1	68.6
Female		
15 to 24 years	62.6	70.5
15 to 17 years	94.6	97.0
18 years	75.6	88.0
19 years	59.7	77.5
20 to 24 years	28.4	50.2

SOURCE: U.S. Bureau of the Census, "Characteristics of American Children and Youth, 1980." *Current Population Reports,* Series P-23, No. 114 (Washington, D.C., 1982).
* Figures for 1960 include persons 14 years of age.

that was efficient for both the husband and wife. In a society where both women and men are part of the paid labor force, however, and in which the conveniences of modern technology make many household tasks less arduous, young men and women do not need each other in this functional sense as much as they did in previous times. Moreover, when sex is tolerated outside the confines of marriage, an additional reason for getting married is weakened (Davis, 1972). Finally, if having a large family (or any children at all) is devalued as a socially desirable goal, or if reproduction itself is tolerated outside marriage, additional social supports for early marriage are eroded. Today American society, like several European societies, clearly is characterized by changing sexual and reproductive norms along these lines, especially among the young (Westoff, 1978; Zelnik et al., 1981).

Other Factors Affecting Exposure to Intercourse

Beyond the age at which people marry and the extent of nonmarriage, several other factors affect the exposure of populations to intercourse. These variables include how much time during the reproductive years *widowed, divorced,* or *separated* people spend after or between conjugal unions. In India, for example, a cultural ban on the remarriage of widows likely has had a dampening effect on fertility. The frequency of divorce varies widely across societies, and its impact on fertility depends not only on its incidence, but also on the frequency and age of remarriage. In the United States, where the divorce rate more than doubled between 1960 and 1982 (from 2.2 to 5.1 divorces per 1000 population), the remarriage rate traditionally has been quite high. By the mid-1970s, however, the remarriage rate began to decline, probably signaling the increased social acceptability of such alternatives to marriage as nonmarital sex, single-parent households, and cohabitation. Thus, divorce or separation does not necessarily mean a lengthy interruption of sexual activity.

Finally, exposure to intercourse also is influenced by ritualistic or ceremonial occasions of a wide variety. *Abstinence* from intercourse can, of course, result from such involuntary causes as impotence or illness. More common, however, are such voluntary practices as abstinence from intercourse following the birth of a child (postpartum abstinence). Voluntary abstinence during pregnancy and menstruation, as well as *sexual taboos* relating to days of the week or ceremonial circumstances, also play a role in determining the frequency of coitus. In medieval Europe, for example, intercourse was proscribed on Mondays, Wednesdays, Fridays, and saints' days, and during all of Lent (Potts and Selman, 1980).

We began our discussion of the importance of marriage with the observation that, since marriage has functioned to regulate sexual behavior in virtually all societies, it constitutes an important factor affecting the exposure of populations to intercourse. But it is not that simple. The emergence of *cohabitation* in such countries as Denmark, Sweden, and more recently the United States signifies a rather dramatic change in the patterns of relations between the sexes and in the social functions of marriage in modern society. Virginity, for example, tends to lose its value in societies characterized by delayed marriage and high rates of divorce and remarriage, and in several modern societies cohabitation is becoming institutionalized as a socially sanctioned arrangement. In the United States, for instance, the number of households maintained by two unrelated adults of opposite sex increased from 523,000 in 1970 to 1,808,000 in 1981 (U.S. Bureau of the Census, 1982). During this time, there also has been a fundamental shift in the age composition of unmarried couples living together with no children. In 1970 a substantial majority of these people were forty-five or more years of age. By 1981, however, 76 percent of the 1.3 million people living together were less than forty-five years old. While unmarried-couple households constitute only 2 percent of all households in the country, the trend in recent years nevertheless has been impressive.

In the modern world, marriage has been losing not only its traditional benefit of socially sanctioned intercourse, but the additional benefit of making children legitimate. The principle of *legitimacy,* discussed in more detail in Chapter 6, is being challenged in the legal systems of several societies, reducing the distinction between children born inside and outside of marriage. Three-fourths of Americans surveyed in a 1978 poll, for example, said that they regarded it as acceptable for a single woman to have and raise a child (Clark and Martire, 1979). All of this means that age at marriage is becoming less important as a determinant of fertility. Rather, family size norms, shaped by the perceptions of individuals and couples as to the relative costs and benefits of children in their societies (in combination with the deliberate use of birth control), are now the most important determinants of fertility on a worldwide basis.

FAMILY SIZE NORMS

Most couples in all societies have wanted to have at least one or two children. Even in highly industrialized societies where birth control is practiced almost universally, and where the enjoyment of sex is largely separated from reproduction, parenthood remains the predominant pattern. Adequate reproduction is of course necessary for the very survival of human societies. Because survival was so problematic through much of human history, it was inevitable that social institutions would develop to promote the bearing and rearing of children. Everywhere, therefore, societies generated cultural and organizational features that maximized the probabilities that women who survived to adulthood would produce children of their own. But while there is clearly a pressure on members of all societies to become parents, in no way does this pressure require men and women to have all the children they could have. The question we must consider now is *how* and *why* the members of societies in different times and places have been motivated to want and to have different numbers of children.

Historical and Primitive Communities

In the past, where conditions of life were harsh and death rates high, correspondingly high birth rates were sometimes necessary for group survival. Many aspects of the social and cultural structure functioned, therefore, to promote high levels of fertility; birth rates throughout the ancient world often must have exceeded 50 per 1,000. But fertility was not always at a maximum level, unrestricted by social factors. Prior to industrialization, for example, even where mortality rates were very high (e.g., where only 50 percent of the children lived to reproductive ages), an average of eight children per woman would have led to a doubling of the population every generation. We know, however, that through most of the centuries prior to the modern era population growth was at very low levels. This knowledge, in combination with evidence from the primitive societies of today, certainly indicates that population growth often was kept in check not only by high death rates but also by such cultural practices as delayed marriage, sexual abstinence, and abortion. In addition, infanticide has been an important instrument for population control throughout most of human history. It would seem that not all births were wanted even in ancient times. Indeed, a review of population patterns in a variety of primitive societies points to abortion as a nearly universal practice, which in combination with infanticide and postpartum abstinence, constituted the basic means for population control in primitive societies (Devereux, 1967). It also seems likely that those who followed such practices did so because of a belief that it was to their benefit to space out their children, or that too many children were detrimental to the interests of the group. In the South Sea island society of Tikopia, for example, the fear of running out of ceremonial food led to strong disapproval of couples who had more than two or three children. The Tikopians, therefore, used celibacy, coitus interruptus, abortion, and infanticide to control their family size (Firth, 1965).

Another interesting example of restricted fertility is that of the !Kung bushmen of the Kalahari Desert in Southern Africa (Kolata, 1974). Until recently their culture had changed little since prehistoric times. Even with an extraordinarily high mortality rate (a life expectancy of only thirty-two years in 1950), the average woman bore no more than five children. The reason for this relatively low fertility (common among hunters and gatherers in general) was the need to adapt childbearing to a nomadic way of life. Mothers were important collectors of food and simply could not carry around, care for, and nurse more than one infant at a time.

Today, most of the !Kung live in agricultural villages, and the structure of their society has changed dramatically. Women have lost some of their previous status as food providers, and the need for long birth intervals has been reduced. Consequently, fertility has increased, and the population is growing more rapidly than in the past.

FERTILITY TRENDS IN THE THIRD WORLD

The world's crude birth rate in 1983 was about 29 per 1,000 population. In an assessment of the world fertility situation in the early 1970s, the United Nations noted that with a few exceptions the less developed countries were those with crude birth rates of 30 or more. This statement accurately describes the world fertility situation today; if anything it understates it. Overall, the crude birth rate in the developing nations is about 33, compared with approximately 15 in the more developed world. A great many developing countries, however, have birth rates much higher than the overall level of 33 per 1,000. Most African countries, for instance, have crude birth rates in excess of 45 (see Chapter 2). The persistence of international fertility differentials between the haves and have-nots, and their projected continuation for perhaps the next several decades, warrants a close examination of the factors associated with this gap in fertility behavior.

According to results obtained in twenty-nine countries by the World Fertility Survey, preferred family size ranges from an average of 3.0 children in Turkey to 8.9 children in Senegal, with an overall average of 4.7 children (see Table 5-2). By regions, the average preferred family size ranges from 7.1 for African nations to 4.0 among the Asian and Pacific countries. The data shown separately for the younger and older women in the developing nations suggest that fertility rates would decline if the younger women could limit their reproduction to the level of their preferences. Nonetheless, most of the averages for preferred family size in Third World nations are much higher than levels needed for even moderate rates of population increase, and they are far above the average 2.2 to 2.5 children women would need to average in these countries to achieve zero population growth. Most important, it should be obvious that families are larger in the developing than in the developed world primarily because parents in Third World societies *want* larger families.

What are the structural and cultural supports for these high fertility norms? We have already noted that high fertility is in part rooted in centuries of past *adjustment to high mortality*. Beyond this, among the strongest inducements to high fertility norms in developing countries are the organizational features of *family and economic life*, the *status of women*, and the cultural supports of *religion*. These factors in combination induce people in developing countries to desire large numbers of children because the societal values of greatest importance are obtained through extended familial and kinship ties rather than through individual means.

This subordination of the individual to the kinship unit has several consequences conducive to high fertility. For one thing, in such a setting the economic cost of rearing children does not impinge solely on the young parents but is spread among other members of the family. Similarly, the time and effort involved in caring for young children do not have to be borne entirely by the parents. Perhaps most important, however, is the simple fact that the more children that a family has, the more people it has to work in the fields and household, to tend the livestock, collect firewood and fetch water, and eventually to contribute to the family income and provide old age security for the parents. Thus, early marriage and early and regular childbearing are strongly encouraged: the prestige and security of the women

Table 5-2
Preferred Family Size among Younger and Older Women in Various Third World Countries, Mid- to Late 1970s

Region and country	Average preferred family size — All women	Age 15–19	Age 45–49	Region and country	Average preferred family size — All women	Age 15–19	Age 45–49
AFRICA				**LATIN AMERICA**			
Kenya	7.2	6.5	8.6	Colombia	4.1	2.7	5.7
Lesotho	6.0	5.7	7.2	Costa Rica	4.7	3.5	6.1
Senegal	8.9	8.8	8.7	Dominican Rep.	4.7	3.4	6.1
Sudan (North)	6.4	5.4	6.5	Guyana	4.6	3.4	5.9
Regional average	7.1	6.6	7.8	Haiti	3.6	2.8	4.3
				Jamaica	4.1	3.3	4.8
ASIA AND PACIFIC				Mexico	4.5	3.8	5.8
				Panama	4.3	3.4	5.1
Bangladesh	4.1	3.7	4.9	Paraguay	5.3	3.7	7.1
Fiji	4.2	2.7	6.1	Peru	3.8	3.1	4.6
Indonesia	4.3	3.3	5.4	Trinidad and Tobago	3.8	3.2	4.8
Korea, Rep. of	3.2	2.8	3.8	Venezuela	4.2	3.0	6.0
Malaysia	4.4	3.9	4.6	Regional average	4.3	3.3	5.5
Nepal	4.0	3.7	4.4				
Pakistan	4.2	4.1	4.6	**MIDDLE EAST**			
Philippines	4.4	3.1	5.6	Jordan	6.3	4.9	7.5
Sri Lanka	3.4	2.6	4.8	Syria	6.1	5.0	7.1
Thailand	3.7	2.9	4.4	Turkey	3.0	2.8	3.1
Regional average	4.0	3.3	4.9	Regional average	5.1	4.2	5.9
				Total average	4.7	3.8	5.7

SOURCE: Robert Lightbourne, Jr., et al., "The World Fertility Survey: Charting Global Childbearing." *Population Bulletin*, 37 (March 1982).

in the family are determined primarily by the number of children they have. Next to barrenness, the worst thing that could happen to a woman is the failure to provide her family with sons. In many parts of the world, the birth of a boy is a cause for celebration while the birth of a daughter is ignored. Even worse, after birth, boys frequently receive better care, a fact reflected in the unusually high mortality rates for female children in several areas of the developing world.

This preference for boys over girls is, of course, related to the *status of women* in society. Virtually no society in the world provides women equal status with men. However, the opportunities for women in most spheres of economic and social activity are especially limited in many of the developing countries. For example, females may be betrothed while they are still children. As adults, women often are denied the right to make legal contracts, to inherit or own property, or to become employed. Larger proportions of women than of men are likely to be illiterate. Confined largely to their homes, Third World women are occupied primarily with housekeeping, field work, and childrearing. Where there are few alternative roles for women, and where social and personal worth are centered around the importance of children, larger families are wanted because they are felt to be needed. We find, therefore, that preferred family size is greatly influenced by a wide range of social and economic forces involved with the process of modernization. Within those areas of developing countries where women are most exposed to modern ideas, preferences are also expressed for the smallest family sizes. In general, rural women and less educated women want more children than do urban and more educated women. Similarly, wives brought into contact through their husbands with professional and managerial occupations desire the smallest family sizes.

Large-family norms tend to persist even after the economic and social conditions responsible for them have changed. Such cultural inertia is frequently sustained by *religious values*, even when there are no specific proscriptions against birth control. The Old Testament injunction to "be fruitful and multiply" has its counterpart in the teachings of several religions predominant throughout the developing world. Islam, especially, has been noted for its close association with high fertility norms (Kirk, 1966). The doctrines of Islam place a high value on sons to continue the family lineage and on large families for old age security. Muslims whose wives are barren are permitted to practice polygamy, and all Muslims are encouraged to remarry after widowhood. Moreover, the social status of women in Muslim nations is relatively low. Women are isolated from many aspects of social life by the practice of *purdah* (seclusion from public life), which prevents their full participation in many educational and employment pursuits.

Current Trends

Demographers disagree over the precise extent to which fertility in developing areas has declined in recent years. They also disagree over the causes of the decline (Demeny, 1979; Tsui and Bogue, 1978). The source of this disagreement lies in the less than perfect nature of the available data and in the complexities of changing fertility behavior.

Data from the World Fertility Survey and other sources, however, permit some generalizations. No fertility decline has occurred in sub-Saharan Africa, where in fact there probably has been a slight increase in fertility in some countries. Egypt and Tunisia in Northern Africa, however, have experienced recent fertility declines (Jamison, 1983). There is also mounting evidence that many of the countries in Asia, the Middle East, and Latin America have experienced declining fertility over the past decade or so. South Asia (which includes India, Bangladesh, and Pakistan) is a very important region of the world where the trend of fertility is less certain: Sri Lanka stands as the only country in this area unquestionably to have experienced significant fertility decline. China and India, by far the world's most populous nations, have followed different paths. In China, the crude birth rate has fallen dramatically, while in India fertility levels remain high. These giant nations are discussed more fully in Chapter 7.

FERTILITY DECLINE IN THE MODERN WORLD

In the middle of the nineteenth century women in most Western European countries, if they married in their early twenties and lived through their reproductive years, would have had between six and eight children. Perhaps four to six of these children would themselves have lived to marry and reproduce. However, as we pointed out earlier, most women in Western Europe did not marry early, and between 10 and 25 percent did not marry at all. Moreover, some women were victims of maternal mortality and others were widowed while still in their fecund years. Thus premature widowhood, delayed marriage, and lifetime celibacy combined to leave nineteenth-century women with fertility well below their potential. Nevertheless, even with late marriage and high mortality, mothers on the average had approximately five children. A century later, fertility throughout the Western world has fallen to a level only about half as high. This shift from high to low fertility (and from high to low mortality), you will recall, is called the demographic transition. It is one of the most important social transformations of modern times. Today the crude birth rates in Western Europe, where the demographic transition began, are typically under 15 per 1,000. In Sweden, for example, which has one of the lowest birth rates in the world today (11 per 1,000 in 1983), the birth rate was in excess of 30 per 1,000 until the later years of the nineteenth century (see Figure 5-4). Most European countries, in fact, had birth rates on the order of 30 or more as recently as the late nineteenth century, and not until the decade immediately preceding the Second World War did birth rates of less than 20 per 1,000 cease to be a rarity. Currently, Europe, North America, Japan, and several other areas of the world are characterized by comparably low levels of childbearing. What caused this momentous shift from high to low fertility?

Throughout this chapter we have approached fertility behavior within a social and cultural context. Fertility, we have argued, is a response to definitions of reality and to perceptions of social worlds shaped by the com-

Figure 5-4
Crude Birth Rate Trends in Sweden: 1750–1980

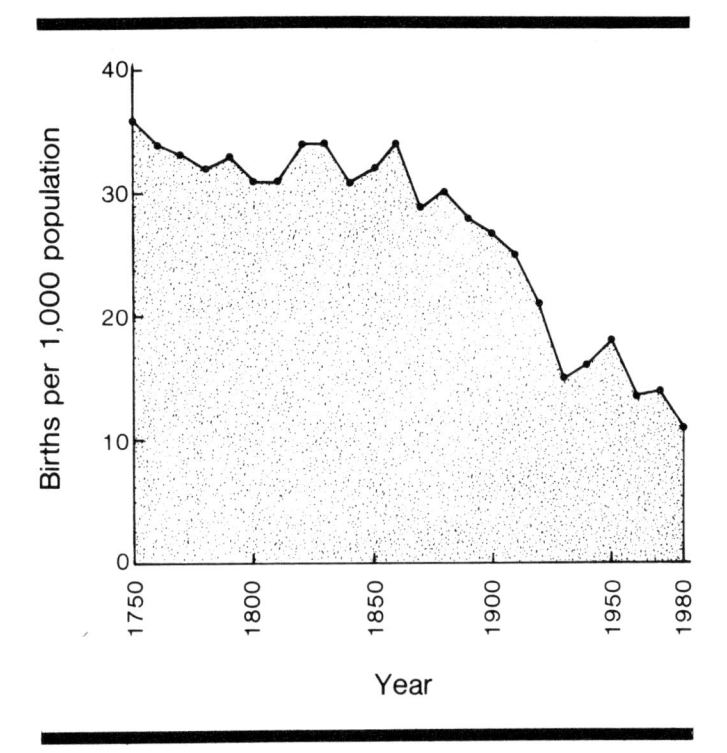

SOURCE: Based on data in Thomas McKeown, *The Modern Rise of Population* (New York: Academic Press, 1976), p. 28; E. G. Stockwell and K. A. Laidlaw, *Third World Development* (Chicago: Nelson Hall, 1981), p. 80; and Population Reference Bureau, *1983 World Population Data Sheet* (April 1983).

munications between people in their daily interactions with one another. Perceptions are subjective, but they are rooted in the objective patterns of culture in which people live their lives. It follows, therefore, that any accounting of the modern fertility decline must link changed motivations for childbearing to changed conditions of social life.

Along these lines, Ansley Coale, a leading American demographer, has studied the kinds of preconditions that are associated with the deliberate, sustained decline in fertility experienced initially by the Western world. He listed three conditions: (1) recognition of the fact that couples have a *conscious choice* regarding fertility; (2) perceptions of *small families as more advantageous* than large families; and (3) the knowledge and availability of effective *means of birth control* (Coale, 1973). All three of these relate to motivation.

The first precondition—the acceptance of the realization that one has a choice regarding fertility—implies a world view in which rational planning for a more or less predictable future is commonplace. We know, however, that even within modern American society, some lives are more aptly characterized by drift, a sense of fatalism, and a perception of the world as more or less chaotic and without meaning. Under these circumstances, the perception of fertility as a conscious, calculated choice hardly seems likely (Groat and Neal, 1967; Neal and Groat, 1980). Rather, children are more likely to be viewed as the result of chance occurrence or of the "will of God."

Coale's second precondition acknowledges the changing motivation for childbearing as a response to changing perceptions of the costs and benefits of children. Several economic demographers have elaborated on this approach by asking us to think of children more or less as "consumer durables" possessing both *utilities* (benefits) and *disutilities* (costs) (Becker, 1981; Easterlin, 1969). To illustrate, some major utilities of children might be the pleasure of having them and watching them grow up, the income they produce for the family or the work they do around the household, and the security they provide for parents in their old age. The disutilities would include such *direct costs* as food, clothing, and shelter, as well as the *indirect costs* of time devoted to childcare responsibilities that otherwise could be used for something else (called "opportunity costs"). The basic idea is that, after balancing the costs and benefits of children, people will be motivated to have small rather than large families, because they will perceive that the direct and indirect costs of large families can interfere with the acquisition of material and nonmaterial things that have become obtainable and socially desirable.

A classic explanation of the fertility decline in England in the latter part of the nineteenth century is cast in terms of this kind of cost-benefit accounting (Banks, 1954). A rising standard of living within a relatively open social structure raised the aspirations and expectations for social mobility among the middle class. To avoid falling back down the social ladder, couples deliberately limited the size of their families. With aspirations higher than incomes, therefore, the benefits of small families won out over the costs of large families. As the concept of family limitation gained currency, the pattern of fertility decline that began in the upper social strata of England eventually spread to all segments of English society. Thus, by extending Coale's third precondition for fertility decline to include the accessibility and the psychological and sociological acceptability of birth control, we see that this third precondition, like the other two, constitutes an important motivation for limiting family size.

Under what conditions of social change in Western Europe did these preconditions for fertility decline appear? An obvious starting point from which to look at the changed motivations for childbearing is the other side

Figure 5-5
Starting Dates of the Downward Fertility Transition in 700 European Provinces, 1780–1969

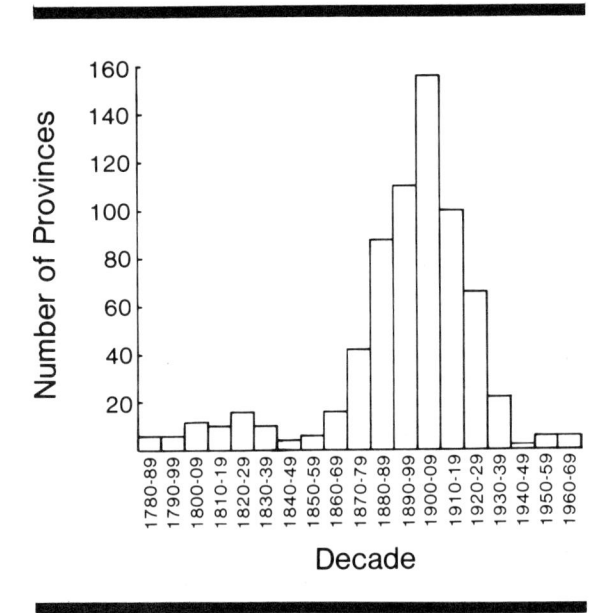

SOURCE: Drawn by authors based on a similar figure in Etienne van de Walle and John Knodel, "Europe's Fertility Transition: New Evidence and Lessons for Today's Developing World," *Population Bulletin,* 34 (February 1980).

of the coin: fertility trends in Third World countries. For example, fertility remains high in many developing countries because of adjustments to high mortality, the importance of extended family and kinship, the low status of women, and religious beliefs. Therefore we would expect to find that, in Europe, changes in some or all of these conditions were associated with reductions in fertility. Indeed, virtually everywhere that massive modernization occurred in Europe, declining fertility *eventually* followed (Teitelbaum, 1975).

Strange as it may seem, however, several changes associated with the emergence and growth of modern urban-industrial society at first had a positive effect on the fertility level. Improved agricultural productivity, for example, and the corollary improvement in the nutritional status of the population, led to declines in infecundity and miscarriage. Increased agricultural efficiency also meant that rural families could now produce enough to feed more children. In addition, at a time when agricultural technology was displacing people from farm occupations, industrial employment in the factory system made it possible for a man to become economically independent at an early age, thereby encouraging earlier marriage.

In spite of these initial effects, the long-run impact of modernization was a reduction in fertility. Most areas of Europe began their fertility transitions between 1870 and 1930 (see Figure 5-5), years that corresponded generally with advances in mortality control, the emergence of the factory system, increased agricultural productivity, the rapid growth of cities, and other features that accompanied the rise of industrialization. As with the cause of mortality decline, changes in both material culture (e.g., factories and mechanized agriculture) and nonmaterial culture were implicated in patterns of declining fertility.

The most significant nonmaterial cultural change was the emergence of a set of attitudes and values that favored smaller families. This *small family ethos* reflected a fundamental transformation in the organization and function of the family in Western society. In part it was associated with a decline in the importance of the family as the primary economic unit. As industrialization progressed, and as the factory system replaced the earlier cottage industries, the necessity of large numbers of children for the economic well-being of the family disappeared or declined, and this eventually led to the rise of the nuclear family rather than the extended kinship group as the dominant productive unit. The decline in the economic significance of large families was accompanied by a decline in their social significance as well. This is reflected in such changes as a lessening of the importance attached to having many sons to ensure perpetuation of the family name, and an increase in the tendency to evaluate an individual on the basis of his or her own accomplishments rather than on the basis of his group membership. In short, values shifted from an emphasis on the well-being of the group to an emphasis on the welfare and development of the individual.

Related to the growth of individualism was the general growth in intellectual freedom caused and further enhanced by the agricultural advances and the Industrial Revolution of the eighteenth and nineteenth centuries. For example, the growing secularization characteristic of the post-Renaissance period saw, among other things, a decline in the importance attached to such biblical commands as "Be fruitful and multiply." Today it is relatively rare to come across a woman who has borne six to eight children, whereas only a few generations ago it was relatively rare to come across a middle-aged married woman who had not borne that many offspring. The epitome of this intellectual development is found in what Max Weber has called the *Protestant ethic*—a system of values and beliefs that is rooted in Calvinism and that places a premium on individual achievement and on a person's ability to exercise a fairly large measure of control over his or her own destiny. The whole Protestant religious revival, in fact, played a key role in upsetting the traditional balance in which dogma and spiritual considerations held primacy over reason and worldly interests, and it brought about a new equilibrium that was generally more favorable toward worldly interests and more inclined to place a positive value on the ability of people to think and act rationally for themselves.

The changing status of women in society provides an interesting illustration of how the growing emancipation of the human mind from traditional beliefs and dogmas had a depressing influence on fertility and family size. An increase in women's rights was one of the many consequences of the growth of intellectual freedom. As more and more women came to regard themselves as equal to men, they naturally demanded a say in determining how many children they would bear, and this had a profound influence on Western fertility reduction. Throughout most of Europe and North America, in fact, women were in the forefront of those who forced the reform of birth control laws. While significant changes in the degree of their personal autonomy occurred very slowly, the changing attitudes of women toward themselves encouraged a much greater receptivity to new ideas, new options, and greater self-confidence. As has been noted elsewhere: "To ignore the changes in the general intellectual atmosphere which made women demand rights as persons is to overlook one of the underlying causal factors in the decline of the birth rate" (Thompson and Lewis, 1965, p. 319). Today, the close relationship between women's status and their desire and ability to plan childbearing is being recognized increasingly by policymakers as well as demographers (Curtin, 1982).

Finally, the overall rising standard of living generated a set of attitude changes that had a significant influence on fertility reduction. As the level of living rose and a better way of life became more easily attainable, more people sought to attain it. In fact, the values of the Protestant revival, with its emphasis on achievement, encouraged such a desire. All else being equal, nonparents are economically better off than parents, and parents of two or three children are better off than parents of five or six children. Thus, the structural changes associated with the transformation from a rural-agrarian to an urban-industrial society ultimately involved a transition in the value of children to parents.

Lessons for the Third World?

Until recently, many demographers believed that the changed motivations for childbearing resulted directly and exclusively from the fundamental shifts in social and cultural life brought about by urbanization, industrialization, and socioeconomic development. We now know, however, that this is not the case. The European Fertility Project—a recent, massive study on European fertility decline involving the detailed demographic analysis of over seven hundred province-size administrative units—has provided strong evidence that sustained fertility declines in Europe began under a much greater variety of socioeconomic and mortality circumstances than was previously thought (van de Walle and Knodel, 1980). In England, for instance, fertility declined only after considerable industrializaton and urbanization had taken place. In France, however, fertility began to decline about 1800 when that nation was still overwhelmingly agrarian. Moreover, in some countries the fertility decline actually preceded the decline in infant mortality. Another important finding is that the available methods of fertility control in pre-transition Europe (e.g., withdrawal, abstinence, abortion) may not have been used extensively because the concept and means of birth control were not yet psychologically and sociologically acceptable to the masses of people. Finally, results of the European Fertility Project suggest that the timing of the fertility decline in Europe may best be explained by the cultural setting of regions and countries that shared common languages, communication networks, religions, and customs. In the words of van de Walle and Knodel (1980, p. 36), "such hard-to-measure factors as changes in the status of women, secularization of attitudes, and the rejection of societal traditions in favor of individual interests may have played a more important role than socioeconomic factors in setting off the West's fertility transition."

Many Third World populations today are characterized by earlier ages at marriage and higher fertility than pre-transition Western European societies. Nevertheless, recent research on European fertility decline has shown that there may be subsets of development changes, far less comprehensive than those that occurred in the West, that can promote motivations for lower fertility in the Third World today (Freedman, 1979). Fertility has already declined in a number of countries and areas that are still in the early stages of development, such as Sri Lanka, the state of Kerala in India, Thailand, and the People's Republic of China. Freedman (1979) has noted that these places have in common a number of significant changes: better health and extended life expectancy, increased educational opportunities for both boys and girls, broad welfare institutions, and relatively well developed communication and transportation systems. With good communication especially, the dissemination of Western ideas may speed up the process by which the extended family in traditional society is replaced by the nuclear family as a distinctive emotional unit, perhaps even prior to economic modernization (Caldwell, 1976). Modern communication may also make the concept and means of family limitation more acceptable to large numbers of people in essentially agrarian settings.

FERTILITY TRENDS IN THE UNITED STATES

The population of colonial America was relatively young, and the opportunities for economic self-sufficiency encouraged young people to marry at an earlier age and to have larger families than their European contemporaries. The annual birth rate during the colonial period was about 55 per 1,000 inhabitants, with women averaging a completed family size of eight or more children. This general pattern of high fertility persisted throughout the first two decades of the nineteenth century (see Table 5-3). Then, in response to the same conditions that were associated with changing fertility in Europe, a fairly rapid decline in fertility began. From a crude birth rate of about 55 in 1820, the annual number of births per 1,000 population was down to 52 in 1840, 44 in 1860, and 40 in 1880 (U.S. Bureau of the Census, 1975). By 1900 the birth rate was close to 30 and the total fertility rate (TFR) was 3.6 births per woman. (The TFR is the average number of children a woman would give birth to in her lifetime if prevailing age-specific birth rates remained constant. See Appendix B).

Official data on U.S. annual births and birth rates go back about seventy-five years and show the generally continuous decline of fertility from 1910 until World War II (see Table 5-4). In 1936 during the Great Depression, the TFR fell to a low of 2.1, and the birth rate was 18.4, an all-time low. This long-term decline in fertility in the United States was part of the demographic revolution that was occurring throughout the Western world as a concomitant of the emergence of modern urban-industrial society. During the economic crisis of the 1930s, many Americans postponed either marriage or childbearing. As employment opportunities improved in the

Table 5-3
Estimated Number of Children per Woman: United States, 1800–1980

Year	Average number of children per woman	Year	Average number of children per woman
1800	6.9	1900	3.6
1820	6.7	1920	3.3
1840	6.2	1940	2.3
1860	5.1	1960	3.6
1880	4.3	1980	1.9

SOURCE: Estimates derived by authors from graphic material presented in William P. Butz et al., *Demographic Challenges in America's Future* (Santa Monica, CA: Rand Corporation, 1982).

Table 5-4
Crude Birth Rates in the United States, 1910–1982

Year	Crude birth rate	Year	Crude birth rate	Year	Crude birth rate
1910	30.1	1935	18.7	1960	23.7
1911	29.9	1936	18.4	1961	23.3
1912	29.8	1937	18.7	1962	22.4
1913	29.5	1938	19.2	1963	21.7
1914	29.9	1939	18.8	1964	21.0
1915	29.5	1940	19.4	1965	19.4
1916	29.1	1941	20.3	1966	18.4
1917	28.5	1942	22.2	1967	17.8
1918	28.2	1943	22.7	1968	17.5
1919	26.1	1944	21.2	1969	17.8
1920	27.7	1945	20.4	1970	18.4
1921	28.1	1946	24.1	1971	17.2
1922	26.2	1947	26.6	1972	15.6
1923	26.0	1948	24.9	1973	14.9
1924	26.1	1949	24.5	1974	14.9
1925	25.1	1950	24.1	1975	14.8
1926	24.2	1951	24.9	1976	14.8
1927	23.5	1952	25.1	1977	15.4
1928	22.2	1953	25.0	1978	15.3
1929	21.2	1954	25.3	1979	15.9
1930	21.3	1955	25.0	1980	15.8
1931	20.2	1956	25.2	1981	15.9
1932	19.5	1957	25.3	1982	16.0
1933	18.4	1958	24.6		
1934	19.0	1959	24.3		

SOURCE: *Vital Statistics of the United States,* 1961, Vol. I (Washington, 1963). Post-1960 data from various issues of *Monthly Vital Statistics Reports* published by the National Center for Health Statistics.

1940s, however, more marriages took place, and some of the deferred births were made up. As expected, the numbers and rates of births spurted upward immediately following the end of World War II in 1945, and by 1947 the total fertility rate was 3.2 children per woman. Then something quite unexpected happened: the birth rate continued at this high level for a decade and more.

The Baby Boom

From its all-time low level of 18 to 19 per 1,000 during the 1930s, the crude birth rate in the United States rose gradually until it reached 23 in 1943.

This moderate increase was followed by two years of declining fertility, and it appeared that the initial fertility recovery following the end of the depression and America's entrance into the war had given way to a revival of the historical downward trend. The declines during the latter years of the war, however, were in part due to the absence of large numbers of men from the country as well as to the deliberate postponement of marriage and childbearing because of the war. The demobilization of the armed forces at the end of the war, during a period of economic improvement, was followed by a sudden and pronounced increase in the birth rate. From a level of 20.4 in 1945 the crude birth rate rose to a peak of nearly 27 per 1,000 in 1947—a level that had not been seen since the early 1920s.

Up to this point the experience of the American population had been consistent with that of other nations in the Western world: fertility declined steadily throughout the nineteenth and early twentieth centuries, reached a low point during the 1930s, then rose to moderately high levels during the immediate postwar period. There, however, the similarity ended. In most European countries the higher postwar birth rates lasted for only one or two years—just long enough to give people a chance to get caught up on the families they had postponed during the earlier depression and war years—and then fertility returned to its low prewar level. In Sweden, for example, the crude birth rate rose from less than 15 per 1,000 during the 1930s to a postwar high of approximately 20 per 1,000 in 1946. But by 1954 it was once again less than 15, and it has remained at or below this low level ever since. In the United States, by contrast, there was a slight dip from 1948 to 1950, but from then until 1957 the crude birth rate remained relatively stable at 25 per 1,000 population.

The years between 1947 and 1957 are usually thought of as the Baby Boom decade, although fertility remained at relatively high levels through the early 1960s. More than 75 million babies were born between 1946 and 1964. In Europe, where the postwar increase in fertility was of much shorter duration, people quickly made up marriages and childbearing they earlier had postponed. Many Americans did the same thing, but they also changed the tempo of their family formation. For example, the average age at marriage declined, and the intervals between marriage and the first and succeeding births were shortened. Thus, childbearing was compressed into a briefer period of time during the early fecund years. Earlier marriage also meant longer exposure to the risk of both wanted and unwanted fertility. Contraception was still far from perfect, and in an era when women's roles were centered in the home rather than in a place of employment, the consequences of a late unwanted pregnancy were probably regarded by many couples as less than devastating. But the Baby Boom also reflected an increase in desired family size. Not only did larger proportions of women marry, but larger proportions of those who married became mothers. The rate of childlessness declined throughout the Baby Boom years.

Economically the postwar prosperity provided an abundance of jobs for the relatively small cohort of young men born during the 1930s. Secure employment, along with other improvements such as expanded health and accident insurance, unemployment compensation, and retirement benefits helped to create an atmosphere of economic optimism. Within this sociocultural context, young couples were encouraged to marry and begin childbearing at an early age. As they moved into their installment-purchased homes in the expanding suburbs, they also opted for a third or fourth child. Sociologically the 1950s also witnessed a strong resurgence of the pronatalist forces of the "feminine mystique" (Friedan, 1963).

It is important to note, however, that the American Baby Boom never really signaled a return to the larger families of an earlier age. On the contrary, throughout the baby boom years there was a decline in the proportions of women having four or more children. What happened, rather, was that larger proportions of young people decided to get married, to marry at younger ages, and to have at least one, two, or three children.

The Baby Bust

By the early 1960s, it was apparent that the postwar baby boom was coming to an end. The peak year was 1957, when the crude birth rate reached 25.3 per 1,000 population and American women gave birth to 4.3 million babies. After that the birth rate declined, slowly at first, then more sharply until by 1965 it had fallen back to the prewar level of less than 20. Many demographers expected the baby boom generation to produce its own baby boomlet in the 1970s as the women in these cohorts entered their childbearing years. Indeed, over the last few years there has been a slight echo effect from the baby boom, reflected in small annual increases in the number of births. Journalistic accounts notwithstanding, however, this was no new baby boom. Rather, the baby boom generation has given the United States its lowest fertility rates in history. The crude birth rates had plunged to less than 15 per 1,000 population by the mid-1970s. And in the late 1970s and early 1980s, total fertility rates were well below the 2.1 births per woman needed to replace the population in the long run. Despite an increase from 36 million to 52 million women in the childbearing ages between 1960 and 1980, the number of annual births fell from over 4 million to just over 3 million by the mid-1970s and rose only to 3.6 million in 1981.

As noted earlier, young Americans are delaying their marriages. The advent of oral contraception, access to safe abortion, increased educational attainment, and the participation of women in the paid labor force, among other things, have also contributed to a postponement of the fewer number of births they eventually expect to have. While the average number of lifetime births expected by American women eighteen to twenty-four years old has remained stable at approximately 2.0, there is increasing evidence of a greater normative acceptance of both voluntary childlessness and the one-child family. Until recently, childlessness was a declining phenomenon in American society. During the 1970s, however, voluntary childlessness increased. In 1982, among all women eighteen to thirty-four years old, 12 percent reported that they expected to remain permanently childless. Among women with four or more years of college the expectations of childlessness increased to 16 percent, and it reached 19 percent among those with five or more years of college (U.S. Bureau of the Census, 1983a). Large proportions of these women are still single, of course, and young women who have remained single have been revising their fertility expectations downward. It seems quite possible, therefore, that 20 percent or more of the women born in the 1950s and 1960s could remain childless. Marriage is the big unknown for single women in these cohorts.

Some of these women and their partners will turn out to have reproductive impairments, and some individuals will commit themselves at young ages to remain childless. Many more individuals and couples will drift into childlessness through a continuous postponement of childbearing right through their reproductive years. Since childlessness is associated with such trends as increased education and the increased economic independence of women, it seems unlikely that rates of voluntary childlessness will decline any time soon. Other young people who want the experience and rewards of parenthood in combination with minimal parental restrictions and responsibilities will opt for a single child. The old stereotypical notion that only children are in some important way disadvantaged has been challenged by recent research (Groat et al., 1980).

One of the major factors underlying the low level of American fertility is unquestionably the high cost of children. Most couples in modern society will continue to want children for the love, novelty, stimulation, and primary relations traditionally associated with the having and rearing of children. But now that the direct out-of-pocket costs of raising and educating a middle-class child are estimated to range between $85,000 and $200,000 (Population Reference Bureau, 1982), more and more young people are deciding to have only one or two children. Beyond the direct maintenance costs (e.g., housing, food, transportation, and clothing) there are also indirect costs in the form of opportunities parents forgo for their children. Examples of opportunity costs are fewer consumption expenditures, a reduction in savings and investment, and the loss of income incurred by a wife or husband who is not working in order to care for a child. The opportunity costs of children for young women who wish to pursue their own careers is, of course, especially important.

The Future of Western Fertility

Fertility has been declining for about a century in most of the Western countries and for longer than that in France and the United States. Viewed in historical perspective, the current low levels of fertility in the Western world are at least partly a continuation of a very long trend. The baby boom was the only major temporary reversal in this long-term trend. But if we could have one baby boom, why not another?

An economic demographer, Richard Easterlin (1980), has argued that there is indeed a cyclical element, connected with cohort size, in fertility fluctuations. For example, children born during the low fertility 1920s and 1930s who came of age after World War II constituted the "good times" cohorts. During the postwar period when the economy was strong and the demand for labor was great, young adults were relatively scarce and their incomes were rising. This encouraged these cohorts to marry early and bunch their two or three children close together; hence the baby boom. When the baby boom cohorts entered the job market in the mid-1960s, however, job competition was more severe and economic conditions were less certain. Young people, therefore, presumably reacted by postponing marriage and having fewer children; hence the baby bust. Looking ahead, by the same logic, as the smaller cohorts of the 1960s and 1970s reach their childbearing ages in the 1990s, there should be another increase in fertility. The greater economic opportunities available to their smaller numbers should once again encourage earlier marriage and higher fertility.

Easterlin's cyclical concept, which is compelling in its logic and in its empirical basis for prediction, nonetheless has been criticized on a number of grounds (Westoff, 1983). Many demographers and sociologists believe that fertility in the developed countries will fluctuate within a rather narrow range at continuing low levels. The total fertility rate is currently about 1.4 children per woman in West Germany and Denmark, and below replacement level in virtually all other Western countries and in much of Eastern Europe. While changing economic conditions may affect the timing of fertility, and thus short-term fluctuations in crude birth rates, the primary forces of social change seem unlikely to generate a significant departure from the very low fertility norms of the 1980s.

These primary forces include the continuing erosion of traditional and religious authority, the increase in individualism, the rise in mass education and mass consumerism, and wide-ranging changes in the institutional arrangements of marriage and the family. The increases in divorce, separation, and out-of-wedlock childbearing, in combination with effective contraception, sterilization, and abortion, constitute a separation of sex from reproduction, a separation of reproduction from marriage, and a weakening of marriage as a "permanent" arrangement between the sexes. As Westoff (1978) has observed, these phenomena are all related in one way or another to the changing status of women—perhaps the most radical change of all affecting fertility. It is noteworthy that two trends—the growing independence of women and their striving for equality with men—are not even close to having run their full course. When we couple these developments with the potential elimination of virtually all unwanted fertility in the modern world by the end of the century, it seems unlikely that we will soon witness a return to significantly larger families.

FERTILITY DIFFERENTIALS

In our earlier discussion of family size preferences in the Third World, we pointed out that rural and less educated women typically want more children than do urban and more educated women, and that women married to men in professional and managerial occupations desire smaller families than do women married to agricultural workers. The study of such differences in fertility, or differential fertility, helps demographers understand the determinants of childbearing and also helps them explain past trends and make predictions about what is likely to happen in the future. In short, fertility differentials enable us to link differences in family size to a variety of socioeconomic and cultural variables.

In the course of the demographic transition from high to low fertility, not all segments of national populations experienced declining fertility at the same time. Rather, subgroups of populations with particular socioeconomic and cultural attributes in common tended to move together toward lower family size norms. In England in the nineteenth century, for example, fertility decline was led by a middle class interested in securing and preserving its economic status. Today in Malaysia, which is populated by three major ethnic groups—Malays, Chinese, and Indians—similarly marked differences in fertility exist between subgroups of the population. The Malays, who have the largest families, are mostly Muslims living in rural areas. The Muslims also have less education than the Chinese, who are largely Buddhists, and the Indians, who are mainly Hindu. Thus different combinations of ethnic, educational, and religious characteristics in Malaysia result in different levels of fertility.

The most urban, educated, and privileged have had the lowest fertility in virtually all societies in which the demographic transition has occurred. The diminishing value of large families has been associated with low infant mortality, the shrinking influence of religion, the diffusion of secular and rational attitudes toward sexual and reproductive decisions, the increasing number of nuclear families, and the availability of effective means of birth control. In most of the Western world nearly all segments of national populations have shared in the overall pattern of fertility decline. Certainly this has been so in the United States (Rindfuss and Sweet, 1977). Yet, as shown in Table 5-5, there are still some important differences in fertility by racial, ethnic, and socioeconomic characteristics.

Table 5-5
Average Number of Births per Woman Age 35–44 by Selected Socioeconomic Characteristics: United States, 1980

Socioeconomic characteristics	Births per woman	Socioeconomic characteristics	Births per woman
Ethnicity		Family income	
White	2.6	Under $10,000	3.5
Black	3.5	$10,000–$14,999	3.0
Spanish Origin	3.1	$15,000–$24,999	2.8
Years of school completed		$25,000 and over	2.6
Elementary 0–7	3.8	Labor force status	
Elementary 8	3.4	In labor force	2.7
High School 1–3	3.3	Employed	2.7
High School 4	2.8	Unemployed	3.3
College 1–3	2.6	Not in labor force	2.9
College 4	2.3	Religion*	
College 5 or more	2.0	Catholic	2.3
Residence		Protestant	2.0
Metropolitan	2.6	Jewish	1.8
Nonmetropolitan	2.9		

SOURCE: U.S. Bureau of the Census, "Fertility of American Women: June 1980." *Current Population Reports,* Series P-20, No. 375 (October 1982).

* World Fertility Survey estimates of number of births per woman standardized by duration of marriage: Elise F. Jones, *Socio-Economic Differentials in Achieved Fertility,* WFS Comparative Studies No. 21 (December 1982).

    To illustrate the difference by race: the fertility rate of blacks has been at a level about 30 percent higher than the rate of whites over the past half-century. Fertility has followed the same trends for both blacks and whites, but the higher black fertility has persisted. Blacks have less education than whites; they also work in less prestigious occupations and earn lower incomes. These facts are undoubtedly implicated in the strong evidence that much of the differential fertility between blacks and whites is due to differences in unwanted fertility (Westoff and Ryder, 1977). Blacks start their childbearing at an earlier age than whites, for example, and thus are exposed to the risk of unwanted births for a longer period of time.

    An important exception to the higher fertility of blacks compared to whites is found among women who have completed four years of college. In 1981 white women aged thirty-five to forty-four who had finished four years of college had borne an average of 2.0 children, while their black counterparts had given birth to an average of only 1.7 children (U.S. Bureau of the Census, 1983b). Why this difference? In order to get ahead people have frequently sacrificed family size. In a society in which racial discrimination remains widespread, black women who wish to earn and use a college education may have to sacrifice more than white women (Weeks, 1981).

Several socioeconomic characteristics are also related to fertility. These differentials can be seen in Table 5-5, which shows the number of births for all American women aged thirty-five to forty-four, and in Table 5-6, which is limited to currently married women under age forty-five in several European countries and in the United States. It is clear that a woman's background has an important influence on her fertility, even within highly industrialized societies. The differentials by education, for example, are clear and consistent. One reason for this is that with increases in education young people postpone marriage and childbearing. But education is also inversely related to family size desires: increased education broadens the horizons of young people and raises the opportunity costs of children. Those with the most education are also more likely to adhere to the requirements of particular contraceptive methods.

Women who live in rural areas typically have more children than those living in urban areas, and we see this trend reflected in the data for several European countries (Table 5-6) as well as by metropolitan or nonmetropolitan status in the United States (Table 5-5). These fertility differences by residence may be understood by a consideration of the ways in which urban life has changed the motivations for family size. For example, there are simply more things that children can help out with in villages and rural areas than in towns and cities. Furthermore, children are not as expensive in farm homes where there may be more space and where at least some of the food is often homegrown. Most important, small town and rural women typically do not have the attractive alternatives to being housewives and mothers that are available to urban women.

Fertility also tends to vary inversely with income, although the relationship is complex. Since people with the highest incomes could afford to have the largest families, why don't they do so? Part of the explanation is that high incomes tend to go with high education and high occupational prestige, which are depressants on fertility. Moreover, rates of unwanted fertility are higher among poorly educated and low income women; thus, upper income women are more likely to have only the children they actually want. Another factor is that as incomes go up, so do the parent's expectations both for their children and for themselves. High income families, for example, are more likely than low income families to provide expensive advantages for their children. Music lessons, summer camp, travel, and a college education, for example, are typical of the expectations that middle- and upper-class parents have for their children. On a final note, we should also recognize that *within* some homogeneous social and occupational subgroups family size is positively related to income (Andorka, 1978). That is, when several other factors affecting fertility are held constant (as within the category of urban, Protestant women married to physicians for

Table 5-6
Average Number of Live Births, Standardized by Duration of Marriage, by Selected Socioeconomic Characteristics in Various Industrialized Countries, Late 1970s

Socioeconomic characteristics	Bulgaria	Czechoslovakia	Finland	France	Italy	Norway	Poland	United States
Intensity of religious feeling								
Strong	...	...	...	2.34	2.15	2.10	...	2.17
Moderate	...	...	...	2.00	1.91	2.08	...	2.17
Weak	...	...	...	1.86	1.69	1.96	...	1.99
Wife's education								
Elementary not completed	2.41	}2.35	}2.01	2.51	2.45	}2.40	2.70	}2.76
Elementary completed	1.74			2.01	1.96		2.32	
Lower secondary	1.55	2.08	1.80	1.86	1.74	2.11	1.95	2.34
Higher secondary	1.50	1.80	1.74	1.79	1.65	1.95	1.71	2.07
Post-secondary	1.37	1.62	1.64	1.66	1.48	1.86	1.55	1.82
Size of current residence								
Village	...	2.16	2.16	2.19	...	2.18	2.47	...
Small town	...	2.14	1.98	1.96	1.98	2.07	2.12	...
Medium town	...	1.87	1.77	2.00	1.93	1.90	1.85	...
Large town	...	1.69	1.61	1.93	1.85	}1.69	}1.66	...
City	...	1.53	1.55	1.77	...			...
Family income								
Very low	1.86	2.10	1.86	2.59	...	2.29	2.19	2.53
Low	1.72	1.82	1.71	2.10	...	2.07	1.94	2.21
Medium	1.62	1.84	1.63	1.85	...	1.98	1.81	2.08
High	1.51	1.95	1.66	1.51	...	1.65	1.80	1.91
Very high	1.49	1.87	1.66	1.57	...	1.68	1.60	1.84
Wife's work history								
Currently working	1.75	1.88	1.78	1.64	1.74	1.90	2.01	1.81
Worked some since marriage	2.11	2.35	2.07	2.24	1.96	2.23	2.18	2.22
Worked only before marriage	2.19	3.01	2.30	2.56	2.15	2.40	2.36	2.58

SOURCE: Elise F. Jones, *Socio-Economic Differentials in Achieved Fertility*, World Fertility Survey Comparative Studies No. 21 (December 1982).

the same number of years), couples in the highest income levels sometimes have higher fertility than those in the lowest income levels. Such findings have led to the so-called *relative income hypothesis,* which holds that a positive relation exists between income and fertility within population subgroups characterized by similar educational and occupational features.

Turning to the expectations of parents for themselves, we must note that the two-earner household has been especially important in changing the decision-making process regarding family size. With the enormous increase in female labor force participation that has occurred in Europe and North America over the past twenty years, the opportunity costs of childbearing have risen tremendously. In societies where large proportions of women want to work after marriage, more and more women are likely to seek higher paying jobs that require professional training. Such training will further depress fertility expectations and desires because it is associated with delayed marriage and postponement of the first birth (Groat et al., 1982). A woman's own economic activity, in fact, is now one of the most fundamental determinants of fertility in the developed world. In general, this is true regardless of education, residence, occupation of the husband, or the husband's income (Jones, 1982). Nonetheless, female work history often has a greater effect on the low status ends than on the high status ends of these other variables. And where labor force participation is not especially incompatible with childbearing, as in some developing countries, the relationship between work history and fertility is much weaker or nonexistent (Weller, 1977).

One of the differentials shown in Tables 5-5 and 5-6 is by religion. In North America, the Netherlands, Belgium, and Great Britain, the fertility of Catholics traditionally has exceeded that of non-Catholics. The fertility of Jews has generally been lower than that of non-Jews. In India, the Parsees have an average family size well below that of other religious groups. Muslim Arabs have lower fertility than Christian Arabs in Lebanon. It is obvious from these examples, therefore, that membership in religious communities can have an appreciable impact on childbearing. The degree of commitment, or intensity of religious feeling, is an important part of this influence.

Some religions are more pronatalist than others, either in their doctrines or in the extent to which they help create a separate group consciousness or discourage the use of birth control. Catholics, for example, traditionally have been encouraged to have as many children as they could educate and support, and they have been discouraged from using modern methods of birth control or abortion. In the 1950s and 1960s in the United States, Catholic fertility was higher (and Jewish fertility was lower) than Protestant fertility even with controls for socioeconomic status. Catholics who had been educated in Catholic schools and who had the greatest involvement in religious activities tended to have the largest family size. In the mid-1960s, however, a clear pattern of convergence in Catholic and non-Catholic fertility was noted, and by 1975 these two groups had quite similar levels of fertility (Westoff and Jones, 1979). Catholics are now contracepting with modern birth control methods at the same high level as non-Catholics. This, in combination with the gradual disappearance of socioeconomic differences between Catholics and non-Catholics, has reduced but not yet eliminated the importance of religion as a determinant of fertility.

SUMMARY

Human births result from sexual intercourse that results in pregnancy, successful gestation, and parturition. An understanding of fertility, therefore, requires an understanding of the complex system of biological and social factors affecting each of these steps. From a strictly biological perspective, most women would be able to give birth to far more children than they actually do. But fertility is never strictly a biological process. Instead, the number of children women will have depends on the prevailing family size norms within the larger social and cultural context of society. These social factors shape the level of fertility by operating through one or more of the intermediate variables: intercourse, conception, and gestation.

All societies regulate sexual behavior through the institutions of marriage and family. Thus, age at marriage and the proportion of females who marry are important factors in determining the level of fertility within a society. Historically, societies based on a nuclear family organization, as in Europe beginning in the sixteenth century, were characterized by relatively late ages at marriage, thereby depressing fertility to lower levels than otherwise would have occurred. Recently, in the United States there has been an increase in the median age at first marriage and a corresponding decrease in the proportion of the population ever married. These changes, which are related to current low levels of fertility, may also be related to important changes in the norms governing premarital sexuality, patterns of marriage and divorce, and out-of-wedlock childbearing.

The crude birth rate in the developing countries today is about 33 per 1,000 population, whereas in the developed world the birth rate is approximately 15. The persistence of international fertility differentials between the haves and the have-nots of the world is due largely to differences in family size preferences, along with the means to realize those preferences, between the two groups of countries. If the younger women in Third World countries could limit their reproduction to the level of their stated preferences, fertility rates in many areas would decline. However, the average preferred family size in many developing countries is much higher than the level needed for even moderate rates of population increase. These high fertility norms reflect past or present adjustments to high mortality and are firmly anchored in the organizational features of family and economic life, the status of women, and the pronatalist influence of religious beliefs.

Fertility in the Western world began to decline a century or more ago in several European countries. Through a process of social change still not completely understood, Western Europeans began to think of fertility as a matter of choice, of small families as more advantageous than large families, and to accept the idea and the means necessary for the deliberate control of their fertility. Thus fertility was affected eventually throughout the Western world by changes in the structure of family and kinship systems, economic life, the status of women, and religious ideologies—in other words, by the complex economic and social transformations which, for lack of a better summary term, we call modernization.

The United States shared this pattern of fertility decline with Western European countries. From an annual crude birth rate of about 55 per 1,000 inhabitants during the colonial period, the American birth rate steadily declined to a low of 18.4 during the Great Depression. With the return of postwar prosperity, the baby boom—a temporary reversal of the century-long fertility decline—sent crude birth rates back up to their highest levels since before the depression years. Nonetheless, the baby boom phenomenon never represented a return to the larger families of an earlier era.

By the early 1960s the baby boom had ended, and fertility in the United States continued to decline through the next decade and has remained at a very low level so far in the 1980s. Delayed marriage, female labor force participation, and the high cost of children are among the factors affecting current fertility. Sterilization, abortion, and highly efficacious contraception are of course the means by which the low fertility norms are realized. To the extent that Western countries in general experience a continuing erosion of religious authority, an increase in individualism, and wide-ranging changes in marriage and family arrangements, fertility is likely to remain at levels near or below the replacement level for an indefinite time. However, fertility is not yet at comparably low levels among all segments of national populations in the Western community. Significant differentials in family size by religion, residence, and socioeconomic status are found in many industrial societies.

REFERENCES AND SUGGESTED READING

Andorka, Rudolf. *Determinants of Fertility in Advanced Societies*. New York: Free Press, 1978.
Banks, J. A. *Prosperity and Parenthood: A Study of Family Planning Among the Victorian Middle Classes*. London: Routledge & Kegan Paul, 1954.

Becker, Gary S. *A Treatise on the Family.* Cambridge, Mass.: Harvard University Press, 1981.

Blake, Judith. "Coercive Pronatalism and American Population Policy." In R. Parke, Jr., and C. F. Westoff, eds., *Aspects of Population Growth Policy.* Washington, D.C.: U.S. Government Printing Office, 1972.

Caldwell, John C. "Toward a Restatement of Demographic Transition Theory." *Population and Development Review,* 2 (September-December 1976): 321–66.

Chandrasekhar, S. *Infant Mortality, Population Growth and Family Planning in India,* 2nd ed. Chapel Hill: University of North Carolina Press, 1975.

Clark, R., and G. Martire. "Americans, Still in a Family Way." *Public Opinion,* 3 (October-November 1979): 16–19.

Coale, Ansley. "Demographic Transition." *Proceedings of the International Population Conference,* Vol. 1. Liege, Belgium, 1973, pp. 53–72.

Curtin, Leslie B. *Status of Women: A Comparative Analysis of Twenty Developing Countries.* Washington, D.C.: Population Reference Bureau, 1982.

Davis Kingsley. "The American Family in Relation to Demographic Change." In Charles F. Westoff and Robert Parke, Jr., eds., *Demographic and Social Aspects of Population Growth.* Washington, D.C.: U.S. Government Printing Office, 1972.

Davis, Kingsley, and Judith Blake. "Social Structure and Fertility: An Analytic Framework." *Economic Development and Cultural Change,* 5 (April 1956): 216–35.

Demeny, Paul. "On the End of the Population Explosion." *Population and Development Review,* 5 (March 1979): 141–62.

Devereux, G. "A Typological Study of Abortion in 350 Primitive, Ancient, and Pre-Industrial Societies." In H. Rosen, ed., *Abortion in America.* Boston: Beacon Press, 1967.

Easterlin, Richard A. "Towards a Socio-Economic Theory of Fertility: A Survey of Recent Research on Economic Factors in American Fertility." In S. J. Behrman and R. Freedman, eds., *Fertility and Family Planning: A World View.* Ann Arbor: University of Michigan Press, 1969.

Easterlin, Richard A. *Birth and Fortune.* New York: Basic Books, 1980.

Eaton, J., and A. Mayer. *Man's Capacity to Reproduce.* New York: Free Press, 1954.

Firth, Raymond. *Social Change in Tikopia.* London: Allen & Unwin, 1965.

Fox, Greer Litton, ed. *The Childbearing Decision.* Beverly Hills, Calif.: Sage, 1982.

Freedman, Ronald. *The Sociology of Human Fertility.* New York: Irvington, 1975.

Freedman, Ronald. "Theories of Fertility Decline: A Reappraisal." *Social Forces,* 58 (September 1979): 1–17.

Friedan, Betty. *The Feminine Mystique.* New York: Dell, 1963.

Glick, Paul C., and Arthur J. Norton. "Marrying, Divorcing, and Living Together in the U.S. Today." *Population Bulletin,* 32 (October 1977).

Groat, H. Theodore, and Arthur G. Neal. "Social Psychological Correlates of Urban Fertility." *American Sociological Review,* 32 (December 1967): 945–59.

Groat, H. Theodore, Jerry W. Wicks, and Arthur G. Neal. *Differential Consequences of Having Been an Only Versus a Sibling Child.* Washington, D.C.: Final Report for the Center for Population Research (NIH), 1980.

Groat, H. Theodore, Jerry W. Wicks, Arthur G. Neal, and Gerry E. Hendershot. *Working Women and Childbearing: United States.* Washington, D.C.: National Center for Health Statistics (PHS), 1982.

Hajnal, John. "European Marriage Patterns in Perspective." In D. V. Glass and D. E. C. Eversley, eds., *Population in History.* London: Edward Arnold, 1965.

Jamison, Ellen. *Fertility Decline in Developing Countries.* International Research Document No. 9. Washington, D.C.: U.S. Bureau of the Census, January 1983.

Jones, Elise F. *Socio-Economic Differentials in Achieved Fertility.* World Fertility Survey Comparative Studies No. 21 (December 1982).

Kendall, Maurice. "The World Fertility Survey: Current Status and Findings." *Population Reports,* 3 (July 1979).

Kirk, Dudley. "Factors Affecting Moslem Natality." In B. Berelson et al., eds., *Family Planning and Population Programs.* Chicago: University of Chicago Press, 1966.

Kolata, G. "!Kung Hunter Gatherers: Feminism, Diet and Birth Control." *Science,* 185 (April 1974): 932–43.

Lightbourne, Robert, Jr., Susheela Singh, and Cynthia P. Green. "The World Fertility Survey: Charting Global Childbearing." *Population Bulletin,* 37 (March 1982).

Neal, Arthur G., and H. Theodore Groat. "Fertility Decision Making, Unintended Births, and the Social Drift Hypothesis," *Population and Environment,* 3 (Fall-Winter 1980): 221–36.

Population Reference Bureau. "Raising a $200,000+ Child." *Intercom,* 10 (November-December 1982): 6–7.

Population Reference Bureau. "1983 World Population Data Sheet." Washington, D.C.: Population Reference Bureau, 1983.

Potts, Malcolm, and Peter Selman. *Society and Fertility.* London: MacDonald & Evans, 1979.

Powers, Mary G., and Joseph J. Salvo. "Fertility and Child Care Arrangements as Mechanisms of Status Articulation." *Journal of Marriage and the Family,* 44 (February 1982): 21–34.

Rindfuss, Ronald R., and James A. Sweet. *Postwar Fertility Trends and Differentials in the United States.* New York: Academic Press, 1977.

Teitelbaum, M. S. "Relevance of Demographic Transition Theory for Developing Countries." *Science*, 188 (May 2, 1975): 420–25.

Thompson, Warren S., and David Lewis. *Population Problems*, 5th ed. New York: McGraw-Hill, 1965.

Tsui, Amy Ong, and Donald J. Bogue. "Declining World Fertility: Trends, Causes, Implications." *Population Bulletin*, 33 (October 1978).

U.S. Bureau of the Census. *Historical Statistics of the United States, Colonial Times to 1970*. Washington, D.C.: U.S. Government Printing Office, 1975.

U.S. Bureau of the Census. *Marital Status and Living Arrangements: March 1981*, Current Population Reports, Series P-20, No. 372 (June 1982).

U.S. Bureau of the Census. "Fertility of American Women: June 1982." Advance Report. *Current Population Reports*, Series P-20, No. 379 (May 1983a).

U.S. Bureau of the Census. "Fertility of American Women: June 1981." *Current Population Reports*, Series P-20, No. 378 (April 1983b).

van de Walle, Etienne, and John Knodel. "Europe's Fertility Transition: New Evidence and Lessons for Today's Developing World." *Population Bulletin*, 34 (February 1980).

Visaria, Pravin, and Leela Visaria. "India's Population: Second and Growing." *Population Bulletin*, 36 (October 1981).

Weeks, John R. *Population: An Introduction to Concepts and Issues*, 2nd ed. Belmont, Calif.: Wadsworth, 1981.

Weller, Robert H. "Demographic Correlates of Women's Participation in Economic Activities." *International Population Conference: Mexico, 1977*. Liege, Belgium: IUSSP, 1977.

Westoff, Charles F. "Some Speculations on the Future of Marriage and the Family." *Family Planning Perspectives*, 10 (March-April 1978): 79–83.

Westoff, Charles F. "Fertility Decline in the West: Causes and Prospects." *Population and Development Review*, 9 (March 1983): 99–110.

Westoff, Charles F., and Elise F. Jones. "The End of 'Catholic' Fertility." *Demography*, 16 (May 1979): 209–17.

Westoff, Charles F., and Norman B. Ryder. *The Contraceptive Revolution*. Princeton, N.J.: Princeton University Press, 1977.

Zelnik, Melvin, John F. Kantner, and Kathleen Ford. *Sex and Pregnancy in Adolescence*. Beverly Hills, Calif.: Sage, 1981.

National health improvement programs are underway throughout the Third World. Here a health inspector takes a blood sample from a child in Somalia.

What is the human life span? This couple in Azerbaijan are celebrating their hundredth wedding anniversary.

WORLD POPULATION

A Gregg County, Texas family in the 1800s. Large families were the norm on the American frontier.

High fertility and large families are a common characteristic of most Third World countries.

172 WORLD POPULATION

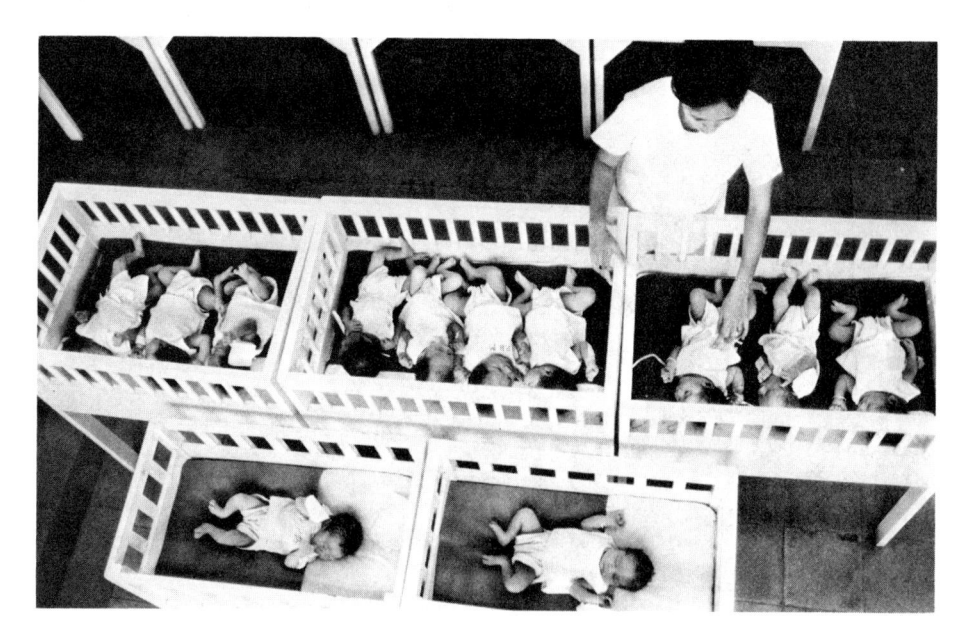

A full maternity ward in Indonesia

An artist's depiction of a pediatrician's office in 1955, during the Baby Boom

WORLD POPULATION 173

An American family decked out for Easter in 1959

In the 1980s, two-child families are the American norm.

FERTILITY CONTROL

6

The World Population Conference held in Bucharest, Romania, in 1974 was the first meeting of national governments on the issue of population. As part of the World Plan of Action adopted by the conference, a special emphasis was placed on the following principle: "All couples and individuals have the basic right to decide freely and responsibly the number and spacing of their children and to have the information, education, and means to do so."*

This "basic right" is not yet a reality for the overwhelming majority of the world's people. It was recently estimated, for example, that fewer than half of the world's population has access to modern contraceptive methods (Segal and Nordberg, 1977). Even in such countries as the United States, where access to contraception and abortion is widespread, fertility control is far from perfect. The ability to control the number of offspring, as well as the timing of pregnancies and childbearing, has been among the most elusive goals for individuals and couples throughout history. On a worldwide basis, people still have remarkably little control over their reproduction.

Fertility control is far from perfect for many reasons. In a general way, we may classify these reasons into those having to do with *motives* and those involving *means*. That is to say (1) people have different motivations or desires for different numbers and spacings of children, and (2) they have different capacities or means (biological, contraceptive, economic, social, psychological, informational, etc.) for meeting their specific reproductive goals.

*From Mauldin, et al., "A Report on Bucharest," *Studies in Family Planning,* 5 (December 1974), p. 1.

In Chapter 5 we concentrated on the ways in which different social and normative structures affect the motivations for family size. We also discussed the importance of variability in exposure to intercourse as an intermediate variable influencing fertility. Our concern in the present chapter is primarily with the means of fertility control as they affect childbearing through the other two intermediate variables of conception and gestation/parturition. Control over fertility, however, always implies combinations of motives and means for *achieving* pregnancy and childbearing as well as for *avoiding* them.

Most couples in all societies have wanted to have at least one or two children. Despite this relatively constant motivation for having at least some children, throughout the world couples have not always known when they married whether they would be able to have any children at all. More important, couples capable of childbearing have seldom known how many children they would have, and even less when they would have them. When we compare the number of children people desire with the number they end up with *(completed family size)*, there are three possible outcomes: fewer children than desired, more children than desired, or the exact number of children desired. When people have fewer children than desired, they experience *deficit fertility*. Having more children than desired involves excess, or *unwanted fertility*. Complete fertility control also implies the capacity to have the desired number of children *when* they are desired. Thus control over the *timing* as well as the *number* of children is involved in our examination of fertility control. We will begin this chapter with discussions of deficit and unwanted fertility, after which we will turn to our main topic—the birth control movement, contraceptive practices, and techniques of fertility regulation.

DEFICIT FERTILITY

In recent years, dramatic advances have been made in the means by which couples with *fecundity impairments* have been able to realize their childbearing goals (McFalls, 1979). The birth of Louise Brown in England in 1978, for example, created headlines throughout the world. All the fuss was justified because baby Louise was the first child in history to be conceived outside her mother's body. The Browns, like millions of other couples, had not been able to conceive a child (in this case due to missing fallopian tubes). Several ripened eggs were therefore removed from Mrs. Brown's ovary and fertilized in a laboratory dish with her husband's sperm. One of these fertilized eggs was then implanted in Mrs. Brown's uterus, the result several months later being a premature but healthy and normal baby girl.

Today we are accustomed to reading newspaper reports of other "test tube" babies, even twins, and stories of multiple births resulting from the treatment of subfecundity with fertility drugs. Yet the problem of subfecundity remains widespread even in highly developed societies. Several studies in the United States (Whelpton et al., 1946; Freedman et al., 1959; Whelpton et al., 1966) have reported that as many as one-third of the married white couples in the childbearing years are subfecund. But whether overall subfecundity is rising or declining in developed nations is unclear, since countervailing factors are operating. For example, venereal disease, which is on the increase, can have a dramatic, damaging impact on reproductive potential. On the other hand, better nutrition and health care can have an equally dramatic and positive impact on the ability to have children. The Old Order Amish, for instance, a traditional religious sect, have been willing to incorporate modern medical technology into their subcultural ways. The result is that Amish fertility has increased and childlessness has declined, during a time in the United States when national trends have been just the opposite (Ericksen et al., 1979).

Subfecundity is much more widespread and has a greater impact on total fertility in the less developed countries. Although Third World fertility is generally much higher than that of industrialized nations, there are some areas within the developing world, primarily in Sub-Saharan Africa, where fertility is relatively low and where childlessness reaches 30 percent (Frank, 1983). The reason for this is that developing societies are so vulnerable to the most important causes of subfecundity: malnutrition and disease. Millions of Third World people are victims of subfecundity related to deficiencies of protein, vitamins, and other forms of chronic undernutrition, as well as the generally poor quality of health delivery systems. In some instances, development projects have made health conditions even worse. Such irrigation projects as the Aswan Dam in Egypt, for example, may provide new breeding grounds for disease-transmitting snails or mosquitoes. In sum, problems of subfecundity throughout the world, but especially in the developing societies, are a major cause of less than perfect fertility control. Millions of men and women who want to have children, or an additional child, cannot have them.

Turning to the brighter side, much is being done to help subfecund couples realize their fertility goals. Beyond the dramatic introduction of the kind of laboratory fertilization techniques that produced Louise Brown, numerous other procedures for treating sexual disorders, hormonal abnormalities, and anatomical anomalies have been developed. Ovulatory failure, for example, caused by hormone deficiency, is now very well understood, and the treatment methods are quite successful. Similarly, microsurgical techniques now offer much hope to infertile men and women with tubal or other physiological abnormalities. As recently as the 1940s, only about 10 percent of all subfecund couples could be helped to have children, while today somewhere between 40 and 60 percent of them can be helped (McFalls, 1979).

Finally, we should acknowledge that such procedures as *in vitro fertilization* and *artificial insemination* (with either the sperm of the husband or that of an anonymous donor) have raised a series of ethical and legal questions. For example, concern has been expressed over the potential for a kind of "technological parenthood" that may be conducive to the exploitation of both children and would-be parents (Rosenblatt, 1983). The use of *surrogate mothers* by couples who desperately want a child is a case in point. In 1983 Americans nationwide read about a microcephalic child born to a surrogate mother who had contracted, for $10,000, to be artificially inseminated with the sperm of a man who was separated from his wife. A deformed baby boy eventually resulted in a controversy over the question of biological, legal, and "moral" parenthood.

UNINTENTIONAL FERTILITY

The other side of the fertility control equation has to do with unintentional pregnancy and childbearing. Far more people are affected by fertility control problems of this kind than of the kind related to infecundity or subfecundity. Moreover, the implications of excess fertility, at both the personal and the societal levels, are likely to be much more serious than those of deficit fertility. Unwanted children, after all, contribute to the perpetuation of family poverty, add to the social and economic costs of various welfare and other programs, and of course magnify problems of population increase in areas of the world that are already overpopulated. In addition, there is evidence that, under certain circumstances, children who are unwanted are at a greater risk of several disadvantages, from nutritional deficiencies to inadequate socialization experiences.

Unwanted Births

By an unwanted birth demographers mean a birth that results from a pregnancy that was not wanted at the time it occurred or at any future time. These are frequently called "number failures," since they refer to births that occur beyond the number that is desired. Wanted births are those that result from pregnancies that are wanted either when they occur or at some other time. Because wanted births can result from pregnancies that were wanted earlier, when they occurred, or later, the wanted category is further divided into planned and mistimed births. Planned births, on the one hand,

Table 6-1
Percentage Distribution of Births to Married Women in the United States, by Planning Status

Planning status	1961–65	1966–70	1970–73	1974–76
Planned	45	57	63	69
Mistimed	31	29	25	23
Unwanted	24	14	12	9

SOURCE: John E. Anderson, "Planning Status of Marital Births, 1975–1976." *Family Planning Perspectives,* 13 (March-April 1981): Table 2. Percents shown in Table are estimates derived from recent national fertility surveys.

are those resulting from pregnancies that are wanted at the time they occur (or were wanted earlier); mistimed births or timing failures, on the other hand, result from wanted pregnancies that occur before they are wanted. When we speak of wanted births, then, we mean births that result either from planned or mistimed pregnancies. *Unplanned births* constitute a final category that includes both timing and number failures.

Unwanted births occur with a wide range of frequency throughout the less developed countries, and they are often a major factor behind fairly rapid rates of population growth. To illustrate, according to data collected from women in eighteen developing countries included in the World Fertility Survey, the proportion of births in the year prior to the survey that were reported as unwanted ranged from 6 percent in Trinidad and Tobago to 44 percent in Jamaica (Lightbourne et al., 1982). It is further estimated that preventing all these unwanted births would have reduced the crude birth rate for the average country from 32 to 24; and, taking all eighteen countries together, it would have reduced the annual rate of population growth by about 40 percent.

Even in the United States, where there is relatively easy access to effective contraception and legal abortion, the number of unwanted births is surprising. According to one recent study, for example, American women from fifteen to forty-four years of age in 1973 would have had 14 million fewer births during their lifetimes if they had given birth only to the children they wanted at the time they became pregnant (Munson, 1977). If only those births had occurred that were wanted at the time of pregnancy, each of these women would have given birth to an average of only 2.1 children rather than the 2.6 they actually had. The data in Table 6-1 clearly point to continued improvement in control over marital fertility (i.e., the percentage of births that were planned has risen steadily since the early 1960s). Nevertheless, in 1975–76 nearly one-third of all births to married women were either mistimed or unwanted. The highest proportions of unwanted births occurred among women who already had at least two children, who had no more than a high school education, who were black, and, most important of all, who were very poor (Anderson, 1981).

Mistimed Births

Because the number of children is usually thought of as more consequential than the timing, the motivations to limit family size tend to be stronger than the motivations to time and space the births. Yet control over the timing and spacing of births is very important at both the societal and individual levels. Postponed childbearing and longer birth intervals reduce period fertility rates and extend the length of generations. Populations, as a result, increase at a slower pace. Average family size may also decline, since successful fertility control at earlier ages is associated with motivations to limit family size at older ages.

Even high fertility societies may exhibit considerable concern with birth spacing. In one highland Guatemalan community, for instance, the women reported an overwhelming desire for five or more children, or "whatever God provided" (Barnett et al., 1971). Nonetheless, virtually all the women expressed preferences for birth intervals of two to three years or more. A frequent reason for such deliberate birth spacing in less developed areas is to maximize infants' chances for survival. Protein deficiency is an important cause of infant mortality in many parts of the Third World. Subsequent pregnancies are therefore frequently postponed through the practice of postpartum abstinence in order that nursing infants will not be denied an adequate diet.

Control over the "tempo" of fertility is especially important in industrial societies, and there is good reason to believe that the birth of the first child is more important in its consequences than the change from one to any higher number of children. The reason why the timing of the first birth is especially crucial is that the first birth has such a strong potential for changing the life course of a couple, and especially of the woman. The first birth marks the onset of parenthood roles and childcare responsibilities. Frequently, it also precipitates entry into marriage itself. In fact, a recent study of six hundred newly married couples revealed that 21 percent of the wives were pregnant at the time of their marriages (Neal et al., 1981).

If the timing of all first births were planned, hasty marriages and illegitimate births would be greatly reduced. Thus greater planning of first births would postpone marriage as well as parenthood. This in turn would provide young people (especially women, since the restrictive effects of childcare are borne disproportionately by them) with more time, free of childcare, in which to continue their education and to develop more intense interests and commitments with respect to occupational and other extra-familial activities. Finally, the broadened perspectives implied by all of this suggest that the desire for many children, or even for parenthood itself, would be reduced, thereby contributing to a reduction in eventual completed family size. Planning the timing of second and higher order births can also be very important to dual-career couples and others who derive financial and psychological rewards from activities apart from family life. Hence, planning one's life necessarily includes the planning of both the number and the timing of one's offspring.

Illegitimate Births

So far, we have concentrated on unintentional fertility within marriage. But births to unmarried women constitute an important proportion of fertility in several countries, including the United States. While some out-of-wedlock births are undoubtedly planned, we can safely assume that the vast majority result from unintentional pregnancies. Births occurring outside the "marital unit," however defined, are commonly referred to as *illegitimate*, a term now in some disrepute because of its degrading connotations.

The principle of legitimacy probably comes as near as any social rule to being truly universal, functioning as it does to allocate responsibility for the socialization of the child and to determine the child's social placement. Because of concern in all societies with how the next generation is to be integrated into a complex system of human relationships, illegitimacy is typically viewed as a threat to the continuity and integrity of society. However, despite strong negative sanctions, the rule of legitimacy is violated to some degree in virtually all societies. In the United States, for example, large numbers of unintentional pregnancies result each year when large numbers of unmarried people engage in unprotected intercourse. Illegitimate births then result if the unmarried, pregnant women fail either to abort the fetus or to marry prior to the birth of the child. During the 1970s, while the number of legitimate births was declining, the number of births to unmarried women increased. This combination of trends resulted in an increase in the proportion of all births that were illegitimate from 11 percent in 1970 to 18 percent in 1980 (National Center for Health Statistics, 1982).

The large numbers of illegitimate births have raised serious questions concerning possible negative consequences for the child, the parents, and society (Hartley, 1975). Infant mortality rates, for example, are higher for the children of unmarried mothers. In addition, the health and emotional stability of children born to unmarried mothers may be at higher risk. While adoption would seem to offer a solution to some of these problems, only a very small proportion of illegitimate children are ever adopted or later legitimated by marriage of the parents. Research also shows that the father of an illegitimate child seldom maintains a lasting relationship with the mother and child, leaving the unwed mother to act as the principal socializing agent in the child's life. These unwed mothers frequently suffer from emotional instability and low self-esteem. Illegitimate children are also more likely than others to be victims of the battered-child syndrome. Finally, while the state may help support an illegitimate child, the amount seldom compares favorably with what an employed father could earn.

Teenage Fertility

There is, unfortunately, a very high correlation between illegitimacy and teenage childbearing, and in many countries these two trends are on the rise. There are several diverse and complex reasons for the increase in out-of-wedlock adolescent pregnancy and childbearing, including earlier sexual maturity and longer periods of time during which young people are together in school and in the labor force prior to marriage. In developing countries, rapid urbanization has helped to weaken traditional social control mechanisms that deter premarital sexuality. Cultural restrictions such as chaperonage and sexual segregation, for example, may no longer be possible or practical. Further, the young people who are or could be motivated to use contraception frequently do not have access to family planning services, which in most developing countries remain oriented toward older, married couples.

Of the approximately 29 million teenagers in the United States in 1978, about 12 million were sexually active. Roughly 80 percent of the males and 70 percent of the females were having intercourse at some point during their teenage years. This sexual activity resulted in well over a million pregnancies, most of which were unintentional. The younger the teenager the more likely that her pregnancy was an accident. Among the 30,000 pregnant girls under age fifteen, for example, virtually none had intended to become pregnant. Altogether in 1978, some 434,000 pregnancies among teenagers ended in abortion, and 362,000 resulted in births conceived out of wedlock. These and other facts on teenage fertility (summarized in Guttmacher Institute, 1981) have been widely publicized in recent years.

If current patterns do not change, 40 percent of young American women can expect to be pregnant at least once during their teenage years. With so many children now living with teenage mothers, nearly half of whom are unmarried, there is a widespread concern over the consequences of early childbearing for both the children and their mothers (Baldwin, 1976). The research on this issue is quite clear: almost all of the health, social, and economic consequences of teenage pregnancy are adverse (Guttmacher Institute, 1981). A young woman's discovery of accidental pregnancy can be a traumatic experience, and pregnancies that result in abortion or miscarriage often are upsetting to the woman, as well as a risk to her health. Pregnancies that result in birth, however, have the most obvious negative consequences. Infant mortality rates are much higher for babies born to women in their teens than for those born to older women, and even when the infant survives, teenage childbearing has several far-reaching consequences for both parents and children. Young parents tend to drop out of school, thereby limiting their opportunities to gain needed occupational skills. Frequently this leads to unemployment or dead-end jobs, with resultant low family incomes. Even if teenage parents marry, they are far more likely than others to become divorced or separated. Ultimately, alone with young children and with only a limited education, many teenage mothers face years of existence on welfare, with incomes well below the officially designated poverty level. As for the children, living in poor one-parent homes is associated with lower IQ and achievement scores, a greater likelihood of repeating grades, and a greater chance of becoming teenage parents themselves.

Why the increase in adolescent pregnancies? Mostly it reflects an increase in the number of teenagers who are sexually active (Zelnik et al., 1981). We live in a society in which young people receive conflicting messages about sex. While society disapproves of adolescent sexuality in general, the media blatantly exploit sex for both advertising and entertainment purposes. Popular teenage heroes and heroines, for example, play up the pleasurable aspects of sex and play down the possible procreative outcomes. We have all witnessed the "slump to the floor" act in a movie or television scene: the hero and heroine look deeply into each other's eyes, madly embrace, and slump passionately to the floor (or couch, bed, boat deck, etc.). At the fade-out, there is little doubt about what is going on. Yet virtually never do the hero and heroine express concern about contraceptive protection. There is a paradox here. The media glorify youth and sexuality while ignoring contraception. In many respects, teenagers do the same thing.

The percentage of unwed sexually active teenage women who use some method of birth control has been increasing (see Table 6-2). That is the good news. The bad news is that the late 1970s also were a time of declining use of the most effective methods such as the pill or IUD and an increase in use of the least effective methods such as withdrawal (Guttmacher Institute, 1981). Moreover, nearly two-thirds of sexually active unwed teenagers report that they *never* use contraception or, if they do, that they practice it inconsistently. Why is this so? In a few cases (less than 10 percent), they are intentionally trying to become pregnant, or are already pregnant. Among the others, however, about 40 percent think, usually mistakenly, that they cannot get pregnant because "it is the wrong time of the month." For those who realize that they can get pregnant, the major reason for nonuse of contraception is that intercourse is not expected at the time it occurs.

Nevertheless, the provision of family planning services to teenagers remains a controversial issue. Some people, in spite of strong evidence to

Table 6-2
Contraceptive Use by Sexually Active Unmarried Women in Metropolitan Areas of the United States, 1976 and 1979

Contraceptive use	1976	1979
Always	29%	34%
Sometimes	36	39
Never	36	27
At first intercourse	38	49

SOURCE: Adapted from Figure 5 in *Teenage Pregnancy: The Problem That Hasn't Gone Away* (New York: Alan Guttmacher Institute, 1981).

the contrary, still believe that sex education and the availability of contraceptives will lead to an increase in teenage pregnancy (Hatcher et al., 1980). But approximately 70 percent of teenage girls seeking family planning services for the first time do so because they think they are already pregnant! Many teenagers have intercourse regularly for several months before they start to use any birth control at all (Guttmacher Institute, 1981). The primary reason for this long delay in starting to use contraceptives is clear: teenagers are afraid their parents will find out. When asked why they chose the family planning clinic they did, teenagers have been equally candid: the clinic would not inform their parents. Withholding family planning services from teenagers, therefore, probably would not result in a decline in the incidence of intercourse but in an increase in unintentional pregnancies. Conversely, given the great number of unintentional teenage pregnancies and their tremendous social, educational, economic, and psychological costs, much more rather than less needs to be done to help teenagers control their reproductive lives. We will return to the issue of public policy—of what more might be done—in Chapter 7.

BIRTH CONTROL THROUGH HISTORY

Unintentional childbearing has been a burden for people all through history, a burden that has fallen most heavily on women, especially poor women. Thus the issue of reproductive choice has always been a part of more general concerns with social and sexual inequality (Gordon, 1976).

In the modern world, neither individuals nor couples can plan their lives with confidence unless they are able to exert control over the number and timing of their children. Yet even in "contracepting" societies like the United States such control is far from complete. Not only the poor but also the young, the ignorant, and the "unlucky" from all walks of life continue to be victimized by unintentional fertility. On a societal level governments are cognizant as never before of the necessity for birth control programs in their arsenals against poverty, malnutrition, and social inequality. Worldwide, if population growth is to be stabilized eventually, approximately 75 to 80 percent of all fecund women must practice contraception on a regular basis (Yinger et al., 1983). Thus contraception and birth prevention have been and remain a continuing concern of humanity.

The story of society's struggle to prevent unwanted births is sometimes amusing and often horrifying (Himes, 1936). Birth control is not a twentieth century discovery. Many modern techniques, in fact, have historical roots that can be traced back for centuries. For example, an Egyptian papyrus dated 1850 B.C. provides a formula for a mixture of crocodile dung and honey to be placed in the vagina for contraceptive purposes. This mixture evidently provided some spermicidal effects in addition to acting as a barrier to sperm.

Other early methods of birth control included devices intended to absorb the sperm. Tampons made of lint and simple sponges were widely used for this purpose until quite recently. Eventually a round cuplike device was designed for placement over the cervix to block the sperm. The first real diaphragm, in fact, may well have been half of a hollowed out pomegranate (Laurensen and Whitney, 1977). Douching and fumigating (i.e., introducing fumes or gases into the vagina) also were used as contraceptive methods. Ancient Egyptian women douched with such substances as wine and garlic, using instruments made from animal horns or bills to administer the solutions. Later, in Europe, douche bags were made of sow bladders with wooden nozzles. The first condoms, which were developed to prevent the transmission of venereal disease rather than to avoid conception, were made from animal guts and bladders.

The simplest method of keeping semen from reaching the egg, of course, was to withdraw the penis before ejaculation. In early history this may well have been the most common method of birth control. Nowadays the dissemination of more effective methods has demoted coitus interruptus to one of the lesser used birth control techniques, although it is still widespread in some places.

European Origins

There is considerable evidence of voluntary restriction of fertility in preindustrial Europe, even though such restriction was frequently at odds with the dominant morals, mores, and philosophies of the societies in which it was occurring. Not until the early nineteenth century did writers begin to describe and recommend the advantages of birth control. The story of their efforts is both poignant and dramatic. Above all, it is the story of progressive men and women who were determined to make it possible for others to exercise control over their reproductive lives (Chandrasekhar, 1981).

One of the first modern scholars to be concerned with the need to control fertility was Thomas Robert Malthus, an eighteenth-century English cleric whose views on population are discussed more fully in later chapters. Malthus expressed his concern within the limits of the conventional morality, and he called for the reduction of fertility through the practice of "moral restraint," by which he meant the postponement of marriage coupled with extended periods of sexual abstinence.

The first unequivocal advocate of birth control as a substitute for moral restraint was Francis Place (Place, 1822). Born into an impoverished English family, Place was keenly aware of the hardships suffered by the working class, and among his scholarly writings was a series of pamphlets, which came to be known as the "Diabolical Handbills," in which he pleaded for birth control as a partial answer to working-class poverty. In addition to coitus interruptus, Place described and recommended a specifically female method: "A piece of soft sponge is tied by a bobbin or penny ribbon, and inserted just before the sexual intercourse takes place, and is withdrawn again as soon as it has taken place."

In the United States, the first attempt to disseminate birth control information is attributed to Charles Knowlton, whose book *The Fruits of Philosophy* (1832) was later to play a dramatic role in the family planning movement. According to an important chronicler of birth control history, Knowlton's "treatment of contraceptive technique is the first really important account after those of . . . two millennia earlier" (Himes, 1936, p. 227). Knowlton stressed the utility of post-coital douching and provided his readers with several formulas.

For the next several decades the birth control movement languished in obscurity, only to be rescued in a sensational way by the publicity attending the trial of two English freethinkers, Charles Bradlaugh and Annie Besant, in the late 1870s. They deliberately tested a court decision banning the sale of Knowlton's *Fruits of Philosophy* which, according to the court, contained "obscene" drawings. Bradlaugh and Besant defiantly republished the Knowlton book and notified the police where and when they would offer it for sale. Arrested, tried, and convicted for publishing a book "calculated to deprave public morals" (Fryer, 1965, p. 164), the two reformers successfully used the attendant publicity to argue for birth control information on behalf of poor women and their children. A week after the sentencing (fines and six-month terms), the case was appealed successfully on a technicality, and Bradlaugh and Besant were soon free to sell Knowlton's book.

The publicity surrounding the Bradlaugh-Besant trial helped foster a significant change in public attitudes, and there was an enormous increase in the visibility and sales of family planning literature. Sales of *Fruits of Philosophy*, which had been less than 1,000 copies a year, rose to over 100,000 in the first three months after the trial and continued at a high level thereafter. In 1877 Besant produced her own book, which she dedicated to "the poor," and in later editions advocated two new methods, the cervical cap and soluble pessaries. From this point on, the manufacture and sale of spermicides, condoms, and diaphragms increased regularly.

Several factors were involved in the subsequent decline in the birth rate in Britain in every year from 1877 to 1918; nonetheless, the wide publicity given the Bradlaugh-Besant trial could not help but make an impact. Attitudes toward birth control were never again to be the same; contraceptive practice in the late nineteenth century was markedly improved, and by the end of the nineteenth century virtually all forms of birth control now used, except oral contraceptives, were being manufactured and distributed. Condoms, spermicides, intrauterine devices, and pessaries were used increasingly; the first human vasectomy was performed around 1893; and abortion, while illegal, was well known.

The Family Planning Movement

It was over the issue of abortion that Margaret Sanger launched her family planning crusade in the United States. In 1916, following a trip to England, Holland, and France looking for reliable information on birth control, Sanger founded her own clinic in New York City. For maintaining this "public nuisance" she spent thirty days in prison. But an idea whose time has come cannot be stopped and, spurred by the efforts of Margaret Sanger and her British contemporary, Marie Stokes, the birth control movement spread throughout the world.

We should keep in mind that by the 1920s and 1930s fertility in Europe, Great Britain, and the United States had already fallen to fairly low levels. Thus, the family planning movement had little impact on the problem of fertility regulation at the societal level. The family planning movement was important, however, in bringing to public attention the unmet needs of the poor, and especially to legitimate what had been happening in private for some time. The movement was also an obvious expression of the political emancipation being sought by women at the time.

The struggle for birth control rights, then, while varying somewhat from one nation or time to another, has evolved into an identifiable doctrine, the key ideas of which have been summarized as follows (Petersen, 1975, p. 516):

1. Control of family size is both physically possible and morally desirable.
2. The ultimate decision whether and when to have children should be made by parents, rather than by fate, or tradition, or church, or state.
3. A relatively small number of children is a social good, both because of favorable effects within the family and because a too rapid population growth is a serious danger to social welfare.

Opposition to Birth Control

The birth control movement, to the present time, has always been shaped by the opposition to it. Over the past century nationalism, socialism, and traditionalism have contributed significant opposition to further spread of the birth control movement (Petersen, 1975). India, for example, eventually became a leader among underdeveloped nations in launching a national birth control program. But immediately following independence, such leaders as Gandhi and Nehru insisted that birth control was either immoral or irrelevant to India's problems. Population growth was frequently associated with national power and prestige, leading ruling elites to regard birth control as outside the realm of national interests. Sometimes nationalism has combined with socialism, as in the Soviet Union and China following their momentous revolutions. For many years, off and on, these communist countries showed considerable hostility toward family planning programs, continuing a long-standing dispute between the followers of Malthus and the disciples of Marx. Malthus argued that overpopulation was the major hindrance to the realization of utopian goals, whereas Marx viewed overpopulation as a by-product of the economic exploitation that characterizes a capitalist system.

The most significant opposition to birth control, however, especially in the Western nations, has always been traditionalism. When people oppose birth control because they perceive it as a threat to the family, or as a form of moral degeneracy, traditional ideologies are nearly always behind their opposition. Throughout much of the twentieth century, for example, many people regarded children as gifts of God. They believed that subjecting reproduction to human will was "unnatural." Thus the idea that couples should actually determine how many children they would have or when they would have them was first expressed by a tiny minority of rebels who often held many other unpopular opinions as well. Annie Besant, for example, was a devoted feminist and later a religious mystic who moved to India (a major road in Bombay is named after her). Charles Bradlaugh was a militant atheist, a freethinker who nonetheless was elected to Parliament, where he served many years despite his refusal to take a religious oath. Thus, the family planning movement, like many other social reforms, was often linked with other sectarian causes: pacifism, vegetarianism, temperance, and the like. The more traditional individuals and institutions were offended by what they perceived as violations of the normative order.

The major institution supporting traditional values regarding family life is, of course, religion. For this reason religious ideology throughout the world is virtually always pro-family and pro-natalist as well. Historically, for example, the major Western religions have directly or indirectly encouraged a pro-natalist and anti–birth control attitude through interpretations of their sacred literatures. Nonetheless, Judaism and Protestantism in most of their variant forms have in the twentieth century moved from a position of tolerance to one of outright advocacy of birth control as a moral duty.

There is still formal opposition to contraception within the Roman Catholic church. This opposition is based on the long, complex, and changing history of the church's teachings on sex and reproduction (Murphy, 1981). While periodic abstinence remains the only acceptable method in the eyes of the church, for all practical purposes there is no longer, if there ever was, a single unified position. Today Catholics in many parts of the world overwhelmingly ignore the church's opposition to contraception. In the United States, for instance, there has been a very strong convergence in contraceptive practices between Catholics and non-Catholics (Groat et al., 1975; Westoff and Ryder, 1977).

Contraception and Abortion

There is no doubt that developments in birth control technology in the late nineteenth and early twentieth centuries were generated through the desire to give individuals greater control over a major social and economic feature of their lives—their reproductive capacity. The notion that a vastly improved technology might permit or even encourage freer sexual activity was not a primary concern. Similarly, the early personalities in the family planning movement, with few exceptions, made a point of disassociating contraception from abortion. Yet it seems logical that once the idea of birth control became accepted it might extend beyond the control of conception. The American writers R. L. Dickinson and L. S. Bryant faced this issue squarely in *Control of Conception* (1938). They pointed out that someday Americans would "frankly face" interruptions of pregnancy for "all reasons," and went ahead to describe the use of a small curette for early abortions. Planned Parenthood, Margaret Sanger's legacy in the United States, eventually incorporated abortion, when public attitudes and legal restraints permitted.

As the traditional distinctions among contraception, sterilization, and abortion have become more or less fused into a broader and less precise category known as fertility control, new controversies have emerged to keep the old conflicts of the family planning movement alive and well. Technologically, we now have such quasi-permanent methods as the pill and, in much of the world, injectable contraceptives, making the distinction between contraception and sterilization less clear. Similarly, post-coital methods such as estrogen injection and "menstrual regulation" have blurred the distinction between contraception and abortion. The potential for using these technological advances to resolve conflicts between personal and social needs, on the one hand, and political and ideological requirements on the other, is worth noting.

CONTRACEPTION TODAY

The early birth control advocates, as we have noted, took pains to disassociate themselves from the notion that improved techniques of fertility control might lead to more liberal sexual mores. In the past couple of decades, however, views on the role of contraception have been transformed. In industrial nations, at least, the great goals of the birth control pioneers had been achieved by the 1960s: informed and highly motivated couples could plan their families with reasonable success. The availability of birth control, therefore, was no longer a major issue for most people, and during the 1960s attention shifted to the *quality* of birth control. New public demands emerged and are still gaining momentum. In short, in countries such as the United States, there has been a dramatic shift in values concerning fertility control (Bumpass, 1973).

When the birth control pill was placed on the mass market in the early 1960s, other contraceptives available at the time were less effective and, above all, were sexually obtrusive. That is, such contraceptives as the diaphragm and the condom, while highly effective if properly used, interfered with the spontaneity of sexual intercourse. So the rapid diffusion of the pill through the population involved both a quantitative change in birth control effectiveness and a qualitative change in expectations that fertility control should be separated from the sex act. The result has been a generation of young people who have come to expect fertility control to be virtually complete and sexually unobtrusive. It is no mere coincidence, for example, that attitudes toward both abortion and sterilization have changed dramatically since the introduction of the birth control pill; as fertility control values have increasingly incorporated concerns with efficacy and convenience, individuals and couples have turned in massive numbers toward these two most effective and sexually unobtrusive techniques.

In the industrial nations there are currently demands for even better birth control techniques, which will be not only effective and unobtrusive, but also even more convenient and free from annoying side effects. These developments largely reflect events in the most economically advanced nations. The situation is somewhat different in the developing world, where existing health and educational delivery systems tend to be weak and overextended. Different technologies from those used in the Western nations—long-acting contraceptive implants, for example—may be more useful and have greater appeal in those parts of the world where fertility has remained at high levels (Schearer, 1977).

The "Perfect" Contraceptive?

Disappointing as it may be, there may never be a single perfect method of controlling fertility. We can enumerate some characteristics of a "good" method, however (Freedman and Berelson, 1976). Certainly everyone wants a contraceptive to be safe, effective, convenient, and inexpensive. Most people also prefer something that does not have to be used at the time of intercourse—in other words something unobtrusive. Needless to say, the method must also be acceptable to cultures with different religious and sexual values. To minimize side effects, the ideal method would also be specific in its interference with a single step in the reproductive process. Ease of manufacture and distribution, and minimal medical or clinical involvement would also be considerations. Finally, people in different stages of the life cycle may have different concerns and requirements. For example, couples must determine preferences for both the timing and number of pregnancies relative to the timing of marriage and the completion of childbearing. The frequency of sexual activity and the potential consequences of contraceptive failure may not be the same for people at different stages of life.

In the United States, after the discovery of the harmful effects of thalidomide taken during pregnancy, extensive requirements were imposed on new drugs, including contraceptive drugs. The requirements, in the interests of public safety, are stringent, making the process of new product development long and complicated. From animal studies through clinical trials, the research and testing process can take fifteen or more years (Segal and Nordberg, 1977). Obviously the pharmaceutical industry has only a limited interest in high-risk research that may have only a very limited profitability. Since the ideal contraceptive should be cheap, for example, and not require repeated purchases, the incentives for private development of contraceptives are somewhat limited. The public sector, therefore, has become increasingly important in the research and manufacture of contraceptives.

METHODS OF FERTILITY REGULATION

We noted in Chapter 5 that there are three basic steps in the reproduction process: intercourse, conception, and gestation. Fertility can thus be regulated by controlling any one of several steps: abstaining from intercourse; preventing conception by means of contraception or sterilization; or by terminating the gestation period by an abortion.

Abstinence

Voluntary abstinence from sexual intercourse is one method of birth control that is socially approved almost everywhere, especially for unmarried young people. Men and women choose abstinence for a variety of moral, religious, and ethical reasons, believing that there are times and circumstances when it is "wrong" to have intercourse. Among nineteen-year-old never-married American women in the late 1970s, for example, approximately one-third had never been sexually active (Zelnick et al., 1979). In some societies nearly all unmarried males and females abstain from intercourse. Sex and intercourse are not the same thing, of course, and sex without intercourse may be viewed as a form of abstinence. This would include such activities as hugging and kissing, petting, mutual masturbation, and oral-genital sex. Many teenagers, in their early experimentations with sex, express themselves sexually without having penis-in-vagina intercourse. Abstinence as a regularly practiced means of birth control, however, certainly seems impractical for most people. And modern contraceptive technology has provided a host of alternatives for sexually active couples.

Contraception

One of the most far-reaching demographic developments taking place in the world today is the change in contraceptive knowledge, attitudes, and practices—what population experts refer to as the KAP of contraception. The trend toward greater adoption and use of contraception has accelerated greatly over the past decade or so. We now find contraception being practiced where it never was before, with people turning increasingly to the newer and more effective methods. In the face of still ominously high birth rates, the upswing in contraceptive use seems to some observers hardly fast enough. Nonetheless, the record of recent years, in combination with widespread legal, moral, and financial support from governments around the world, certainly allows room for encouragement.

Contraceptive Awareness and Use

Since the mid-1970s the World Fertility Survey (WFS) has been collecting data on reproductive knowledge, attitudes, and practices from both developed and developing countries around the world (Lightbourne et al., 1982). Among the many important preliminary findings of this massive research endeavor are data showing that knowledge about contraception is fairly widespread. Except in four countries—Lesotho, Senegal, Sudan, and Nepal—80 percent or more of the married women had heard of at least one method of contraception, and overwhelmingly, those women were aware of at least one modern, effective method.

What about contraceptive use? In sharp contrast to the developed countries where nearly three-fourths of fecund married couples are using contraception, the proportion of users in the developing countries was as low as 3 percent in Nepal, with an overall average among twenty-nine countries of only 32 percent. Fertility, however, is still lower in these countries than it might otherwise be because of another practice documented by the WFS. Specifically, the overwhelming majority of women in the developing world breast-feed their babies, thus extending the period of natural infertility after birth and lengthening the intervals between births. Among the most rural and illiterate peasantries, therefore, much of the current restraint on fertility comes from the traditional practice of breast-feeding (in combination with some postpartum abstinence). Because breast-feeding is declining in most Third World nations, some demographers have predicted an increase in marital fertility in such places as Pakistan, Bangladesh, and Kenya unless contraceptive use can replace breast-feeding rapidly enough to compensate for this trend.

In addition to the overall contraceptive use rate, there are substantial differences between developed and developing societies with respect to the age of the user and the method used. In the United States, for example, married women from fifteen to nineteen are five times more likely than their counterparts in the Third World to use contraception. The pattern of contraceptive use by age shown in Figure 6-1 suggests that women in the United States (and other developed countries) use contraception to time and space births as well as to prevent childbearing altogether, while in developing countries women are more likely to initiate contraception only after having the number of children they want.

Even though there is widespread awareness of modern methods of contraception, 31 percent of the contracepting women in the WFS devel-

Figure 6-1
Age Patterns of Contraceptive Use among Currently Married, Fecund Women, Late 1970s

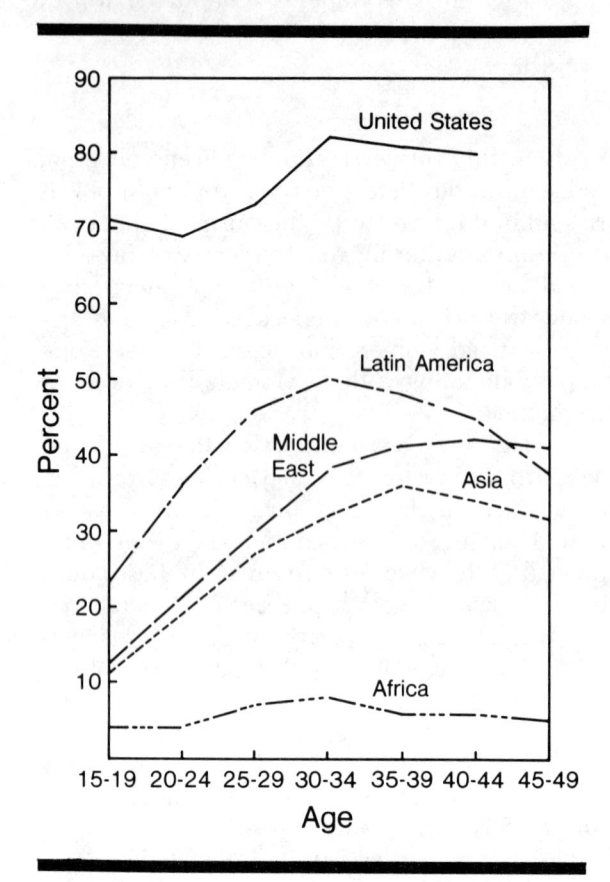

SOURCE: Redrawn by authors from a similar figure in Robert Lightbourne et al., "The World Fertility Survey: Changing Global Childbearing." *Population Bulletin,* 37 (March 1982).

oping nations were using inefficient or traditional methods. The highest proportions of contraceptors using inefficient means (categorized by the WFS as including douche, rhythm, withdrawal, abstinence, and "other") were in the countries of Africa (46 percent) and the Middle East (40 percent), while the lowest proportions were in Asia (25 percent) and Latin America (27 percent).

There is also a wide variation in the specific methods used from country to country. For example, only 5 percent of the contraceptors in Sri Lanka use the pill, compared with more than 50 percent in Indonesia, Sudan, and

Syria. On the other hand, female sterilization is very rare (1 percent) in Indonesia but relatively common in Sri Lanka (29 percent). Among the traditional methods, withdrawal is extremely rare in Senegal (1 percent) but very common in Turkey (44 percent).

In sharp contrast to the techniques used in the developing world, the pill, IUD, and condom are the most popular methods in the United States and most of the Western European countries. Where the widespread use of such inefficient methods as withdrawal and rhythm is reported—Bulgaria, Romania, Hungary, and some other East European countries—abortion is used as a major backup method of birth control.

Contraceptive Use in the United States

During the past two decades contraception has become not only commonplace but nearly universal among married couples in the United States. In 1960, for example, approximately 50 percent of currently married women were using contraception. This figure was 65 percent in 1970; and by 1980 approximately 70 percent of all married couples were using some contraceptive method (Mosher, 1981).

Data from the National Survey of Family Growth in 1976 (Mosher, 1981) indicated that roughly 49 percent of the married couples with wives fifteen to forty-four years of age were using nonsurgical methods of contraception, whereas 19 percent of the wives or husbands had been surgically sterilized. Most of the nonusers of contraception were pregnant, postpartum, or trying to become pregnant (13 percent), or unable to become pregnant due to noncontraceptive sterility (11 percent). The remaining 8 percent were not using contraception because of fecundity impairments, religion, or indifference to possible pregnancy.

Among couples using nonsurgical techniques in 1976, the pill was by far the most popular method (46 percent), with the condom (15 percent) and IUD (13 percent) running a distant second and third. Both younger (age fifteen to twenty-nine) and older (thirty to forty-four) wives were contraceptively protected in nearly equal proportions in the 1970s, although the methods used by each age group were quite different. Contracepting wives under thirty relied most heavily on the pill, while older women relied to a much greater extent on sterilization. Thus nearly all married couples at risk of unintended pregnancy are now using the most effective methods. However, there is still room for improvement. This is reflected indirectly in the remaining though narrowing differences in contraceptive use by family income, religion, and education (see Figure 6-2), and in differentials among these subcategories in the types of contraception being used (Ford, 1979). Nonetheless, married couples in the United States since the mid-1970s have been well protected against unintentional childbearing, compared with couples in the past. For that matter, so have several million widowed, di-

Figure 6-2
Percent of Currently Married Women 15 to 44 Years of Age, by Contraceptive Status and Education: United States, 1976

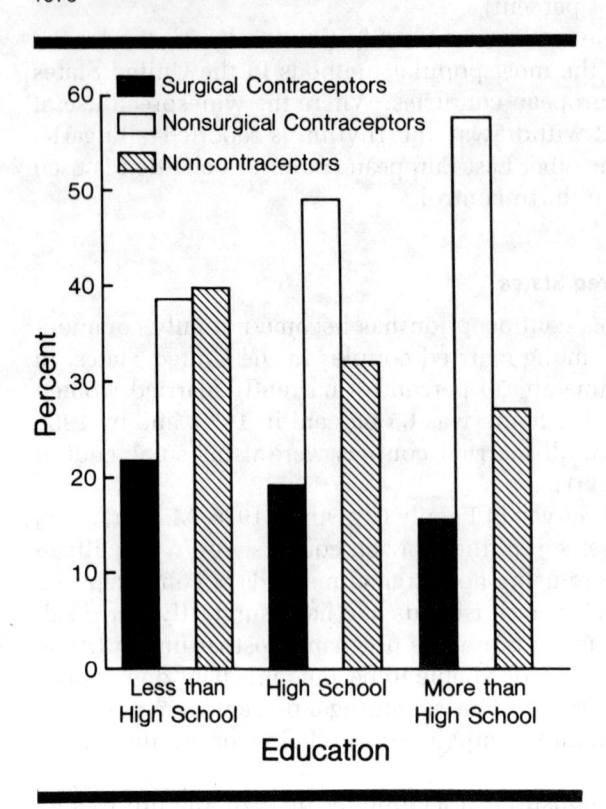

SOURCE: Redrawn by authors from a similar figure in William D. Mosher, "Contraceptive Utilization," *Vital and Health Statistics,* 23:7 (March 1981).

vorced, and separated women still in their childbearing years, 40 percent of whom were using nonsurgical methods and 14 percent of whom were contraceptively sterile in 1976 (Mosher, 1981).

Contraceptive Effectiveness

Once the decision is made to use contraception, the next question is which contraceptive to use. Typically, such matters as side effects, cost, convenience, and safety will enter into the decision-making process. Many people, however, are most interested in the effectiveness of different methods. Contraceptives vary in their effectiveness even when used exactly as they should be used, without error or omission. The *theoretical effectiveness* of a method is its maximum effectiveness under ideal circumstances. Human beings do very few things perfectly, however. Some people do not follow directions as carefully as others, or are more careless, or forgetful, or more likely to take risks. Beyond the theoretical effectiveness of contraception there is *use effectiveness*, which takes into account the characteristics of the user as well as those of the contraceptive method. Use effectiveness measures always combine method failure (e.g., a leaky condom) and use failure (e.g., forgetting to take the pill).

One of the most striking findings of research on contraceptive effectiveness has been the impact of intentions regarding fertility on the actual effectiveness people experience with a particular method: couples who intended to *delay* further (wanted) pregnancies are much more likely to experience contraceptive failure than couples who use contraception to *prevent* further (unwanted) pregnancies. Thus the motivation of the couple is obviously a powerful variable in the use effectiveness of different contraceptive methods. Failure rates (i.e., the percent of users who become pregnant during the first year of use) among delayers and preventers as reported by one recent study are shown in Figure 6-3.

Figure 6-3
Percent of Married Women 15 to 44 Years of Age Who Experienced Contraceptive Failure during the First Year of Use, by Contraceptive Intent and Method: United States, 1970–73

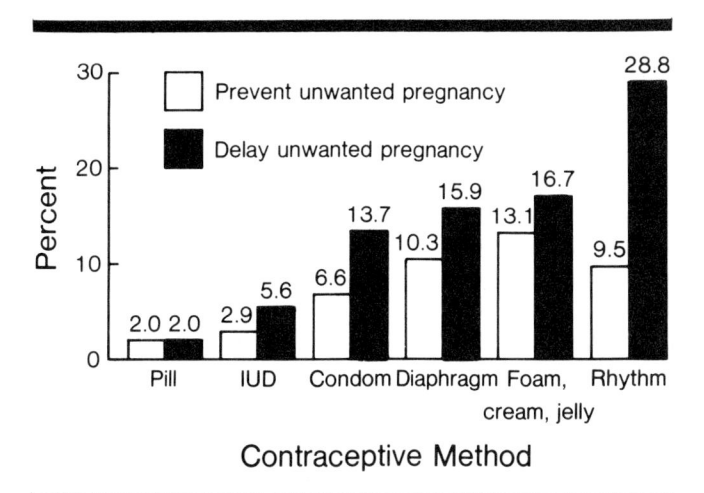

Contraceptive Method	Prevent unwanted pregnancy	Delay unwanted pregnancy
Pill	2.0	2.0
IUD	2.9	5.6
Condom	6.6	13.7
Diaphragm	10.3	15.9
Foam, cream, jelly	13.1	16.7
Rhythm	9.5	28.8

SOURCE: Redrawn by authors from a similar figure in Barbara Vaughan et al., "Contraceptive Efficacy among Married Women Aged 15 to 44 Years," *Vital and Health Statistics,* 23:5 (May 1980).

The reader should keep in mind that failure rates have been measured in several different ways, with different results. Instead of concentrating on the effectiveness of one particular method, therefore, attention should be directed to the effectiveness of different methods relative to one another. In the following discussion of various methods, we will give use effectiveness values that incorporate the results from different studies (summarized in Hatcher et al., 1980). These effectiveness rates, expressed as a percentage, refer to the approximate number of pregnancies resulting during the first year of use for one hundred women using the method.

Nonprescription Methods

The major contraceptive alternatives available in the United States without a doctor's prescription are the condom, various spermicides, withdrawal, and periodic abstinence or rhythm.

Condom. The condom, or "rubber," is the only highly effective method of contraception for men. Condoms are relatively inexpensive and easy to obtain and use. A cylindrical sheath worn over the erect penis, the condom, usually made of latex, is available in several types. Most condoms are rolled, and many have reservoirs at the end to receive the semen. If properly used, high-quality condoms can be very effective. The failure rate, however, due to misuse and nonuse, is around 10 percent. Condoms will eventually deteriorate if they are carried around in a wallet where they are exposed to body heat. The requirements of this method also include some preparation and planning, and a brief interruption of lovemaking. Men may also complain about a reduction in pleasure.

The major advantages of the condom are its safety and ready availability to almost everyone, including minors. More are being sold each year through mail order, which now accounts for approximately one-sixth of the condom market (Hatcher et al., 1980). Finally, condoms offer effective protection against veneral disease, a particular advantage for teenagers and young people who may have several sexual partners prior to marriage.

Spermicides. Vaginal contraceptives provide another highly accessible and theoretically effective method of contraception. Modern foams, creams, and jellies contain both spermicidal chemicals that immobilize or destroy the sperm, and inert base materials that physically block the entry of sperm into the cervix. Spermicides come in a variety of forms, including creams inserted by syringelike applicators, manually inserted suppositories and foaming tablets, and aerosols that produce a dense foam of carbon dioxide. Creams and jellies are not recommended for use without a diaphragm (Hatcher et al., 1980).

Because there are so many ways in which foams can be used carelessly or improperly, actual user effectiveness is much lower than one might think. For example, running out of foam can be a problem. A spare should always be on hand, because with many brands there is no way to tell how nearly empty the container is. Failure can result from using too little foam, from having intercourse without using foam each time, from forgetting to shake the container vigorously, from douching too soon after intercourse, and of course from not taking time out from lovemaking to use the foam at all. All these combine to produce a failure rate for actual users of 20 to 25 percent or higher. Nonetheless, spermicides, like condoms, have the advantage of being available in drug stores everywhere without prescription. The disadvantages of this method include its messiness and having to wait while it melts or spreads. The relatively high failure rate can be dramatically reduced by using foam in combination with a condom.

Withdrawal. Withdrawal, or coitus interruptus, is the world's oldest method of contraception and is still widely used, particularly in some Islamic societies. Withdrawal costs nothing, has no known side effects, and is always available as a method. Yet family planning professionals virtually always emphasize its single greatest disadvantage: a failure rate of 20 to 25 pregnancies per 100 women a year among actual users. The reason for this relatively high failure rate (about the same as for foam) is that the method demands so much self-control. For the male to withdraw his penis from his partner's vagina just before ejaculation requires that he interrupt coitus at precisely the point at which it is becoming most pleasurable for him. Thus failure to withdraw is the main reason for the low use-effectiveness rate of this method. There is also the possibility that sperm from the pre-ejaculatory fluid may escape into the vagina before the penis is withdrawn, especially following a recent ejaculation. Semen deposited near the vagina, needless to say, can also result in a pregnancy.

Nevertheless, withdrawal has been used by so many different peoples for so long that we cannot deny its importance as a form of birth control. Some demographers believe it to have been the major method responsible for European fertility decline in the eighteenth and nineteenth centuries. Indeed, recent data from the World Fertility Survey show that in France withdrawal is still a widely used contraceptive method among couples over age thirty-four and second to the pill among younger people (Leridon, 1979).

Periodic Abstinence (Rhythm). Couples who are educated about the menstrual cycle and the various signals of ovulation are able to pinpoint days during which they can have intercourse with a very low risk of pregnancy. Couples can also use *fertility awareness techniques* to determine when a backup method of birth control may be warranted, or to plan a pregnancy more effectively. For maximum effectiveness, different signs and patterns of fertility awareness techniques should be checked against each other. Since this method depends on abstinence from intercourse during the fertile period of a woman's menstrual cycle, the major techniques of this method are designed to help calculate the precise time of ovulation. These calculations are generally based on the assumption that sperm can survive for seventy-two hours after intercourse, that ova can be fertilized for twenty-four hours after ovulation, and that ovulation occurs fourteen days, plus or minus two days, prior to the beginning of a menstrual period. Thus very little equipment is needed (a calendar and a thermometer), there are no expenses or side effects, and the method is acceptable to religious groups that oppose some or all of the other methods. On the minus side, these techniques require careful training, record keeping, and the motivation to practice periodic abstinence. Women with irregular cycles may also have some difficulty with the calendar and temperature techniques.

There are three distinct procedures for practicing this form of birth control. The *calendar method* entails recording menstrual records over an extended number of months. The earliest ovulation is estimated by subtracting eighteen days from the shortest cycle. By subtracting eleven days from the longest cycle a similar estimate is made of the latest day on which ovulation is likely to occur. This procedure determines the range of the fertile period during which abstinence must be practiced.

The *temperature method* is based on the rise in basal body temperature (BBT) following ovulation. A person's BBT is determined by taking the temperature, during rest at the same time each day. The BBT tends to rise as ovulation occurs and remains high until the next menses. Three days of a sustained increase in the BBT is typically taken as evidence that ovulation has occurred. Since the BBT rises only *after* ovulation has occurred, the woman assumes that her fertile days are over only after her BBT has risen and remained at an elevated level for three full days. Thermometers with widely spaced markings designed for this procedure are available in most pharmacies.

The *cervical mucus* method relies on the fact that most women are able to notice changes caused by hormonal variations in the amount and nature of vaginal wetness. By following her own cycle and noting her own usual pattern, a woman can obtain distinctive evidence that ovulation is occurring from the changes in the cervical mucus. Because estrogen and secretion levels are low immediately following menstruation, the vagina tends to be somewhat dry at that time. The color and consistency of the cervical secretions then change as estrogen levels increase. Just prior to and following ovulation, when the woman is fertile, the discharge increases in volume and becomes quite slippery and clear. Thus by carefully noting changes in viscosity and color, the time of ovulation can be noted with considerable accuracy. The *symtothermal method,* which combines the mucus and temperature methods, gives women information from both sources and provides greater effectiveness than either of the two methods used alone. The nature of mucus secretions tells women when ovulation is about to occur, and the BBTs tell them when it has taken place.

Because these techniques of "natural" birth control are so dependent on the precise determination of the fertile period, there is considerable interest in the potential for technological improvements in the ways of measuring changes in both temperature and the cervical mucus. Some recent studies have indicated very low failure rates for the symtothermal method among couples who wanted to prevent any further pregnancies (Weeks, 1981). Thus there is little doubt that, when used properly by highly motivated couples, the method can be very effective indeed. The range of use effectiveness rates for these fertility awareness techniques, however, suggest twenty to thirty pregnancies per one hundred women during the first year of use. The World Health Organization concluded in a 1978 report that the mucus method, both alone and in combination with the BBT method, is "relatively ineffective" (Hatcher et al., 1980). The suspicion however, is that more accidental pregnancies result from risk-taking by couples during the fertile period than from the difficulties couples have in determining the timing of the fertile period.

Prescription Methods

The major contraceptive alternatives in this category are the pill, the intrauterine device (IUD), and the diaphragm.

The Pill. In some countries the oral contraceptive, or the pill, may be purchased through commercial outlets without medical supervision. In the United States, however, the pill is one of three methods of contraception available only through medical prescription. Worldwide, the pill is now used by tens of millions of women, and is currently the most popular form of contraception in the United States. The pill is virtually 100 percent effective if always used exactly as directed. As with other theoretically effective methods, however, actual use is not always "exactly as directed," the result being a user failure rate of 4 to 10 percent (Hatcher et al., 1980). The pill can be used incorrectly, skipped because of side effects, or simply forgotten. Nonetheless, if it were not for its side effects the pill would come very close to being an ideal contraceptive. Because of the side effects, however, the pill is not suitable for many women.

Many different varieties of pills are manufactured throughout the world, differing in size, relative quantities of estrogen and progestin, chemical structure, and effects on the body. The most popular combination type of pill (containing both estrogen and progestin) works by inhibiting ovulation and thickening the cervical mucus as well as changing the uterine lining in ways that are hostile to sperm and, should an ovum be released anyway, hostile to the implantation of the egg. There are also sequential pills, with some tablets containing only estrogen and others containing a combination of hormones. Pills containing only progestin, the so-called mini-pills, are also available. These low-dose progestin pills are sometimes prescribed for women who may experience severe side effects from estrogen. Since ovulation is not necessarily suppressed, the effectiveness of the mini-pill depends on its capacity to make cervical mucus hostile to sperm, to interfere with the fertilization and implantation processes, and to frustrate ovum transport. Mini-pills are slightly less effective than combination pills.

Because the hormones in birth control pills affect many parts of the body, it is not surprising that various side effects are often associated with their use. Beyond the relatively minor and often transient side effects associated with initial use of oral contraceptives (e.g., nausea, breast tenderness, spotting, and weight gain), much more serious adverse reactions have been attributed to the pill. For example, there is an increased tendency among pill users of blood clotting, resulting in higher risks of heart attack and stroke. Women with histories of high blood pressure, diabetes, and blood clotting usually are advised not to use the pill. Similarly, women over the age of thirty-five and women who smoke should not use the pill because of higher risks of stroke, clotting disorders, and heart attack.

The other side of the story is that since 1960, when the pill was first approved and marketed, there have been major improvements, primarily a lowering of the dosages of steroids. Moreover, the pill has been associated with several beneficial side effects, such as relief from irregular or painful menstruation, control of acne, and treatment of ovarian cysts. Couples using the pill sometimes report greater sexual enjoyment as well, presumably because of the reduced fear of pregnancy and the sexually unobtrusive nature of the pill.

Another pill is sometimes used as an emergency measure following unprotected midcycle intercourse. This *morning-after pill* contains a large dose of diethystilbestrol (DES). The woman takes it within the first seventy-two hours after intercourse and continues to take it for five days. This synthetic estrogen frequently causes nausea and vomiting, and DES is a known cause of vaginal cancer in young women whose mothers took it during pregnancy. For these reasons, the morning-after pill is never considered a method for regular use. If and when a safe post-coital pill becomes available, it would have special advantages for women who have infrequent and sporadic intercourse—teenagers, for example. Meanwhile, alternative birth control options open to women seeking morning-after treatment include a morning-after IUD insertion or, following a late period, *menstrual extraction*. Menstrual extraction, or menstrual regulation, is a preemptive endometrial aspiration which, if performed prior to a pregnancy diagnosis, is sometimes useful to women who may be uncomfortable with the idea of abortion (Hatcher et al., 1980). This procedure sometimes involves use of a substance called "prostaglandin" to create an endocrinal imbalance and thereby bring on the appearance of menstruation.

The Intrauterine Device (IUD). Intrauterine contraception began with the observation that a foreign body in the uterus prevents pregnancy. The IUD evidently works by interfering with implantation by making the uterus hostile to either the sperm or the fertilized egg. Exactly what occurs is not precisely known. IUDs came to be regarded favorably during the early 1960s, after the development of new materials such as plastics and stainless steels made it possible for the device to be left in the uterus indefinitely. Today's IUDs are highly reliable, and since women can make relatively few errors using IUDs, the use effectiveness (90 to 94 percent) approximates the theoretical effectiveness (95 to 99 percent). Characteristics of the IUD include ease of insertion and removal, minimal side effects, and the use of a location aid such as a "tail" or string that extends into the vagina and can be felt by the wearer herself. Perhaps forty or more different types of IUDs are in use today, varying in size, shape, and material, with one thing sometimes being improved at the expense of another. Small size, for example, tends to reduce pain and bleeding, but may increase the risk of expulsion. Common shapes are coils, loops, rings, and Ts.

The major advantage of the IUD is obvious: prolonged protection without having to take further action on a regular basis or prior to each act of intercourse. Hence the motivation of the user, in theory, does not have to remain at a high level over an extended time. This characteristic led many family planners to believe that the IUD eventually would have a dramatic impact on the world's birth rate. It may yet, since many millions of women worldwide do indeed use the IUD. But various side effects such as cramps and bleeding, along with the tendency of younger women who have never given birth to expel the devices, have no doubt adversely affected the popularity of this contraceptive method.

The Diaphragm. The diaphragm is a dome-shaped device made of soft rubber or plastic sealed over a circular steel spring. Invented in the nineteenth century, the diaphragm at one time was the most popular form of birth control used by women in the United States. The device, which is worn inside the vagina during intercourse, serves both as a container for spermicides and as a mechanical barrier that blocks the entry of sperm into the cervix. Each diaphragm must be individually fitted so that the dome fits snugly over the cervix. Since they do not always fit tightly enough to prevent the entry of sperm, diaphragms should always be used in combination with spermicides. Following intercourse, the diaphragm and spermicide are left in place for several hours to allow time for the spermicide to do its job. After removal, the diaphragm is simply washed, dried, and stored in its container. When used properly, the diaphragm results in only about three pregnancies a year per one hundred users. Unfortunately, this method requires that attention be paid to contraception before each act of intercourse. Thus diaphragms left in dresser drawers, or used carelessly, contribute to an actual use failure rate of between 15 and 20 percent.

A smaller device, thimble-shaped and usually made of plastic, is widely used in Europe but not in the United States. This *cervical cap*, as it is called, works by providing a greater mechanical block against sperm than does the diaphragm.

Sterilization

One of the most dramatic developments of contraceptive choice over the past decade has been the increased popularity of surgical sterilization. By the late 1970s more than 80 million couples worldwide, about one in every ten of reproductive age, were estimated to have been sterilized for contraceptive purposes (Nortman, 1977). In the United States sterilization is now the leading method of birth control among couples with wives older than thirty. Larger proportions of non-Catholic than Catholic couples have been contraceptively sterilized, however; and male sterilization is much more common among white than among black couples.

Sterilization has an obvious advantage: it is a one-time procedure that can virtually guarantee a couple for life against pregnancy. But sterilization also has its limitations: its permanence, surgical nature, and initial expense. In addition, there is often some stigma attached to this method, related to its history of use for eugenic and punitive reasons. There are also misconceptions about the nature of this procedure, and many people from all walks of life, in developing and developed nations alike, falsely identify sterilization with castration and a loss of sexual appetite. Taking these limitations of sterilization into account, the rapidity with which it has spread throughout the world is indeed remarkable.

Female Sterilization

Women can be sterilized by removal of the ovaries or the uterus, or by blocking the fallopian tubes. Until recently, hysterectomy (removal of the uterus), which involves major surgery, was the most common method of sterilization for women. Since the 1960s, however, simplified procedures have permitted female sterilization with local anesthesia on an out-patient basis. Three different procedures are currently used to block the fallopian tubes: abdominal or vaginal *tubal ligation*, and *laparoscopy*. The latter involves the insertion of a coagulating instrument through a tiny incision in the lower abdomen, after which each tube is seared or a small portion of it is removed. The safety, minimal discomfort, and low cost of this technique account for its increased popularity in Europe and the United States (Hatcher et al., 1980).

Male Sterilization

The cutting of the male's sperm-carrying duct, the vas deferens, is a minor surgical procedure called a *vasectomy*, now routinely performed in physicians' offices and out-patient clinics. The operation is relatively simple, is often done with a local anesthetic, and lasts no more than ten or twenty minutes. A small incision is made in the scrotum, permitting the physician to coagulate, tie, or clip the vas, first on one side and then the other. Following a vasectomy, the male continues to produce sperm, but they are unable to move from the testicles to the penis, and are simply absorbed into the body.

Both tubal ligation and vasectomy are very highly effective methods of birth control, but neither is 100 percent effective. In rare instances, for example, a physician will mistakenly identify a round ligament as a fallopian tube; or in the case of males the ends of the vas will sometimes rejoin. Sterilization should always be considered a permanent procedure. Nonetheless, depending on the circumstances of the initial surgery and the skill of the surgeons, both tubal ligations and vasectomies can sometimes be reversed (Segal and Nordberg, 1977; Hatcher et al., 1980).

Induced Abortion

Induced abortion is probably the most widely used method of birth control throughout the world. Despite strong condemnation by governments, religious bodies, and the medical community in many countries, each year millions of women obtain abortions, legally or illegally, sometimes at great expense and often at great personal risk to life and health. Abortion is the termination of pregnancy before the fetus has become viable—in other words, prior to the time the fetus is capable of independent life outside the uterus. Traditionally, the medical community has considered viability to be reached after twenty-eight weeks of gestation, calculated from the first day of the last menstrual period. In actual practice, both pregnancy duration and fetal weight are taken into account in any presumption of viability.

Different techniques for abortion are used at different stages of pregnancy and according to the preferences of the woman and her physician (Hatcher et al., 1980). Vaginal evacuation, which entails emptying the uterine contents by either scraping (dilation and curettage) or suction (vacuum aspiration), is the major technique for induced abortion. Other procedures include the injection of saline (or some other substance) into the uterus in order to initiate preventive labor. Sometimes, in cases of very advanced pregnancy, surgical evacuation is necessary. Because most legal abortions are now performed early in gestation, under sanitary conditions, and with competent medical supervision, the mortality risk is now lower for abortion than for giving birth.

The legal status of abortion among developing and developed countries around the world ranges from abortion on request to complete prohibition (U.S. Bureau of the Census, 1983). As of 1980, according to a summary by Tietze (1981), 9 percent of the world's population lived in countries where abortion was totally prohibited; 19 percent lived where abortion was allowed only to save the life of the pregnant women; 10 percent lived where abortion was permitted on broader medical grounds or when pregnancy resulted from rape or incest; 24 percent lived where abortion was allowed for a variety of social and economic reasons (such as being poor or unmarried); and 38 percent of the world's population lived in countries that allow abortion on request without need for specifying reasons. These data demonstrate graphically how far the world's nations have moved toward legal abortion since 1920, when the Soviet Union became the first country in the world to legalize abortion on request.

Why the worldwide trend toward legalization of abortion? On the individual level, women from time immemorial have resorted to abortion, often illegally and at great risk, for a wide range of personal reasons. The principal arguments in favor of legal abortion relate to health (especially to reduce the risks associated with illegal abortion), social justice (giving the poor as well as the rich access to safe abortion), and the notion that women should have control of their own bodies (Nortman, 1977). Only a handful of countries (e.g., India and China) offer abortion in their national family planning programs. Nonetheless, abortion and contraception should be viewed as complementary in society's efforts to reduce fertility. If the fertility levels of Third World populations are to approximate in general the replacement levels characteristic of most developed nations, contraception must be supplemented by induced abortion. For example, in order to limit lifetime births to 2.2 per woman, at least one abortion per woman is required in a population practicing moderately effective contraception. And an average of 0.2 abortions per woman would be expected even if highly effective (but less than perfect) contraception were practiced (Tietze and Bongaarts, 1975).

There is tremendous variability in the number of legal abortions from country to country (see Table 6-3). In the United States, where legal abortions now number over 1.5 million a year, a large proportion of women obtaining abortions are teenagers. About one-third of U.S. abortion seekers are under age twenty, another third are between twenty and twenty-four, and one-third are twenty-five and older. Nearly 80 percent of the women seeking abortion are unmarried. Compared with other industrialized nations, the United States has a high concentration of abortions among unmarried and younger women (Henshaw and O'Reilly, 1983).

Until 1967, abortion in the United States was justified only on very narrow grounds—to save the pregnant woman's life or to protect her health. A few states liberalized their abortion laws in the late 1960s and early 1970s, and abortion became legal in all states following the 1973 Supreme Court ruling that states could interfere in the abortion decision only to ensure the medical health and safety of the woman. Since then religious leaders, politicians, feminists, and the larger public have continued to debate the ethical, medical, and legal issues related to abortion. The center of the controversy over the right to abortion is the state of the fetus: Is it living or not

Table 6-3

Legal Abortions per 1,000 Women Age 15–44, 1978

Country	Abortions per 1,000 women	Country	Abortions per 1,000 women
Scotland	8.0	Denmark	22.3
Canada	11.3	United States	28.2
England, Wales	11.4	Singapore	28.9
Finland	15.8	Czechoslovakia	29.1
Tunisia	16.5	Hungary	37.0
Norway	18.4	Cuba	52.1
Sweden	19.4	Bulgaria	68.3
Germany, West	21.4		

SOURCE: Adapted from Table 2 in Christopher Tietze, *Induced Abortion: A World Review, 1981*, 4th ed. (New York, N.Y.: Population Council, 1981).

living, human or not human? Many religious and ethical leaders, for instance, consider the fetus a human being from the time of conception. In contrast, feminists and others regard the fetus not as a human being but as a part of the pregnant woman's body, and they believe the woman should have the right to make decisions about it. These conflicting beliefs are reflected in the continuing polarization of public opinion. Immediately following the 1973 Supreme Court decision, public attitudes shifted toward a more favorable attitude toward abortion. Now, however, there is a growing organized opposition to abortion, whose members are pushing for more restrictive legislation of several kinds, including a constitutional amendment that would virtually prohibit abortions altogether. Meanwhile, abortion continues to be an extremely important means of birth control for the American people. Consequently, it continues to affect the woman who has the abortion, the father of the aborted fetus, and their families. Many women, following abortion, are left with a sense of relief and freedom; others feel guilty and depressed. Most people involved in an abortion probably have to deal with some combination of these reactions, either from within themselves or from other persons. However, such alternatives to abortion as entering a forced marriage, giving a child up for adoption, bearing an out-of-wedlock child, or adding an unwanted child to one's family also seem likely to be accompanied by social and psychological problems for the woman, the child, and the family (David, 1982). As long as the American public continues to assess the abortion controversy in terms of "morality" or "truth," conflicting sentiments within individuals as well as within the body politic are likely to continue.

The Next Twenty Years

Although the revolution in birth control technology of the last two decades has had a great impact on fertility behavior and attitudes, it is likely that we will see the development of even better methods in the years ahead. If improvements continue to be made and a greater number and variety of techniques become available, it seems probable that many more couples will have access to some method of birth control that meets their needs.

A recent survey by the U.S. Office of Technology Assessment (1982) detailed the status and prospects for different contraceptive methods over the next twenty years. Highly likely before 1990, according to this report, are safer, lower-dose oral contraceptives and improved IUDs that can remain in place for five to ten years. Injectable steroids that will provide protection for up to six months are also in the offing. An injectable contraceptive called Depo-Provera is already available and widely used in many countries, although it has not yet been approved for use in the United States. The implantation of steroid capsules under the skin is also a realistic short-term possibility, as is the greater use of prostaglandin drugs for nonsurgical abortion. On a more mundane level, sperm-killing sponges, spermicide-impregnated condoms, and even biodegradable condoms are some of the other likely options. By the year 2000 several additional possibilities might well be available, including anti-pregnancy vaccines for both men and women as well as simplified and reversible sterilization procedures.

SUMMARY

Worldwide, people have remarkably little control over their reproduction. For example, while most couples in all societies want to have at least one or two children, they seldom know when they marry whether they will be able to have any children at all. Fecundity impairments affect millions of couples throughout the world, but they are especially prevalent in the developing countries where malnutrition and disease are widespread. Much is being done, however, to help subfecund couples realize their fertility goals. Procedures for treating sexual disorders and hormonal abnormalities, for example, have contributed to the increasing probabilities that subfecund couples can be helped to have children. And the once dramatic procedures of in vitro fertilization and artificial insemination have become relatively common in several countries.

The other side of the fertility control problem has to do with unintentional pregnancy and childbearing. Far more people have this kind of fertility control problem than the kind related to fecundity impairments. Unwanted children contribute to family poverty, add to the costs of welfare programs, and magnify problems of population growth in already overpopulated areas of the world. In several Third World countries, the prevention of all unwanted births would reduce the birth rates significantly. Even in the United States, the number of unwanted pregnancies is surprisingly great. Illegitimate and teenage childbearing, for example, most of which is unintentional, currently constitutes an important proportion of American fertility. The large numbers of births to unmarried teenagers have raised serious questions about possible negative consequences for the child, the parents, and society. Despite these concerns, however, the provision of family planning services to teenagers remains a controversial issue.

Unintentional fertility has been a burden for people all through history. To plan their lives with confidence, individuals and couples must be able to exert control over the number and timing of their births. Yet it was not until the nineteenth century that writers began to describe and recommend birth control methods. The struggle for birth control began in Europe but expanded to the United States in the early twentieth century when Margaret Sanger launched the family planning movement in New York City. Various kinds of opposition to the movement, based largely on traditional ideologies, have helped to shape the movement from its origins up to the present time.

In the United States, where contraception among married couples is now almost universal, people have come to expect fertility control to be both complete and sexually unobtrusive. Partly because of this, especially since the advent of the pill, there has been a dramatic change in attitudes toward sterilization and abortion. Individuals and couples have turned in massive numbers toward these methods of birth control. Nonetheless, there is a great need for even better birth control techniques—effective and sexually unobtrusive yet free from annoying or dangerous side effects. And while there may never be a "perfect" contraceptive, it is likely that we will see much safer, lower-dose oral contraceptives, injectable steroids, and other improved birth control technologies within a decade or so.

REFERENCES AND SUGGESTED READING

Anderson, John E. "Planning Status of Marital Births, 1975–1976." *Family Planning Perspectives*, 13 (March-April 1981): 63–70.

Baldwin, Wendy H. "Adolescent Pregnancy and Childbearing—Growing Concerns to Americans." *Population Bulletin*, 31 (September 1976).

Barnett, C. R., J. Jackson, and H. Cann. "Child-Spacing in a Highland Guatemala Community." In S. Polgar, ed., *Culture and Population*. Cambridge, Mass.: Shenkman, 1971.

Besant, Annie. *The Law of Population: Its Consequences, and Its Bearing upon Human Conduct and Morals*. London: T. Fisher Unwin, 1877.

Bumpass, Larry L. "Is Low Fertility Here to Stay?" *Family Planning Perspectives*, 5 (Summer 1973): 67–69.

Chandrasekhar, S. *"A Dirty, Filthy Book."* Berkeley: University of California Press, 1981.

David, Henry P. "Eastern Europe: Pronatalist Policies and Private Behavior." *Population Bulletin*, 36 (February 1982).

Dickinson, R. L., and L. S. Bryant. *Control of Conception: An Illustrated Medical Manual*. London: Tindall and Cox, 1938.

Ericksen, Julia, Eugene Ericksen, John Hostetler, and Gertrude Huntington. "Fertility Patterns and Trends among Old Order Amish." *Population Studies*, 33 (July 1979): 255–76.

Ford, Kathleen. "Contraceptive Utilization: United States." *Vital and Health Statistics*, 23:2 (September 1979).

Frank, Odile. "Infertility in Sub-Saharan Africa: Estimates and Implications." *Population and Development Review*, 9 (March 1983): 137–44.

Freedman, Ronald, and Bernard Berelson. "The Record of Family Planning Programs." *Studies in Family Planning*, 7 (January 1976).

Freedman, Ronald, Pascal Whelpton, and Arthur Campbell. *Family Planning, Sterility, and Population Growth*. Princeton, N.J.: Princeton University Press, 1959.

Fryer, Peter. *The Birth Controllers*. London: Secker and Warburg, 1965.

Gordon, Linda. *Woman's Body, Woman's Right: A Social History of Birth Control in America*. New York: Grossman, 1976.

Groat, H. Theodore, Lynn G. Knisley, and Arthur G. Neal. "Contraceptive Nonconformity among Catholics." *Journal for the Scientific Study of Religion*, 14 (December 1975): 60–74.

Guttmacher Institute. *Teenage Pregnancy: The Problem That Hasn't Gone Away*. New York: Alan Guttmacher Institute, 1981.

Hartley, Shirley Foster. *Illegitimacy*. Berkeley: University of California Press, 1975.

Hatcher, Robert A., Gary K. Stewart, Felicia Stewart, Felicia Guest, David W. Schwartz, and Stephanie A. Jones. *Contraceptive Technology 1980–81*. New York: Irvington, 1980.

Henshaw, Stanley K. and Kevin O'Reilly. "Characteristics of Abortion Patients in the United States, 1979 and 1980." *Family Planning Perspectives*, 15 (January-February 1983): 5–16.

Himes, Norman E. *Medical History of Contraception*. Baltimore: Williams & Wilkins, 1936.

Knowlton, Charles. *The Fruits of Philosophy*. London: Freethought, 1832.

Lauersen, Niels, and Steven Whitney. *It's Your Body: A Woman's Guide to Gynecology*. New York: Playboy Press, 1977.

Leridon, H. "Contraceptive Practice in France in 1978." *International Family Planning Perspectives*, 5 (1979): 25–27.

Lightbourne, Robert J., Susheela Singh, and Cynthia P. Green. "The World Fertility Survey: Changing Global Childbearing." *Population Bulletin*, 37 (March 1982).

McFalls, Joseph A., Jr. "Frustrated Fertility: A Population Paradox." *Population Bulletin*, 34 (May 1979).

Mauldin, W. Parker, Nagli Choucri, Frank W. Notestein, and Michael Teitelbaum. "A Report on Bucharest." *Studies in Family Planning*, 5 (December 1974): 357–95.

Mosher, William D. "Contraceptive Utilization: United States, 1976." *Vital and Health Statistics*, 23, 7 (March 1981).

Munson, Martha. "Wanted and Unwanted Births Reported by Mothers 15–44 Years of Age: United States, 1973." *Vital and Health Statistics, Advance Data*, 9 (August 1977).

Murphy, Francis X. "Catholic Perspectives on Population Issues II." *Population Bulletin*, 35 (February 1981).

National Center for Health Statistics. "Advance Report of Final Natality Statistics, 1980." *Monthly Vital Statistics Report*, 31 (November 1982).

Neal, Arthur G., H. Theodore Groat, and Jerry W. Wicks. *Family Formation and Fertility Control in the Early Years of Marriage*. Final report prepared for the Center for Population Research, NIH (1981).

Nortman, Dorothy. "Changing Contraceptive Patterns: A Global Perspective." *Population Bulletin*, 32 (August 1977).

Petersen, William. *Population*, 3rd ed. New York: Macmillan, 1975.

Place, Francis. *Illustrations and Proofs of the Principle of Population*. London: Privately printed, 1822.

Presser, Harriet B. "Perfect Fertility Control: Consequences for Women and the Family." In Charles F. Westoff et al., eds., *Toward the End of Growth*. Englewood Cliffs, N.J.: Prentice-Hall, 1973.

Rosenblatt, Roger. "The Baby in the Factory." *Time*, February 14, 1983, p. 90.

Schearer, S. Bruce. "The Status of Technology for Contraception." In John Money and Herman Musaph, eds. *Handbook of Sexology, III: Procreation and Parenthood*. New York: Elsevier, 1977.

Segal, Sheldon J., and Olivia Schieffelin Nordburg. "Fertility Regulation Technology: Status and Prospects." *Population Bulletin*, 31 (March 1977).

Tietze, Christopher. *Induced Abortion—A World Review, 1981*. New York: Population Council, 1981.

Tietze, Christopher, and John P. Bongaarts. "Fertility Rates and Abortion Rates: Simulations of Family Limitation." *Studies in Family Planning,* 6 (May 1975): 114–20.

U.S. Bureau of the Census. "International Fertility Indicators." *Current Population Reports,* Series P-23, No. 123 (February 1983).

U.S. Office of Technical Assistance. *World Population and Fertility Planning Technologies: The Next 20 Years.* Washington, D.C.: Government Printing Office, 1982.

Weeks, John R. *Population: An Introduction to Concepts and Issues,* 2nd ed. Belmont, Calif.: Wadsworth, 1981.

Weller, Robert H., and Leon F. Bouvier. *Population: Demography and Policy.* New York: St. Martin's, 1981.

Westoff, Charles F., and Norman B. Ryder. *The Contraceptive Revolution.* Princeton, N.J.: Princeton University Press, 1977.

Whelpton, Pascal, Arthur Campbell, and John Patterson. *Fertility and Family Planning in the United States.* Princeton, N.J.: Princeton University Press, 1966.

Whelpton, Pascal, and Clyde Kiser. *Social and Psychological Factors Affecting Fertility.* New York: Milbank Memorial Fund, 1946–1958.

Yinger, Nancy, Richard Osborn, David Salkever, and Ismail Sirageldin. "Third World Family Planning Programs: Measuring the Costs." *Population Bulletin,* 38 (February 1983).

Zelnick, Melvin, Y. J. Kim, and John F. Kantner. "Probabilities of Intercourse and Conception among U.S. Teenage Women, 1971 and 1976." *Family Planning Perspectives,* 11 (May-June 1979): 177–83.

Zelnick, Melvin, John F. Kantner, and Kathleen Ford. *Sex and Pregnancy in Adolescence.* Beverly Hills, Calif.: Sage, 1981.

A course for midwives in Iraq

Pakistani students receiving instructions in methods of family planning

Learning about sterilization in Bangladesh

WORLD POPULATION 213

Birth control pioneer Margaret Sanger in 1917

Anthony Comstock (1844–1915), founder of the New York Society for the Suppression of Vice, staunch opponent of the family planning movement. *Opposite:* An early 20th-century cartoon depicting Anthony Comstock detecting vice

ANTHONY AT WORK

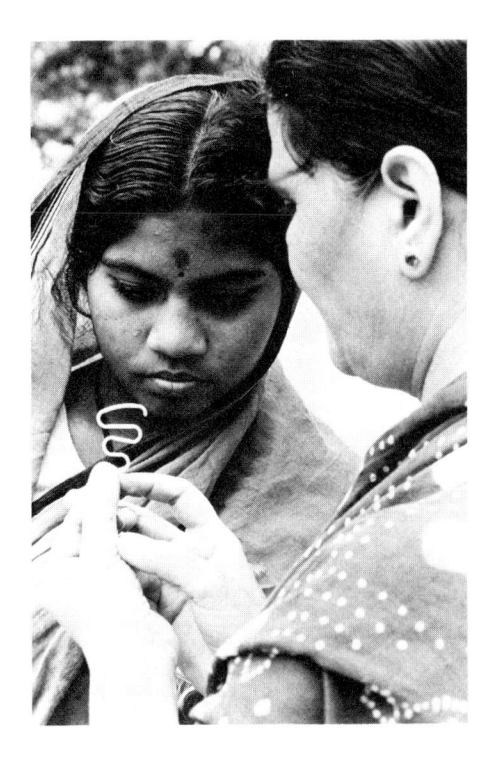

An intrauterine device is explained to an Indian mother.*

A Balinese song-and-dance drama illustrates the theme of family planning.

WORLD POPULATION 215

FERTILITY AND PUBLIC POLICY

7

We began Chapter 6 by referring to the widely endorsed principle that couples have a right to have the number of children they want, and no more. The implications of this principle, ideally, would involve public efforts to help couples avoid having unwanted and unplanned children as well as efforts to accommodate the needs of couples who, due to fecundity impairments, cannot have the number of children they desire. The latter problem has typically been ignored, since government-sponsored policies have usually emphasized family planning programs designed to help people avoid excess fertility rather than to help people overcome deficit fertility. Nonetheless it seems likely, especially in the low fertility, highly developed countries, that public policy will be directed increasingly toward enabling couples to realize their family size goals by taking steps to reduce involuntary subfecundity or sterility. The development of new drugs to reduce the occurrence of spontaneous abortion would be a step in this direction, as would the control of sterility-causing diseases and the improvement of surgical techniques to correct reproductive impairments. Government-sponsored research in the areas of in vitro fertilization and artificial insemination, as well as the establishment of infertility clinics, could also help people realize their reproductive goals. In addition, social and legal changes could make the adoption of children a more viable option for couples who cannot have children of their own. In some states, for example, adopted children still are not granted a legal and social status equal to that of natural children.

The major focus of programs to help couples achieve their desired fertility is the government-sponsored family planning program. These are generally education and service programs that distribute contraceptive information and supplies to the public. Such programs are oriented primarily toward helping people have only those pregnancies and births that they want, when they want them—in other words, to help couples avoid unwanted and unplanned childbearing. The basic intent of many family planning programs, therefore, is to promote family well-being by providing access to modern methods of birth control. Strictly speaking, the manifest concern of such programs is usually to improve the quality of maternal and child health and enhance basic human rights rather than to achieve a specific demographic objective such as a lower birth rate. However, any program that increases people's awareness of and access to birth control methods cannot help having some impact on the birth rate. In point of fact, whether they intend to or not, all governments have some indirect effect on both individual and aggregate levels of fertility as a result of a wide variety of socioeconomic policies relating to such nondemographic issues as education, taxation, employment, and economic development.

THE UNITED STATES

Although the United States has no "official" fertility policy, several recommendations designed to help couples avoid unintentional fertility and to maintain freedom of choice were put forth by the Commission on Population Growth and the American Future (1972). The Commission, proposed by President Nixon in 1969, was established to assess the implications of population growth in the United States and to make recommendations on how best to cope with it. The resulting recommendations included a wide variety of components related to the quantity and quality of the American population. With respect to fertility control, however, the Commission specifically recommended that abortion be legalized and made available on request, a change that did in fact take place after the Supreme Court decision in 1973. Another recommendation was that the nation give the highest priority to research in reproductive biology and to the search for improved methods by which individuals could control their fertility. Two additional recommendations were, and remain, highly controversial in nature. According to the Population Commission, sex education should be available to everyone, and all states should permit minors to receive birth control information and services.

The dramatic upsurge in the incidence of adolescent premarital intercourse during the past decade, and the consequent problems of unintentional teenage fertility, especially out-of-wedlock childbearing, have continued to focus public attention on the issues of sex education and birth control services to unmarried young women. Many people still believe that teaching young people about sex encourages their early experimentation with it. Some also believe that access to family planning and abortion services leads to early and promiscuous sexual encounters. Further, while some improvement in contraceptive use among teens has been noted, the major progress in fertility control among unmarried teenagers apparently has been due to an increased reliance on abortion (Campbell, 1980).

Given the political constraints implied by the nature of the problem, what can and should be done to reduce more effectively the incidence of unwanted teenage pregnancy and childbearing? One opinion currently gaining adherents in some quarters is that the families of teenagers need to be integrated into family planning delivery systems as partners in preventive efforts. This approach emphasizes the potential for parental influence over the decision by teenagers to engage or not to engage in early premarital sexual activity (Mecklenburg and Thompson, 1983).

A quite different position holds that, while parents should be encouraged to communicate with their children and to guide them toward responsible sexual decisions, the larger normative trends apparent in American society make it very difficult, if not impossible, for most young people to resist imitating the attitudes and behavior that they see exhibited by adults. From this point of view, the powerful pressures exerted by peers and the media to become sexually active at an early age, prior to marriage, seem unlikely to be overridden by parental influence. Those who support this position would like to see even greater extensions of birth control services for unmarried adolescents. This position also implies a much greater use of school and other community institutions for the delivery of information on sex, reproduction, and contraception, as well as the explicit incorporation of birth control concerns into the popular media directed at the adolescent market. These steps would, of course, come into conflict with many parental and community attitudes and values, making the advocacy of such programs a politically risky venture.

In the United States, programs related to such domestic fertility issues as teenage pregnancy and birth control services for the poor are administered primarily by agencies within the Department of Health and Human Services. American interest in the control of fertility at the societal level, directed at the Third World, is another matter. Assistance to developing countries that are trying to lower their levels of fertility is administered largely through the Agency for International Development. Thus while the United States has no official fertility policy, per se, American involvement in fertility issues both at home and abroad is quite far-reaching.

CONTROLLING SOCIETAL FERTILITY

Helping individuals realize their fertility goals is quite a different matter from trying to attain a given level of fertility or population size at the societal level. Thus we need to distinguish between individual fertility goals and the demographic needs and requirements of particular societies. Societies that are striving for a given level of fertility, for example, will not necessarily reach that level through broad welfare programs designed to help couples exercise their right to have only the number of children they want. That is, left to their own choice, couples may decide to have an average family size that may or may not be consistent with governmental definitions of what constitutes a desirable level of fertility. For this reason, many countries today are attempting to manipulate their national birth rates through specific policies aimed at the *motivations* for family size goals as well as the *means* by which those goals may be realized. Such policies may be either pronatalist or antinatalist in nature.

Before moving on to a discussion of specific kinds of population policies, we need to acknowledge that national leaders as well as scholars differ sharply in their views about the importance of population growth as a factor affecting rates of economic growth; and, to the extent that population growth is seen as a problem, they also differ about what should be done about it. We can identify the adherents of two basic positions with respect to the impoverished nations of the Third World: (1) those who view rapid population growth as one of the major obstacles to national economic development (the Malthusian position); and (2) those who view population growth as relatively less important than inequalities within and between countries caused by past and continuing economic exploitation of the poor masses by the ruling elites and exploitation of the poorer countries of the Third World by the modern industrialized nations of the West (the Marxist position). Those who adhere to the Malthusian position regard high fertility and rapid population growth as an important contributing *cause* of world poverty. Accordingly, they see the reduction of fertility and the slowing down of population growth rates as major challenges facing the less developed countries today. Adherents of the Marxist position perceive the high birth rates prevailing throughout the Third World as *symptoms* rather than causes of their poverty; they see as the major challenge the reduction of national and international economic inequalities through a redistribution of resources, wealth, and opportunities. They assert that when greater economic parity is achieved, fertility will fall and population growth eventually will cease to be a factor in world economic development.

The international aspects of these two perspectives, which are described more fully in Chapter 8, came into sharp conflict at the 1974 World

Population Conference in Bucharest; since then, however, there has been a gradual convergence of views. Although substantial differences in emphasis still exist, those who regard rapid population growth as a problem to be brought under control also see the need to work toward economic parity and improvements in levels of living as a means to facilitate this control. Similarly, many of those governments that call for a redistribution of the world's wealth also see the need to relieve the symptoms of high fertility and rapid population growth.

Once a government decides that it needs an official policy aimed at slowing down population growth through a reduction in the national birth rate, it has a variety of options open to it. Before discussing these options, however, we will look at the other side of the coin: those governments that are concerned about declining rates of population growth and that have adopted pronatalist policies in an effort to increase their birth rates.

PRONATALIST POLICIES

It may seem strange, in a world where the overriding concern is with problems of overpopulation, that several countries are deliberately trying to increase their birth rates through pronatalist policies in the hope of increasing the size of their populations. Yet this is precisely what Argentina, Bolivia, France, Uruguay, and a number of East European countries have recently tried to do (United Nations, 1980). To date, however, it has been mainly the centrally planned economies of Eastern Europe, which are essentially closed to immigration, where governments have offered direct incentives to encourage larger families (David, 1982).

In the early 1960s, while much of Europe was experiencing a slight increase in fertility, the birth rate was falling or threatening to fall below replacement level in several of the East European countries, including Romania, the German Democratic Republic, Czechoslovakia, Hungary, and Bulgaria (see Table 7-1). This fertility decline coincided with a surge in legal abortions following a wave of legislation permitting abortion for a broad range of social conditions, or simply on request. Governments in several countries were shocked by the unwelcome sharp decline in fertility and population growth rates; they feared future labor shortages, aging populations, and the prospect of national "suicide." As a result, policymakers responded by taking active pronatalist measures, including the restriction of abortion and the implementation of stepped-up programs that operated both directly and indirectly to ease the financial burdens of parenthood. To illustrate, several countries increased their family allowances (monthly pay-

Table 7-1
Crude Birth Rates in Selected East European Countries, 1950–80

Year	Bulgaria	Czechoslovakia	German Democratic Republic	Hungary	Romania
1955	20.1	20.3	16.7	21.4	25.6
1956	19.5	19.8	16.2	19.5	24.2
1957	18.4	18.9	15.9	17.0	22.9
1958	17.9	17.4	15.9	16.0	21.6
1959	17.6	16.0	17.1	15.2	20.2
1960	17.8	15.9	17.2	14.7	19.1
1961	17.4	15.8	17.7	14.0	17.5
1962	16.7	15.7	17.5	12.9	16.2
1963	16.4	16.9	17.6	13.1	15.7
1964	16.1	17.1	17.2	13.1	15.2
1965	15.4	16.4	16.5	13.1	14.6
1966	14.9	15.6	15.7	13.6	14.3
1967	15.0	15.1	14.8	14.6	24.6
1968	16.9	14.9	14.3	15.0	26.7
1969	17.0	15.5	14.0	15.0	23.3
1970	16.3	15.9	13.9	14.7	21.1
1971	15.9	16.5	13.8	14.5	19.5
1972	15.3	17.4	11.8	14.7	18.8
1973	16.2	18.9	10.6	15.0	18.2
1974	17.2	19.9	10.4	17.8	20.3
1975	16.6	19.6	10.6	18.4	19.7
1976	16.5	19.2	10.8	17.5	19.5
1977	16.1	18.7	13.3	16.7	19.6
1978	15.5	18.4	13.9	15.7	19.1
1979	15.3	17.8	14.0	15.0	18.6
1980	14.3	16.2	14.6	13.9	18.0

SOURCE: Henry P. David, "Eastern Europe: Pronatalist Policies and Private Behavior," *Population Bulletin,* 36 (February 1982). On the one hand, note the impact of restrictions on abortion adopted by Bulgaria (1968, 1972, and 1973), Czechoslovakia (1962 and 1973), Hungary (1974), and especially Romania (1966). On the other hand, note the drop in the GDR birth rate when that country approved abortion on demand in 1972.

ments to families with children), augmented birth payments and paid maternity leaves, and gave specific attention to the encouragement of second and third births in order to reverse the growing popularity of one-child families. Large families of four or more children, however, typically were not encouraged on the grounds that such large families might lower the quality of family life.

Most of the socialist countries of Eastern Europe, including the Soviet Union, currently have explicit pronatalist cash-incentive programs. The financial incentives for childbearing in the German Democratic Republic (GDR), to take an example, are among the most generous in the world (David, 1982). Birth grants, paid at birth for all children, are about $500. Family allowances are paid monthly, increasing in value with each additional child. These allowances can be quite substantial, ranging to a high for a six-child family of nearly 30 percent of the average monthly wage. In addition, some newly married couples are entitled to interest-free loans for the purchase of housing or furnishings. The debt is reduced after the birth of a first and second child, and canceled after the birth of a third child, provided this birth occurs within eight years after the loan is granted. Paid maternity leave with cash allowances has been extended also, and there is guaranteed re-employment after voluntary unpaid maternity leave of up to three years. Further, working mothers with two or more children are eligible for slightly reduced work weeks at full pay. Finally, the GDR's network of subsidized child-care facilities is one of the most extensive in the world.

How effective are programs such as those in the German Democratic Republic? In the mid-1970s, while fertility was falling dramatically in most of the industrial countries, birth rates were relatively stable or rising in several socialist countries with strong pronatalist policies. Many policymakers believe that this trend was the result of their pronatalist programs. However, while there is little doubt about the immediate positive impact on birth rates of the sudden restrictions on abortion (e.g., the birth rate in Romania rose from 15 per 1,000 in 1966 to 25 in 1967 following the adoption of abortion restriction legislation), the role of economic incentives is much more difficult to evaluate. Many observers, citing recent downturns in fertility in several of these countries, have serious doubts about any long-lasting effects of cash-incentive programs on completed family size. In Romania, for example, the fertility increase that resulted when the 1966 abortion restrictions caught people off guard was only temporary, and in 1980–81 the birth rate was only 18 per 1,000; and in the GDR, despite its elaborate incentive program, the 1980–81 birth rate was only 14 per 1,000. In the GDR the death rate was also 14 per 1,000, so that the annual population growth rate was zero (Population Reference Bureau, 1983). The main effect of these pronatalist policies, therefore, seems to be the successful persuasion of couples to have first and second births sooner than they would otherwise have had them (David, 1982). The incidence of third births, toward which many of the pronatalist policies are clearly directed, seems not to be greatly affected.

Why have these pronatalist policies not been more successful? As a starting point, we should recognize that national economic necessity in these countries virtually requires the full participation of most women in the production of goods and services. Further, given the prevailing wage levels, families need two incomes to attain the standard of living most couples aspire to. Between 70 and 85 percent of women in several Eastern European countries are employed outside the home, for example, greatly exceeding the 50 to 55 percent rate of female labor force participation in the United States. Yet, despite the fact that these socialist countries were among the first to decree the emancipation of women and the principle of sexual equality, male chauvinism persists, and public services have not yet caught up with the realities of massive female employment. Regardless of financial incentives from the government, therefore, societal conditions make child rearing very difficult for women. The basic conflict between child care and a woman's desire and need to work is compounded by the reluctance of most husbands to help with household chores and by the shortages of time-saving appliances and convenience services. Consequently wives frequently must devote many hours each day to shopping, cleaning, and cooking in addition to their paid employment (David, 1982). Under these circumstances, many women have concluded that having only one or two children will allow them to have the satisfactions of parenthood while at the same time permitting them to enjoy a better life-style. In sum, the experience of Eastern Europe suggests that policies to motivate couples to have more children are likely to be only moderately successful when couples are determined to have only one or two children.

ANTINATALIST POLICIES

Policies to increase fertility seem anachronistic now that mortality is generally low and the dominant concern is with high rates of population growth. Indeed, far more nations are trying to decrease their fertility rates than to increase them. *Antinatalist policies*, broadly defined, include both explicit and implicit measures designed to reduce fertility directly or indirectly. The United States, for example, has no explicit or official fertility policy; yet the government is actively engaged in providing large subsidies for family planning programs. This is characteristic of the developed Western nations where the current low levels of fertility represent the culmination of a long history of fertility control and decline. In the face of mounting economic, political, and environmental problems relating to global population pressures, most organized opposition to birth control practices and movements in the Western world eroded in the 1960s. Following this, government efforts to support family planning were extended to foreign aid programs in developing countries, led by Sweden in 1960 and the United States in 1965.

By 1981 the family planning programs of many developing nations were funded substantially by the governments of industrialized nations or by international agencies (Nortman, 1982).

Today, in many European nations as well as in Canada, Australia, and New Zealand, family planning services and supplies are either free or subsidized, and are available to the general population through national health, welfare, or family planning systems. In the United States, federal funding for family planning services, designed especially to help eliminate unwanted childbearing by making contraception available to the poor and disadvantaged, has been provided since 1967. In assessing the relationship between established national family planning programs and low birth rates, however, it must be remembered that in both the United States and Europe fertility declined long before governments became involved in any way with the provision of birth control services. In fact, fertility declined in spite of many legal obstacles to the free choice of the means of fertility control. In this country, for example, the Comstock Law of 1873, named after Anthony Comstock, the founder of the New York Society for the Suppression of Vice, led to the seizure of many thousands of books on family planning and contraception (Westoff and Westoff, 1971); and some states still had anti–birth control laws (known as Little Comstock Laws) on their books as late as the 1960s. In other Western nations as well, fertility decline predated the removal of legal restrictions to abortion and the development and diffusion of modern contraceptives such as the pill. As we pointed out earlier, the major reason for the fertility decline in the West was the change in people's motivations for having children. Accessibility to improved birth control methods has contributed to fertility decline only in recent decades. Today, however, both the *means* by which people can limit their family size and their *motivations* for doing so need to be considered in national antinatalist programs in the developing countries of the world.

Although both dimensions of fertility control—the means and the motives—should be considered in attempts to reduce national birth rates, the actual practice in most countries today is to give priority to manipulating the means rather than the motives. This distinction between means and motives, although analytically useful, is not clear-cut. There is an obviously close relationship between them: the better the means of fertility control, the less motivation is required to use them; conversely, very highly motivated people can effectively reduce their fertility by using even crude methods of birth control. Nonetheless, we can still distinguish between two kinds of policies: (1) those that emphasize the availability of means or methods of birth control (these are typically regarded as *family planning programs*), and (2) those that strive to change peoples' motives for childbearing while at the same time providing them with the means to limit births (these are said to go "beyond family planning"—Berelson, 1969).

PROVIDING THE MEANS:
NATIONAL FAMILY PLANNING PROGRAMS

The most common and popular kind of policy for lowering fertility is the family planning approach, which makes birth control information, supplies, and services as widely available as possible to the general population. The rationale for this strategy involves several assumptions regarding the likely demographic impact of family planning programs on national birth rates (Nortman, 1982). The basic assumption behind family planning policies is that, despite high fertility rates and various cultural inducements to have large families, much fertility in Third World countries is unwanted. Therefore, the reasoning goes, family planning programs should be capable of satisfying the need for methods of birth prevention. Further, family planners believe that the legitimization of birth control practices by governments, in combination with information and education campaigns, helps to create additional demand for family planning services.

In 1960 only two countries in the world, India and Pakistan, had officially supported and organized family planning programs. Two decades later, seventy-two countries in the developing world, encompassing well over 90 percent of its population, either had launched family planning programs of their own or had given their support to private groups such as those affiliated with International Planned Parenthood. The majority of these nations view family planning as a means of reducing their birth rates in the interest of economic development. An almost universally endorsed rationale for government support of family planning, however, revolves around such issues as health, family welfare, and the rights of people to have access to the means of controlling their reproduction.

One of the most appealing features of the family planning approach is its voluntary nature. Moreover, family planning programs have the advantage of being almost universally acceptable because of their emphasis on voluntary parenthood as a human right, freedom of choice with respect to birth control, and the avoidance of unwanted childbearing as a maternal and child health issue. This means that government leaders can advocate family planning with relatively little political risk. Another politically appealing quality is that family planning is a gradual effort that can be implemented fairly inexpensively (Berelson, 1969).

There is little doubt that the elimination of unwanted childbearing, even in the United States, would have a marked negative impact on fertility. In the Third World the impact would be even more striking. Data from the World Fertility Survey show that in many developing countries large proportions of fecund married women want no more children. Many others report not wanting their last child or their current pregnancy (see Table 7-2).

Table 7-2

Estimated Reduction in Birth Rates if All Unwanted Births Were Prevented

Region and country	Percent of births not wanted in year before survey	Crude birth rate average 0–3 years before survey	Crude birth rate if unwanted births eliminated
Asia and Pacific			
Bangladesh	37.6	40	25
Fiji	9.5	31	28
Indonesia	13.8	32	28
Korea, Rep. of	22.2	29	23
Philippines	22.7	34	26
Sri Lanka	28.2	28	20
Latin America and Caribbean			
Colombia	34.5	34	21
Costa Rica	26.6	27	20
Dominican Rep.	36.4	40	25
Guyana	34.3	29	19
Jamaica	44.0	28	16
Panama	31.6	28	19
Paraguay	11.2	32	28
Peru	42.6	36	21
Trinidad and Tobago	6.5	22	21
Venezuela	25.3	34	25
Middle East			
Jordan	21.6	45	35
Turkey	28.8	32	23
Total average	26.8	32	24

SOURCE: Robert Lightbourne, Jr., Susheela Singh, and Cynthia P. Green, "The World Fertility Survey: Changing Global Childbearing." *Population Bulletin,* 37 (March 1982). Adapted from Table 16.

The implications of all this seem clear: family planning programs, to the extent that they can tap into this unmet need for contraceptive services, have the potential for lowering birth rates and decreasing rates of population growth.

There are several well-documented cases of recent substantial fertility declines in the developing world. Most notable are the two city-states of Hong Kong and Singapore, along with Taiwan, South Korea, Malaysia, Sri Lanka, Fiji, Mauritius, Costa Rica, and Chile, most of which are island or peninsula nations (see Table 7-3). Some of these nations have very close economic and political ties to the United States. Others have economies that are thriving in comparison with those of most of the Third World. All have government-supported family planning programs, and all have relatively rapid rates of economic development. They also are quite small countries,

Table 7-3
Recent Fertility Declines in Selected Developing Countries

Country	Crude birth rates						
	1950	1955	1960	1965	1970	1975	1980–81
Chile	34	35	34	32	26	25	22
Costa Rica	47	51	47	45	33	30	29
Fiji	40	39	40	33	29	28	28
Hong Kong	34	36	36	30	20	18	17
Malaysia	...	47	41	38	34	31	31
Mauritius	50	41	39	35	26	25	26
Singapore	45	44	38	31	23	17	17
South Korea	45	45	41	36	36	29	25
Sri Lanka	40	37	40	33	29	29	28
Taiwan	43	45	40	33	27	25	23

SOURCE: United Nations, *Demographic Yearbook* (various years). Estimates for 1980–81 from Population Reference Bureau, *1983 World Population Data Sheet* (Washington, D.C., 1983).

which means that their impressive fertility declines have not had much impact on world rates of population growth. Further, because social and economic development occurred at the same time that family planning programs were expanding, there is no way to determine precisely the relative influence on fertility of the one as opposed to the other. Taiwan and Korea, for example, have often served as showcases for the presumed efficacy of the family planning approach; yet in both nations a temporal analysis of the data shows that the birth rate was in fact declining before they adopted national family planning programs (1959 in Taiwan and 1961 in South Korea). In Taiwan, in fact, the government did not actually adopt an official antinatalist policy until 1968, at which time the crude birth rate was substantially lower than it had been in the early 1950s. Singapore represents still another good example (see Figure 7-1). That country adopted a very strong antinatalist program in the late 1960s, yet by the time this program was implemented the birth rate had already declined by nearly 50 percent.

All of the countries listed in Table 7-3 have well established family planning programs, and all of them have clearly experienced some fairly remarkable declines in fertility in recent years. However, it is difficult if not impossible to measure how much of the decline is due to the adoption of national family planning programs and how much is merely the continuation of earlier declines that were generated by increasing levels of social and economic development. Overall, it seems probable that in several countries organized family planning programs did little more than help to accelerate or sustain a fertility decline that was already under way or that would have occurred anyway. Certainly this important contribution cannot

Figure 7-1
Crude Birth and Death Rate Trends: Singapore, 1950–80

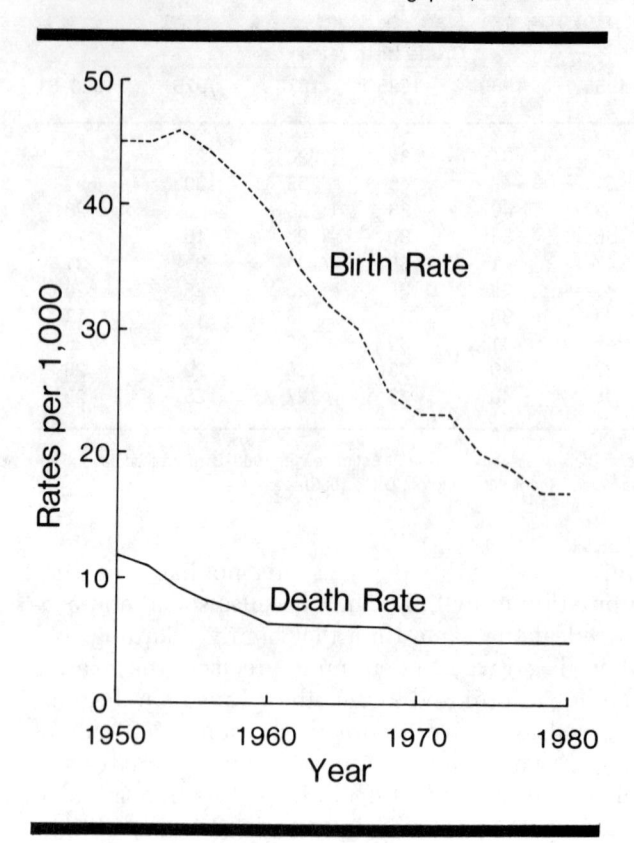

SOURCE: Based on data contained in various issues of the annual *Demographic Yearbook* of the United Nations.

be ignored, but the fact remains that the downward trend in fertility was generally well underway before the establishment of the national family planning programs.

In 1980 there were ninety-two developing nations with populations of at least one million, but more than 80 percent of all Third World people lived in only sixteen countries with a combined population exceeding 2.5 billion, representing more than half of all the world's people (see Table 7-4). The People's Republic of China alone, with its 1,023 million inhabitants, accounted for nearly 30 percent of the people in the developing countries and slightly more than one-fifth of the entire world population. On a global scale, the success or failure of policies to control population growth

Table 7-4
Population Size and Crude Birth Rate Trends in the Sixteen Largest Developing Countries

Country	Estimated population, mid-1983 (in millions)	Crude birth rates Late 1960s	1980–81	Percent decline
People's Republic of China	1,023.3	33	23	30%
India	730.0	43	36	16
Indonesia	155.6	48	32	33
Brazil	131.3	38	31	18
Bangladesh	96.7	51	49	4
Pakistan	95.7	51	43	16
Nigeria	84.2	50	50	0
Mexico	75.7	44	32	27
Vietnam	57.0	38–50	37	...
Philippines	52.8	45	34	24
Thailand	50.8	43	26	40
Turkey	49.2	40	31	23
Egypt	45.9	44	43	2
Iran	42.5	45	43	4
South Korea	41.3	39	25	36
Burma	37.9	40	38	5

SOURCES: *Demographic Yearbook, 1970* (New York: United Nations, 1971); and *1983 World Population Data Sheet* (Washington, D.C.: Population Reference Bureau, 1983).

will ultimately depend on these larger countries. These nations exhibit an enormous diversity in culture, ethnicity, socioeconomic development, population policy, and levels of fertility. Two of them, Nigeria and Brazil, have no policies to reduce population growth rates, although both have recently moved toward support of family planning for reasons of human rights and public health. Burma, where contraceptives are not readily available to the general population, has a pronatalist stance, but the remaining countries in this group have adopted measures of one kind or another to reduce their population growth rates.

The experience of these key countries in recent years has been mixed. Since the late 1960s, very strong fertility declines (30 percent or more) have occurred in Indonesia, South Korea, Thailand, and the People's Republic of China. Indonesia, a country with very low per capita income and a low rate of economic growth, embarked on a massive family planning program in 1968. This program is considered one of the most vigorous in the world, and consequently the number of family planning "acceptors" has been quite high, especially in Java and Bali (Mauldin, 1980). Fertility declines have also been impressive (20–29 percent) in Mexico, the Philippines, and Turkey, but in the remaining countries they have declined much more modestly (Brazil, India, and Pakistan) or scarcely at all (Bangladesh, Burma, Egypt, Iran, and Nigeria).

India

The family planning program in India is especially interesting, and critical, because of its huge population (its approximately 730 million people make it the second largest nation in the world) and because of its extremely low level of social and economic development. India was a world pioneer when, in 1952, it became the first country in the world to adopt a population policy deliberately structured to reduce its population growth rate (Demerath, 1976).

After an initial period of underfinancing and very slow development, India's family planning program was revitalized in the mid-1960s. Despite the largely free distribution of contraceptives through family planning clinics, the birth rate had not responded. Accordingly, the Indian government, with help from the Ford Foundation, reorganized its efforts in 1963 and again in 1966, trying to extend family planning services to its overwhelmingly peasant, village population. A demographer, S. Chandrasekhar, eventually was named Minister of State for Health and Family Planning. Under his leadership, more use was made of the mass media, abortion was legalized, and men were offered transistor radios if they would undergo voluntary vasectomies. Male sterilization, because of its permanence and relatively low cost, has been especially emphasized by the Indian government (see Figure 7-2). Between 1956 and 1981, in fact, more than 33 million sterilizations, two-thirds of them vasectomies, were performed throughout the country. As of the early 1970s, however, the birth rate had still not yet declined (Visaria and Visaria, 1981). At this point one of the most aggressive, though short-lived, family planning drives in history was initiated by Prime Minister Indira Gandhi. With soaring inflation, declining food production, and ubiquitous strikes, Mrs. Gandhi declared emergency rule in the summer of 1975. As part of this emergency rule, during which time civil liberties were suspended, thousands were arrested, the press was censored, and family planning was given a very high political commitment. With the full support of the prime minister, the goals of the family planning program were quickly accepted by most other political and government leaders, especially in the Hindi-speaking northern heartland of the country. Most of the states actually declared that they could do better than merely comply with the official sterilization targets for 1976–77. Consequently, while the official target called for 4.3 million sterilizations, the actual achievement was 8.3 million—over three times the 2.7 million sterilizations performed in 1975–76. The estimated proportion of couples protected by modern birth control

Figure 7-2
Annual Number of Sterilizations: India, 1965/66—1980/81

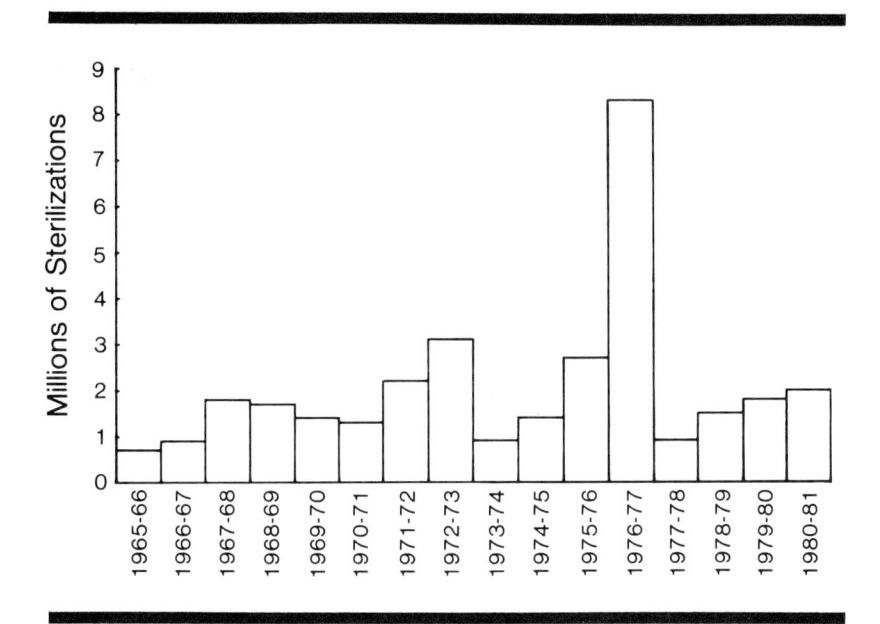

SOURCE: Based on data in Pravin Visaria and Leela Visaria, "India's Population: Second and Growing," *Population Bulletin*, 36 (October 1981).

methods rose from 17 percent to 24 percent in only one year (Visaria and Visaria, 1981).

This sterilization program constituted only a portion of some sixteen population policy statements announced in 1976. In addition to increasing the size of payments (about $19) to sterilization patients with two or fewer children, the government permitted states to compel sterilization for couples with four or more children. Other measures included raising the minimum legal age of marriage, making financial assistance to state governments partially dependent on family planning performance, and setting priorities for improved female literacy.

Although some state and local administrators adopted measures that went far beyond these official policy measures, most of them had not yet been implemented when the entire campaign collapsed. Some of these more extreme proposals included such positive incentives as raises in salary for being sterilized. Negative incentives ranged from mild to cruel. In the destitute state of Bihar, for example, public food rations were denied to families with more than three children. Teachers in Uttar Pradesh were told to be sterilized or lose a month's salary. And in the state of Maharashtra legislation was passed, though never put into effect, calling for compulsory sterilization of couples with three or more children. These and other measures, along with numerous rumors of coercion, resulted in a strong popular backlash that was a major factor in the defeat of Mrs. Gandhi's government in 1977. The new government did not dismantle the family planning program, but it did shift the emphasis toward voluntary compliance and renamed the program "family welfare." Family planning workers were demoralized, and program achievements reached a low ebb. Nonetheless, despite the understandable attempts of Mrs. Gandhi, who was elected again in 1980, to maintain a low profile on family planning during her first years back in office, a mild recovery in family planning activities has been noted. While the current level of fertility in India is not known with much precision, there seems to be little doubt that the crude birth rate, now estimated to be in the mid-30s, is well below traditional levels of 40 or more that prevailed a few years ago. At the same time, there also seems to be little doubt that India will still have to cope with an annual addition of 13 to 14 million people to its population, even if its family planning program fully recovers.

The question, then, is what might the government of India do, beyond what it has already tried, to achieve more rapid and substantial declines in fertility? The population policy statements issued in 1976 and 1977 included measures that would move toward a more comprehensive approach to the related problems of population growth and economic development. Among these proposed measures were an even higher minimum legal age of marriage, the improvement of women's educational levels and children's nutrition, the use of group incentives for village councils and other opinion leaders, and above all an emphasis on the importance of motivating the population to a greater acceptance of smaller families. India seems clearly poised to move beyond family planning, but with a population of 730 million people increasing at a rate of 2.1 percent a year, its task is a prodigious one.

CHANGING THE MOTIVATIONS: BEYOND FAMILY PLANNING

The assumptions on which family planning programs are based have led many demographers to question their ultimate efficacy for lowering birth rates in Third World countries (Davis 1967; Demerath, 1976; Groat and Perry, 1968). Because fertility decline depends so much more on the motivations for family size than on the means of birth control, programs that ignore the family size desires of their populations, as India's program did until quite recently, seem unlikely to have much impact on fertility. Even if all births were perfectly planned, fertility rates would not come down to replacement level anywhere in the world unless people wanted to have small families. Planned families, in other words, can be large as well as small. Nevertheless, the implicit assumption of family planning programs is that by preventing *unwanted* fertility the birth rate will be reduced to a level consistent with a society's demographic needs and goals. Millions of couples throughout the world do indeed have more children than they want; therefore, increasing people's knowledge about and access to modern methods of birth control can be of great practical and humanitarian value in helping to reduce the individual and societal burdens of unwanted childbearing.

But what if the number of children couples want to have is still higher than a government's fertility target? Given the mortality levels in most developing nations, for instance, an average family size of 3.5 children would produce an annual growth rate of 1.2 percent. The point, of course, is that desired levels of fertility, even if realized, may not be compatible with the attainment of reduced rates of population growth. As one American demographer noted several years ago, "there is no reason to expect that millions of decisions about family size made by couples in their own interest will automatically control population for the benefit of society" (Davis, 1967, p. 732).

The conclusion of many demographers, and increasingly of national governments, is that family planning is a necessary starting point, but not sufficient by itself to curb high rates of population growth within many of the large, impoverished Third World countries. For this reason, efforts that go beyond family planning, by engineering social change that might alter family size desires, are gaining increased attention.

How can governments change the family size motivations of their populations? In an earlier chapter, we discussed the social factors that result in motivations for smaller families. The reason why people desire large families instead of small families is that they perceive the benefits derived from large families to outweigh the costs. Because perceptions of benefits and costs of childbearing are woven into the social fabric of all societies—that is, into the cultural and structural foundations of social life in all its forms—non–family planning approaches to fertility control necessarily imply substantial institutional change. Fertility levels in all societies are founded on family size norms, which in turn are the products of sociocultural environments. To change the family size norms, therefore, policy measures that go beyond family planning must emphasize changes in the pronatalist features of social organization. For example, if the institutional arrangements of society reward people for marrying at an early age and having four or five children, then family planning alone is unlikely to lead to small family norms. However, if the system of institutional incentives and disincentives can be changed, as happened in the natural course of economic development in the West, perhaps new family size norms will replace the old.

The magnitude of change implied by a non–family planning approach to fertility reduction is awesome. Changing the motivations for childbearing involves changing the ways in which people perceive their social worlds, and hence their adaptations to their environments on an everyday basis. An extreme position along these lines would hold that nothing short of complete societal modernization will result in long-term declines in family size (Goldscheider, 1971). This is consistent with the famous slogan, coined by the Indian delegation to the World Population Conference in 1974, that "development is the best contraceptive." Most of the arguments for this theory are based on the Western experience with fertility decline, sometimes in combination with the notion that Third World countries are victims of Western economic policies that actually hinder indigenous development and foster a continued dependency of the poor nations on the rich nations. Be this as it may, to argue that nations should develop economically in order to reduce their birth rates is an oversimplification. After all, most poor countries with antinatalist policies are trying to control their fertility in order to increase their rates of economic development. Broadly based development efforts are needed in combination with extensive family planning services.

In Chapter 5 we noted evidence that there may be subsets of development change, far less comprehensive than those that occurred in the West, that can promote norms for smaller families. An example of this would be changes in the economic and social structures that would result in better health and extended life expectancy. In addition, improved literacy and educational opportunities for both girls and boys would lay the groundwork for modifications in traditional sex roles and for patterns of delayed marriage. Increased female labor force participation of some kinds could also provide alternatives for women to the dominant values and rewards of family life and help to promote greater sexual equality. Further, the development of communication facilities may have the potential for making the concept of family limitation more acceptable to largely agrarian populations. Even if incomes are not raised appreciably, changes in the opportunity structure that encourage fuller participation in social and political life, and that provide more equal benefits from that participation, may result in lower fertility. The state of Kerala in India, for instance, has achieved the most dramatic fertility decline in that nation. The average income is low, but it is relatively equal in its distribution. Moreover, public services and political organizations are broadly accessible to many people, and basic education is widespread. Under these and similar circumstances, there is evidence that motivations for large families will change (Repetto, 1981). On the other hand, the most striking examples of successful programs that have gone beyond family planning have combined institutional change with some powerful, even coercive, sets of incentives and disincentives.

Singapore, a tiny Southeast Asian republic with a population of less than three million, was formerly a British colony. In the 1960s, shortly after Singapore became independent, the government grew concerned over the probability that rapid population growth would interfere with the new nation's economic development (Salaff and Wong, 1978). To meet this challenge, a traditional family planning program of contraceptive services, delivered through clinics and hospitals, was instituted. In 1969, when the downward trend in the birth rate appeared to have leveled off (see Figure 7-1), a program of strong disincentives was added to the family planning effort. To encourage couples to keep the number of their children down to one or two, several measures were adopted to "punish" couples who exceeded this limit. Among these disincentives were higher maternity costs for each successive birth, the assignment of third and higher-order children to low priorities for school enrollment, the withdrawal of paid maternity leave following the birth of the second child, the assignment of low housing priorities for large families, and the withdrawal of income tax allowances for more than three children. Further, the government has enacted legislation that requires male and female foreign workers who wish to marry Singaporeans to agree to undergo sterilization after the birth of their second child. Failure to comply means suspension of permission to work in the country as well as the loss of other privileges.

The impact of these rather coercive disincentives on fertility in Singapore is readily apparent: between 1970 and 1980 the birth rate declined by another 25 percent. Even more dramatic is the trend in the total fertility rate (the average number of children per woman): from a level of 4.5 in the mid-1960s it fell to only 1.8 children per woman in 1982 (Population Reference Bureau, 1983). In noting this truly remarkable reduction in fertility, however, we must remember that it was achieved by a very small population that is 100 percent urban and that has one of the highest per capita gross national products in all of Asia. On a much more impressive scale, the People's Republic of China, which encompasses more than one-fifth of the world's population, has moved in the same direction as Singapore.

The People's Republic of China

China, with a population now exceeding one billion, is the world's first country to formulate a deliberate and comprehensive policy designed to reach zero population growth by the year 2000, or as soon thereafter as possible. Because of the sheer magnitude of China's population, and because of widespread curiosity over the ways in which vast social and economic transformations have affected its demographic features, demographers (as well as the general public) have become increasingly fascinated by the accumulating evidence of successful fertility control in this giant nation (Aird, 1981; Chen and Kols, 1982; Demerath, 1976; Tien, 1981 and 1983).

The perceived need to slow population growth in the interest of economic development did not come easily or quickly to the Marxist government that rose to power in China in 1949. On the eve of the Communist party's rise to power, Chairman Mao Zedong denied that any serious population problem existed or even could exist in a communistic society. Malthusian concerns over population growth were called "absurd." Policies began to change within a few years, however, and by 1957 Mao was advocating the need for zero population growth. This change of mind resulted in part from the findings of the first national census, in 1953–54, which revealed a population of nearly 600 million. Other survey data disclosed a crude birth rate of 37 and a crude death rate of 17, yielding a natural increase rate of 2 percent per year (Chen and Kols, 1982).

Spurred on by these data, the government officially endorsed birth control and opened the first clinics in 1956. These efforts were very short-lived, however, as they were interrupted by the political and economic dislocations of the Great Leap Forward. In 1962 a second family planning campaign (called "birth planning" by the Chinese), was started. With strong backing from the central government, there followed national symposia on birth planning, growth rate targets, liberalized abortion and sterilization laws, and measures designed to promote contraceptive use and to encourage late marriage. This campaign might have had some effect but, like the first, it was cut short by further disruptions, this time brought on by the Cultural Revolution. Red Guards shut down factories and disrupted distribution networks, effectively cutting off the supply of contraceptives. Further, the party lost administrative control over the age at marriage, and people no longer felt restricted in this regard (Chen and Kols, 1982).

Following the restoration of order, a third birth planning movement was lauched in 1971. At this time all citizens were asked by their national leadership to abide by the three new reproductive norms of *later*, *longer*, and *fewer*. "Later" referred to a later age at marriage: the minimum recommended ages for marriage varied between rural and urban areas, and were generally higher than the legal minimum age of marriage, which was twenty-two for males and twenty for females in 1980. "Longer" meant a longer time between births, and "fewer" referred to fewer children. Originally this meant two for urban and three for rural couples, but in 1977 this was changed to mean no more than two for everyone.

By the mid-1970s the Chinese government began setting yearly targets for each province, and the provinces in turn allocated birth quotas to their jurisdictional counties, with the process continuing downward through the communes and production brigades to the production teams (see Figure 7-3). At this level the community determined which couples would be permitted to have children during the coming year. In 1982 this birth planning

Figure 7-3
Organization of Administrative, Political, and Birth Planning Units in Rural China

Administrative level	Population size of typical unit	Chinese Communist party unit	Birth planning unit
Nation	900,000,000–1,000,000,000	Politboro	State birth planning commission and birth planning staff office of state council
Province (or autonomous region or municipality)	2,000,000–90,000,000	Provincial party committee	Provincial birth planning committee and provincial birth planning staff office
County	400,000–600,000	County party committee	County birth planning committee and county birth planning staff office
Commune	15,000–50,000	Commune party committee	Commune birth planning committee and full-time birth planning cadres
Production brigade	1,000–3,000	Brigade party branch	Brigade birth planning leading group
Production team	250–800	Party cadres	Part-time birth planning workers

SOURCE: Adapted from Figure 2 in Pi-Chao Chen and Adrienne Kols, "Population and Birth Planning in the People's Republic of China," *Population Reports,* 25 (January-February 1982).

procedure included the issuance of "planned birth cards" to couples selected for childbearing by the local committees. Couples who are not issued birth cards are expected to avoid becoming pregnant or, if they do, to have an abortion. Since an ineligible couple's defiance of the norms means that another, eligible couple may have to postpone having a child, eligible community members have a vested interest in the compliance of their fellow citizens. Accordingly, there are strong peer pressures for conformity.

Officially, the birth planning program in China is committed to persuasion rather than coercion. Methods of persuasion include the use of slogans, posters, television and radio broadcasts, pamphlets, editorials, public exhibits, plays, songs, meetings, and study groups. Beyond these persuasion techniques, there are positive incentives to practice birth control. Contraceptives, sterilizations, and abortions are free, for example, and sterilizations may earn extra "work points," which are the equivalent of income in the rural communes where they determine personal shares of food and supplies.

The One-Child Family

The fourth birth planning campaign is the current drive for one-child families begun in 1979. This program is designed to achieve zero population growth in two stages, first convincing couples not to have a third child and then convincing couples not to have a second child. The government's call for one-child families is a compromise between demographic goals and social realities. The natural rate of population increase could not possibly be reduced to zero in two decades without many people remaining childless. The one-child family, therefore, is probably the most extreme reduction in fertility the people would tolerate (Chen and Kols, 1982).

To promote the one-child family norm an elaborate system of incentives and disincentives is now operative throughout China, with specific details left to provinces, counties, and even brigades. The goal is to have as many couples as possible sign a pledge to have only one child. Upon signing, couples receive a certificate that entitles them to benefits specified by local law. These incentives vary from place to place, but include supplementary monthly payments and food rations, free health care, preference for housing and jobs, free and preferential education for children, and higher retirement pensions (Population Reference Bureau, 1981; Tien, 1983). There are also penalties, which vary widely by locale, for not complying with the one-child policy. Examples of disincentives include the requirement to return previously earned stipends or work points, reductions in monthly wages, the denial of free medical care and education for the children, and ineligibility for job promotions.

As one would expect, this campaign for one-child families is not without its difficulties (Tien, 1983). Without an adequate system such as our Social Security, for example, parents in China still look to their children for care in their old age. But if an only son marries an only daughter, the couple can live with and take care of only one set of parents. Further, most Chinese couples also want at least one son, so it remains to be seen how many parents with an only daughter will be willing to stop at one child. Just how strong this son preference really is, in fact, has been highlighted by recently reported infanticides among one-child certificate holders whose first child was a daughter.

It has long been generally accepted throughout the world that governments have the right to establish certain national goals and to implement policies affecting individual behavior to achieve these goals. Examples with which we are all familiar include various vaccination programs aimed at improving national health, as well as literacy goals and laws pertaining to compulsory education. We noted in Chapter 6, however, that a major doctrine of the Western family planning movement has been that childbearing decisions should be made by parents rather than by fate, tradition, church, or state. Moreover, the World Population Conference in 1974 reaffirmed the basic right of couples and individuals to decide for themselves the number

Table 7-5
Vital Rate Trends in the People's Republic of China*

Year	Rates per 1,000 population		
	Birth	Death	Natural increase
1965	38.1	9.6	28.5
1966	35.2	8.9	26.3
1967	34.1	8.1	25.7
1968	35.8	8.3	27.5
1969	34.3	8.1	26.2
1970	33.6	7.6	26.0
1971	30.7	7.3	23.4
1972	29.9	7.7	22.3
1973	28.1	7.1	21.0
1974	25.0	7.4	17.6
1975	23.1	7.3	15.8
1976	20.0	7.3	12.7
1977	19.0	6.9	12.1
1978	18.3	6.3	12.0
1979	17.9	6.2	11.7
1980	17.0	6.3	10.7

SOURCE: H. Yuan Tien, "China: Demographic Billionaire," *Population Bulletin,* 35 (April 1983).

* Many demographers feel that these rates, which are based on data issued by the Chinese government, overestimate the amount of progress that has been made, especially for the most recent years. Although the situation is certainly much better than it was in the 1960s, some demographers today would place the 1980 Chinese birth rate in the low 20s and its annual rate of population growth at close to 1½ percent. The *1983 World Population Data Sheet* of the Population Reference Bureau, for example, gives 1980-81 crude birth, death, and natural increase rates of 23, 8 and 15 per 1,000 respectively.

and spacing of their children. Under these circumstances, does a government's right to establish national goals allow it to limit parenthood in the long-run interests of the society? While the implications of such awesome state authority may seem ominous, the government of China clearly has answered in the affirmative.

To date, the Chinese birth planning programs appear to have been successful. Although estimates vary, it now appears that China has reduced its birth rate from somewhere in the middle 30s in 1970 to the low 20s in 1982 (see Table 7-5). Such a fertility decline over the course of a decade is without precedent among large developing countries. Moreover, the possibility of still further declines is suggested by the fact that millions of one-child couples have pledged to have no more children. The transferability of this approach to other Third World countries, however, is highly questionable. Several features of the Chinese accomplishment are, after all, clearly unique: the strong commitment of the national leaders to birth planning, their powerful authority over all levels of government, and the absence of any major political opposition. Above all, birth planning in China has also been linked to a revolutionary restructuring of social and economic institutions, the roles of women, family life, and the work place. While the specific measures adopted by the People's Republic of China may not be applicable in other developing countries, it is very likely that the greatest success in fertility reduction will be achieved by those governments that integrate traditional family planning programs into similar programs that seek a radical restructuring, at the grass roots level, of traditional social and cultural values and practices.

SUMMARY

The right of couples to have the number of children they want—no more and no fewer—ideally implies public efforts to help couples overcome fecundity impairments and to help couples avoid unplanned and unwanted fertility. Especially in the low fertility countries, it seems probable that there will be an increase in government-subsidized research directed toward helping couples who are frustrated in their efforts to have children. By far the major thrust of public policy to help people achieve their desired fertility, however, is through government-sponsored family planning programs.

Strictly speaking, the manifest intent of these programs is to promote maternal and child health and to enhance human rights rather than to lower the birth rates. The United States, for example, has no official fertility policy, even though the government is involved in several ways with the development and distribution of fertility control services. The public issue of how best to reverse the dramatic upsurge in teenage pregnancy is a case in point; yet precisely what the government can and should do to reduce the incidence of teenage pregnancy remains highly controversial.

Helping individuals realize their fertility goals is not the same thing as trying to manipulate societal levels of fertility or rates of population growth. For this reason, we need to distinguish between *individual* fertility goals on the one hand and the demographic needs and requirements of *societies* on the other. The governments of several countries today, for example, are deliberately trying to increase their national birth rates through pronatalist policies of various kinds. Fearful of the implications of continued low fertility, these countries have initiated programs of financial incentives to encourage young couples to have more than one or two children. So far the results of these efforts have been, at most, uncertain.

Among nations desiring to alter their fertility rates, far more are trying to decrease them than to increase them. Today both the *means* by which people may limit their family size and their *motivations* for doing so are taken into account by antinatalist programs in several developing countries. Nonetheless, demographers typically distinguish between policies that emphasize the availability of birth control technologies (family planning programs) and those that strive to change people's motivations for childbearing by going "beyond family planning." The most common and popular kind of policy for lowering fertility is the family planning approach. Many Third World countries are now using family planning in their attempts to reduce national birth rates. In some of these countries, mostly small and relatively advanced economically, birth rates have fallen dramatically. On a global scale, however, it is in the larger nations that the success or failures of policies to control fertility ultimately must be evaluated.

The world's two most populous nations, India and China, are especially interesting in this regard. India was a pioneer in family planning when in 1952 it became the first country to adopt a deliberate antinatalist population policy. After one of the most intense family planning drives in history, however, the program ultimately collapsed in the late 1970s with the defeat of the government's ruling party. Meanwhile, the Indian birth rate remains at well over 30 per 1,000 population.

The People's Republic of China clearly has gone beyond family planning in its attempts to change the motivations for childbearing in addition to providing the means for limiting family size. With a population exceeding one billion, China is the first country in the world to formulate a deliberate and comprehensive policy to reach zero population growth by the year 2000, or as soon thereafter as possible. After an uncertain beginning, China's national leaders are now asking the Chinese people to abide by three new reproductive norms: later marriage, longer intervals between births, and fewer children. An important part of the current campaign is the drive for one-child families, backed up by an elaborate system of incentives and disincentives to motivate people to have only one child. To date the Chinese program to control fertility appears to have been successful. Whether or not such a comprehensive program could be utilized by other Third World nations, however, is uncertain.

REFERENCES AND SUGGESTED READING

Aird, John S. "Fertility Decline in China." In Nick Eberstadt, ed., *Fertility Decline in the Less Developed Countries*. New York: Praeger, 1981.
Berelson, Bernard. "Beyond Family Planning." *Studies in Family Planning* 38 (1969): 1–16.
Campbell, Arthur A. "Trends in Teenage Childbearing in the United States."

In C. S. Chilman, ed., *Adolescent Pregnancy and Childbearing: Findings From Research* (Washington: U.S. Government Printing Office, 1980).

Chen, Pi-Chao, and Adrienne Kols. "Population and Birth Planning in the People's Republic of China." *Population Reports* 25 (January-February 1982).

Commission on Population Growth and the American Future. *Population and the American Future* (Washington, D.C.: 1972).

David, Henry P. "Eastern Europe: Pronatalist Policies and Private Behavior." *Population Bulletin*, 36 (February 1982).

Davis, Kingsley. "Population Policy: Will Current Programs Succeed?" *Science* 158 (1967): 730–39.

Demerath, Nicholas J. *Birth Control and Foreign Policy: The Alternatives to Family Planning.* New York: Harper & Row, 1976.

Finkle, Jason L., and Barbara B. Crane. "The Politics of Bucharest: Population, Development, and the New International Economic Order." *Population and Development Review*, 1 (September 1975): 87–114.

Goldscheider, Calvin. *Population, Modernization, and Social Structure.* Boston: Little, Brown, 1971.

Groat, H. Theodore, and Joseph B. Perry, Jr. "Population Control as a Motivational Problem." *Ohio Journal of Science*, 68 (1968): 219–25.

Kent, Mary Mederios, and Ann Larson. *Family Size Preferences: Evidence from the World Fertility Surveys.* Washington, D.C.: Population Reference Bureau, 1982.

Li, Wen L. "Temporal and Spatial Analysis of Fertility Decline in Taiwan." *Population Studies* 27 (1973): 97–104.

Mauldin, W. Parker. "Population Trends and Prospects." *Science* 209 (1980): 148–57.

Mecklenburg, Marjory E., and Patricia G. Thompson. "The Adolescent Family Life Program as a Prevention Measure." *Public Health Reports* (January–February 1983): 21–29.

Nortman, Dorothy L. *Population and Family Planning Programs: A Compendium of Data Through 1981.* New York: Population Council, 1982.

Population Reference Bureau. "China's One-Child Population Future." *Intercom* (August 1981): 1.

Population Reference Bureau. *1983 World Population Data Sheet* (April 1983).

Repetto, Robert. "The Effects of Income Distribution on Fertility in Developing Countries." In Nick Eberstadt, ed., *Fertility Decline in the Less Developed Countries.* New York: Praeger, 1981.

Salaff, J., and A. Wong. "Are Disincentives Coercive? The View from Singapore." *International Family Planning Perspectives and Digest* 4 (1978): 50–55.

Tien, H. Yuan. "Changing Population Policy Approaches in China." *Intercom* (October 1981): 10–11.

Tien, H. Yuan. "China: Demographic Billionaire." *Population Bulletin*, 38 (April 1983).
United Nations. *World Population Trends and Policies: 1979 Monitoring Report*, Vol. 1 (New York: United Nations, 1980).
Visaria, Pravin, and Leela Visaria. "India's Population: Second and Growing." *Population Bulletin*, 36 (October 1981).
Westoff, Leslie Aldridge, and Charles F. Westoff. *From Now to Zero*. Boston: Little, Brown, 1971.

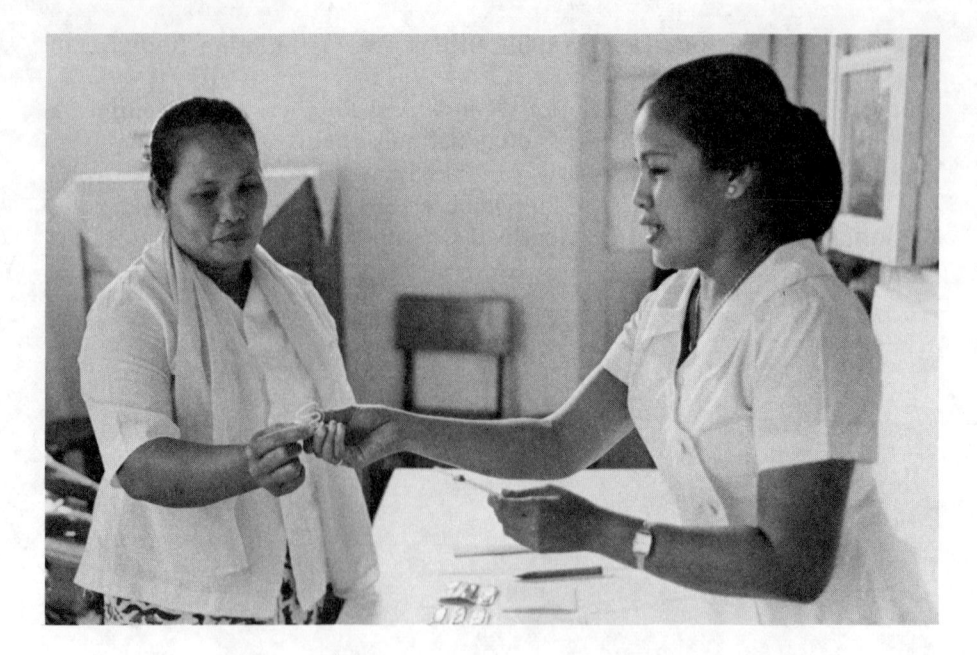

In Indonesia, a nurse at a family planning clinic provides a woman with an intrauterine device.

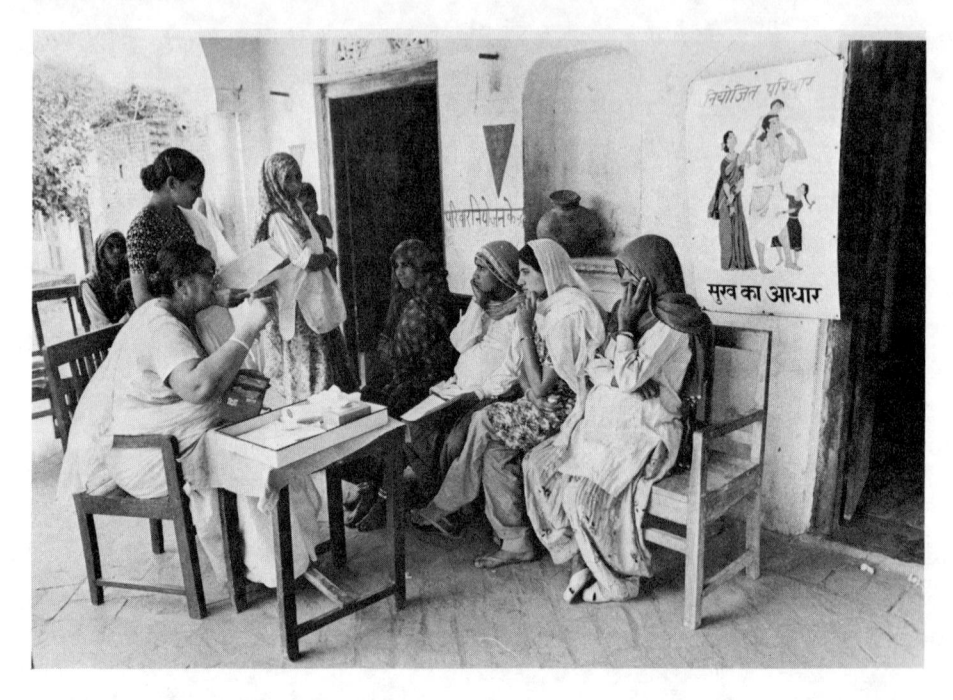

Indian wives listen attentively to a lesson in reproductive biology.

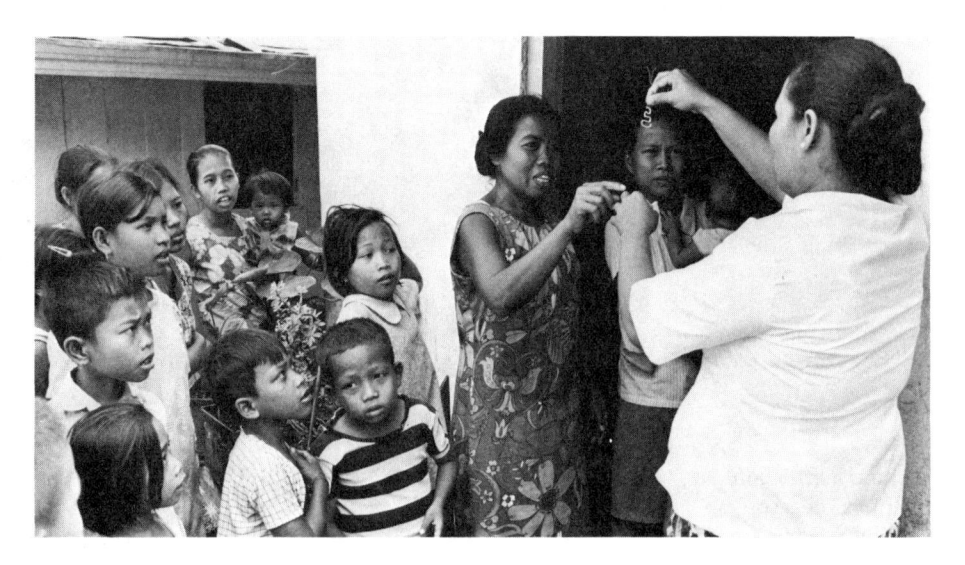

Children watch as a family planning worker explains to Indonesian wives the proper use of an intrauterine device.

Indian poster: "A Small Family Is a Happy Family."

WORLD POPULATION

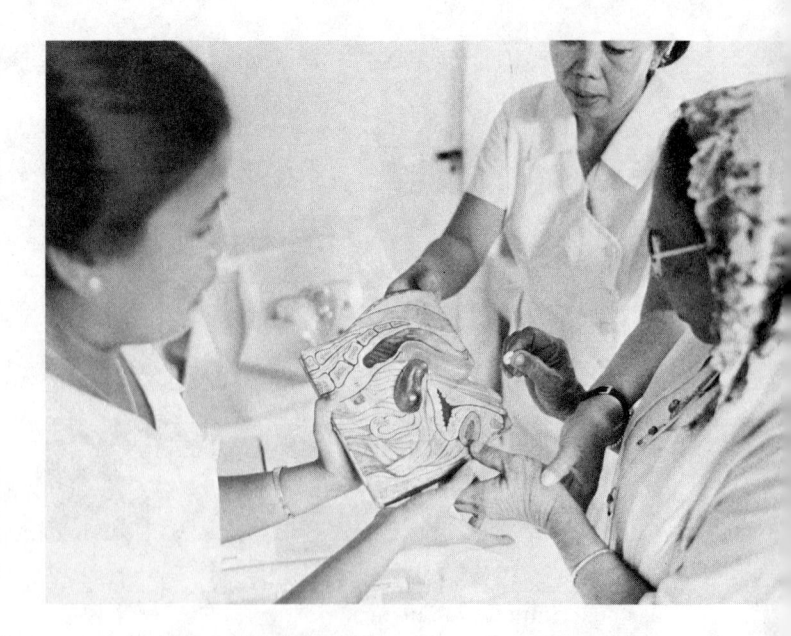

Women learn about the physiology of conception at a village family planning clinic in Indonesia.

A family planning worker describes contraceptives in an Indian village.

246   WORLD POPULATION

In the People's Republic of China, one-child families are encouraged by the government.

A grandfather with his grandson in the People's Republic of China

WORLD POPULATION 247

PROBLEMS OF THIRD WORLD POPULATION GROWTH

8

Estimates prepared by the United Nations (1980, p. 9) indicate that approximately 90 percent of the world's population growth is taking place in those less developed countries of the Third World that are already having difficulty supporting their present numbers. The most outstanding characteristic of these rapidly growing countries is their widespread poverty and very low levels of living and material well-being. To illustrate, recent estimates indicate that annual per capita income, translated into the purchasing power of U.S. dollars, was only $860 in the less developed countries taken as a whole as compared with $8,130 in the more developed countries (see Table 8-1). Incomes were considerably lower in Africa than in other less developed nations, while Latin America was somewhat better off than either Asia or Africa. This pattern generally holds true for all indexes of development: Latin America, where most of the countries have been politically independent for several generations, ranks highest; Asia ranks second; and Africa, where most nations have only recently received their independence and where the drive toward modernization is only just beginning, ranks at the bottom.

Although income is the most common measure of national development, it is important to realize that poverty means much more than just low income. Defining poverty solely in terms of per capita income glosses over the adverse conditions that characterize the daily lives of many of the people in such areas. For the masses of the people living in Third World countries today, poverty is much more than having a low income. It is often being hungry a good part of the time and having to subsist on a diet that is not only low in calories but frequently deficient in basic nutrients. It is a high

Table 8-1

Per Capita GNP, 1980: Physical Quality of Life, Late 1970s

Area	Per capita GNP (U.S. dollars)	Physical quality of life index*
World	$ 2,620	65
More developed areas	8,130	92
North America	11,240	95
Europe	7,990	93
USSR	4,550	91
Oceania	7,600	86
Less developed areas (excluding China)	860	55
Africa	770	33
Asia	920	58
Latin America	1,910	71

SOURCES: Population Reference Bureau, *World Population Data Sheet, 1979* and *1982*.
* The greater this index, which falls between the limits of 0 and 100, the better the overall quality of life.

rate of morbidity associated with malnutrition and the lessened ability of the body to resist various disease-causing microorganisms. It is a high level of infant and childhood mortality; an acute shortage of medical and paramedical personnel to provide needed health care; a high rate of illiteracy and a shortage of schools and teachers to remedy this situation; living in shanties and hovels that lack electricity, running water, toilet facilities, or even such basic home furnishings as chairs, beds, and cooking and eating utensils. In short, poverty is a state of severe deprivation with respect to virtually everything that we in the United States and the other developed countries regard as essential for maintaining even a minimally adequate level of living. A person who has not actually seen and smelled poverty may not understand how depressing and debilitating it can be; yet the majority of the people in the world today live under such conditions.

A somewhat more revealing picture of living conditions in these poverty-ridden countries is provided by a measure known as the Physical Quality of Life Index (PQLI). This index, which was devised by the Overseas Development Council as a means of providing a summary measure of the overall well-being of a population, is based on three indicators: infant mortality, life expectancy at age one, and literacy. The PQLI ranges within the theoretical limits of 0 and 100, with 100 indicating the highest level of living. Table 8-1 shows that the PQLI for the less developed countries as a whole was 55 compared with 92 for the more highly developed countries of Europe and North America. Once again Africa ranked lowest among the major Third World regions: nine African countries had a PQLI of less than 20, and in three countries (Guinea-Bissau, Mali, and Niger), it was less than 15 (Population Reference Bureau, 1979). At the other extreme, overall living levels were determined to be highest (PQLI 96–97) in the Netherlands and in the Scandinavian countries.

While it would be simplistic and naive to cite rapid population growth as the only cause of the massive poverty found throughout the Third World, it is a fact that there is a very strong association between overpopulation and poverty. It is also true that programs specifically designed to solve one of these problems will generally have a mollifying influence on the other. In this chapter we will take a closer look at the relationship between population growth and economic development in the developing countries today, paying particular attention to the problems associated with feeding the expanding millions. We will also discuss the implications of the population–food crisis for world peace.

POPULATION GROWTH AND ECONOMIC DEVELOPMENT

In the past economic development often encouraged population growth. We saw in Chapter 2, for example, that rudimentary economic development in the form of a more abundant and varied food supply laid the groundwork for the initial mortality declines that started the European demographic transition of the eighteenth and nineteenth centuries. Today, however, in many less developed countries mortality declines and rising rates of population growth have occurred in the absence of any real economic progress. As a result, attention has come more and more to focus on the converse relationship, or on the question of how population growth affects economic development.

With respect to this question, one school of thought has long maintained that population growth should be viewed as a stimulus to economic development. Those who have taken this position have generally started from the premise that all societies establish some sort of equilibrium or balance between the size of their population and the carrying capacity of their environment (Wilkinson, 1973; Abernethy, 1979)—that is, they increase in numbers until they reach a size that, given the existing level of technology and the nature of the resource base, could theoretically be maintained indefinitely at a given level of living. If population grows to a size that exceeds the carrying capacity of the environment, the society has three options: (1) it can accept the added numbers and reduce its level of living accordingly (a course of action that most people will resist); (2) it can relieve the added pressure on the environment by having the surplus population move away (a not infrequent occurrence among some primitive peoples, as long as there is some place to move to); or (3) it can reorganize itself in order to increase production.

In the third course of action economic development occurs as a response to population growth, and human history is replete with illustrations that would lend support to the validity of this causal connection. It is argued, for example, that the emergence and development of agriculture at the start of the Neolithic era was a necessary response to a situation in which population had increased to a point where it threatened to exceed the carrying capacity of the environment. Similarly, the well-known economist Colin Clark (1967) has attributed the start of the Industrial Revolution in England and other European countries to increased population pressure, reasoning that mortality decline and the associated increase in the rate of population growth created a demand for more resources, and this growing demand encouraged the technological innovations that led to increases in productivity.

This perspective has most recently been defended by the economist Julian Simon in his highly controversial book, *The Ultimate Resource*. Simon argues that, while population growth may be harmful in the short run, in the long run "per capita income is likely to be higher with a growing population than with a stationary one, both in more developed and less developed countries" (Simon, 1981, p. 6). This optimistic conclusion is based on two premises: (1) the more people there are, the greater will be the pressure to find solutions to the short-run problems such as a dwindling food supply; and (2) the more people there are, the more likely solutions will be found because more brains will be at work on them. As proof of this argument Simon cites the historical fact that the standard of living of the human population has risen along with the size of that population since the beginning of recorded time.

A careful reading of *The Ultimate Resource* reveals a number of flaws in Simon's argument. For one thing, it is based on a serious misreading of history. The implication of his argument is that population growth "caused" the increase in the standard of living when in fact the long-run trend has been one in which an increase in the standard of living has, by lowering the death rate, "caused" the population to increase. More important, however, arguments such as those of Simon and Colin Clark are based on an undifferentiated conception of time and space in which developments in European history become the basis for assessing the growth and development potential of Asia, Africa, and Latin America today. It is a fact that the very rapid economic growth that characterized Europe and North America during the eighteenth and nineteenth centuries was accompanied by a substantial increase in the population; and one may indeed argue that population growth, by encouraging innovation and technological change, helped to stimulate past economic development in the now highly industrialized nations of the Western world. It does not follow from this, however, that population growth will necessarily stimulate economic growth among the present less developed countries. For one thing, it must be remembered that the situation in the Third World today is substantially different than it was when the economy and population of the European community were expanding (Birdsall, 1980). For example, annual population growth rates in industrializing Europe seldom exceeded 1 or 1½ percent, compared with the growth rates of 2 to 3 percent a year that have prevailed throughout most of the less developed world since the end of World War II. These more rapid rates have not only meant a doubling of their numbers in twenty to thirty-five years but have also led to an increasing concentration of the population at the younger, nonproductive ages. This situation not only slows down per capita productivity but also burdens the countries with the need to spend larger amounts of their scarce capital on consumption items such as health services and education. It also creates the momentum for continued rapid population growth. In other words, the younger a population, all else being equal, the lower the death rate and the higher the birth rate and resulting rate of natural increase. Further, unlike the situation in the eighteenth and nineteenth centuries, the rapidly growing less developed countries today have not been able to get any relief from population pressures through emigration.

For these reasons, the evolving situation in many developing countries during the past several years has been one in which population growth has clearly not been a stimulus to any significant economic progress. On the contrary, there has emerged a growing debate among scholars concerning whether or not population growth may instead be acting as a major obstacle to economic development in the Third World today. That there is a relationship between these two processes is clearly indicated by the fact that population growth rates are fastest in the poorest countries; this is especially evident in the World Bank data presented in Table 8-2. Although these estimates provide only a rough approximation of economic conditions and trends in various countries, and although there will be exceptions where individual countries are concerned, the aggregate picture is very clear: the rate of economic development, as measured by the annual rate of increase in per capita income, declines sharply as the rate of population growth increases.

Population Growth as an Obstacle to Development

It is an indisputable fact that population growth today is occurring at a faster rate in those countries where incomes and associated levels of living are lowest. Two things are disputed, however: (1) the nature and strength of the causal connection between population growth and poverty, and (2) the

Table 8-2

Average Annual Growth Rates in Per Capita Real GNP in Countries Grouped According to Annual Rates of Population Growth, Late 1970s

Average rate of population growth (percent)	Average annual rate of increase in per capita GNP*
Less than 1.0	3.7% (33)
1.0–1.9	2.6 (32)
2.0–2.9	2.3 (60)
3.0 or more	0.7 (33)

SOURCE: Calculated by authors from data published in *1980 World Bank Atlas* (World Bank, 1981).
* Numbers in parentheses indicate number of countries on which average GNP growth rates are based.

most appropriate measures for dealing with overpopulation and poverty. On the simplest level one can identify two basic perspectives on the relationship between population and poverty (Weeks, 1981, p. 25–32): the *Malthusian* perspective, which sees population growth as a major contributing cause of Third World poverty; and the *Marxist* perspective, which sees no necessary causal connection between population growth and economic status and which regards both overpopulation and poverty as being caused by the exploitation of labor under a capitalist system of production.

The Malthusian Perspective

The Malthusian perspective on population and poverty is derived from the writings of Thomas Robert Malthus, an English clergyman and political economist of the late eighteenth and early nineteenth centuries. Although his famous *Essay on the Principle of Population*, first published in 1798, dealt primarily with the relationship between population growth and the food supply, a broader interpretation of his theory identifies population growth as a major cause of poverty and misery. Drawing on the works of earlier writers, particularly Adam Smith, Malthus argued that human populations are impelled by nature to reproduce up to the limits that could be supported by the carrying capacity of the environment. The poor in particular overproduce themselves, creating a surplus of labor, which then forces wages down and perpetuates their poverty. In other words, the reproductive behavior of the lower classes is responsible for their poverty; thus, the solution to poverty is seen to lie in a reduction in the rate of population growth among the poor. Malthus, a conservative clergyman who was also writing years before the advent of modern methods of birth control, suggested that the only way this could occur would be for the poor to refrain from marriage and sexual intercourse. However, he doubted that they would be sufficiently motivated to behave in such a virtuous manner; thus, there would always be poverty in human society.

Although contemporary scholars reject both Malthus's notion of a natural law that impels human reproductive behavior and his insistence on sexual abstinence as the solution to problems of overpopulation, many still subscribe to his basic belief that population growth is a major cause of poverty. Such persons, who are often labeled neo-Malthusians, are strong advocates of the need for the widespread adoption of birth control to stem the tide of what they see as runaway population growth throughout the less developed countries. They regard a rapid rate of population growth as a major obstacle to economic development, and they see little hope of overcoming poverty and generating economic growth anywhere in the Third World unless fertility levels are sharply reduced and population growth rates are brought under control.

The Marxist Perspective

The Marxist perspective is rooted in the nineteenth-century socialist writings of Karl Marx and Friedrich Engels. These scholars completely rejected Malthus's claim to a natural law concerning the tendency for population to outstrip resources and instead promoted the theory that the existence of poverty depends on the social and economic organization of society. Specifically, they regarded overpopulation and poverty as being synonymous with the unemployment that was a necessary consequence of a capitalist mode of production. Under capitalism the wealthy owners of the means of production exploit the workers in order to maximize their own profits. They then invest these profits in machinery that replaces human labor, thus creating unemployment. In a socialist society, on the other hand, where ownership of the means of production is shared, the fruits of production will be more equitably distributed so that there are no population problems. The solution to overpopulation and poverty is thus seen to lie in a shift away from a capitalist to a socialist mode of production.

In more recent years this classical Marxist perspective has been incorporated into what has come to be known as "world systems theory" (Wallerstein, 1974). According to this theory, the causes of the pronounced economic inequalities that exist today between the developed nations of the Western world and the underdeveloped countries of the Third World are intimately related to the historical causes of the development of the West (Frank, 1969)—that is, development and underdevelopment are seen as two aspects of the same process. Before there were developed countries, there were no underdeveloped countries. All countries were at one time undeveloped. Then, beginning in the fifteenth century as the Western Europeans spread out and colonized all parts of the world, the European countries and those largely of European origin such as the United States began to undergo rapid economic development largely because they were in a position to exploit the resources (human as well as natural) of other nations that now began to emerge as underdeveloped. In other words, this theory asserts, the developed world has achieved its present high level of living largely at the expense of the now underdeveloped countries of Asia, Africa, and Latin America. Historically, the Europeans disrupted the traditional ways of life in these Third World countries, appropriated their economic assets, and forced them into close dependent relationships with one or another of the emerging colonial or imperialist powers. Moreover, the economic domination of the less developed countries by the industrial powers is seen as continuing today under the label of neo-colonialism. Adherents of this neo-Marxist position believe that the solution to the problems of poverty in the Third World today lies in ending the economic exploitation and in redistributing the world's wealth—not in such simplistic measures as slowing down population growth.

This basic Marxist position—that there are no population problems, only economic problems—has often caused difficulties for contemporary Marxist governments, which have had to reconcile their ideological position with events taking place in the real world. The Soviets, for example, have been hard pressed to explain why their own population trends resemble those of the developed Western bloc countries, while rapid population growth has continued to be a source of problems for many Third World nations with socialist governments. Furthermore, this position was a major factor behind Soviet bloc opposition to the early efforts of the United Nations to provide birth control assistance to the developing countries. Soviet leaders frequently argued that the so-called population problem in the Third World was nothing more than a red herring set up by the Western capitalist countries to divert attention away from the more basic political and economic roots of world poverty. The real problem, they insisted, required a radical restructuring of the world economic system.

This call for a New International Economic Order (NIEO) became a dominating force at the first major World Population Conference sponsored by the United Nations and held in Bucharest in August 1974. In opposition to the conference planners, primarily representatives of Western bloc nations who saw population growth as a serious obstacle to economic development, a small but vociferous group of representatives from Third World countries argued that population problems were not a cause but a consequence of underdevelopment, and that attention should be focused on eliminating economic inequality rather than controlling population growth:

> They took the view that if the West claims to be committed to curbing population growth in order to facilitate economic development, then

for the same end it should be equally if not more committed to restructuring the international economic system and to paying "fair" prices for the products of the developing nations. If the West claims to be concerned about people of the developing nations having too many children, then it should be more concerned about its own "excessive" consumption of raw materials that cannot be replenished. If the West claims to be concerned about malnutrition and starvation in the Third World, then it is not enough to urge that fewer children be born; it is equally essential that the rich countries "more equitably" distribute their abundant food supplies (Finkel and Crane, 1975, pp. 104–05).

Although there has been no loss of commitment to the struggle for international economic parity, the harsh reality of rapid population growth and continued poverty throughout the less developed countries, even among those whose governments are based on a Marxist-socialist philosophy, has in recent years led to a softening of the traditional ideological opposition to birth control. In some nations, most notably the People's Republic of China, efforts to reduce fertility and slow down the rate of population growth have become official government policy. However, this does not mean that Marxists have altered their basic perspective. Although they may now be taking a more realistic approach to the total development problem, they still see poverty as a necessary consequence of capitalism, and they believe that the ultimate answer to Third World development lies in a redistribution of the world's wealth.

How Population Growth Impedes Development

Various arguments and ideologies aside, many experts regard the rapid population growth rates now prevailing throughout much of Asia, Africa, and Latin America as serious obstacles to efforts to develop national economies and improve the overall well-being of a majority of the world's people. Even those who adhere to the Marxist perspective need not close their eyes to the problems associated with rapid population growth. Using a simple analogy, they can look upon poverty as a disease for which a cure is being sought. At the same time they can look at rapid population growth as a painful symptom of this disease. No rational argument can be offered for not trying to relieve the symptom while working on the ultimate cure (economic development).

Most scholars today would agree that, although it may not be the cause of their poverty, continued rapid population growth in the poorer countries will seriously hamper national development efforts. In general, population and income trends throughout the world clearly suggest that income levels rise faster in countries where population growth is occurring most slowly (see Table 8-2). Also, persistent rapid rates of population growth are likely to exert a depressing effect on the rate of economic development in the countries concerned (Stockwell and Laidlaw, 1981, pp. 103–05). Countries where population growth is rapid must spend a larger proportion of their national income on providing basic necessities rather than using it for more productive purposes. Many countries, for example, must use potential food surpluses to feed expanding populations instead of trading the food on the world market in exchange for needed capital. Similarly, by aggravating existing food shortages, rapid population growth may lead to an increase in malnutrition and various deficiency diseases, thereby significantly reducing the productive efficiency of the labor force. This lower productivity due to poor health can jeopardize the quality of the next generation, perpetuating their low income status in a vicious circle of poverty.

Population growth increases the need and demand for all manner of public services (welfare, education, housing, health facilities, etc.), thus causing the government to divert capital to the provision of these services rather than to invest it in more productive endeavors. Population growth also tends to depress wages while increasing the costs of various goods and services, thereby putting an even greater strain on the poorer people in the countries affected.

Rapid population growth that hampers social and economic welfare improvements may also lead to political turmoil within nations and/or wars between nations, in both instances causing resources to be diverted away from general development programs. Similarly, population growth often creates pressure toward unemployment, particularly if this growth is accompanied by agricultural advances and the associated displacement of farm labor. Paradoxically, because the youthful segment of the population is expanding most rapidly, population growth generates a high ratio of dependent consumers to producers at the same time that it generates pressures toward unemployment. Among other things, this situation could lead to an increase in internal unrest and tension.

In many cases, rapid population growth increases the need for foreign aid, thus building up a greater national debt and prolonging a state of financial dependence on the aid-granting nations; to the extent that continued population growth hampers development efforts in the low income countries it leads to a widening of the gap between rich and poor nations, thereby increasing jealousy and resentment in the poor nations, and heightening international tensions.

The list could be extended further. The main point, however, is very simple: at any given level of economic development the more people there are, the less there will be available for each individual. Among the poor countries of the Third World today it is safe to say that population growth accentuates virtually every problem with which they must contend. Poor health, low education, poverty, low per capita productivity, unemployment, inadequate diets, rapid urbanization, housing shortages—all become increasingly serious as population continues to expand, and all become increasingly more costly and more difficult to alleviate. And the situation does not look as if it is going to improve much in the very near future. An overall population growth rate in excess of 2 percent a year could cause the population of the developing areas of the Third World to double in about thirty years. Thus, shortly after we enter the twenty-first century there could be twice as many people in these countries, all of whom have to be fed, clothed, housed, educated, and so forth. Since many of the countries involved are already seriously deficient in their ability to provide for these basic human needs, the prospect of continued rapid population growth must be regarded as a serious obstacle to their future development. As long as birth rates remain high and population continues to grow rapidly, many of the countries in Asia, Africa, and Latin America will find themselves in a situation where they will have to run as fast as they can just to stay in the same place. They will have to achieve very substantial increases in national income just to maintain the wide economic gap that already exists between the rich and the poor nations of the world.

The simple fact of the matter is that a disproportionate share of the population growth taking place in the world today is concentrated in the developing regions that are least able to cope with it. Most of the poor countries are in the midst of major efforts to improve their economic condition, but all too often any potential gains in economic status are wiped out by rapid and increasing rates of population growth. As we noted in Chapter 2, these increasing rates of population growth are the result of remarkable success in controlling death in the virtual absence of any real fertility control. As long as this situation persists, as long as birth rates do not decline, the rate of population growth in the less developed regions can be expected to remain high, with the unfortunate consequence of prolonging, if not even widening, the absolute gap between the rich and the poor nations of the world.

As long as population growth continues, the only real result of technological gains and so-called economic progress in the developing countries will be an increase in the number of people these nations are capable of supporting at existing low levels of living. This can hardly be called progress! Continued population growth means only that the years ahead will see more and more people living at marginal levels of subsistence, more and more people leading impoverished lives characterized by the steady erosion of human rights and individual freedom, more and more people with less and less to lose and more and more to gain from the overthrow of the existing order. Not everyone would agree that the population crisis is the most serious problem confronting the world today, but most would agree that the successful development programs in the coming years will be those that have as one of their major goals the slowing down of population growth through the deliberate reduction of fertility.

Population Growth and the Family

The discussion so far has focused on the general kinds of problems that rapid population growth creates for the society as a whole. While this societal level is probably the most important as far as overall economic development is concerned, one should not ignore the adverse consequences that rapid growth can have for the families and individuals of the society. The point here is that high fertility and the resultant large families tend to have a relatively detrimental effect on individuals, especially children, and this detrimental effect will be greater in a poor, less developed country than in a more highly developed country (Birdsall, 1980). The larger the family, all else being equal, the less money will be available on a per capita basis for such things as health care, food, and education. Thus, children from large families are more likely to be less healthy, to experience learning difficulties, and to grow up to be unskilled adults who are less capable of earning a good livelihood and are thus likely to perpetuate poverty into the next generation. Repeated childbirth can also have an adverse effect on the health of the mother, which can carry over into the life of the entire family. This, too, can contribute to the perpetuation of poverty. A sickly mother is able to give less attention to the care and nurture of her children, who accordingly will experience less than optimal social and emotional development.

This is not to say that poverty is a necessary cause of high fertility and large families, or vice versa. Nevertheless, there is a definite association, and the available evidence clearly indicates that certain aspects of poverty do contribute to high fertility. Some of these are high infant mortality, which motivates couples to have many children in the hope that a sufficient number of them will survive to support the parents in old age; inadequate education of women; a need for the economic contribution that children can make to the family; and ignorance of or lack of access to modern methods of contraception. Thus, rapid population growth does have generally adverse consequences for society as a whole, and the less developed the society, the more serious the adverse consequences and the more likely the ill effects of poverty will be transmitted from one generation to the next. Once again, then, the evidence clearly supports the position that a major aspect of any Third World development program must focus on efforts to reduce fertility and family size and slow down the rate of population growth.

Population Growth and Age Structure

A leading authority on population and poverty in the developing world noted recently that the negative association between population growth and economic development is based on two assumptions. The first is the assumption of diminishing returns, which says that as numbers increase, each individual worker produces less in relation to the land and capital he or she

Figure 8-1
Percent of Population under Age 15 and under Age 5, c. 1980

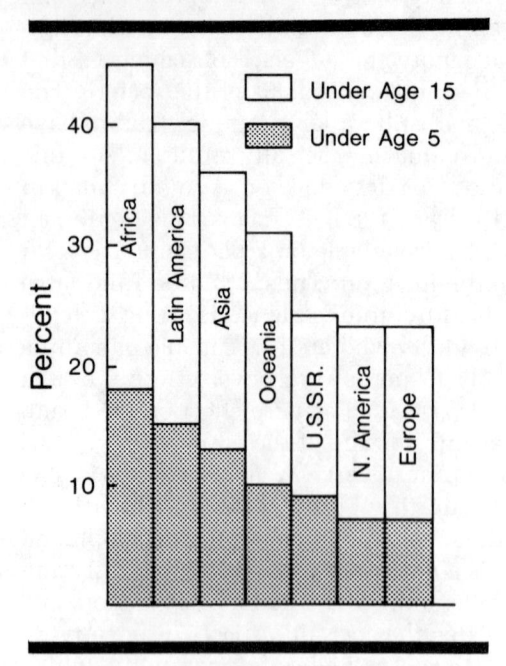

SOURCE: Population Reference Bureau, *1982 World's Children Data Sheet* (April 1982).

has to work with. Second, it is assumed that as population grows, and especially as the number of dependent children increases, living expenses will increase and savings will go down, thus restricting the amount of money available for investment in education and physical capital such as housing, roads, and factories (Birdsall, 1980). However, the validity of these assumptions depends on a wide variety of other factors such as the availability of natural resources, the level of technological development, and the degree to which labor can be substituted for capital. Because of the relevance of these other factors, it is difficult to specify the main effect of population growth on the economy. However, one aspect of the pattern of rapid population growth in the developing areas does have fairly straightforward consequences for the overall economy of the poor countries, and that is its effect on the age structure of the population.

To make a somewhat oversimplified generalization concerning the relationship between age composition and economic growth in low income countries: the younger the population, the more capital will have to be diverted from production to consumption purposes, and the more difficult will be the overall development problem. The available data, which indicate that the population in the less developed regions is considerably younger than that of the more highly developed areas of the world, clearly reveal the seriousness of this demographic obstacle to development. According to recent estimates, only 23 percent of the population in the more developed regions is under fifteen years of age, as compared with 42 percent in the less developed regions (Population Reference Bureau, 1982a). Among the less developed areas the proportion of the population under age fifteen ranges from 36 percent in Asia to 45 percent in Africa (see Figure 8-1). This fraction exceeds 45 percent in many Third World countries, and in a few of them (e.g., Jordan, Kenya, Rwanda, Zimbabwe), 50 percent or more of the population falls into this youthful age group.

The comparative youthfulness of the populations of the less developed countries is especially apparent in the proportion of the population under age five. The size of this age group varies from 7 percent of the population in Europe and North America to 18 percent in Africa. In several African countries fully one-fifth of the population is made up of children under five years of age.

A most useful device for analyzing the age structure of any population is the population pyramid. This graphic device permits the analyst to tell at a glance what the age distribution of a population is, by sex, and it also reveals a great deal about past demographic trends in the population and their probable consequences. Figure 8-2 shows recent population pyramids for Sweden and Mexico superimposed on each other. As is customary in such pyramids, age is plotted vertically (in this figure five-year age groups are used), males are depicted on the left and females on the right, and the percentage is plotted, separately for each sex, along the base line. Such pyramids can also be constructed on the basis of absolute numbers rather than percentages, but the use of percentages facilitates comparison. Thus, in Figure 8-2 the bars on either side of the center line represent the percentage of the population in each specified age–sex group. A glance at this figure clearly reveals the typical differences in the age structure of more developed and less developed societies. Sweden's bullet-shaped pyramid depicts a developed society that is relatively old and stable, whereas the pattern for Mexico shows the pronounced youthfulness of the population and depicts its heavy growth potential. The aging of the 1978 female child population under fifteen years of age, for instance, will lead to a doubling of the number of potential young mothers in that country by the end of the century.

The explanation for the pronounced youthfulness of the Third World populations must be sought in the present pattern of rapid population growth resulting from declining mortality, especially in infancy. When death rates decline, especially death rates among infants and young children, while birth rates remain high, the effect is a marked increase in the number and pro-

Figure 8-2
Age–Sex Structure of Sweden and Mexico, 1978

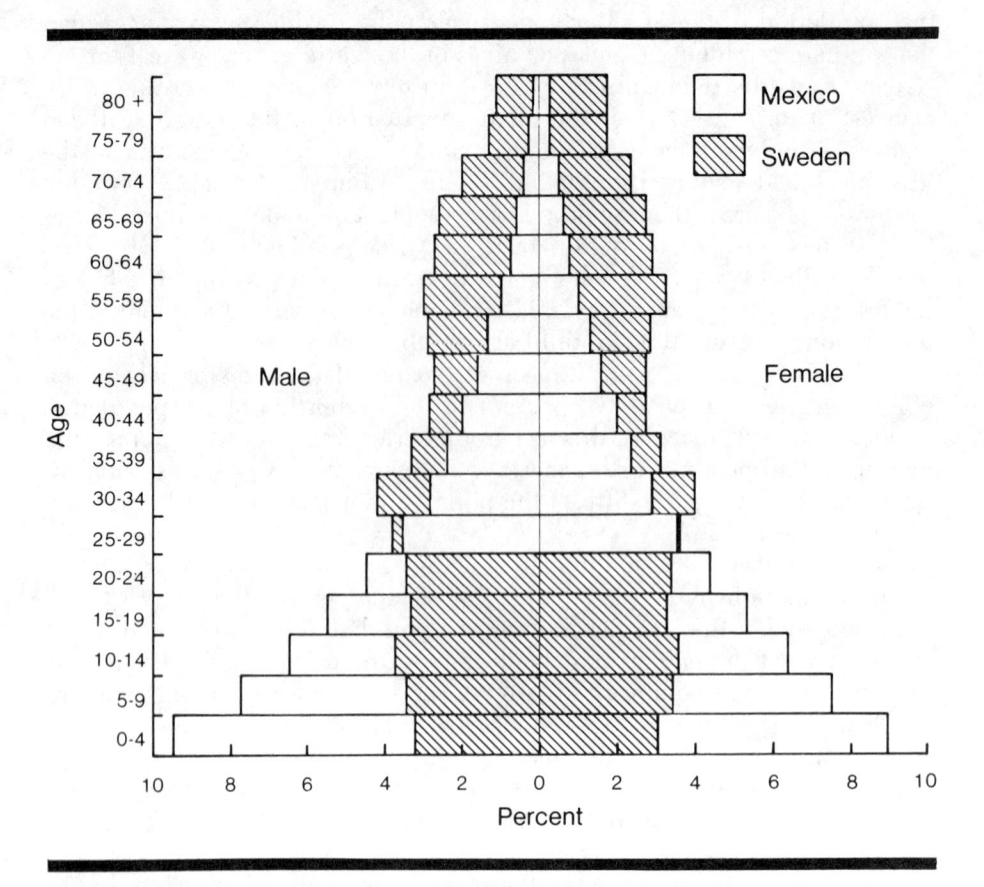

SOURCE: Based on data in *Demographic Yearbook, 1979* (New York: United Nations, 1980).

portion of youth in the population. Since young people are primarily consumers (not only of food but also of other essential services such as health and education), such an increase in the number of youth greatly intensifies the dependency burden on the rest of the population. This means that a smaller proportion of adult workers have to bear a larger burden of support, and it also means that resources that might have been used to support various development programs must be used instead to provide for the needs of the young. Furthermore, when the surviving infants reach working age, a corresponding increase will occur in the already serious problems of unemployment and underemployment.

Finally, in addition to creating serious social and economic problems in the developing areas by putting greater pressure on limited educational facilities, for example, or by diverting capital to necessary maintenance expenses, the present heavy burden of youth dependency may also have serious political implications. The young people, with all their youthful ideals and ambitions, are the least committed to the maintenance of the status quo, and this most volatile segment of the population in the developing world is most likely to react violently to a situation in which continued failure and increasing frustration are the major by-products of the so-called revolution of rising expectations. Uncommitted and dissatisfied young people have in the past been a major source of social unrest and political instability in many countries, and their rising numbers pose the same threat today in many areas of the developing world. Because internal political stability is an important requisite for national economic development, the present age structure of the population in many Third World countries must be regarded as an especially serious aspect of the overall development problems they face.

In summary, over and above the great disparity in population growth rates between the rich and the poor countries, the major demographic trend of the 1980s will be the growing influence of greatly increased numbers of young people in the developing areas who will be asserting themselves socially, economically, and politically during this period (Piotrow, 1980, p. 4). Moreover, this heavy burden of youth dependency and the problems associated with a youth-dominated society will remain as long as fertility remains high. (When the recent birth cohorts reach adulthood, they will have proportionately more children, if fertility does not fall, and the increasing population will be characterized by the same high ratio of children to adults.) Hence, there is even greater urgency to reduce the level of fertility in today's developing nations—not only to slow down the present growth rates but also to alter the youthful composition of the population and thereby lessen the momentum for continued rapid growth in the years to come.

POPULATION AND FOOD

The world food situation is one of the most serious problems confronting the developing nations today. The problem of feeding the people of the world is as old as the human race itself, and there is every indication that it is going to remain a serious problem for some time to come. Although agricultural production has kept pace with population growth on a world level, the population is fast outstripping its food supply in many areas today, and already serious food shortages will become much more acute during the 1980s.

The Malthusian Principle

One of the first persons in the modern era to call attention to the problem of the relationship between population growth and the food supply was the British clergyman and economist, Thomas Robert Malthus, whom we mentioned earlier. Writing in England at the close of the eighteenth century, Malthus formulated a "principle of population" based on two postulates and one assumption. The two postulates were: (1) people cannot live without food, and (2) the human sex drive is very strong and is not likely to diminish. Because the sex drive is so strong and pervasive, Malthus believed that the human race would always be in danger of increasing its numbers at a faster rate than it could increase the food supply. More specifically, Malthus assumed that population was capable of increasing exponentially, doubling itself every twenty-five years or so, whereas the best one could anticipate with respect to food production was an arithmetic rate of increase. In Malthus's words:

> . . . the power of population is infinitely greater than the power in the earth to produce subsistence for man. Population, when unchecked, increases in a geometrical ratio. Subsistence increases only in an arithmetical ratio. A slight acquaintance with numbers will show the immensity of the first power in comparison of the second (Malthus, 1959, p. 5).

The "immensity of the first power in comparison of the second" is clearly illustrated by the following progressions:

Population (geometric progression): 1 . . . 2 . . . 4 . . . 8 . . . 16 . . .
Food (arithmetic progression):   1 . . . 2 . . . 3 . . . 4 . . . 5 . . .

The second term of the above progressions indicates that the increase in the food supply is keeping pace with the growth of population. The third term, however, is obviously untenable as it indicates a population size (4) in excess of the food supply (3). Clearly, something has to happen to prevent population from growing beyond the number that can be sustained by the available food supply.

In order to keep the size of the population within the limits set by the ability to produce food, Malthus believed that some check to population growth would always be necessary. He explicitly recognized two such checks: *positive checks* such as war, famine, and disease, which would hold population size down by increasing the number of deaths; and *preventive checks*, by which he meant "moral restraint," or such things as delayed marriage and total sexual abstinence outside marriage, which would control population size by reducing the number of births.

Based on his two postulates, the assumption, and the perceived need for checks to curtail population growth, Malthus formulated a three-part "principle of population," which can be summarized as follows:

1. The size of the population is limited by the size of the available food supply.
2. Because of the strong human sex drive, any increase in the food supply will be followed by an increase in population, unless something happens to prevent it.
3. The various things that can happen to prevent population from increasing fall into one of two categories: "moral restraint" (preventive checks) or "vice and misery" (positive checks).

Although implicit in this principle of population is the clear provision that people could, by exercising moral restraint, keep population size within the limits set by the food supply, Malthus himself was not very optimistic about this happening. He regarded the human sex drive as so powerful that people would be unlikely to exercise such moral restraint; hence, he foresaw a world in which war, disease, and periodic famine would always be with us to maintain population size within the limits that could be supported by the available food supply.

Not surprisingly, the Malthusian principle of population was not received with open arms when it was first published in 1798. The late eighteenth century in Europe was a period of widespread optimism concerning humanity's future, and philosophers and social critics were coming to believe that people were perfectible and easily capable of creating a better world for themselves. In this atmosphere, the unmitigated pessimism of "Parson Malthus" was decidedly unwelcome, and its appearance generated a literary controversy that carried over into the field of economics and lasted well into the nineteenth century. During the late nineteenth century, however, a declining death rate and increasing rates of population growth were accompanied by tremendous social and economic advances that contributed to substantial increases in the level of living. In light of these developments there seemed little justification for being concerned with the doomsday theories of an eccentric English clergyman, and the world appeared more or less to forget Malthus.

Present Situation

Since the end of World War II, there has been a reawakening of concern over the old Malthusian hypothesis that the human race is doomed to a miserable existence because of the continuing tendency for population to press upon the limits of the food supply. The reason for the renewed concern lies in the new transitional growth pattern that has emerged in the less developed countries (see Figure 2-4) and in the resulting rapid acceleration in the rate of world population growth. Coupled with this rapid increase in the number of people in the world there has been a growing awareness of the limits to the earth's productive capacity, an awareness that has been reinforced by the existence of chronic food shortages in many parts of the world as well as periodic acute famines in some of the poorest areas (most notably in sub-Saharan Africa). Although the much heralded "green revolution" of the late 1960s was able to ameliorate the world food crisis temporarily, it fell far short of being the miraculous solution that some hoped it would be. The increased per acre production made possible by the high yield varieties of wheat and rice depends heavily on large amounts of chemical fertilizer, pesticides, and water. Many of the less developed countries have simply not been able to provide these necessities. Many fertilizers, pesticides, and herbicides are petroleum-based, and modern irrigation systems require fuel for pumping the water. The OPEC price increases of the early 1970s seriously impaired the ability of the poorer countries to participate in this so-called green revolution. By the time the less developed countries had paid for their oil imports (up from $3.7 billion in 1972 to $15 billion in 1974), they had little capital left with which to buy the other chemicals and nutrients that the high yield intensive farming required; and countries like India have been unable to afford the amount of fertilizer needed in order to maximize their agricultural output.

On a world level the problem may not appear to be critical. The years since 1950 have witnessed some tremendous increases in food production—increases that have in fact been more than enough to offset population growth. The problem, however, is that these increases have not been evenly distributed. Most of the increases in food production have occurred in the more developed countries of Europe and North America, whereas the population increases have been greatest in the less developed countries. Thus, while per capita food production has remained relatively stable on a global level, it has fallen considerably in many parts of the world. Between 1965 and 1973, for example, the annual rate of population growth exceeded the annual rate of increase in agricultural production in at least forty-two of the less developed countries of Asia, Africa, and Latin America (International Bank, 1976); and by the middle of the 1970s it was generally agreed that the world food situation had reached crisis proportions (Brown, 1982). The magnitude of the problem at that time can be illustrated by considering the international variations in the *per capita food supply index*. According to this index, which is a measure of both the quantity and quality of a person's diet, the amount and type of food consumed each day by the average person throughout the world in 1974 was equivalent to less than two American-type meals (see Table 8-3); and in some areas the average person's diet

Table 8-3
Population and Food

Area	Annual rate of increase in: Population (1979)	Annual rate of increase in: Grain yields (1970–78)	Per capita food supply index*
WORLD	1.9%	1.9%	1.8
Africa	2.9	0.6	1.2
Upper Volta	2.2	−0.3	1.1
Nigeria	3.3	−1.4	1.0
Chad	2.3	−4.4	0.8
Liberia	3.3	0.8	0.7
Ethiopia	2.6	1.4	1.1
Asia	2.1	1.9	1.2
Bangladesh	2.7	1.6	0.9
Thailand	2.3	−1.0	1.2
Philippines	2.2	0.6	0.9
PRC	2.0	1.1	1.1
Latin America	2.5	1.8	1.7
Bolivia	2.6	0.6	0.9
Peru	2.8	0.1	1.4
Mexico	2.8	1.6	1.8
North America	0.9	2.2	3.6
Europe	0.4	3.7	3.2

SOURCES: Environmental Fund, *World Population Estimates;* data sheets for 1978 and 1979.
* Based on a measure of total calories available and the per capita protein supply. This measure can be interpreted as the number of average U.S. meals available per person per day.

was well below the equivalent of only one American-type meal per day! Still other estimates prepared by the Food and Agricultural Organization of the United Nations indicate that in the early 1970s approximately one out of every four persons in the less developed world had a diet that fell below the minimum nutritional level. Even more tragic, it was estimated that as many as 50 percent of all young children in the developing countries suffered from some degree of malnutrition (Population Reference Bureau, 1982b).

More recent trends do not offer much encouragement. One set of estimates indicates that worldwide cereal grain production during the 1970s increased at an average annual rate of 1.9 percent, more or less keeping pace with the rate of world population growth (see Table 8-3). However, because there was already so much hunger in the world, there has been little if any improvement in the living conditions of the majority of the human race.

More significantly, a number of countries have been characterized by annual rates of population growth far in excess of recent rates of increase in grain yields; and in a few of the more serious cases grain production yields have actually been declining. In both Africa and Latin America, for example, where annual population growth rates are highest, the early 1970s witnessed a decline in per capita food production (Ridker and Cecelski, 1979); and by the summer of 1978, a reported twenty-eight countries encompassing some 230 million people had experienced abnormal food shortages, mostly as a result of shortfalls in food production during the preceding year (Population Reference Bureau, 1978). Food supplies were continuing to shrink in 1980, as agricultural production in the less developed countries rose by only 1.3 percent, compared with a population increase of about 2 percent. Dwindling supplies means higher prices, and as we entered the 1980s the World Bank estimated that nearly a billion people in the world did not have enough money to maintain an adequate diet (Population Reference Bureau, 1982a). Moreover, serious food shortages were being reported in a number of sub-Saharan African countries; emerging food reserves in the world were considerably lower than the level recommended by the Food and Agricultural Organization (FAO) of the United Nations; the director general of the FAO characterized the world food situation as "extremely dangerous"; and Lester Brown, a noted authority on the world food situation, wrote that mounting pressure on global food resources was one of the major threats facing human society and that this pressure "demanded immediate attention" (Brown, 1981, p. 5). While it is certainly not true that half the world is starving to death, as some hysterical alarmists would have us believe, it is generally agreed that hundreds of millions of people in the world today are not getting enough proper food to lead fully active, healthy lives. Moreover, there are isolated pockets of the globe, largely in Africa, where tens of millions of people do periodically suffer from severe famine (Eckholm and Record, 1976, pp. 10–11). Clearly, the problem of maintaining a balance between numbers and resources, which concerned Malthus nearly two centuries ago, is still with us today.

Although global gains in food production have so far kept pace with world population growth, this delicate balance is becoming more and more difficult to maintain, and it is apparent that feeding the world's growing population will continue to pose serious problems in the years ahead. A recent presidential commission report in fact states that the worsening world food situation is becoming so serious that, if nothing is done to prevent it, the last two decades of the twentieth century could see the emergence of a food crisis of substantially greater proportions than the energy crisis of the 1970s (President's Commission on World Hunger, 1980). Moreover, the major recommendation of this report is that the United States make the elimination of hunger the primary focus of its relationships with the developing countries.

Prospects for Increasing Food Production

The problem of imbalance between the number of people and the size of the food supply could be solved in two obvious ways: increase the food supply and/or decrease the rate of population growth. Many approaches offer some potential for increasing the amount of food resources available in the world. These include increasing the amount of land devoted to agricultural production; increasing per acre yields through the use of high yield variety seeds and the adoption of other modern farming techniques; developing and exploiting new sources of food such as algae derivatives and other ocean products; and reducing food losses due to spoilage and pests.

Although such efforts do have some potential for increasing the world's food supply, they are at best short-run solutions; taken by themselves they will not solve the crisis but merely postpone it for a while. One reason for this is that the efficacy of many of these approaches to increased food production is overrated. We have already seen, for example, the financial constraints of realizing the increased per acre yields that are technically feasible using the new high yield varieties of wheat and rice. Still another problem that needs to be noted in relation to efforts to increase food production concerns the effect that such efforts have had on the quality of the environment and the resource base in many parts of the world (van der Tak et. al., 1979, pp. 28–29). For example, slash-and-burn agriculture, overcopping, overgrazing, and subsequent wind and water erosion have seriously threatened the food producing capacity in vast areas of Africa, Asia, the Middle East, and Latin America, and increasing demands for cropland, firewood, and timber have caused a 20 percent reduction in the world's forest coverage since 1950. This loss of forestation represents a twofold problem: on the one hand, the destruction of surface vegetation reduces the source of our oxygen and destroys the ecosystem needed to maintain a variety of wildlife; on the other hand, the loss of water-holding ground cover has resulted in millions of tons of irreplaceable topsoil being washed into the sea. In some areas of the world the massive water requirements of modern agriculture and industry are creating serious water shortages, while in other areas the fish catch has been leveling off due both to overfishing and to the pollution of spawning beds. In short, the efforts in recent decades to increase the food supply have also meant a sharp increase in the rate of basic resource depletion and pollution, thus steadily worsening an already serious situation.

The other side of the problem, of course, is the simple fact that the potential consumers of any food increases are already alive. That is, since a large portion of the world's people are already living close to bare subsistence levels, any increases in food production will be quickly absorbed by the already existing surplus population. It may be comforting to realize that increases in world food production have kept pace with increases in population in the recent past, but this has not led to any increases in per capita food consumption. For that to occur the available food supply must be increased at a *faster* rate than the size of world population. One of the ironic aspects of the situation here is that increases in the rate of population growth could be generated by the mortality reductions that generally accompany increases in the quantity and quality of the food supply. With the number of people in the less developed world already increasing by about 70 million persons per year, it is clear that a major task in the years ahead is to achieve some sort of check on population growth. To be of value in reducing world hunger, increases in food production must be accompanied by declines in the rate of population growth (i.e., by declines in the number of births). As was noted in a report by the United Nations published more than twenty years ago:

> It seems evident that the problem of achieving the needed increases in food production during the next decades would be made easier, and the risk of failures would be diminished, if the population were to increase less than is indicated by the projections of present trends for the economically less developed regions of the world. . . . With few exceptions, the experts who have studied this question agree that the outlook would be far more favorable if the present rates of population increase in the underdeveloped countries could be slowed down by moderation of birth rates. In fact, some experts hold that unless the growth of population becomes slower in the near future, there is little hope of improving the conditions of life in many of these countries, and even to hold the present low levels of living may prove to be difficult (United Nations, 1962, p. 43).

More than two decades later many experts are still of the opinion that significant improvements in per capita food supply are not likely to be achieved at all until population growth rates in the developing countries have been reduced (Johnson, 1976). Further, one leading expert on world food resources has recently stated unequivocally that future food needs will *not* be met if global population growth continues as projected (Brown, 1982), and this pessimistic outlook has been borne out by the latest (1983) study of the Food and Agricultural Organization of the United Nations. Based on data from 117 countries, this study concluded that there are very real limits to the food production potential of the less developed countries, and that by the year 2000 as many as 65 of them would be unable to produce enough food to feed their populations. It should be patently obvious that as long as the Malthusian tendency persists for population to grow as rapidly as does the means of subsistence, then all the talk about achieving increases in food production and raising levels of living in the poor countries is sheer fantasy. Although many authorities anticipate that existing levels of per capita food production will be maintained through the end of the century, after that it will become more and more difficult for food output growth to keep pace with continuing population growth, thus highlighting the need for concerted efforts to bring an end to the current world population explosion.

One other point deserves to be made in relation to the adequacy of the world's food supply, and that concerns its distribution. Simply put, disproportionate shares of the world's food resources are produced in the more highly developed countries, and the bulk of the emergency reserves are stored in the warehouses of a few major producing nations. The United States, for example, contains about 5 percent of the world's population, but it produces slightly more than 10 percent of the world's meat, nearly 50 percent of the world's corn, and more than two-thirds of the world's soybeans. We not only produce a huge surplus, but we also consume much more than people in the less developed countries do. It is estimated, for example, that the average American consumes about 2,000 pounds of grain per year, most of it indirectly in the form of meat, poultry, eggs, and milk (i.e., animals are fed the grain and then we eat the animal products). In a country like India, by contrast, the average person consumes only about 400 pounds of grain per year, most of it directly in the form of bread and cereal products. In other words, the average American consumes roughly five times more grain per year than the average Indian. The difference of course is due to the fact that it takes several pounds of grain to produce a single pound of animal product (e.g., roughly 8 pounds of grain are needed to produce 1 pound of beef); and one implication of this differential is that even a slight modification in the diet of Americans and other industrialized peoples could theoretically free up billions of tons of grain per year for export to the less developed countries. Such a notion is oversimplified in that it ignores various political and economic considerations as well as the logistical problems of distributing the food surpluses, but the fact remains that a significant dimension of the present world food crisis (and the crisis with respect to many of the earth's other resources as well) can be traced to the extraordinarily high consumption levels in the industrialized countries.

One other aspect of the food problem that needs to be mentioned is the maldistribution of food *within* countries. In many Third World nations food surpluses are exported in order to acquire much needed foreign capital; in others food is disproportionately allocated to urban areas in order to promote and maintain political stability; and in still others food surpluses, either produced at home or received through foreign aid, are bought up by private speculators who reap large profits at the expense of their own countrymen. Even in the richly endowed United States it is estimated that some 30 million people live in poverty households, and that the majority of them suffer seriously because they cannot afford to maintain an adequate diet (Schwartz-Nobel, 1981). Tragic as it may seem, the fact is that much of the hunger in the world today, even in countries blessed by food surpluses, is the result of indigenous economic and/or political policies. The obvious implication of this situation is that solving the present world food problems will require some major policy changes within the developing countries themselves. Such political considerations aside, it is clear that the poorer nations of the world today face a serious challenge to prevent population from increasing at a faster rate than food production does, and meeting this challenge will entail a reduction in fertility through a wider adoption of modern birth control techniques. The alternative will be a continuation of and perhaps even an increase in the poverty, misery, and hunger that now mark the majority of the world's population.

Implications for World Peace

Before concluding this discussion of the world food problem some attention must be given to its implications for the maintenance of world peace. Hungry people are dissatisfied people, and in the past it has not been unusual for such people to attack their neighbors and confiscate their food for themselves. On a national level, the German and Japanese imperial expansions during the 1930s and 1940s clearly illustrated what can happen when a country becomes dissatisfied with its share of the world's wealth. More recently, dissatisfaction within have-not nations has been demonstrated by the border disputes between India and Pakistan, Bangladesh, and the People's Republic of China; between Honduras and El Salvador; between Argentina and the United Kingdom; between Iran and Iraq, and throughout the Middle East in general; and by the various internal conflicts in places like Ethiopia, Cambodia, Nicaragua, and El Salvador. Such conflicts are likely to become even more frequent during the 1980s as pressures on world food supplies continue to mount.

Food shortages were not a major threat to world peace in the preindustrial world, but today, when hungry peoples have or are trying to develop industrial power, such shortages could become a real threat to peace. In the developing countries of Africa, Asia, and Latin America, large segments of the population already live very close to the subsistence level. Moreover, population is growing so rapidly in these areas that any increases in food production serve mainly to permit a greater number of people to subsist at the same low level. Should this situation continue, particularly if it gets worse (as it very well might), it could act as a potent force against world peace. This is not meant to imply that an imbalance between numbers and the available food supply is necessarily a cause of war. Such an imbalance did not lead India to start a war during the critical food shortages of 1966 (although who is to say it would not have happened if other nations with food surpluses had not been ready and willing to help?). Neither is overpopulation a sufficient cause for war. A starving people who do not possess the industrial and military wherewithal to carry on modern warfare are not likely to start World War III. But hunger has been a contributing cause to war in the past and could become even more so during the coming years, particularly as hungry nations such as India, Indonesia, Egypt, Pakistan, and others continue to develop industrially (and militarily).

One can conclude, therefore, that the problem of feeding the hungry people of the world is not one to be solved only for humane reasons. Nor should we do everything we can simply because of a sense of moral or ethical obligation to help our fellow human beings. Rather, the solution of this food problem should be regarded as a fundamental precondition for the very survival of the world as we know it.

POPULATION GROWTH AND NONFOOD RESOURCES

The problems that the less developed countries of the Third World face with respect to the balance between population size and growth and the availability of other nonfood resources are much less pressing than the food problem. On the one hand, many of these nations are especially well endowed with particular resources. The oil reserves in several of the low income countries (Nigeria, Indonesia, Venezuela, and several of the Middle East Arab nations) are a prime example, but they are far from the only one. Other nations have large and valuable reserves of such mineral resources as bauxite, copper, zinc, manganese, tin, and other metals for which there is a large and growing world demand. In fact, the presence of these resources often led to their earlier domination and exploitation by the emerging European states, and that former colonial status is at least partly responsible for their current status as less developed nations. Many of these countries in fact are not exploiting the natural resources they have available because they have not developed the industries to process them. The colonizing nations developed these countries to serve as suppliers rather than users of their raw materials. The problem, then, is not an inadequate supply of important natural resources in the developing countries; it is their need to achieve greater control over and a more appropriate utilization of existing resources to benefit their own economies rather than those of the more highly developed industrialized nations. The establishment of OPEC to control the price and distribution of oil resources can be cited as an illustration of how the developing countries can make better use of their particular natural resource base.

Another reason why nonfood resources do not represent such a serious issue for Third World countries today (even for those nations that are not particularly well blessed in this regard) can be found in the many technological advances that have been and are still being made. One outcome of such advances is that many resources that were once very important will play a much more limited role in economic development in the future. Progress in transportation, for example, makes it much easier today to redistribute basic resources and raw materials from one area to another. To cite another illustration, the development of synthetic substances has greatly reduced the significance of some raw materials such as rubber. Further, continued progress in technology can be expected to reduce the importance of still other natural resources in the years to come. The development of either nuclear or solar energy, for example, will reduce much of the pressure on the supply of fossil fuels. Much of this optimism with respect to nonfood resources is, however, predicated on the assumption that the richer developed countries will take more active steps to share their knowledge, wealth, and technology with the less developed countries (e.g., by removing trade barriers or expanding foreign assistance programs). It also assumes that the various mineral resources will not be soon exhausted as world consumption levels continue to increase. Whether or not either of these assumptions is justified remains to be seen. Nevertheless, it does appear that the developing countries of the Third World face a much more auspicious future with respect to nonfood resources than they do with respect to food.

Energy Sources

One critical exception to what might appear to be a relatively optimistic assessment of the situation in the Third World with respect to population growth and nonfood resources is energy. Food is the basic source of energy in human society, and for countless thousands of years it was the only source we consumed. However, beginning first with the discovery of fire and the burning of wood for heat and cooking, the total daily energy consumption on our planet has steadily risen. The biggest increase, of course, came with industrialization and the increasing utilization of fossil fuels (coal, oil, and gas), and the highly developed industrialized nations are the heaviest consumers of these primary energy resources today. To illustrate, one recent study has estimated that annual per capita energy consumption in the United States in 1975 was 332 million Btu (British thermal units, or the amount of heat required to raise one pound of water one degree Fahrenheit). This rate was 136 million Btu in other industrialized countries, but it was only 11 million Btu in the less developed countries (Council on Environmental Quality, 1980).

The problem with respect to energy is that the primary fossil fuel sources that provide most of it are effectively nonrenewable, and they are presently being used at a rate that could lead to their depletion within a few decades. In view of the consumption differences, it is obvious that this problem cannot be traced to the less developed countries. Nevertheless, it is a problem with which they will increasingly have to contend. Given the current rate of population growth (1.7 percent a year), the number of people on our planet will double in forty-one years. Thus, we would have to double our output of all material goods in forty-one years just to maintain present consumption levels. However, the countries of the Third World do not want to *maintain* present consumption levels; they are striving very hard to develop their societies and *increase* their level of living. This means that, as in the case of food, we will have to increase productivity at a much faster rate than the population is growing and this will require an ever increasing use of dwindling energy supplies.

In short, while the growing energy crisis has its roots in the more developed industrialized countries, the projected growth of the population in the less developed countries (a doubling in about thirty years) *and* the anticipated increases in their per capita consumption levels will greatly intensify the problem in the years ahead. This is certainly not to say that the less developed countries are not entitled to a much greater share of the world's energy resources or that they should not strive for industrial development and a higher level of living. However, it does indicate one more way in which population growth is putting increasing pressure on the carrying capacity of our planet; and it does highlight the importance (urgency!) of increasing our efforts both to conserve energy through more efficient use and to find new supplies of old sources (oil, coal, gas) as well as develop new safe and effective sources of energy. At the same time it highlights the importance of increasing our efforts to reduce fertility levels and bring Third World population growth under control. While it is true that most of the increased utilization of consumable resources in the world today reflects increasing levels of per capita consumption rather than population growth, an interaction effect (especially in the less developed countries) is producing more people with higher levels of consumption. As with all of the problems discussed in this chapter and elsewhere, the energy crisis will not be solved by an end to population growth. However, the slower the rate of population growth the easier the energy problem will be to deal with.

PROSPECTS FOR SLOWING POPULATION GROWTH

As we have just pointed out, the various problems confronting the less developed countries during the coming years would be substantially easier to cope with, and the risk of failure would be considerably diminished, if their rates of population growth would slow down. Experts have long been aware of this problem, and since the end of World War II more and more scholars in a variety of disciplines have focused their attention on finding ways to reduce the birth rates in Third World countries, thereby slowing down what have often been described as runaway rates of population growth. The early efforts were not very successful, however, and the trend since the 1950s has been for population growth rates to increase. As described in Chapter 2, this increase was due largely to a steady and sometimes very rapid decline in the death rate while the birth rate remained relatively stable at fairly high levels. In many cases, the rising growth rate was further enhanced by increases in the birth rate, which reflected improvements in the overall health status of the population concerned and associated declines in spontaneous abortions and involuntary sterility.

During the past few years, however, it has become clear that the rate of world population growth has been declining. A fairly stable annual rate of 2 percent from the late 1950s through the early 1970s has most recently declined to an estimated 1.7 percent a year. Part of this decline reflects the very low birth rates in the United States and the highly developed countries of Western Europe, but it also reflects some significant fertility declines in a number of the less developed countries, notably in the People's Republic of China, South Korea, Taiwan, Malaysia, Indonesia, Thailand, the Philippines, Sri Lanka, Costa Rica, Colombia, and Mexico. These recent trends and the associated decline in the overall growth rate have prompted some people to take a very optimistic position and to assert that the family planning efforts of the past two decades are finally starting to pay off. Such persons believe that the less developed countries of the Third World are well on their way to achieving a stationary population and that *if* recent fertility trends continue, the world population crisis will soon be solved (Tsui and Bogue, 1978). However, as indicated in earlier discussions of fertility control and current growth trends, there are many reasons for tempering this optimistic view. For one thing, growth rates have not shown any inclination to decline in most of the less developed countries, and in many of them—particularly in Africa—they have even been increasing. Furthermore, some would argue that taking such an optimistic position is dangerous because it might lead to a lessening of concern and a corresponding relaxation of efforts to reduce national birth rates. For example, in his October 1979 address to the board of governors of the World Bank, Robert McNamara not only called such optimism a "very dangerous misunderstanding" but also went on to stress that "The current rate of decline in fertility in the developing countries is neither large enough, nor rapid enough, to avoid their ultimately arriving at stabilized populations *far in excess of more desirable—and more attainable—levels*" (McNamara, 1979; emphasis added). He went on to note that if the present *modest* rates of fertility decline continue, world fertility will not reach replacement level for another forty years, and a stationary population will not be achieved until seventy years after that, at which time (2090) world population would finally be stabilized at approximately 10 billion people—well over twice as many as there are today.

The key question is not whether Third World fertility levels will fall and world population growth will slow down. Rather, the basic issue is one of timeliness. Birth rates will decline at some point, and population growth rates will slow down throughout the less developed countries. But how rapidly will birth rates fall? How soon will runaway population growth come to an end? Will population growth rates slow down in time to ease the process of development and avert many of the calamities such as widespread famines, depletion of natural resources, increasing domestic unrest and violence, and a return to the higher death rates of the past that some observers have been predicting will be the outcome of continued rapid population growth? These are questions for which there are no clear answers. Although some demographers are more optimistic than others about the future course of population growth and its effects in the developing world, almost all would agree that waiting for the "natural" gradual decline in fertility of the classical transition model that paralleled the socioeconomic development of Western Europe during the nineteenth century would be a naive and unrealistic response to the present world demographic situation. Further, most would also agree that specific policies and programs to reduce fertility and the rate of population growth should continue to be an important component of national development plans.

The need for continued concerted action in reducing fertility is further emphasized by the fact that, as high as they already are, there is a very real possibility that the future will see even higher population growth rates. One reason is that many of the less developed nations where mortality is still fairly high are in the midst of ambitious programs for improving sanitation, public health, and medical care, and as a result, they might well achieve further substantial mortality reduction in the years ahead. As long as birth rates remain high, these mortality reductions will mean an even greater widening of the current demographic gap and will increase the rate of population growth in the countries concerned. Such a development would clearly intensify the already critical population obstacle to economic growth in these areas. An even worse tragedy would be a deterioration in the economic situation caused by too rapid population growth and a consequent failure to achieve the additional mortality declines that are biologically possible.

In this same connection we must again emphasize that many of the modernizing forces now in progress could lead to even higher birth rates (Petersen, 1975, pp. 642–43). The same improvements in health status that could bring about further mortality declines could also enhance fertility by reducing the rate of miscarriage and the incidence of involuntary sterility.

Again, the resulting increases in the rate of population growth would seriously aggravate the demographic and economic problems confronting the areas affected. There are no easy answers to the population problems in the Third World, but it is clear that we must continue to focus attention on them, and that we must continue to encourage and assist the less developed countries in their ongoing efforts to reduce their fertility and stabilize their rates of population growth.

SUMMARY

As we entered the 1980s, there were nearly 3.5 billion people living in the less developed countries of Asia, Africa, and Latin America. The overall growth rate in these regions was 2.1 percent a year, a rate that would double the number of Third World inhabitants in thirty-four years. Thus, shortly after we enter the twenty-first century there could be twice as many people in these countries who have to be fed, clothed, housed, educated, and so forth. Since many developing countries are already seriously deficient in their ability to provide for these basic human needs, the prospect of continued rapid population growth must be regarded as a serious obstacle to their future development.

While population growth is certainly not a necessary cause of poverty, it is nonetheless clear that by far the greatest numerical growth taking place in the world today is concentrated in the less developed regions that are least able to cope with it. These poor countries are at the same time in the midst of major efforts to improve their levels of living, but all too often they find that their efforts are frustrated by population increases that cancel out potential economic gains. These rapid rates of population growth are due to fairly recent and pronounced declines in death rates while birth rates have generally remained at traditional high levels. As long as fertility remains high in these countries the rate of population growth can also be expected to remain high, and the unfortunate consequence of persistent rapid population growth will be a perpetuation, if not even a widening of the deep economic gulf that now separates the rich and the poor nations of the world.

As long as increases in productivity continue to be absorbed by increasing numbers of people, the poorer countries of the world will make no real economic progress. All that can come from this situation is an increase in the absolute number of persons whose basic needs have to be met, an increase in the difficulty of meeting these basic needs, and (if the needs are not met) an increase in political instability and heightened international tensions. Although an end to population growth will not in and of itself bring an end to the problems associated with world poverty, it is difficult to imagine any solution emerging as long as population growth continues to be so rapid. Even those who are more optimistic about the future situation with respect to population and resources in the world would generally agree that population growth needs to be halted. While it won't eliminate world poverty, an end to population growth will certainly slow down the rate at which poverty and its related problems are increasing. Furthermore, it will make efforts to solve the many problems that much easier, and it will reduce the absolute size of the world population that will ultimately have to be maintained on this finite planet of ours.

REFERENCES AND SUGGESTED READING

Abernethy, Virginia. *Population Pressure and Culture Adjustment.* New York: Human Sciences Press, 1979.

Birdsall, Nancy. "Population Growth and Poverty in the Developing World." *Population Bulletin,* 35 (1980).

Brown, Lester R. "World Food Resources and Population: The Narrowing Margin." *Population Bulletin,* 36 (1981).

Brown, Lester R. *Population Policies for a New Economic Era.* Worldwatch Paper 53. Washington, D.C.: Worldwatch Institute, March 1983.

Clark, Colin. *Population Growth and Land Use.* New York: St. Martin's, 1967.

Cockcroft, James D., et al. *Dependence and Underdevelopment.* New York: Anchor/Doubleday, 1972.

Council on Environmental Quality. *The Global Report to the President: Entering the Twenty-First Century,* Vol. 1. Washington, D.C.: U.S. Government Printing Office, 1980.

Eckholm, Erik, and Frank Record. *The Two Faces of Malnutrition.* Worldwatch Paper 9. Washington, D.C.: Worldwatch Institute, December 1976.

Finkel, Jason L., and Barbara B. Crane. "The Politics of Bucharest: Population, Development, and the New International Economic Order." *Population and Development Review,* 1 (September 1975): 87–114.

Frank, Andre G. *Latin America: Underdevelopment or Revolution.* New York: Monthly Review Press, 1969.

Gilland, Bernard. "Considerations on World Population and Food Supply." *Population and Development Review,* 9 (June 1983): 203–11.

Heer, David M. *Society and Population,* 2nd ed. Englewood Cliffs, N.J.: Prentice-Hall, 1975.

Humphrey, Craig, and Frederick Buttel. *Environment, Energy, and Society.* Belmont, Calif.: Wadsworth, 1982.

International Bank for Reconstruction and Development. *World Tables, 1976.* Baltimore: Johns Hopkins University Press, 1976.

Johnson, D. Gale. "Food for the Future: A Perspective." *Population and Development Review,* 2 (March 1976): 1–19.

Malthus, Thomas Robert. *Population: The First Essay.* Ann Arbor: University of Michigan Press, 1959.

McNamara, Robert S. Annual Presidential Address to the Board of Governors of the World Bank. Belgrade, Yugoslavia (October 2, 1979). Rept. in *Population and Development Review,* 5 (December 1979): 736–39.

Murdock, William W. *The Poverty of Nations: The Political Economy of Hunger and Population.* Baltimore: Johns Hopkins University Press, 1980.

Petersen, William. *Population,* 3rd ed. New York: Macmillan, 1975.

Piotrow, Phyllis T. *World Population: The Present and Future Crisis.* Foreign Policy Association, Headline Series 251 (October 1980).

Population Reference Bureau. *Intercom,* 6 (June 1978).

Population Reference Bureau. *1979 World Population Data Sheet* (April 1979).

Population Reference Bureau. *Intercom,* 8 (October 1982a).

Population Reference Bureau. *1982 World's Children Data Sheet* (April 1982b).

Population Reference Bureau. *Intercom,* 10 (February 1982c).

President's Commission on World Hunger. *Overcoming World Hunger: The Challenge Ahead* (Washington, D.C.: Government Printing Office, 1980).

Ridker, Ronald G., and Elizabeth W. Cecelski. "Resources, Environment, and Population: The Nature of Future Limits." *Population Bulletin,* 34 (August 1979): 3–39.

Schwartz-Nobel, Loretta. *Starving in the Shadow of Plenty.* New York: McGraw-Hill, 1981.

Serron, Luis A. *Scarcity, Exploitation and Poverty: Malthus and Marx in Mexico.* Norman: University of Oklahoma Press, 1980.

Simon, Julian L. *The Ultimate Resource.* Princeton, N.J.: Princeton University Press, 1981. See also the Review Symposium of this book in *Population and Development Review,* 8 (March 1982): 163–77.

Stockwell, Edward G., and Karen A. Laidlaw. *Third World Development: Problems and Prospects.* Chicago: Nelson-Hall, 1981, Chapter 3.

Tsui, Amy Ong, and Donald J. Bogue. "Declining World Fertility: Trends, Causes, Implications." *Population Bulletin,* 33 (October 1978).

United Nations. *Population and Food Supply.* New York: United Nations, 1962.

United Nations. *Concise Report on the World Population Situation in 1979.* New York: United Nations, 1980.

van der Tak, Jean, Carl Haub, and Elaine Murphy. "Our Population Predicament: A New Look." *Population Bulletin,* 34 (December 1979).

Wallerstein, Immanuel. *The Modern World System: Capitalist Agriculture and the Origins of the European World Economy in the Sixteenth Century.* New York: Academic Press, 1974.

Weeks, John R. *Population: An Introduction to Concepts and Issues,* 2nd ed. Belmont, Calif.: Wadsworth, 1981, Chapters 2 and 10–14.

Weller, Robert H., and Leon F. Bouvier. *Population: Demography and Policy.* New York: St. Martin's, 1981, Chapter 2.

Wilkinson, Richard S. *Poverty and Progress.* New York: Praeger, 1973.

Thomas Robert Malthus. His *Essay on Population* (1794) ignited a controversy that continues to this day.

The triumph of death. War, famine, and disease have historically been the ultimate checks on population growth.

Karl Marx, the founder of modern communism, was an ardent critic of the Malthusian principle of population.
Below: an anti-Malthusian cartoon in the early 19th century

Children and poverty are the dominant characteristics of many Third World countries.

A UNICEF nutrition consultant presents a nutrition demonstration for village women in Mali.

A doctor examines children for *kwashiorkor*. In some parts of Africa this protein deficiency disease has reached epidemic proportions.

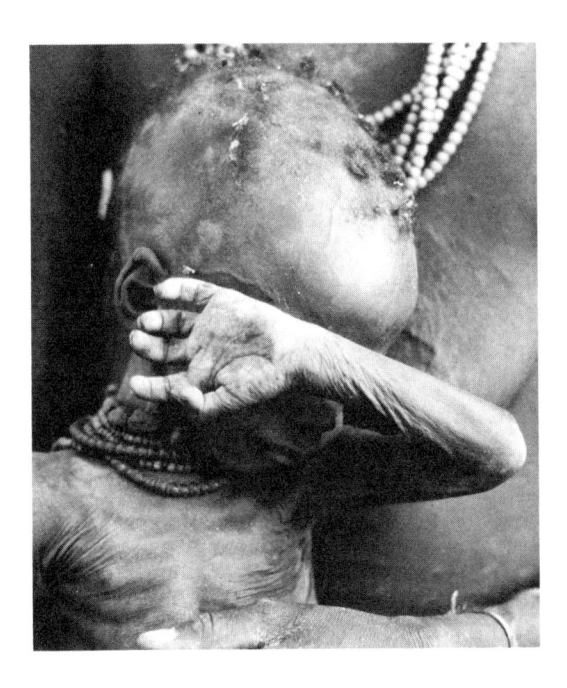

A severely malnourished child in Uganda, 1980

HUMAN MIGRATION

9

The third and final demographic process is migration, the movement of people from one geographic area of residence to another. We have left the discussion of migration until last for several reasons. First, it is a much more complex process than either fertility or mortality. It is neither inevitable (like mortality) nor necessary for the continued survival of the species (like fertility). Hence, individual motivation plays a much greater role in determining migration, and an adequate understanding of migratory behavior must include a consideration of the reasons why people move. Second, births and deaths are generally fairly easy to pinpoint in space and time, or in terms of where and when they occur. Migration, however, takes place between areas over time and is thus more difficult to define.

Finally, the study of migration is made more complicated by the difficulty of acquiring the relevant data. Statistics on fertility and mortality are more or less readily obtainable from local or federal vital records, but such records are not available for migration in most countries. A few countries do have continuous population registers; persons wishing to move must fill out migration certificates or permits that are somewhat analogous to birth and death certificates, and in such countries migration trends and differentials can be studied in much the same manner as are fertility and mortality trends. But in the majority of nations, including the United States, where there is no such registration system, data on the mobility trends in the population and the characteristics of migrants must be obtained from other sources—for example, from census data on place of birth cross-tabulated by place of residence—which for many purposes are not as adequate as birth and death records.

SOCIAL SIGNIFICANCE OF MIGRATION

The importance of migration as a topic of study goes far beyond its role as one of the basic processes of population change. It is both a source of problems for society and a major factor in social progress. From a sociological point of view, for example, migration often creates problems of *assimilation*, the process whereby the beliefs, customs, and behavior patterns of one group are merged with those of another, generally larger group. These problems are reflected in such things as the existence of ethnic ghettos, marginal men (people caught between the conflicting values of two cultures), and higher incidences of deviant behavior among migrant groups. Although not all of the world's ills result from a loss or breakdown of primary associations, the necessity of abandoning familiar surroundings for a new and perhaps strange environment when one migrates often leads to personal and social disorganization; so it is not surprising to find that migrants are often characterized by higher rates of delinquency, adult crime, mental illness, prostitution, divorce, and other social ills.

Related to this is the frequent tendency for migration to be a source of *social conflict*, particularly if the migrants differ ethnically from the dominant native group, and if the natives see their traditional culture and way of life as threatened by the migrants. In Great Britain, for example, there has been a growing movement to curtail immigration from former and present commonwealth territories (e.g., India, Pakistan, the West Indies) out of fear that the country is "being swamped by people of a different culture" (Population Reference Bureau, 1978). A series of brutal attacks against Algerian workers in France in 1973 was attributed to a perceived association (encouraged by the French government) between immigration and unemployment (Newland, 1979). In the United States economic competition has at various times generated violence toward Irish Catholic immigrants, imported Chinese laborers, Mexican aliens, and, most recently, Vietnamese shrimp fishermen along the Gulf Coast. The growing number of illegal aliens entering this country, the bulk of whom are Hispanic, is also generating hostility in some areas. Some people in the United States, in fact, see all foreigners as a threat to "our American way of life" and would like to put a stop to all immigration.

On the more positive side, migration has historically served as a major mechanism bringing people from diverse cultures (with different customs, knowledge, skills, technology) into contact with one another. Although this occasionally has had adverse consequences (as illustrated by the destruction that accompanied the Mongol invasions of Europe, or the arrival of the Spaniards in Peru and Mexico), this intermingling and interstimulation of diverse groups has generally exerted a positive influence on the growth and development of human civilization. Thus, human migration may be regarded as a major mechanism of social and cultural diffusion.

Migration has also played a key role in helping humanity maintain a more or less even balance between the distribution of numbers and resources. In the pre-industrial world the number of people who could be supported in a given area was determined largely by the food-producing capacity of that area. If the population increased to the limits that could be supported, it became necessary for some people to migrate to a new area: the alternative was for the surplus to be killed off in some fashion (e.g., war, disease, or starvation). In more modern times, the role of migration in maintaining a balance between numbers and resources is illustrated by the rural-to-urban movement of the population. As improved agricultural techniques reduce employment opportunities in rural areas, surplus farm workers move to the cities where the growth of nonagricultural industries creates jobs to absorb them. Similarly, the decline of foreign immigration to this country after the First World War created a large number of employment opportunities in many of the industrial centers of the urban Northeast, and this influenced the emergence and growth of a major movement of blacks out of the southern states. And most recently the rapid economic growth and development of the Sun Belt has generated a new migration stream to the southern and southwestern areas of the United States. Because it serves to redistribute numbers in relation to available resources and opportunities, migration is often referred to as The Great Equalizer.

From a purely demographic viewpoint, migration is, of course, significant because it is one of the three major processes through which changes in population size, composition, and distribution are effected. The population of the United States, for example, would hardly be as large as it is today had it not been for the millions of European immigrants of the past two centuries. Moreover, since migrants are usually younger than the general population, areas that are losing people through emigration (rural farm areas, for example) will find their populations becoming older than those of areas into which migrants are moving. In the early days of the twentieth century, when large numbers of persons were entering the United States from Europe (an average of roughly a million immigrants each year during the decade preceding the First World War), the median age of the population was about twenty-four. This compares to a median age of thirty in 1960, several years after the adoption of restrictive immigration legislation—despite the age-lowering effects of the unusually high birth rates that prevailed throughout the 1950s. Finally, as already indicated, the vast shift in the distribution of population from rural to urban areas as industrial development progresses is brought about largely by migration.

DEFINITIONS AND CONCEPTS

There are many different types of migration and many different ways of defining it. All types have two things in common, however. First, all migration entails the movement of individuals or groups from one area of residence to another with a view toward a *permanent change of residence*. This eliminates tourists, college students, military personnel, and others who may move into or out of particular areas but who generally do not have any permanent impact on the size, composition, or distribution of the population. Moreover, persons in these groups do not consider themselves migrants. They have generally maintained basic social ties (family, friends, job) in another area, and they plan to return home sometime in the future. Accordingly, when we use the term "migration" we are referring to a change of residence that is intended to be permanent and that results, therefore, in a definite change for the population in both the sending and the receiving areas.

The second factor that marks all types of migration is distance. The concept of migration always implies some measure of *distance* between the old and the new area of residence. Thus, someone who moves to a new house in the same neighborhood or community is not generally considered a migrant. Rather, persons who change their place of residence *within* a specified area are conventionally designated as *local movers*, as opposed to *migrants* who move *between* communities. Local movement is of course very important for the life of the community within which it occurs. It may alter the overall distribution of population as well as the size and composition of various subunits. These changes could have significant implications for a variety of local problems and issues (provision of public utilities, consumer markets, housing supply, school facilities, etc.). However, such local movement is qualitatively different from what we commonly regard as migration because it does not affect the size or composition of the overall resident population, nor does it entail the social disruption that one generally associates with migration (e.g., leaving a job and friends, breaking family ties).

In short, all migration involves residential mobility, but not all residential mobility will be regarded as migration. To qualify as migration a move must be (1) a *permanent* move, and (2) a move of enough *distance* to entail breaking ties in one area and reestablishing them in another.

Types of Migration

A common distinction is made between *group* migration (such as the exodus of Moses and the Hebrew tribes out of Egypt, or the more recent movement of the Mormons in this country to Utah) and *individual* or family migration (foreign immigration to the United States, or the worldwide cityward movement away from declining rural areas). Most migration in the modern era has been individual and has involved the movement of persons and their immediate families rather than large groups of people. This is in contrast to the pre-industrial era when the survival of the individual was so much more dependent on the group and when migration more often involved the movement of larger groups, such as entire clans or tribes.

Another way of looking at migration is to consider whether it is *voluntary or involuntary*. Much of the group migration that occurred in the ancient world was forced in that the exhaustion of the environment's food-producing capacity necessitated a move to a new habitat. Some examples of forced migration in the modern era are the nineteenth-century slave trade, the westward movement of the Mormons in search of freedom from religious persecution, the deportations carried out all over Europe by the government of Nazi Germany during World War II, the hundreds of thousands of refugees forced to flee the various wars in Asia and the Middle East during the 1970s, and the expulsion of thousands of Ghanaian workers from Nigeria in 1983. In contrast to these are those migrations in which there is no element of force, in which individuals or groups move not because they have to but because they want to and because they believe they can better their life chances by moving. In contrast to forced migration, voluntary migration is often the result of some positive pull toward a new and perhaps better home. Although there are exceptions—dramatically illustrated by the presence even today of large numbers of refugees from war or political oppression—most migration in the world nowadays tends to be individual and voluntary, and it is largely motivated by positive factors.

Internal and International Migration

Perhaps the most basic distinction made in the definition of migration is in terms of whether movement occurs between different countries *(international migration)* or within the borders of a single country *(internal migration)*. Most migration in the world today is internal migration—the *voluntary* internal movement of *individuals* who are pulled to areas of greater opportunity. International and internal migration are further distinguished by the terms applied to migrants. On the international level, a person who enters a given country is called an *immigrant*, whereas a person who leaves a country is called an *emigrant*. On the internal level, however, a person who moves into one area from another area in the same country is called an *in-migrant*, whereas a person who leaves one area for another within the same national territory is called an *out-migrant*. The use of this distinct terminology simplifies discussions of migration patterns for areas (like the United States) where there has been a good deal of international and internal migration.

Migratory moves could be classified in many other ways. One could distinguish among migrants on the basis of *distance* covered by the move (for example, long- versus short-distance migration), or one could distinguish in terms of the type of areas between which migration takes place (rural-to-urban, urban-to-urban, etc.). In the 1950s an American demographer formulated a classification of migration based on a combination of the forces impelling particular moves and on whether they preserve an old or create a new way of life—in other words, a classification based on both the determinants and the consequences of particular moves (Petersen, 1958).

One could go still further and identify more specific types of migrants such as refugees, migrant farm workers, illegal aliens, or even *transmigrants* (persons whose move from one area of origin to a specific area of destination takes place in stages—such as Europeans who migrate to the United States by way of Canada). However, this international–internal dichotomy is generally regarded as the major classification of migration. For one thing, it provides a ready scheme for discussing those movements that alter the distribution of world population (international migration) as opposed to more localized movements that have only a slight impact on the world population situation but can have profound significance for the local areas involved. For another thing, it is a dichotomy into which all other types of migration can be fitted. Most of this chapter will focus on international migration; internal migration and its role in population redistribution will be discussed in Chapter 11.

Causes of Migration

An important aspect of migration study focuses on the reasons why people move. On the simplest level it can be said that people move because they believe that life will be better for them in a different area. That is, in the absence of force, a person's decision to migrate will be based on a subjective evaluation of the relative advantages and disadvantages of two areas: the area of current residence and the area to which a move is being contemplated.

The most common framework that is used in the causal explanation of migration behavior is the *push–pull theory*. According to this theory people move from a particular *area of origin* to a particular *area of destination*, either because some set of forces or circumstances drives them out of the old habitat (*push* factors), or because a different set of forces or circumstances attracts them to a new area (*pull* factors). Some of the more common push factors are religious or political persecution, ethnic discrimination, depletion of natural resources, lack of employment opportunities, and natural disasters such as a drought, flood, or earthquake. Some of the factors that pull people to an area are desirable employment opportunities, a favorable climate, or a greater degree of freedom and equality of treatment.

More often than not, migration will involve both push and pull factors in some degree, with the magnitude and location of the two complementary forces determining the volume and direction of migratory streams. (A *migration stream* is a large number of people who, over a period of time, move from a common area of origin to the same area of destination.) For example, to explain the causes of the nineteenth century's Great Atlantic Crossing, during which some 20 million persons migrated from Europe to the United States, one can cite a number of significant push factors in the various sending countries: political and religious persecution, economic instability, and rural overpopulation as major advances in agricultural technology reduced the size of the farm labor force more rapidly than the surplus could be absorbed into still infant industries. Balanced against these push factors were the strong pull forces exerted by the United States: political and religious freedom, rapid economic expansion, the availability of large tracts of undeveloped land, and a reservoir of relatively high-paying jobs in developing industries. To cite more recent examples, the large numbers of Cubans and Haitians who have migrated to southern Florida have been motivated by both a push factor (poverty and/or political oppression) and a pull factor (the promise of political freedom and better economic opportunities).

To say that migration streams such as those noted above occur because people are pushed out of one area at the same time they are pulled to another area is somewhat of an oversimplification. Push and pull forces will exist in both areas. Thus, the potential migrant will have to assess the relative strengths of a combination of factors, and the decision to migrate may also involve some sacrifice on the part of the migrant. For example, people may be pushed out of one area by the existence of religious persecution, but they may also be drawn to the same area through close personal ties with family and friends or perhaps because of a good job. Similarly, people may be pulled to a particular area because it offers more and better economic opportunities, but the area in question may have an undesirable location or be characterized by a forbidding climate. What potential migrants have to do then is add up the various pluses and minuses for the area of origin and for alternative areas of possible destination, and base their decisions on whether the balance of push and pull factors favors moving or staying.

One other point needs to be made with respect to the decision to migrate. A number of *intervening obstacles* will have to be overcome before a move can take place between

(Lee, 1966). Some of these obstacles may be merely inconveniences (e.g., a geographic barrier such as a mountain or an ocean or a great distance that must be crossed); others may be more serious (e.g., political barriers such as the Berlin Wall designed to keep people in, or restrictive laws in the desired area of destination that aim to keep people out). Personal characteristics may also intervene to influence a migration decision. That is, whether a person elects to stay in one area or move to another will depend in part on his or her age, health, marital status, number and age of children, their health, and so forth. The seriousness of particular intervening obstacles will of course vary from person to person. A barrier that appears almost insurmountable to one person will seem trivial to another. The point is that the decision to migrate depends on a great many considerations: the personal characteristics of the individuals contemplating a move, the characteristics of the areas of origin and destination, the nature and magnitude of intervening obstacles, and, perhaps most important, the individual's subjective perception of the relative advantages and disadvantages of making the move in question. It should thus be clear that an adequate explanation of the causes of any individual move or migration stream will entail much more than a simple enumeration of push factors in the area of origin and pull factors in the area of destination.

MIGRATION IN HISTORY

Little can be said about specific migration trends in prehistoric times, but it is generally acknowledged that the roving of primitive peoples in search of game gradually led to the dispersion of the human population away from its origins in Africa to all parts of the earth (McNeill, 1978). By about 8000 B.C. all areas of the world, from Siberia to Tierra del Fuego, are believed to have been settled, and the natural carrying capacity of our planet was probably reaching a saturation point. At this time various peoples in different parts of the world began to intensify their search for food, first by diversifying their diet and then by developing agriculture to produce their food on a regular basis. The major civilizations of antiquity emerged in those areas most suitable to agricultural development (in the fertile river valleys of the Tigris-Euphrates, the Nile, the Indus, and the Yellow rivers), and the rise and fall of these and subsequent civilizations were closely correlated with various migrations, often associated with the conquest of one group by another and associated shifts in the distribution of human populations.

We can identify a number of specific currents of migration that contributed to the emergence, maintenance, and growth of modern civilization. For example, the movement of urban merchants to peripheral or frontier areas in search of trade goods and markets contributed to the spread of commerce and the growth of cities. Similarly the movement of rural peasants to the emerging cities compensated for the very high death rates that prevailed in urban areas, which were, until fairly recently, very unsanitary and inhospitable places in which to live (McNeill, 1978; Pirenne, 1946). However, not until the seventeenth century did migration begin to change significantly the pattern of world population distribution. Beginning with the colonization of the United States in the 1600s and lasting through the closing of the American frontier and the adoption of immigration restrictions early in the twentieth century, European peoples, spurred by accelerating rates of population growth at home, spread out to all corners of the globe. In some areas, such as Asia and most of Africa, they merely established administrative outposts to oversee their various commercial ventures, but in other areas they displaced the indigenous inhabitants and established colonies that continued to attract new settlers and that eventually emerged as modern nation-states. For example, migration from Europe played a major role in the growth and development of Argentina and Brazil and all of the major English-speaking countries: Australia, Canada, New Zealand, South Africa, and the United States.

Historically, international migration out of both Asia and Africa was relatively small when compared with the mass European exodus of the nineteenth century, and it was substantially different in character. Much emigration from Asia involved indentured service or some kind of contract labor. During the late nineteenth century, for example, after the abolition of slavery, Indian laborers were recruited to places as diverse as East Africa, Fiji, and Trinidad; Japanese and Filipinos went to Hawaii; and Chinese came to the West Coast of the United States. In the twentieth century, with the end of the intercontinental flow of indentured labor, such migration continued on a small scale within Asia. Indians and Chinese especially settled in fairly large numbers in other Asian countries, and descendants of the Chinese can today be found distributed throughout the region.

Intercontinental migration from Africa in the past was singularly different in that most of it was involuntary and involved the forced transportation of human beings to be sold as slaves. From the sixteenth century until the abolition of slavery in the nineteenth century it is estimated that as many as 11 million Africans were forcibly enslaved and sent to the New World. Moreover, there is evidence to suggest that some clandestine sale of Africans continues to this very day.

In terms of numbers, the movement of European peoples to North America during the eighteenth and nineteenth centuries, particularly to the United States, clearly stands out as the major international migration stream of the modern era, and it marks the first significant impact of migration on the distribution of population after the initial dispersion of the human species in antiquity. When the people of Europe began to move, the United

States did not exist as a nation, and the territory it now covers was very sparsely settled. Today, however, we are the fourth largest nation in the world, and our citizens can trace their ancestry to all corners of the globe. It can truly be said, then, that if it were not for international migration, the United States as we know it today would not exist. The role that migration has played in the growth and development of American society is the subject of the following section.

IMMIGRATION TO THE UNITED STATES

The vast majority of all Americans are immigrants or the descendants of earlier immigrants (or colonists). Even Native Americans are descendants of wandering bands of pre-Neolithic peoples who migrated from Asia across the Bering Strait land bridge thousands of years before the first Europeans came to our shores. It is eminently clear, therefore, that immigration has been a most persistent and most pervasive influence in the development of the United States. It may even be said that the whole of American history has been molded by the successive waves of immigrants who responded to the lure of the New World. The labors of the immigrants and their descendants transformed an almost unoccupied continent into the world's richest and most powerful nation. Other countries (Australia and Argentina, for example) have experienced heavy immigration, but no country has received such a large and diverse number of immigrants as the United States has. Moreover, in no country, with the possible exception of Israel in the post–World War II years, has immigration had the pervasive influence on population growth and socioeconomic development that it has had in America.

The United States has passed through three distinct phases or eras of immigration and is currently in the midst of a fourth. These eras, which are discussed more fully in the following sections, are: (1) initial colonization and early settlement; (2) the mass immigration of the nineteenth century; (3) the era of federal restrictions on immigration; and (4) the current period of controlled immigration.

Colonization and Early Settlement: America before 1820

The first major era of immigration to the United States lasted roughly from the arrival of the first settlers in the early seventeenth century until the end of the Napoleonic Wars early in the nineteenth century. Although no official statistics exist to show the exact numbers of migrants, the evidence indicates that immigration during this early period of American history did not involve a very large number of people. For one thing, when the first federal census was taken in 1790, well over a century and a half after the first settlers landed, only about 4 million people were enumerated. Given the relatively high birth rates of the early colonists (50 to 55 per 1,000), it is highly unlikely that the population would have been that small if there had been any large-scale immigration.

There are a number of reasons why the volume of immigration was relatively small during the seventeenth and eighteenth centuries. Among the most important are: (1) the lack of a really strong pull prior to the Industrial Revolution and the opening of the American West; (2) poor transportation for the difficult Atlantic crossing; (3) ignorance, especially among landlocked European peasants, of the nature of conditions in the colonies; and (4) restrictions on emigration in a number of European countries of origin (many European governments, for example, looked upon emigration as a loss of potential soldiers and taxpayers).

Although this first era of immigration did not involve a very large number of people, it did have a special significance for the type of society into which the United States ultimately developed. Specifically, this early immigration laid the foundations for what is popularly called the American way of life. The United States has long been regarded (at least by Americans) as the classic land of equality and opportunity for all peoples; this "American ideal," with its religious and political freedom and its emphasis on a classless society, is largely an outgrowth of the initial pattern of immigration and settlement. With regard to freedom of thought and belief, it may be noted that the United States was initially settled by basically bigoted groups who came in search of religious freedom but who themselves were frequently intolerant of those who held dissenting views. As the number and diversity of religious groups seeking asylum increased, however, it became impossible for one group to dominate another; hence a tolerance of diverse views emerged more or less by necessity. With regard to the equality-for-all ideal, the important point is that colonial America had an almost limitless supply of land; virtually everyone could become a property owner. Although the early United States had a social structure resembling that of Europe, the widespread ownership of land made class lines less rigid. And since land was the basis of political power as well as wealth in the preindustrial world, the relative ease with which it could be obtained inhibited the rise of a landed aristocracy and virtually assured the development of our democratic form of government. In short, the fact that the United States was a sparsely settled country with plenty of available land, plus the diverse nature of early colonial settlement, virtually necessitated the emergence and development of America as a land of social, political, economic, and religious freedom.

Mass Immigration: 1820–1919

Shortly after the War of 1812, immigration to the United States began to assume mass proportions. The volume of immigration began to swell at this time for several reasons. On the one hand, various push factors were operating in the European countries of origin: rural overpopulation, economic instability, political unrest, and so on. On the other hand, very strong pull forces were exerted by a rapidly expanding American economy, particularly during the last half of the nineteenth century. At this time, according to the authors of a demographic history of the United States,

> The great land areas beyond the Mississippi were available for agricultural use. Rapid industrialization created major demands for unskilled labor to work in factories, build canals and roads, and later railroads, and carry on many tasks not yet mechanized. At this same time conditions in Europe were becoming more improved, and more and more people learned of the opportunities in the United States. Improved transportation within Europe facilitated movement to the coast, while steamships permitted quicker, safer, and cheaper passage across the ocean than had sailing ships of earlier days (Taeuber and Taeuber, 1958, p. 52).

This era of mass immigration lasted roughly one hundred years, from about 1820, when attempts to collect immigration statistics were first initiated, to 1920, when the emergence of restrictive legislation led to a sharp decline in foreign immigration. During this century it is estimated that close to 35 million aliens entered the United States (see Table 9-1). During the first decade of this era (1820–1829) the number of immigrants averaged slightly more than 15,000 a year. This figure rose rapidly and substantially as the country expanded westward, until it surpassed 300,000 per year during the decade preceding the Civil War. Immigration declined slightly during the war years but thereafter continued to increase at a rapid rate. By the beginning of the twentieth century the average number of immigrants per year was in excess of 800,000, and it remained at roughly this level until America's entry into World War I, whereupon the era of mass immigration came to a sudden halt.

In discussing this century of mass immigration, it is customary to divide it into two periods: pre–Civil War and post–Civil War. This distinction is significant not only because it tells us *when* immigrants came but also because it tells us *where* they came from. Although the vast majority of the immigrants during this century came from Europe (80 percent or more each decade), one can identify two fairly distinct groups: those who arrived prior to the Civil War decade (1860–69) came almost entirely from northern and central Europe (the British Isles, Germany, Scandinavia), whereas

Table 9-1
Number of Immigrants to the United States in Each Decade since 1820

Years	Number of immigrants	Percent*	Years	Number of immigrants	Percent*
1820–29	151,636	1.5	1900–09	8,202,388	10.8
1830–39	572,716	4.5	1910–19	6,347,380	6.9
1840–49	1,479,478	8.7	1020–29	4,295,510	4.1
1850–59	3,075,900	13.3	1930–39	699,375	0.6
1860–69	2,278,612	7.2	1940–49	856,608	0.6
1870–79	2,742,137	7.1	1950–59	2,499,268	1.7
1880–89	5,248,568	10.5	1960–69	3,213,749	1.8
1890–99	3,694,294	5.9	1970–78	3,875,653	1.9

SOURCE: U.S. Bureau of the Census, *Historical Statistics of the United States: Colonial Times to 1970* (Washington, D.C., 1975). Data for 1970s are from the 1978 *Annual Report of the Immigration and Naturalization Service* (Washington, D.C., 1980).
* These values express the number of immigrants during each decade as a percentage of the total population at the beginning of the decade. The trend in these percentages clearly illustrates the changing importance of immigration as a factor in American population growth. See text for explanation.

the postwar decades saw a larger and larger proportion of immigrants coming from the countries of eastern and southern Europe (the Baltic countries, Poland, Italy, and the Balkans). These two groups are generally designated as the *old immigrants* (those who came earlier from north central Europe) and the *new immigrants* (the later arrivals from southeast Europe). This shift in the place of origin of U.S. immigrants beginning after the Civil War is also significant because it marked a major turning point in the official immigration policy of the United States, for at this point agitation on the part of the native population to restrict foreign immigration really began.

The volume of immigration to the United States from particular countries of origin was determined by the whole process of socioeconomic and demographic change that spread across Europe during the nineteenth and twentieth centuries. Given that the pull forces in the New World remained more or less constant throughout the period of mass migration, the major factors influencing emigration from Europe were (1) rapid population growth as a declining death rate created a widening gap between levels of fertility and mortality; (2) innovations in agricultural technology that displaced large segments of the rural farm labor force; (3) land reform programs (such as the British Enclosure Acts and the French Primogeniture Laws) that aggravated the displacement of the rural population; and (4) widespread urban unemployment as emerging industries failed to expand rapidly enough to absorb the excess population. These developments occurred first in the British Isles and in the countries of Northwest Europe that had already established social, cultural, and economic ties with the young republic on the other side of the Atlantic. It is thus not surprising that these parts of the world were the first to contribute to the mass immigration of the nineteenth century: at the time of the Civil War, roughly nine out of every ten U.S. immigrants were coming from the north central part of Europe, mostly from Germany, Great Britain, and Ireland (see Table 9-2 and Figure 9-1).

In the ensuing decades, however, the situation changed radically. On the one hand, these socioeconomic and demographic changes began to spread across Europe to the south and east where they created a tremendous push to emigrate. On the other hand, the push from the countries of Northwestern Europe began to decline. In part this happened because their developing industries began to reach maturity and were thus more able to absorb surplus populations. Another reason was that the birth rate began to fall, thus slowing down the rapid rate of population growth that had character-

Figure 9-1
Percent of American Immigrants Coming from North Central and Southeast Europe since 1820

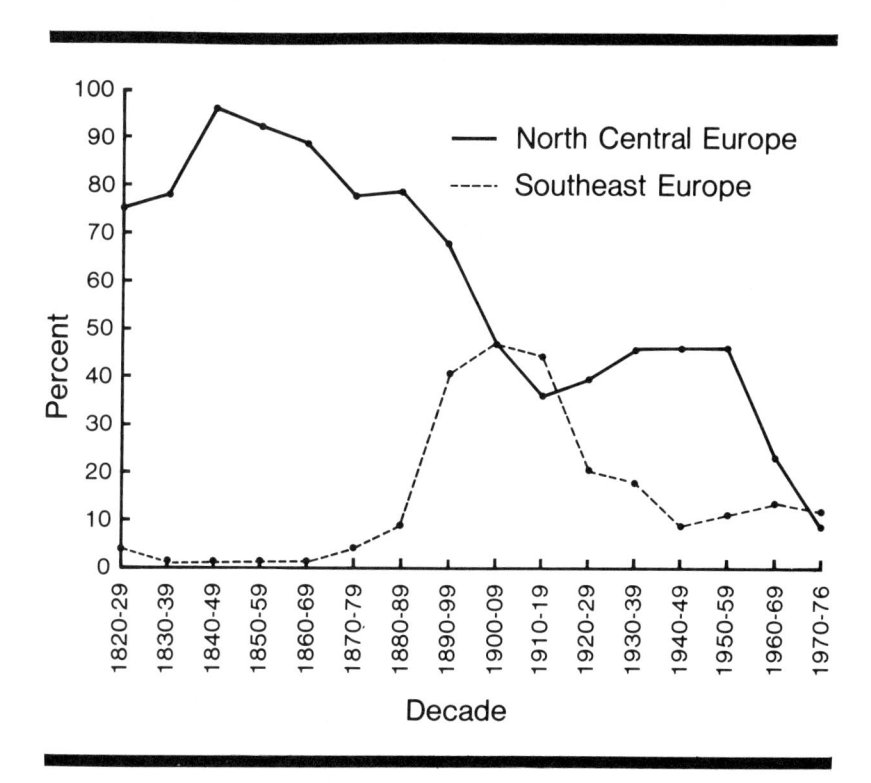

SOURCE: Based on data presented in Table 9-2.

Table 9-2
Percent of American Immigrants Coming from Specified Areas of Origin since 1820

Years	All areas	Total	Northwest Europe[1]	Central Europe	Eastern Europe	Southern Europe	Asia	Africa	Oceania	Other America	All other
1820–29	100	77.3	70.1	4.5	0.1	2.5	*	*	*	7.5	15.2
1830–39	100	78.9	54.5	23.3	0.1	1.0	*	*	*	5.5	15.6
1840–49	100	96.0	68.7	27.0	...	0.3	*	*	*	3.5	0.4
1850–59	100	93.0	57.6	34.7	...	0.7	1.3	*	*	3.0	2.7
1860–69	100	90.2	54.2	35.0	0.1	0.9	2.6	*	*	6.3	0.9
1870–79	100	82.1	48.4	30.0	1.3	2.4	4.9	*	0.4	12.6	...
1880–89	100	88.4	45.0	34.3	3.6	5.5	1.3	*	0.2	10.0	...
1890–99	100	96.9	33.8	33.0	12.5	17.6	1.6	*	0.1	1.0[2]	0.4
1900–09	100	93.1	18.1	28.4	20.2	26.4	2.9	0.1	0.2	3.4	0.2
1910–19	100	79.7	14.8	20.9	19.2	24.7	3.1	0.1	0.2	16.9	...
1920–29	100	60.0	20.7	19.1	4.1	16.1	2.6	0.1	0.2	37.0	...
1930–39	100	63.7	19.9	26.0	2.4	15.4	2.6	0.3	0.5	32.9	...
1940–49	100	55.2	28.5	17.6	0.8	8.3	4.0	0.8	1.7	38.3	...
1950–59	100	56.3	17.3	28.2	0.4	10.5	5.3	0.5	0.5	36.9	0.5
1960–69	100	35.4	13.1	9.8	0.5	12.1	11.0	0.7	0.7	52.1	...
1970–76	100	21.6	5.1	4.3	1.3	10.8	30.7	1.6	1.0	45.1	0.0

SOURCE: Prepared by authors from data published in U.S. Bureau of the Census, *Historical Statistics of the United States: Colonial Times to 1970* (Washington, D.C., 1975), and the *1977 Annual Report of the Immigration and Naturalization Service* (Washington, D.C., 1977).
[1] *Northwest Europe:* Great Britain, Ireland, Scandinavia, Netherlands, Belgium, Luxembourg, Switzerland, and France; *Central Europe:* Germany, Poland, Czechoslovakia, Yugoslavia, Hungary, and Austria; *Eastern Europe:* USSR, Latvia, Estonia, Lithuania, Finland, Romania, Bulgaria, and Turkey; *Southern Europe:* Italy, Spain, Portugal, Greece, and other European nations not elsewhere classified.
[2] No data on immigration from Mexico between 1886 and 1893.
... Less than 0.1 percent.
* Included in "All Other."

ized these countries during the early years of the nineteenth century. With these developments came a gradual shift in the source of United States immigrants. During the 1880s only 63 percent of European immigrants to America came from Great Britain, Ireland, and Germany. This trend continued throughout the remainder of the nineteenth and into the twentieth century, and during the 1910 decade these three countries accounted for only 15 percent of all European immigrants whereas the proportion coming from the south and east (Italy, Poland, Russia, and the Baltic states) was up to 46 percent.

Restricted Immigrations: 1920–1965

After World War I there was another pronounced change in the character of American immigration. The nature of this change is revealed by: (1) a sharp drop in the total *number* of immigrants, and (2) a shift in their *place of origin* back to the earlier pattern where the largest single group of immigrants came from North Central Europe. (During the 1930s Great Britain, Ireland, and Germany alone accounted for 47 percent of the European immigrants.) Unlike earlier immigration trends, however, this change was not caused by either socioeconomic or demographic developments in either Europe or the United States. On the contrary, the era of mass immigration came to an end at a time when the push from Southeastern Europe was at its height, and the decline in the volume of immigrants was determined largely by legislative developments in the United States.

From the days of earliest settlement until well into the twentieth century, immigration to the United States was relatively unrestricted. Attempts had been made fairly early to exclude particularly undesirable people such as convicts, the mentally incompetent, and prostitutes, and some legislation had been aimed specifically at keeping out Asians (e.g., the Chinese Exclusion Act of 1882 and the 1907 Gentlemen's Agreement with the government of Japan); however, there was no real national immigration policy in the United States until after the First World War. At that time the federal government began to implement a policy that placed severe restrictions on immigration. This in itself would not necessarily be any cause for concern. Rather, the tragic aspect of these restrictions was the basis on which persons were barred. Specifically, the decade of the 1920s marks the beginning of an era that saw ethnic and racial discrimination become official government policy in a nation where freedom and equality supposedly prevailed for all persons.

The main reason for the emergence of a restrictive immigration policy lies in the shift in the source of American immigrants, and the adoption of restrictive legislation may be regarded as both an economic and a sociocultural response to the *new immigration* from Southeast Europe. When the new immigrants began to arrive in increasing numbers toward the end of the nineteenth century, the United States had more or less completed its transition from a rural-agrarian to an urban-industrial society. The vast majority of immigrants arriving at this time from Southeast Europe were rural peasants. When the agricultural peasants from North Central Europe had arrived during earlier decades, the United States was still largely an agricultural country; hence the *old immigrants* had settled in quite readily. The new peasants, however, did not fit very well into the industrial mold of American society for a number of reasons: (1) most of them were illiterate and possessed no industrial skills; (2) all were poor; (3) the American frontier was closing, which meant that large tracts of cheap agricultural land were no longer available; (4) the new immigrants were easily identified by their strange languages, customs, modes of dress, and so forth (whereas many of the old immigrants had come from the British Isles and were barely distinguishable from the natives); and (5) labor was becoming organized in this country, and organized labor was very much opposed to the immigration of poor foreigners who would be willing to work for lower wages and would thus have a depressing effect on wages in general. For such reasons, people all over the country began to show concern over the hordes of "strange and ignorant peasants" flocking to our shores, and movements to restrict immigration began to gain strength. The growing agitation eventually led to the adoption of ethnically discriminatory legislation, which remained until the mid-1960s as part of the law of the land.

The first major piece of restrictive legislation came toward the end of the First World War. In response to the growing agitation, Congress set up its first large-scale immigration commission out of which came the Immigration Act of 1917. Among the many provisions of this act were: (1) the establishment of an Asiatic Barred Zone to exclude Asians; (2) the designation of Ellis Island as a clearinghouse for all European immigrants; and (3) the adoption of a literacy test requirement that banned illiterate persons from entering the country. In view of the fact that most potential immigrants from Southeast Europe were illiterate (full-scale industrial development and its accompanying emphasis on education had not yet evolved in that part of the world), one can regard the literacy test requirement of the 1917 legislation as a deliberate attempt to limit immigration from this part of the world. Nevertheless, the literacy test was aimed at individuals rather than groups; the attempt to improve the "quality" of immigrants by restricting on a group, or ethnic, basis was—except for Asians—still a few years away.

Agitation for even more stringent restrictions continued to mount after World War I had ended. To the earlier socioeconomic motives (fear that immigrants would depress wages, or general aversion to the "strange" ways and customs of the alien peasants) were added political motives. The postwar period was characterized by a growth of antiforeignism ("Let Europe take care of its own problems," and so forth), and this was aggravated by a growing fear of the "Red Menace" in Russia. Many bills designed to bring about sharp reductions in immigration were introduced to the Congress at this time, and out of all the legislative efforts came the now infamous Immigration Act of 1924, which not only substantially lowered the number of immigrants to be allowed into the country each year but also established the basic pattern of the *national origins system* whereby ethnic characteristics became the basis for restricting immigration. On the one hand, the 1924 act established an annual quota of 150,000 immigrants. On the other hand, it set quotas for each country based on the number of people enumerated in the census of 1890 who were born in each country. Since most of the foreign born in 1890 were from Northwest Europe (approximately one-third were born in the British Isles), this provision clearly amounted to discrimination against those countries of Southeast Europe that had, as of 1890, sent only a very few nationals to the United States.

The Immigration Act of 1924 contained provisions for even more stringent restrictions to go into effect as of July 1, 1929. The legislation that became official American policy in 1929 also authorized the admission of about 150,000 immigrants per year. Furthermore, it reaffirmed ethnic discrimination by setting quotas for each country determined not on the basis of the number of American residents born in that particular country but on the basis of the proportion of the *total* white population of 1920 who could trace their *national origins* to that country. This specification of national origins, or ancestry, as the criterion for setting quotas clearly implied a belief that some ethnic groups are superior to others. Moreover, the use of total whites rather than just the foreign born as the base population for setting quotas clearly discriminated against the new immigrants who had not been in this country long: they had not had time to produce the second and third generations that the old immigrants had produced and that helped to increase the quotas allotted to the old immigrant countries of Northwest Europe.

The restrictive legislation of the 1920s had a profound effect on the total volume of immigration to the United States. In contrast to the 1.3 million aliens admitted in 1907 (the peak year during the era of mass immigration), the number of immigrants arriving each year between 1929 and the change in our immigration laws in the mid-1960s exceeded 300,000 only twice (in 1956 and 1957), and in most years it was well below 250,000. Ironically, however, the national origins quota system did not achieve its desired end; the ultimate purpose of this legislation was to restore an ethnic composition of immigrants similar to that of the white population of the United States in 1920, but this purpose has never been realized. To illustrate, roughly 80 percent of the total immigration quota was allotted to the countries of Northwest Europe, but these countries have accounted for only about 40 percent of all immigrants admitted since 1920. One reason for this is that high-quota countries like Great Britain and Ireland have seldom filled their quotas. Another reason is that the United States has received a large amount of *non-quota immigration*. On the one hand, countries exempted from quota regulation during this period (e.g., Mexico and other Western Hemisphere nations) have contributed a great deal more to total immigration than was initially anticipated: between 1930 and 1965 roughly one-third of all immigrants to the United States came from the Western Hemisphere (see Table 9-2) as compared with the 6 percent that was expected under the national origins legislation. On the other hand, a fairly large number have been allowed in under special legislation provisions (such as the Displaced Persons Act of 1948 and the 1963 Refugee Relief Act), and the majority of these persons were from Southeastern Europe. To illustrate, of the more than 600,000 European refugees admitted to the United States between 1945 and 1965, nearly three-fourths came from the Southeast European countries of Poland, 154,000; the Baltic states of Latvia, Estonia, Lithuania, 74,000; Italy, 62,000; Hungary, 60,000; Yugoslavia, 45,000; the USSR, 38,000; and Romania, 21,000 (Smith, 1966).

The national origins system was never very popular among American liberals (even President Eisenhower, a fairly conservative Republican president, publicly criticized it), and it was opposed from many sides all the while it was in effect. The struggle for repeal was not an easy one, however. Following the end of the Second World War, as the East–West cold war developed, the U.S. Congress passed the 1952 McCarran-Walter Act, which perpetuated the system of ethnic discrimination. This act slightly increased the total annual quota to 154,647 (determined as one-sixth of 1 percent of the 1920 white population), but the allocation of quotas was still determined by the national origins formula laid down in 1929. Agitation for the repeal of this discriminatory legislation continued to mount in the United States, and throughout the 1950s and early 1960s this agitation gained strength as more and more people came to realize that our immigration legislation was not helping our image as a world leader. Both the East Europeans and the peoples of the less developed countries of Asia and Africa were, of course, affronted by a policy that excluded them from immigration on the basis of more or less arbitrary racist principles. A number of countries (e.g., the Philippine Republic) used official diplomatic channels to point out "certain irritating inequalities" in our immigration laws.

In the face of such arguments it became more and more apparent that the restrictionist view that any sovereign nation has the right to regulate immigration as it sees fit was not the strong arguing point it had been during the isolationist days of the 1920s. Rather, it became more and more obvious that the United States could not afford to ignore the opinion of other countries, and that for the sake of our national interests we had to try to establish and maintain a maximum of friendly cooperation among all nontotalitarian powers. This growing moral and political pressure on the United

States eventually had the desired effect in the summer of 1965. At that time Congress adopted a new immigration policy that struck down the national origins quota legislation and finally put an end to what had long amounted to an officially sanctioned policy of ethnic discrimination. According to the Immigration and Nationality Act of 1965, the national origins system was scrapped as of July 1968; however, this did not mark any return to the relatively unrestricted immigration of an earlier era. This act also established an overall ceiling on the annual number of immigrants to be accepted (290,000), and it established general quotas of 170,000 for the Eastern Hemisphere, with a limit of 20,000 from any one country, and 120,000 for the Western Hemisphere, with no limit for any one country. This act was later amended to lower the numerical quota to 270,000 a year and to remove the hemispheric distinction and impose a 20,000 maximum quota on *all* countries.

Controlled Immigration: After 1965

Four basic characteristics have marked United States immigration since the legislative changes of the mid-1960s. First, despite an official numerical limit of 270,000 the number of legal arrivals each year, exclusive of refugees, has generally been in excess of 400,000, mainly because of the large number who come in each year who are not subject to numerical quotas (e.g., rela-

Table 9-3
United States Immigration Data, 1981

Legal immigrants (not including refugees)	480,000
(Quota)	(329,000)
(Nonquota)	(151,000)
Refugees	217,000
Total legal immigrants (legal plus refugees)	697,000
Estimated number of illegal immigrants	100,000 to 500,000+
Total number of immigrants	
Assuming 100,000 illegals	797,000
Assuming 500,000 illegals	1,197,000
Total immigration (legal, refugees, illegal) as a percent of annual population growth, 1981	
Assuming 100,000 illegals	29%
Assuming 500,000 illegals	43%

SOURCE: Adapted from E. M. Murphy and P. Cancellier, *Immigration: Questions and Answers* (Washington, D.C.: Population Reference Bureau, 1982).

tives of U.S. citizens). In 1981, for example, there were 329,000 quota immigrants plus 151,000 who were exempt from quota limits, yielding a total number of 480,000 legal immigrants for that year (see Table 9-3). When the number of refugees and estimates of illegal immigration are added, the number of new arrivals amounts to about one million persons and represents anywhere from 30 to 40 percent of our annual population increase.

Second, the removal of quotas based on national origins has resulted in a dramatic shift in the source of immigrants. Prior to the 1960s over half of all immigrants came from Europe, whereas today less than one-quarter are of European origin. The largest share of immigrants to this country today come from Latin America, but by far the biggest change with respect to the origin of immigrants is in the number and proportion coming from Asia (see Figure 9-2). Given the relative lack of pressure to emigrate in the more highly developed European countries, it is very likely that Asians and Latin Americans will continue to dominate U.S. immigrants. In this connection one might wonder about the very small proportion coming from Africa. In part this may reflect the newness of independence and the particularly low degree of modernization characterizing most African states, as well as the Africans' reluctance to leave their homes and become part of a minority racial group in a white-dominated society. All this may change in the years ahead, however, as rapid population growth generates increasing pressures to emigrate and as rising levels of development create more people willing to consider emigration as a means of individual advancement.

A third major characteristic of the immigration situation in the United States today is the large and increasing number of refugees who have been admitted. Recognizing the need to assume a greater role in trying to alleviate the world refugee problem, the U.S. Congress passed the Refugee Act of 1980, which laid down guidelines for admitting persons who had been forced to flee their homes because of political persecution or natural disaster. The definition of "refugee" is still somewhat limited, however, in that it includes those fleeing Communist countries but omits persons who might want to escape from right wing dictatorships in Latin America. Our government officials cite this distinction (thus promoting charges of racism) when justifying the admission of Cuban exiles while trying to restrict the entrance of Haitians. In any case, the effect of this legislation change is clearly revealed by the number of refugees admitted to permanent residency in 1980 (367,000—of whom 135,000 were Cuban and Haitian special entrants) and in 1981 (217,000).

Whether or not such a high level of refugee immigration continues remains to be seen. Beginning in 1983 the annual refugee quota will be set each year by the President in consultation with Congress. The size of the quota could vary widely from year to year based not only on the number and severity of conflicts that may erupt around the world but also on the economic situation and climate of public opinion within this country.

Figure 9-2
Changing Origin of American Immigrants since 1960

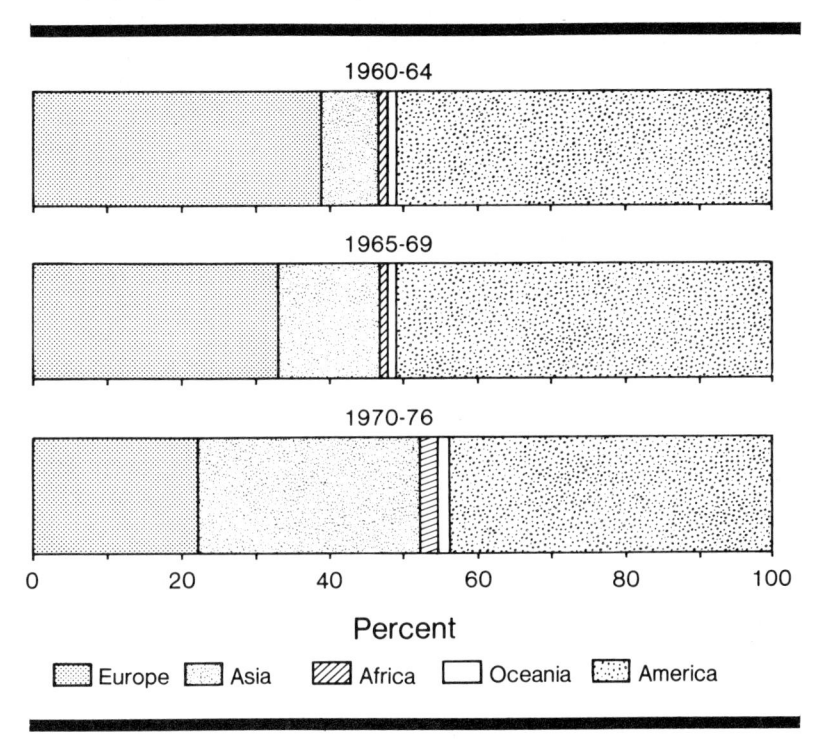

[Bar chart showing percentage origin of American immigrants for periods 1960-64, 1965-69, and 1970-76, with categories: Europe, Asia, Africa, Oceania, America]

SOURCE: Based on data contained in the sources cited for Table 9-2.

Finally, American immigration in recent years has been characterized by a rapid and sizable increase in the number of illegal aliens entering the country. Further, given the widespread poverty in Latin America (where most illegal immigrants come from) and the political turmoil characterizing a number of countries in the region, this trend is likely to continue to pose a problem for the United States for sometime to come.

Because they are in this country illegally, these immigrants are unrecorded. Therefore, it is difficult to assess the magnitude of the problem with any degree of accuracy. Estimates of the number of undocumented aliens presently residing in the United States range from 3 to 6 million; some place it as high as 10 to 12 million. Similarly, estimates of the number of illegals arriving each year vary from 100,000 to 500,000 or more. We do know that about a million persons (well over half of whom are Mexican) are apprehended trying to enter the country each year, but we do not know how many of these are the same people being caught more than once. Moreover, there is no way of knowing how many of those who do not get caught plan to remain or how many simply want to work for a short time and then return home.

Illegal immigration is a highly emotional issue in the United States and is frequently cited as being responsible for many of our economic troubles. Illegal aliens take jobs away from our citizens, one often hears, and they place a heavy strain on welfare programs and other community service agencies, such as schools. Opponents of these charges argue that the jobs the aliens take are so arduous (back-breaking farm work and textile sweatshop labor) and pay so little that most Americans would refuse to accept them. Further, aliens are less likely than citizens to apply for welfare or other services out of a fear of being caught and deported. The relative merits of these opposing arguments notwithstanding, the fact is that illegal immigration is becoming a matter of serious concern in the United States today, and as this was being written Congress was considering a number of proposals. These include such actions as strengthening border patrols, requiring employees to provide proof of citizenship or of legal residence, imposing fines on American firms or businessmen who knowingly hire illegal aliens, and subjecting persons who recruit illegal immigrants to criminal prosecution. The specific policies or regulations that will eventually be adopted remain to be seen, but one can be sure that much more effort will be put into the control of illegal immigration than has been done in the past.

CONSEQUENCES OF MIGRATION

Because there are so many different kinds of migration between areas that differ widely in so many respects, it is not possible to draw a single generalization that will sum up all the consequences of human migration. Such consequences can be felt in different areas of life (social, demographic, economic, political), and they can be considered both on the individual and societal level in either the area of origin or the area of destination. On the level of the individual one can study the consequences of migration on the lives of those who actually migrate as well as on the lives of those left behind in the area of origin. To illustrate, if an area is losing population due to migration, those who remain behind may benefit because of a decline in competition for various opportunities and resources; conversely, they may suffer adverse consequences, especially if the human exodus is accompanied by economic decline and the loss of various services—as in fact has happened in many parts of rural America. On the other hand, the individual migrants generally experience an improvement in some aspect of their life (e.g., a better job, more political freedom, greater social equality); at the same time they may have to contend with certain problems such as the hostility of the native population in the new home, the trauma of leaving friends and family behind, the necessity of learning a new language or otherwise becoming adjusted to a new environment, and so forth.

Consequences of Out-Migration

While such consequences are important, especially for the individuals who experience them, a much more significant aspect of migration is the overall demographic and structural impact it has on the society as a whole in the areas of origin and destination. Historically, migration has been a means of maintaining a balance between the size of a population and its resource base (food supply, employment opportunities, etc.), and migration out of an area has often been a response to the pressure of increasing numbers on limited resources. In such situations, migration has generally had a beneficial impact on the area of origin. The exodus from Ireland during the potato famine of the 1840s, the movement today of excess laborers from Egypt and Jordan to other oil-rich nations in the Middle East and from Greece and Turkey to more developed countries in Northwest Europe, and the movement of surplus numbers out of rural areas undergoing agricultural modernization—all represent examples of how a society may benefit from out-migration. Such benefit, it may be noted, derives not only from the reduction in population pressure caused by migration but also from the cash remittances that migrants frequently send back to the area of origin. Such remittances from migrants working abroad have become a major source of foreign exchange and a crucial element in the balance of payments for many countries (e.g., in the late 1970s Jordan, Portugal, Turkey, and Yemen all received more from migrant remittances than they earned fom exports); and without them these countries would have a great deal of difficulty meeting their import bills (Newland, 1979).

The precise consequences of migration for any area will depend in large part on *migrant selectivity,* or on the characteristics of those who migrate. An area that is overpopulated, for example, may benefit from out-migration and a resulting reduction in population pressure. However, a disproportionate number of those who move tend to be members of the more productive adult age groups. Thus areas that have experienced migration loss may find themselves peopled largely by young children and older persons, thereby increasing the overall burden of economic dependency. Similarly, if the more highly educated and skilled workers are overrepresented among migrants, then areas of origin may suffer the loss of their most talented members. A problem confronting many of the less developed countries today, for example, is the so-called brain drain—the emigration of skilled labor and scientific personnel. This brain drain represents a double loss to the countries affected—the loss of the investment made in the education and training of the emigrants, and the loss of their potential productivity and contribution to national growth and development.

Consequences of In-Migration

The consequences of migration for areas of destination will also vary with the number and especially the characteristics of the migrants. On the one hand, since migrants tend to be concentrated at the adult working ages, areas receiving migrants will generally experience an increase in economic productivity. On the other hand, if the economy of the receiving area is a highly developed one but the migrants are largely unskilled, then their arrival may contribute to an increase in unemployment and a corresponding decline in per capita earnings. Similar negative effects can result if the number of arrivals is too large or if they come at too fast a rate to be absorbed into the economy. These opposite economic consequences of migration can be illustrated by the recent experience of Hong Kong and Saudi Arabia. In Hong Kong the large influx of refugees from the Chinese mainland was a major contributor to rising unemployment in the early 1970s (Bouvier et al., 1977); whereas in Saudi Arabia, as well as in a number of other Middle Eastern OPEC nations, economic growth and development have clearly been enhanced by the immigration of large numbers of foreign workers (Nagi, 1982).

Depending on how different the migrants are from the native population in terms of cultural background, race, language, and economic status, their arrival may create various social problems of adjustment and assimilation. In all cases migrants will have a demographic impact not only on the overall size of the population but on its composition as well. For example, the arrival in South Florida of large numbers of refugees from Cuba and Haiti during the late 1970s has had a profound impact on the ethnic and economic characteristics of the population in that area.

This discussion clearly indicates the wide range of consequences that migration may have for any given area of destination. In the following section attention is focused on a more thorough analysis of a specific case: the impact that foreign immigration has had on the growth and development of the United States.

SOME CONSEQUENCES OF AMERICAN IMMIGRATION

Foreign immigration has had and continues to have many and varied consequences for the United States. In this section we shall consider briefly the effect of immigration on population growth and economic growth, the social and cultural contributions that immigrants have made to our society, and some of the problems we have had to face as a result of immigration from other societies and cultures.

Immigration and Population Size

One of the most obvious consequences of immigration is its effect on population size. It is only natural to deduce that emigration leads to a reduction in population size, whereas immigration brings about an increase. In the short run this deduction would certainly be valid, but in the long run it is questionable. No one can refute the impact of migration on the ethnic composition of the United States today, but there has long been disagreement concerning its impact on size. On the one hand, history has shown that population losses due to migration have soon been replaced by natural increases (an excess of births over deaths) resulting from either a rise in the birth rate or a drop in the death rate. This should be kept in mind when considering migration as a possible solution to the problems of overpopulation plaguing many of the economically less developed nations in the world today. Although emigration may be of value as a temporary solution to give these young economies a chance to get started (as it was for many European countries during the nineteenth century)—provided the potential migrants could find a welcome somewhere—the only long-run solution to current problems of overpopulation is to reduce the rate of population growth through the rational control of fertility.

Turning to the opposite issue, scholars in this country have long debated the effect of foreign immigration on the size of the U.S. population. Opposing those who argue that immigration was a major factor in American population growth have been men like Francis Walker, a nineteenth-century conservative who wrote numerous essays and magazine articles criticizing our then relatively free immigration policy. Walker maintained that immigration had little or no effect on the long-run growth of the population because one of its consequences was to encourage a reduction in the level of native fertility. The general argument was that for every immigrant there would be one less baby born to the native group; thus, rather than contributing to population growth, immigration merely lowered the "quality" of the population by replacing a "native son" with a "foreigner."

Since the birth rate in the United States was declining at a time when the volume of immigration was climbing toward its peak during the late nineteenth and early twentieth centuries, it is difficult to refute such xenophobic arguments. There is in fact some validity to them if one realizes that immigration, by hastening industrialization and urbanization, did contribute indirectly to fertility decline. Even so, these arguments can be criticized because of their failure to consider adequately one crucial fact: most of the immigrants were young adults who came to this country at a time when an expanding economy was desperately in need of a larger labor force. In the absence of immigration, the needed labor would not have been available—because the native births that the critics argue would have taken place in the absence of immigration would not have contributed to the adult work force until a generation later. The most significant point, then, does not concern the question as to whether the population of the United States today would be as large if there had not been such heavy immigration during the nineteenth and early twentieth centuries. Rather, the important point is that this mass immigration did have a positive impact on the economic growth of the nation. This subject will be considered in greater detail in the following section.

One final point concerning the impact of immigration on the demographic structure of the population relates to composition. America today is a "nation of nations" in that it comprises people whose ancestors came from all over the world. Out of this mingling of widely different sociocultural backgrounds has come a unique kind of Americanism that is homogeneous by virtue of its heterogeneous background. Most Americans today, for example, when asked what their origin is, can list a number of different countries in which their various ancestors were born. Added to this overall heterogeneity are the specific contributions of individual immigrants. This topic will also be discussed more fully later in this chapter.

Immigration and Economic Growth

One aspect of American immigration that merits special consideration is the role it has played in the economic growth and development of the nation. We noted earlier that the economic prosperity of the United States was a major factor motivating people to leave their homelands during the nineteenth century and migrate to the "land of opportunity." But this heavy immigration was also a major factor behind the rapid economic growth of the nation during that era. Immigration provided a continuous supply of fresh labor when and where it was most needed. In other words, the relationship between immigration and economic growth in the United States has traditionally been a two-way relationship: economic growth has encouraged immigration, and this immigration has promoted further economic growth.

This positive relationship does not always exist, and there have been many historical instances where too large a volume of immigration has had the opposite effect: it has retarded economic growth. In both West Germany and Israel during the postwar decade, for example, the influx of refugee immigrants was so great that it placed a severe strain on the economy, and it was several years before this immigration provided an impetus to economic expansion. Whether or not immigration is favorable for the economy of any country depends on that nation's *carrying capacity* (i.e., the capacity of a given country to absorb additional laborers, either through immigration or through natural increase, without putting a serious strain on the economy). The postwar economies of West Germany and Israel were just getting off the ground when the flood of incoming refugees arrived, and the immigrants tended to slow down rather than promote economic development. In nineteenth-century America, however, the economy was very well developed for that time, and its rate of expansion was in large part determined by the rate at which labor became available. A few countries today (Canada, for example) might likewise benefit from immigration that would increase the size of the labor force and permit a more optimal development of available natural resources. For the most part, however, potential immigration areas are virtually nonexistent today because so few nations are willing to accept significant numbers of immigrants. Moreover, in those few instances where immigrants are actively sought, their number and characteristics are rigidly controlled. Even in the United States, where the ethnic basis of our national immigration policy has finally been removed, the number of immigrants we will accept each year is limited, and preference is given to doctors, engineers, chemists, and others who possess various technical skills. Thus, although the United States certainly benefited from the mass immigration of a previous era, it is doubtful if the world will ever again witness migration on a comparable scale.

Sociocultural Contributions of Immigrants

Most discussions stress, with some justification, the economic consequences of immigration for the historical growth and development of the nation. But we should not neglect the fact that the immigrants also made many contributions to American social and cultural development. For one thing, the heavy immigration of unskilled peasants occurred at a time when the United States was undergoing a rapid transition to an urban-industrial society, and this immigration was a major factor contributing to the maintenance of a highly mobile and open class society during the nineteenth and early twentieth centuries. Thus, one contribution of immigration was its role in the emergence of America as the classic example of a "classless" democratic society with virtually unlimited opportunities. Similarly, as we have mentioned, whatever homogeneity exists in the United States today is not solely the outgrowth of our colonial American heritage. Rather, it is the result of the interstimulation between the native-born population and the millions of immigrants who came from vastly different social and cultural backgrounds. These diverse traditions were mingled with one another and ultimately synthesized into a new cultural tradition that was uniquely

American. Another significant contribution of immigration, then, is the role it has played in promoting societal growth by necessitating a synthesis of differences.

The sociocultural contributions of immigration become more apparent when considered on an individual level. What would American music be like today, for example, without the benefit of immigrants such as Béla Bartók, Jascha Heifetz, José Iturbi, Serge Koussevitzky, Fritz Kreisler, Sergei Rachmaninoff, Arthur Rubinstein, Leopold Stokowski, Igor Stravinski, Arturo Toscanini, Bruno Walter, and Irving Berlin—to cite just a few? Similarly, who can deny the influence on the American theater and movie industry of immigrants like William Fox, Otto Preminger, Max Reinhardt, and the Warner brothers? And who is to say where America would stand as a world power today if it had not been for the work of immigrants such as Albert Einstein, the atomic scientists Enrico Fermi and Edward Teller, and rocket scientist Wernher von Braun? In every field of endeavor, in fact, immigrants have left their mark.

To cite a few others who have come to the United States and made significant contributions to their various fields: Sholem Asch, Lion Feuchtwanger, and Erich Maria Remarque in literature; Salvador Dali and Karl Bittner in art; Jacob Riis and Joseph Pulitzer in journalism; Felix Frankfurter in law; Victor Borge, Greta Garbo, and Jean Herscholt in entertainment; Bruno Rossi in physics; Knute Rockne in athletics; Igor Sikorsky in aeronautics; Bronislaw Malinowski in anthropology; Florian Znaniecki and Pitirim Sorokin in sociology. The list could go on for hundreds of pages (thousands of pages if we were to include the contributions of the sons and daughters of immigrants), but the few we have cited should be sufficient to illustrate the point: immigration has played a major role in the sociocultural development of America and the American way of life, as well as in the economic growth of the nation.

Problems Created by Immigration

Although no one would deny the importance of immigration in the growth of the United States, it did create its share of problems for the society. In the first place, whenever two or more diverse cultural groups come into close contact, they must develop some sort of composite culture incorporating various attitudes, values, behavior patterns, and so on. This usually means that the smaller group must modify many of its beliefs and traditions to accommodate those of the larger dominant group. This transformation process (the various degrees of which are denoted by such terms as *accommodation, adjustment, assimilation,* and *integration*) is a difficult, often painful process that entails both personal and social readjustment to new situations. In general, the magnitude of the problems involved reflects the extent of the differences between the minority and majority groups. Where differences in such obvious traits as language and skin color are minimal, the adjustment process will be relatively easier. Where such differences are pronounced, adjustment will be slower and more difficult to achieve—if it is achieved at all. The most obvious illustration of this is the American black who even after hundreds of years, and in the face of some fairly strong civil rights legislation since the 1960s, has not yet been able to become fully assimilated into American society.

Most people know that the death rate is higher among many ethnic minorities (native blacks and Hispanics and various foreign-born white groups) and that these groups have higher rates of crime and delinquency, prostitution, illegitimacy, and other manifestations of personal and social disorganization. Although statistics bear this out, they do not reveal the most important fact: *the greater incidence of deviant behavior on the part of minorities is not an inherent ethnic trait but is a reflection of the problems encountered in the assimilation process.* Broadly speaking, two basic sources of problems attend the assimilation of an ethnic minority group: (1) rejection by the dominant group; and (2) resistance by the minority group. The former leads to such things as the segregation of minorities in ghettos where differences are reinforced. It also leads to other discriminatory practices. For example, many nineteenth-century help-wanted ads carried the note "No Irish Need Apply," and discrimination against black Americans was legal until the 1960s. Racist attitudes persist even today. All of these, of course, cause resentment among members of the minority and may encourage lack of respect for the majority laws. This in turn causes a greater incidence of lawlessness and other forms of deviant behavior.

The other source of problems is resistance to assimilation on the part of the minority group, which often does not want to modify any of its traditions. This is most prevalent among the older foreign born, and it is frequently a source of intergenerational conflict within immigrant groups. The nature of this conflict is represented by the marginal man, who is caught between two conflicting cultural groups. The native-born children of immigrants have often found themselves caught between the Old World of their parents and the New World in which they are trying to make their way. Often the marginal person facilitates assimilation by acting as a bridge between the two cultures. Not infrequently, however, such a person may seek to escape the conflict by rejecting both cultures. This rejection generally takes the form of some socially deviant behavior (crime, prostitution, drug addiction), and basically this marginal group accounts for the generally greater incidence of personal and social disorganization among immigrant ethnic groups.

Widespread marginality resulting from the efforts of older immigrants to maintain their cultural traditions may often occur because they have had unpleasant experiences in their dealings with the larger society. Many immigrants came to this country not knowing the language, not having much money, and not possessing any technical skills, and they frequently encountered a native population that regarded their poverty and lack of knowledge of American ways as a sign of laziness and stupidity. The immigrants' only defense against such hostility was to retreat into the security and understanding of their own group. The implication here is that the immigrants' resistance to assimilation is itself often a result of the dominant native group's resistance to the newcomers. This suggests that assimilation can best be achieved not by trying to force immigrants to adopt American ways but by accepting them as social equals and encouraging their active participation in American society.

In talking about assimilation and the problems encountered by various ethnic groups in the United States, it is important to distinguish between *structural assimilation* and *cultural assimilation*. Structural assimilation refers to integration into the external features of society (i.e., the extent to which members of a minority group come to resemble the dominant group in terms of such things as level of educational attainment, occupational composition, and income levels), whereas cultural assimilation is concerned with the extent to which the immigrant minority adopts the prevailing beliefs, values, and life-style of the native population. Historically, structural assimilation has been more difficult to achieve than cultural assimilation has. In fact, the ease with which a particular group could achieve cultural assimilation was a major determinant of the speed and success of structural assimilation. For example, the early immigrants to this country from Northwest Europe had a much easier time being assimilated into white Anglo-Saxon Protestant America than did the later immigrants from Southern and Eastern Europe with their vastly different cultures, languages, and religions. However, there is evidence that this situation has improved somewhat since the early days of the present century. This was clearly illustrated in 1960 when John F. Kennedy, the descendant of Irish Catholic immigrants, was elected President of the United States. In part, the immigrants have themselves to thank for this increased tolerance of ethnic differences: despite the barriers and hostility they frequently encountered, these later immigrants succeeded in becoming "Americanized" (i.e., culturally assimilated), thus demonstrating to the native population that many of their fears were groundless. Unfortunately, it is just as clear that this tolerance has not been extended to include a number of native groups, notably blacks and some Hispanics, as well as some of the more recent immigrants from Southeast Asia. These groups, because of their distinctive physical characteristics, are unable to "disappear" into the general population; even though they may achieve complete cultural assimilation, their ethnic visibility continues to be a major determinant of prejudice and discrimination and a major obstacle to their full structural assimilation into American society.

It is worth noting here that the various fears that underlie ethnic prejudice and discrimination in the United States today are likely to be as groundless as those that generated the earlier hostility toward the immigrants from Southeast Europe. The higher incidence today among blacks and other ethnic minorities of drug addiction, unemployment, illegitimacy, and juvenile delinquency does not reflect loose morals or laziness. Rather, it reflects economic and social frustration and a resentment against being treated as second-class citizens. This suggests that a more equitable treatment of these minorities would lead to a substantial modification of the deviant behavior patterns that the bigots of our society so piously point to in justifying their discriminatory practices.

Overview

Many volumes, a few of which are cited at the end of this chapter, have been written on the consequences of immigration for the growth and development of the American nation. In this section we have indicated very briefly what some of the major consequences of this immigration have been. It is difficult to visualize an America as rich and as powerful as it is today without the immigration of past years. Moreover, there is no reason to anticipate any reduction in the significance of the contributions to be made by the immigrants coming today and who may come in future years. Perhaps this knowledge will help promote a greater tolerance among the American population for groups of people whose language sounds strange to our ears, whose customs seem a little unorthodox, or whose skin is a different color. A greater tolerance of such differences will greatly reduce the unfavorable consequences of immigration and very likely speed up the realization of positive contributions.

INTERNATIONAL MIGRATION IN THE WORLD TODAY

Two distinctive kinds of migration are taking place between countries in the world today: (1) the voluntary movement of individuals or families, primarily in response to differences in economic opportunity; and (2) the involuntary movement of refugees who, for one reason or another, have been forced to leave their homeland.

Refugee Migration

Refugees have always existed, but only since World War I have they existed in large enough numbers to constitute a problem for human society. At that time, the redrawing of a number of national boundaries in Europe, internal political strife in many countries, and the rise of fascist dictatorships created several sizable refugee migration streams. Among these were the 1.5 million Russian nationals who fled the aftermath of the 1917 Revolution, the 323,000 Armenians who fled the persecutions that followed the fall of the Ottoman Empire and the rise of Turkish nationalism, and the thousands of Spaniards who sought refuge in France and other countries after the Spanish Civil War.

Millions more refugees were created by World War II and its aftermath, in Asia as well as in Europe. Millions fled westward as communist rule took hold in the several countries of Eastern Europe. About 5 million Japanese in once conquered territories were repatriated back to Japan. A massive population transfer involving some 12 to 14 million people took place between India and Pakistan following partition in 1947. And the establishment of the People's Republic of China in 1949 caused hundreds of thousands of Chinese to flee the mainland and go to Taiwan, Hong Kong, and Macao. In more recent times, thousands more refugees have been created each year by smaller wars or internal revolutions in Afghanistan, Angola, Cambodia, Cuba, El Salvador, Ethiopia, Hungary, Korea, Somalia, Uganda, and Vietnam, to name just a few. Then, in 1983, an economic crisis in Nigeria caused by a glut on the world oil market led that country to expel hundreds of thousands of people, mostly Ghanaians whose labor had been needed and welcomed at an earlier time. Moreover, since political turmoil and periodic economic crises are likely to continue to be a fact of life in the world today, especially among the less developed countries, the problem of refugees will likely be around for many years to come.

Voluntary Migration

Although the post–World War II years have witnessed a marked increase in the number of political refugees seeking asylum outside their native land, the dominant motivation behind international migration in the world today is economic: people move from areas of low economic development and limited opportunities to areas of higher economic development and more opportunities. Thus, on a broad regional level Asia, Africa, and Latin America have all been areas of emigration whereas North America and Oceania have been areas of immigration (United Nations, 1980). Europe, too, has experienced a net migration loss, but it has been much smaller than that characterizing the less developed regions. Moreover, within the broad regions mi-

Table 9-4
Selected Migration Streams in Europe and the Middle East, 1975–76

Country of origin			Country of destination		
Europe	**Belgium**	**France**	**Federal Republic of Germany**	**Switzerland**	**United Kingdom**
Greece	10,000	...	178,800	5,165	10,500
Italy	96,000	199,200	276,400	261,566	56,500
Portugal	6,000	360,700	63,600	4,144	3,000
Turkey	16,000	31,200	527,500	15,168	4,500
Yugoslavia	3,000	42,200	390,100	24,110	8,500
Middle East	**Kuwait**	**Libya**	**Oman**	**Qatar**	**United Arab Emirates***
Egypt	37,600	175,000	5,300	2,700	12,700
India	21,500	2,000	24,800	19,800	73,000
Jordan	47,700	7,000	2,600	1,700	6,400
Pakistan	11,000	5,000	20,200	14,500	94,000
Syria	16,500	15,000	1,500	400	3,400
Yemen	11,400	...	1,000	2,600	3,500

SOURCE: United Nations, *World Population Trends and Policies: 1979 Monitoring Report* (New York, 1980).
* Rough estimates.

gration streams flow from poorer to more modern countries. In North America, for example, migrants flow from Mexico to the United States. In Europe, where much international migration today represents the temporary exchange of labor in "guest worker" programs, migration streams flow from the more traditional Southeastern countries such as Greece, Italy, Yugoslavia, to the more industrialized nations in the Northwest such as France, West Germany, Switzerland (see Table 9-4). A similar situation exists in the Middle East where temporary migrant workers move from the more overpopulated countries of Egypt, Jordan, and Syria to Libya and the oil-rich nations on the Persian Gulf. In some of the latter countries, the volume of immigration has been so large that foreign laborers represent a large majority of the total labor force. In the mid-1970s, for example, immigrant labor accounted for roughly three-fourths of total employment in both Kuwait and Qatar and nearly 90 percent in the United Arab Emirates.

Information on international migration trends within Africa is sketchy, partly because much of it is seasonal and partly because it is largely unorganized and subject to less control than in other parts of the world. However, as would be expected, those streams that can be identified also flow from the less developed to the more developed countries of the region (e.g., from the drought-stricken Sahel countries of Mali and Upper Volta to Senegal and especially to the Ivory Coast where foreign nationals constituted slightly more than 25 percent of the economically active population in 1975).

Perhaps most important, international migration is much more controlled today than it was during the free mass migration days of an earlier era. Many countries now have official policies, if not rigid laws, aimed at regulating the movement of people across their national boundaries. This topic is the subject of the final section of this chapter.

POPULATION POLICY AND THE FUTURE OF INTERNATIONAL MIGRATION

International migration policies have the general objective of regulating the number and/or the type of people moving into or out of a country. For example, the National Origins legislation that governed immigration to the United States from 1924 to 1968 sought not only to restrict the total number of immigrants to this country but also (especially) to control their ethnic background. The United States is not the only country that has adopted such regulatory legislation. Among the various efforts to regulate the volume and direction of international migration one can identify four basic kinds of policies based on whether they seek to encourage or restrict either immigration or emigration.

Immigration Policies

A recent survey of 158 countries around the world found that 42 countries had policies governing immigration (see Table 9-5). Of these, 32 were characterized as restrictive whereas only 10 had policies favoring a higher level of immigration.

Policies that encourage immigration include such incentives as paying transportation expenses, making land available free or at a very low cost, assisting immigrants in finding housing and employment, and providing various services (e.g., language instruction) to facilitate the adjustment process. Among the countries having policies that favor more immigration are Argentina, Australia, Bolivia, Israel, Saudi Arabia, and South Africa.

It must be noted that favoring immigration is not the same as having an open-door policy, and countries that do encourage immigration are generally interested in attracting particular kinds of people to whom differential consideration is given. Israel, for example, automatically grants citizen-

Table 9-5
National Views and Policies on Immigration and Emigration, 1978

Government's views and policies	World	More developed regions	Less developed regions
Total number of countries	158	42	116
View and policy on immigration:			
Viewed as not demographically significant	116	27	89
Policy favoring higher rate	10	2	8
Policy to maintain current rate with strict control	16	2	14
Policy to reduce future immigration but maintain already established immigrant population	16	11	5
View and policy on emigration:			
Viewed as not demographically significant	103	31	72
Policy favoring higher rate	6	2	4
Policy to maintain current rate	24	1	23
Policy to reduce future emigration	25	8	17

SOURCE: United Nations, *Concise Report on the World Population Situation in 1979* (New York, 1980).

ship to Jewish immigrants, whereas non-Jews have to apply for citizenship in much the same manner as do immigrants to the United States. Australia provides another example. Although it has an official policy of nondiscrimination on the grounds of race or nationality, Australia has established certain selection criteria for immigrants, such as particular occupational skills, that give considerable preference to white Europeans over Asians. It should also be noted that all such policies that encourage immigration are very tenuous and, as the history of immigration policy in the United States clearly illustrates, they can change very quickly in response to internal economic, demographic, or political change.

Policies that *restrict immigration* do so either by placing a ban on aliens entering the country or by severely limiting the rights of those who do come in (e.g., requiring foreigners to live in specified areas, limiting access to certain occupations, prohibiting immigrants from becoming citizens or engaging in political activity). Those countries that place a ban on aliens entering may do so absolutely. The Soviet Union, for example, admits virtually no foreign immigrants. Instead of an absolute ban, nations may place some limitation on the number of legal immigrants who will be allowed in during a single year. Both Canada and the United States restrict immigration this way. Often such numerical limitations are combined with various priority criteria that have the effect of discriminating against certain kinds of people. Such criteria usually result in preference being given to more highly educated persons or persons with particular occupational skills, to relatives of current residents, or to members of some particular ethnic group. One of the factors used to determine an immigrant's admissibility to Canada, for example, is the ability to speak either English or French.

Sometimes restrictions will be imposed with the deliberate aim of keeping out particular groups of people. This was clearly the purpose of much of the earlier immigration legislation in the United States (e.g., the Chinese Exclusion Act). The present restrictions on immigration to the United Kingdom from other Commonwealth countries stem largely from the fact that those who immigrated before restrictions were imposed were predominantly nonwhite peoples from Asia, Africa, and the West Indies.

Emigration Policies

The survey cited earlier found 55 countries with policies aimed at regulating emigration, the vast majority of which sought to maintain emigration at its present level or else reduce it. Only 6 countries had policies that encouraged its citizens to emigrate.

Those few nations that encourage emigration generally do so for either economic or political reasons. A number of North African countries, for example, either encourage or facilitate emigration as a means of easing unemployment—an economic reason. Cuba, for political reasons, has long encouraged dissidents to leave. In 1980, for instance, the Castro government literally dumped thousands of its citizens onto boats to seek refuge in the United States. On an extreme level, repressive internal policies aimed at particular segments of a population often lead to large-scale emigrations. A case in point was the appearance of the Vietnamese "boat people" after the North took over the government of that country in 1975.

Policies that restrict emigration are generally adopted for economic reasons: governments do not like to see their citizens leave and take the potential productivity of their labor with them, particularly if they possess some specialized skill. The most dramatic modern example of a policy aimed at preventing people from leaving a country is the Berlin Wall, erected by the Soviets and East Germans in the early 1960s to stem the tide of refugees fleeing to the West. The USSR also has a history of trying to prevent the permanent emigration of its citizens. Until the early 1970s it was virtually impossible for college graduates to leave, and those who were permitted to emigrate had to pay an exit fee—sometimes as much as $30,000—depending on the amount and kind of education they had received. Even today, the Soviet Union makes it difficult for Jews to emigrate.

The Future of International Migration

As long as social, economic, and political inequalities exist, there will be pressures to migrate. Whether or not such migration actually takes place, however, will depend on a number of contingencies, one of which will be government policy. Restrictions on emigration will repress some potential movement, but the most important limiting factor will be the lack of a place to go. Strong pressures to emigrate will likely exist for some time to come in the poorer, less developed countries where population is growing most rapidly, but the hard truth of the matter is that there are no longer vast areas of sparsely populated land such as were available to the European emigrants in the eighteenth and nineteenth centuries. Moreover, those nations that do have the economic capacity to absorb additional peoples all place some restrictions on immigration, and such restrictions are likely to become even more severe as the industrial nations become more concerned about population growth, resource utilization, and environmental quality. Hence, despite continued pressures, international migration is not likely to be a significant force in the world of the future—certainly not to the extent that it has been in the past.

SUMMARY

Migration, the third basic demographic process, is generally defined as a *permanent change of residence* enough distance away from home so that the migrant experiences a change in both the physical and social environment. Defined as such, migration is an important social variable as well as a major source of population change. It is significant not only because of its effect on the size and characteristics of population in both sending and receiving areas but also, perhaps especially, because of its impact on a variety of other social, economic, cultural, and political issues.

One can distinguish among migrants on the basis of whether they move from one country to another (international migration) or within the political confines of a single nation (internal migration). Although people move from one area to another for many reasons, the primary motivating force behind both internal and international migration is an economic one: people generally move for the specific purpose of enhancing the opportunities available to them or otherwise improving their overall level of living.

Throughout antiquity migration played a major role in the dispersion of the human population around the world, and it has been a basic force in promoting the growth and development of modern civilization. In more recent times, it was the major process behind the expansion of the European peoples in the eighteenth and nineteenth centuries and the spread of European culture and civilization to all corners of the globe. The United States in particular owes much of its character to the successive waves of foreign immigrants who flocked to its shores during the past three centuries.

The history of immigration to the United States can be divided into four major eras: (1) the era of colonization and initial settlement, lasting from the early seventeenth century until about 1820; (2) the nineteenth century era of mass immigration, lasting from about 1820 until the end of World War I; (3) the national origins era of federal restrictions on immigration, lasting roughly from 1920 until 1965; and (4) the post-1965 era of numerically controlled immigration. The number of legal immigrants admitted annually under current legislation was nearly 700,000 in the early 1980s, of whom approximately one-third were refugees admitted over and above the quota limitations.

One aspect of the American immigration system that has been growing more serious in recent years is the problem of illegal aliens. Anywhere from 100,000 to more than half a million persons are believed to enter this country illegally each year; they, together with the legal immigrants, account for between 30 and 40 percent of our total annual population growth.

Although the consequences of international migration can vary markedly depending on the volume and direction of particular streams, it is reasonably safe to conclude that they are generally positive, both on the level of the individual migrant who more often than not experiences an economic gain, and on the larger societal level where migration frequently functions to maintain a balance between the distribution of human resources in relation to needs and opportunities. This is certainly true in the world today where the bulk of the migration that does take place, excluding refugee migration, flows from areas of low economic development and limited opportunities to areas of greater development and more opportunities.

The existence of international differences in opportunity will likely persist, thus continuing to be a potent motivating force for international migration. However, movement across national political boundaries is subject to a great deal of control today, and future migration will be determined largely by the nature and severity of restrictive policies in both countries of potential emigration and potential immigration as will the volume and direction of any streams that emerge.

REFERENCES AND SUGGESTED READING

Bentley, Judith. *American Immigration Today: Pressures, Problems, Policies*. New York: Julian Messner, 1981.

Bouvier, Leon F. *The Impact of Immigration on U.S. Population Size.* Washington, D.C.: Population Reference Bureau, 1981.

Bouvier, Leon F., et al. "International Migration: Yesterday, Today, and Tomorrow." *Population Bulletin,* 32 (September 1977).

Handlin, Oscar. *The Uprooted.* New York: Grosset & Dunlap, 1951.

Handlin, Oscar, ed. *Immigration as a Factor in American History.* Englewood Cliffs, N.J.: Prentice-Hall, 1959.

Keeley, Charles B. *U.S. Immigration: A Policy Analysis.* Washington, D.C.: Population Council, 1979.

Kritz, Mary M., et al., eds. *Global Trends in Migration: Theory and Research on International Population Movements.* Staten Island, N.Y.: Center for Migration Studies, 1981.

Lee, Everett S. "A Theory of Migration." *Demography,* 3 (1966): 47–57.

McNeill, William H. "Human Migration: A Historical Overview." In W. H. McNeill and R. S. Adams, eds., *Human Migration: Patterns and Policies.* Bloomington: Indiana University Press, 1978: 3–19. This entire volume is recommended to persons interested in the importance of migration as a social process.

Murphy, Elaine M., and Patricia Cancellier. *Immigration: Questions and Answers.* Washington, D.C.: Population Reference Bureau, 1982.

Nagi, Mostafa H. "Development with Unlimited Supplies of Capital: The Case of OPEC." *The Developing Economies,* 20 (March 1982): 3–20.

Newland, Kathleen. *International Migration: The Search for Work.* Worldwatch Paper 33. Washington, D.C.: Worldwatch Institute, November 1979.

Petersen, William. "A General Typology of Migration." *American Sociological Review,* 23 (June 1958): 256–66.

Pirenne, Henri. *Medieval Cities.* Princeton, N.J.: Princeton University Press, 1946.

Population Reference Bureau. *Intercom,* 6 (May 1978).

President's Commission on Immigration and Naturalization. *Whom We Shall Welcome.* Washington, D.C.: U.S. Government Printing Office, 1953.

Smith, Richard F. "Refugees." *Annals of the Academy of Political and Social Science,* 367 (September 1966).

Taeuber, Conrad, and Irene B. Taeuber. *The Changing Population of the United States.* New York: John Wiley, 1958.

Taeuber, Conrad, and Irene B. Taeuber. *People of the United States.* Washington, D.C.: U.S. Bureau of the Census, 1971.

Thomlinson, Ralph. *Population Dynamics: Causes and Consequences of World Demographic Change,* 2nd ed. New York: Random House, 1976, Chapters 12–14.

United Nations. *Trends and Characteristics of International Migration,* ST/ESA/SER.A/64. New York: United Nations, 1979.

United Nations. *World Population Trends and Policies: 1979 Monitoring Report*, Vol. I. New York: United Nations, 1980.

Weeks, John R. *Population: An Introduction to Concepts and Issues*, 2nd ed. Belmont, Calif.: Wadsworth, 1981, Chapter 7.

Weller, Robert H., and Leon F. Bouvier. *Population: Demography and Policy*. New York: St. Martin's, 1981, Chapters 8 and 12.

POPULATION GROWTH IN THE UNITED STATES

10

When the European population explosion began in the middle of the seventeenth century, the United States did not exist as a nation. In fact, the areas that our country now comprises were very sparsely populated. At that time, it is estimated that the population of the entire North American continent numbered no more than a few hundred thousand Native Americans dispersed throughout the land and a handful of European colonists scattered along the eastern seaboard and in Mexico. Not until midway through the eighteenth century did the first million people of European descent accumulate in what is now the United States. Since then, however, the population has doubled and redoubled at a rate that is astounding.

During the late colonial and early national period, the population of the United States increased at an average rate of 3 percent a year—a rate that doubled the population every twenty-five years. Numbers more than quadrupled between 1800 and 1850, more than trebled from 1850 to 1900, and nearly doubled from 1900 to 1950. Throughout the 1950s and early 1960s the population increased at an annual rate of nearly 2 percent, adding close to 3 million persons each year. During more recent years, however, the rate of growth and the size of the annual increment have fallen off considerably. Between 1960 and 1970 the average annual growth rate was down to 1.4 percent, adding nearly 2.4 million people to the population each year, and from 1970 to 1980 the annual growth rate was down to only 1.1 percent. Even with this relatively low rate of growth, however, the number of Americans continued to increase by slightly more than 2.2 million persons a year, and there is every reason to expect that this level of increase will continue well into the twenty-first century.

While this numerical increase may be the most dramatic demographic development for the United States, the growth of our nation has been accompanied by a number of other significant changes in both the composition and the distribution of the population. For example, the average age of the population has gradually increased over the years, our ethnic makeup has become more heterogeneous, the level of education has risen substantially, and the economic structure of the labor force has shifted steadily away from one based on agriculture to one based on a high level of industrial development. This economic transformation has been accompanied by a corresponding steady shift in the distribution of the population away from small rural communities to larger urban centers; more recent years have witnessed a greater dispersal of the urban population away from the core cities to the suburbs; and our entire history has been characterized by a gradual westward expansion of the population.

We will give further consideration to the trends and problems associated with the distribution and composition of the population in Chapters 11 and 12. In this chapter we shall describe past and present population growth trends in the United States and discuss some of the problems that our society faces as a result of population size and growth trends.

HISTORICAL GROWTH TRENDS

When the first federal census was taken in 1790, the population of the United States numbered less than 4 million (see Table 10-1). It passed the 100 million mark between 1910 and 1920, and by 1960 it was more than 200 million. The most recent census in 1980 enumerated more than 226 million Americans, and mid-decade estimates indicated a population in this country in excess of 235 million. In the relatively short time since its formation as a nation, the population of the United States has grown from a few million to over 200 million, and today this country is the fourth most populous nation in the world, after the People's Republic of China, with 1,012 million people; India, with 667 million; and the USSR, with 263 million (U.S. Bureau of the Census, 1980). The entire history of the human race records no other population as having grown to such a size and at such a rate over a comparable span of time.

The population of an area can change in only two ways: through reproduction (the balance between births and deaths) and through migration (the movement of people into or out of an area). In the earlier discussion of trends in world population size and growth, we needed only to consider

Table 10-1
Population Growth Trends in the United States, 1790–1980

Date	Population	Average annual rate of growth each decade (percent)
1790	3,929,214	...
1800	5,308,483	3.5
1810	7,239,881	3.6
1820	9,638,453	3.3
1830	12,866,020	3.4
1840	17,069,453	3.3
1850	23,191,876	3.6
1860	31,443,321	3.6
1870	38,558,371	2.3
1880	50,189,209	3.0
1890	62,979,766	2.6
1900	76,212,168	2.1
1910	92,228,496	2.1
1920	106,021,537	1.5
1930	123,202,624	1.6
1940	132,164,569	0.7
1950	151,325,798	1.5
1960	179,323,175	1.9
1970	203,211,926	1.3
1980	226,504,825	1.1

SOURCE: U.S. Bureau of the Census, *1970 Census of Population,* Final Report PC(1)-A1, *Number of Inhabitants: U.S. Summary* (Washington, D.C., 1971); and *1980 Census of Population and Housing,* Advance Report PHC80-V-1, *United States Summary: Final Population and Housing Counts* (Washington, D.C., 1981).

the reproductive component of population change. On a national level, however, one must consider the effect of both reproduction and migration. This is particularly true in the United States where, beginning with its initial settlement by the nomadic bands who crossed back and forth over the Bering Strait land bridge thousands of years ago and continuing even today, population growth has been significantly influenced by migration.

Reproduction and migration have exerted different influences at different times in this country; thus an adequate understanding of United States population trends can be obtained only by considering the nation's growth during distinct phases or time periods. In general, it can be said that the nation has passed through five distinct phases of population growth: the colonial period, the frontier era, the early twentieth century, the interwar years, and the baby boom period.

Colonial Growth Phase

The first phase of American population growth, the colonial phase, covers the period from the initial colonization and settlement until about 1820. Although the numbers involved were small, this initial period was characterized by extremely rapid rates of population growth. Rising immigration from Europe during the later years of this period began to make some contribution, but for the most part the rapid growth rates of this phase were the result of very high rates of natural increase. The early settlers married more frequently and at a younger age than their European contemporaries, which meant that a larger proportion of the population was married and that each married couple was exposed for a longer time to the likelihood of bearing children. The longer exposure to the risk of childbearing, coupled with the fact that large families were considered an asset in conquering the wilderness, meant that birth rates were very high and often approached the maximum of which the human race is biologically capable (50 to 55 per 1,000). While the United States was in this phase of its growth it is estimated that the population increased, on the average, at a rate of 3½ percent a year.

Frontier Growth Phase

Growth continued to be rapid during the frontier phase, which lasted from about 1820 until the end of the nineteenth century. Reproduction rates were high during these years, but were declining as a falling birth rate began to narrow the demographic gap. At the same time, however, immigration from abroad swelled to tremendous proportions (see Table 9-1 in Chapter 9 and Figure 10-1). During the 1820s, for example, immigrants accounted for only 4 percent of the population increase, but this proportion rose steadily over the ensuing years, exceeding one-third by the 1850s, and it remained at a fairly high level throughout the rest of the century. As noted in Chapter 9, rapid population growth on the European side of the Atlantic, agricultural advances that displaced large segments of the rural European population, and an expanding frontier with seemingly limitless opportunities in this country, all combined to bring about one of the greatest population transfers in history: between 1820 and the end of the nineteenth century it is estimated that close to 20 million people entered this country from Europe.

A closer examination of Table 10-1 suggests that this frontier growth phase can be subdivided into two periods: the pre–Civil War years, during which high birth rates and rising immigration served to maintain average annual growth rates at about 3½ percent a year; and the post–Civil War years, during which the rapid fertility decline that accompanied industrial development was enough to offset the high immigration rate and reduce annual

Figure 10-1
Percent of U.S. Population Increase Due to Immigration, 1820–1976

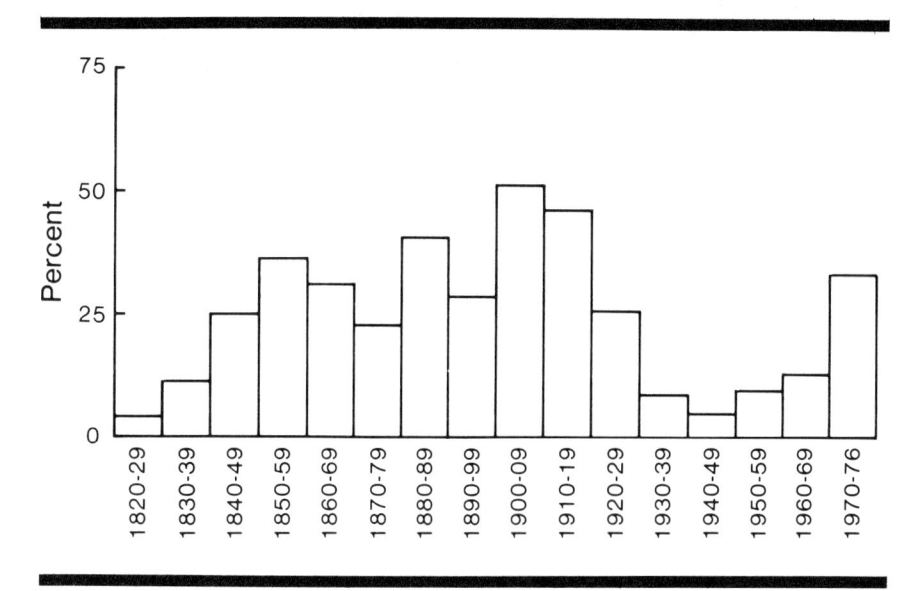

SOURCE: Based on data in Tables 9-1 and 10-1.

growth rates to roughly 2½ percent. Numerical growth was substantial during this second phase. All in all, this period saw the population of the United States grow from slightly less than 10 million to over 75 million—more than a sevenfold increase during a scant eighty years.

Early Twentieth-Century Growth Phase

During the third historical growth phase, lasting roughly from 1900 to 1925, the rapid rates of growth that had prevailed during the nineteenth century continued their downward trend. The reproduction increase began to level off as a steadily declining birth rate brought the United States nearer to the completion of its demographic transition; and, as a result of the disruptive effects of World War I in Europe and the increased agitation for restrictive legislation here at home, the volume of European immigration declined until it was a fraction of what it had been previously. Immigration as a factor in population growth peaked during the first decade of the century, at which time immigrants accounted for slightly more than half (51 percent) of the total numerical gain, but during the 1920s this fraction was cut in half. Reflecting these developments, growth rates during this period amounted to only 2 percent a year, compared with average annual growth rates in excess of 3 percent throughout most of the nineteenth century. Nevertheless, because of the larger population base, numerical increases continued to be substantial. During the early decades of the present century the size of the U.S. population increased by about 1.5 million per year as compared to an average annual increment of roughly 833,000 during the frontier growth phase. It was during this growth phase that the American population surpassed the 100 million mark.

The Interwar Years

The next phase, lasting from about 1925 until America's entry into the Second World War, saw growth rates continue to decline—only now the decline was much more rapid than before. On the one hand, the Immigration and Nationality Act of 1924 sharply curtailed immigration from abroad: the number of immigrants arriving each year fell from an average of over 800,000 during the 1900–09 decade to less than 70,000 during the 1930s; and between 1930 and 1939 immigrants accounted for less than 10 percent of the total population gain. On the other hand, as the country slid into a severe economic depression, the long-term fertility decline speeded up and the birth rate reached an unprecedented low level, falling to less than 20 per 1,000 for the first time in our history. During the years immediately preceding World War II, the population of the United States increased at a rate of less than 1 percent a year, the annual increment fell way below 1 million persons per year, and it appeared that the era of rapid population growth had come to an end. Beginning in the mid-1940s, however, this downward growth trend underwent a significant and substantial reversal.

The Baby Boom Era

The end of the Second World War marked the beginning of a fifteen-year growth spurt in the United States (1945–60). Although the continued existence of restrictive legislation meant that the volume of immigration remained a mere fraction of its former size (immigration accounted for well below 10 percent of the annual growth throughout this period), the historical decline in fertility underwent an unexpected and substantial reversal. From an all-time low level of about 18 live births per 1,000 population during the 1930s, the birth rate rose to a level of 26.2 per 1,000 in 1947 and remained at about 24 to 25 per 1,000 until the late 1950s. This unexpected phenomenon, popularly known as the baby boom, caused the rate of population growth to increase from less than 1 percent a year during the 1930s to well over 1½ percent a year during the 1950s. Although the growth rates

Table 10-2
Vital Statistics: United States, 1900–1980

Year	Crude birth rate	Crude death rate	Crude rate of natural increase
1900	32.3	17.2	15.1
1905	...	15.9	...
1910	30.1	14.7	15.4
1915	29.5	13.2	16.3
1920	27.7	13.0	14.7
1925	25.1	11.7	13.4
1930	21.3	11.3	10.0
1935	18.7	10.9	7.8
1940	19.4	10.8	8.6
1945	20.4	10.6	9.8
1950	24.1	9.6	14.5
1955	25.0	9.3	15.7
1960	23.7	9.5	14.2
1965	19.4	9.4	10.0
1970	18.4	9.5	8.9
1975	14.8	8.9	5.9
1980	15.8	8.7	7.1

SOURCE: *Historical Statistics of the United States, Colonial Times to 1970,* Part I (Washington, D.C.: U.S. Bureau of the Census, 1975). Rates for 1975 and 1980 are from *Monthly Vital Statistics Reports,* 29:31 (September 1981) and 30:12 (March 1982).

that prevailed during the postwar decade were much lower than those experienced during the nineteenth century, their application to a substantially larger population base brought about some really dramatic numerical increases. The nearly 50 million people added to the population between 1940 and 1960, for example, accounts for nearly half of the total population gain of the entire twentieth century. Furthermore, although the baby boom has long been over, its effects are still with us, and they will continue to be with us for some time to come.

Post–Baby Boom Growth Trends

The late 1950s were characterized by two major developments with regard to fertility and mortality trends in the United States (see Table 10-2 and Figure 10-2). On the one hand, the long-term downward trend in mortality was halted and the death rate became more or less stabilized at a relatively low level. On the other hand, the postwar baby boom came to an end and the birth rate began to decline. The combined effects of these two devel-

Figure 10-2
Crude Birth and Death Rates: United States, 1900–1980

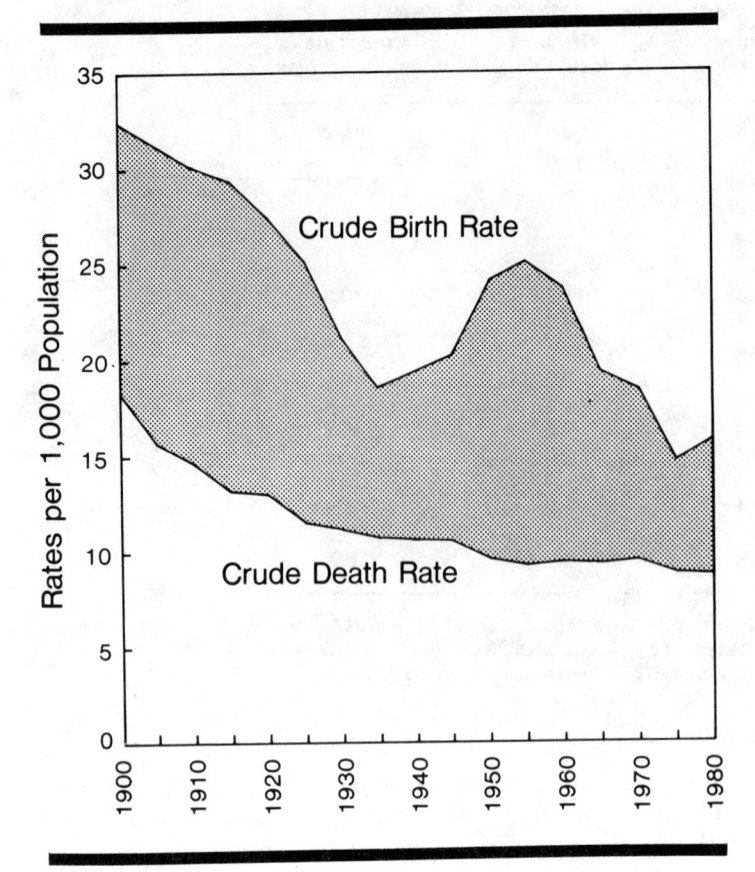

SOURCE: Based on data in Table 10-2.

opments, particularly the latter, has been a steady and fairly pronounced decline in the *crude rate of natural increase*. (This rate is computed simply as the difference between the crude birth rate and the crude death rate and is defined as the net number of people added to the size of a population each year for every 1,000 members of that population.) During the 1950s the impact of the postwar baby boom resulted in annual growth rates on the order of 1½ percent a year, but by 1965 this rate had fallen to 1 percent, a level it had not occupied since the early years of World War II. The birth rate continued to decline throughout the 1960s and into the 1970s, reaching its lowest level in history in 1975–76, at which time the American birth rate was only 14.8 per 1,000 population and the natural increase rate of the population was just over 0.6 percent a year.

Since the impact of foreign immigration continued to be almost negligible until after 1970, the decline in the rate of natural increase meant a decline in the overall rate of population growth. Between 1960 and 1970 the population of the United States increased at an average rate of 1.4 percent a year, compared with an annual growth rate of 1.9 percent during the 1950s, and during the most recent intercensal decade the overall growth rate was, despite the growing influence of immigration, only 1.1 percent a year.

The drop in the annual growth rate of the American population since 1960 has been so rapid and so substantial that in spite of the steadily increasing population base to which it has applied there has been a marked reduction in the number of people being added each year. Between 1950 and 1960, as the baby boom was peaking, the population of the United States increased at the rate of about 3 million persons per year. Between 1960 and 1970, however, the gain of 24.3 million persons amounted to an average annual increase of only 2.4 million; and during the most recent decade, 1970 to 1980, the average number of people being added to our population each year was down to 2.2 million. Thus, as the 1970s came to an end, it became clear that the postwar baby boom was only a temporary disturbance in the modern demographic balance of a country that has completed its demographic transition.

The pronounced slowdown in our population growth behavior since the early 1960s is most dramatically revealed by the trend in the *total fertility rate*. This rate, which for any specified time period is defined as the average number of children each woman would ultimately bear if the prevailing fertility patterns did not change, was as high as 3.7 at the height of the baby boom in the late 1950s. Twenty years later, however, it was down to a level of about 1.8 births per woman. The magic number of zero population growth is estimated to be 2.1 children per woman, so American fertility had fallen to such a low level that we were not replacing ourselves, and as of 1980 we appeared to be on the verge of becoming a zero growth society.

FUTURE GROWTH OUTLOOK

Despite appearances, and the fact that the 1980 level of fertility and childbearing was well below the replacement level, the United States is far from becoming a zero growth society. Nor is it likely to become one in the very near future—certainly not in this century (Bouvier, 1975). As the United States entered the 1980s its numbers were increasing at a rate of about 2 million persons per year, and there was every indication that numerical growth would continue to be substantial for several decades. According to the U.S. Bureau of the Census (1977), our population in the year 2000 could number anywhere between 245 and 287 million inhabitants, and could be as high as 300 million a generation later.

Two factors explain why our population will continue to increase for many years to come: immigration and the youthfulness of the population. First, the elimination of national quotas in the Immigration and Naturalization Act of 1968, and other modifications of laws since then, and large numbers of refugees such as the Vietnamese boat people and the more recent Cuban exiles have meant that immigration is again becoming an important component of American population growth. The number of legal immigrants arriving each year was nearly 500,000 in 1981, equivalent to one-fourth of the annual natural increase. To this number must be added the illegal immigrants, whose exact number is unknown, although some estimates have placed it as high as a million each year. If it really was this high, then our population was actually growing at a rate of nearly 3 million persons per year (a rate equal to that prevailing at the height of the baby boom), and approximately one-half of our growth was being contributed by immigration. Actual numbers notwithstanding, the point is that net immigration does contribute substantially to the growth of the U.S. population today, and we will never become a zero growth society as long as this level of immigration persists. While it may seem selfish and even un-American to talk about ending one of our great democratic traditions by closing our borders to foreign immigrants, we will hear this topic discussed more and more in the years to come. Pressure was already mounting in the early 1980s to tighten up border restrictions on the large number of Haitians seeking political asylum in South Florida, and there is little reason to anticipate any relaxation of such pressure in the foreseeable future. It seems unlikely, at this time anyway, that we will ever see a day when all immigration is completely cut off, but we might very possibly see the adoption of increasingly restrictive legislation and tighter policies aimed at controlling the number of immigrants to fit the needs of the society (e.g., to offset the population declines that would ultimately occur if fertility remains below the replacement level).

The second factor ensuring that numerical growth will continue to be substantial for some time to come lies in the age structure of the American population. The larger birth cohorts born during the postwar baby boom (1945–60) have now reached the young adult ages where new family formation takes place, and the impact that they will have could be considerable. To make a contrast with an earlier generation, the number of women at the major childbearing ages (20–34 years) was only 17 million in 1960, and these relatively few women who had been born during the interwar growth phase of relatively low fertility contributed so much to the baby boom. By 1980, however, the number of women at these main reproductive ages was nearly 29 million, meaning that there were 12 million more potential mothers than there had been a generation earlier! Even if the fertility of these baby boom cohorts remains at or below replacement levels, the fact that there are so many more women at the childbearing ages means that they will contribute substantially to the numerical growth of the population during the remainder of the century. Any increase in the present level of fertility, even a moderate increase up to a bare replacement level, would add even more to the projected growth of our population. What all this means, as indicated earlier, is that the baby boom of the 1950s continues to exert a significant influence on our population. Its full impact has not been felt yet, and will not become fully apparent until the members of this cohort have all passed through the childbearing ages. This will not occur until the late 1990s, however, by which time the number of Americans could easily exceed 250 million.

It is of course impossible to say for certain what the population of the United States will be at any particular time in the future. That depends on the volume of immigration, a large part of which is an unknown quantity, and on the number of children the baby boom cohorts decide to have during the 1980s and 1990s. However, we can make tentative projections based on certain assumptions pertaining to the current growth situation. For example, given a replacement level fertility of an average 2.1 children per woman, as well as a continuation of the present level of legal immigration, the population of the United States will reach the 300 million mark in about forty-five years (Bouvier, 1975). In the unlikely event that immigration were to be curtailed completely and fertility were to remain at the replacement level, the United States would still not reach zero population growth (ZPG) until about the year 2035, at which time our population would be about 270 million. Finally, if immigration were curtailed and fertility were to remain at its 1980 below-replacement level of about 1.8 children per woman, the current age structure would ensure that our population would still continue to grow for the next fifty to sixty years and would exceed 250 million by the time we did achieve ZPG. Thus, there is little doubt that we can look forward to a continued increase in our numbers for a long time to come, and that when (if?) we achieve ZPG, we will achieve it with a population that is much larger than the nearly 227 million enumerated in the 1980 decennial census. To illustrate the range of possibilities open to us, Table 10-3 presents some alternative estimates, prepared by the U.S. Bureau of the Census, of the size of the American population through the year 2050.

PROBLEMS OF POPULATION SIZE AND GROWTH

Official concern over population growth and related problems in the United States emerged during the 1960s, and the past ten to fifteen years have witnessed the emergence and growth of the environmental movement, the founding of a national society to promote zero population growth, and the

Table 10-3
Projections of the U.S. Population, 1980–2050

Year	Population in thousands		
	Lowest series	Middle series	High series
1980	226,505	226,505	226,505
1990	245,507	249,731	254,686
2000	255,638	267,990	282,339
2010	260,669	283,141	311,061
2020	261,605	296,339	341,907
2030	256,090	304,330	370,810
2040	244,989	307,952	399,425
2050	230,813	308,856	428,664
Projection Assumptions			
Lifetime births per woman	1.6	1.9	2.3
Life expectancy by 2050	76.7	79.6	83.3
Annual net immigration (in thousands)	250	450	750

SOURCE: U.S. Bureau of the Census, "Projections of the Population of the United States: 1982–2050 (Advance Report). *Current Population Reports,* Series P-25, No. 922 (October 1982).

publication of an increasing number of books expressing varying degrees of alarm over the future well-being of our nation with respect to population, resources, and the environment. Among other things, this growing concern led to the establishment in 1969 of a presidential commission to study the problems of population growth and the American future. In the summary report issued by the commission in 1972, the most overriding conclusion is that the traditional growth ethic of "the more the better" is no longer appropriate for our society and that no substantial benefits would result from the continued growth of the nation's population. The report further concludes that the ultimate goal of improving the quality of life for all our citizens could best be accomplished with a slowdown in the rate of population growth. More recently, a conference of the leaders of sixty major environmental and population groups, held in Washington in January 1981, reached even stronger conclusions. The final conference report noted that

> Current trends of rapid population growth, wasteful resource consumption, and abuse of the environment seriously endanger the global base for all human activity. . . . We believe this situation constitutes nothing less than a threat to U.S. national security and to the future well-being of the American people (Population Reference Bureau, 1981).

The final statement of this conference went on to recommend that Congress formulate a national policy aimed at stabilizing our population, and that it create an Office of Population Policy within the executive branch to coordinate present and future government activities pertaining to population research and education, family planning, immigration policy, and other population-related issues. In this section we shall explore more fully some of the problems that lie at the base of this growing national concern.

The first point to make here perhaps is this: whether or not a given area or country can be said to have a population problem does not depend solely on the size of its population but on the nature of the balance between numbers and resources in relation to technology and tastes. That is, population problems are defined by the relationship among population size, available resources, the level of technology, and the prevailing standard of living that influences the level of resource consumption. At first glance, then, it may appear somewhat incongruous to suggest that the United States has a problem insofar as the size and growth of its population are concerned. After all, the nation as a whole is the wealthiest in the world; technological progress has been and continues to be fairly rapid; and our people are living at a level of material comfort and well-being never before experienced by a people and not now experienced by any other country. However, the very nature of this high level of living, which we have come to take so much for granted, lies at the base of what is in fact a very serious problem. Although the overall population picture in the United States may indeed appear rosy in contrast with the depressing situation found throughout much of the rest of the world, it could be very dangerous to our long-run national welfare if we let complacency or naive optimism obscure the potential crises facing the nation.

Population and Resources

In sharp contrast to the situation throughout much of the Third World, the United States does not now face a serious food crisis, nor is it likely to face such a crisis in the foreseeable future. Indeed, the dietary problems that do exist in our country are problems of overeating, particularly animal fats and sugars. The people of the United States have the fullest bellies in the world and do not have to live with chronic food shortages and the constant threat of famine, but this does not mean that no problem exists. On the one hand, as population growth has outstripped food production in other areas of the world, the United States, along with a few other food surplus nations, has had to assume an ever increasing role in making up these food deficits by exporting surplus foods to Third World nations. In the 1960s, for example, we experienced a serious "grain drain" as a result of our increasing efforts to help feed the hungry millions in the poorer countries, and these exports virtually eliminated the huge surpluses that resulted from the once perennial problem of overproduction. By 1970 we had increased our grain reserves again to the point where they amounted to about three months of world consumption needs, but by the middle of the decade these reserves had fallen back to only about a thirty-day supply (Brown, 1976). In the early 1980s, however, they were on the increase again. The nation still has, and will continue to have for a long time to come, an abundance of food of every kind, but fluctuations such as we have experienced in the volume of surpluses can upset the price structure, and when that happens, it tends to have a general destabilizing effect on the economy as a whole.

One other aspect of the food situation in the United States needs to be mentioned, and that is the nature of our consumption patterns and their relevance for the larger world food crisis. Specifically, on a per capita basis Americans consume a disproportionate share of the world's food. It is estimated, for example, as we pointed out earlier, that the average American today consumes around 2,000 pounds of grain a year; by contrast, the average per capita grain consumption on the Indian subcontinent is only about 400 pounds a year. In other words, the average American consumes roughly five times as much basic grain food as the average inhabitant of India or Bangladesh. The reason for such a large discrepancy lies in the simple fact that in India and Bangladesh most of the grain is consumed directly in the form of bread and cereal, whereas most of the grain consumed in the United States is eaten indirectly: 80 to 90 percent of the grain consumed in this country is eaten by animals (cattle, chickens, pigs), which then provide us with a variety of animal food products such as steak, pork chops, milk, and eggs. When one realizes that it takes about 8 pounds of grain to produce a pound of beef, one sees the quarter-pounder that one American eats for lunch as the equivalent of a two-day grain supply for one Indian.

The seriousness of our consumption problem takes on even greater dimensions when it comes to nonfood resources. One reason for this is that many of these resources exist in a fixed quantity and will ultimately be exhausted. For example, according to one recent assessment, many of the earth's major metal resources could be used up well within the readers' lifetime; if consumption rates continue to increase at projected levels, they will be exhausted much sooner (see Table 10-4). A second potential problem lies in the fact that we in the United States are consuming the world's resources at a disproportionately high rate. One commonly hears that Americans, who constitute slightly more than 5 percent of the world's population, account for about 30 percent of the world's resources that are consumed in a given year. Some people would put this estimate still higher, but even the most conservative estimates would place the consumption figure at around 20 percent. Whatever the figure, the simple fact of the matter is that the people of the United States have long consumed, and continue to consume, much more than their fair share of the world's raw materials. At the turn of the century our country was producing substantially more nonfood raw mate-

Table 10-4

Estimated Life Expectancy of Selected Metal Resources at Two Different Rates of Consumption

Metal	Life expectancy in years — At 1976 rates of consumption	At projected rates of consumption
Silver	20	17
Zinc	26	19
Mercury	22	21
Lead	37	25
Tungsten	52	31
Tin	41	31
Copper	63	36
Nickel	86	43
Platinum	110	44
Manganese	164	56
Iron	172	62
Aluminum	312	63
Chromium	377	80

SOURCE: Council on Environmental Quality, *The Global Report to the President: Entering the Twenty-First Century,* Vol. I, *The Summary Report* (Washington, D.C.: U.S. Government Printing Office, 1980).

rials than it was consuming, but since the end of the Second World War we have been consuming more than we have produced. Furthermore, our heavy reliance on foreign imports has been increasing.

The most blatant example of our dependence on foreign resources, an example with which we are all too painfully familiar, is the situation with respect to crude petroleum. To illustrate, statistics published in *Statistical Abstracts of the United States* (97th ed.) reveal that in 1950 our domestic production of crude petroleum amounted to nearly 2 billion barrels whereas we consumed roughly 2.4 billion barrels (i.e., a consumption level about 20 percent in excess of production). By the mid-1970s, however, the estimated domestic consumption of crude petroleum (6 billion barrels) exceeded domestic production (3.2 billion barrels) by 90 percent!

Although the situation with respect to petroleum may be the most vivid example of what has been happening, it is certainly not the only one. It is an unhappy fact that the United States today must import a substantial portion of the raw materials it uses, and, as in the case of petroleum, the volume of imports has grown steadily as rapid industrial expansion has continually increased the demand for raw materials. In 1975, for example, again citing data from *Statistical Abstracts* (97th ed.), we had to import approximately 30 percent of the iron we used (compared with 15 percent in 1960);

we had to import 85 percent of our aluminum (compare 68 percent in 1960); 64 percent of our zinc (46 percent in 1960); 73 percent of our mercury (25 percent in 1960); and 54 percent of our tungsten (32 percent in 1960). All totaled, the value of our foreign imports of fuel and metals exceeded the corresponding value of exports by $1.3 billion in 1960, but by 1974 this trade deficit amounted to $15.2 billion. That is, in a fourteen-year period our import-export deficit experienced more than a tenfold increase—an increase that has clearly been reflected in our steadily rising cost of living.

With the obvious exception of petroleum, the reserves of which some estimates say could be exhausted within fifty years, the United States has not yet encountered any serious difficulties in finding raw materials. In noting this, however, we must keep three important considerations in mind. First, continued industrial expansion to meet the needs of our present and future population means that our domestic demand for all kinds of raw materials can be expected to increase. Second, and especially crucial in view of our increasing dependence on foreign imports to supply many of our raw materials, the nations that provide many of these resources are themselves undergoing industrial expansion. As this process continues their own domestic demands for industrial raw materials can be expected to increase, thus reducing the amounts available for export. Third, a major problem concerning our needed resources in the years ahead does not stem so much from their decreasing supply as it does from the fact that we have become increasingly dependent for supplies on a world where growing political instability poses a very serious threat (Iranian oil is only the most obvious recent case in point). In other words, diminishing supplies of the world's nonrenewable resources, coupled with increasing competition for them in a politically unstable world will make it increasingly difficult, and much more costly, for us to secure the resources necessary to maintain the comfortable life-style to which we have become accustomed.

To sum up: the demand for both food and nonfood resources increases steadily as the population grows. Although the United States is certainly not on the verge of becoming one of the hungry nations of the world, the raw materials situation is serious and could become critical. The production of many important raw materials has already started to falter (e.g., the production of bauxite aluminum ore fell by 2 percent between 1960 and 1974), while the cost of recovering others has increased considerably—two trends that can be expected to continue as supplies diminish even farther. The unhappy truth is that the supplies of many of the basic raw materials on which our industrial society is so heavily dependent are nonrenewable. They exist in limited quantities, and increasing demands will inevitably lead to their exhaustion at some point in the future. There is clearly a major need to reorder priorities and make some significant changes in our consumption patterns and life-style. The question is whether the needed changes will be made in time to forestall a serious deterioration in our level of living.

One other point needs to be made. Although our discussion here has been limited to the United States, much of it is just as relevant to the other modern industrial nations in both the Eastern and Western blocs. That is, with respect to many of the earth's resources, the problem is not so much one of too many people as it is one of very high rates of consumption by a relatively small percentage of the world's population. Further, just as consumption levels have been increasing in the United States, so too have they been increasing in many of the other industrial nations. Consumption levels in the more developed countries have been rising not only in an absolute sense but also in a relative sense, and this rise is contributing to a widening of the already pronounced economic gap between them and the less developed countries of the Third World. In light of this situation, the Marxist perspective on population and poverty and the more recent call for a new international economic order discussed in Chapter 8 take on more poignancy.

The Lifeboat Ethic Reconsidered

We pointed out in an earlier chapter that some people would apply the lifeboat ethic to the problem of world population and nonrenewable resources (Hardin, 1974). Adherents of this ethic view the world as a full lifeboat with limited provisions tossing aimlessly on the open sea. The boat is so overcrowded, in fact, that it cannot afford to take on any more passengers and indeed may have to reduce the present number in order to ensure the survival of those who remain. The lifeboat, of course, is a metaphor for the overcrowded earth. Just as the boat must not take on more passengers, so the earth must end population growth and reduce its size if we are to avoid disaster. Since the cause of the present rapid growth situation has been an upset in the old demographic balance (as we gained greater control over mortality), it follows that population growth can be stopped only by reestablishing a demographic balance. This can be done either by allowing death rates to rise to their earlier high level or by reducing birth rates to match the present low mortality level. There is little doubt as to which solution is to be preferred. Indeed most countries in the world today have some kind of policy that seeks to reduce fertility through the widespread adoption of birth control.

Efforts to control population growth, however, deal with only one side of the problem. In light of the differences in consumption levels between richer countries and poorer developing nations, we might suggest a different analogy. Instead of an overcrowded lifeboat, we can look at the earth as a luxury ocean liner in which one-fourth of the passengers are traveling in style in the first-class section while the remaining three-fourths are suffering varying degrees of deprivation in the second-class section. Is it unreasonable to ask the first-class passengers to limit their consumption somewhat in order to help those in second-class to increase theirs? It may not be unreasonable, but it is probably not very realistic to look for any such development in the foreseeable future. Be that as it may, the point we are making and want to stress is simply this: it is very important that world population growth be brought under control as soon as possible, but we must not expect that such a simple thing as an end to population growth will by itself solve the many pressing and complex problems that the population explosion has created and is creating on this small planet. The population problem is basically an economic problem, and solving it will require coming to grips with such things as the uneven distribution of production in relation to the world's wealth and resources, international trade barriers, the vestiges of colonialism, and other geopolitical issues. Fewer people and a slower rate of growth may make solutions easier to achieve, but we must not look to an end to population growth as the panacea for all our problems.

The Quality of American Life

Although we can ill afford to close our eyes to the severe problems of poverty and hunger that exist in many parts of the Third World today, we in the United States clearly do not face comparable crises in the foreseeable future as a result of population growth. Instead of threatening life itself, population growth has had and will continue to have its greatest impact on the *quality* of American life. More specifically, the most significant consequence of continued population growth in the more affluent nations such as ours will be the erosion of many of the personal freedoms and pleasures that we have achieved as part of our increasingly high level of economic development. In fact, some have long argued that this erosion has been under way for years (Day and Day, 1964), and that as population continues to increase, the people of the United States will be less and less able to enjoy many of the aesthetic pleasures that we have come to regard as major rewards of our increasing affluence.

Loss of Open Spaces

One of the most obvious problems created by overpopulation is lack of space, particularly space for recreation. Although a walk along a littered public beach on a Monday morning after a hot summer weekend may cause the cynic to wonder just how much we really appreciate the beauty of our natural environment, the fact is that Americans have long been lovers of the great outdoors. Our appreciation for natural beauty and our desire to preserve it is attested to by the vast amounts of public lands set aside for parks and other recreational purposes. The problem, however, is that the amount of available land is finite; yet the continued growth of population (not to mention the trend toward shorter working hours and increased leisure time) increases the need for parks, beaches, picnic grounds, camping areas, and plain wilderness. In the areas surrounding larger American cities, green meadows and rolling hills have been bulldozed away to make room for Levittown-type residential areas and blacktop parking lots for sprawling suburban shopping malls. Nowhere is this more apparent than in the great urban sprawl of the Northeast. This megalopolis (Gottman, 1961), forming a triangle with Portland, Maine, in the north, Chicago in the west, and Washington, D.C., in the south, was home for nearly 100 million Americans in 1980 (close to 45 percent of the total population). For many of these people, a Sunday afternoon drive in "the country" has become an event of the past.

Although the efforts of some farsighted individuals and groups have ensured that some open spaces still exist, the spaces are woefully inadequate to meet the aesthetic and psychological needs of the people and will become even more so as numbers continue to increase. As we entered the 1980s more and more Americans found themselves spending their vacations at increasingly overcrowded lake and mountain resorts and at increasingly overcrowded camping areas (if they were lucky enough to get in). Anyone who has recently taken a family winter vacation to Walt Disney World in Florida or tried to drive from Boston to Cape Cod for a weekend in July or August does not need to be told just how serious this situation is becoming. For a while in the 1950s, various wilderness areas continued to offer some sanctuary from the pressures of modern urban society, but the growing popularity of family camping and backpacking has destroyed even this. It is no longer possible, for example, to hike the mountain trails of Vermont and New Hampshire without encountering numerous other persons searching for solitude; and one often has to line up for hours—sometimes even days—waiting for a campsite in a state or national park. What is happening in this respect was most vividly described in an article in the *Wall Street Journal* (June 24, 1966), which noted that if one had visited scenic Yosemite National Park that summer and climbed to a mountainous vantage point overlooking the valley below, one would have beheld a magnificent panoramic view of a veritable sea of tents and trailers. The article went on to describe the scene in even more unhappy detail:

> The damp night air, heavy with a pall of eye-watering smoke, is cut by the blare of transistor radios, the clatter of pots and pans, the roar of a motorcycle, and the squeals of teen-agers. Except for hundreds of shiny aluminum trailers and multi-colored tents squeezed into camping areas, this might be any city after dark. . . . At dawn and dusk even fresh air is a rare commodity in these crowded campgrounds. Then, when the air is still, smoke from thousands of cooking fires hangs over these areas . . . and the heavy wood smoke brings tears to the visitors' eyes.

This is living? Yosemite has not grown any larger, but each year more and more Americans, with more money to spend and more leisure time in which to spend it, have come to visit it and other national parks and vacation areas. Rapid population growth during the postwar decades of rising prosperity has greatly increased the need for readily available space and recreational facilities; at the same time, finite land resources make these needs even more difficult to fill. The problem had become so serious by the mid-1970s that many national parks were forced to impose a two-week limit on the use of camping sites. The problem will not lessen as the population continues to grow during the next several decades.

Rising Costs

Another dimension of the population problem confronting Americans today is an increase in costs, not only with respect to basic resources but also with respect to a myriad of other services that we have increasingly come to take for granted. What most of us today would regard as the minimum requirements for a decent level of living—garbage collection, air and water purification, traffic control, police and fire protection, schools, libraries, hospitals, roads, and the myriad of other public-supported social services—today cost more and more merely to maintain, let alone to improve. Moreover, when one considers such things as the increasing pollution of many of our major waterways, one sees that the problem of maintenance gives way to the problem of re-creating what has already been lost. Fresh air is already a thing of the past for residents of many American cities, which are today surrounded by a haze of atmospheric pollution. Despite rising gasoline prices and projected energy shortages, our roadways continue to be overtaxed by an ever increasing number of vehicles. Many municipal hospitals are struggling to stay solvent as equipment costs and other expenses mount; soaring costs of higher education are making the much sought after college degree more expensive to acquire; many young Americans have given up on the dream of owning their own home as building costs and interest rates have soared; public health and welfare agencies have too few workers and inadequate budgets to cope efficiently with the rising problems of our burgeoning urban centers; the shortage of physicians and other trained professionals (e.g., nurses, teachers, physical therapists, social workers) is daily becoming more acute . . . and so on ad infinitum. The sad truth of the matter is that in many areas—not only in recreation but also in the more vital areas of health, education, and welfare—the quality of American life already shows signs of deteriorating. Continued increases in the size of the population will make it increasingly necessary to spend more and more money on every kind of public service, and as maintenance costs rise, it will become more and more difficult to achieve any progress in raising the standard of living. The ultimate outcome of this, unfortunately, could very easily be a pronounced speeding up of the already visible deterioration in the quality of American life.

Environmental Pollution

The quality of American life is also threatened by the growth of industry and the spread of environmental pollution. Although it would be naive to single out population growth per se as the cause of the progressive deterioration of the environment, there is an undeniable association between increasing numbers and industrial expansion: the more people there are, the greater the demand for the products of our industry; and the greater the level of industrial production the greater the pressure on the absorptive capacity of the environment. Problems of environmental pollution are most dramatic when they involve some highly emotional issue such as the dumping of radioactive materials or other toxic waste products (e.g., dioxin), or the destruction associated with such practices as strip-mining; however, the less publicized issues may be just as serious, if not more so. Air pollution, for example, represents an increasingly serious problem throughout the country, especially in the urban areas where roughly three-quarters of the American people live. Areas of population concentration today are usually areas of industrial concentration wherein the atmosphere is daily clouded by smoke pouring from the smokestacks of hundreds of factories. Despite numerous attempts to control this problem, the majority of our citizens live in areas where air pollution continues to pose a serious hazard to health and well-being. Large concentrations of population also mean more houses with chimneys adding their fuel waste to the problem, and as population increases there is a correspondingly greater need for more public incinerators to dispose of the increasing amount of waste material.

And then there is the automobile! In addition to the traffic problem it has created in many cities during the post–World War II years, the automobile has contributed substantially to the growing volume of impurities in the air we breathe. The problem has become so severe in some areas that smog has come to be regarded as a normal part of life. This is perhaps most dramatically revealed by the fact that the Pollutant Standard Index (PSI), which most of us had not even heard of a decade ago, has today become a regular item on the televised evening weather report in most large American cities, along with such other data as temperature, precipitation, and barometric pressure. In some areas the problem is so severe that *thermal inversions* are not uncommon. (A thermal inversion occurs when a mass of cool air flows over a hot air mass, preventing the latter from rising, thus trapping air pollutants over an area.) These inversions create serious health hazards and cause numerous victims, especially among the very young and the elderly, to be hospitalized for respiratory ailments. Despite a growing public concern and an increase in various state and federal legislative efforts to control the problem, air pollution continues to be a fact of life in many parts of the United States. This not only has major economic consequences (e.g., the increasing costs of trying to maintain a relatively pollutant-free atmosphere), but it also has serious consequences for the health of our population. Over and above the less serious problems such as itching and burning eyes and general nose and throat irritation, the continuous exposure to air pollutants and their accumulation in the body must be recognized as a slow poisoning process that significantly increases the risk of acquiring and dying from such respiratory illnesses as bronchitis, emphysema, and lung cancer (Ehrlich and Ehrlich, 1970).

Even less dramatic are the potential long-run damaging effects of air pollution on the earth's ecosystem (Julian, 1980, pp. 532–33). There is some evidence, for example, that the fluorocarbon gases commonly used in spray cans may be contributing to a breaking up of the earth's protective ozone layer. This ozone layer, which surrounds our planet about ten to thirty miles above sea level, acts to screen out many of the harmful ultraviolet rays of the sun. If this protective covering were to be broken up it would lead to a much higher worldwide incidence of skin cancer and crop failure, and it could also influence changes in the world's climate.

The steadily increasing amount of carbon dioxide in the atmosphere represents still another phenomenon that could affect the earth's temperature. It is estimated that the amount of carbon dioxide in the atmosphere has increased by about 25 percent during the past century, and it is estimated that unless effective preventive measures are found it is likely to increase by another 25 percent shortly after we enter the twenty-first century. Many scientists are concerned that such a buildup of carbon dioxide could produce a "greenhouse effect" in the atmosphere, trapping heat near the earth's surface and raising the average temperature. According to these scientists, such a temperature increase, even if only a few degrees, could cause the polar ice caps to melt, leading to disastrous flooding along coastal areas. Clearly then, the contamination of our air by various industrial pollutants has already contributed to a deterioration in the overall quality of American life, and it threatens to cause even greater damage in the years to come.

Population growth and industrial expansion in the United States during the twentieth century have also had serious consequences for the quantity and quality of the *water* supply. The hydrologic cycle continually renews this vital resource (as water in our rivers, streams, and oceans evaporates into the atmosphere where it then condenses and falls back to earth as rain), but serious problems exist nevertheless. On the one hand, the factory that pollutes the air often pollutes the water as well; it has even been said of Americans today that the world's cleanest people "bathe in scented fats and drink a factory's slime" (Gordon, 1965, p. 110). Another aspect of this problem is *thermal pollution*. Thermal pollution results when factory wastes, especially those from nuclear power plants, are sufficiently warmer than the rivers and streams into which they are dumped so that they raise the temperature of the water. Such thermal pollution can be ecologically devastating, contributing to major fish kills and causing the death of many cold-blooded animals which are unable to adjust to the temperature change. Still other aspects of this problem that have been dramatically revealed in recent years include the destruction of marine life, both real and potential, resulting from oil spills, and the physical damage done to humans who have eaten fish and other aquatic foods poisoned by the discharge of toxic chemicals such as mercury.

Considering the more direct impact of increasing numbers of affluent consumers, a growing population means an increase in the amount of waste created every day, and many municipal sewers are today dumping waste into rivers and streams at rates far in excess of what is considered optimal to maintain pure water. The problem is further intensified by modern technology, which gives today's consumer a wide variety of labor-saving devices such as washing machines, garbage disposals, and dishwashers that not only increase the demand for water but also contribute toward its pollution. In some areas the situation is so acute that if pollution is not more effectively controlled, existing treatment and purification facilities will soon be incapable of producing potable water.

It bears repeating here that no one should be naive enough to regard population growth as a direct cause of increasing environmental pollution. The nature and amount of such pollution is not so much a function of the absolute number of people as it is of their level of affluence and their associated patterns of consumption. Further, emphasis on population alone ignores the very important political dimension to the problem: far too much environmental pollution exists in the United States today (and in other industrialized nations as well) because of the unregulated and irresponsible activities of corporate producers vis-à-vis uncontrolled industrial burning and the expulsion (or deliberate dumping) of toxic waste products. In short, industry pollutes the environment not because of growing numbers of people, but because the society has allowed it to by its failure to adopt sufficiently strong environmental protection programs. It is going to take the adoption and strict government enforcement of strong legislative measures, not simply an end to population growth, to bring these pollution problems under control. However, it can be said at the same time that a growing population increases the seriousness of the problem in general, and that continued population growth will make the ultimate solution that much more difficult—and more costly—to achieve.

The Threat to Individual Freedom

Perhaps the most serious threat to the quality of American life is found in the area of individual freedom. Americans have long cherished their privacy—as witness the western pioneer who decided it was time to move when the smoke from his neighbor's fire became visible. And our love of the basic democratic freedoms (of speech, thought, assembly, travel, and so on) is well attested to by the wars we have fought (in other countries as well as at home) to protect them. But today we stand in real danger of losing much of this cherished freedom and privacy.

The democratic institutions we know and love so well are today being challenged from two directions, both of which are intimately related to the numerical increase in population. On the one hand, we are challenged from without by the ever present danger of an "explosion" among the seething masses in the world's less developed areas. On the other hand, we are challenged from within by the growth of formal organization and bureaucracy with its emphasis on conformity and its deemphasis on the individual and individuality.

The External Threat

The implication of the present population crisis for world peace has already been noted in an earlier discussion of the political aspects of the world food situation (see Chapter 8); nevertheless the problem is sufficiently serious to merit further attention. The tensions and political instabilities generated by explosive population growth in the economically less developed nations have a very special significance in the contemporary world because the split between the haves and the have-nots cuts across the cleft between communist and noncommunist nations of the developed world. That is, many of the Third World developing countries that are today struggling to raise their level of living remain uncommitted in the East–West power struggle that has emerged since the end of World War II. In their efforts to generate sustained economic growth, these poorer nations of Africa, Asia, and Latin America are faced with a choice between the Western *evolutionary* way or the communist *revolutionary* way. If the nations that elect the communist route to development demonstrate that they can achieve their goal sooner and more efficiently than those who elect to follow a more democratic process, then the ideological basis of our Western way of life will be open to serious challenge from the Third World. It is not sufficient for people in the West to sit complacently by, comforting themselves with the belief that the communist approach is doomed to failure (a belief that is not necessarily true). The struggling nations must be offered all the help possible, not only in developing their economies but also in reducing their birth rates and slowing down their rates of population growth. Success or failure in the East–West struggle may well hinge on the ability of the nations involved to control their rate of population growth. In order to promote world stability and facilitate the preservation of our own freedom it therefore behooves us to do everything in our power to aid the development process in the countries of Asia, Africa, and Latin America.

East–West ideological power struggles aside, the problem of Third World population growth and poverty is likely to be a major cause of growing international tensions and political instability throughout the remainder of this century. Within many of these countries, rapid population growth is closely associated with rising unemployment, falling wages, and increasing poverty, particularly in the urban centers where the natural increase of the population is being augmented by a fairly heavy volume of rural-to-urban migration. That is, many developing countries are witnessing the growth of an increasingly volatile urban proletariat that makes growing demands for such basic services as housing, education, and health care. Efforts to meet these demands generally mean that scarce capital has to be diverted from other areas, often to the detriment of overall development plans, and this in turn often aggravates the already depressed economic situation (Stockwell and Laidlaw, 1981, pp. 96–97). Failure to meet these demands leads to increasing unrest and, in many cases, increasing violence, perhaps even revolutionary action: witness Iran in 1979, and Nicaragua, El Salvador, and Lebanon in the early 1980s, to cite only some of the more recent trouble spots. While such internal violence does not necessarily pose a direct threat to the peace and stability of American society, there can be no denying the profound impact it has on our lives, and we can anticipate that future conflicts of this nature will continue to have a profound impact on our lives in the years ahead.

The Internal Threat

The second threat to individual freedom in the United States—the threat from within—is less dramatic and consequently more insidious than the external one. This threat arises from the simple fact that societal life necessarily becomes more complex as numbers increase. For one thing, an increase in numbers creates the need for more organization, which means, in effect, the further enhancement of group or societal values rather than individual values. The trend toward increasing complexity of organization has been pronounced in the United States during the postwar period, and a continuation of this tendency could lead to such an encroachment on personal freedom as to approximate totalitarianism.

As numbers increase, so does the need for police and fire protection, educational facilities, sanitation control, health and welfare programs, and so on. Such services are not as important to the smooth functioning of smaller groups, and where they are necessary they can generally be handled on an individual level. As the populatioin grows, however, the task of providing such services becomes too large to be carried out on an individual basis, and collective action becomes more and more necessary. As collectivities increase in importance, the freedom of the individual declines proportionately.

The impact of population growth on greater control of the individual (and consequent loss of individual freedom) can be seen in a number of ways. The more numbers increase, the greater the need for formal laws to regulate more and more aspects of human behavior. Our behavior is already controlled in many ways: traffic speed laws, stop signs and lights; requirements for a license to marry, drive a car, hunt, fish, and so on. Such seemingly insignificant control measures could become considerably more widespread if the population grows much larger. Many communities throughout the nation, for example, have suddenly found themselves faced with numerous problems resulting from haphazard land development and have recently established planning and zoning commissions and created legislation (building codes, zoning restrictions) in an effort to achieve more orderly development. The controls adopted could become even more stringent if population continues to increase. In this respect, the years ahead could see the use of privately owned land (if land is allowed to remain privately owned!) becoming further and further circumscribed. As one American couple suggested several years ago,

> Eventually, there could be no such thing as a "family farm" or a "place in the country"—or, under still greater pressure of numbers, even a backyard—whose owner could be allowed the luxury of determining for himself how he wanted to use it, whether to use it for growing flowers instead of for the production of food or minerals. In these more extreme conditions, the right of eminent domain would become little more than a museum piece; the idea that a man's home was his castle, something of a wry joke (Day and Day, 1964, p. 69).

Increasing control over the individual is also felt in the need for greater centralization. As numbers continue to swell, and particularly as population density continues to increase, the autonomy that many local communities now cherish will have to be sacrificed to the dictates of regional needs. In the northeastern metropolitan belt, where localities run into and overlap one another in what is fast becoming a virtually uninterrupted urban chain along the entire length of the Atlantic Coast, the idea that one community can exist and function independently of its neighbors begins to seem ridiculous. Given this situation, the future of autonomous communities acting independently of one another is virtually doomed, and it is readily apparent that some sort of new government unit is needed, with sufficient powers to plan and administer a wider geographical area.

Still another indication of the deleterious impact of population growth on individual freedom is the widening gulf between the individual and the various groups controlling his or her destiny. Such groups are not limited to those governmental bodies that run the country but also include the managing elite of labor unions, educational institutions, religious bodies, and corporations. When Andrew Jackson was President, any American could call at the White House and expect to be received cordially. The idea of a President today trying to welcome every complainant or well-wisher is horrendous to contemplate. Similarly, a generation ago it was not unusual for college professors to entertain their classes at home. Today's student, however, is likely to have to wait in line for long periods of time just to obtain his grade from a graduate assistant! Both of these illustrations reflect the impact of simple increases in sheer numbers. This gap between the individual and members of formal organizations with which he or she is associated does not necessarily damage the operation of the organizations concerned. But it does mean that individuals have progressively less control over decisions concerning their own welfare, and it is a major cause of the increasing alienation that some scholars see as a growing malaise of contemporary urban-industrial society.

It should be clear that in a large and increasing population, the individual is not only more and more constrained to follow the dictates of the group; he or she also has less and less of a say in determining these dictates. As was noted with respect to the problem of environmental pollution, population growth is certainly not the only cause of the deemphasis on the individual in the modern era. It is, however, a major component of the coalition of forces that have transformed this society from one in which individual values are paramount to one in which the group dominates. As one observer noted more than two decades ago,

> The urbanization of society, the collectivization of economic activity into huge corporate concentrates with the accompanying trade unions, the change in nature of government from the "nightwatchman State" to the "Security State," the rapid depletion of natural resources, the dangers from hostile ideologies and national power centers, the rise of mass democracy and the trend toward equality—all of these and more merge into an unmistakable movement away from individualism to a new type of society, one in which the person qua individual tends to be submerged into a congeries of collectivities (Miller, 1960, p. 615).

There can be little doubt that population growth is a major contributor to all these trends, and as long as it persists it will continue to contribute to a further depersonalization of the individual. As long as population continues to grow, we can anticipate increasing control over individual actions, principally through the expansion of government programs and activities. But even though greater control is inevitable, the magnitude and severity of the increase is still an open question: just how stringent this control will be depends on how soon the population of the United States becomes stable. The more people there are when the population becomes stabilized (as eventually it must, given the finite qualities of the earth), the greater will be the control exercised over individual activities. Thus, it would clearly be to our advantage to adopt and adhere to a positive population policy that aims for a population sufficiently small so that it would produce the conditions (economic, political, and social) that will enable us to maintain a society in which democratic values are maximized. This view was clearly expressed in the report of a recent presidential commission to examine the role of population in America's future (Commission on Population and the American Future, 1972). A major conclusion of this commission was that the United States would not benefit substantially from continued population growth and that we should work toward the development of a national policy for social development in which population factors would receive major consideration. As yet we have not moved very far in the direction recommended by the commission. Nevertheless, the fact of the matter is that numerical stability must come soon in the United States if we are to maintain, let alone extend, the traditional high quality of our American way of life. Greater control may be inevitable, but the smaller the ultimate population the less stringent (and therefore less painful) the controls will be.

Limitations of Zero Population Growth

The argument for ending population growth as a means of alleviating many problems requires some clarification. Such a clarification is all the more necessary in view of the fact that we seem to be moving toward the attainment of zero population growth (ZPG) in the United States. In a perfect ZPG society, age-specific birth and death rates remain constant so that the size and age–sex structure of a population remains stationary from one year to the next. (The characteristics of this ideal stationary population are discussed in Appendix C). Some people regard ZPG as a potential threat to our national well-being. Some, for example, worry that zero population growth will lead to zero economic growth; others see it as contributing to a decline in our military strength; and still others see population pressure as a potent stimulus to scientific and technological innovation, and they look upon ZPG as likely to cause a considerable slowdown in, if not a complete halt to, the rate of human progress.

Such fears are fairly easy to counter: (1) per capita buying power, not numbers of consumers, determines the rate of economic growth, and a stationary population with proportionately fewer dependent children and more working adults should generate more discretionary income than a rapidly growing one; (2) military might cannot be equated with population size in an era of rockets, satellites, and nuclear technology; and (3) it is naive to assume that people will stop being interested in improving the quality of their lives simply because there is no pressure to do so.

Even more worrisome, perhaps, is the contrary position that ZPG, by reducing pressure on resources and the environment, will bring with it some magical solution to the many social, economic, and political problems confronting American society today. Such is definitely not the case. As we stressed in our reconsideration of the lifeboat ethic, an end to population growth will not, by itself, solve anything. In order to reduce air pollution, for example, we need to control factory emissions and develop a more fuel-efficient automobile engine, not reduce the number of people. Given a society that is committed to scientific and technological progress, the most we can expect from ZPG is a slowing down of the rate at which the many population-related problems are increasing; this, one may hope, will make it a little bit easier to cope with those problems.

SUMMARY

As of 1980 the population of the United States numbered nearly 227 million people, and it was growing at the relatively modest rate of 1.1 percent a year. Although immigration had once again emerged as a major contributor, most of our growth reflected an excess of births over deaths. However, there was some basis for wondering how long this excess would characterize our population. The sharp reduction in fertility since the mid-1960s and its persistence at a relatively low level has made it clear that the growth spurt occasioned by the postwar baby boom is clearly over. Moreover, the level of reproduction was so low that we were well on our way to becoming a zero growth society.

Coupled with the fact that our internal growth is well under control is the fact that, despite the increasing instability of our economy during the late 1970s, the people of the United States continue to enjoy the highest level of living of any nation in the history of the world. In other words, with respect to population size and growth and our future well-being, we are substantially better off than the many poverty-stricken Third World nations in Asia, Africa, and Latin America. Nevertheless, this does not mean that our country is free of population problems. On the one hand, the past growth of our population is already having an impact on the quality of American life; and the continued growth that is projected for the next couple of generations can only intensify many of the population-related problems with which we now have to contend.

On the other hand, the United States does not exist in a vacuum but is part of a larger world society in which population growth trends in one part have various social, economic, and political ramifications throughout all other parts. We live in a world today that is highly interdependent and that is becoming more so every year. To ignore this fact is to court disaster. The problem of rapid population growth in the Third World countries of

Asia, Africa, and Latin America has emerged as one of the most critical problems facing the human race today, and it will likely continue to be a critical problem for several decades to come. Vast efforts have already been put forth to reduce fertility and slow down the rate of population growth in these developing countries, and some limited success has indeed been achieved. However, considerable efforts in this direction will continue to be required for the remainder of this century, if not longer. Added to this is what many believe to be the need, indeed the moral imperative, for the people of the United States and other highly industrialized countries to curtail sharply their unnecessarily high and often wasteful levels of consumption of the world's resources (van der Tak et al., 1979). More than the well-being of the people in the poor countries is at stake; the well-being of all of us hangs in the balance, and it is very much in the best interests of all of us to exert the massive efforts that are and will be required to bring about an end to the present population explosion in the less developed countries and to achieve some semblance of socioeconomic parity throughout the world.

REFERENCES AND SUGGESTED READING

Bouvier, Leon E. "U.S. Population in 2000—Zero Growth or Not?" *Population Bulletin*, 30 (1975): 3–30.

Breiver, Michael. "The Changing U.S. Farmland Scene." *Population Bulletin*, 36 (December 1981).

Brown, Lester R. "World Population Trends: Signs of Hope, Signs of Stress." Worldwatch Paper 8. Washington, D.C.: Worldwatch Institute, October 1976.

Butz, William P., et al. *Demographic Challenge in America's Future*. Santa Monica, Calif.: Rand Corporation, 1982.

Commission on Population Growth and the American Future. *Population and the American Future*. Washington, D.C.: U.S. Government Printing Office, 1972.

Council on Environmental Quality. *The Global Report to the President: Entering the Twenty-first Century*, Vol. I, *The Summary Report*, Washington, D.C.: U.S. Government Printing Office, 1980.

Day, Lincoln H. "What Will a ZPG Society Be Like?" *Population Bulletin*, 33 (June 1978): 3–38.

Day, Lincoln H., and Alice Taylor Day. *Too Many Americans*. New York: Dell, 1964.

Ehrlich, Paul R., and Anne H. Ehrlich. *Population, Resources, Environment*. San Francisco: W. H. Freeman, 1970.

Gordon, Mitchell. *Sick Cities.* New York: Penguin, 1965.

Gottman, Jean. *Megalopolis: The Urbanized Northeastern Seaboard of the United States.* Cambridge, Mass.: MIT Press, 1961.

Hardin, Garrett. "Living in a Lifeboat." *Bio-Science,* 24 (October 1974): 561–68.

Humphrey, Craig, and Frederick Buttel. *Environment, Energy and Society.* Belmont, Calif.: Wadsworth, 1982.

Julian, Joseph. *Social Problems,* 3rd ed. Englewood Cliffs, N.J.: Prentice-Hall, 1980.

Miller, Arthur S. "Some Observations on the Political Economy of Population Growth." *Law and Contemporary Problems,* 25 (Summer 1960): 614–29.

Omran, Abdel R. "Epidemiologic Transition in the U.S." *Population Bulletin,* 32 (May 1977): 3–42.

Ophuls, William. *Ecology and the Politics of Scarcity.* San Francisco: W. H. Freeman, 1977.

Osborn, Frederick. *Population: An International Dilemma.* Princeton, N.J.: Princeton University Press, 1958.

Population Reference Bureau. *Intercom,* 9 (February 1981).

Population Reference Bureau. "U.S. Population: Where We Are; Where We're Going." *Population Bulletin,* 37 (June 1982).

Ridker, Ronald G., and Elizabeth W. Cecelski. "Resources, Environment, and Population: The Nature of Future Limits." *Population Bulletin,* 34 (August 1979): 3–39.

Schnaiberg, Allan. *Environment: From Surplus to Scarcity.* New York: Oxford University Press, 1980.

Stockwell, Edward G., and Karen A. Laidlaw. *Third World Development: Problems and Prospects.* Chicago: Nelson-Hall, 1981.

U.S. Bureau of the Census. *Historical Statistics of the United States: Colonial Times to 1970.* Washington, D.C.: U.S. Government Printing Office, 1975.

U.S. Bureau of the Census. "Projections of the Population of the United States: 1977 to 2050." *Current Population Reports,* Series P-25, No. 704 (July 1977).

U.S. Bureau of the Census. *World Population 1979—Summary—Recent Demographic Estimates for the Countries and Regions of the World.* Washington, D.C.: U.S. Government Printing Office, 1980.

U.S. Bureau of the Census. "Estimates of the Population of the United States to November 1, 1980." *Current Population Reports,* Series P-25, No. 895 (January 1981).

van der Tak, Jean, Carl Haub, and Elaine Murphy. "Our Population Predicament: A New Look." *Population Bulletin,* 34 (December 1979): 3–46.

Weller, Robert H., and Leon F. Bouvier. *Population: Demography and Policy.* New York: St. Martin's, 1981.

Immigrants arriving at Ellis Island in 1923 . . .

. . . and being examined for trachoma. If found, trachoma meant rejection by the New World.

Completion of the transcontinental railroad in 1869 greatly facilitated the westward movement of the American population.

Political upheavals and crises continue to create refugees throughout the world.

Americans are a highly mobile people. Approximately 20 percent change their places of residence each year.

Slum dwellings in the black village of Cross Roads, South Africa

WORLD POPULATION

It is estimated that several hundred thousand Mexicans enter the United States illegally each year.

In the 1960s, the Baby Boomers came of age in the United States.

INTERNAL MIGRATION AND POPULATION REDISTRIBUTION

11

No one can deny the general role that international migration has played in dispersing the human population over the face of the earth, nor would anyone undervalue its more specific contribution to the growth and development of a number of modern nation states (e.g., Israel, Argentina, and the English-speaking countries of North America and Oceania). Moreover, it should be clear from Chapter 9 that international migration continues to be a major force in the world today, not only for economic reasons (as is illustrated by the guest worker exchange programs that have been established among many countries) but also because of its political importance (as is illustrated by the many problems associated with refugees and illegal aliens). At the same time, however, an equally important demographic phenomenon, perhaps a more important one, is the movement of population within the boundaries of nations. Many less developed countries, for example, are today facing serious problems because of excessive migration out of rural areas into already overcrowded urban centers. Even in more advanced societies a variety of problems can be caused or exacerbated by this pattern of internal migration.

In this chapter we shall consider (1) general mobility within the United States, (2) the major changes internal migration has brought about and is bringing about in the distribution of the American population, and (3) some internal migration and population redistribution trends and problems in other countries.

POPULATION MOBILITY IN THE UNITED STATES

Added to the fact that immigration from abroad has played a major role in the growth and development of the United States is the equally significant fact that there has always been a substantial volume of residential mobility within the country. Each new year sees the center of population move farther westward as the people become more evenly dispersed through the land, and each new year sees an increase in the proportion of the population living in or near large urban areas of the country. Within the urban areas, migration trends recently have brought about a shift in the balance of the population from the older central cities to the newly developing suburban fringe areas. Beginning in the 1970s internal mobility has played a major role in the accelerated rate of population growth in the rapidly developing Sun Belt areas in the southern and western United States.

The extent to which Americans are a mobile people is well illustrated by the fact that 45 percent of the persons five years old and over living in the United States in 1980 were living in a different house from the one they had lived in five years earlier (see Table 11-1). Other estimates indicate that approximately one out of every five persons in this country moves from one house or apartment to another every year, and about one in twenty moves from one county to another. Although it has long been known that repeated movement by the same people accounts for part of the high annual mobility rate in the United States (Goldstein, 1958; Taeuber et al., 1968), it is a fact that not more than 2 or 3 percent of the adult population spend their entire lives in the same house or apartment, and perhaps not more than 10 to 15 percent live their entire lives within the same county. Thus, while we may not be a "race of nomads" or a "nation of strangers" as some popular writers have suggested (Packard, 1972; Toffler, 1970), it is eminently clear that Americans move around a great deal. In this section further consideration will be given to the overall mobility status of our population as well as to differences in the mobility level of particular subgroups and to some of the problems related to present patterns of residential mobility. Before discussing trends and differentials, however, it is necessary to become acquainted with some of the basic mobility concepts currently in use in the United States.

Mobility Concepts Defined

Because residential mobility is one of the fundamental mechanisms of population change, a knowledge of the extent to which people are moving, the characteristics of movers, and their respective areas of origin and destination is necessary for an adequate understanding of the developments that

Table 11-1

Percent Distribution of the American Population in the Spring of 1960, 1970, and 1980 by Residence Five Years Earlier

Residence 5 years earlier	1960	1970	1980
Total age 5 and over			
Number (in thousands)	159,004	186,094	202,216
Percent	100.0	100.0	100.0
Same house (nonmovers)	49.9%	53.0%	53.0%
Different house in U.S. (movers)	48.9	45.6	45.1
Same county	29.8	23.3	25.8
Different county (migrants)	17.4	17.1	19.3
Same State	8.5	8.4	10.2
Different State	8.9	8.6	9.1
Abroad	1.3	1.4	1.9

SOURCE: U.S. Bureau of the Census, *1970 Census of Population,* Final Report PC(1)-C1, *General Social and Economic Characteristics: United States Summary* (Washington, D.C., 1972); and "Geographic Mobility: March 1975 to March 1980," *Current Population Reports,* Series P-20, No. 368 (December 1981). The category of "Movers" in 1960 and 1970 includes persons who moved but whose place of earlier residence was not reported.

are taking place in any population. For this reason the United States Bureau of the Census periodically collects information designed to measure population mobility. Aside from the data on the state of birth of the native population that have been collected at each census since the middle of the nineteenth century (see Appendix B), internal migration statistics are derived from the responses to census or survey questions on current place of residence cross-tabulated by place of residence at some specified earlier date. Such questions have been asked annually since 1947 as part of the *Current Population Survey* (see Appendix A), and they have been included on each decennial census since 1940. One of the questions on the 1980 census schedule, for example, asked for usual place of residence on April 1, 1975, of persons who were five years old or over on April 1, 1980. The extent of mobility in the population was then determined by comparing the answers to this question to usual place of residence at the time of the census.

In classifying the population according to mobility status, the Bureau of the Census identifies three main categories:

1. *Nonmobile Persons* (nonmovers): This category includes all persons reported as living in the same house at both the time of the survey or census and at the earlier specified date.

2. *Mobile Persons* (movers): This category consists of all persons whose residence at the time of the census or survey was in a "different house in the United States" from that of the earlier specified date. Such mobile persons are further subdivided into *intracounty movers*, or persons who lived in a different house but whose place of residence at the two dates in question was in the same county; and *intercounty movers*, or *migrants*—persons whose place of residence at the two dates was in a "different county." These intercounty migrants were subdivided into *intrastate migrants* (persons who moved to a different county within the same state) and *interstate migrants* (persons who moved to a different county in a different state).
3. *Movers from Abroad:* This group consists of persons, either citizens or aliens, living in this country at the time of the census or survey, whose place of residence at the specified earlier date was outside the United States. This group includes persons who were living either in an outlying area under the jurisdiction of the United States or in a foreign country. These persons are distinguished from the general category of movers who moved from one place to another within the United States.

Mobility Status of the American Population

The general mobility status of the United States population in the spring of 1960, 1970, and 1980 is depicted in Table 11-1. Of the slightly more than 202 million persons five years old and over living in the nation at the most recent date, roughly 107 million (53 percent) were living in the same house they had lived in five years earlier. During the same period (1975–1980), some 52 million persons had changed their place of residence within a single county (roughly one-fourth of the eligible population), and another 39 million persons (19 percent of the population) had moved across county lines. This migration was fairly evenly divided between intrastate and interstate movers, with a slightly larger proportion (10 percent as opposed to 9 percent of the total population age five and over) moving within the same state. Finally, nearly 2 percent (3.8 million people) of those persons five years old and over had been living outside the boundaries of the United States in 1975. All in all, some 91 million persons, 45 percent of the nation's population age five and over in 1980, were living in a different house from the one in which they had lived in 1975.

Although there have been a few minor changes in the relative size of the various categories, one of the more remarkable observations to be drawn from the data in Table 11-1 is that the general pattern of mobility has re-

Table 11-2
Interregional Migration and Metropolitan-Nonmetropolitan Migration in the United States (in thousands)

	Region				All areas	
	Northeast	North Central	South	West	Metropolitan	Nonmetropolitan
1965–70						
In-migrants	1,273	2,024	3,142	2,309	5,457	5,809
Out-migrants	1,988	2,661	2,486	1,613	5,809	5,457
Net migrants	−715	−637	+656	+696	−352	+352
1970–75						
In-migrants	1,057	1,731	4,082	2,347	5,127	6,721
Out-migrants	2,399	2,926	2,253	1,639	6,721	5,127
Net migrants	−1,342	−1,195	+1,829	+708	−1,594	+1,594
1975–80						
In-migrants	1,106	1,993	4,204	2,838	5,993	7,337
Out-migrants	2,592	3,166	2,440	1,945	7,337	5,993
Net migrants	−1,486	−1,173	+1,764	+893	−1,344	+1,344

SOURCE: U.S. Bureau of the Census, "Geographic Mobility: March 1975 to March 1980," *Current Population Reports,* Series P-20, No. 368 (December 1981).

mained fairly stable over time. For all three dates, roughly 45 percent of all Americans age five and over were classified as mobile (i.e., were living in a different house than they had lived in five years earlier), and roughly one out of five was living in a different house in a different county. The "different county" migrants were distributed fairly evenly among intrastate and interstate migrants, and at all three dates between 1 and 2 percent of the eligible population had been living outside the boundaries of the United States five years previously. Thus, while such trends as the increasing rate of female labor force participation and the associated greater commitment of women to their own careers, as well as the overall aging of the population (see Chapter 12), are likely to mitigate against any sizable increase in the propensity to move, it is clear that the relatively high level of mobility long characteristic of the United States population has not shown any signs of declining.

While the overall level of mobility appears to be fairly stable, the same cannot be said for the volume and direction of particular mobility streams (see Table 11-2). In recent years, for example, there has been a pronounced increase in the volume of migration out of the Northeastern and North Central regions into the West and especially into the South where, since the early 1970s, the black exodus has undergone a marked reversal. There has also been a notable slowdown in the long-term trend toward an increasing migration loss to metropolitan areas and a corresponding increasing net gain to nonmetropolitan areas, particularly in the Sun Belt states. The significance of such migration streams lies largely in the impact that they have on the overall distribution of the population. This topic is discussed more fully later in this chapter.

Differential Mobility

Although Americans in general are very mobile, not all segments of the population are characterized by the same mobility patterns. Over the years, for example, small but fairly consistent differences have been observed in the level of mobility by both *sex* and *race* (see Table 11-3). Males are slightly more mobile than females, with the differential increasing with distance covered. Blacks have a slightly higher overall mobility rate than whites, but blacks are characterized by a notably greater amount of short distance (intercounty) movement.

The slightly higher rate of mobility among American males has traditionally been explained by the fact that men in our Western culture have always enjoyed a greater freedom to travel than women have. More specifically, the higher rate of mobility among males was influenced by such things as the fairly large number who were in the armed forces, the cultural role of the male as the family breadwinner, which made it more likely that men would move around more in search of better job opportunities, and the greater

Table 11-3
Mobility Status of U.S. Population by Sex and Color

Residence in 1975 compared with 1980	Male	Female	White	Black
Total age 5 and over Number (in thousands)	97,567	104,648	175,185	23,037
Percent	100.0	100.0	100.0	100.0
Same House	52.1	53.8	53.3	52.8
Different House in U.S.	45.6	44.4	45.0	45.8
Same County	25.8	25.7	24.8	33.0
Different County	19.8	18.7	20.2	12.7
Same State	10.4	9.9	10.7	6.4
Different State	9.4	8.8	9.4	6.3
Abroad	2.1	1.6	1.5	1.5

SOURCE: U.S. Bureau of the Census, "Geographic Mobility: March 1975 to March 1980," *Current Population Reports,* Series P-20, No. 368 (December 1981).

tendency for males to attend college, especially at longer distances from home. Given all these factors, it is surprising that the sex mobility differential is as small as it is. One reason it is not larger is that when men move they generally take their families with them, and their wives and children also show up as movers in the mobility statistics. In more recent times the growth of the women's movement has offset many of the factors that earlier contributed to higher male mobility, and it is likely that both of these phenomena will serve to keep the sex mobility differential at its present modest level.

The higher rate of mobility among blacks, particularly the notably higher incidence of short-distance movement, is likely a reflection of the generally greater instability characteristic of the American black family, and especially the many inequalities that still exist in our society, making it necessary for black people to move around more in search of a better job, improved housing conditions, and so on.

Figure 11-1
General Mobility Rate* by Age: United States, 1980

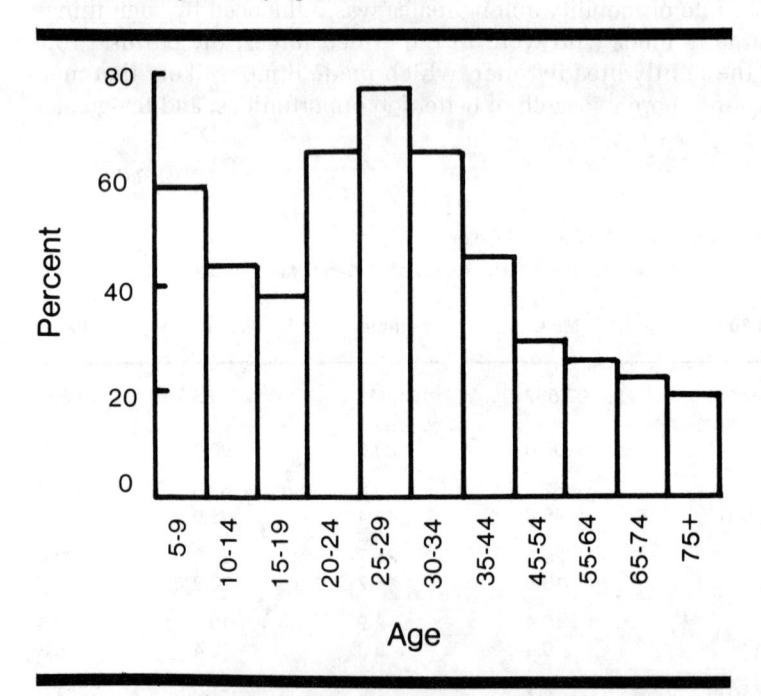

SOURCE: Based on data in U.S. Bureau of the Census, "Geographic Mobility: March 1975 to March 1980," *Current Population Reports,* Series P-20, No. 368 (December 1981).
*Percent of 1980 population living in a different house in 1975.

Age

One important variable according to which mobility rates differ is age. The overall pattern of this differential is clearly depicted in Figure 11-1. It is readily apparent that the young adult population is by far the most mobile age group in the United States. More than seven out of ten persons twenty-five to twenty-nine years of age in 1980 had changed their place of residence sometime during the preceding five-year period. As age increased beyond thirty years, the percentage of movers decreased. Slightly more than six out of ten persons thirty to thirty-four years of age were living in a different house in 1980 than they had lived in five years earlier. At age thirty-five to forty-four this figure decreased to slightly more than four out of ten. At ages forty-five to fifty-four it was slightly less than three in ten, and from fifty-five to seventy-four only about two in ten had changed their place of residence between 1975 and 1980. In the oldest age group, seventy-five and over, the proportion of movers was slightly less than two out of ten. At the other end of the age cycle, nearly 60 percent of the children five to nine years of age had moved during the five years preceding 1980, and roughly four out of ten children age ten to nineteen had changed their place of residence between 1975 and 1980.

This general pattern is fairly consistent for all moves, whether they occurred within the same county, between counties in the same state, or between states. Mobility rates reach a peak during the twenties and then decline with age up to age seventy-five. The high rate of mobility among persons in their twenties is due to this being the age when young people leave the parental home, marry, and establish homes of their own. The decline in mobility at succeeding ages reflects a trend toward greater stability as persons develop strengthening social and economic ties to a particular job or community, whereas the higher rate of mobility of children is coincidental with that of their parents. Naturally there are exceptions to these rules. Not all young people leave home when they mature; some persons never achieve a stable relationship in a community; and some jobs entail a higher degree of mobility than others. For the majority of persons, however, this general pattern applies.

Socioeconomic Status

Mobility rates also tend to vary directly with socioeconomic status. For example, the survey carried out by the Bureau of the Census in the spring of 1980 revealed that fully one-third of the mobile workers were employed at professional or managerial jobs and that over half of these high-status workers had moved during the preceding five years. More significantly, the data depicted in Figure 11-2 reveal a marked differential by education: the higher a person's education the greater the amount of mobility. Differentials such as these suggest that areas of out-migration might be experiencing a quali-

Figure 11-2
General Mobility Rate* by Level of Educational Attainment: United States, 1980

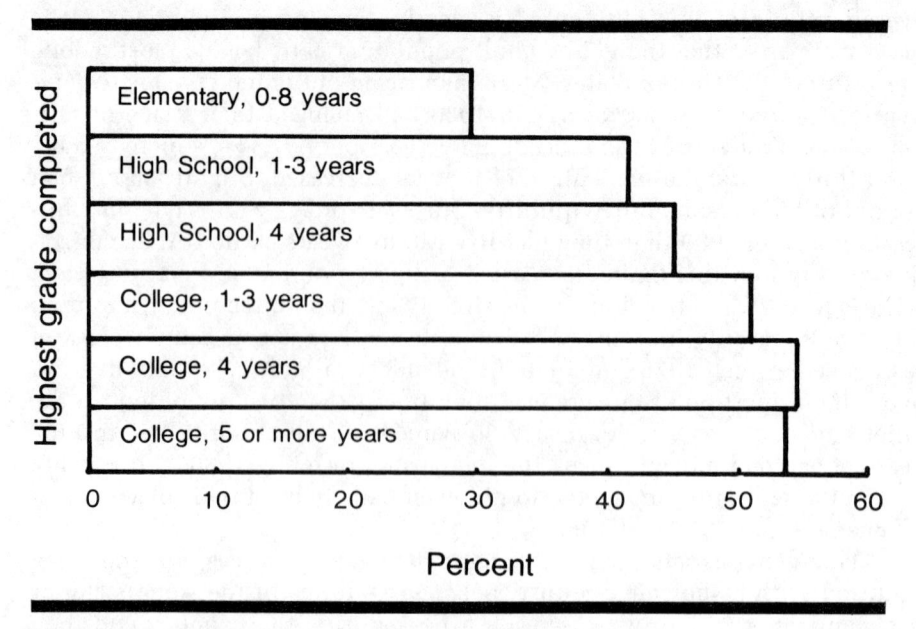

Highest grade completed	Percent
Elementary, 0-8 years	~30
High School, 1-3 years	~41
High School, 4 years	~44
College, 1-3 years	~51
College, 4 years	~54
College, 5 or more years	~53

SOURCE: Based on data in U.S. Bureau of the Census, "Geographic Mobility: March 1975 to March 1980," *Current Population Reports,* Series P-20, No. 368 (December 1981).
*Percent of 1980 population living in a different house in 1975.

tative as well as a simple quantitative loss. One instance in which this is a fact is represented by the economic decline of many urban centers in the United States during the post-World War II era as the more well-to-do members of the population have moved out of the cities into the surrounding suburbs. The implications of this movement will be discussed more fully in a later section of this chapter. On a somewhat positive note, however, we should also point out that much of the internal mobility in our society today entails a general interchange between areas and it has relatively little impact on the communities involved. In today's modern, highly specialized industrial society, migration has become a routine part of the career development of many people, and streams of migration between areas often reflect little more than a circulation of persons whose moves are associated with their life cycle stages more than with real differences in economic opportunity.

To summarize briefly, the propensity to migrate is not distributed evenly among all segments of the population. In the United States the most pronounced differences are those associated with the life cycle and socioeconomic status, and whether or not a given individual decides to move at any time will in large measure be a function of his or her age and level of educational attainment. Such a decision will most often be associated with a change in marital or family status or with a change of job (or spouse's job).

PROBLEMS RELATING TO POPULATION MOBILITY

The high rate of mobility of the American people is not without its problems. Although a detailed discussion of the variety and complexity of such problems is beyond the scope of this book, we can identify a few broad areas and cite some specific examples to indicate the kinds of problems that may arise as a consequence of population mobility. To this end, the various mobility-related problems may be grouped into three broad categories: (1) problems that relate to the generally high degree of mobility in the *population as a whole*; (2) those that relate to the impact of mobility on the *individuals* involved; and (3) those that relate to the impact of mobility on the *communities* involved.

The High Rate of Mobility

To begin with, it may be noted that with roughly 20 percent of the population moving each year, Americans are among the most highly mobile people in the world. Historically this has proven to be a definite economic advantage in that it has helped to balance the distribution of numbers in relation to available resources as the nation has grown and expanded. By dispersing people from one section of the country to another, it has also helped to create a relatively homogeneous society. This relatively high degree of mobility creates numerous problems, however. The basic problem is the difficulty in preparing and maintaining adequate estimates of the population of local areas, and this seriously impedes the effectiveness of a wide variety of local, state, regional, and national planning organizations. For example, it hampers businessmen who want to identify the size and characteristics of particular consumer markets, and it can complicate the work of economic development agencies trying to keep track of the size and occupational skills of the labor force in various areas. A similar dilemma faces the various groups whose task it is to (1) plan for the utilization and conservation of local natural resources such as land and water, (2) evaluate the adequacy of existing schools, hospitals, and other community services, (3) provide for the housing and other needs of older persons, and so forth. In short, persons or groups who want to know something about the size and composition of local populations in order to have a sound basis for devising programs have their efforts severely complicated by the high mobility of the American population.

Such problems are minimal at the time of decennial censuses, and their existence during interim periods is mainly due to the absence of a systematic program of data collection. Until current mobility data become more readily available for local areas in this country, problems of high mobility such as those cited above will continue to exist.

Problems for the Individual

From a more purely sociological perspective, interest focuses on the effects of mobility on the individuals who move and on the communities between which they move. In part, the problems here are similar to the problems foreign immigrants had to face (cultural shock, adapting to a new environment, marginality, ethnic ghettos, and so on). We will consider the individual level first.

Since people often cite some sort of economic reason for moving (a new job, better housing), migration frequently results in an improvement in an individual's economic situation. But this is not always the case, as is clearly revealed by the experience of migrant farm workers and by the existence of chronic poverty in the ethnic ghettos of many of our large urban centers.

Discounting the economic impact, a number of other frequent corollaries of population mobility may be noted. For one thing, the incidence of personal and social disorganization (e.g., crime, divorce, prostitution, drug addiction, illegitimacy, alcoholism) is higher among mobile persons than among the more sedentary segments of the population. Mental health has been studied extensively in this country, and the results of these investigations clearly show that the incidence of mental disorders is substantially higher among migrants than among nonmovers.

Migration (particularly group differences in migration) may also be indicative of other social and economic problems in the nation. The greater mobility of blacks, for example, is a sign of greater instability among that segment of the American population, as reflected in the greater incidence of mental disorders among them. This greater instability is in turn the result of the ethnic discrimination that has historically made it necessary for blacks to move around more in order to find good jobs, decent housing, and so forth.

Problems for the Community

With respect to the impact of mobility on the community, the most general observation is that heavy in-migration is often an indicator of economic growth and development, whereas heavy out-migration more commonly signifies a decaying socioeconomic environment. With regard to the community of destination, in-migration can also create problems. It may cause a housing shortage, overcrowding in the schools, or a widening gap between various public service needs (police and fire protection, hospital facilities, public utilities) and the services actually provided. For the most part, the nature of mobility-related problems in any community reflects the particular characteristics of the in-migrants. Conflict in one degree or another often results when the new arrivals differ sharply from the old residents (vis-à-vis the contrast between foreign immigrants and the native population or between whites and blacks). But even less obvious variations such as difference in age or in the stage of family cycle can lead to conflict concerning such things as the need for new schools, hospitals, old age and other welfare programs, and so forth.

To illustrate, if the in-migrants are young married couples, the receiving community is faced with the task of having to provide adequate housing and educational facilities. Some settled rural and suburban communities in the United States had their traditional social organization drastically upset during the postwar years by the influx of large numbers of exurbanites with their demands for new and improved schools, better roads, and increased public services. Conversely, the in-migration of older persons increases the need for specialized housing and for expanded health and welfare programs. When there is a heavy influx of blacks or members of some other ethnic minority group, the receiving community must contend with a wide variety of social problems resulting not only from the cultural shock entailed by migration but also from the discriminatory treatment frequently meted out by the dominant group. Such problems are reflected most vividly in the widespread poverty and higher incidence of various forms of personal and social disorganization in the ethnic ghettos of our larger cities. The seriousness of such problems in contemporary urban America cannot be overemphasized.

As far as communities of origin are concerned, the impact of migration is often the converse of the impact on the communities of destination. If young people are moving out, for example, the need for school facilities is reduced at the same time that the size of the tax base is decreased for the support of other basic community services. A loss of population may frequently be regarded as a reflection of a pathological situation and a sure indication that some problem needs attention. The large-scale movement of blacks out of the South into northern cities prior to the 1970s not only created problems in the receiving areas but also reflected the pronounced lack of economic opportunities for blacks in the South—particularly the rural South. Similarly, the long-term movement of middle-class Americans to the suburbs is due not only to the pull of the aesthetic features of a nonurban environment but also to a very strong push out of the crowded, dirty, and noisy cities—many of which are well on their way to becoming large urban slums. And in the 1970s the movement out of the larger northern industrial centers into the Sun Belt has been both an index of and a stimulus to the economic expansion of the Sun Belt. It has also exacerbated a variety of problems associated with rising unemployment and local population decline in a number of northern cities. Clearly, to say that mobility has no significant impact other than to redistribute people in relation to resources is naive. Mobility creates problems and continues to play a pervasive role in the growth and development of American society.

MIGRATION AND POPULATION REDISTRIBUTION

When the first federal census was taken in 1790, as we have said, there were roughly 4 million people in the United States. Virtually all of them lived on a relatively narrow strip of land running north and south along the eastern seaboard, and nearly all of them (95 percent) lived in small rural communities. This is radically different from the situation in 1980. At the time of the most recent census, only 55 percent of the population was living in the eastern part of the country, and approximately three-fourths of all Americans were living in large metropolitan areas. These fundamental changes in the pattern of settlement could only have been effected through migration. Although differences in the rate of natural increase have always existed among the various areas of the nation, such differences have never been great enough to bring about changes in population distribution as substantial as these. In essence, then, when one talks about trends and changes in the spatial distribution of the American population one is talking primarily about trends in the volume of human migration between geographic areas.

Of the many streams of migration that have prevailed (some of which still prevail) between various areas in the United States, four stand out as having exerted a particularly profound influence on the distribution of the population over the land area. Two of these streams have been associated with significant shifts in the overall regional distribution of the population, or of one segment of it, whereas two have altered the basic structure of the local community throughout the nation. The two major regional migration trends and the distribution changes associated with them are (1) the east-to-west trend and (2) the black exodus from the South. The other two streams are (3) the historical rural-to-urban trend and (4) the suburbanization trend, which has most recently been augmented by a movement back to rural areas.

The East-to-West Trend

One of the most significant migratory trends in this country has been the east-to-west dispersion of the population. The initial settlement of the na-

Table 11-4
Regional Distribution of the Population of the United States, 1790–1980

	Percent of total population living in			
Year	Northeast	North Central	South	West
1790	50.1	...	49.9	...
1800	49.6	1.0	49.4	...
1810	48.2	4.0	47.8	...
1820	45.2	8.9	45.9	...
1830	43.1	12.5	44.4	...
1840	39.6	19.6	40.7	...
1850	37.2	23.3	38.7	0.8
1860	33.7	28.9	35.4	2.0
1870	31.9	33.7	31.9	2.6
1880	28.9	34.6	32.9	3.6
1890	27.6	35.6	31.8	5.0
1900	27.6	34.6	32.2	5.7
1910	28.0	32.4	31.9	7.7
1920	28.0	32.1	31.2	8.7
1930	27.9	31.3	30.7	10.0
1940	27.2	30.4	31.5	10.9
1950	26.1	29.4	31.2	13.3
1960	24.9	28.8	30.7	15.6
1970	24.1	27.8	30.9	17.1
1980	21.7	26.0	33.3	19.1
Percent change, 1970–80	0.2	4.0	20.0	23.9
Population per square mile	301	78	86	25

SOURCE: U.S. Bureau of the Census, *United States Census of Population: 1960,* Final Report PC (1)-1A, *Number of Inhabitants: United States Summary* (Washington, D.C., 1981); and *1980 Census of Population and Housing,* PHC80-V-1, *Final Population and Housing Unit Counts: U.S. Summary* (Washington, D.C., 1981).

tion was largely confined to the Atlantic coastal belt, but from the time the nation achieved its independence it has been characterized by a continuous westward expansion. The nature of this east-to-west redistribution of the population is clearly revealed by the statistics in Table 11-4 and Figure 11-3 showing the percentage of the population living in each of four broad regions at every census since 1790. The states and geographic divisions that make up these four regions are shown in Figure 11-4.

For about two hundred years after initial colonization early in the seventeenth century, there were no major shifts in the distribution of the American population. At the time of the first census in 1790, the entire European population was still settled along the Atlantic Coast, more or less

Figure 11-3
Percent Distribution of the Population of the United States by Region, 1790–1980

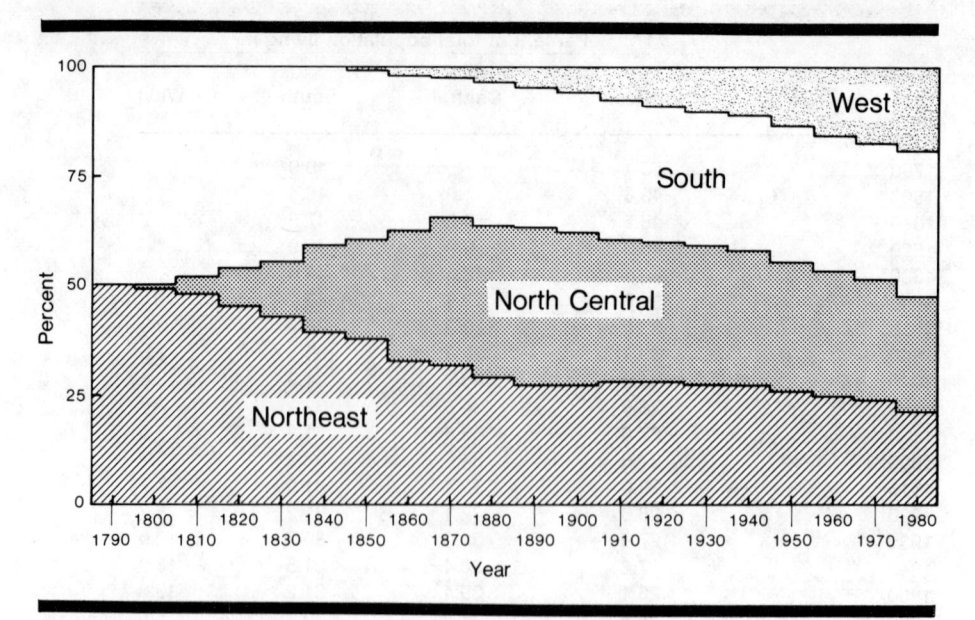

SOURCE: Based on data in Table 11-4.

evenly divided between the Northeast and the South. But after 1800 the increasing congestion in what was still largely an agrarian society began to encourage westward migration, and each subsequent decade has seen a smaller and smaller proportion of the population living in these two eastern regions.

When this westward movement first began, it was not a movement to the Far West. Instead, it was largely a settling of the central part of the nation. Not until after the Civil War was there any sizable settlement on the West Coast. At this time the impetus to westward migration provided by the completion of the transcontinental railroad was reinforced by the passage of the Homestead Laws. These laws, the first of which was enacted in 1862, provided large tracts of farmland at relatively little cost to persons who agreed to occupy, cultivate, or otherwise improve the land within a specified period of time. The purpose of these acts was to encourage the settlement of the whole country as well as to increase food production to enhance the strength of the nation. Their success is attested to not only by the rapid westward expansion of the population during the late nineteenth and early twentieth centuries but also by the rapid emergence of the United States as the wealthiest and one of the most powerful nations in the world.

The dispersal of the population from the area of initial settlement toward the West is still taking place today. During the most recent intercensal decade, for example, the population of the West increased by approximately one-fourth, or six times as fast as the North Central region and nearly a hundred times faster than the almost stationary Northeast. The South also emerged as a rapid growth area between 1970 and 1980, increasing by one-fifth as a result of an emerging migration trend toward the Sun Belt.

Although the West may be the fastest growing region, the fact that it was so late in getting started, compared with other regions, means that it is still the least populated section of the country. In 1980 the West accounted for only 19 percent of the total national population, and it had a density of only 25 persons per square mile. The South had the largest share of the population in 1980 (33 percent), followed by the North Central area (26 percent). In spite of having the largest share of the nation's population, both of these regions had relatively low man–land ratios. In 1980 the number of people per square mile was only 78 in the North Central states and only 86 in the South. In the North Central area this is partly a reflection of later settlement; in the South it is partly a reflection of the earlier emphasis on plantation agriculture and thus a delayed industrial growth.

In marked contrast to the other three regions, the Northeast, where one-fifth of the American population lives, had a population density of 301 persons per square mile. This clearly reflects not only the earlier settlement of

Figure 11-4
Geographic Regions of the United States

this part of the country but also the fact that American industrial development began in this region; hence it was the first to experience large-scale urban growth and expansion. The point is that the historical westward expansion and the recent movement to the southern states has not been accompanied by any marked thinning out of the northeastern population. Furthermore, since the major financial centers and industrial complexes continue to be concentrated in the Northeast, it is unlikely that these trends will lead to any significant thinning out in the years immediately ahead. What can be expected, rather, is a further spreading out of the area of concentration. Under present trends (and there appears to be little likelihood that these will change in the near future), this expansion will have its greatest impact in the West and South, and the years ahead will witness a steady increase in the size and density of the population in these two regions of the country.

Migration to the Sun Belt

A major trend in recent years has been the emergence of a strong net migration stream into the Sun Belt. This region, which has been formally defined as comprising the eleven states of the Deep South (Alabama, Arkansas, Georgia, Florida, Louisiana, Mississippi, North Carolina, Oklahoma, South Carolina, Texas, and Virginia) plus Missouri and the three southwestern states of (Arizona, California, and New Mexico), is today the most rapidly growing area in the nation. The growth of this region is bringing about a radical change in the redistribution of the United States population, and in 1980, for the first time, the combined population of the South and West exceeded that of the two northern regions. Among other things this has meant a shift in the regional balance of power in the nation. In 1970, a full 225 of the 435 members of congress represented states in the Northeastern and North Central regions, compared with 210 from the South and West, but the reapportionment based on the most recent 1980 census has reversed this balance. Today a majority of the congressional representatives (227) come from the South and West, while the minority (208) come from Northeastern and North Central states; and 1984 marks the first time that more delegates from the South than from any other region attended the national political conventions. Given traditional southern conservatism, such a shift in the balance of power could have a significant influence on the dominant political ideology of the nation. Alternatively, to the extent that the large number of in-migrants from the more liberal northern states serve to dilute this traditional conservatism, the shift in political dominance could have little or no effect on the national ideology. This remains to be seen. What is certain, however, is that the regional interests of the South and West will exert a greater influence on national policy than they did in the past.

The emergence of the strong net migration gain to the Sun Belt, which reflects both a decline in migration out of the region as well as an increase in the volume of in-migration, has been influenced by a number of factors. Although some negative push factors are at work (such as economic decline and rising unemployment in many of the older industrial centers of the North), the major cause of the migration is the pull of the South. Among the many pull factors are (1) the *aesthetic characteristics* of the region—the mild southern climate with its year-round outdoor casual life-style contrasts very favorably with the severe northern winters, especially in the eyes of older retirees; (2) *technological changes*, such as the widespread adoption of air conditioning, which have made even the most oppressive areas and times of the year fairly tolerable; and (3) the new *political climate*—the racial situation of the New South has improved markedly since the 1960s, and today many blacks have joined the mainstream of southern economic and political life.

As with most major migration streams, a major pull factor has been (4) the changing *economic character* of the South. The relocation of many northern firms and the rapid growth of the energy industry have created many new job opportunities for in-migrants and old residents alike, and this has substantially reduced the long-standing economic gap between the South and the rest of the nation. To this must be added the generally lower cost of living (lower home heating costs, for example) as well as the fact that state and local taxes are generally lower in the South than in the Northeastern and North Central states. All of these factors have coalesced in recent years to make the South a more attractive place in which to live than it has been in the past, and this explains the substantial increase in migration to the Sun Belt as well as its emergence as the fastest growing region in the United States.

The heavy volume of migration into the Sun Belt has not been without its problems. Both sending and receiving areas, for example, have had to face some severe economic pressures. On the one hand, given the nature of differential migration, many sending areas in the North have had to contend with losing many of their younger, better-educated, and more productive people. This in turn has led to a shrinking tax base and, in many northern areas, the emergence of very serious fiscal crises. On the other hand, the receiving areas in the South face problems of rapidly escalating costs of providing education, housing, and other needed services for the flood of new residents, and of dealing with myriad other problems (urban sprawl, traffic congestion, environmental degradation) associated with rapid population growth. Since there is no evidence that this new migration trend will change in the foreseeable future, we can anticipate a continuation if not an intensification of these problems in both the sending areas and the receiving areas of the Sun Belt.

The Exodus of Blacks from the South

The black population of the United States has always been concentrated in the South. This, of course, reflects the historical development of a plantation–slave economy in that region. To illustrate, in 1790 there were roughly 757,000 black people in the United States, of whom well over 90 percent were slaves living in the South (U.S. Bureau of the Census, 1975). In recent years, however, there has been a pronounced tendency for the black population to become more evenly dispersed throughout the nation. Although black migration out of the South began almost immediately after the Civil War, it was not a large movement at first, partly because agricultural employment opportunities were relatively good in the South, and partly because the heavy foreign immigration to northern industrial centers during the latter part of the nineteenth century meant greater competition there for nonagricultural employment. Thus, during the late nineteenth century blacks felt no very strong push out of the South and no significant pull to northern industrial centers.

Shortly after World War I the situation began to change. On the push side, continued technological progress made agricultural employment opportunities more and more scarce in the South. On the pull side, the restrictive federal legislation adopted during the early 1920s caused a sudden and drastic fall in the volume of foreign immigration, thus increasing the availability of unskilled and semiskilled industrial jobs in northern cities— jobs for which southern blacks were actively recruited. As a result, black migration out of the South began to gain momentum (see Table 11-5). By 1930 the proportion of blacks living in the South had declined to less than 80 percent. This figure was below 70 percent in 1950, less than 60 percent in 1960, and only 53 percent in 1970. Since 1970, however, the momentum of the black exodus from the South has been halted as part of the new Sun Belt migration stream, and during the 1970s the persistent decline in the percentage of blacks living in the South ceased, and the corresponding increase in the Northeast reversed itself while the trend in the North Central region also stabilized. Only the West experienced a continued increase in the proportion of blacks in its population.

The Rural-to-Urban Trend

A third major trend in the growth and development of the United States has been a shift in the distribution of the population from rural to urban areas. This urbanization trend is revealed in two basic ways: (1) by an increase in the number and size of urban places, and (2) by an increase in the number and proportion of the population living in urban places. According to the first federal census, there were only twenty-four urban places in the

Table 11-5
Distribution of the Black Population: United States, 1860–1980

Year	Total black population	Northeast	North Central	South	West
1860	4,441,830	3.5	4.1	92.2	0.1
1870	4,880,019	3.7	5.6	90.6	0.1
1880	6,580,793	3.5	5.9	90.5	0.2
1890	7,488,676	3.6	5.8	90.3	0.3
1900	8,833,994	4.4	5.6	89.7	0.3
1910	9,827,763	4.9	5.5	89.0	0.5
1920	10,463,131	6.5	7.6	85.2	0.7
1930	11,891,143	9.6	10.6	78.7	1.0
1940	12,865,518	10.6	11.0	77.0	1.3
1950	15,042,286	13.4	14.8	68.0	3.8
1960	18,871,831	16.0	18.3	59.9	5.8
1970	22,580,289	19.2	20.2	53.0	7.5
1980	26,488,218	18.3	20.2	53.0	8.5

Percent living in:

SOURCE: U.S. Bureau of the Census, *Historical Statistics of the United States: Colonial Times to 1970* (Washington, D.C., 1975); and *1980 Census of Population and Housing*, PHC 80-V-1, *Final Population and Housing Counts: U.S. Summary* (Washington, D.C., 1981).

United States in 1790, and they contained only 5 percent of the population. Since that time there has been a continuous increase in the number of urban places and a continuous shift in the distribution of the population away from rural areas to the emerging cities (see Table 11-6 and Figure 11-5). The urban fraction passed the 50 percent mark during the second decade of the present century, and by 1980 approximately three-fourths of the American population was living in one of more than 8,700 urban places (see Note to Table 11-6).

Another indication of pronounced urbanization is the change in the size of urban places. In 1790 only 5 of the 24 urban places had populations of 10,000 or more, while none had as many as 50,000 inhabitants. In 1980, however, there were 2,903 places with 10,000 or more inhabitants, and there were 463 places whose population exceeded 50,000.

The pervasive significance of the rural-to-urban migration trend is further revealed by the fact that it has cut across other major distribution trends. The westward expansion, for example, had a pronounced rural-to-urban character. In 1860 the West contained roughly 2 percent of the American population, of which only 6 percent was urban (compared with 20 percent for the total United States). One hundred years later, however, this region was more urban than the nation as a whole, and at the time of the 1980 census only 19 percent of the American people were living in the West, but

Table 11-6
Urbanization Trends in the United States, 1790–1980*

Year	Number of urban places	Percent of population living in urban places	Number of urban places with population over: 10,000	50,000
1790	24	5.1	5	0
1800	33	6.1	6	1
1810	46	7.3	11	2
1820	61	7.2	13	3
1830	90	8.8	23	4
1840	131	10.8	37	5
1850	236	15.3	62	10
1860	392	19.8	93	16
1870	663	25.7	168	25
1880	939	28.2	223	35
1890	1,348	35.1	354	58
1900	1,737	39.1	440	78
1910	2,262	45.7	597	109
1920	2,722	51.2	752	144
1930	3,165	56.2	982	191
1940	3,464	56.5	1,077	199
1950	4,764	64.0	1,262	232
1960	6,041	69.9	1,891	332
1970	7,062	73.5	2,301	396
1980	8,765	73.7	2,903	463

SOURCE: U.S. Bureau of the Census, *1980 Census of Population,* Final Report PC80-1-A1, *Number of Inhabitants: United States Summary* (Washington, D.C., 1983).

* As originally defined by the Bureau of the Census, the term "urban" was used to refer to all incorporated places of 2,500 or more inhabitants. This initial definition was based on the assumption that politically defined city limits would embrace virtually all persons who were living under conditions that may be regarded as truly urban. By the middle of the twentieth century, however, as more and more people moved out of the cities into the surrounding fringe areas, it became increasingly apparent that this assumption was untenable and that a change in the basic definition of "urban" was needed. Accordingly, a new definition was formulated for the census of 1950, in which provision was made to include other places that could be regarded as essentially urban in character (for example, unincorporated places of 2,500 or more inhabitants as well as incorporated places). The effect of this definition change was to increase both the number of urban places and the size of the uban population. Under the old rules, 59.6 percent of the population would have been living in 4,054 urban places in 1950.

84 percent of the West's population was urban, compared with only 74 percent for the total United States.

Like the east-to-west movement of the population as a whole, the dispersal of the black population out of the South was largely rural-to-urban. In 1920, when the black migration was just beginning to gain momentum, only about a third of the blacks in America were living in urban areas, com-

Figure 11-5
Urban and Rural Population of the United States, 1790–1980

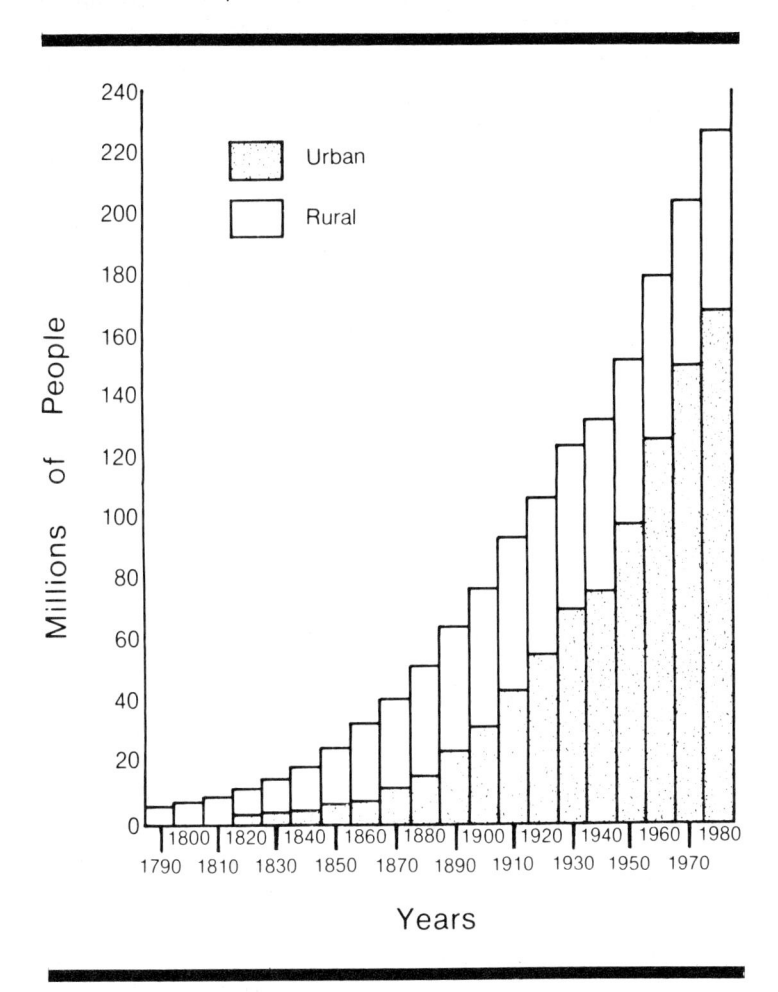

SOURCE: Based on data in U.S. Bureau of the Census, *1980 Census of Population*, PC80-1-A1, *Number of Inhabitants: U.S. Summary* (Washington, D.C., 1983).

pared with 51 percent for the population as a whole. By 1980, however, blacks were markedly more urbanized than the general population. To illustrate, at the time of the 1980 census 58 percent of the black population lived in metropolitan centers as compared with only 25 percent of whites.

This urbanization trend is, of course, a natural accompaniment to the basic transformation of the United States from an agrarian economy to a highly industrialized one. Although completely comparable statistics on industrial development are not available for all periods in American history, the general significance of this transformation is relatively easy to document. In 1820, for example, before the Industrial Revolution had made much headway in this country, slightly more than seven out of every ten gainful workers in the United States were employed in agricultural industries. By 1870 this proportion was down to slightly more than half, and at the end of the nineteenth century only 37 percent of the American work force was employed in agriculture. In 1940, the last year for which comparable data are available, agricultural industries accounted for only 17 percent of the gainful workers in the United States.

When related statistics for more recent years are considered, the same general trend is apparent. To illustrate, the proportion of the economically active population represented by farmers and farm workers declined from 38 percent in 1900 and had dropped to only 3 percent by 1980. Clearly, the basic economic trend of the first two centuries of American history has been the transformation from an agrarian to an industrial society. The basic demographic trend has just as clearly been a redistribution of the population from declining rural farm areas to growing urban industrial areas.

The Rural Renaissance

The 1970s witnessed the emergence of two new significant trends in internal migration and the pattern of population redistribution. One, of course, was the movement to the Sun Belt; the other was an unexpected reversal in the traditional rural-to-urban migration stream and a corresponding growth of rural and small town populations. To illustrate, between 1970 and 1980, the rural population of the United States, which had declined from 1950 to 1970, increased at a rate of 9 percent, only slightly below that of the urban population (12 percent) (U.S. Bureau of the Census, 1983).

The effect of this reverse migration flow on differential growth patterns is most clearly illustrated by what has happened to the metropolitan–nonmetropolitan population. Recognizing that there were substantial differences in the life cycle and characteristics of those urban dwellers who lived in places of three or four thousand inhabitants and those who lived in much larger centers, the U.S. Bureau of the Census began, in 1940, to identify large urban concentrations as *metropolitan areas*. As presently defined, these metropolitan areas (now called "standard metropolitan statistical areas" or SMSAs) are large urban agglomerations that generally include a central city or cities of fifty thousand or more, the county or counties in which the central city is located, and adjacent counties that are sufficiently integrated with the socioeconomic life of the central city to qualify as part of its area of influence. As of 1980 there were 318 such areas in the United States. As the data in Table 11-7 clearly reveal, the 1970–80 decade witnessed a pronounced change in the growth trends of the metropolitan and nonmetropolitan areas. Prior to the 1970s and in line with the continuing urbaniza-

Table 11-7
Population of the United States by Metropolitan and Nonmetropolitan Residence, 1950–80*

Year	Total population	Metropolitan population	Nonmetropolitan population
1950	151,325,798	104,172,853	47,152,945
1960	179,323,192	131,318,714	48,004,478
1970	203,302,020	153,693,767	49,608,253
1980	226,545,805	169,430,623	57,115,182
Percent change			
1950–60	18.5	26.1	1.8
1960–70	13.4	17.0	3.4
1970–80	11.4	10.2	15.1

SOURCE: Adapted from data published in U.S. Bureau of the Census, *State and Metropolitan Area Data Book, 1982* (Washington, D.C., 1983).
* Based on 1980 definition of 318 areas.

tion trend, the metropolitan population increased at a much faster rate than did the population of nonmetropolitan areas. Between 1970 and 1980, however, the nonmetropolitan growth rate was half again as high as that of the metropolitan areas.

This reversal in the magnitude of metropolitan–nonmetropolitan growth rates reflects the fact that since the late 1960s the nonmetropolitan areas of the country have ceased to be areas of out-migration and have instead been experiencing a substantial net migration gain (Morrison and Wheeler, 1976; U.S. Bureau of the Census, 1981). A number of factors can be cited to explain the reversal of this historical migration flow. Among them are the automobile and a growing superhighway network that has made previously remote areas more readily accessible, the availability of cheaper land, general life-style considerations, and the decentralization of industry and manufacturing (Morrison, 1977). This decentralization is especially important because it has created jobs in nonurban areas where employment opportunities did not exist before, thus lessening one of the traditional push factors in rural areas and making them economically more attractive places in which to live.

This renewed growth in rural America has not been without its price, however, and many of the once idyllic, pastoral smaller communities of the United States have begun to experience some of the problems commonly associated with urban areas (e.g., crime and delinquency, traffic congestion, environmental pollution). Further, like the rapidly growing areas of the Sun Belt, many of the smaller nonmetropolitan communities in the United States now face problems of rising costs of providing the basic services needed by the newcomers. Since there is little indication that the current rural growth trend will cease in the foreseeable future, such problems of change and adjustment can be expected to increase.

The Suburbanization Trend

The recent reversal in the magnitude of the metropolitan–nonmetropolitan growth rate is the latest manifestation of the final major migration trend to effect a basic change in the settlement pattern of the American population—suburbanization. The term "suburbanization" refers to the expansion of the urban community beyond its politically defined boundaries as a result of the movement of urbanites out of the larger cities into the surrounding suburban towns. This deconcentration trend, which recent research indicates has also begun in many nonmetropolitan areas (Lichter and Fuguitt, 1982), began early in the twentieth century but did not gain much momentum until after the Second World War, when the automobile really came into its own as a major means of transportation. The causes of the growing suburban movement in the postwar period may be sought in such things as higher incomes, an urban housing shortage, and a desire for a more aesthetic environment in which to raise a family, but the automobile played the key role in facilitating the movement. Widespread use of the automobile, accompanied by the construction of a vast, interconnected network of superhighways and expressways, has greatly extended the borders of the urban community. By permitting persons who work in cities to live greater distances from their place of employment, the automobile led to the emergence of a new type of community—a city-region or *metropolitan community* in which the population is widely dispersed over a large area far beyond the boundaries of the central city (McKenzie, 1933).

This most recent trend has modified significantly the pattern of population distribution within the built-up urban sections of the country. The nature of this shift is clearly revealed by the data in Table 11-8. In 1950, when 63 percent of the American people were living in metropolitan areas, 57 percent of the metropolitan population was living in the large central cities. Since then the city population has declined consistently: it fell below 50 percent in the early 1960s, and by 1980 only 40 percent of the metropolitan population was living in the central cities.

The nature and magnitude of the suburbanization trend is also revealed by the differential rates of increase within metropolitan areas. Between 1950 and 1960, for example, the total population residing in metropolitan areas increased by slightly more than one-fourth (26 percent). Within these areas, however, the central city population increased by only 12 percent, compared with an increase of 46 percent in the surrounding suburban area. During the most recent intercensal decade, which was marked by a

Table 11-8

Population of Standard Metropolitan Statistical Areas in the United States, 1950–80 (in thousands)

SMSA Area	1970 definition (243 areas) 1950	1960	1970	1981 definition (323 areas) 1970	1980
SMSA total	94,579	119,595	139,419	153,694	169,405
Inside central cities	53,696	59,947	63,797	67,850	67,930
Outside central cities	40,883	59,648	75,622	85,843	101,475
Percent of total population living in SMSAs	62.5	66.7	68.6	75.5	74.7
Percent of SMSA population living in central cities	56.7	50.1	45.7	44.1	40.1

SOURCE: U.S. Bureau of the Census, *1970 Census of Population,* Final Report PC(1)-A1, *Number of Inhabitants: United States Summary* (Washington, D.C., 1971); and "Population Profile of the United States: 1981," *Current Population Reports,* P-20, No. 374 (September 1982).

substantial slowdown in the rate of overall metropolitan growth, the internal growth differential has persisted: between 1970 and 1980 the central city population remained virtually unchanged while the size of the metropolitan population living outside central cities increased by 18 percent.

One other point should be noted with respect to this general trend: *suburbanization has been primarily a white middle-class phenomenon.* Between 1970 and 1980, all of the increase in the white population of metropolitan areas occurred in the suburban ring: the number of whites living in the centers actually declined by 12 percent (see Table 11-9). In sharp contrast, approximately half of the growth of the black metropolitan population took place in central cities. The consequence of these differential patterns of growth has been to promote greater racial disparity between urban centers and their surrounding suburbs: in 1970, blacks constituted 20 percent of the metropolitan central city population, and by 1980 this figure had risen to 25 percent. Moreover, given the decidedly lower socioeconomic status of the black population as a whole (see the discussion of income differentials in Chapter 12), these trends have also widened the gap between city and suburb with regard to per capita wealth. In short, many cities in the United States today, where the increasing numbers of American blacks are being augmented by similar increases in the Hispanic population, are on the verge of becoming islands of ethnic poverty—slum cities surrounded by affluent suburbs. More than one expert has suggested that this growing difference in racial composition between the core cities and their suburban

Table 11-9

Population of the United States in Metropolitan and Nonmetropolitan Areas, by Race, 1970 and 1980 (in thousands)

Area and race	1970	1980	Percent change
White	177,749	188,341	6.0
Metropolitan areas	133,574	138,044	3.3
Central city	53,100	47,014	−11.5
Suburb	80,474	91,029	13.1
Nonmetropolitan areas	44,175	50,297	13.9
Black	22,580	26,488	17.3
Metropolitan areas	17,872	21,474	20.2
Central city	13,546	15,301	13.0
Suburb	4,326	6,173	42.7
Metropolitan area	4,708	5,014	6.5

SOURCE: U.S. Bureau of the Census, "Population Profile of the United States, 1981," *Current Population Reports,* P-20, No. 374 (September 1982).

rings, combined as it is with such a marked discrepancy in socioeconomic characteristics (education status, unemployment levels, income, housing conditions, etc.), lies at the bottom of many of the problems plaguing our society today (National Commission on the Causes and Prevention of Violence, 1969).

We should also note, however, that recent urban renewal efforts in a number of cities have resulted in a phenomenon called *gentrification:* higher status whites are moving back into renovated urban houses and displacing lower status black persons. So far, gentrification has not involved very large numbers of people, but the trend appears to be a growing one (Spain, 1980). Should it continue, and should it gain momentum, it could significantly enhance the overall economic status of those cities in which it occurs.

INTERNAL MIGRATION IN OTHER COUNTRIES

Statistics on internal migration for other countries of the world are much less readily available than are those pertaining to births and deaths. Moreover, even when data on the residential mobility of the population are available, they are often not comparable from one country to another. Many countries, for example, collect statistics on the number of people moving between administrative areas during some specified interval of time (Shryock et al., 1976; Chapter 21), but even when the time interval is the same, there are wide variations in the type and size of the administrative units (counties and states in the United States, provinces in the Netherlands, departments in France, etc.). Some attempts have been made to examine international differences in geographic mobility, however, and the results indicate that Americans are not unique in having a high rate of internal migration. In a study of geographic mobility in seven countries around 1970, for example, both Australia and Canada were found to have general mobility levels as high as or higher than those observed in the United States (U.S. Bureau of the Census, 1976). Conversely, Great Britain, Japan, and especially Taiwan and Ireland were characterized by much lower rates of mobility (see Table 11-10). These differences can largely be explained in terms of past experiences of particular countries as well as the present level of industrial development. On the one hand, the high mobility countries (Australia, Canada, the United States) are all relatively young English-speaking countries where immigration has played a major role in overall growth and development, and where large size and ample supplies of land early established a migration tradition. The lower mobility rates in Great Britain and Japan, on the other hand, reflect the fact that they are old, established countries with limited land resources. Finally, the lowest rates of mobility are found in those countries that are least developed industrially (Taiwan and Ireland), and where a large proportion of the population is still tied to a specific locality because of its dependence on agriculture.

Table 11-10
General Mobility Rates in Seven Countries, c. 1970*

Country	Percent age 1 and over moving during a single year	Percent age 5 and over moving during a five-year interval
Australia	15.7	48.4
Canada	NA	44.3
Great Britain	11.1	35.9
Ireland	4.3	NA
Japan	12.0	35.8
Taiwan	9.1	NA
United States	18.6	43.2

SOURCE: U.S. Bureau of the Census, "The Geographic Mobility of Americans: An International Comparison." *Current Population Reports,* Series P-23, No. 64 (Washington, D.C., 1976).
* Excludes movers from abroad.
NA Not available.

Rural-to-Urban Migration

While it may be difficult to find comparable data on the overall volume of internal migration taking place in the world today, it is possible to identify at least one pervasive stream: the movement of people away from rural farm areas to urban centers. Here again direct estimates of the extent of this movement are difficult to come by; however, migration trends can easily be inferred by examining differences in the rate of growth among the various geographical subdivisions of a country. Assuming that there are no major differences in the reproductive behavior of the population in various areas, differences in overall growth rates can largely be attributed to migration. For example, when one compares the rate of growth of urban and rural areas (see Table 11-11), the prevalence of this urbanization trend is readily apparent: with the exception of the two Scandinavian countries, urban growth rates are everywhere substantially greater than those of rural areas.

Further consideration of the growth rates shown in Table 11-11 reveals that there are also some notable differences with respect to the magnitude of the rural-to-urban migration trend. Although national differences in the definition of "urban" detract from the comparability of these data, it is clear that the rate of urbanization is generally most pronounced among the less developed countries of Africa, Asia, and Latin America. Throughout these regions, in fact, excessive migration out of rural areas into already overcrowded urban centers has been creating serious social and economic problems, and many countries have adopted policies aimed at diverting rural migrants away from the major urban centers and dispersing them to other less densely settled areas.

Migration, Urbanization, and Economic Development

In the historical experience of the industrialized countries of Europe and North America, the movement of people away from rural areas to the cities was so closely associated with the process of economic growth that urbanization came to be regarded as both an index of and a stimulant to economic development. On the one hand, since large population aggregates cannot exist without some means of livelihood, the growth of cities indicates, at the very least, some minimum development of opportunities for nonagricultural employment. On the other hand, the growth of cities provides concentrations of the manpower needed for the further growth and expansion of nonagricultural activities. Given this Western experience, the rapid urbanization now taking place in many of the less developed areas might be regarded as an indication that economic growth is taking place and as a potential stimulus to continued economic growth. However, closer examination of the nature of the urbanization process currently under way in many of these areas reveals that this is not necessarily true and that the

Table 11-11

Percent Increase in Urban and Rural Areas, 1970–1978/79

Country	Urban	Rural
Africa		
Benin	41.6	25.6
Chad	93.6	8.8
Egypt	25.8	14.8
Zambia	74.1	14.5
Zimbabwe	49.1	37.4
Latin America		
Brazil	43.6	9.1
Chile	29.7	−0.1
Dominican Republic	53.0	7.1
Panama	41.9	22.4
Asia		
Bangladesh	87.1	22.7
India	32.3	17.9
Iran	46.6	4.8
Syria	44.1	22.8
Europe		
Bulgaria	20.0	−14.0
Finland	−3.7	16.1
Hungary	6.2	1.2
Norway	−30.2	72.6
Poland	18.2	−4.8
Romania	28.6	−6.3
Spain	27.9	−13.7
USSR	19.1	−6.1

SOURCE: *1979 Demographic Yearbook* (New York: United Nations, 1980). Percentages calculated by authors.

role of the city in relation to economic growth needs to be reassessed. Pursuing this further, it is possible to distinguish at least three ways in which the urbanization process now taking place in the less developed areas differs from the historical experience of the now industrialized nations: these relate to (1) cause, (2) type, and (3) effect (Stockwell and Laidlaw, 1981, pp. 89ff).

Cause

As we noted in Chapter 9, people usually move from one area to another in order to find better opportunities for themselves. Thus, any migration stream can generally be explained in terms of a combination of push factors (such as a high level of unemployment) and pull factors (such as an abundance of employment opportunities). In the historical experience of the more developed countries both sets of factors were usually present, so that the rural-to-urban migration stream performed the dual function of reducing overpopulation in rural areas at the same time that it provided the workers needed for the expanding urban industries. The problem with respect to many developing countries today, however, arises from the fact that the traditional rural push is as strong as ever (if not stronger, given the much higher rates of population increase prevailing throughout the developing world); but the existence of the urban pull forces is more felt than real. That is, rural peasants are flocking to the cities in search of jobs that are not there. In contrast to the past, when economic development and the growth of industry were the underlying causes of rural-to-urban migration, in many parts of the developing world today, rural-to-urban migration takes place in the absence of comparable industrial development, and this same rural-to-urban migration frequently acts as a major obstacle to the overall development process.

Type

In the developed countries of Europe and North America, the process of urbanization generally involved the growth and development of a large number of cities, many of which were characterized by a more or less specialized function, such as government administration (Washington, D.C.), commerce (Boston and New Orleans), heavy industry (Detroit, Gary, and Pittsburgh), or insurance and finance (Hartford and New York). The result was the development of a functionally integrated urban network, or system of cities. In marked contrast to this pattern, much of the urban growth that has been taking place in many underdeveloped areas in recent years has been concentrated in a single large city of a sort that has come to be called a *primate city*. While it is rare for a single city in a modern industrial country to contain as much as 20 to 25 percent of the urban population, statistics published by the World Bank indicate that this fraction is often on the order of 55 to 60 percent in less developed countries, and in some instances as much as 80 percent of the urban population resides in the single largest city (see Table 11–12).

These primate cities, it must be noted, owe their existence in large measure to the colonial experience of the past. They are the easily accessible *metropolises* in which the Western colonial powers established the administrative apparatus for governing the colony and exploiting the resources of the *satellite* areas of the country (Frank, 1969). Once established as the major centers of economic activity, they became magnets for the indigenous population, enhancing their own growth and development at the expense of the rest of the nation. Moreover, many of them continue today to have a parasitic effect on the indigenous economy.

Table 11-12
Percentage of the Urban Population Living in the Largest City, 1980

Developed countries	% in largest city	Developing countries	% in largest city
Belgium	14%	Angola	64%
Canada	18	Benin	63
Czechoslovakia	12	Costa Rica	64
France	23	Guinea	80
Germany, Dem. Rep.	9	Iraq	55
Germany, Fed. Rep.	18	Kenya	57
Netherlands	9	Lebanon	79
Poland	15	Mozambique	83
Sweden	15	Panama	66
United Kingdom	20	Saudi Arabia	64
United States	12	Senegal	65
USSR	4	Thailand	69

SOURCE: International Bank for Reconstruction and Development, *World Development Report, 1982* (Washington, D.C., 1982).

Effect

The significance of the "cause" and "type" differences in the urbanization process taking place in many developing areas today lies in their effect on national economic growth. Despite certain advantages (e.g., ready access to world markets, the presence of a large labor pool), a great deal of evidence has been amassed concerning the potential detrimental effects of the tendency for a single large city to draw a disproportionate share of the rural-to-urban migrants. To illustrate, these so-called primate cities tend to monopolize the professional and skilled personnel (teachers and doctors, for example), leaving other areas without many needed services; by draining off rural resources while returning little if anything to the rural markets, they tend to command more than their fair share of the national income; because they attract all of the available labor pool, they discourage industrial dispersion and the growth of other cities; and they tend to be the center of all major cultural activities (theaters, colleges and universities, museums, etc.), leaving the rest of the country in a barren state.

A major problem, of course, is the relative lack of productive employment opportunities in the large cities, as a result of which the rural-to-urban migration stream often does little more than effect a transfer of rural poverty to urban areas; in many nations it has even contributed to greater urban poverty. When a surplus of poor workers compete for a limited number of unskilled low-paying jobs, the effect is to depress incomes even more, and the hundreds of thousands of unskilled urban laborers and service workers constantly find their low wages bid even lower by the waves of new migrants who flock to the cities from depressed rural areas. This problem is further exacerbated by the age composition of the rural-to-urban migrants: for the most part they are younger than the general population, and their influx into the urban areas increases the heavy burden of dependency and the potential for economic and political instability.

In addition to flooding the labor market, depressing wages, and increasing the ranks of the unemployed, the rapid growth of the urban population may have a more direct harmful effect on national development programs. In many countries, the growth of a large urban proletariat has created needs and demands that must be met, often at the expense of more productive investments. That is, funds that might otherwise have been used to finance various programs to promote national development must be diverted to the provision of food and basic services such as public health, housing, and education for the masses.

Based on these observations, it can be concluded that the relation between city growth and economic development is no longer as clear-cut as it once seemed. Whether or not urbanization promotes economic development will depend on the nature of the urbanization and on the type of city that emerges. It can also be suggested that when city growth occurs in the absence of sufficient industrial development, and when it is concentrated in one or two large primate cities, as indeed appears to be happening in many of the developing areas, then its influence on economic development may actually be negative rather than positive.

INTERNAL MIGRATION POLICIES

The basic goal common to all internal migration policies is some kind of population redistribution, and nations will try to achieve their goal through various programs that aim to encourage growth in some areas while discouraging it in others. According to one recent survey, the vast majority of the world's countries, both developed and developing, expressed some dissatisfaction with the distribution of their populations, and most had some kind of program aimed at modifying the situation (United Nations, 1980). The most commonly perceived problem throughout the world was that of relieving congestion in large urban areas and dispersing population more evenly throughout the country. In the more highly developed countries the issue was primarily one of fine-tuning the distribution of population in order to reduce regional economic inequalities and extend an already high level of living to all inhabitants. In the less developed countries, however, the issue was often one of bringing about a radical change in current migration trends and in the prevailing pattern of population distribution.

The various policy programs that a government may adopt in order to influence rural-to-urban migration and population distribution can be grouped into three general categories: (1) those that seek to slow down or *halt* migration out of rural areas; (2) those that seek to *redirect* rural out-migrants away from major urban centers to smaller cities or sparsely populated frontier areas; and (3) programs that seek to *reverse* the traditional flow pattern by encouraging migration from urban to rural areas. Short of using force (as in the radical resettlement program in Cambodia/Kampuchea in the late 1970s), or of placing some kind of legal restrictions on internal mobility (such as those the government of South Africa imposes on its nonwhite citizens), the various programs that may be implemented to halt, redirect, or reverse the traditional flow entail some effort to reduce the social and economic inequalities between rural and urban areas that prompt much of the migration taking place. In Latin America, for example, several countries have tried to curtail rural out-migration by implementing various land reform programs in the countryside, and/or by improving the quality of rural services (housing, schools, health care, etc.); Indonesia has a financial incentive program to encourage residents of densely populated Java to move to more sparsely settled areas on Sumatra and other outer islands; and a number of countries in all the major regions are presently involved in programs either to relocate existing urban industries or to build new factories in rural areas in an effort to provide more economic opportunities in sparsely settled parts of the nation.

Very often some combination of programs will be implemented in an effort to achieve some specified policy goal. Poland, for example, has tried to decentralize its population by putting limits on the number of factory jobs in large urban areas and by transferring some plants away from Warsaw to more remote cities. Similarly, the Ivory Coast has a program that aims to slow down the rural exodus by stimulating agriculture and agriculture-related employment opportunities and improving conditions in rural areas, and it plans to create a network of medium-sized towns in order to counteract movement to the larger urban centers.

Historically the United States has implemented a number of programs that have had an effect on the volume and direction of migration streams and on the overall pattern of population distribution. In some instances the effect has been the direct result of a program that was deliberately adopted to achieve a specific policy goal (e.g., one purpose of the Homestead Acts in the nineteenth century was to encourage settlement in the interior of the country); in other cases the effect has been the indirect result of some other program (e.g., the suburbanization trend was clearly enhanced by the post–World War II highway construction program). To the extent that such policies exist today, however, they are confined to local efforts either to increase population by bringing in new people or to slow down the rate of growth. On the one hand, a community may offer various tax concessions to attract new industries and thereby encourage growth. On the other hand, a number of municipalities have recently tried to curtail expansion by limiting building permits and placing moratoria on new housing construction. On a national level, there is no official policy with respect to internal migration and population distribution in the United States today. Although a recent study group has recommended that Congress review the situation with a view toward formulating some kind of national policy (Select Committee on Population, 1978), nothing of significance has as yet been forthcoming. Rather, in line with our basic beliefs in economic and political freedom, the unofficial policy is one in which the government keeps its hands off and lets the normal play of the market determine the changes necessary to maintain a relative balance between population and resources (opportunities).

Although the United States has so far done little to develop a formal national policy pertaining to internal migration and population distribution, it is safe to assume that such policies will continue to play a role in the overall development efforts of many countries, especially throughout the Third World. The nature and success of such policies will depend on a variety of factors: geographic region, level of economic development, degree of urbanization, and especially the extent to which the economy is centrally planned as opposed to being a free market economy (i.e., where the economy is centrally planned the government can intervene much more directly in the population redistribution process). One thing is certain, however: as long as marked differences in living levels and life-styles continue to characterize rural and urban areas, pressures to migrate will persist. As the lyrics of an old song remind us, "How ya gonna keep 'em down on the farm, after they've seen Paree?"

SUMMARY

Internal migration functions today as the basic process underlying changes in the spatial distribution of population within any politically defined area. Much internal mobility, like international migration, is economically motivated: people move from areas of limited opportunities to areas where opportunities are greater and where the overall level of living is higher.

An especially high rate of internal migration has long been and continues to be a major characteristic of the American population. About 20 percent of the population changes its place of residence every year, and within a five-year interval close to half of the American people will move from one house to another. Although mobility rates are generally high, certain categories of people are more likely to move than others. Young adults, for example, and more highly educated persons have mobility rates that are substantially higher than the general average. The fact that different types of peoples are more likely to move than others means that the internal migration process affects not only the overall spatial distribution but also the composition of the population in both sending and receiving areas.

Rapid changes in either the size or the composition of a population as a result of movement into or out of an area can create serious problems of adjustment, both for the individual migrants and for the community at large. For the most part, however, the impact of internal migration is positive: individual migrants enhance their life-style, and the society is able to maintain a relative balance between the spatial distribution of its population and its resources.

In the United States four major historical trends have altered the distribution of the population over the land area. Two of these reflect fundamental regional shifts: the gradual westward dispersion of the population away from the initial settlement areas along the east coast, and the twentieth-century movement of blacks out of the rural south to the northern urban industrial centers. The other two reflect a basic shift in our economy and in the structure of the American community: the long-term movement of the population out of rural agrarian areas to urban industrial centers, and the more recent shifting of the population within urban areas away from the core cities out into the expanding suburbs.

During the 1970s, two new trends have become apparent. First, the emergence of a major migration stream from the Snow Belt to the Sun Belt has reversed the long-term movement of population out of the South. Second, the post–World War II suburbanization trend has extended beyond the metropolitan suburbs into nonmetropolitan areas away from any large city.

Although wide variations exist in rates of internal migration around the world—variations that reflect different historical antecedents and/or current levels of economic development—a nearly universal trend today is the movement of people from rural to urban areas. In a number of the lesser developed regions urbanization has been taking place so rapidly that it has seriously exacerbated the general development problem, and a number of countries have adopted or are considering policies to regulate the volume and direction of internal migration. Such policies notwithstanding, it is likely that internal migration streams in all countries of the world will continue to flow from areas with limited opportunities to areas where people perceive greater opportunities and the chances of a better life for themselves.

REFERENCES AND SUGGESTED READING

Beier, George J. "Can Third World Cities Cope?" *Population Bulletin*, 31 (December 1976).

Biggar, Jeanne C. "The Sunning of America: Migration to the Sunbelt." *Population Bulletin*, 34 (March 1979).

Bogue, Donald J. *The Population of the United States.* New York: Free Press, 1959, Chapters 14 and 15.

Brown, David, and John M. Wardwell. *New Directions in Urban-Rural Migration: Population Turnaround in Rural America.* New York: Academic Press, 1980.

Chalmers, James A., and Michael J. Greenwood. "The Economics of Rural to Urban Turnaround." *Social Science Quarterly,* 61 (September 1980): 524–44.

DeJong, Gordon F. "The Impact of Regional Population Redistribution Policies on Internal Migration." *Social Science Quarterly,* 62 (June 1981): 313–23.

Frank, Andre G. *Latin America: Underdevelopment or Revolution.* New York: Monthly Review Press, 1969.

Gilbert, Alan, and Joseph Gugler. *Cities, Poverty and Development: Urbanization in the Third World.* New York: Oxford University Press, 1982.

Goldstein, Sidney. *Patterns of Mobility, 1910–1950.* Philadelphia: University of Pennsylvania Press, 1958.

Goldstein, Sidney. "Facets of Distribution: Research Challenges and Opportunities." *Demography,* 13 (November 1976): 423–34.

Gordon, Mitchell. *Sick Cities.* New York: Penguin, 1965.

Heaton, Tim B., and Glenn V. Fuguitt. "Dimensions of Population Redistribution in the United States Since 1950." *Social Science Quarterly,* 61 (September 1980): 508–23.

Lichter, Daniel T., and Glenn V. Fuguitt. "The Transition to Nonmetropolitan Deconcentration." *Demography,* 19 (May 1982): 211–21.

Long, Larry H. *Population Redistribution in the U.S.: Issues for the 1980s.* Washington, D.C.: Population Reference Bureau, 1983.

McKenzie, Roderick D. *The Metropolitan Community.* New York: McGraw-Hill, 1933.

Morrison, Peter. *Current Demographic Changes in Regions of the United States.* Santa Monica, CA: Rand Corporation, 1977.

Morrison, Peter A., and Judith P. Wheeler. "Rural Renaissance in America?" *Population Bulletin,* 31 (October 1976).

National Commission on the Causes and Prevention of Violence. *Violence in America: Historical and Comparative Perspectives* (Washington, D.C.: U.S. Government Printing Office, 1969).

Packard, Vance. *A Nation of Strangers.* New York: David McKay, 1972.

Population Reference Bureau. "U.S. Population: Where We Are; Where We're Going." *Population Bulletin,* 37 (June 1982).

Pryor, Robin J., ed. *Migration and Development in South-East Asia.* New York: Oxford University Press, 1979.

Select Committee on Population. *Domestic Consequences of United States Population Change.* Washington, D.C.: U.S. Government Printing Office, 1978.

Shryock, Henry S., Jacob S. Siegel et al. *The Methods and Materials of De-*

mography: Condensed ed. by E. G. Stockwell. New York: Academic Press, 1976.

Simmons, Alan B. "Slowing Metropolitan City Growth in Asia: Policies, Programs and Results." *Population and Development Review,* 5 (March 1979): 87–104.

Spain, Daphne. "Indicators of Urban Revitalization: Racial and Socioeconomic Changes in Central-City Housing." In Shirley B. Laska and Daphne Spain, ed., *Back to the City: Issues in Neighborhood Renovation.* Elmsford, N.Y.: Pergamon Press, 1980.

Stockwell, Edward G., and Karen A. Laidlaw. *Third World Development: Problems and Prospects.* Chicago: Nelson-Hall, 1981.

Sundquist, James L. *Dispersing Population: What America Can Learn From Europe.* Washington, D.C.: Brookings Institution, 1975.

Taeuber, Irene B., and Conrad Taeuber. *People of the United States in the 20th Century.* Washington, D.C.: U.S. Bureau of the Census, 1971, Chapters 2, 3, and 12–15.

Taeuber, Karl E., Leonard Chiazze, Jr., and William Haenszel. *Migration in the United States: An Analysis of Residence Histories.* Public Health Monograph No. 77. Washington, D.C., 1968.

Todaro, Michael P. *Internal Migration in Developing Countries.* Geneva, Switzerland: International Labor Organizations, 1976.

Toffler, Alvin. *Future Shock.* New York: Bantam Books, 1970.

United Nations. *World Population Trends and Policies: 1979 Monitoring Report,* Vol. I. New York: United Nations, 1980.

U.S. Bureau of the Census. *Historical Statistics of the United States: Colonial Times to 1970.* Washington, D.C.: 1975.

U.S. Bureau of the Census. "The Geographical Mobility of Americans: An International Comparison." *Current Population Reports,* Series P-23, No. 64. Washington, D.C.: 1976.

U.S. Bureau of the Census. "Geographic Mobility: March 1975 to March 1980." *Current Population Reports,* Series P-20, No. 368 (1981).

U.S. Bureau of the Census. *1980 Census of Population,* PC80-1-A1, *Number of Inhabitants: U.S. Summary* (1983).

Weeks, John R. *Population: An Introduction to Concepts and Issues,* 2nd ed. Belmont, Calif.: Wadsworth, 1981, Chapters 7 and 12.

Weinstein, Jay A. *Demographic Transition and Social Change.* Morristown, NJ: General Learning Press, 1976.

Weller, Robert H., and Leon F. Bouvier. *Population: Demography and Policy.* New York: St. Martin's, 1981, Chapters 8 and 12.

Wilkinson, Kenneth, James G. Thompson, Robert R. Reynolds, Jr., and Lawrence M. Ostresh. "Local Disruption and Western Energy Development: A Critical Review." *Pacific Sociological Review,* 25 (July 1982): 275–96. Also recommended are the several following "Commentaries" in this debate on the impact of boom town growth on community social and economic life.

High fertility and declining mortality have created very young populations throughout the Third World.

Working mothers and their children in Malawi

A resting place for the elderly poor in Sierra Leone . . .

. . . and in the United States. By the year 2000, an estimated 13 percent of Americans will be over 65.

After weathering the "me" generation, postwar Baby Boomers have a fresh outlook on marriage.

In the 1980s, over half the adult women in the United States work outside the home.

Women drawing water from the village pump in the Chetta district of Calcutta

A Chicago family poses in its apartment. Poverty and large families often go together.

WORLD POPULATION 403

POPULATION COMPOSITION

12

The term "population composition" refers to those characteristics and traits of a population that can be observed and measured at any one point in time: the proportion age sixty-five and over, the number of children enrolled in school, the percent of adults possessing particular occupational skills, the number of families with income below $20,000 a year, the number and percent of men and women who are married, nonwhite, foreign born, and so on. In the examination of such characteristics the simple numbers begin to take on meaning, and we come to find out what a society is really like: the kinds of people it comprises, its likely tastes and attitudes, its productive potential, its basic needs and potential problems, and so forth.

The general topic of population composition is very broad, and its nature and significance varies substantially from one society to another. Accordingly, it will not be possible within the limited scope of this volume to delve very deeply into the topic. Rather, in this final chapter we shall try to illustrate the importance of population composition by presenting a brief description and analysis of some of the major characteristics of the American people. Generally speaking, the characteristics that are of most interest in the study of population can be grouped into two broad classes: (1) those that pertain to the *demographic* structure of a population, such as age and sex, and (2) those that relate to its *socioeconomic* composition, such as occupation and income. We will also discuss the basic trends and issues associated with selected aspects of these two broad categories as they pertain to the population of the United States.

DEMOGRAPHIC CHARACTERISTICS

The discussion of the demographic structure of the United States population will be divided into three sections: (1) age and sex, (2) marital status and living arrangements, and (3) ethnic characteristics. In each of these sections attention will be focused on (1) a brief discussion of the general social significance of the characteristic in question, (2) a description of the historical trends leading up to the present situation in the United States, and (3) a discussion of some of the consequences (problems) of the prevailing situation for the well-being of the society as a whole.

Age and Sex Structure

The most fundamental feature of any population is the distribution of its members according to age and sex. Almost any aspect of human behavior—from subjective attitudes and physiological capabilities to objective characteristics such as income, labor force participation, occupation, or group membership—will vary with age and sex. In addition, the specific needs of a given society, both now and in the future, will in large part be determined by the age–sex structure of its population. Despite some converging trends in industrial societies, women generally differ from men in the kinds of jobs they hold, the length of time they remain in the labor force, the income they earn, their consumption patterns, and their attitudes toward various social and economic issues. Similarly, a population composed mainly of young people will differ from one with a high proportion of older members in its productive capacity, its needs and problems, and its outlook and mode of life. The measurement of labor force efficiency and the determination of productive capacity are based on the number of persons within the active adult ages, compared with the number of persons outside these ages, both young and old. The adequacy of facilities such as housing, schools, and convalescent hospitals depends, respectively, on the number of young people who are marrying and starting families, the number of children at school and pre-school ages, and the number of older persons. Since women have a lower death rate than men, and since only women at certain ages can bear children, the levels of fertility and mortality and the rate of natural increase in any population are directly related to its age and sex composition. The number of elderly people in a society has important implications for problems of old age security, such as jobs for older workers, medical and health benefits, and pensions for the aged. For reasons such as these, a knowledge of a population's age–sex structure, how that structure came into being, and what its consequences are likely to be is essential both for determining present needs and for planning with respect to the future needs of a population.

Age Composition

The data in Table 12-1 highlight the major trends in the age and sex composition of the American population during the twentieth century. Considering age first, one of the most convenient ways of telling whether a population is "young" or "old" and how its age composition has been changing is to examine the proportions of the population falling into particular age groups. Here, it is useful to designate three broad age groups that may be assumed to correspond roughly to the three major stages of the life cycle: youth (under twenty years), adulthood (twenty to sixty-four years), and old age (sixty-five years and over). The percentage of the population in these three broad age groups at each census since 1900 clearly reveals the basic changes that have occurred in each stage of the life cycle during this century.

Prior to the 1940–50 decade, a major trend was a fairly consistent decline in the proportion of the population under twenty years of age. At the beginning of the twentieth century, 44 percent of all Americans fell into this age group, but by 1940, after several decades of declining birth rates, this proportion had fallen to about one-third. Since 1940, however, the erratic pattern of fertility has resulted in two reversals of this trend. First, the postwar baby boom led to an increase in the proportion of youth during the 1950s; second, the sharp declines in fertility since the mid-1960s have led to another decline, and by 1980 the proportion of youth in our population had fallen to less than one-third.

For the adult ages, the effect of the fluctuating fertility trend of the present century was the reverse of its effect on the relative size of the youth group. As the proportion of youth fell during the years of declining fertility, the proportion of the population twenty to sixty-four years of age increased; from 1940 to 1960, as a consequence of the higher fertility of the postwar baby boom, the percent of the population falling into these active adult ages declined; and since 1960 the return to fertility decline has led to a resurgence of the earlier upward trend.

By far the most important difference between the 1980 population and the population at the beginning of the century is the proportion of elderly persons. In 1980, the percentage of the population over sixty-five years of age was nearly three times as great as it was in 1900: it was 11 percent in 1980 as opposed to only 4 percent at the turn of the century. In terms of absolute numbers, the change has been even more striking. In 1900, there were slightly more than 3 million persons age sixty-five and over in the nation, but by 1980 this number had swelled to nearly 25 million.

Table 12-1
Selected Age–Sex Characteristics of the United States, 1900–1980

Year	Percent in broad age groups			Index of aging*	Males per 100 females
	Under 20	20–64	65 and over		
1900	44.3	51.6	4.1	11.8	104.4
1910	41.9	53.8	4.3	13.4	106.0
1920	40.8	54.5	4.7	14.6	104.0
1930	38.8	55.8	5.4	18.4	102.5
1940	34.4	58.8	6.8	27.3	100.7
1950	34.0	57.9	8.1	30.2	98.6
1960	38.5	52.3	9.2	29.7	97.0
1970	37.9	52.2	9.9	34.6	94.8
1980	31.9	56.9	11.2	49.8	94.5

SOURCE: U.S. Bureau of the Census, *1970 Census of Population,* Final Report PC(1)-B1, *General Population Characteristics: United States Summary* (Washington, 1972); and *1980 Census of Population and Housing,* Supplementary Report PHC80-51-1, *Provisional Estimates of Social, Economic and Housing Characteristics* (Washington, D.C., 1982).
* Number age sixty-five and over per 100 under fifteen years of age.

The marked aging of our population, which is the most consistent demographic trend of this century, is especially well measured by the *index of aging,* which may be defined as the number of persons age sixty-five and over per 100 children under fifteen years of age. As shown in the fourth column of Table 12-1, prior to the 1950–60 decade the aging index increased during each decennial interval, with the increase being particularly marked between 1920 and 1940. In 1950 there were 30 persons age sixty-five and over per 100 under fifteen years in the nation, as opposed to only 12 in 1900. That is, during the first half of the twentieth century, the number of older persons relative to the number of children in the population nearly tripled.

Although partly due to the drying up of the immigration stream following the adoption of federal restrictive legislation, the pronounced aging of the population between 1900 and 1950 was largely the result of the cumulative effects of the historical decline in the birth rate. Contrary to popular belief, the increasing proportion of elderly persons was not related to the pronounced decline in the death rate that has also taken place during this century. In fact, the fraction over sixty-five today would be larger and the average age of the population greater if mortality had not declined during the twentieth century. Although the increase in the absolute number of older people was indeed the consequence of improvements in death control, the fact that declines in mortality were greatest among infants and young children meant that a larger proportion of babies survived, and this larger proportion who remained alive actually served to retard the aging of the population.

The relationship of declining fertility to population aging is readily apparent from the fact that the greatest increase in the index during the first half of the century occurred between 1930 and 1940, or during the depression decade when birth rates hit their lowest level. By the same reasoning, the much smaller increase from 1940 to 1950 and the slight rejuvenation (i.e., a decline in the index) between 1950 and 1960 reflect the high levels of fertility that prevailed from the end of World War II through 1960. Similarly, a resumption of fertility decline "caused" the sharp increases in the index of aging during the most recent census intervals, particularly during the 1970s when the birth rate fell to a level even lower than it had been during the Great Depression. As a result of the recent sharp fertility declines, the index of aging in the United States has risen by 68 percent since 1960, and in 1980 there were roughly 50 persons age sixty-five and over per 100 under fifteen years of age. Thus, with the exception of the temporary interruption caused by the postwar baby boom, the long-term trend has clearly been for the American population to become older. Moreover, this trend seems likely to continue for some time to come: the U.S. Bureau of the Census has estimated that by the year 2020 the number of persons age sixty-five or older could be as high as 40 million (Bouvier et al., 1975). Thus, in contrast to the late 1950s and 1960s, when the major social issues were largely youth-related (e.g., overcrowded schools, rising juvenile delinquency, the emergence of a middle-class drug culture, political activism on college campuses), the 1980s and beyond will see a society in which greater attention will have to focus on such problems as medical and health care for the aged, increasing costs of Social Security and other benefits, jobs for older workers, and other programs dealing with post-retirement activities and interests.

Sex Composition

With regard to the sex composition of the population, the most significant conclusion to be drawn from the statistics in Table 12-1 is that the United States is more and more becoming a female-dominated society. The sex composition of the population is commonly measured by the *sex ratio*, or the number of males per 100 females. Reflecting the heavy volume of immigration (especially male immigration) during the late nineteenth and early twentieth centuries, the sex ratio of the United States was on the rise until 1910: at that time there were 106 males for every 100 females in the population. Since then, the sex ratio has declined fairly consistently, and in 1980 there were only 94.5 males for every 100 females in the United States.

The long-term decline in the American sex ratio can be explained largely

Figure 12-1
Sex Ratios by Age: United States, 1980

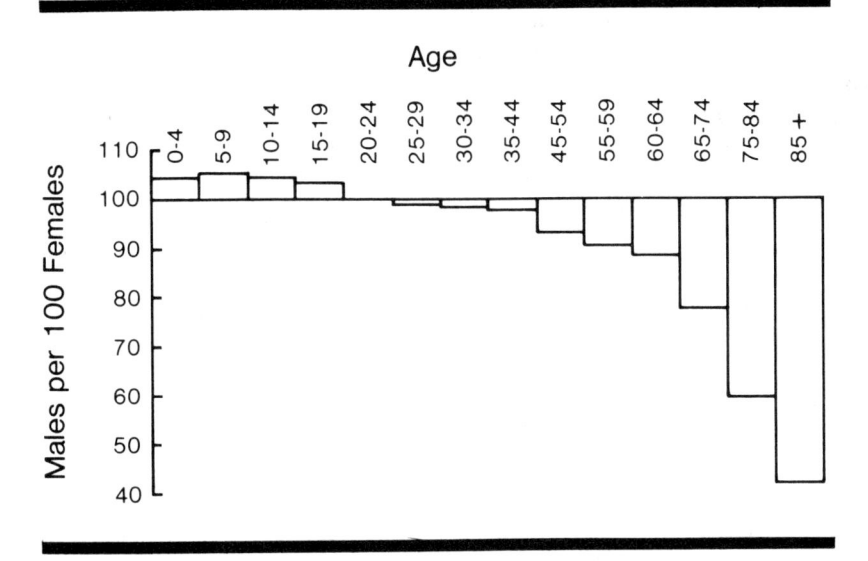

SOURCE: Based on data in U.S. Bureau of the Census, *1980 Census of Population and Housing*, Supplementary Report PHC80-S1-1, *Provisional Estimates of Social Economic and Housing Characteristics* (Washington, D.C., 1982).

in terms of differential mortality. Simply put, the marked declines in mortality during the present century have been more pronounced for women than for men, thus reducing the relative number of males in the population. Moreover, since this mortality differential seems likely to persist, there is little prospect for any significant increase in the sex ratio in the future. On the contrary, it appears that American women will continue to outnumber men in the years ahead.

Because of migration selectivity, the magnitude of the sex ratio varies markedly among the various sections of the country. The general rural-to-urban migration trend, for example, has involved more females than males, with the result that rural areas are generally characterized by a preponderance of males while there is a female excess in urban areas. There is, however, a great deal of intercity variation. In the Washington, D.C., area, for example, where employment opportunities for women are unusually high, the sex ratio in 1980 was only 86. This contrasts sharply with cities characterized by large military populations or heavy industry bases where the sex ratio generally shows a preponderance of males. To illustrate, in 1980 males outnumbered females by a ratio of 106 to 100 in San Diego, and by a ratio of 121 to 100 in Groton, Connecticut.

The sex ratio bears an interesting relationship to age (see Figure 12-1), and the United States today has at least one problem relating to age variations in sex composition. For some little understood biological reason, more boys are born than girls. Thus there is a preponderance of males in the population at the younger ages. From the very first moment of life, however, death takes a greater toll among men than among women. Thus the initially high sex ratio is gradually decreased by mortality as the older ages are approached. To illustrate, in 1980 the sex ratio of persons under five years of age in the United States was approximately 105. At the younger adult ages (twenty to twenty-four) when most people tend to marry, the two sexes were evenly balanced, but thereafter there was an ever increasing preponderance of females in the population: the sex ratio was 96 at ages thirty-five to thirty-nine; by ages sixty-five to seventy-four it had fallen below 80; and among persons eighty-five and older there were only 42 males for every 100 females in the United States.

A major implication of this situation relates to the care of older persons. In an earlier era when the American family was more multifunctional than it is today, the care of the elderly was not a matter for public concern. As the role of the family has become more centered around bioaffectional functions, however, its earlier broad functions concerning such matters as education, protection, welfare, and so on, have been transferred to outside agencies in the community. One corollary of this development has been an increase in welfare programs and legislation for the elderly. Given the pronounced sex imbalance at the older ages, it is clear that contemporary problems of caring for the elderly are primarily problems of caring for *elderly women*—a significant fact to bear in mind in planning for the types of nursing homes, housing projects, medical care programs, and other facilities and services necessary to meet the needs of our aging population.

Age Composition Problems

The atypical and radically changing age structure of the American population represents one of the most important demographic developments of the past half-century. It has been and will continue for some time to be a major factor underlying a number of dislocations and associated problems in our society. In this section we will take an even closer look at the nature and implications of our changing age composition.

The nature of our changing age structure, which reflects the erratic trend in the American birth rate during the past forty to fifty years, is especially well illustrated by the population pyramids presented in Figure 12-2. A *population pyramid*, it will be remembered, is a standard graphic device for describing the age–sex composition of a population. As is customary in such pyramids, age is plotted on the vertical axis, males are depicted on the

Figure 12-2
Population Pyramids: United States, 1940, 1960, and 1980

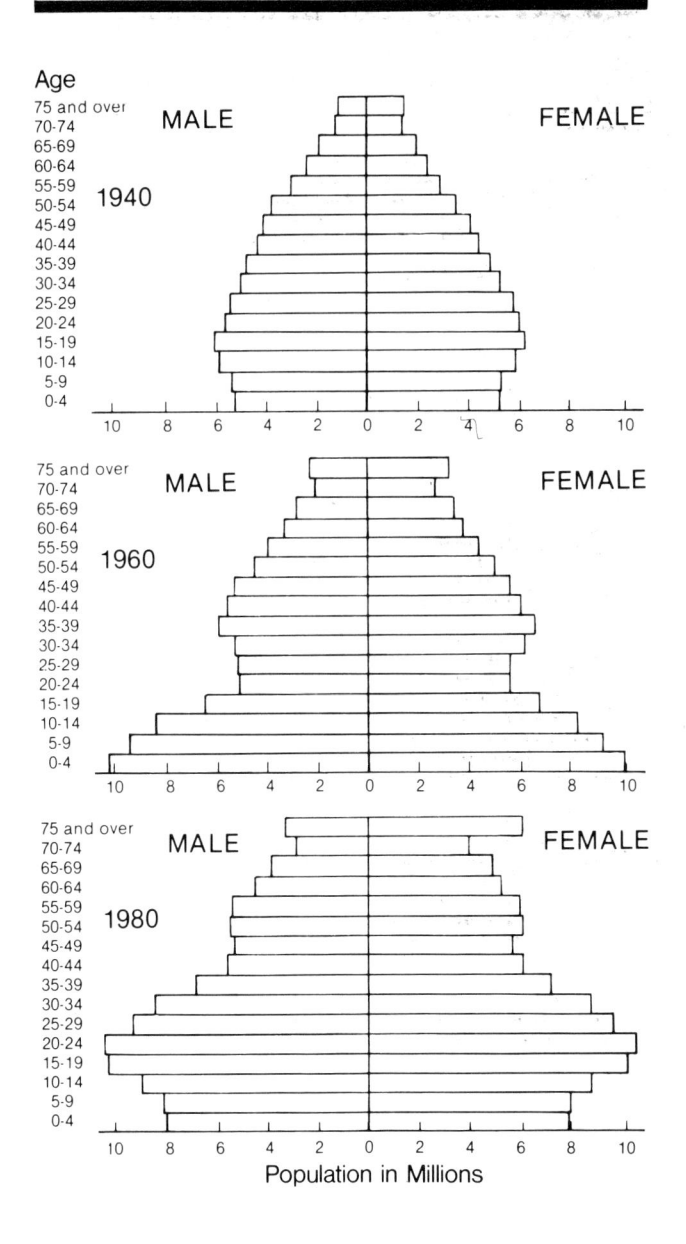

SOURCE: Based on data contained in the sources cited for Table 12-1.

left and females on the right, and the number (or percent) of people is plotted for each sex along the horizontal axis. Thus, the bars on either side of the center vertical represent the size of specified age–sex groups.

Careful examination of the pyramids in Figure 12-2 clearly reveals the nature and implications of the fluctuating fertility trend of the past several decades. Among these are (1) the very low fertility of the 1930s (note the relative deficit of persons under ten years of age in the 1940 pyramid and the smaller cohorts at subsequent twenty-year age intervals in 1960 and 1980); (2) the postwar baby boom (note the successively larger cohorts in the 1960 pyramid from age fifteen to nineteen, those born from 1940 to 1944 and on down; and note the subsequent bulge in the 1980 pyramid at ages fifteen to thirty-four; and (3) the revival of the long-term fertility decline since the mid-1960s (note the decline in the size of the cohorts under 15 years of age in the 1980 pyramid).

These changes in the age structure of our population have already created a number of dislocations in American society, and they will continue to do so in the years ahead as the various bulges and gaps pass through different stages of the life cycle. During the 1950s, for example, as the first of the baby boom cohorts reached school age, it became necessary to expand educational facilities at a rapid rate to accommodate the steady increase in the student population: expansion became necessary at the elementary level in the early 1950s, at the secondary school level in the late 1950s and early 1960s, and at the college level in the mid-1960s. More recently, as the number of births has been declining so sharply, the "supply" of elementary school facilities has begun to exceed the "demand," and many municipalities in the late 1970s and early 1980s were faced with the unhappy task of having to cut back on staff and even close down some schools.

The postwar baby boom has clearly had the greatest impact on our society in recent years, and the impact will continue to be profound in the years to come as this "fateful bulge" progresses through the life cycle (Bouvier, 1980). Some of its effects will be beneficial; others may create problems. For example, the much bemoaned increase in crime, notably juvenile delinquency, since the 1960s has been due in part to the substantially larger numbers at the high crime ages (fifteen to twenty-four), but as the baby boom cohorts age during the 1980s and are followed by the smaller numbers from the "baby bust" generation, crime rates should subside. The same can be said for the higher rates of unemployment, motor vehicle accidents, and other social phenomena that are more prevalent among young people. A decline in unemployment as the baby boom comes to dominate the active adult ages could, in addition to its earlier noted potential for generating another population growth spurt, enhance the growth of the economy (by generating higher per capita incomes, increasing demands for housing and other family consumption goods, revitalizing the lagging elementary educational system, etc.). On the other hand, the larger number of workers competing for jobs could have a negative impact on the economy by promoting higher unemployment or, at best, slowing down rates of upward job mobility.

The strains on the Social Security fund in the early 1980s are in part a result of the smaller numbers of people at the major productive ages (the survivors of the pre-1940 birth cohorts), but these pressures should be considerably relieved in the coming decades, both because of the smaller number of retirees to be expected from the depression generation and also because of the substantial increases in the number of workers coming from the baby boom generation. Conversely, by the second decade of the twenty-first century we could be facing another very serious crisis as the larger baby boom cohorts reach retirement age and have to be supported by the much smaller baby bust cohorts that are following behind them. One can, in fact, identify a number of areas where the passing of one large group and its succession by a much smaller one has already created and will continue to create various problems for the entire society or for particular segments of it (e.g., the obviously declining demand today for all kinds of baby products). For example, as we entered the 1980s the problem of declining enrollments that had been plaguing elementary school officials was beginning to be felt in the high schools, and all over the country college and university administrators were gearing up for an anticipated enrollment crunch beginning around 1984–85. Similarly, as we faced a definite and measurable decline in the number of young men in the population, there was talk about the effect this might have on the ability of the military: could it continue to maintain itself on a voluntary basis, or would it become necessary to reinstate the draft? Looking even further ahead, in general terms we can anticipate an increase in a wide variety of issues and problems—over and above those pertaining to retirement support—applying to an aging population: increasing conservatism, health problems, jobs for the elderly, leisure time activities, and so forth. All of these will have to be faced and dealt with by the relatively smaller number of working adults who will come from the baby bust cohorts.

The important point to stress here is that we know the present age structure of the population, and we can easily project what the structure will be at various points in the future. Knowing this we should be able to anticipate many of the future needs and problems of the society and gear up to deal with them.

As a final word we should emphasize that the social, economic, and political problems facing countries of the world today differ markedly depending on the overall age composition of their populations. This can be illustrated quite dramatically by the two extreme pyramids presented in Figure 12-3. On the one hand, Kenya, with its high birth and death rates, exhibits the traditional pyramidal structure of a rapidly growing population whose major needs and problems will be heavily youth-oriented. Sweden, on the other hand, is characterized by an age structure that is generally typ-

Figure 12-3
Population Pyramids of Kenya (top) and Sweden (bottom), c. 1970

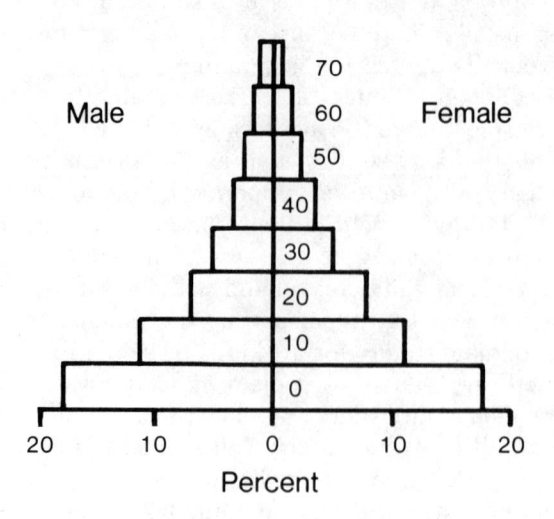

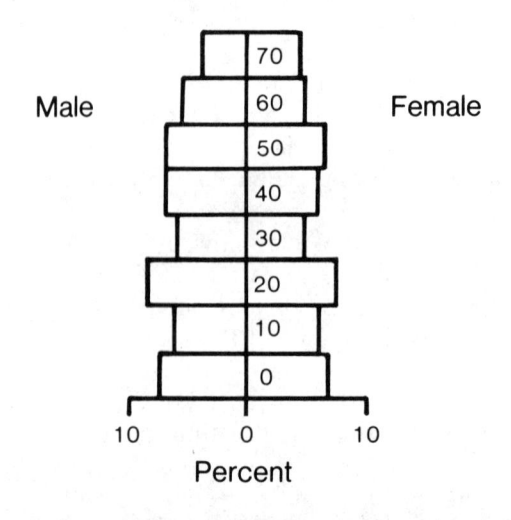

SOURCE: Based on data published in *1973 Demographic Yearbook* (New York: United Nations, 1974).

ical of low birth and death rate populations that are approaching a zero growth rate, and where the needs and problems of the elderly are of major concern.

It should also be apparent that the overall age structure and associated problems can vary substantially from one area of a given country to another. In the United States, for example, it should not take much imagination to realize that the particular needs and problems of a retirement community (Cocoa Beach, Florida) will differ substantially from those of a city containing a fairly large military population (Groton, Connecticut), and especially from those of a college town such as Bowling Green, Ohio (see the five-year age group pyramids depicted in Figure 12-4).

Figure 12-4
Population Pyramids (Five-year age groups) of Three American Cities, 1980

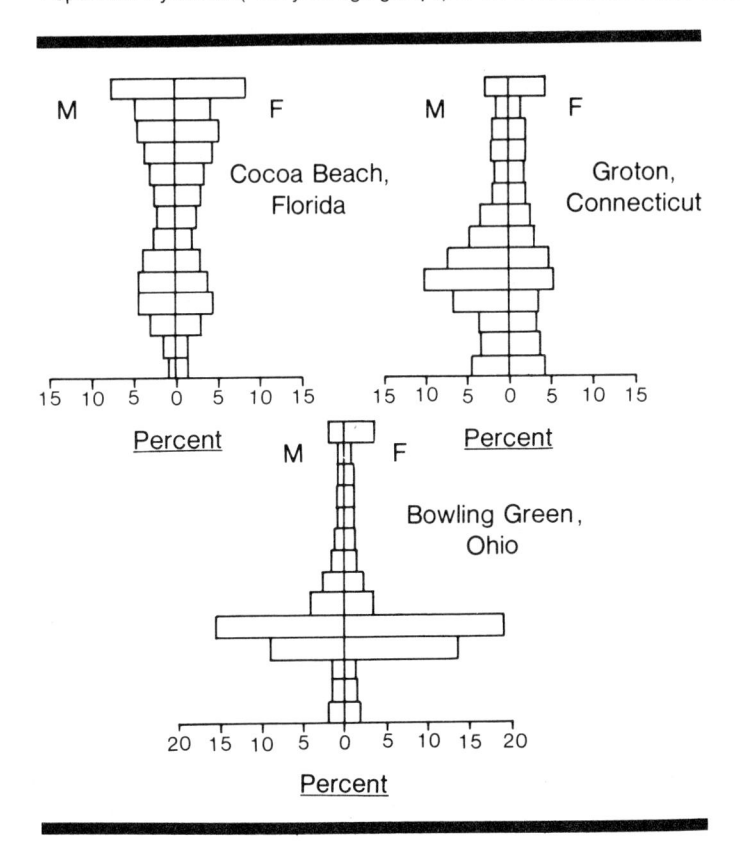

SOURCE: Based on data published in the state reports of the *1980 Census of Population,* Final Report PC 80-1, *General Population Characteristics* (Washington, D.C., 1982–83).

Marital Status and Household Living Arrangements

The topics of marital status and household living arrangements lead into the much broader and sociologically very significant subject of the structure and function of the family in our society. Here, however, we shall limit ourselves to a discussion of a few selected statistics to indicate some basic trends that have emerged in the United States today and to provide some insight into the possible implications of such trends for the future of American society.

Marital Status

The distribution of a population according to marital status has both socioeconomic and demographic significance. On the socioeconomic side, marital status composition will influence the nature of housing needs in a community, the type of consumer goods purchased, the adequacy of existing recreational facilities, and so on. Marital status is an important determinant of such things as where people live, whether or not they work, the kinds of groups they belong to, and what they do during leisure hours. Marital status is also known to be related to various forms of deviant social behavior: in general, the incidence of crime, suicide, mental illness, and automobile accidents is lower for married than for unmarried persons. On the demographic side, married persons have lower death rates than the unmarried, and birth rates tend to vary with the proportion who are married. Also, married persons are more likely to settle down than are unmarried persons; hence one might expect the rate of residential mobility to be greater in communities having a large proportion of unattached persons. Thus, like age and sex, marital status is intimately associated with a great many aspects of human behavior.

Trends in the marital status of the American population since 1920 are depicted in Table 12-2. According to these data, several important developments have taken place in this century, particularly since 1940. Until that time, the proportion of persons who were married had remained relatively stable at about six out of ten. Then, at the close of the Second World War, this proportion rose sharply, partly as a result of the rush to "make up" marriages that had been postponed earlier because of the depression and the war, and partly as a result of the "moving ahead" of marriages that would otherwise have occurred at a later time. This latter trend is indicated by a steady decline in the average age at marriage between 1940 and 1950. It is clear, however, that since 1960 the marriage boom has run out of steam: age at first marriage has risen again, and by 1980 the proportion of married persons had fallen to 62 percent for males and only 58 percent for females. There are a number of reasons for this letup. Among them is the continued pressure on young people to obtain a higher education, the increasing par-

Table 12-2
Distribution of the Population by Marital Status: United States, 1920–80

	Percent age 15 and over who are:			
Sex and year	Single (never married)	Now married (including separated)	Widowed	Divorced
Male				
1920*	35.1	59.3	4.8	0.6
1930*	34.1	60.0	4.6	1.1
1940	33.2	61.2	4.3	1.3
1950	24.9	68.9	4.2	2.0
1960	23.2	71.1	3.5	2.2
1970	26.4	67.7	3.1	2.8
1980	29.9	62.2	2.5	5.4
Female				
1920*	27.3	60.6	11.1	0.8
1930*	26.4	61.1	11.1	1.3
1940	25.8	61.0	11.5	1.7
1950	18.5	67.0	12.0	2.4
1960	17.3	67.4	12.4	2.9
1970	20.6	62.8	12.7	3.9
1980	23.0	57.5	12.3	7.2

SOURCE: Data for 1920–1970 from U.S. Bureau of the Census, *Historical Statistics of the United States, Colonial Times to 1970* (Washington, D.C., 1975); data for 1980 from *1980 Census of Population and Housing*, PHC80-S1-1, *Supplementary Report: Provisional Estimates of Social Economic and Housing Characteristics* (Washington, D.C., 1982). Percentages calculated by authors.
* Totals on which percentages were based included a "Not Reported" category.

ticipation of women in the labor force, and the emergence of a trend for young people to live together in nonfamilial situations. In addition to these, a "marriage squeeze" emerged in the 1970s: since women generally marry men slightly older than themselves, a sharp rise in the number of births such as occurred during the baby boom years leads, a generation later, to a shortage of marriageable men relative to the number of women.

These marked fluctuations in the proportion married over the past forty years have had, and continue to have, a pronounced impact on American society. Most significantly, the earlier marriage boom and more recent marriage bust were major factors underlying the subsequent boom and bust in the American birth rate, and they are thus indirectly responsible for all the dislocations and problems associated with the radical changes in age structure discussed above.

The trend in the years to come will depend on many factors, but it seems reasonable to assume that any future fluctuations in the percentage of married persons will be much smaller than those of the past two generations. On the one hand, one might anticipate a slight increase in the proportion married as the pending reversal of the marriage squeeze enhances marriage opportunities for women. On the other hand, this potential may be dampened by the growing economic independence and greater social freedom that women have recently come to enjoy in our society. An especially important factor here will be the state of the American economy: a marked improvement in economic conditions could lead to an increase in marriage rates, but an economic slump like that of the late 1970s and early 1980s could lead to even further declines in the proportions of married persons. Another factor will be the trend with respect to the number of unmarried couples living together: this number tripled during the 1970s (rising from roughly half a million in 1970 to nearly 2 million in 1981), and it is expected to increase still further during the 1980s. Although numerically small, the projected increase in the number of such couples could continue to have a depressing effect on the overall marriage rate.

The trends in the proportion who are single (never married) can largely be understood in the context of the changes that have occurred in the percent married, but the situation with respect to widowed and divorced persons requires further comment. In the first instance, it is apparent that the percent of females who are widowed has changed only slightly over the years while the percentage of widowed males has undergone a consistent decline. This has been due both to the widening of the sex mortality differential in evidence until the most recent period and to the greater tendency for males to remarry after the death of a spouse. Either way, the effect is to create a situation in this country where the proportion of widowed females is nearly five times as great as the proportion of widowed males. As indicated earlier, this means that many of the problems relating to older persons in the United States today are primarily problems of elderly women. Moreover, as long as the sex mortality differential prevails, this situation and its associated problems will persist.

With respect to the divorced population, the data in Table 12-2 reveal a sharp upward trend, especially during the 1970s. The causes of this trend, which is another factor contributing to a decline in the proportion married, must be sought in such things as the increasing liberation of women in American society, the decline in fertility and family size, the increasing emphasis on romantic love, the decline in the importance of the family as a major production as well as consumption unit, and a relaxation of traditional sexual mores. The relative importance of these contributing causes is debatable, as is their long-run effect on the overall well-being of our society. One can argue, however, that the broken homes that result from divorce are disproportionately represented among the various social problems in the United States today. Broken families, for example, are associated with a greater incidence of crime and mental illness. Since a large proportion of divorces involve children, the harmful effects of marital dissolution are not limited to the contending adults. Thus, juvenile delinquency is much higher among children of divorced parents than among children of more stable families. Although part of this relationship may be due to divorce and delinquency having the same underlying causes (e.g., poverty), evidence also suggests that children of divorced parents are more likely to experience feelings of insecurity and that this can lead to truancy, running away, and other forms of deviant social behavior. Although there is reason to anticipate a slowdown in the rate at which divorce has been increasing in our society, as contributing factors such as the rate of increase in female labor force participation slow down, there is no reason to expect this trend to reverse itself in the foreseeable future. Thus, it is possible that the proportion of the population that is divorced will continue to rise over the next several years, and this will mean the persistence of, and perhaps even an increase in the incidence of the various social problems associated with broken homes.

Household Characteristics

The changing marital status distribution of the American population coupled with an increasing number of young adults leaving their parental home to live independently has resulted in the increasing fragmentation of the American household. Two marked trends may have serious repercussions

Table 12-3
Selected Household Characteristics of the United States, 1970 and 1980 (in thousands)

Household characteristics	1970	1980	Percent increase
Number of households	63,401	79,108	24.8%
Family households	51,456	58,426	13.5
Married couple	44,728	48,180	7.7
Other, male householder*	1,228	1,706	38.9
Other, female householder*	5,500	8,540	55.2
Nonfamily households	11,945	20,682	73.1
Population in households	199,030	217,482	9.3
Average per household	3.14	2.75	−12.4
Population in family households	185,592	192,860	3.9
Percent of household population	93.2	88.7	xxx

SOURCE: U.S. Bureau of the Census, "Household and Family Characteristics: March, 1980," *Current Population Reports*, Series P-20, No. 366 (September 1981).
* "Householder" is a new term developed to replace the older "head of household." In the past, the husband was always designated as the head of a husband–wife family, but under the new definition the householder may be identified as either the husband or the wife.

for our society. First, the number and proportion of nonfamily households in the United States has increased substantially (see Table 12-3). Such households (consisting of persons who live alone or with nonrelatives) rose from 12 million in 1970 (19 percent of all households) to nearly 21 million in 1980, at which time they constituted 26 percent of all households. This has been associated with a corresponding decline in average household size—from 3.14 persons per household in 1970 to 2.75 in 1980. Second, among family households (two or more persons related by birth, marriage or adoption who occupy their own separate housing unit) there has been a very substantial increase in one-parent families, particularly those in which a female is head of the household. In other words, those family types and living situations that are most likely to be associated with various social problems in our society have increased at a rate that is markedly disproportional to the rate of increase in the number and proportion of traditional husband–wife family households. Lest anyone draw too negative a conclusion from this observation, however, we must stress that the overwhelming majority of the American people (89 percent of the household population in 1980) continues to live in a traditional family setting.

Ethnic Characteristics

The particular ethnic group to which a person belongs has a significant effect on a great many aspects of his or her life. Although the deterministic nature of inherent ethnic characteristics may be minimal from a biological perspective, the fact remains that characteristics such as race, color, and national origins exhibit a marked relationship to a number of socioeconomic and demographic variables. These factors have always been extremely important in determining where persons have been allowed to live, where they have been permitted to attend school, the type of job skills they could acquire, the kinds of jobs available to them, the amount of money they could earn, and so forth. No one can deny, for example, the inferior treatment meted out to blacks and members of other nonwhite ethnic groups in our time. These inequalities, in turn, have led to other group differences—in educational attainment, in the prevalence of deviant behavior, and in the levels of fertility and mortality, among others. The observable racial and ethnic differences in such things as prostitution, illegitimacy, crime, mental health, birth and death rates, and so on are not due to differences in ethnic background. Instead, they are due to differences in the nature and availability of opportunities to participate in the mainstream of American life. Many social problems that have arisen at various periods of American history have, in fact, been directly traceable to the kind of treatment the dominant native white group has meted out to different ethnic minorities.

Table 12-4
Percent of the Population in Specified Ethnic Groups: United States, 1900–1980

Year	Percent nonwhite Total	Black	Other	Percent foreign born
1900	12.3	11.6	0.7	13.7
1910	11.3	10.7	0.6	14.8
1920	10.5	9.9	0.6	13.2
1930	10.4	9.7	0.7	11.6
1940	10.4	9.7	0.7	8.8
1950	10.7	9.9	0.7	6.9
1960	11.4	10.5	0.9	5.4
1970	12.5	11.1	1.4	4.7
1980*	13.8	11.7	2.0	6.2

SOURCE: U.S. Bureau of the Census, *1970 Census of Population,* Final Report PC(1)-B1, *General Population Characteristics: U.S. Summary* (Washington, D.C., 1972); Final Report PC(1)-D1, *Detailed Characteristics: U.S. Summary* (Washington, D.C., 1973); and "Preliminary Estimates of the Population of the United States by Age, Sex and Race: 1970 to 1981," *Current Population Reports,* Series P-25, No. 917 (July 1982).
* Data published in the 1980 census reports may not agree with those shown here because of a change in the procedure for reporting race. The figures shown here have been adjusted to make them consistent with those for 1970 and earlier years.

Since color and national origin are so closely associated with many of the problems facing American society today, we should have some understanding of the major trends in the ethnic composition of the population (see Table 12-4). When the first federal census was taken in 1790, nonwhites, the vast majority of whom were black slaves, accounted for roughly one-fifth of the American population. Thereafter, the proportion declined consistently until it reached a low of 10 percent during the early years of the twentieth century. This decline occurred in spite of the fact that the nonwhite rate of natural increase has generally been much higher than the corresponding white rate, and it can only be explained by reference to migration trends. On the one hand, the end of the slave trade during the early nineteenth century put a stop to the "immigration" of blacks. On the other hand, the nineteenth century was characterized by a steady rise in the volume of free immigration from Europe. These two developments meant that the nonwhite population grew almost entirely through natural increase, whereas the white population grew by both natural increase and immigration.

This explanation is further supported by more recent developments: ever since federal legislation drastically curtailed immigration during the

1920s, the proportion of foreign born in the population has undergone a sharp decline (i.e., the low volume of immigration has meant that the older foreign born have not been replaced when they died). Conversely, the proportion of nonwhites in the population has increased slightly. These two opposing trends have not affected the existence of ethnic group problems, but they have altered their nature somewhat. During the early days of the twentieth century the foreign born were most intimately associated with prevailing social problems; today nonwhites, and especially the blacks, are most characteristically associated with ghettos and the higher incidence of poverty, illegitimacy, crime, divorce and desertion, and so forth. Again we must stress that the higher incidence of deviant behavior does not reflect any inherent biological differences between whites and nonwhites. Rather, it reflects the great disparity in socioeconomic status of the two color groups. We will consider these differences more fully in the following section on socioeconomic characteristics.

One final point needs to be made about the changing ethnic composition, and that concerns the recent upturn in the percent foreign born and an associated change in the composition of the nonwhite population. Although blacks have long constituted the major portion of the nonwhite population, the size of their majority fraction has been decreasing since the 1960s. This is due to the change in immigration laws that permitted an increase in Asian immigration, and also to the large numbers of refugees from Southeast Asia during the late 1960s and early 1970s. To illustrate the magnitude of this development: blacks increased by 41 percent between 1960 and 1980 but the "other nonwhites" increased by nearly 200 percent during the same interval. As a result, the proportion of blacks in the nonwhite population fell from 92 percent in 1960 to 85 percent in 1980.

The Hispanic Population

Perhaps the most dramatic development with respect to the ethnic composition of the American population in recent years has been the marked increase in the number and proportion of persons of Spanish origin. The number of Hispanics in this country increased from 9.3 million in 1970 to 14.6 million in 1980. This represents an increase of 57 percent during the decade (compared with 18 percent for blacks and 6 percent for the white population), and it has resulted in a notable increase in the proportion of Hispanics in the population. In 1980, this ethnic group represented nearly 7 percent of the population (up from 4.5 percent a decade earlier), and if illegal aliens were included, the figure could have been as high as 10 percent.

Although part of the reason for the emergence of Hispanics as the fastest growing minority in the United States lies in their higher fertility, most of their increase has come about in response to the changes in our immigration laws discussed in Chapter 9. Since the 1960s, roughly half of all legal immigrants (as well as the vast majority of illegals) have come from other nations in the Western Hemisphere, with the largest single group coming from Mexico.

The dominance of Mexicans in our Hispanic population is, of course, partly a function of our historical expansion, which incorporated vast amounts of territory that once belonged to Mexico, and partly a result of physical proximity. The extent of this dominance is clearly revealed by a survey conducted by the U.S. Bureau of the Census in the spring of 1980. This survey found that 60 percent of the Hispanics were of Mexican origin, 14 percent were Puerto Rican, 6 percent were Cuban, 8 percent came from other countries throughout Central and South America, and 12 percent were classified as "other Spanish," including persons whose origin was unknown or not reported (U.S. Bureau of the Census, 1981).

Since Hispanics are such a distinctive cultural-religious group, an increase in their numbers will necessarily have some influence on the nature of our society. For example, because of their higher fertility and the fact that most of them are Catholic, their increase might lead to a widening of what has recently been a narrowing Catholic–non-Catholic fertility differential. Moreover, on a local level an increase in the Hispanic segment of the population may create a variety of problems reflecting such things as the language barrier, prejudice and discrimination on the part of the dominant Anglo group, and the personal and social disorganization often associated with minority group status and/or cultural marginality. In the long run, however, there is no reason why we cannot expect persons of Spanish origin, like members of other ethnic groups, to make positive and significant contributions to the growth and development of our society.

SOCIOECONOMIC CHARACTERISTICS

Here we will examine the educational and income status of the American population and the characteristics of the labor force, focusing on the sociological significance of particular characteristics as well as on the historical trends that have led to the present situation.

Education

A vitally important feature of any modern society is the educational status of the population as reflected in (1) the number and proportion of young persons currently enrolled in school at various levels and (2) the number of years of schooling completed by persons who have finished their formal education. To begin with, educational status indicates the extent to which the labor force is getting the more highly trained technicians it needs to carry out the increasingly complex tasks of an expanding industrial society. Moreover, since only literate persons with some background in history, government, and other related subjects can clearly understand the issues at stake and can vote intelligently, the level of educational attainment also indicates how well we have prepared our young people to participate in the political life of our democratic society. The educational level of a community is closely related to its economic and political attitudes, its consumer buying habits, its social status relative to that of other population groups, and its attitudes and opinions covering a wide area of human social life. The level of school enrollment is also a measure of the adequacy of educational facilities, and points out where expansions or cutbacks may be desirable, or even necessary. Finally, differential levels of educational attainment within a population point out the degree to which the opportunities and advantages of education are being shared equally by all members of the society.

School Enrollment Trends

Considering school enrollment first, the data in Table 12-5 show the size of the school age population and the number and proportion of young people enrolled in school at various ages at ten-year intervals since 1950. According to these data, the major trend prior to the 1970s was a steady and substantial increase in the size of the school population. This enrollment increase was due not only to the growth of the total population at these ages (which increased from 47 to 76 million between 1950 and 1970); it is also due to an increase in *school enrollment rates* (the percentage of the school-age population that is enrolled in school). In 1970, some 74 percent of five- to twenty-four-year-olds were enrolled in school. This compared to a national enrollment rate of only 63 percent in 1950, and it represents an increase of 18 percent in school enrollment rates during that twenty-year period.

During the 1970s the upward trend in the size of the American school population came to an abrupt halt. Due to a decline in both the number of school-age persons and the overall enrollment rate, the 1970s saw the size of the school population decline by nearly 3½ million, or by slightly more than 5 percent.

The trends in school enrollment during the past several decades have not been the same for all ages and levels of enrollment. The greatest numerical increase during the years from 1950 to 1970 characterized the group five to thirteen years of age (roughly equivalent to the elementary school age population), whereas the greatest proportional increase characterized the college age group (eighteen to twenty-four years old). The high school age

Table 12-5
Selected School Enrollment Data: United States, 1950–80

Year	Total, age 5–24 years	Age groups 5–13	14–17	18–24
Total Persons (in thousands)				
1950	46,725	22,374	8,479	15,871
1960	59,566	32,727	11,261	15,578
1970	76,194	36,695	16,116	23,383
1980	73,601	30,044	15,427	28,130
Enrolled in School (in thousands)				
1950	29,216	19,208	7,115	2,894
1960	42,728	29,296	9,844	3,587
1970	56,241	33,753	14,945	7,543
1980	52,249	29,604	14,411	8,234
Percent Enrolled				
1950	62.5	85.8	83.9	18.2
1960	71.7	89.5	87.4	23.0
1970	73.8	92.0	92.7	32.3
1980	71.0	98.5	93.4	29.3

SOURCE: U.S. Bureau of the Census, *1970 Census of Population, General Social and Economic Characteristics:* Final Report PC(1)-C1, *United States Summary* (Washington, D.C., 1972); and "School Enrollment: Social and Economic Characteristics of Students: October 1980," *Current Population Reports*, Series P-20, No. 362 (May 1981).

group, ages fourteen to seventeen, ranked second in terms of both numerical and percentage gains between 1950 and 1970. During the 1970s the number enrolled at the college ages continued to increase, although the gains were much smaller than in earlier years; but the number of high school students and especially the number of elementary students declined sharply. The declines at these ages were sufficiently large to offset the gains at the college level, thus bringing about a reduction in overall school enrollment during the 1970s.

Although changing enrollment rates have certainly had an impact on the number enrolled in school, particularly at the college ages, the key to understanding the major changes in the American school population lies in the fluctuating birth rate of the past several decades. At ages five to thirteen, for example, the pronounced increase in the enrolled population from 1950 to 1960 and the more moderate increase from 1960 to 1970 reflects the impact of the postwar baby boom and the continuation of relatively high levels of fertility throughout the 1950s. Most recently, the end of the baby boom and the substantially smaller cohorts born since the mid-1960s have brought about a decline in the size of the elementary school age population, despite a marked increase in the enrollment rate at these ages between 1970 and 1980.

At the high school ages, large increases occurred in the school population between 1950 and 1960, and especially between 1960 and 1970, again reflecting the progressive aging of the baby boom cohorts; but from 1970 to 1980, despite a slight increase in the enrollment rate, the first of the smaller baby bust cohorts began to enter this age group bringing about a slight decline in the number of fourteen- to seventeen-year-olds enrolled in school.

At the college ages, in contrast to the other two groups, changes in the rate of enrollment rather than in the size of the base population have had the greatest impact on the number in school. This is especially well illustrated by the trend from 1950 to 1960 when the number of eighteen- to twenty-four-year-olds enrolled in school increased by roughly one-fourth, despite a small decline in the total population at these ages (a decline that reflected the aging of the smaller birth cohorts of the 1930 depression decade). Between 1960 and 1970 the college population in the United States experienced a very substantial increase, due to an increase both in the enrollment rate and in the number of young adults as the aging baby boom cohorts displaced the smaller depression cohorts at these ages. From 1970 to 1980, however, population growth took over as the sole contributor to rising enrollment: during this decade the number enrolled at ages eighteen to twenty-four years grew by 440,000 (6 percent) despite a 12 percent *decline* in the enrollment rate—a decline that is at least in part due to the deterioration of the national economy during the late 1970s.

Looking ahead, we can easily project that the 1980s will be characterized by a pronounced decline, first, in the number of high school students and, later, in the number enrolled in college. Even if high school enrollment rates, already at 94 percent, rise further and even if college enrollment rates revert to their previous high level, the substantial population declines that can be anticipated as the smaller birth cohorts of the late 1960s and 1970s progressively age through their teens and into their twenties will be sufficient to bring about sizable reductions in the number of students.

The problems that began to plague elementary schools during the 1970s (declining enrollments, shrinking budgets, teacher and staff layoffs, school closings, etc.) were starting to be felt in the high schools by 1980. All over the country, college administrators were gearing up to meet the problems associated with the projected decline in their enrollments. Clearly the age composition changes that have resulted from the erratic fertility trend over the past several decades have had a profound impact on American society, and they will continue to do so for some time to come.

A more detailed discussion of this topic would note that the pattern of school enrollment is not the same for all segments of the American population. Enrollment rates tend to be highest for men, whites, and urban dwellers, and lowest for women, members of ethnic minorities, and rural residents. As we will see, however, the significance of these and other enrollment differentials lies in the associated differences in levels of educational attainment.

Educational Attainment

The enrollment in school of more and more persons for longer periods of time will have an obvious impact on the educational level of a population. As the data in Table 12-6 reveal, the educational attainment status of the American population has increased markedly over the years. As of 1980 the median number of school years completed by persons twenty-five years old and over in the United States was 12.5, or 45 percent higher than the 8.6 years that had prevailed forty years earlier. The proportion of adults who had completed high school, including those who went on to college, rose from slightly less than one-fourth in 1940 to just over two-thirds in 1980, while the proportion who had completed four or more years of college rose from 5 to 16 percent. At the other end of the scale, the proportion of per-

Table 12-6

Educational Attainment of the U.S. Population Age 25 and Over*

Year	Median school years completed	Less than 5 years elementary**	High school graduates	College graduates
1940	8.6	13.5	24.1	4.6
1950	9.3	10.8	33.4	6.0
1960	10.6	8.3	41.1	7.7
1970	12.1	5.5	52.3	10.7
1980	12.5	3.5	67.7	16.4

Percent with specified levels of educational attainment

SOURCE: U.S. Bureau of the Census, *1970 Census of Population,* Final Report PC(1)-C1, *General Social and Economic Characteristics: United States Summary* (Washington, D.C., 1972). The 1980 data actually refer to 1979 and were obtained from "Educational Attainment in the United States: March 1979 and 1978," *Current Population Reports,* Series P-20, No. 356 (August 1980).

* Statistics pertaining to the educational attainment of the population are here based on adults age 25 and over. The reason for this is that many people below these ages are still in school and have not yet completed their education. By the time they have reached age 25, most people have completed the amount of education to which they aspire, which they can afford, or which they have been required to obtain for their chosen occupation.

**Labor force experts define persons who have completed less than 5 years of elementary school as *functionally illiterate;* that is, they are not equipped to perform anything but menial tasks that require little or no technical skill.

Figure 12-5
Percent High School Graduates, by Age: United States, 1979

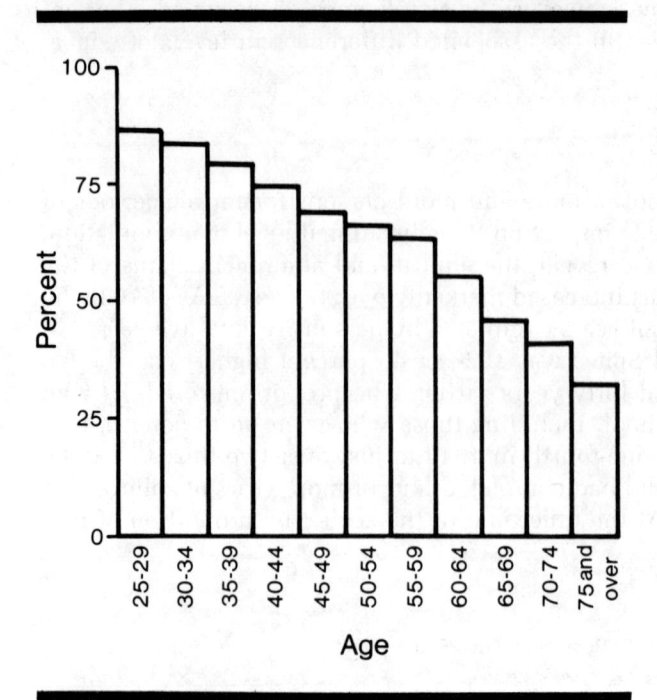

SOURCE: Based on data in U.S. Bureau of the Census, "Educational Attainment in the United States: March 1979 and 1978," *Current Population Reports,* Series P-20, No. 356 (August 1980).

sons who had completed less than five years of elementary school had been cut by three-fourths. This latter trend in part reflects the dying off of foreign-born persons who immigrated to this country during the late nineteenth and early twentieth centuries. On the other hand, the increase in the proportion of high school and college graduates reflects the growing tendency during the postwar era for more and more people to stay in school beyond the ages of compulsory attendance. Together, these two trends have combined to cause a substantial rise in the overall level of educational attainment in the United States.

The rise in the educational status of the population over time can be viewed more clearly by examining current differences by age. Data collected by the Bureau of the Census in 1979, for example, showed that among persons seventy-five years old and over (i.e., persons who attended school a few generations ago), only 33 percent were high school graduates (see Figure 12-5). Of persons sixty to sixty-four (who were educated about two generations ago), 55 percent had finished high school. At ages forty to forty-four (persons whose schooling was completed roughly one generation ago), 75 percent were high school graduates. For the youngest age group, twenty-five to twenty-nine years, most of whom had only just passed through the educational system, 86 percent had completed a minimum of four years of high school.

Educational Differentials

In spite of the overall improvement in the level of educational attainment in the United States, marked differences continue to characterize the various subgroups in the population (see Table 12-7). For example, American men have a slightly higher level of educational attainment than women, with the differential being largely due to differences at the college level. The proportions of functional illiterates and high school graduates are similar for both sexes, but men clearly predominate at the highest level of educational attainment where they outnumber female college graduates by a ratio of roughly two to one.

Table 12-7
Educational Attainment Differentials for Specific Sex, Ethnic, and Residence Groups: United States, 1979

Demographic characteristics	Median school years completed	Less than 5 years elementary	High school graduates	College graduates
Male	12.6	3.7	68.4	20.4
Female	12.4	3.2	67.1	12.9
White	12.5	2.7	69.8	17.2
Black	11.9	9.6	49.3	7.8
Spanish origin*	10.3	17.7	41.9	6.6
Metropolitan areas	...	2.4	72.3	16.3
In central city	...	3.4	67.7	14.9
Outside central city	...	1.8	75.7	17.3
Nonmetropolitan areas	...	3.8	63.7	11.1
Nonfarm	...	3.9	63.8	11.4
Farm	...	3.2	63.1	8.3

SOURCE: U.S. Bureau of the Census, "Educational Attainment in the United States: March 1979 and 1978." *Current Population Reports,* Series P-20, No. 356 (August 1980).
* Persons of Spanish origin may be of any race.
... Not available.

The educational attainment of blacks and especially that of Hispanic Americans is substantially lower than that of the white population, with the differential being most pronounced at the extreme levels. At the lowest level the proportion with less than five years of elementary schooling was more than three times as great among blacks as whites, and among persons of Spanish origin this proportion was more than six times as great as among whites. At the other extreme, the proportion of whites who were college graduates was more than twice that of blacks and nearly three times that of Hispanics.

Among residence groups, the highest educational level was found in the metropolitan areas, most notably among suburban dwellers, whereas the lowest educational attainment characterized the farm population in the nonmetropolitan parts of the country.

These data on educational attainment clearly indicate that our system of free public education, at the elementary level first and later at the high school level, continues to be a major strength of the United States. Coupled with this has been the emergence and expansion of the land grant college system, which has provided low-cost higher education to qualified youth. The aim of these institutions has been twofold: (1) to provide an opportunity for education to young people who otherwise—because of economic status, ethnic background, or social class—might have been forced to live out their lives in obscure mediocrity; and (2) to provide the society with the more highly trained workers necessary for continued rapid scientific and technological progress. That these institutions have been successful in increasing school enrollment and raising the overall level of educational attainment in the United States has been amply demonstrated in the preceding discussion. However, while there is good reason to be proud of past accomplishments, the persistence of several marked differentials emphasizes that there is still ample room for improvement. Although individual variations make it unlikely that the day will ever come when all persons graduate from college, it does seem realistic to aim for such goals as the elimination of differentials (such as those associated with sex and race) that result from various kinds of discriminatory treatment rather than from group differences in ability or incentive.

Income Characteristics

Income is an extremely sensitive index of the economic well-being of a population. To the extent that income levels are rising or declining, we can assume that the overall standard of living of a population is also rising or declining. Moreover, income differences among members of a population reflect many other basic differences—in educational attainment, technical skills, physical and mental abilities, discriminatory wage scales, and so forth.

Table 12-8

Distribution of Families by Level of Income:
United States, 1960, 1970, and 1980

Income levels	Percent distribution of families		
	1960	1970	1980
All levels	100.0	100.0	100.0
Under $2,500	17.5	6.6	2.1
$ 2,500–$ 4,999	24.5	12.5	4.1
$ 5,000–$ 7,499	28.4	15.2	6.2
$ 7,500–$ 9,999	15.2	16.6	6.5
$10,000–$12,499	7.5	15.8	7.3
$12,500–$14,999	3.1	11.0	6.9
$15,000–$19,999	2.1	13.1	14.0
$20,000–$24,999	0.8	4.6	13.7
$25,000 and over	0.9	4.6	39.3
Median income:			
Current dollars	$ 5,620	$ 9,867	$21,023
Constant (1980) dollars	15,637	20,939	21,023

SOURCE: U.S. Bureau of the Census, "Money Income and Poverty Status of Families and Persons in the United States: 1980," *Current Population Reports,* Series P-60, No. 127 (August 1981).

Income differentials are also major determinants of still other differences relating to such things as the quantity and quality of food consumed, place of residence and condition of housing, family size and living arrangements, use of leisure time, and levels of morbidity and mortality. Because of this pervasive influence, a knowledge of the income characteristics of a population—and especially of existing differentials in the ability to purchase needed goods and services—is particularly essential for an adequate understanding of a society and its problems.

The income status of the American population has both positive and negative aspects. On the positive side, recent years have seen a marked increase in income levels, and more families are earning more money today than ever before. To illustrate, between 1960 and 1980 the median income of families in the United States increased from $5,620 to $21,023, or by 274 percent (see Table 12-8). In noting this increase in dollar income, however, it is necessary to keep in mind that the cost of living has also risen substantially over the years, especially during the years of double-digit inflation in the 1970s; thus, only part of the dollar increase represents a gain in *real income,* or in the purchasing power of the dollar. When price changes are taken into consideration, the magnitude of the increase in family income levels becomes noticeably less. In terms of constant (1980) dollars, for

Figure 12-6
Percent of the Population Living in Families with Income below the Poverty Level: United States, 1960–80

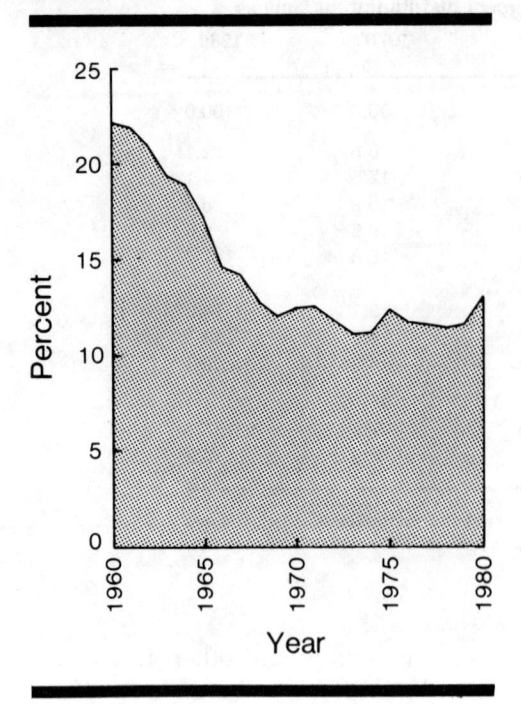

SOURCE: Based on data in U.S. Bureau of the Census, "Money Income and Poverty Status of Families and Persons in the United States: 1980." *Current Population Reports,* Series P-60, No. 127 (August 1981).

example, the increase in the median income of American families between 1960 and 1980 would have been from $15,637 to $21,023—an increase of only 34 percent. Further, taking inflation into account shows that the bulk of the increase in real income (98 percent) occurred during the 1960s. That is, there was virtually no change in real family income during the 1970s. Nevertheless, it is still worth stressing that the 1980 income level represents a substantial increase in the buying power of the American population over what it was in 1960.

Of greater significance, perhaps, is the fact that the increase in median income since 1960 has been accompanied by a major shift upward of families along the entire income scale. On the other hand, the proportion of families with annual incomes of less than $10,000 declined from slightly more than four-fifths in 1960 (85.6 percent) to well below one-fifth (18.9 percent) in 1980. Families with incomes in excess of $25,000 a year, on the other hand, increased from less than 1 percent to 39 percent between 1960 and 1980. Clearly, the years since 1960 have witnessed a marked improvement in the income status of the population.

An especially good index of the relative income status of the American population at any point in time is the *poverty rate,* or the percentage of the population living in families where the annual income is less than the officially defined poverty level. Families are classified as being above or below the poverty level on the basis of an index developed by the Social Security Administration. This poverty index is determined solely by the amount of cash income needed to meet the basic food consumption needs of families of varying size and composition, and it is updated each year to reflect changes in the cost of food. In 1959, the earliest year for which such data are available, an estimated 22 percent of the American people were living in families whose income was below the poverty level. During the 1960s, however, as the nation launched a massive "war on poverty," this rate declined dramatically (see Figure 12-6). The percentage of the population living in poverty families fell below 15 percent in 1965, and by 1973 it had fallen to an all-time low of 11 percent. During the remainder of the 1970s, reflecting both a slowdown in national economic growth and cutbacks in many of the federal poverty relief programs set up in the 1960s, this proportion remained fairly stable between 11 and 12 percent; but after 1979 both the number and proportion of people living in poverty families increased sharply. This latest increase, which reflects the worsening recession of that time, raised the 1980 poverty rate up to 13 percent and pushed the number of Americans living in poverty families to over 29 million; in 1982 nearly 34 million people (15 percent of the population) were living below the poverty level.

Income Differentials

The discussion so far has provided only a very general picture of the income characteristics of the American people, and it has not considered the substantial differences in income levels among various subgroups in the population (see Table 12-9). One of the most important income differentials in the United States has long been associated with race. In 1980 the median annual income of white families in this country ($21,904) was 73 percent greater than the corresponding median for black families ($12,674), and it exceeded that of Hispanic families ($14,717) by 49 percent. This ethnic group income differential—which reflects past as well as some present discrimination in such things as educational opportunity, employment status, and wage scales—is underscored by the differential poverty rate. In 1980, only

Table 12-9
Selected Family Income Characteristics of Specified Subgroups in the Population: United States, 1980

Population subgroups	Median income	Percent with income below poverty cutoff
All families	$21,023	10.3%
White	21,904	8.0
Black	12,674	28.9
Spanish origin	14,717	23.2
Nonfarm	21,151	10.2
Farm	15,755	14.0
Married-couple families	23,141	6.2
Wife in paid labor force	26,879	...
Wife not in paid labor force	18,972	...
Male householder,* no wife present	17,519	11.0
Female householder,* no husband present	10,408	32.7
Males, age 15 and over	12,530	17.4
Females, age 15 and over	4,920	27.4

SOURCE: U.S. Bureau of the Census, "Money Income and Poverty Status of Families and Persons in the United States: 1980," *Current Population Reports,* Series P-60, No. 127 (August 1981).
* See note to Table 12-3.
... Not available.

8 percent of white families had an income below the official poverty cutoff level, as compared with poverty rates of 23 and 29 percent respectively for Spanish-origin and black families.

The income characteristics of families also varied noticeably between the two basic residence areas. Reflecting the higher salaries generally characteristic of nonagricultural occupations, the 1980 median income of nonfarm families was 34 percent greater than that of farm families. The relatively disadvantaged position of the nation's farm population is further revealed by comparing the proportion of families receiving incomes that were less than the poverty level: 10 percent for nonfarm families as opposed to 14 percent for farm families.

Two particularly noteworthy income differentials in the United States today reflect two recent trends that have characterized the American family. First, a major trend over the past several years has been an increase in *two-earner families* as a larger number and proportion of married women have chosen to work outside the home. As would be expected, two-earner families have a substantially higher median income ($26,879) than do families in which the wife is not a member of the paid labor force ($18,972). This trend toward an increase in female labor force participation is discussed more fully in the following section.

The second trend of recent years has been an increase in the number of *one-parent families,* especially in the number of female-headed families: as of 1980 one-parent families with a female head outnumbered those with a male head by a ratio of five to one. The significance of this trend for our society derives from the existence of a pronounced sex differential in income. To illustrate, the 1980 median income of adult males was more than 2½ times greater than that of females. Similarly, the median income of one-parent families with a male head was 68 percent higher than that of female-headed families, and the poverty rate for the latter (33 percent) was three times that of male-headed families (11 percent). Among the reasons for this sex differential are (1) more females than males hold part-time jobs; (2) more females have seasonal or temporary employment; (3) it is not uncommon for women to receive lower wages for performing the same tasks done by men at higher rates of pay; and (4) there are more older widows than widowers who do not work and whose only income is a small pension or Social Security check each month.

Age, in fact, is a very important variable as far as income is concerned (see Table 12-10). The pattern of the relationship between age and income approximates a normal curve: incomes start out low at the youngest ages, increase very rapidly up to a maximum level at ages forty-five to fifty-four, and then decline with advancing age. This age-and-income relationship is relatively simple to explain. On the one hand, the middle age groups where incomes are highest represent the most productive years of a person's life—

Table 12-10

Median Income of Households by Age and Education of Householder: United States, 1980

Age of householder*	Median income	Education of householder*	Median income
15–24	$12,710	Elementary: less than 8 years	$ 7,900
25–34	19,336	Elementary: 8 years	10,121
35–44	23,626	High school: 1–3 years	12,756
45–54	25,120	High school: 4 years	18,777
55–64	19,546	College: 1–3 years	20,736
65 and over	8,780	College: 4 years or more	28,047

SOURCE: U.S. Bureau of the Census, "Money Income and Poverty Status of Families and Persons in the United States: 1980," *Current Population Reports,* Series P-60, No. 127 (August 1981).
* See note to Table 12-3.

years that are usually characterized by a steady advancement in one's chosen vocation. At the younger ages, especially under twenty years, incomes are low partly because there is a great deal of part-time and seasonal employment at these ages, and partly because those persons who do hold full-time jobs have only recently entered the labor force and have not yet worked their way up the income scale. At the other extreme, incomes are lower at ages sixty-five and over because many persons at these ages have retired from active participation in the labor force and must subsist on small incomes from Social Security or some other pension program.

One other notable income differential merits consideration. Earlier in this chapter we noted the advantages of higher education from the point of view of the society as a whole (e.g., the higher the educational level of a population, the better equipped it is to perform the increasingly complex tasks of an expanding industrial society). The advantages of higher education are not limited to the society, however, but also accrue to the individual. There is in fact a pronounced direct association between individual incomes and level of educational attainment in the United States. The magnitude of this association is strikingly revealed in Table 12-10. The median annual income in 1980 of persons who had completed at least four years of college was $28,047. This was roughly 50 percent higher than the median income of persons whose education had stopped after graduating from high school ($18,777). It was more than twice as high as that of persons who attended but did not graduate from high school ($12,756), and it was nearly four times as high as the median income of the so-called functional illiterates, or persons who completed less than five years of elementary school ($7,900). Such impressive income differentials should cause young Americans to think seriously before they drop out of high school to "make some money." Although not all persons are prepared to undertake college study, most people are capable of finishing high school; and the available data strongly suggest that, in terms of subsequent financial returns, the time spent in acquiring a high school diploma is definitely time well spent.

We must stress an important point in concluding this section: although we are the richest country in the world, and although our incomes have been increasing, we have by no means eliminated poverty from our society. On the contrary, several marked differentials in income status still prevail. Furthermore, these income differentials are closely related to other differences in the lives of particular groups (such as differences in both the quantity and nutritional quality of food consumed, conditions of housing, health status, and ability to purchase medical care and other needed services); and they clearly emphasize that there are still a number of battles to be won in the war on poverty if all citizens are to benefit equally from living in our increasingly affluent society.

Labor Force Characteristics

Labor force analysis interests a great many persons for a variety of reasons. Sociologists, for example, may look at the trend with regard to women in the labor force and investigate topics such as the changing role of women in society and the effects of the working wife on fertility and family size, child-rearing attitudes and practices, juvenile delinquency, and general lifestyle of the family. Government personnel and agencies seeking to alleviate unemployment problems need to know something about the number and distribution of unemployed persons as well as the occupational skills they possess. The number of available workers and their occupational skills are important factors to be considered by businessmen who may be contemplating the expansion or relocation of industries; by political scientists who are concerned with the balance of power in the world today; and by labor economists who may be interested in a wide variety of topics such as the relationship between residential and occupational mobility, the changing importance of particular occupations in the society, variations in the rate of retirement from one occupational group to another, and so forth.

On a more general level, the size and distribution of the labor force and the characteristics of its members can reveal a great deal of information about a given population—how it has organized itself to earn its livelihood, the social and economic well-being of its members, and its potential for industrial expansion. Moreover, changes over time in the size and composition of the labor force also reflect changes in the level of economic well-being and reveal the emergence of new patterns of economic and social organization.

Since 1967 the labor force in the United States has been defined as all persons age sixteen years and over who are currently working at a specific job, either full- or part-time *(employed)*, or who—although without a job at the moment—want to work and are actively looking for some form of regular employment *(unemployed)*. The labor force is composed of many diverse types. It includes all persons who receive a monetary return for their labors, whether they are fixed-salary employees, hourly-wage workers, or self-employed professional people such as doctors, lawyers, and shopkeepers. In addition, it includes unpaid family workers who perform gainful work for at least fifteen hours a week but who receive no money income (such as the son who helps out on the family farm or the woman who helps her husband tend the grocery store). Finally, members of the armed forces are included as part of the labor force, although as a group they are often excluded when concern is limited to an analysis of the *civilian labor force*. Not included in the labor force are (1) dependent children, (2) persons doing unpaid family work for less than fifteen hours a week, (3) women who have no job other than keeping house, (4) students who are not working, (5) inmates of institutions, such as jails or hospitals, and (6) persons who are retired or who are unable to work because of ill health or for some other reason (e.g., resident aliens who do not have a work permit).

A major trend in the United States over the past several decades has been a substantial increase in the size of the labor force (see Table 12-11). As compared with 53 million workers in 1940, the 1960 labor force of the nation numbered nearly 70 million, and by 1980 there were roughly twice as many people in the labor force (106 million) as there had been in 1940. As might be expected, most of this increase is due to the overall growth of the population. To illustrate, between 1940 and 1980 the total adult population of the United States increased from slightly more than 101 million to nearly 166 million, or by approximately 63 percent.

Although the increase in the size of the labor force has been due largely to the growth of the population as a whole, this should not obscure the fact that there has also been some increase in the *labor force participation rate* (i.e., the percentage of the adult population that is in the labor force). In 1940 the labor force participation rate in the United States was 52 percent. It has increased slowly but steadily since that time, and by 1980 nearly two-thirds of the adult population (64 percent) was in the labor force. This in-

Table 12-11

Labor Force Status of the Adult Population:
United States, 1940, 1960, and 1980

Labor force status	(Population in thousands)		
	1940	1960	1980
Total adult population*	101,458	126,277	165,693
In the labor force	53,011	69,877	105,505
(percent)	52.2	55.3	63.6
Armed forces	306	1,733	2,093
Civilian labor force	52,705	68,144	103,412
Employed	45,070	64,639	96,566
Unemployed	7,634	3,505	6,846
(percent)	14.5	5.1	6.6
Not in the labor force	48,447	56,399	60,188

SOURCES: U.S. Bureau of the Census, *U.S. Census of Population: 1960,* Final Report PC(1)-1C, *General Social and Economic Characteristics: United States Summary* (Washington, D.C., 1962). Data for April 1980 are from Bureau of Labor Statistics, *Employment and Earnings,* 27:5 (May 1980).

* Data for 1940 and 1960 are for all persons age 14 and over, while data for 1980 are for the noninstitutional population age 16 and over; hence, the latter are not completely comparable to the former. However, since both the number of 14- and 15-year-olds and the institutional population included in 1940 and 1960 represent such a small fraction of the totals, these discrepancies are unlikely to affect the basic trends revealed in the table.

Figure 12-7
Percent of Adult Population in the Labor Force, by Sex: United States, 1940, 1960, and 1980.

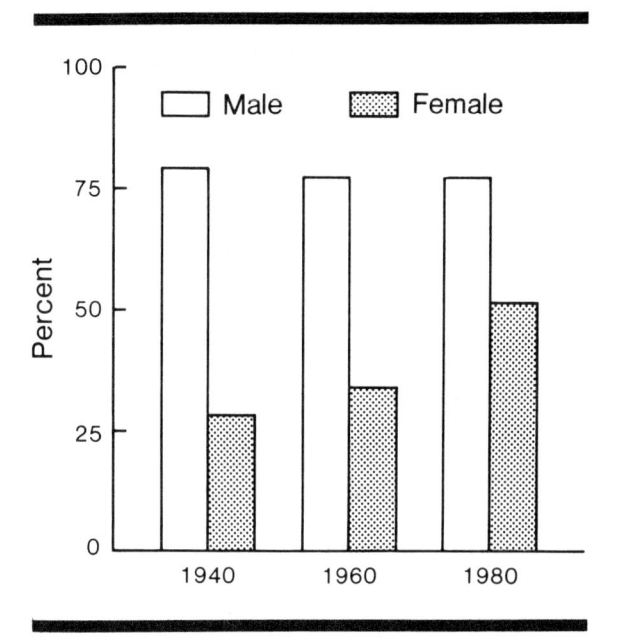

SOURCE: Based on data from sources of Table 12-11.

crease in the overall rate of labor force participation is due entirely to an expansion of employment opportunities for women and a corresponding increase in female employment (see Figure 12-7). The labor force participation rate for males has remained fairly stable over the years, but the proportion of females in the labor force has risen steadily: it increased from roughly one-fourth in 1940 to more than one-third in 1960, and by 1980 just over half (51 percent) of the women in America were in the labor force.

The vast majority of the workers in the United States are in the civilian labor force. However, although they make up only a small fraction of the total labor force, the number and proportion of persons in the armed forces have increased substantially over the years—from 306,000 (0.5 percent) in 1940 to 2.1 million (2 percent) in 1980. This growing importance of the military in our economy is, of course, a reflection of the persistence of the East–West cold war as well as the various brush-fire hot wars (e.g., in South Korea and Vietnam) in which the United States has been involved since the 1940s.

With respect to the *unemployment rate* (the percent of the civilian labor force that is unemployed), it is apparent that there has been a substantial decline since 1940 when the country was just emerging from a severe economic depression. It must be stressed, however, that this fairly volatile measure varies, often markedly, from month to month and year to year; thus, comparing three rates so widely separated in time as those in Table 12-11 really does not reveal much about the changing viability of the American economy.

Finally, it may be noted that a substantial proportion of the adult population is classified as "not in the labor force." A breakdown of this group in 1980 would show that it consisted primarily of housewives (52 percent) and persons who were either going to school (15 percent) or who were disabled (5 percent). The remainder consisted of persons who were not in the labor force for "other" reasons (e.g., persons who did not want to work at that time, as well as *discouraged workers,* or those who had been unable to find work for so long that they had stopped looking). Although the number of persons in this category has increased in recent years, the proportion of the adult population that they represent has undergone a slight decline—from 48 percent in 1940 to 44 percent in 1960, to only 36 percent in 1980. This declining proportion is of course complementary to the increase in the rate of labor force participation, and like that increase it reflects the greater tendency for women to join the labor force today than a generation ago.

Occupational Composition

One of the most notable developments in recent years has been a pronounced change in the occupational structure of the American labor force (see Table 12-12). Two changes in particular stand out. First, there has been a substantial reduction in the number and proportion of farm workers in the nation. Second, among nonfarm workers there has been a marked increase in the importance of white-collar occupations and a corresponding decline in the significance of blue-collar occupations. Historically, blue-collar workers have always outnumbered white-collar workers, and have done so to a substantial degree. In 1940, for example, blue-collar workers outnumbered white-collar workers by a ratio of three to two. This gap has gradually narrowed over the years, however, and during the most recent period the white-collar group has emerged as the dominant segment of the nonfarm labor force.

These two trends—the decline in the size of the farm labor force, and the shift away from the lesser-skilled nonfarm occupations—have been in evidence for several generations, and they reflect the increasing mechanization, bureaucratization, and spread of automation in a society that is daily becoming more complex. In particular, they reflect a fundamental reorganization of our mode of gaining a livelihood, necessitated by the rapid technological progress of the twentieth century. Moreover, since this process of technological change is a continuous one in which new occupations are

Table 12-12

Occupational Distribution of Employed Persons:
United States, 1940, 1960, and 1980

Occupational class	1940	1960	1980*
Total employed	100.0	100.0	100.0
Farm occupations	18.6	6.4	2.6
Nonfarm occupations	81.4	93.6	97.4
Total nonfarm workers	100.0	100.0	100.0
White-collar workers	*40.4*	*46.3*	*53.7*
Professional and technical	9.8	12.6	16.8
Managers, officials, proprietors	10.0	9.4	11.2
Clerical workers	12.1	16.2	19.3
Sales workers	8.5	8.1	6.4
Blue-collar workers	*59.6*	*53.7*	*46.3*
Craft and kindred workers	14.2	15.2	13.4
Operatives	22.2	20.7	14.6
Service workers	14.6	12.5	13.8
Nonfarm laborers	8.6	5.4	4.6

SOURCE: U.S. Bureau of the Census, *U.S. Census of Population: 1960,* Final Report PC(1)-1C, *General Social and Economic Characteristics: United States Summary* (Washington, D.C., 1962). Data for 1980 (April) are from Bureau of Labor Statistics, *Employment and Earnings,* 27:5 (May 1980).

* Data for 1940 and 1960 are for all persons age 14 and over, while data for 1980 are for the noninstitutional population age 16 and over; hence, the latter are not completely comparable to the former. However, since both the number of 14- and 15-year-olds and the institutional population included in 1940 and 1960 represent such a small fraction of the totals, these discrepancies are unlikely to affect the basic trends revealed in the table.

constantly being created while others become obsolete, it is likely that these trends will continue in the years ahead.

Labor Force Differentials

The various subgroups in the population exhibit different labor force characteristics, and these differences often reflect the existence of major social problems. For example, rates of labor force participation and unemployment vary systematically with age: the former is distributed normally whereas the latter approximates a J-shaped curve, being especially high at the younger ages (see Table 12-13). The age differences in labor force participation are easily understandable and do not really represent a problem. There are some notable variations by sex and color, but the general pattern is the same: labor force participation rates are relatively low at the younger ages because so many are still attending school; they increase substantially in the early

Table 12-13
Labor Force Participation and Employment Status of the Population 16 Years Old and Over, by Age, Sex, and Color: United States, April 1980

Age	White Male	White Female	Black and other Male	Black and other Female
Percent in Labor Force				
Total, 16 and over	78.2%	51.0%	70.6%	52.3%
16–17	49.6	41.6	23.9	20.0
18–19	71.8	60.6	54.7	39.8
20–24	86.3	69.0	80.7	58.3
25–34	95.9	65.9	90.3	68.7
35–44	96.3	65.3	88.6	68.5
45–54	92.1	59.2	84.8	61.1
55–64	73.9	41.9	61.4	44.7
65 and over	19.3	8.1	18.3	9.9
Percent of Labor Force Unemployed				
Total, 16 and over	6.0	5.8	12.3	12.1
16–17	16.8	16.1	32.5	35.5
18–19	12.2	11.2	25.1	29.0
20–24	10.8	7.6	20.0	21.0
25–34	6.2	5.7	13.1	11.6
35–44	3.6	4.2	7.6	8.0
45–54	3.3	3.8	5.7	6.5
55–64	3.3	3.1	7.5	5.3
65 and over	2.6	3.1	11.2	2.3

SOURCE: Bureau of Labor Statistics, *Employment and Earnings,* 27:5 (May 1980).

twenties as more and more people complete their education and enter the work force; and they remain at generally high levels until about age fifty, at which time they start to decline as people begin to reach retirement age.

In contrast to labor force participation, the pattern of unemployment does indicate some specific problem areas. Although the rate of unemployment can vary markedly over time, as the economy fluctuates between periods of inflation and recession, the general pattern of differentials does not change, and a major feature of this pattern is the very high unemployment rate for teenagers, especially black teenagers. In the spring of 1980, roughly 16 percent of all whites age sixteen to seventeen years and a third of all blacks at these ages were unemployed; at ages eighteen to nineteen the corresponding percentages were 11–12 percent for whites and 25–29 percent for blacks. These high youth unemployment rates largely reflect the fact that these are ages when people start to leave school and enter the labor force for the first time, and many of these sixteen- to nineteen-year-olds are probably still looking for their first full-time job.

Men and women differ notably with regard to labor force participation, but they have fairly similar unemployment rates. On the other hand, whites and blacks have fairly similar rates of labor force participation but markedly different levels of unemployment. The sex differential does not represent a serious problem and is just what one would expect to find. The reason for this is twofold. First, the role of women in our society has long been culturally defined as one of dependence, and for the most part women have not been required to earn their own living. Second, and perhaps more important, in spite of the growth of the women's movement and the general increase in female employment, the fact remains that the biological role of the female with regard to bearing children, and her related housekeeping responsibilities, have been and will probably continue to be major factors restricting the employment activities of many women and reinforcing the traditional cultural attitude that "a woman's place is in the home."

The white–black unemployment differential, however, is cause for concern. The fact that black unemployment was substantially higher than that of whites in virtually every age–sex group provides a real basis for the often heard remark that blacks are "the last to be hired and the first to be fired." This differential is in part due to racial prejudice and continued discrimination in hiring practices (in spite of the growth of affirmative action programs), but it is also a reflection of the more objective characteristics of black people such as their lower level of educational attainment and their relative lack of occupational skills. Of course, these characteristics are themselves a result of past discrimination. For example, a low level of educational attainment is partly due to a lack of adequate educational opportunities and facilities, and this lack of a good education means that many occupational skills are more difficult to acquire.

As with overall labor force participation and employment status, the various subgroups in the population differ notably with regard to their occupational composition. The major differences in the United States today relate to sex and color and are illustrated by the percentages shown in Table 12-14. A major differential relates to the proportion of employed persons working at white-collar or blue-collar occupations. More than six out of every ten working women were employed in white-collar occupations in 1980, compared with only four out of ten males. The difference was also marked between the color groups; slightly more than half of the employed whites were working at white-collar jobs in 1980, compared with just under 40 percent for the black population. The preponderance of white-collar workers among employed females is due mainly to the large numbers of women employed in clerical occupations; the smaller proportion of blacks

Table 12-14
Occupational Distribution of Employed Persons Age 16 and Over, by Sex and Color: United States, April 1980

Occupation	Both sexes White	Both sexes Black	All races Male	All races Female
Total employed	100.0	100.0	100.0	100.0
White-collar workers	54.0	39.1	42.3	65.7
Professional and technical	16.8	12.8	15.8	17.1
Managers, officials, proprietors	11.7	4.8	14.0	6.8
Sales workers	6.7	2.8	6.1	6.4
Clerical workers	18.8	18.6	6.4	35.4
Blue-collar workers	43.3	59.1	54.1	33.3
Craftsmen	13.4	9.7	21.4	1.8
Operatives	13.5	19.1	16.9	10.6
Service workers	12.2	23.6	9.0	19.6
Nonfarm laborers	4.2	6.7	6.8	1.3
Farmers and farm laborers	2.7	1.8	3.8	1.0

SOURCE: Bureau of Labor Statistics, *Employment and Earnings,* 27:5 (May 1980).

in the white-collar category reflects the heavy concentration of black workers in the lesser skilled blue-collar occupations—particularly as operatives and service workers.

In concluding this section it is worth noting that the occupation differences just described are closely related to education and income differences: a person's income is in large part determined by the nature of his or her occupation; and the occupation is influenced a great deal by the amount of education a person has. The implication of this interrelationship is that as long as all persons in our society do not have access to the same educational opportunities, the United States will continue to be faced with a social, cultural, and economic imbalance among large segments of the population.

INTERNATIONAL DIFFERENCES IN POPULATION COMPOSITION

Although our primary focus in this chapter has been on trends and differentials with respect to various characteristics of the American population, we should at least make reference to some of the profound compositional differences that exist among the nations of the world. Recognizing that there is a great deal of internal variation within countries, just as there is within our own United States, the most significant differences are those that exist between the more developed countries of the Western world and the less developed countries of Asia, Africa, and Latin America (see Table 12-15). The more developed nations generally resemble the United States in that they have an aging population, a nuclear family structure, a high level of school enrollment and educational attainment, an industrial economy with a fairly elaborate division of labor, and a relatively high level of personal income. The less developed countries, on the other hand, tend to be characterized by a much younger age composition, an extended family structure, low levels of school enrollment and educational attainment, an agricultural economy with a less developed division of labor, and relatively low income levels.

While such broad generalizations have some limited validity, it must be stressed that each individual country, whether developed or developing, will have its own particular compositional features and problems, and an adequate understanding of the sociodemographic situation in any country will require a thorough knowledge of its unique composition. The brief examination of the composition of the U.S. population presented here will, it is hoped, enhance the reader's appreciation of the importance of this fundamental demographic variable.

Table 12-15
Selected Characteristics of More Developed and Less Developed Countries, Late 1970s

Characteristic	More developed countries	Less developed countries
Percent under age 15	23%	41%
Percent age 65 and over	11%	3%
Primary enrollment ratio*	103	78
Percent literate	99%	52%
Percent of GNP originating in agriculture	4%	19%
Percent of labor force in agriculture	9%	49%
Per capita GNP (U.S. dollars)	$8,657	$728

SOURCE: International Bank for Reconstruction and Development, *World Tables, 1980* (Baltimore: Johns Hopkins University Press, 1980).
* Number in primary school per 100 age 6–11 years. Ratio exceeds 100 in more developed countries where primary enrollment is virtually universal and where the number of enrollees exceeds the number at ages 6–11 because some of the former are under age 5 or over age 11.

SUMMARY

It is through the study of its specific characteristics that one comes to know and understand the social and economic life of a population. Among the many compositional features of any human population, two categories are most relevant for population analysis: demographic characteristics such as age, sex, color, and marital status; and socioeconomic characteristics such as education, income, and labor force status. In this chapter we have presented selected statistics for the United States pertaining to both categories, and we have discussed briefly some of the problems associated with the current and changing composition of our population.

In many respects, age structure is the most important of the several compositional variables, because so many of the other social and economic characteristics of a society, as well as the levels of the basic demographic processes will vary with its age composition. It is also important because the overall age structure of its population is a major determinant of the various needs and problems confronting any society. Many of the social and economic dislocations recently experienced in the United States, for example, as well as those that can be projected for the foreseeable future, are clearly related to marked annual fluctuations in the number and proportion of persons in particular age groups.

Among the major demographic trends in evidence in the United States in the 1980s are an aging trend, marked by an increase in the number and proportion of elderly people; a slight fragmentation of the American family, indicated by such things as a decline in the marriage rate, an increase in divorce, and a tendency for more and more people to maintain separate or nontraditional households; and a relative increase in the predominance of Asians and especially persons of Spanish origin among ethnic minorities. While none of these trends is necessarily problematic in and of itself, they are all indicative of basic social and cultural changes that are taking place in our society today and that will have an impact on the nature of the society in which we will live tomorrow.

The United States is also experiencing some noteworthy changes with respect to various socioeconomic characteristics of the population. Some of these changes relate to one or another of the major demographic trends (e.g., fluctuations in the pattern of school enrollment are largely a function of the changing age structure, whereas the increase in female labor force participation may be both a cause and an effect of the changes in marital status and household living arrangements). Others are indicative of some basic changes that are taking place in our general life-style and standard of living (e.g., the increasing level of education, the increase in and more equitable distribution of income, and, again, the increase in the number and proportion of working women). Still others reflect developments in the economic organization of a society that is moving rapidly into a post-industrial era (e.g., the progressive decline in the importance of blue-collar occupations and the corresponding increase in the demand for professional and technical workers).

An important point to keep in mind with respect to these socioeconomic trends, particularly those that reflect an improvement in our overall level of living, is that they have not characterized all segments of the population to the same extent. Pronounced socioeconomic differentials still characterize a number of subgroups in our society, most notably the various ethnic minorities, and the task of narrowing such group differences in socioeconomic well-being continues to represent a major challenge for the American people.

REFERENCES AND SUGGESTED READING

Bouvier, Leon F. "America's Baby Boom Generation: The Fateful Bulge." *Population Bulletin*, 35 (April 1980).

Bouvier, Leon F., and Cary B. Davis. *The Future Racial Composition of the United States*. Washington, D.C.: Population Reference Bureau, 1982.

Bouvier, Leon F., et al. "The Elderly in America." *Population Bulletin*, 30 (3) (1975).

Butz, William P., et al. *Demographic Challenges in America's Future*. Santa Monica, CA: Rand Corporation, 1982.

Glick, Paul C., and Arthur J. Norton. "Marrying, Divorcing, and Living Together in the U.S. Today." *Population Bulletin*, 32 (October 1977).

Jones, Landon. *Great Expectations: America and the Baby Boom*. New York: Coward, McCann & Geoghegan, 1980.

Population Reference Bureau. "U.S. Population: Where We Are, Where We're Going." *Population Bulletin*, 37 (June 1982).

Reid, John. "Black America in the 1980s." *Population Bulletin*, 37 (December 1982).

Soldo, Beth J. "America's Elderly in the 1980's." *Population Bulletin*, 35 (November 1980).

U.S. Bureau of the Census. "Persons of Spanish Origin in the United States: March 1980 (Advance Report)." *Current Population Reports*, Series P-20, No. 361 (May 1981).

U.S. Bureau of the Census. "Population Profile of the United States: 1980." *Current Population Reports*, Series, P-20, No. 363 (June 1981). This periodic publication of the Bureau of the Census provides a useful description of major trends and changes with respect to various characteristics of the American population.

Waite, Linda J. "U.S. Women at Work." *Population Bulletin,* 36 (May 1981).
Weeks, John R. *Population: An Introduction to Concepts and Issues.* Belmont, CA: Wadsworth, 1981, Chapters 8, 9, and 12–14.
Weller, Robert H., and Leon F. Bouvier. *Population: Demography and Policy.* New York: St. Martin's, 1981, Chapters 9 and 10.

POSTSCRIPT

The number of people living on our planet is rapidly approaching 5 billion, and it will very likely exceed 6 billion by the time we enter the twenty-first century. Many of the social, economic, and political problems that exist throughout the world today are intimately related to the prevailing population situation, and the future course of population will have an important impact on the lives of all of us. We in the United States may not have to contend with the severe poverty, chronic food shortages, and social unrest found throughout much of the Third World today, but the trends and changes now taking place in our population will exert a major influence on the overall nature and quality of the life that we lead and that we pass on to our children and grandchildren.

As we pointed out in the Introduction, the primary purpose of this book has been (1) to describe some of the more important *population trends*, past and present, in the world in general and in the United States in particular, (2) to explain the underlying *determinants*, or causes, of the various trends, and (3) to indicate briefly their *consequences* in terms of the kinds of problems that have been caused by or are otherwise closely associated with these major demographic developments. We hope that this broad overview will provide the reader with a basic demographic perspective that will permit him or her to understand better and adjust more easily to our evolving society, but we also wish to emphasize two important caveats.

First, our discussion obviously does not represent an exhaustive coverage of this very important subject. The demographic variable has so many dimensions and so many different problems are associated with each dimension that is is not possible to do justice to the topic in the pages of a single volume. Although none of the more serious population problems has been neglected in this book, space limitations have made it difficult to discuss any one of them in great detail. For example, we talked at length about the Third World problem of population growth and economic development, but we barely mentioned such important contributing factors as previous colonial status or the existence and nature of current international trade barriers. Similarly, we noted the existence of marked differences in family income as representing a major problem in the United States today, but we did not investigate the chronic causes of low income or the many other problems that confront those who live in severe poverty in the midst of an otherwise affluent society. Some problems have been barely mentioned in passing: for example, the political aspects of the international food supply situation, guest worker programs and the international migration of labor in a number of European and Middle East countries, the higher rates of all forms of deviant social behavior in urban slum areas. Still other problems have not been discussed at all: internal migration trends and population redistribution policies in Europe today, and the problem of *underpopulation,* or not having enough people to permit the optimal development of available resources. We have tried to compensate for these limitations, however, by providing those readers who wish to pursue particular topics in greater depth with a list of suggested readings at the end of each chapter.

Second, and perhaps most important, we must emphasize the dynamic nature of the demographic variable. Population, like many other aspects of human society, is in a constant state of change; and as a nation's population changes, the nature and magnitude of that nation's population problems change. The issue of freedom of choice with respect to fertility and family size, for example, was once confined to official opposition to the use of birth control, but today it includes the evolution in a few countries of official population policies that come close to imposing compulsory birth control. Within the United States, the population problems a generation ago included such things as the rapid growth that resulted from the baby boom, a youth-dominated society, continued metropolitan expansion, the inequities of our national origins immigration laws, and the progressive decline of the South. In the 1980s, however, we are concerned with the potential impact of the baby bust, a rapidly aging society, the resurgence of growth in nonmetropolitan areas, the influx of refugees and illegal aliens, and the rapid expansion of the Sun Belt.

Looking to the future, we can anticipate a continuation of the aging trend in the United States, a trend that will become especially pronounced toward the end of the century as the larger cohorts of the earlier baby boom move into the older age groups. On a world level there are very encouraging signs that birth rates are finally starting to fall in many of the less developed areas, but any optimism here must be tempered by a knowledge that the marked mortality declines of the past two decades mean that the number of potential mothers will continue to increase very rapidly throughout the remainder of the century. Furthermore, even though population growth rates may slow down, expectations will continue to rise in the developing countries, putting an ever increasing strain on the carrying capacity of our small planet and intensifying the already serious problems of resource conservation and environmental pollution.

In conclusion let us emphasize that the purpose of our book has been to alert and educate, not to scare. We do not regard the future with dread or dismay, and we do not want to paint a doomsday picture of what lies ahead for the human race. However, we do believe that population trends will continue to pose major problems, for the world and for our society, and that forewarned is forearmed. We certainly make no claims that reading our book will make one an expert in matters of population. But we do hope that our readers will go away with a better understanding and appreciation of the intimate interrelationship between population change and social change, and that this enhanced awareness will make them a little better prepared to comprehend the society in which they live and a little better able to cope more efficiently with its problems.

NATURE AND SOURCES OF POPULATION DATA

APPENDIX **A**

The first step in the study of human population is to learn something about the kinds of data that form the basis for such study and where these data are commonly obtained. Given the definition of demography presented in Chapter 1, one can identify two basic kinds of demographic data: (1) statistics on the number of people in the population *(size)* classified into various categories of *composition* and *distribution* at any given point in time; (2) statistics on the ongoing occurrence of those basic events (birth, death, and change of residence) that lead to changes in population over time. Although there are many ways of obtaining them, these two fundamental kinds of statistics are derived primarily from two corresponding major sources of data: (1) a *census* (a head count of a population aggregate at one point in time), or (2) *vital statistics* (official government records on the number of vital events, such as births and deaths, taking place in a population over time). A number of other sources (e.g., population registers and a variety of public and privately sponsored sample surveys) provide the demographer with an abundance of information on particular populations and on the determinants and consequences of demographic behavior. This appendix will be devoted to a brief consideration of some of these major sources of population data.

POPULATION CENSUSES

A census may be defined simply as a head count of the population in a particular society, taken in order to ascertain its size, composition, and distribution at a certain time. Somewhat more elaborate is the definition used by the United Nations: "A census of population may be defined as the total process of collecting, compiling and publishing demographic, economic and social data pertaining, at a specified time or times, to all persons in a country or delimited territory" (United Nations, 1953, p. 3). Defined in this manner, a population census can be likened to an instantaneous photograph of the traits and characteristics of a particular population at a specified point in time. When a census is taken at regular intervals, it serves to provide a series of still pictures depicting the growth and development of the population over time.

A census is generally carried out by the government to collect basic information on the many characteristics of the population that can then be used to guide various policy decisions and planning activities. Although census-taking is still a relatively new development in many areas of the world, it is today generally recognized that the information provided by a census is essential for the orderly management of any society, and that census-taking constitutes one of the major bookkeeping tasks of a government.

History of Census-Taking

Governments have long been interested in the number and characteristics of the people who make up the societies over which they rule, and efforts to obtain such information by means of some kind of population census are of very ancient origin. Some fragmentary evidence exists to indicate that censuses were taken thousands of years before the Christian era in Babylonia, China, and Ancient Egypt, and the Bible contains numerous accounts of census-taking, from the post-exodus command given to Moses to "Take the sum of all the congregation of the children of Israel" (Numbers 1:1–3) to what is perhaps the best known, the story of the Nativity (Luke 2:1–7). One of the more significant biblical accounts of a census was the one taken by King David in 1071 B.C. David wanted to know how many subjects he ruled and so, at the urging of the devil and despite the warnings of Joab, he took a census of Israel: "And God was displeased with this thing; therefore he smote Israel" (I Chronicles 21:7). The displeasure expressed by God over this act of David's was to be cited in eighteenth-century England by those who opposed the establishment of a national census in that country.

Despite its relatively ancient origins the evolution of the modern census was a gradual one. The earlier censuses were limited both by their lack of regularity and their limited coverage. Most of them were very narrowly focused, generally being concerned with ascertaining the potential number of fighting men or with determining who was eligible to pay taxes and how much they should pay. Such reasons are hardly designed to encourage public cooperation, and it can be safely assumed that these early censuses lacked much in the way of accuracy.

Shortly after the dawning of the modern era in the seventeenth century, census-taking begins to come into its own as an important source of information to aid government administration. A census was taken in the Virginia colony as early as 1624–25, and the following 150 years saw numerous enumerations conducted throughout colonial America as well as in the Canadian provinces of Quebec and Nova Scotia. Censuses of various types and scope were also conducted during this period in numerous states and provinces throughout Europe and in parts of Asia, but it remained for the first United States census in 1790 to mark the birth of modern census-taking. Although Sweden is generally credited with taking the first modern national census in 1749, it was not until the Founding Fathers of the United States wrote the requirement of a decennial census into the Constitution that census-taking became established and recognized as a regular function of government.

The American Population Census

A census of population has been taken in the United States every ten years since 1790. The basic purposes for which the census was established in the Constitution (Article I, Section 2) were to determine the number of representatives each state should send to the Congress and to decide upon the apportionment of direct tax revenues. Although the census was initially conceived to be a simple head count of the population, James Madison amended the first census act to authorize the collection of information on age, sex, and occupation. Occupation was not included in 1790, but some information on age and sex was collected, thus establishing a precedent for subsequent enumerations.

Over the years as our society has become larger and more complex the need for additional data has grown. In response to this growing need, the scope and coverage of the census has been expanded, with the changing content reflecting the emergence of different national issues and problems. In the mid-nineteenth century, for example, as the population started to expand westward at a fairly rapid rate, a question on the state of birth of the native population was included in the census to enable officials to measure the volume and direction of internal migration streams. The growing concern generated by the upsurge of foreign immigration early in the twentieth century led to the inclusion of several questions on citizenship and national origins on the 1920 census questionnaire. Following the dislocations experienced during the Great Depression of the 1930s, additional questions on population mobility, employment status, and earnings were added to the 1940 census. The 1960 census saw the addition of questions pertaining to place of work and means of transportation to work, and the 1970 census included new questions on occupational activity and vocational training. The most recent census in 1980 asked new questions pertaining to ancestry, language proficiency, travel time to work, car pooling, and work and unemployment. A list of the population and housing items included in the 1980 census is presented in Table A-1.

A glance at Table A-1 shows that the 1980 census did not collect data on all the topics from all persons in the population. Ever since 1940, in fact, a large part of the American census has been conducted on a sample basis. In 1980, only six questions were asked of all persons while the bulk of the data collected were obtained from a 20 percent sample of households. Taking the bulk of the census on a sample basis has made it possible to increase the scope of the census without unduly increasing the costs or the time and effort required to conduct the census. Other innovations (e.g., the use of pre-coded questionnaires, taking the census largely by mail, the utilization of high-speed computers and other electronic equipment) have reduced the time required to collect and collate the information and greatly enhanced the capacity of the census to generate the basic data on which so many federal activities and programs are based.

Responsibility for conducting the decennial census rests with the U.S. Bureau of the Census, a division of the Department of Commerce and a permanent part of the federal bureaucracy since 1902. The most recent census was taken in the spring of 1980. On March 28 of that year the U.S. Postal Service delivered a census questionnaire to each household in the country: 80 percent of the households received the short form of the questionnaire containing the 100 percent items, whereas 20 percent received the longer form containing all the sample item questions. In most instances the questionnaires were left with instructions that they be filled out and mailed back on April 1, but in some sparsely settled areas where it was not feasible to prepare an advance address list, the questionnaires were picked up by an enumerator. The basic field work for the census was virtually completed by late summer of 1980, at which time the massive task of collating and tabulating the data on 226 million Americans living in 88 million households was begun. Although the simple head count data on the population of the fifty states needed for reapportionment was completed and transmitted to the President, as required by law, by January 1, 1981, several years were required to make all the tabulations and prepare the data for release in its various forms.

Published Reports

The results of the 1980 population census are published in two basic volumes. Volume I, *Characteristics of the Population*, consists of separate reports for each of the fifty states, the District of Columbia, various outlying

Table A-1
Major Topics Covered by the 1980 Census of the United States

Population items	Housing items
Items collected from every household (100%)	
Household relationship	Number of units at address
Sex	Complete plumbing facilities
Race	Number of rooms
Age	Whether unit is owned or rented and whether part of a condominium
Marital status	Value of home
Spanish/Hispanic origin or descent	Monthly rent
	Vacancy status
Items collected from a sample of households (20%)	
School enrollment	Type of unit
Educational attainment	Stories in building and presence of elevator
Place of birth	Year built
Citizenship and year of immigration	Year moved into this house
Current language and English proficiency	Farm residence
Ancestry	Acreage and crop sales
Residence five years ago	Source of water
Activity five years ago	Sewage disposal
Veteran status and period of service	Heating equipment
Presence of disability or handicap	Fuels used for house heating, water heating, and cooking
Children ever born	Cost of utilities and fuels
Marital history	Complete kitchen facilities
Employment status last week	Number of bedrooms
Hours worked last week	Number of bathrooms
Place of work	Telephone
Travel time to work	Air conditioning
Means of transportation to work	Number of automobiles, vans, and light trucks
Persons in car pool	Homeowner shelter costs for mortgage, real-estate taxes, and hazard insurance
Year last worked	
Occupation and industry	
Class of worker	
Work in 1979 and weeks looking for work in 1979	
Amount of income by source and total income in 1979	

SOURCE: Charles P. Kaplan and Thomas L. VanValey, *Census '80: Continuing the Factfinder Tradition* (Washington, D.C.: U.S. Bureau of the Census, 1980).

territories such as Guam, Puerto Rico, and the Virgin Islands, and a summary report for the United States. Each of these reports consists of four sections or chapters:

Part A, *Number of Inhabitants*, contains the final population counts for each state and for its major political and statistical subdivisions: counties (urban and rural parts), Standard Metropolitan Statistical Areas (SMSAs), urban areas, all towns or minor civil divisions, census county divisions, all incorporated places, and unincorporated places of 1,000 inhabitants or more.

Part B, *General Population Characteristics*, contains statistics on the 100 percent items (age, sex, race, etc.) for states and their various political and statistical subdivisions.

Part C, *General Social and Economic Characteristics*, contains statistics on those items collected on a sample basis (see Table A-1). Data are given for states and for some of the major political and statistical subdivisions.

Part D, *Detailed Characteristics*, contains data on most of the sample population items presented in much more detail than in Part C and/or cross-tabulated by age, sex, race, and other characteristics. Data in these sections are shown for states, SMSAs, and some of the larger cities.

Volume II, *Special Reports*, consists of a series of special subject reports that provide more extensive statistics on such topics as fertility and child spacing, Americans living abroad, education and vocational training, various ethnic subgroups (e.g., blacks, American Indians, Hispanics), state of birth and population mobility, occupation and industry of the labor force, marital status, household and family composition, and so forth. These reports present detailed data and cross-tabulations largely on a national and regional level, although some contain data for states and SMSAs.

In addition to these two basic volumes the Bureau of the Census prepares and publishes several volumes for each state containing data on housing characteristics as well as several reports for larger metropolitan areas that combine population and housing items. In recent years these published reports have been supplemented by a growing use of computer tape and microfiche files, both of which increase the amount of data that can be made available to consumers at a reduction in cost and especially in storage space. All in all, the many reports and data files that have been created for a variety of administrative and research purposes represent a tremendously rich source of information about ourselves and our society, the value of which will touch on all of our lives at one time or another.

The various publications of the Census Bureau are generally available in college and university libraries or they can be obtained through one of the offices of the bureau's Data User Services Division. In addition, many states are now participating in the State Data Center Program whereby a cooperative arrangement is made between the Bureau of the Census and a designated state agency for the purpose of assisting local governments and other groups who need data for local areas.

Importance of the Census

As noted earlier, the basic purpose of the census is to provide the population figures needed to define the congressional districts within the states from which members of the U.S. House of Representatives are elected. But the use and value of the census extends far beyond simple reapportionment. Its next most important use, perhaps, is in determining how much money is to be returned to the states. The distribution of billions of dollars each year in the form of block grants as well as funds earmarked for particular programs is based on information provided by the census: some child welfare and education funds are distributed to states on the basis of the number of children under twenty-one years of age; adult education funds depend on the number over eighteen with less than five years of schooling; various programs for the elderly are funded on the basis of the number over sixty or sixty-five; some revenue-sharing funds are allocated on the basis of the number of poverty families in an area, and so forth.

The census is also an important source of information on a variety of community needs. Schools, police and fire protection, hospitals, water and sewage treatment facilities, roads, etc., all must be planned for; and adequate planning requires information on the size, composition, and distribution of the local population. Businessmen use census data to locate labor markets and to identify consumer product needs (should one invest in baby carriages or wheel chairs?). Finally, census data are an important source of information on various trends and emerging changes that may have serious implications for the social and economic life of the society: changing marital patterns and living arrangements could affect the future of the family and the rate of population growth; changes in the number and proportion of young people will have implications for the adequacy of existing educational facilities and services; changes in the spatial distribution of the population may herald important shifts in the center of economic power; changing ethnic composition will have an effect on the cultural life in some areas; and so forth. All in all, the census is by far the best and richest source of information about our society—information that is essential for the orderly management of the social, economic, and political life of the country.

The Current World Census Situation

By the middle of the nineteenth century the importance of official statistics for understanding and administering government affairs began to be widely accepted in the more developed countries of Europe and North America. During the period from 1855 to 1864 censuses were conducted in twenty-four countries comprising an estimated 17 percent of the world's population (Linder, 1959). The number of countries taking a population census increased slowly throughout the late nineteenth and early twentieth century, but since the end of the Second World War, largely due to the persuasive efforts as well as the technical and financial assistance of the United Nations, there has been a sharp increase in census-taking. As part of the 1960 world census program, for example, 150 enumerations were carried out between 1955 and 1964, covering nearly 70 percent of the world's people. It is estimated that between 55 and 60 percent of the world's population was covered by the 183 censuses conducted between 1965 and 1974 (United Nations, 1974); the smaller percentage covered in 1965–74 is due mainly to the omission of the People's Republic of China from the estimates. However, a number of countries in the less developed regions have not yet taken a census—partly because the governments feel less pressure for the statistics a census could produce, but mostly because they lack the technical skills, the administrative capacity, and especially the money required to take a modern census. Nevertheless, the United Nations as well as a number of other national and international organizations (such as the Agency for International Development) are still working toward this goal. The effectiveness of their continuing efforts to promote national census-taking is seen by the fact that over 200 enumerations were planned as part of the 1980 World Population and Housing Census Program spanning the decade from 1975 to 1984 (United Nations, 1980). If all these enumerations are completed as planned, we will, for the first time in history, come close to achieving the goal of "complete coverage" of the number, distribution, and characteristics of the world's population.

VITAL STATISTICS

Vital statistics are official government records pertaining to birth, death, and changes in an individual's civil status (e.g., marriage, annulment, divorce) during his or her lifetime. The basic purpose of such records is a legal one. An official birth record is needed to establish proof of citizenship and to prove one's age in order to obtain a driver's license, purchase alcoholic beverages, or apply for Social Security retirement benefits; an official death record is required in order to settle an estate or collect on a life insurance policy; marriage records establish legal paternity and prove the legitimacy of children; a divorce record establishes the right to remarry, and so forth. Over and above their value to the individual as legal documents, however, vital statistics taken collectively have come to represent a major source of data for the study of human populations.

Vital statistics are generally obtained through some sort of registration system in which the fact, place, and date of the particular events are recorded at the time of their occurrence. More important, from a social demographic perspective, a number of other facts—such as age, sex, race, place of residence, occupation, education—are generally recorded at the same time. These data on the characteristics of persons experiencing particular events greatly enhance the value of vital statistics as a source of continuous up-to-date information on various trends and changes taking place in a population, and make them an indispensable tool for demographic analysis. Just as a number of censuses taken at regular periodic intervals provide a series of still photographs depicting the stages of population growth and development at specific points in time, vital statistics may be likened to a motion picture of the changes taking place in a population over time. In an analogy suggested by Walter Willcox, a major American demographer of the twentieth century, just as the life of a plant or animal cannot be adequately studied using only a series of still pictures taken at various intervals of growth, the life of a population cannot be adequately studied unless the periodic censuses are supplemented by vital statistics.

History of Vital Statistics Registration

Compared with census-taking, vital statistics registration is of fairly recent origin. In the United States, for example, we have had a census every ten years since 1790, but we have had complete national registration of births and deaths only since 1933. Census-taking, as we have seen, dates back hundreds of years before the dawn of the Christian era, but not until the Middle Ages did people make any real attempt to collect data on the vital events occurring in a population. Moreover, these early efforts were nothing like present-day registration systems. Rather they were the unsystematic and uncoordinated work of ecclesiastical authorities—parish priests keeping track of the number of baptisms, weddings, and funerals that occurred among their parishioners. Not until the early sixteenth century was there any effort to coordinate these local efforts (Shryock et al., 1976, pp. 20–21). The first major development came in 1532 when, in an attempt to keep track of plague deaths, the city of London passed an ordinance requiring parish priests to maintain burial records for weekly "bills of mortality." A few years later every Anglican priest in England was required by civil law to maintain weekly records of weddings and baptisms. Three centuries later, in 1837, civil authorities assumed responsibility for registering these events, and a central records office was established; not until 1839 was the first official government report on vital statistics published in England.

Other modern Western nations also began to establish systems for maintaining vital statistics records. In 1563 the Council of Trent made the registration of marriages and baptisms a law of the Catholic church, and registration systems were shortly thereafter established in many European countries as well as in their New World colonies. Compulsory *civil* registration of vital events dates from the early seventeenth century in the Scandinavian countries, and there is evidence that in Japan and China some form of civil registration dates as far back as the seventh century A.D. Today, most of the developed countries have fairly well established systems of civil registration that yield relatively complete data on the number and characteristics of the vital events occurring in their populations. Among the less developed countries, however, registration systems are much less complete (or even nonexistent), and the quality and accuracy of the data that are available from them varies considerably from country to country.

Vital Statistics Registration in the United States

The registration of vital statistics in the United States has primarily been the responsibility of states and a few cities, and was not even a matter of concern to the federal government until late in the nineteenth century. For this reason the establishment of a national registration system came much later in this country than the establishment of a national census.

In 1639 the Massachusetts Bay Colony created legislation that required the recording of births, deaths, and marriages, and it is generally credited with being the first political entity both to include such registration as an integral part of an overall administrative-legal system and to transfer responsibility for maintaining the records from the clergy to the civil authorities. Other states and a few cities gradually followed the lead of Massachusetts, but many of the early systems were voluntary and were often grossly incomplete. The registration of deaths began to improve first, largely as an outgrowth of the broader public health movement, and in 1880 the U.S. Bureau of the Census began to collect copies of death certificates from those states and cities where the coverage was judged to be reasonably complete. However, the role of the federal government in maintaining a national registration system does not really begin until 1900. At that time a model state law was recommended, a standard death certificate was adopted, a Death Registration Area was set up comprising those states that complied with the federal guidelines, and an annual series of reports on mortality was initiated.

In 1915 the Bureau of the Census also established a Birth Registration Area for the collection and compilation of birth statistics. At first only ten states and the District of Columbia qualified for inclusion in either registration area (i.e., followed the recommended procedures and were judged to be at least 90 percent complete in the registration of the deaths, or births, that occurred). However, as more states met the qualifications they were added to one area or the other, and by 1933 all the states except Alaska had been admitted to both registration areas (Alaska was not admitted until 1950). Thus, although some national data on mortality and fertility are available as far back as 1900 (for deaths) and 1915 (for births), only since 1933 have the annual reports of vital statistics in the United States included birth and death statistics for the entire country.

The national registration of marriages (and divorces) has lagged far behind that of births and deaths. Although some historical data on simple counts of the number of events are available for some areas going back to the middle of the nineteenth century, national registration areas for marriages and divorces were not established until 1957 and 1958, respectively.

Published Reports

Responsibility for the national registration systems originated with the Bureau of the Census but now lies with the National Center for Health Statistics in the Department of Health and Human Services. This agency is responsible for compiling and publishing the three volumes of the annual (since 1937) report of *Vital Statistics of the United States*. The present organization of these volumes is as follows:

Volume I, *Natality*, contains detailed statistics on births and birth rates, by various characteristics (sex of child, age of mother, birth order, legitimacy status, etc.), for the nation as a whole, for states and major geographic subdivisions, and—although less detail is given—for counties and urban places of ten thousand or more population.

Volume II, *Mortality*, consists of two basic parts: Part A contains death statistics (deaths and death rates by cause for specific age–sex–race groups) for the larger geographic areas of the country, as well as a section on life tables (see Appendix C), and Part B contains more detailed cross-tabulations for the national level as well as statistics for smaller areas.

Volume III, *Marriage and Divorce*, contains data for the United States total and for the registration area as well as some statistics for states and counties, by age, color, and various other characteristics such as type of ceremony (religious or civil), previous marital status, duration of marriage, and the number of children involved in a divorce.

In addition to these annual reports, the National Center for Health Statistics also publishes a *Monthly Vital Statistics Report* based on a sample of records obtained from state offices. Like the publications of the Census Bureau, these and other reports of the National Center for Health Statistics are normally found in most college and university libraries.

Immigration Statistics

Many governments also collect and publish statistics on the number of immigrants arriving at and the number of emigrants departing from official ports of entry and stations on land borders. These statistics are based on such things as the number of passports issued, exit and entry visas, work or residence permits applied for, and so forth; and they are generally more complete and accurate for arrivals who apply for permanent settlement than they are for nationals who elect to emigrate from their country of origin.

Immigration and emigration statistics for the United States are today maintained by the Immigration and Naturalization Service in the Justice Department. Although a continuous series of federal statistics on immigration dates back to 1820, no official attempts were made to collect statistics on the number of people leaving the country until much later (1892). Even today the data for visa applications are compiled and published for alien arrivals only (both immigrant and nonimmigrant) in the *Annual Report of the Immigration and Naturalization Service*. These annual reports contain a summary table showing the number of immigrant arrivals by year since 1821, and detailed tabulations of current immigrants by such characteristics as age, sex, marital status, occupation, county of birth, immigrant classification status (refugee, quota immigrant, nonimmigrant alien, etc.), place of intended residence, and so forth. They also contain some current statistics on the number of aliens excluded or deported and the reasons for such decisions.

In addition to its annual report, the Immigration and Naturalization Service also publishes a quarterly *INS Reporter*, which contains articles on selected topics of demographic interest such as the U.S. refugee policy, border patrol activities, changes in immigration laws or regulations, and alien smuggling.

SAMPLE SURVEYS

For many demographic research purposes official population census data and vital statistics are of limited value. Both, it must be remembered, are established and supported by the government in order to obtain information needed for administrative or legal purposes, and many of the data collected are not relevant for understanding the determinants and consequences of population trends (e.g., the death certificate entry pertaining to whether a decedent was buried or cremated, or such census items as veteran status, number of persons sharing a car pool, or the type of fuel used for heating and cooking). Conversely, and more important, many of the data that professional demographers might like to have at their disposal are of limited administrative value and are not collected. In the United States, for example, neither the decennial census nor the standard birth and death certificates now in use contain questions pertaining to religion, an important variable influencing fertility behavior; nor do they collect any information on health care knowledge and practices that might help explain variations in mortality levels among particular subgroups in the population.

In many parts of the world, particularly among the less developed countries, official population statistics are often lacking entirely, and even where they exist their completeness and accuracy may be open to serious question. The value of the population census is further limited by its infrequency. A census is most commonly taken only once every ten years (at least in part because of the enormous amount of work involved and the costs of taking a complete census), and new population trends may emerge between the census dates that could have important implications for a number of government programs.

For reasons such as these, there has been a growing tendency to rely on sample surveys as a means of gathering a wide variety of population data. In countries lacking an adequate vital statistics registration system, for example, sample surveys have been used to provide estimates of the number of births and deaths occurring in a year. In more highly developed countries sample surveys have been used to supplement registration data by collecting information on such things as the number of children ever born who are still living, the number of children women want or expect to have in the years to come, the prevalence of particular chronic or disabling conditions, and so forth.

A recent example of a major international effort to collect important demographic data using the sample survey approach is the World Fertility Survey (WFS) being undertaken by the International Statistical Institute in collaboration with a number of other international agencies. The WFS, which began in the mid-1970s, is an ongoing program designed to assist interested countries, particularly the less developed ones, in carrying out nationally representative, internationally comparable surveys of human fertility behavior. The specific aims of the project are to help the participating countries acquire the scientific information to describe and interpret the fertility behavior of their population, and to increase their capacity to do fertility research and other demographic work. As of 1981 some sixty-four nations (forty-four of which were developing countries) had participated or were participating in this program, and a number of individual country reports had already been publsihed. When completed, the combined results of these national surveys will greatly enhance our knowledge and understanding of the state of human fertility throughout the world.

In the United States, efforts to collect survey data in order to increase our understanding of fertility behavior go back to the 1930s when the major pioneering study of social and psychological factors affecting fertility was carried out in Indianapolis. These efforts continue today in the National Survey of Family Growth, a periodic survey undertaken by the National Center for Health Statistics (NCHS) to collect up-to-date information on trends and determinants of human fertility, family planning practices, and related maternal and child health issues. This agency also periodically conducts a number of other surveys to obtain supplementary information on fertility and mortality as well as on various health characteristics of the population. The results of these surveys, along with other methodological and analytical reports pertaining to vital statistics trends in the United States, are published by NCHS in several series of reports with the general title *Vital and Health Statistics*.

The Current Population Survey

A major source of up-to-date statistics on the population situation in the United States is the Current Population Survey (CPS), a sample survey conducted every month by the U.S. Bureau of the Census for the primary purpose of collecting national data on the occupation and employment status of the American labor force. In addition to the basic labor force data (which are published by the Bureau of Labor Statistics in its *Monthly Labor Review*), different supplementary questions on various population topics are included each month. These supplementary questions provide the data for the Census Bureau's *Current Population Reports*, a series of annual reports on marital and family status, households and families, metropolitan and nonmetropolitan residence, population mobility, characteristics of the farm population, school enrollment, educational attainment, the black population, and consumer income.

In addition to these regular annual reports, there are supplementary reports every two years or so on fertility and voting behavior, as well as occasional reports on such subjects as religion, the Spanish population, characteristics of youth, and poverty in the United States. Finally, in a special P-25 Series of its *Current Population Reports* the U.S. Bureau of the Census publishes periodic "estimates and projections" of the population of the United States and some of its major subdivisions.

CONTINUOUS POPULATION REGISTERS

In addition to the vital events of birth and death, many national governments also maintain systems for recording various other facts pertaining to the members of their populations. When such systems are established and maintained on a continuous basis they are called *continuous population registers*. Such registers are of two types. The first type is the *universal population register*, which attempts to collect various statistics pertaining to all members of a population on a permanent basis. Where such a register exists, a person is generally entered into the system at birth, with other significant characteristics (e.g., educational attainment, occupation) or changes in his or her life (e.g., marriage, change of residence) being added when appropriate. Universal population registers are relatively rare, and are found primarily in a few Scandinavian and Far Eastern countries, although some East European countries have established them in recent years. They have generally been set up for identification and administrative control purposes, and only rarely have they been used for purposes of population research. In some countries, however, data from the registers have proven useful in providing current population estimates for local areas and for deriving statistics on internal migration patterns.

The second type, the *partial population register,* is much more common. In contrast to the universal register, which attempts to cover all persons in a population on a continuous basis, the partial register is established for specific administrative purposes; it collects statistics pertaining only to those persons directly affected by the specific administrative program. Examples of some common partial population registers are national Social Security systems, lists of welfare recipients, voter lists, tax office records, lists of persons eligible for military draft, consumer rationing programs, lists of resident aliens, and so forth. Such partial registers are of less research value than universal registers because they are limited to specific subgroups in a population, but they may be useful for some specific purposes. Social Security records, for example, may be useful and have been used as a source of data on internal migration patterns of the labor force.

SOURCES OF POPULATION DATA

Nations that take a population census and/or maintain some kind of registration system generally publish their statistics in a variety of official reports, much like the reports of the U.S. Bureau of the Census and the National Center for Health Statistics. Often these reports can be obtained directly from the data-collecting agencies in the various countries, through embassy offices, or through university libraries. However, by far the most convenient and readily available source of international population data are the annual *Demographic Yearbooks* that have been published by the United Nations each year since 1948. These yearbooks contain several tables that are published annually showing summary data for the world and its major regions, and the most up-to-date statistics available on the size, age and sex composition, and urban–rural distribution of the population in all countries of the world, as well as recent data on births, deaths, marriages and divorces, and international migration. In addition, each annual issue is devoted to one special topic (e.g., mortality statistics, fertility trends, recent population censuses) and contains extensive tables dealing with that particular topic.

In our own country, the U.S. Bureau of the Census publishes a very valuable source of data in its *Statistical Abstract of the United States*, an annual volume that contains summary data on various characteristics of the American population as well as on a wide variety of other topics of national interest. It also publishes an occasional volume of *Historical Statistics of the United States from Colonial Times*, which contains extensive time series of many of these same data. Moreover, in addition to providing statistics on the population of the United States, the Census Bureau maintains an International Demographic Data Center that publishes periodic reports containing demographic profiles of selected developing countries, and every two years since 1975 it has published a detailed summary report on *Recent Demographic Estimates for the Countries and Regions of the World*.

The Population Reference Bureau, a privately funded research organization in Washington, D.C. publishes an annual *World Population Data Sheet* containing summary demographic data for all the countries and major regions of the world. This organization also publishes *Intercom*, a monthly news magazine that summarizes recent world population trends and developments, as well as a *Population Bulletin*, each issue of which is devoted to a thorough description and analysis of some important population topic. Somewhat similar to this bulletin in presenting concise discussions of major population issues are the occasional *Worldwatch Papers* of the Worldwatch Institute, another Washington-based independent research organization.

Other professional publications that contain analyses of various population trends and problems are *Demography*, the official journal of the Population Association of America; *Population Studies*, published by the Population Investigation Committee at the London School of Economics and Political Science; *Population and Development Review*, a quarterly journal sponsored by the Population Council; and the *International Migration Review*. The Population Council also periodically publishes other population-related reports, among which is *Studies in Family Planning*, a monthly journal devoted to a description of family planning programs and efforts throughout the world.

In addition to these professional journals, a number of other magazines deal with various population topics. Most notable of these are *Family Planning Perspectives* and *International Family Planning Perspectives*, both published by the Alan Guttmacher Institute; and *American Demographics*, a monthly magazine that analyzes and interprets current American population trends for the benefit of applied users.

Finally, a particularly valuable source of information is the *Population Index*, a quarterly publication of the Office of Population Research at Princeton University, which contains short articles of current interest and, most important, an extensive bibliography of current research in all areas of demographic interest. This publication, as well as the others mentioned above, are generally available in college and university libraries.

LIMITATIONS OF OFFICIAL STATISTICS

It is very important, especially for beginning students, to be aware that no census, survey, or registration system for collecting population data is ever completely free of error. The two most common kinds of errors in official statistics are errors of coverage and errors of reporting. *Errors of coverage* result from the simple fact that data-collecting systems sometimes include persons they should not or, more likely, omit persons whom they should have included. In the early American censuses, for example, slaves and especially Native Americans were often underenumerated.

Persons who are erroneously included generally reflect double counting (e.g., persons temporarily absent from home at the time of an enumeration may be counted both at their usual home and at their temporary place of residence). The opposte kind of mistake, an error of omission, may occur for a variety of reasons. Some persons may be missed in a census because they were not at home when the enumerator called; some may deliberately avoid being counted (e.g., criminals, illegal aliens); there may be inadequacies in the design of the census itself (incomplete household listings, inaccurate maps, confusing instructions); census schedules may be lost or misplaced; some respondents may either deliberately or inadvertently neglect to answer all the questions; or errors can be made in the final processing of the data (errors in coding, transcription, tabulation, sample inflation). Even in the United States, which has a long-standing census tradition and a very sophisticated census operation, an estimated 2 to 3 percent of the total population was not counted in recent censuses, and for some areas (notably the larger cities) and groups the estimated undercount was even higher.

Errors of coverage in registration systems may arise because people fail to report births or deaths, either because of ignorance or for a specific reason—such as a wish to avoid registration fee or tax that may be involved—or they may arise because of inadequacies in the system itself. Even when particular events are registered, coverage may be incomplete because not all the information asked for was provided. A person filling out a death certificate, for example, may not know the major occupation of the decedent, or where he or she was born.

Errors of reporting are simply wrong answers to the questions asked. They may arise because the person recording or transcribing the information makes a mistake, or they may occur because respondents give inaccurate responses to some questions, either deliberately or out of ignorance. In populations where illiteracy levels are very high, for example, people may not know the exact date of their birth or even how old they are, and when asked to report their age their "guesstimates" tend to be rounded off to some convenient number. The extent to which this occurs is revealed by the single-year-of-age statistics from the censuses in many less developed countries, which show large concentrations of people at ages ending in 0 or 5, and a marked deficiency of people at other ages.

Still other people may deliberately lie when filling out a census or vital statistics form. A respondent may lie about his or her income to avoid paying taxes; a woman may lie about her marital status so that her child will not bear the stigma of illegitimacy; a man may lie about his age to avoid military conscription, and so forth.

Although no official data source will ever be completely accurate, it is fairly safe to assume that errors of coverage and/or reporting will be less serious in the more highly developed countries and that they are likely to increase as the level of societal development goes down. This is not to say that the official statistics available for the less developed countries are of no value for population research; it does mean, however, that one should exercise a great deal of caution in using them for anything other than the simplest kinds of analyses.

The Definition Problem

One final problem concerning the use of official statistics in population research needs to be mentioned—the problem of the *comparability of definitions* of basic concepts, either among different countries at one point in time or within the same country over time. To take a simple illustration, data for the early 1970s indicate that the proportion of the population living in urban areas was 27 percent in Liberia but only 15 percent in Madagascar (United Nations, 1975). However, concluding from these data that Liberia is more urban than Madagascar is limited by the fact that in Liberia "urban" is defined as "having a population of 2,000 inhabitants," whereas in Madagascar an urban place is defined as a "center having more than 5,000 inhabitants." The larger cutoff point in Madagascar would by itself be sufficient to reduce the urban fraction in that country relative to that of Liberia. Among other countries the definition of "urban" ranges from as low as 400 inhabitants in Albania to 10,000 or more in Greece, thus making the task of comparing countries in terms of their level of urbanization much more complicated than might appear at first glance. Other topics where differences in the definition of key concepts may impair international comparability of data are labor force status, literacy, marital status, mobility of the population, household composition, and overall fertility levels.

An illustration of how changes in a definition over time can influence conclusions based on official population statistics is provided by the procedure for enumerating college students in the United States. Prior to 1950 students were counted as residents of their parental home but from 1950 on they have been enumerated as residents of the town in which they are attending college. This meant that for some small college towns the census counts showed a substantial increase in the size of the total population between 1940 and 1950, an increase that could have prompted all sorts of erroneous conclusions pertaining to population growth trends if one were not aware of the change in the definition of place of residence for students. Other census concepts that have experienced important definition changes in the United States include the labor force, the nonwhite population, and the mobility status of the population.

In short, whenever official statistics are used for demographic analyses one has to consider not only the probable completeness and accuracy of the data being used but also, where any kind of comparative analysis is contemplated, the degree to which key concepts are defined in the same way.

REFERENCES AND SUGGESTED READING

Benjamin, Bernard. *The Population Census.* New York: Social Science Research Council, 1970.

Francese, Peter K. "The 1980 Census: The Counting of America." *Population Bulletin,* 34 (September 1979).

Grove, Robert D., and Alice M. Hetzel. *Vital Statistics in the United States, 1940–1960.* National Center for Health Statistics, 1968, Chapter I.

Kaplan, Charles P., and Thomas L. VanValey. *Census '80: Continuing the Factfinder Tradition.* Washington, D.C.: U.S. Bureau of the Census, 1980.

Linder, Forest E. "World Demographic Data." In P. M. Hauser and O. D. Duncan, eds., *The Study of Population.* Chicago: University of Chicago Press, 1959.

Shryock, Henry S., Jacob S. Siegel, et al. *The Methods and Materials of Demography,* condensed ed. by E. G. Stockwell, ed. New York: Academic Press, 1976, Chapters 2 and 3.

United Nations. *Principles and Recommendations for National Population Censuses.* Statistical Papers, Series M, No. 27, 1953.

———. *Handbook of Vital Statistics Methods.* Studies in Methods, Series F, No. 7, 1955.

———. *Handbook of Population Census Methods.* Studies in Methods, Series F, No. 5 (Three Volumes), 1958–59.

——. *Methodology and Evaluation of Population Registers and Similar Systems.* Studies in Methods, Series F, No. 15, 1969.
——. *Demographic Yearbook, 1973.* New York: United Nations, 1974.
——. *Demographic Yearbook, 1974.* New York: United Nations, 1975.
——. *Demographic Yearbook, 1979.* New York: United Nations, 1980.
Weeks, John R. *Population: An Introduction to Concepts and Issues,* 2nd ed. Belmont, Calif.: Wadsworth, 1981, Chapter 1.

MEASURING THE DEMOGRAPHIC PROCESSES

APPENDIX **B**

Although a thorough knowledge of demographic methodology is not essential for the general study of world population trends and problems, one should be familiar with a few basic measures if one is to understand fully even the simplest newspaper accounts of population phenomena. In this appendix, accordingly, we will describe and illustrate some of the more common techniques for measuring the basic demographic processes.

For some purposes (e.g., evaluating the adequacy of various community services) we will want to know the *absolute* number of vital events taking place in a population. However, in order to present meaningful comparisons between different populations in time and space it is necessary to take into consideration the *relative* size of the populations being compared. This is usually done by means of a *rate* of one kind or another. A rate, which is basically a proportion, may be defined as the ratio of the number of times a given event actually occurred, during a specified time in a specified place, to the number of times it could have occurred:

$$\text{Rate} = \frac{\text{Number of events}}{\text{Number of possible events}}$$

In order to avoid fractions and facilitate description and discussion, demographers commonly calculate such rates by multiplying the quotient derived from the basic ratio by some constant—usually 1,000. This computational procedure and its significance will become clearer in the following discussion of some specific death rates.

MEASURES OF MORTALITY

Death rates measure the extent to which the impact or *force of mortality* prevents the members of a population from attaining the maximum age to which they are biologically capable of living (Weeks, 1981, p. 128). Several different rates are commonly used to measure the effect of mortality on a population, most of which are based on data obtained from a combination of census and vital statistics sources.

Crude Death Rate

The simplest and most frequently used measure of mortality is the *crude death rate* (CDR), which is defined as the number of deaths in a year per 1,000 persons in the population. It is calculated by dividing the number of deaths occurring in a calendar year by the total population in the year (usually defined as either the midyear population or the average number of people who were alive during the year), and multiplying this quotient by 1,000:

$$\text{CDR} = \frac{\text{Number of deaths in a year}}{\text{Midyear population}} \times 1{,}000$$

To take a specific illustration, estimates prepared by the U.S. Bureau of the Census and the National Center for Health Statistics show a 1978 midyear (July 1) population in the United States of 222,585,000 persons, and 1,927,788 deaths during the year. Thus,

$$\text{CDR} = \frac{1{,}927{,}788}{222{,}585{,}000} \times 1{,}000 = 8.7$$

This rate tells us that in 1978 there were 8.7 or nearly 9 deaths for every 1,000 people in the United States.

The highest death rates in the world today are found in the less developed countries of the Third World, particularly in Africa where it is not uncommon to find CDRs in excess of 20 per 1,000. Most of the modern industrial countries of Europe have CDRs ranging from 8 to 12, whereas some areas of Latin America and East Asia have death rates as low as 5 or 6 per 1,000. For the most part, death rates this low are associated with high levels of fertility and reflect recent declines in mortality among infants and young children so that the overall age of the population is fairly young. It should be stressed, in fact, that the crude death rate is significantly influenced by the age composition of a population, and that observed differences in death rates may be more a function of differences in age composition than in the actual force of mortality. To illustrate, in 1977 the United

Table B-1

Age-Specific Death Rates for Guatemala and the United Kingdom, 1977

Age	Guatemala	United Kingdom
All ages	11.2	11.7
0–4	32.6	3.0
5–14	2.8	0.3
15–24	2.9	0.6
25–34	4.0	0.7
35–44	6.0	1.7
45–54	8.5	5.4
55–64	16.5	14.1
65 and over	53.5	60.9

SOURCE: Calculated by authors from data contained in the 1979 *Demographic Yearbook* (New York: United Nations, 1980).

Kingdom had a crude death rate of 11.7 per 1,000—slightly higher than the 11.2 found in Guatemala (see Table B-1). One can certainly not ascribe the lower CDR in Guatemala to a higher level of living and better health conditions. Rather, Guatemala has a lower CDR because its population is much "younger." Less than 4 percent of its population was over sixty-five years of age, the ages at which death is more likely to occur, while in the United Kingdom nearly 15 percent of the population was in this elderly group. Because its population was so much "older," the United Kingdom had a higher proportion of deaths in the total population than did Guatemala, even though living levels and general health conditions were considerably better in the United Kingdom.

Thus, while the crude death rate may be an accurate measure of the rate at which deaths are occurring in a given population, the fact that it is so sensitive to differences in age composition means that it is not a valid measure of the relative force of mortality per se in different populations. In order to measure the relative force of mortality more accurately one must make use of mortality rates that take age differences into account. There are generally two ways in which this is done—either by calculating death rates separately for each specific age group in the population being compared or by calculating an overall "age-adjusted" death rate.

Age-Specific Death Rates

Age-specific death rates are calculated by the same general formula as the CDR, except that the formula is applied to each age group separately. Thus, for persons age twenty to twenty-four, the age-specific death rate in a given year would be calculated as follows:

$$\frac{\text{Number of deaths to persons age 20-24}}{\text{Midyear population age 20-24}} \times 1{,}000$$

When such rates are calculated for all age groups, more valid comparisons of the real difference in the force of mortality among populations can be made. This is clearly apparent from the death rates presented in Table B-1. Although the United Kingdom had a slightly higher CDR than did Guatemala, the fact that the age-specific death rates in the latter were generally much higher than those in the United Kingdom clearly indicates that the force of mortality was much heavier in Guatemala.

In addition to age, the discussion of mortality differentials in Chapter 4 notes that death rates can vary markedly with other demographic characteristics, particularly sex. Except under very special circumstances, the death rate of men has always been higher than that of women; hence, substantial differences in the proportion of men and women could also influence the level of the crude death rate. For this reason, age-specific death rates are frequently calculated separately for each sex.

Race or ethnicity is another factor that may be associated with mortality differences, although in this case the mortality differences are largely due to race or ethnic differences in economic status and life-style rather than innate biological factors. Nevertheless, for populations that have a substantial ethnic segment it is common to calculate age-specific rates separately by race as well as by sex.

Age-Adjusted Death Rates

Measuring variations in the force of mortality among several different population groups can become very cumbersome and time-consuming if one first has to calculate and then try to analyze several sets of age-specific death rates. Accordingly, it would be desirable to have an overall summary index of the level of mortality that has been adjusted to eliminate the influence of age composition. There are numerous statistical procedures for calculating such *age-adjusted death rates* (see Shryock et al., 1976, pp. 235–44). While it is not necessary for purposes of this volume to be familiar with these more complex statistical techniques, one should be aware that such rates can be calculated and that they give a simple and accurate picture of the relative mortality levels characterizing different population groups. This can be illustrated easily by considering the mortality differences between the white and nonwhite segments of the American population (see Table B-2). In 1978 the crude death rate of the white population was 9.0 per 1,000 as compared

Table B-2

Death Rates by Age and Race: United States, 1978

Age	White	All Other
All ages	9.0	8.1
0–1	12.1	24.6
1–4	0.6	1.0
5–14	0.3	0.4
15–24	1.1	1.4
25–34	1.2	2.5
35–44	2.1	4.7
45–54	5.6	9.9
55–64	13.4	20.9
65–74	29.6	36.2
75–84	71.6	75.6
85 and over	153.2	92.3
Age-adjusted death rate	5.8	8.0

SOURCE: National Center for Health Statistics, *Monthly Vital Statistics Report*, 29:6, *Final Mortality Statistics, 1978* (September 17, 1980).

with a nonwhite rate of 8.1 per 1,000. However, the age-specific rates clearly show that nonwhites are subjected to a much greater risk of mortality at nearly every age. Further, this differential risk of mortality is clearly and simply revealed by the age-adjusted death rates: 5.8 for whites and 8.0 for nonwhites.

While age-adjusted death rates are a better measure of the relative force of mortality characterizing different populations, it must be stressed that they are not true death rates. Such adjusted rates are nothing more than the result of statistical manipulations that control for differences in the age composition of populations. For all of its limitations as a measure of the force of mortality, the crude death rate is an accurate measure of the rate at which any given population is losing members through death.

Infant Mortality Rate

Another measure of mortality that is free from the direct influence of age composition, and which is a particularly useful measure of general health conditions, is the *infant mortality rate* (IMR). The IMR is defined as the number of deaths under one year of age in a calendar year per 1,000 live births. As such it measures the probability that a newborn baby will survive the hazards of infancy and live to celebrate its first birthday. It is calculated simply by dividing the number of deaths under age one in a year by the corresponding number of live births and multiplying by 1,000:

$$\text{IMR} = \frac{\text{Deaths under age 1}}{\text{Live births}} \times 1,000$$

To illustrate, in Guatemala in 1977 there were 284,513 live births and 21,897 deaths to infants under one year of age. Thus, the 1977 infant mortality rate of that country was as follows:

$$\frac{21,897}{284,513} \times 1,000 = 77.0$$

This means that 77 out of every 1,000 infants could be expected to die before reaching their first birthday (i.e., 7.7 percent of all infants die before attaining age one).

The significance of this rate as an overall index of the health and well-being of a population can be seen when one compares the 1977 IMR of Guatemala (77 per 1,000) with the 1977 IMR of the United Kingdom (14 per 1,000). Despite the lower crude death rate in Guatemala (see Table B-1) the two nations' IMRs clearly reflect the poorer health conditions and consequent greater force of mortality in Guatemala than in the United Kingdom. Note the similar situation with respect to the 1978 mortality differences among the white and nonwhite segments of the American population (see Table B-2).

Another measure that reflects the force of mortality in infancy is the *mean expectation of life at birth*. This measure is defined as the total number of years of life that will be lived, *on the average*, by persons born at some specified time under a particular set of mortality conditions. This measure, which is derived from the life table, is discussed more fully in Appendix C.

Neonatal and Postneonatal Mortality

Because the risk of mortality is higher during the first few hours and days of life than in later months, and because different causes account for the bulk of the deaths at the earlier and later ages of infancy, it is fairly common practice in studies of infant mortality to break up the conventional infant mortality rate into two separate components: *neonatal mortality*, or deaths occurring to infants under one month of age, and *postneonatal mortality*, or deaths between the ages of one month and one year. In each instance the mortality rate is calculated as 1,000 times the ratio of the deaths in the appropriate age category to the annual number of live births:

$$\text{Neonatal death rate} = \frac{\text{Deaths under 1 month}}{\text{Live births}} \times 1{,}000$$

$$\text{Postneonatal death rate} = \frac{\text{Deaths at ages 1 to 11 months}}{\text{Live births}} \times 1{,}000$$

Since the denominator is the same in each of these computations, and since the sum of the two numerators is equal to the total number of infant deaths, the sum of the neonatal and postneonatal death rates will be equal to the overall infant mortality rate.

Cause of Death

People die from different causes. Moreover, the relative frequency of particular causes may vary substantially from one population to another, and this variation will have important implications for the overall level of mortality. In general, the cumulative force of mortality is greater in less developed societies where various infectious and parasitic diseases (e.g., tuberculosis, malaria, influenza, and pneumonia) are major causes of death. It becomes less as improvements in general health conditions are accompanied by a decline in the incidence of death from the infectious diseases and a corresponding increase in mortality from such degenerative causes as cancer and heart diseases. Accordingly, an adequate analysis of the mortality conditions prevailing in a given population must consider the relative impact of particular causes of death. One of the most common ways to do this is to calculate *cause-specific death rates*. A cause-specific death rate is conventionally defined as the number of deaths from a given cause or group of causes during a year per 100,000 of the midyear population; a larger constant is used here because of the relatively small number of deaths from many causes. Expressed as a formula:

$$\text{Death rate for Cause } i = \frac{\text{Deaths due to Cause } i}{\text{Midyear population}} \times 100{,}000$$

To illustrate, there were 8,181 deaths due to malignant neoplasms (cancer) in Finland in 1975. The estimated population at that time was 4,717,724. Substituting these values in the above formula:

$$\frac{8{,}181}{4{,}717{,}724} \times 100{,}000 = 173.4$$

This tells us that for every 100,000 people in Finland in 1975 there were 173 deaths due to cancer.

In situations where population base data are not available (a not uncommon occurrence, especially with respect to less developed countries), the relative impact of particular causes of death can be measured by means of *cause-specific death ratios*. These ratios simply denote the percentage of all deaths due to a particular cause or group of causes, and they are calculated like any percentage as 100 times the ratio of the number of deaths from a particular cause to the total number of deaths:

$$\frac{\text{Deaths due to Cause } i}{\text{Total deaths}} \times 100$$

In Finland in 1975 there were a total of 43,853 deaths. Thus, the cancer death ratio would be calculated thus:

$$\frac{8,181}{43,853} \times 100 = 18.7$$

This tells us that nearly 19 percent of all deaths in Finland in 1975 were caused by some form of cancer.

MEASURES OF MORBIDITY

Three basic measures pertain to disease and illness in a population: (1) measures of the number of people who contact a disease (incidence rates); (2) measures of the number of people who have a disease (prevalence rates); and (3) measures of the frequency at which people who contact a particular disease die from that disease (case fatality rates).

Incidence Rates

The incidence rate is the number of persons who contact a specific illness or disease during a given time period, generally a calendar year, per 1,000 population:

$$\text{Incidence rate} = \frac{\text{Number of persons developing a disease}}{\text{Population}} \times 1,000$$

In the United States in 1977 there were approximately 85.6 million reported cases of influenza, and an estimated midyear population of 218.7 million persons. Thus, the 1977 incidence rate for influenza was as follows:

$$\frac{85.6}{218.7} \times 1{,}000 = 391.4$$

This means that 391 out of every 1,000 Americans (roughly 4 out of 10 persons) contacted some form of influenza in 1977.

Prevalence Rates

The prevalence rate is based on the total number of persons who have a particular disease during a given year—new cases that have their onset during the year as well as all previously existing cases. Like the incidence rate it is defined as the number of cases of a disease per 1,000 persons:

$$\text{Prevalence rate} = \frac{\text{Number of persons who have a disease}}{\text{Population}} \times 1{,}000$$

In the United States in 1973, according to the National Center for Health Statistics, there were 4.2 million persons with diabetes. The midyear population was estimated at 211.9 million; hence the 1973 prevalence rate for diabetes is calculated as

$$\frac{4.2}{211.9} \times 1{,}000 = 19.8$$

That is, in 1973 nearly 20 out of every 1,000 Americans (2 percent of the population) had diabetes.

Case Fatality Rate

The case fatality rate, which is a measure of the killing power of particular diseases, is defined simply as the proportion of persons contracting a disease who die of that disease. It is calculated as 100 times the ratio of deaths from a given disease to the number of cases of the disease:

$$\text{Case fatality rate} = \frac{\text{Deaths from a particular disease}}{\text{Number of persons developing a disease}} \times 100$$

To illustrate, in the United States during the three years from 1959 to 1961 1,192 people had tetanus, of whom 756 died (Dauer et al., 1968, Appendix A). The case fatality rate for tetanus for this period is calculated as follows:

$$\frac{756}{1,192} \times 100 = 63.4$$

This means that nearly two-thirds of all persons who contacted tetanus died from it. The data for measles during this period were 1,276,000 cases, 1,199 deaths, and a case fatality rate of 0.1 percent. The differences in the killing power of these two diseases is clearly evident: although measles is much more common and widespread, tetanus is obviously much more deadly.

MEASURES OF FERTILITY

Several different measures are commonly used to determine the fertility level of a population. Most of them, like most measures of mortality, are based on data obtained from a combination of census and vital statistics sources; however, a number of techniques involving only data from a census or sample survey can be used to estimate the number of children that women are having. Either way, one must keep in mind that the resulting fertility measures, like all demographic measures, are only as good as the amount and quality of the data on which they are based; the conscientious student will always give some attention to an evaluation of the source and data base of any such estimates. In this section we shall briefly describe some of the more common measures of human fertility and reproduction.

Measures of fertility are of two general types: *period rates*, which are cross-sectional rates that measure the level of fertility during a given period of time, usually a single year; and *cohort rates*, which are based on data for a number of calendar years and which measure changing patterns of childbearing for a single group over time. The rates described in this section are basically period rates, though some of them can be modified to cohort rates.

Crude Birth Rate

The simplest and most frequently used measure of human fertility is the *crude birth rate* (CBR). This rate is analogous to the crude death rate and is defined as the number of live births occurring per 1,000 people in a given population during a calendar year. It is calculated quite simply by dividing the annual number of births by the midyear population and multiplying the quotient by 1,000:

$$\text{CBR} = \frac{\text{Annual number of births}}{\text{Midyear population}} \times 1{,}000$$

To take a simple illustration, let us assume a society has 1,350 births in a given year and a midyear population of 62,575. The crude birth rate is then calculated:

$$\text{CBR} = \frac{1{,}350}{62{,}575} \times 1{,}000 = 21.5$$

The highest crude birth rates in the world in 1980–81 were found in the less developed countries of Africa and parts of Asia, where it is not uncommon to find CBRs in excess of 45 to 50 per 1,000. At the other extreme, a number of the low fertility countries of Northwest Europe have CBRs as low as 10 to 12 per 1,000. The 1980 crude birth rate in the United States of roughly 16 per 1,000 represents a moderately low level of fertility.

Although it is the most commonly used measure of fertility, the usefulness of the CBR is limited because it does not take into account the fact that only women at certain ages can have babies. Should there be marked differences in the age–sex composition of particular populations the CBR could give a seriously distorted picture of the fertility differences between them. Suppose, for example, that there are two populations containing 62,575 people; in each population there are 1,350 births in a year. Both populations thus have the same CBR (21.5). One of them, however, consists of 31,000 women and 31,575 men, whereas the other is made up of 20,000 women and 42,575 men. Therefore, we certainly cannot say their fertility levels are comparable. Rather, it is clear that in the latter population the smaller number of women would need to have a much higher level of fertility to produce the same number of babies as the women in the former population, which has nearly equal numbers of men and women. The problem could be even further complicated if there were marked differences in the ages of the women in the two populations.

General Fertility Rate

Since the age and sex composition of a population exerts such a strong influence on the level of its CBR, certain refinements have to be introduced to minimize this influence and provide measures that are more useful for comparative fertility analyses. One of the simplest of these refined measures is the *general fertility rate* (GFR), which is defined as the number of births occurring in a year per 1,000 women at the childbearing ages (generally assumed to be ages fifteen to forty-four years):

$$\text{GFR} = \frac{\text{Annual number of births}}{\text{Number of women age 15–44}} \times 1{,}000$$

To illustrate the difference between the CBR and GFR one need only consider the recent fertility trend in the United States. According to estimates prepared by the National Center for Health Statistics, the CBR in this country rose from 14.9 in 1973 to 16.2 in 1980 indicating nearly a 9 percent jump in fertility during that period. However, the GFR for both years was 69.2 births per 1,000 women ages fifteen to forty-four years, indicating no difference in fertility at the two dates. The reason for the increase in the CBR lies in an increase in the proportion of women who were in the childbearing ages—from 42 percent in 1973 to 46 percent in 1980. That is, the larger proportion of childbearing women at the most recent date served to inflate the CBR, even though no change was observed in the actual level of female fertility.

Age-Specific Birth Rates

Perhaps the most refined measures to use in comparative fertility analyses are *age-specific birth rates*. Such rates are defined and calculated as the number of births in a year to women of a specified age per 1,000 women at that age. Thus, for women age twenty to twenty-four, the age-specific birth rate would be calculated this way:

$$\frac{\text{Number of births to women age 20–24}}{\text{Total number of women age 20–24}} \times 1{,}000$$

Such rates are very useful in pointing to meaningful differences in the fertility behavior of various populations. For example, in 1970 the United States age-specific birth rate was 168 for women age twenty to twenty-four years and 145 for women age twenty-five to twenty-nine years, but in 1978 both these age groups had rates of 112 births per 1,000 women. This clearly indicates that the general decline in American fertility during the 1970s was notably more pronounced for the younger women.

Total Fertility Rate

Although age-specific birth rates are very useful in the comparative analysis of fertility behavior, they can become very cumbersome if one is interested in several different populations at several different points in time. Accordingly, it is desirable to have a summary measure that is based on them but that is simpler and more convenient to analyze. One such summary measure is the *total fertility rate* (TFR), which is defined as the weighted sum of the age-specific birth rates. If these rates are calculated for single years of age, the TFR is obtained simply as their sum; otherwise it is calculated as the sum of the birth rates at each age interval multiplied by the number of years in the interval. Letting n represent the number of years in an age interval,

$$\text{TFR} = \Sigma \,(\text{Age-Specific Birth Rate} \times n)$$

In comparative fertility analyses the TFR is interpreted as the total number of children each woman will have, on the average, if the prevailing age-specific birth rates do not change; it is commonly used as a measure of completed family size. According to estimates prepared by the Population Reference Bureau, the TFR of the United States, as defined above, was 1,800 in 1978, which can be interpreted to mean either that 1,000 women will bear 1,800 children during their reproductive years (assuming that 1978 birth rates remain constant), or that each woman will have an average of 1.8 children. To illustrate the marked differences in fertility levels in the world today, the same source has estimated that TFRs in the late 1970s ranged from a low of 1.4 in West Germany to a high of 8.1 in Kenya.

Cohort Fertility

Although the total fertility rate is commonly interpreted as an estimate of completed family size, this interpretation is based on the assumption that observed age-specific birth rates will not change. We know that they do change, however, and we need some way to take these changes into account. Cohort fertility analysis provides one solution. Cohort fertility measures are calculated by following a group of women through their reproductive ages and are based on age-specific birth rates they actually experienced at specific ages rather than those prevailing at a given time. To illustrate, in contrast to the TFR, which estimates completed family size as the sum of a cross-sectional schedule of age-specific birth rates, actual completed family size would be derived by summing weighted age-specific birth rates over time. For example, in Table B-3 the sum of the rates identified in the first column would be the 1950–54 TFR, a period rate interpreted as an estimate of completed family size based on the assumption of constant fertility. In contrast, the sum of the rates indicated along the diagonal, multiplied by 5 or the number of years in each age interval, would represent an estimate of the actual completed family size in 1980 of the cohort that began its fertility behavior at age fifteen to nineteen in 1950–54.

Cohort fertility measures are far from perfect (e.g., they do not reflect current fertility), but they are essential tools for understanding trends and differentials in fertility behavior. For the most part, the fertility measures encountered by the beginning student of population will be period rates, and the student will generally not have to be concerned with how the var-

Table B-3
Illustration of Period versus Cohort Fertility Rates

	Age-specific birth rates for particular years					
Age	1950–54	1955–59	1960–64	1965–69	1970–74	1975–79
15–19	xxx	—	—	—	—	—
20–24	xxx	xxx	—	—	—	—
25–29	xxx	—	xxx	—	—	—
30–34	xxx	—	—	xxx	—	—
35–39	xxx	—	—	—	xxx	—
40–44	xxx	—	—	—	—	xxx

ious cohort rates are calculated or applied in more sophisticated demographic analyses. However, all students should be aware of the fundamental distinction between period and cohort rates, and they should be especially aware of the limitations inherent in any period rate based on cross-sectional data. All such rates do is measure the impact of a given schedule of age-specific birth rates on the age structure of a given population at one given point in time. It is especially important to be aware of this limitation when interpreting the reproduction rates described in the following section.

Reproduction Rates

Reproduction rates are concerned with measuring the extent to which a given population is replacing itself through natural processes. The simplest and most commonly used of such measures is the *crude rate of natural increase* (CRNI), which is defined simply as the difference between the crude birth and death rates:

$$CRNI = CBR - CDR$$

If a given population has a birth rate of 25 and a death rate of 10, then its crude rate of natural increase is $25 - 10 = 15$, which means that for every 1,000 people in a population there will be 15 additions in a given year as a result of the difference between the annual number of births and deaths.

Although the CRNI, like the CBR and CDR, is conventionally determined per 1,000 people, it is more common, when using it, to shift the decimal point one place to the left and speak in terms of numbers added per 100 (or percent). Thus, in the above illustration, a CRNI of 15 would generally be interpreted as a natural increase rate of 1½ percent per year.

Two other fairly common measures of reproduction with which students should be familiar are the *gross reproduction rate* (GRR) and the *net reproduction rate* (NRR). The GRR is simply a modification of the TFR wherein the age-specific birth rates are calculated on the basis of female births only. The rationale for restricting the rate to female births is that since only women can have babies a more realistic measure of the reproductive potential of a population will be the extent to which the women of today are producing daughters to bear children in the next generation.

In calculating the gross reproduction rate, two options are available. One can either calculate age-specific female birth rates and derive the GRR as their weighted sum in much the same way as the TFR is derived, or one can simply calculate a conventional TFR and then multiply it by the percentage of births that are female. To illustrate, 48.7 percent of the births in the United States in 1978 were female. Using this fraction in connection with the TFR cited above one can estimate the 1978 gross reproduction rate as follows:

$$GRR = 1,800 \times .487 = 877$$

This can be interpreted to mean that given the fertility level prevailing in 1978, every 1,000 American women would ultimately give birth to 877 daughters (an average of .88 daughters per woman), a number that was considerably less than the number required for replacement (i.e., replacement fertility can be defined as one daughter per woman).

In making this interpretation one must keep in mind the limitation of the GRR: it is based on cross-sectional age-specific rates, and as these rates change over time, the number of daughters the women will bear will also change. As a measure of population replacement the GRR is further limited by the fact that not all the babies that are born will survive to bear children. Some will die in infancy, and others will die at various ages under forty-five years. Thus, to measure the current replacement level of a population more accurately it is necessary to control for the effects of mortality. This is done by calculating the *net reproduction rate* (NRR), which is defined as the number of daughters a cohort of women will ultimately bear on the assumption that observed female age-specific birth *and* death rates remain unchanged throughout the lifetime of the cohort. (See Appendix C for an illustration of how to calculate the NRR.) Because it allows for the fact that some of the female infants will die before reaching the end of the childbearing years, the NRR will always be smaller than the GRR, with the magnitude of the difference increasing with the level of infant mortality. Where infant mortality is relatively low, as in the United States, the difference will be very small: according to the calculations presented in Table C-2, the 1978 NRR was .85 as compared with a GRR of .87.

Fertility Measures from Census and Survey Data

We have noted that some fertility measures are based solely on data gathered in a census or sample survey. One such measure is the *child–woman ratio*, also known as the *fertility ratio*, which is defined as the number of children under five years of age per 1,000 women at the childbearing ages in a given year:

$$\text{Child–woman ratio} = \frac{\text{Total age 0–4}}{\text{Women age 15–44}} \times 1,000$$

Using estimates prepared for the United States in 1975,

$$\text{Child–woman ratio} = \frac{13,141,000}{47,164,000} \times 1,000 = 279$$

This figure compares with child–woman ratios of 404 in 1970 and 563 in 1960; and, although this ratio is limited in that it is also influenced by mortality (especially infant mortality) and female migration, it reflects the profound changes that have occurred in the fertility behavior of the American population during the past two decades.

Although the child–woman ratio is the most common census-based measure of fertility, recent years have seen the development of numerous others. Most such measures, which have come into use as developments in computer technology have permitted some rather sophisticated refinements in cohort fertility analysis, entail extensive manipulation of statistics on the number of women at the childbearing ages in relation either to number of own children or to the number of children ever born (Shryock et al., 1976, pp. 301–10). However, students at a beginning level need not be concerned with the data collection and calculation procedures involved in the derivation of those measures.

MEASURES OF MIGRATION

Migration, especially migration that takes place within the borders of a single country, has always been the most difficult process to measure. Most nations make some attempt to keep track of people entering or leaving their political territory, but only rarely are systematic efforts made to collect and maintain official statistics on the number and type of people who change their place of residence within a country or on the origin and destination of such residential moves. Thus, a good deal of the work in migration analyses consists of estimating and/or compiling the basic data on the number and characteristics of migrants.

A variety of sources and techniques are available to demographers to provide estimates of migration. While it is not appropriate to go into them too deeply in the present context, it is desirable for students to have some understanding of where the basic data come from. Generally speaking, there are two ways that such data can be obtained: they can be obtained *directly* by asking people where they lived at some earlier date, or they can be obtained *indirectly* as the residual component of some total population change.

Direct Migration Estimates

The decennial census of the United States contains two items that provide data on internal migration in this country. The first is a question on *state of birth* which, when compared with state of residence at the time of the census, provides a basis for identifying the following three categories of people:

1. Nonmigrants—those who are living in the state in which they were born.
2. In-migrants—those living in each state who were born elsewhere.
3. Out-migrants—those who were born in one state but are living in another at the time of the census.

These data, which have been available at each census since the mid-nineteenth century, are shown for each state and major geographic area, and for various subgroups within the population. They are the primary source of a wealth of data on the timing, origin, destination, volume, and characteristics of the major migration streams that have occurred and are presently occurring in the United States (e.g., the historical westward movement of the population, the dispersal of blacks from the South, the more recent movement from the Snow Belt to the Sun Belt).

Since 1940 these state-of-birth data have been supplemented by data obtained from a question pertaining to *place of residence at some earlier specified date*. In 1980, for example, one of the items on the sample questionnaire asked people where they lived on April 1, 1975. By cross-tabulating place of residence at the time of the census with place of residence five years earlier it is possible to devise estimates of more recent migration trends for more localized areas in much the same way that lifetime migration estimates are derived from state-of-birth data. Similar annual estimates of internal migration are available on a broader regional level from the Current Population Survey, which each March asks a sample of the population where they were living on March 1 one year ago. Much of the information we have on current migration trends and differentials in the United States is obtained from these earlier residence data.

Indirect Migration Estimates

Indirect estimates of migration are those that are obtained by first measuring the total amount of change in a population between two points in time and then separating out that portion of the change that can be accounted for by the natural processes of birth and death. The *residual change* that cannot otherwise be accounted for is then assumed to be due to migration. The two most common residual techniques for estimating net migration are the *survival rate method* and the *vital statistics method*. In the survival rate method, which is illustrated more fully in Appendix C, estimates of net migration are obtained by (1) using appropriate age-sex specific survival rates to estimate the number of people who could be *expected* to survive from one census to another, (2) comparing the number of expected survivors to the number actually *enumerated* in each specific age–sex group, and (3) attributing the difference between the expected and enumerated population to migration.

The *vital statistics method*, which yields an estimate of net migration for the total population of an area (i.e., for all age groups combined) requires counts of a population (by sex and race if desired) at two consecutive censuses and complete counts of the number of births and deaths during the intercensal interval. These known values are substituted in the following equation, which is then solved for the unknown migration component:

$$P_2 = P_1 + B - D + M$$

In this equation P_2 represents the population at the most recent census (Time 2); P_1 is the population at the earlier census (Time 1); B and D are the number of births and deaths that occurred between the two censuses; and M represents the contribution of migration to population change during the intercensal interval. Now, by simple algebraic transposition this equation can be rearranged to estimate migration as follows:

$$M = (P_2 - P_1) - (B - D)$$

To illustrate this procedure, the population of Arkansas as enumerated in two censuses was 1,786,272 (P_1) in 1960 and 1,923,295 (P_2) in 1970. Between the two census dates there were 400,627 births and 192,735 deaths in Arkansas. Substituting these values in the preceding equation:

$$M = (1{,}923{,}295 - 1{,}786{,}272) - (400{,}627 - 192{,}735)$$
$$M = -70{,}869$$

This tells us that between 1960 and 1970 the effect of migration into and out of Arkansas was a net loss of approximately 71,000 persons.

Migration Rates

There are three basic migration rates that are analogous to the crude birth, death, and natural increase rates. They are the in-migration rate, the out-migration rate, and the net migration rate.

In-Migration Rate

The in-migration rate, which is analogous to the birth rate in measuring additions to a population, is the number of people moving into an area per 1,000 population of the area in a given time, usually one year:

$$\text{In-migration rate} = \frac{\text{Number moving into an area}}{\text{Population of area}} \times 1{,}000$$

This rate can refer either to the number of *international migrants* crossing a specified political boundary for the purpose of taking up residence in a new country, or it can refer to the number of *internal migrants* moving into a political or geographic subdivision within a given country. When it refers to international migration, it is called an "immigration rate" to differentiate it from the more general in-migration rate. To illustrate, there were 373,326 legal immigrants to the United States in 1970. The estimated midyear population for that year was 205,052,000. Thus the 1970 immigration rate can be calculated as follows:

$$\frac{373{,}326}{205{,}052{,}000} \times 1{,}000 = 1.82$$

This indicates that in 1970 there were nearly 2 immigrants to the United States for every 1,000 residents.

Out-Migration Rate

The out-migration rate is analogous to the crude death rate and can be defined as the number of people leaving an area per 1,000 population in a year.

$$\text{Out-migration rate} = \frac{\text{Number moving out of an area}}{\text{Population of area}} \times 1{,}000$$

Table B-4

Native-born Population of Ohio by State of Birth and State of Residence, with Net Gain or Loss Through Interstate Movement, 1960 and 1970

	Living in Ohio Total	Born in other state (in-migrants)	Born in Ohio but living in other state (out-migrants)	Net migration gain or loss (IM)–(OM)
1960	9,085,041	2,350,459	1,666,486	+683,973
1970	9,904,589	2,538,985	2,041,458	+497,527
Net migration change, 1960–70	...	+188,526	−374,972	−186,446
Annual average, 1960–70	9,495,000	+18,900	−37,500	−18,600

SOURCE: U.S. Bureau of the Census, *State of Birth,* PC(2)-2A, *U.S. Census of Population, 1960* (Washington, D.C., 1963); and *1970 Census of Population* (Washington, D.C., 1973).

The out-migration rate can also refer either to the number of people crossing a political boundary to establish permanent residence in another country *(emigration rate),* or to the number of people moving out of a subdivision within a given country. To illustrate, using the state-of-birth data we can estimate that an average of 37,500 native-born Americans moved out of Ohio each year between 1960 and 1970 (see Table B-4). The estimated average size of the native population of Ohio during the decade was 9,495,000; thus, an average annual rate of migration out of Ohio during the 1960s can be calculated as follows:

$$\frac{37,500}{9,495,000} \times 1,000 = 3.95$$

This means that between 1960 and 1970 Ohio lost an average of nearly 4 persons per 1,000 population per year.

Net Migration Rate

The net migration rate is analogous to the crude rate of natural increase and is calculated simply as the difference between the in- and out-migration rates. In the Ohio illustration, for example, the average number of people moving into the state each year between 1960 and 1970 was 18,900, yielding an annual in-migration rate of

$$\frac{18{,}900}{9{,}495{,}000} \times 1{,}000 = 1.99$$

The average annual net migration rate for this decade can now be calculated in either of two ways:

$$\frac{(\text{Number of in-migrants}) - (\text{Number of out-migrants})}{\text{Average Population}}$$

$$\frac{(18{,}900) - (37{,}500)}{9{,}495{,}000} = -1.96$$

or,

$$(\text{In-migration rate}) - (\text{Out-migration rate})$$
$$(1.99) - (3.95) = -1.96$$

That is, between 1960 and 1970 the native-born population of Ohio experienced a net migration loss amounting to approximately 2 persons per 1,000 population per year.

REFERENCES AND SUGGESTED READING

Dauer, Carl C., et al. *Infectious Diseases.* Cambridge, Mass.: Harvard University Press, 1968.

Haupt, Arthur, and Thomas T. Kane. *Population Handbook.* Washington, D.C.: Population Reference Bureau, 1981.

Shryock, Henry S., Jacob S. Siegel, et al. *The Methods and Materials of Demography,* condensed ed. by E. G. Stockwell. New York: Academic Press, 1976.

Weeks, John R. *Population: An Introduction to Concepts and Issues,* 2nd ed. Belmont, Calif.: Wadsworth, 1981, pp. 87–93, 128–130, 371–76.

Weller, Robert H., and Leon F. Bouvier. *Population: Demography and Policy.* New York: St. Martin's, 1981.

THE LIFE TABLE

APPENDIX **C**

Persons engaged in population research frequently hold widely differing opinions as to the most significant determinants and consequences of particular population trends. All such persons, however, will tend to agree on one basic point: the most versatile and valuable analytical tool of demographic research at their disposal is the *life table*. Although it is basically a death probability table originally developed in connection with the study of mortality, the life table today is used in virtually all phases of research dealing with trends and changes in human populations. On the simplest level, the analysis of *fertility* trends and differentials, the description of prevailing patterns of *migration*, and the preparation of *population estimates* and *projections* are all facilitated by the use of the life table. On a more sophisticated level, life tables can be extremely useful in the study of trends and differentials in such things as school enrollment and labor force participation; they have been used to measure the economic cost to society of particular causes of death; and they are the basis for the construction of complex analytical models to illustrate potential future population growth and change, and to provide various population estimates where official data are lacking or otherwise deficient (Shryock et al., 1976).

DESCRIPTION OF THE LIFE TABLE

The life table is a convenient method of summarizing the lifetime mortality experience of a single cohort. It describes the life and death history of a group of persons from the time they are born until they have all died. Such life tables can be either one of two types. They can be hypothetical, in that they can describe what the mortality experience of a given birth cohort would be *if*, throughout the lifetime of the last survivor, it was subjected to the age-specific death rates prevailing at the time of its birth. On the other hand, life tables can represent a real description of the mortality conditions that actually characterized a group of people as they progressed through life.

Quite obviously, these two life tables present very different pictures of mortality. The first type, the *current life table,* is the better known and the more commonly used of the two. It describes the mortality conditions prevailing at one particular point in time. Since no single cohort has actually experienced or is likely to experience this particular pattern of mortality throughout its life span, the current life table presents a hypothetical pattern of mortality conditions. Such a table merely shows the combined effect of the mortality experiences of many different existing cohorts on one newborn cohort.

The second type of life table, the *cohort* or *generational life table,* presents a historical record of what has actually occurred. It is a factual summary of the mortality that actually characterized a particular cohort born many years in the past, and characterized only that cohort and no other. Because of this limited character (and also because the historical mortality data needed for their construction are often imperfect or entirely lacking), cohort life tables are used much less widely in demographic analyses than are current life tables. Accordingly, since they are more frequently encountered, we will deal primarily with current life tables.

Current Life Tables

The current life table is a method of describing, in summary form, the mortality experience of a single generation or birth cohort that is subjected, throughout its lifetime, to a constant set of age-specific death rates (generally those prevailing at the time the cohort was born). Such a table selects a starting population and follows it throughout its entire lifetime. The table takes the death rates characterizing a given population at a given time and describes the mortality experience that would characterize persons born at that time (the probability of dying at specific ages, the average number of years each member can expect to live, the proportion who will still be alive at successive ages, etc.). The assumption is made that these observed age-specific death rates will remain unchanged throughout the lifetime of the cohort. The current life table, then, is a life history of a hypothetical birth cohort as it is diminished gradually over the years by deaths. Beginning at birth and continuing until all have died, the cohort loses a predetermined proportion at each age, thus representing a situation that is artificially contrived. Defined as such, the life table derives its value from the fact that it depicts the mortality conditions inherent in the prevailing age-specific death rates (i.e., the mortality conditions that would ultimately emerge if the prevailing age-specific death rates persisted at a constant level for an indefinite period of time).

Explanation of the Columns

The 1978 life table of the female population of the United States (Table C-1) is a current life table. It depicts the life and death history that would characterize a group of American women who were exposed, throughout their lives, to the age-specific female death rates prevailing in the United States in 1978. Let us now examine each of the columns in this table and describe the basic calculations involved in constructing a current life table.

Column 1 (Age, x to x + n). The first column in any life table is the age column, and every entry in the life table refers to some particular age or age interval. Age is defined very strictly in a life table. The age column is denoted by the symbols x to x + n, where x refers to an *exact* age (the lower limit of an age interval), and n refers to the number of years within the age interval. In a complete life table constructed for single years of age, n would always be equal to one year. In the abridged table used here for illustrative purposes, however, the first interval, which is for persons under 1 year of age (x = 0, n = 1), is the only interval where n is equal to 1 year. The second interval is for persons between the ages of 1 and 5 years (x = 1, n = 4), and all other intervals are for 5-year age groups (n = 5). In the first interval, where x = 0 and n = 1, the age referred to is the interval between birth *up to but not including* age 1; where x = 1 and n = 4, the interval includes persons between exact age 1 *up to but not including* age 5; where x = 5 and n = 5, the interval is from exact age five *up to but not including* exact age 10, etc. Each value in the life table, as will soon be noted, refers to either of two aspects of age—either to the exact age x or to the interval between ages x to x + n.

Column 2 (Mortality Rates, $_nq_x$). The second column in the life table depicted here contains the mortality rates characterizing the population group for which the table is being constructed. These mortality rates, denoted by the symbol $_nq_x$, are computed from basic population data and death statistics, and indicate the probabilities that a person who reaches any given age x will die before attaining age x + n. The mortality rate for American females at ages forty to forty-five years, for example ($_5q_{40}$ = .0106), tells us that slightly more than 1 percent of all women who survive to age forty will die before reaching forty-five years of age. Mortality rates, then, refer to the whole age interval, rather than to the exact age marking the beginning of the interval.

Although these mortality rates are similar to age-specific death rates, they differ conceptually: mortality rates refer to an initial base population

Table C-1
Abridged Life Table for the Female Population of the United States, 1978

Age interval	Proportion dying	Of 100,000 born alive		Person-years lived		Average remaining lifetime
Period of life between two exact ages stated in years (1)	Proportion of persons alive at beginning of age interval dying during interval (2)	Number living at beginning of age interval (3)	Number dying during age interval (4)	In the age interval (5)	In this and all subsequent age intervals (6)	Average number of years of life remaining at beginning of age interval (7)
x to $x+n$	$_nq_x$	l_x	$_nd_x$	$_nL_x$	T_x	$\overset{\circ}{e}_x$
0–1	0.0122	100,000	1,224	98,934	7,718,382	77.2
1–5	.0024	98,776	234	394,554	7,619,448	77.1
5–10	.0014	98,542	137	492,339	7,224,894	73.3
10–15	.0012	98,405	121	491,753	6,732,555	68.4
15–20	.0028	98,284	272	490,787	6,240,802	63.5
20–25	.0033	98,012	328	489,254	5,750,015	58.7
25–30	.0036	97,684	355	487,562	5,260,761	53.9
30–35	.0044	97,329	428	485,642	4,773,199	49.0
35–40	.0064	96,901	617	483,068	4,287,557	44.2
40–45	.0106	96,284	1,022	479,030	3,804,489	39.5
45–50	.0169	95,262	1,615	472,510	3,325,459	34.9
50–55	.0258	93,647	2,413	462,545	2,852,949	30.5
55–60	.0381	91,234	3,475	447,939	2,390,404	26.2
60–65	.0591	87,759	5,187	426,535	1,942,465	22.1
65–70	.0813	82,572	6,710	397,033	1,515,930	18.4
70–75	.1284	75,862	9,741	356,263	1,118,897	14.7
75–80	.2125	66,121	14,051	296,800	762,634	11.5
80–85	.3178	52,070	16,546	219,198	465,834	8.9
85 and over	1.0000	35,524	35,524	246,636	246,636	6.9

SOURCE: *Vital Statistics of the United States, 1978*, Vol. II, Section 5, *Life Tables* (Hyattsville, Md., National Center for Health Statistics, 1980).

whereas age-specific death rates are based on the average population during a specified time interval. It is therefore necessary to apply a transformation equation to convert one into the other. While certain refinements may be introduced to calculate $_1q_0$ to correct for the very skewed distribution of deaths during infancy, mortality rates can be derived from death rates using the following formula:

$$_nq_x = \frac{2(n)(_nM_x)}{2+(n)(_nM_x)}$$

In this formula $n=$ the number of years in an age interval and $_nM_x=$ the age-specific death rate per person rather than per 1,000 persons. To illustrate, for ages 1–4 years ($n=4$) the 1978 age-specific death rate for American females was .000599. Substituting in the preceding equation,

$$_1q_4 = \frac{2(4)(.000599)}{2+(4)(.000599)} = .00239$$

Similarly, for ages 5–9 ($n=5$) where the observed death rate was .000278,

$$_5q_5 = \frac{2(5)(.000278)}{2+(5)(.000278)} = .00138$$

and so on for all age intervals up to age 85 and over, where the probability that persons who reach that age will eventually die is obviously equal to unity ($q_{85}=1.0$).

Column 3 (Life Table Survivors: l_x). The first entry in this column is called the *radix* of the life table, and gives the total number of live births in the cohort for which the table is being constructed. Although it would be possible to construct a life table based on the actual number of births during a given period, the most common procedure is to select a standard number, usually 100,000, to represent the radix. This facilitates comparisons between life tables depicting the mortality conditions of different population groups. The remaining entries in this column, after the radix, refer to the number of persons out of the original 100,000 who survive to successive *exact* ages. For example, $l_{65}=82,572$ means that out of 100,000 females born in 1978 in the United States, 82,572 will still be alive at age 65. Since the table is based on a standard 100,000 births, the entries in this column also reveal what proportion will still be alive at successive ages. For example, $l_{65}=82,572$ indicates that if the 1978 mortality pattern does not change, then slightly more than four-fifths of all infants (82.6 percent) can be expected to survive until they are 65.

Column 4 (Life Table Deaths: $_nd_x$). The fourth column of the life table, denoted by the symbol $_nd_x$, shows the number of deaths that will occur in the cohort during each age interval. For example, $_5d_{20}=328$ means that of the 98,012 women who survive to age 20 ($l_{20}=98,012$), some 328 will die before the cohort as a whole reaches age 25.

In the construction of a life table, Columns 3 and 4 are calculated simultaneously. Beginning with the radix or first entry in the survivorship column, the number of deaths in each age interval ($_nd_x$) and the corresponding number who survive to the next age interval (l_x) are derived simultaneously from the basic mortality rates ($_nq_x$). To illustrate, the number who will die before attaining 1 year of age ($_1d_0$) is obtained by applying the mortality rate for the population under one year ($_1q_0$) to the number of births in the initial cohort (l_0):

$$(_1q_0)(l_0) = {_1d_0}$$
$$(.01224)(100,000) = 1,224$$

The next entry in the l_x column, or the number who survive to age 1 (l_1), is obtained simply as the difference between the number in the original cohort (l_0) and the number who died during the first age interval ($_1d_0$):

$$l_0 - {_1d_0} = l_1$$
$$100,000 - 1,224 = 98,776$$

This procedure is continued until all of the values for l_x and the $_nd_x$ columns have been entered:

$$\text{Ages 1-4: } (_4q_1)(l_1) = {_4d_1}$$
$$\text{Ages 5-9: } l_1 - {_4d_1} = l_5$$
$$(_5q_5)(l_5) = {_5d_5}$$
$$\text{Ages 10-14: } l_5 - {_5d_5} = l_{10}$$
$$(_5q_{10})(l_{10}) = {_5d_{10}}, \text{ etc.}$$

Column 5 (Number of Years Lived within Each Age Interval: $_nL_x$). The fifth column of the life table shows the number of person-years lived during an age interval by those members of the original cohort who survived to enter that interval. For example, $_5L_{35}=483,068$ means that the 96,901 persons who survived to exact age 35 ($l_{35}=96,901$), lived a total of 483,068 years between the time they reached 35 up until the cohort as a whole attained age 40. The values in this column are obtained by a method of interpolation between successive values of l_x. They are roughly equivalent to the arithmetic mean of the two l_x values marking off a given age interval (weighted by the number of years in the interval), and are derived on the assumption that all deaths within a given age interval are evenly distributed throughout that interval. To illustrate, if there were no deaths between exact ages 35 and 40, then the 96,901 survivors to age 35 would each live five years during the interval, or a total of 484,505 years (96,901 times five years). There were 617 deaths during the interval, however ($_5d_{35} = 617$), so that only 96,284 persons actually survived to age 40 ($l_{40} = 96,284$). If all of these deaths had occurred precisely at the time the cohort reached age 35, then there would have been only 96,284 persons living during the interval. Each of these would have lived 5 years, making a total of 481,420 person-years lived during the interval (96,284 times five years). The deaths did not occur precisely at age 35, however, but took place at various times during the interval; some died at age 36, others died at age 37, etc. Thus, the total number of person-years actually lived during the interval must fall somewhere between 481,420 and 484,505, which it in fact does: $_5L_{35} = 483,068$.

Although a somewhat more sophisticated procedure was used in calculating the national female life table included here, it is possible (and fairly common practice) to make the assumption that deaths in an age interval are evenly distributed throughout the interval, and then calculate the number of person-years lived in an age interval using this formula:

$$_nL_x = (n)(l_x - \tfrac{1}{2}d_x)$$

If this formula was used in the preceding example for American women age 35–40 years the following results would have been obtained:

$$_5L_{35} = (5)(96,901 - \frac{617}{2})$$

$$_5L_{35} = 482,963$$

This compares with a value of 483,068 in Table C-1, and is a difference of only 105 person-years (0.02 percent).

For the first year of life, where the assumption of an even distribution of deaths is clearly not applicable (i.e., the vast majority of all infant deaths occur during the first few weeks after birth), the preceding formula should not be used. A number of alternative procedures may be used to calculate the number of person-years lived during the first interval; but for developed countries where infant mortality is reasonably well under control, perhaps the simplest procedure is to use the following formula (Weller and Bouvier, 1981, p. 334):

$$_1L_0 = l_0 - (.9)(_1d_0)$$

In this example,

$$_1L_0 = 100,000 - (.9)(1224)$$

$$_1L_0 = 98,898$$

This compares to a volume of 98,934 in Table C-1—a difference of only 35 years, or 0.03 percent.

At the oldest age, where the interval is open, still another method must be used to derive an estimate of the number of person-years lived. The most common procedure here is to calculate the desired value as the ratio of the number of survivors at age 85 to the death rate for persons age 85 and over:

$$L_{85} = \frac{l_{85}}{M_{85}}$$

Had this approximating procedure been used in the present illustration, the results would have been $(35,524) \div (.135412) = 262,340$ person-years lived at ages 85 and over by those women who survived to age 85.

Column 6 (Total Number of Years Lived by the Cohort from Age x until All Have Died: T_x). Each member of the cohort of 100,000 live births will live a specified number of years. Some, of course, will die in infancy; others, however, will live 70, 80, or even 90 years, and a few will live even longer. The total number of years the cohort will live as a whole from birth until all have died is represented by the first entry in the sixth column of the life table (T_0). Each subsequent entry in this column indicates the total years of life remaining to the survivors at each succeeding exact year of age. For example, $T_{35} = 4,287,557$ means that the 96,901 persons who survive to exact age 35 ($l_{35} = 96,901$) will live a total of 4,287,557 more years before the last survivor has died.

For age 85 and over, the number of years to be lived "in this and all subsequent intervals" is obviously identical to the number of years lived "in the age interval." That is,

$$L_{85} = T_{85}$$

For all other ages the total number of years that remain to be lived by the survivors to any given age x is simply the cumulative sum of the number of years lived during the age interval x to x+n by the survivors to age x, *plus* the number of years lived in all succeeding intervals. To illustrate, if 219,198 years are lived during the interval 80–84 years by persons who survive to age 80 ($_5L_{80} = 219,198$), and if persons who survive to age 85 live an additional 246,636 years before all have died ($L_{85} = 246,636$), then the number of years of life remaining to survivors at exact age 80 (T_{80}) is $219,198 + 246,636 = 465,834$ years. Similarly:

$$T_{75} = {}_5L_{75} + {}_5L_{80} + L_{85}$$
$$T_{70} = {}_5L_{70} + {}_5L_{75} + {}_5L_{80} + L_{85}, \text{ etc.}$$

Column 7 (Average Remaining Lifetime: $\overset{o}{e}_x$): The values in the last column of the life table indicate the number of years, on the average, that will be lived by *each* survivor to exact age x. For example $\overset{o}{e}_{65} = 18.4$ years means that each woman who survives to age 65 can expect to live an average of 18.4 more years. Again, the relationship between the entries in this column and the entries in columns 3 and 6 should be obvious. If 82,572 women survived to age 65 ($l_{65} = 82,572$), and if the survivors to exact age 65 can expect to live a total of 1,515,930 years before all have died ($T_{65} = 1,515,930$), then the average number of years that each individual survivor can expect to live is computed simply as:

$$8_{65} = \frac{T_{65}}{l_{65}} = \frac{1,515,930}{82,572} = 18.4$$

The most important entry in this column, perhaps the most important single entry in the entire life table, is the first entry, $\overset{o}{e}_0$. This entry is the *expectation of life at birth*, and tells how long, on the average, each individual in the birth cohort would live if the age-specific death rates prevailing at the time of birth remained constant throughout the cohort's lifetime. Thus, it is one of the most meaningful measures available for use in comparing the relative mortality conditions characterizing different population groups.

THE STATIONARY POPULATION

The preceding discussion of the life table columns is based on the conventional interpretations of the life table as the death history of a hypothetical cohort as it passes through life experiencing the age-specific death rates prevailing at the time of its birth. An alternative interpretation is to conceive of the life table in terms of the stationary population concept. A *stationary population* is one in which the annual number of births and deaths is the same so that the size of the population remains constant (i.e., stationary) from year to year. That population would ultimately rise if a constant number of births occurred each year, and if each birth cohort was, throughout its life, subjected to the same unchanging set of age-specific death rates. In constructing a conventional life table, it is customary to start with 100,000 live births and subject them to the observed age-specific death rates prevailing at the time of birth until all are dead. Now, *if* these age-specific death rates did not change, and *if* each year there was an additional 100,000 live births, *then, by the time all of the initial cohort had died there would be a population of unchanging size in which each year there were 100,000 live births and 100,000 deaths*; that is, a *stationary population*.

The idea of the stationary population can be explained quite simply by means of a hypothetical illustration. Suppose, for example, that there are 100,000 live births in one year, and that these births are subjected to a mortality rate during the first year of life of 25 per 1,000. At the end of the first year of life, then (according to the death history interpretation of the life table), there would be $100,000 - [(100,000)(.025)] = 97,500$ survivors from the original cohort, or a total population of 97,500 individuals all one year of age. According to the stationary population interpretation, however, the end of the first year of life would see the addition of another 100,000 live births, yielding a population of 97,500 persons one year of age *plus* 100,000 newborn infants, or a total population of 197,500:

	Death History	Stationary Population
Start of 1st year, age 0	100,000	100,000
Start of 2nd year, age 0	. . .	100,000
age 1	97,500	97,500

To continue this illustration, suppose that there were 100 annual deaths during the age interval 1–2 years. Then, at the end of the second year of life, according to the death history interpretation, there would be a population of $97,500 - 100 = 97,400$ persons two years of age. Viewed in terms of the stationary population, however, the end of the second year of life would see a population of 97,400 two-year-olds who had survived from the first cohort, *plus* 97,500 one-year-olds who had survived from the second cohort, *plus* a third cohort of still another 100,000 live births:

	Death History	Stationary Population
Start of 1st year, age 0	100,000	100,000
Start of 2nd year, age 0	. . .	100,000
age 1	97,500	97,500
Start of 3rd year, age 0	. . .	100,000
age 1	. . .	97,500
age 2	97,400	97,400

And so forth until all of the original cohort had died, at which time the 100,000 live births each year would be matched by an equal number of deaths, and the stationary population would be in effect.

While these two interpretations of the life table (the death history and the stationary population) in no way conflict with each other, they may be confusing to the beginning student unless he or she distinguishes carefully between them. The major difference between the two interpretations consists of a slight modification in the meaning of some of the life table columns when the stationary population interpretation is used. There would be no change in the interpretation of x to x+n, $_nq_x$, or $\overset{o}{e}_x$, but the other columns would take on a slightly different meaning. The most significant change would be in the $_nL_x$ column. In a death history, the entries in this column indicate the number of person-years lived during a specified age interval by the survivors at the start of the interval. In terms of the stationary population these values represent the number of persons who would be alive at any time in the age interval. That is, this column represents the age distribution of the stationary population at any one point in time. The interpretation of the remaining columns would be as follows:

l_x The number of persons who reach the beginning of the age interval *each year.*

$_nd_x$ The number of persons who die *each year* within the specified age interval.

T_x The number of persons who at any time are alive at age x and over, with T_o representing the total size of the stationary population.

Each of these two interpretations has its special uses in demographic analysis. The stationary population interpretation, for example, is used in comparative mortality measurement and in studies of population structure; the death history interpretation is used in various kinds of mortality analysis, and in the calculation of survival rates for use in estimating population, net migration, and reproductivity. Some of these more common uses are illustrated in the following section.

USES OF THE LIFE TABLE

While an extensive consideration of the many uses of life tables in demographic analysis is far beyond the scope of this introductory volume, a few simple examples can be presented to demonstrate its value and versatility in areas other than mortality analysis.

Net Reproduction Rate

In Appendix B, the net reproduction rate (NRR) was introduced as a measure of generational replacement. It is defined specifically as the number of daughters that will be born to a cohort of women under the assumed conditions of unchanging age-specific birth and death rates. A net reproduction rate of 1.0 indicates an average of one daughter per woman and means that

Table C-2
Computation of Reproduction Rates for the United States, 1978

Age of mother	Age-specific birth rates*	Person-years lived in age interval $_nL_x$	Estimated births (col. 2) × (col. 3)
(1)	(2)	(3)	(4)
15–19	.0524	490,787	25,717
20–24	.1123	489,254	54,943
25–29	.1120	487,562	54,607
30–34	.0591	485,642	28,701
35–39	.0189	483,068	9,130
40–44	.0039	479,030	1,868
Total 15–44	.3586	...	174,966

Female birth percent $= \dfrac{\text{female births}}{\text{total births}} = \dfrac{1{,}623{,}885}{3{,}333{,}279} = .487$

TFR = 5 × sum of age-specific birth rates = 5 (.3586) = 1.79

GRR = TFR × female birth percent = 1.79 × .487 = .87

NRR $= \dfrac{\text{sum of estimated births}}{100{,}000} \times$ female birth percent

$= \dfrac{174{,}996}{100{,}000} \times .487 = 1.75 \times .487 = .85$

* SOURCE: *Monthly Vital Statistics Report,* Advance Report, *Final Natality Statistics, 1978* (Hyattsville, Md., National Center for Health Statistics, 1980).

a cohort is replacing itself exactly. A value greater than 1.0 indicates the extent to which a cohort is overproducing itself and a value of less than 1.0 indicates that the fertility of a population has fallen below replacement level. If fertility remains below the replacement level for a protracted period of time, and in the absence of any migration, the population will eventually begin to decline.

In order to calculate an NRR we need to know (1) the age-specific birth rates, (2) the proportion of births that are female, and (3) the number of females who will survive to bear children at specified ages. The first two values are obtained from conventional vital statistics sources; the number of survivors is obtained from the stationary population column ($_nL_x$) of an appropriate life table. Once these data have been gathered the computation of the NRR is a relatively simple matter.

Table C-2 illustrates the procedure for calculating the gross and net reproduction rates for the United States in 1978. Column 1 of the table denotes age intervals; column 2 contains the 1978 age-specific birth rates; column 3 shows the number of women who will survive to have babies in each age interval (taken from column 5 in Table C-1); and column 4, obtained by multiplying the figures in columns 2 and 3, indicates the total number of births that the women will have at each age. The gross reproduction rate (GRR), defined more fully in Appendix B, is simply the total fertility rate (TFR) adjusted for the proportion of births that are female (.487 in this illustration). Thus, in our example in Table C-2 the TFR, which is an estimate of the total number of children each woman will bear, is calculated as the sum of the age-specific birth rates in column 2 multiplied by 5, or the number of years in each age interval (TFR=1.79); and the GRR is derived as the product of the TFR and the percent of births that are female (GRR=1.79×.487=.87). In a somewhat similar manner the NRR is calculated by first summing up the total number of births to all women (column 4), dividing this sum by 100,000 (the size of the initial life table cohort) to estimate the number of births per woman, and multiplying this value by the female birth percent. Following these steps yields a 1978 NRR for the United States of .85 daughters per woman. This rate is less than 1.0, which means that if the prevailing age-specific birth and death rates remain unchanged, the cohort of women born in 1978 will not replace themselves during their reproductive years.

A final word of caution: neither the GRR nor the NRR should be regarded as predictive. All that either measure does is take cross-sectional birth rates (and death rates in the case of the NRR) and project future childbearing performance on the assumption that the rates will remain constant. However, these rates do not remain constant, particularly the age-specific birth rates, and any changes in the base pattern of either fertility or mortality in the years ahead will lead to a level of reproduction that differs markedly from that indicated by the 1978 rates.

Survival Rates

A particularly useful measure that can be derived from a life table is the rate at which persons in a population are surviving from one age group to another. Such survival rates are easily calculated from the stationary population column ($_nL_x$) as the ratio of the number of survivors in an age interval to the number in the preceding interval. To illustrate, the rate at which American women were surviving the age interval 55–60 years in 1978 can be calculated as follows:

$$\frac{_5L_{60}}{_5L_{55}} = \frac{426{,}535}{447{,}939} = .9522$$

This tells us that under the mortality conditions prevailing in 1978, some 95 percent of the women alive at ages 55–60 years will still be alive at ages 60–64 years. (Note that survival rates can also be calculated from the sur-

Table C-3
Illustrative Use of Survival Rates in Estimating Migration and Projecting a Base Population

Age	Enumerated population, 1975	Age-specific survival rates	Estimated population, 1980	Enumerated population, 1980	Estimated migration, 1975–80	Projected population, 1985
0–4	500	.95	...	500	...	...
5–9	400	.90	475	480	+5	475
10–14	300	.85	360	350	−10	432
15–19	200	.80	255	250	−5	298
20–24	100	...	160	175	+15	200

vivorship column, l_x, to measure the rate of survival from one specific age to another).

Migration Estimates and Population Projections

Survival rates have a number of important uses in formal demographic analysis. Two of the more common uses are in estimating migration and in projecting future populations. To take a simple illustration, consider the hypothetical data presented in Table C-3. In the case of migration, survival rates are used to project a base population from one date to another on the assumption that there will be *no migration*. Any difference between the projected population and the number actually enumerated at the later time is then attributed to migration. Thus, if there were 500 persons at ages 0–4 in 1975 and the five-year survival rate for this age group is .95 there will be $500 \times .95 = 475$ survivors at ages 5–9 in 1980. If the population actually enumerated at ages 5–9 in 1980 is 480, it would indicate 5 more people than could have survived from the earlier date, and these 5 additional persons are counted as net in-migrants. Following this procedure for the other age groups in our example results in estimated migration losses of 10 and 5 respectively at ages 10–14 and 15–19 years, and a net migration gain of 15 at ages 20–24.

A simple projection of the population at some future date can be arrived at in a similar manner. In this case, by making the assumption that the 1975–80 survival rates will not change, the number of survivors in 1985 is projected in the same manner as the 1980 estimates were derived. These projected survivors represent an estimate of what the population would be in 1985 if in fact survival rates do not change (i.e., if mortality levels remain constant) *and* if there is no net migration gain or loss. In formal demographic analyses the procedures are generally much more complex than those just described (e.g., other calculations may be introduced to derive estimates of the youngest group, or adjustments will be made to add in some kind of migration component), but the examples presented here should suffice to illustrate the potential uses and value of life table survival rates.

REFERENCES AND SUGGESTED READING

Shryock, Henry S., Jacob S. Siegel, et al. *The Methods and Materials of Demography*, condensed ed. by E. G. Stockwell. New York: Academic Press, 1976. Chapter 15 of this text describes life tables and procedures for constructing them, but illustrative uses of life tables in various areas of demographic analysis are found throughout.

Weeks, John R. *Population: An Introduction to Concepts and Issues*, 2nd ed. Belmont, Calif.: Wadsworth, 1981, pp. 371–76.

Weller, Robert H., and Leon F. Bouvier. *Population: Demography and Policy*. New York: St. Martin's, 1981, pp. 333–43.

PICTURE CREDITS

Franklin Watts, Inc., is grateful to Diane Raines Ward of Carousel and Patrick Bunyan of the American Heritage Library. All the phototgraphs are from the files of the United Nations, unless otherwise noted below.

Pages 88–91: Egyptian wall painting-Metropolitan Museum; *The Plague*-Walters Art Gallery; L. Pasteur-French Embassy; A. Fleming-National Library of Medicine

Pages 171–174: Texas family-Brown Brothers; Stephan Dohanus' *Pediatrician's Office*-Rubin Collection; Easter family-UPI

Pages 213–215: M. Sanger-UPI; A. Comstock-Pach; Cartoon-New York Public Library

Pages 282–285: T. Malthus-National Portrait Gallery; *Triumph of Death* - Palazzo Sclafoni, Palermo; K. Marx-German Information Center; Thai children-Carey Winfrey; Malthus cartoon-Bettmann Archive

Pages 358–361: Ellis Island-National Archives; Railroad-Union Pacific Railroad; Bulletin board-Viviane Holbrook, Wheeler Pictures; Moving day-J. R. Eyerman, *Life* magazine; Mexican immigrants-Steve Smith, Wheeler Pictures; Baby boomers-Enrico Ferorelli, Wheeler Pictures

Pages 400–403: African children-Carey Winfrey; Old people on bench-Carey Winfrey; Woman working-Enrico Ferorelli, Wheeler Pictures

SUBJECT INDEX

Abortion, 189–190, 207, 230, 237
    Eastern Europe, 195, 220, 222
    induced, 41, 205–207
    spontaneous, 131
    United States, 206–207
Abstinence, 142, 144, 192
Accidents, deaths from, 84
Acute diseases. See Infectious diseases.
Adolescent pregnancy. See Teenage fertility.
Africa, population growth trends, 42–46, 248
Age, 405–408
    cause of death, 96
    effects on fertility, 336–337
    life cycle, 406
    at marriage, 137–141, 154, 157
    in relation to:
        education, 424, 427
        employment status, 442
        fecundity, 131
        income, 435
        labor force participation, 441
        mobility, 368, 369
        mortality, 94–102, 474
        nativity, 422
    social significance of, 405
Age pyramid. See Population pyramids.
Aging, of population, 407–408, 415
    index of, 407
    problems of, 413
Agricultural Revolution, 66
Air pollution, 71, 347–348
    See also Environmental pollution.
Aliens, 307–308, 422
Antinatalism. See Population policy.
Antisepsis, 70
Artificial insemination, 178

Asepsis, 70
Asia, population growth trends, 46–49, 248
Asian Flu, 79
Asiatic Barred Zone, 302
Assimilation of immigrants, 287, 314–317

Baby Boom, 54, 156–158, 332–333, 412–413
    echo boom, 158
Baby Bust, 158–159
Basal body temperature, method of birth control, 200
Besant, Annie, 186, 188
"Beyond Family Planning," 232
Bills of Mortality, 461
Birth, defined, 58, 130
    See also Fertility.
Birth control. See Family planning movement; Fertility control.
Birth order, 131
Birth rate, defined, 27, 482, 484
Birth Registration Area, 462
Black Death, 64
Black population in the U.S.
    fertility, 162
    growth trends, 421–422
    internal migration, 380, 381, 387–388
    mortality, 108–110
    socioeconomic characteristics, 430, 433, 442
Bradlaugh, Charles, 186
Brain Drain, 309
Breast feeding, as a means of birth control, 193
Brown, Louise, 176

Calendar method (birth control), 200
Calvinism, 152

Cancer, 83
   and cigarette smoking, 84, 106, 125
Cardiovascular diseases, U.S. trends in, 81, 82–84
Caribbean area population
   growth trends, 50–51
Carrying capacity, 250, 293, 313
Cause of death, 59–60
   age differences, 96
   endogenous, 59, 82, 84, 98, 99
   exogenous, 59, 82, 84, 98, 99
   infant mortality, 98–100
   mortality stabilization, 81
   sex differences, 105–106
   U.S. trends, 82–84, 107, 120
   See also specific causes
Census. *See* Population censuses.
Central cities,
   growth trends, 386–388
Cervical cap, 203
Cervical mucus method (birth control), 200
Child spacing, 175, 180
Child–woman ratio, 488
Childlessness, 158
China, People's Republic of, 3, 7, 32, 47, 148, 154, 188, 228, 229, 235–240, 272, 276, 318
   population policy, 235–240
      one-child family, 238–240
Chinese Exclusion Act, 301, 322
Chronic diseases,
   changing importance of, 120
   trends in, 82–84
Cohabitation, 142
Cohort fertility, 482, 485–486
Coitus interruptus, 185, 199
Color. *See* Race.
Comestock, Anthony, 224
Communicable diseases. *See* Infectious diseases.
Completed family size, defined, 131
Composition. *See* Population composition.
Conception,
   exposure to, 133
Condom, 198
Contraception. *See* Fertility control.
Contraceptive awareness, 193
Contraceptive effectiveness, 196–198
   measurement of, 197
Contraceptive use, 193–195
   in the United States, 184, 194, 195–197
Cultural assimilation, 316
Cultural change,
   fertility decline, 152
   material/nonmaterial, 65, 152
   mortality decline, 65–68
Cultural contribution of immigrants, 313–314
Current Population Survey, 110

DDT, 67, 71, 74
Death rate:
   age-adjusted, 476–477
   age-specific, 475–476
   cause, specific, 82, 479
   in Colonial America, 77
   defined, 27, 58, 60, 474
Death ratio, 480
Death registration in the U.S., 76–77
Death Registration Area, 72, 462
Deficit fertility, 176–178
Demographic balance, defined, 34
Demographic data. *See* Population data
Demographic gap, 36
Demographic processes, 13–14
   See also Fertility; Mortality; Migration.
Demographic transition, 33, 34*ff*
   accelerated, 41
   classical model, 34–38
   less developed countries, 38–41
   stages of, 36–38
   Sweden, 40–41
Demographic variables, 12
Demography, 12
   defined, 17
   formal demography, 14, 16
   relevance to sociology, 19
   social demography, 14, 15–16
Density, 377
Dependency, economic, 261, 262
Depo-Provera, 208
Depopulation, European fear of, 200
Developed countries:
   age composition, 413, 414
   fertility, 132
   fertility decline, 38, 148–153
   mortality, 72
   population growth trends, 52, 53–54
Developing countries:
   demographic transition in, 38–41
   fertility trends, 144*ff*
   food consumption levels, 265–268
   internal migration, 389, 394
   population growth and economic development, 250–258
   population growth trends, 6, 32–33, 38–41, 248, 251–258, 276–277
   urbanization, 390–394
   See also specific regions.
Diaphragm, 203
Dioxin, 71
Disincentives, fertility, 235
Displaced Persons Act, 304
Distribution. *See* Population distribution.
Division, geographic, 337
   differential growth trends, 375–379
Doubling time, 28, 32

Echo boom, 158
Economic development, and population growth, 227, 250–258
Education:
    advantages of, 430, 436
    social significance of, 423–424
Educational attainment:
    group differences in, 429–430
    in relation to:
        age, 428
        income, 436
    trends, 427–428
Elderly population, 407–408
    international variations in size, 413–415
Ellis Island, 302
Emigrant, 290
Emigration policies, 321, 322
Endogenous causes of death, 59, 82, 84
    in infancy, 98–99
Energy consumption, problems of, 340–342
    in less developed countries, 274–275, 342
Environmental pollution, 5, 71, 347–349
Epidemic diseases, 64–65, 72
    1918 influenza epidemic, 65, 79
Errors in demographic data, 469–471
Ethnic characteristics, 420–423
    basis for discrimination, 303–305
    regional variations, 380, 381
    See also Nativity; Race.
Europe, population growth trends, 52, 53–54
European Fertility Project, 154
European marriage pattern, 138
European population explosion, 31
Excess fertility, 176, 178
Exogenous causes of death, 59, 82, 84
    in infancy, 98, 99
Expectation of life. See Life expectancy.
Exposure to intercourse, 136–143
Extended family, 138

Family, 419
    influence on fertility, 138, 153
    one child family, 238–240
    one parent family, 435
    two income family, 434
Family planning. See Fertility control.
Family planning movement, 187–189
    European origins of, 185–186
    United States, 187
Family size norms, 131, 134, 135, 143–144, 146, 233, 236
    historical, 144–145
    religious influence, 147
    small family ethos, 152
    status of women, 147
Famine, 63
    modern threat of, 268

Fecundity, 131
    impairments, 176, 177, 216
Fertility:
    cost-benefit analysis, 150, 159, 233
    definitions and concepts, 130–132
    disincentives, 235
    factors affecting, 130, 132*ff*
    future outlook, 154, 159–169
    measurement of, 482–488
    timing of, 176, 178, 180–181
    trends in:
        developed country, 148–153, 220–221
        developing countries, 144–148, 227, 229, 239, 276
        United States, 155*ff*
    See also following specific topics.
Fertility and family size, 134–135, 155, 233
    attitudes toward, 134, 176, 188
    in developing societies, 144, 145
    nonwhite, 162
    religion, 147, 165–166
Fertility awareness techniques, 199–201
Fertility control:
    age, 183, 194, 195, 196
    antinatalist policies toward, 223–224
    attitudes toward, 186, 190, 218
    current legislation, 191, 206
    history of, 184–190
    India, 188, 206, 225, 230–232, 234
    individual *versus* societal fertility, 218, 219, 233
    in less developed countries, 144, 193–195, 206
    means *versus* motivation, 175, 195–197, 219, 224
    methods of, 192*ff*, 208
    moral restraint, 186, 264
    nonprescription methods, 198–201
    official American policy toward, 217, 223
    opposition to, 188–189, 224
    People's Republic of China, 188, 206, 228–229, 235
    perfect contraception, 191
    prescription methods, 201–203
    primitive methods, 185
    pronatalist policies toward, 220–223
    religion, 165–166, 189, 204
    Singapore, 226–227, 235
    United States, 186, 187, 191, 195–197, 201, 204, 217, 223–224
    See also specific methods (e.g., Condom).
Fertility decline:
    Asia, 47
    baby bust, 158–159
    below replacement level, 158, 220
    effects on age composition, 407–408
    historical trend, 148–53

industrialization, 152, 155
Latin America, 49
less developed countries, 147–148, 276
more developed countries, 148–153
mortality decline, 136, 145
prospects for in less developed countries, 154, 276–277
role of contraception, 158, 226–229
Sri Lanka, 41, 154
status of women, 153
Sweden, 40, 148, 149
United States, 156
urbanization, 152, 154, 155
Fertility differentials, 161ff
female labor force participation, 164, 165
international differences, 162, 163–165
race, 162
religion, 162, 164, 165–166
significance of, 161
socioeconomic status, 163, 164
urban-rural residence, 163, 164
Fertility increase, as a response to development, 36, 277
Fertility inducements, 6, 146–147
Fertility levels:
  determinants of, 130, 131, 180
  influence of:
    age composition, 137
    family size norms, 131, 143–144
    family type, 138
    religion, 152–153, 423
    social structure, 6, 145–146
  in less developed countries, 144–145
  in relation to mortality levels, 34, 129, 136, 143–144, 145
  in the United States, 155ff
  pre-historical, 143–144
  See also Fertility; Fertility decline; Fertility differentials.
Fertility ratio, 488
Fetal mortality, 58, 131
Fleming, Alexander, 70
Food and Agricultural Organization, 6, 268, 270
Food supply, 267
  fertility, 151–152
  mortality, 63, 65, 66, 72
  problems of, 249, 256–257, 263ff, 271, 339–340
  prospects for increasing, 265–266, 269–272
  uneven distribution of, 266–268, 271
Forced migration, 290, 318
Foreign born. See Nativity.
Foreign stock. See Nativity.
Fossil fuels, depletion of, 274
Freedom, population as a threat to, in the United States, 349–354
Functional illiterate, 436

General fertility rate, 483
Gentleman's Agreement, 301
Gentrification, 388
Geographic mobility. See Internal migration.
Germ theory, 70, 71
Germany, Democratic-Republic, 220, 222, 322
Gestation, defined, 130
Gestation variables, 134
Green Revolution, 266
Gross National Product (GNP), per capita, 249, 253
Gross reproduction rate, 487
Guest worker programs, 319

Head of household. See Householder.
Health. See Morbidity.
Heart disease, 82, 83, 96
Hispanic population, United States, 422–423, 430, 433
Homestead Laws, 376, 395
Household, 419–420
Householder, 419
Housing, and mortality, 64
Hua Guofeng, 3
Hutterites, 132

Illegal immigration, 306, 307–308, 336, 422
Illegitimacy, 143, 181
Illness. See Morbidity
Immigrant, 290
  See also Immigration
Immigration, United States, 295ff
  causes of, 297–299
  colonization, 295–296
  consequences of, 296, 310–317
  current legislation, 305–308
  economic growth, 312–313
  illegal, 306, 307–308, 336, 422
  mass migration, 297–301
  problems of, 314–317
  population growth, 310–312, 331
  quotas, 303–304
  restriction of, 301–305
  social and cultural contributions of, 313–314
  See also Immigration policies.
Immigration and Naturalization Service, 464
Immigration policies, 320–322
  Great Britain, 287, 322
  United States, 301–308
  U.S.S.R., 321
Immunization, 69–70, 78
Immunology, 69
Income, 430–436
  differentials, 433–436
  international differences, 248
  mortality, 113–115

per capita, 248, 249, 251, 253
  real income, 431–432
  social significance of, 430–431, 436
  trends, 431–433
India, 7, 49, 137, 142, 148, 154, 188, 225, 234, 271, 272, 273
  population policy, 230–232
Industrial Revolution, 31, 35, 66, 251
  See also Industrialization.
Industrialization:
  effects on fertility, 152
  mortality, 66–67
Industrialized countries. See Developed countries.
Infant mortality, 5, 60, 74, 76, 97–102, 103, 183
  cause of death, 98–100
  color, 108
  in developing countries, 73, 100–102, 113
  socioeconomic status, 60, 113–115
  trends in the United States, 97–100
  in U.S.S.R., 101–102
Infant Mortality Rate, 74, 477–478
Infanticide, 144
Infectious diseases, 69, 78, 100, 120
Infecundity, 131
Influenza, 1918 epidemic, 65, 79, 80
In-migrant (In-migration), 291, 309–310, 491
Intercourse, exposure to, 136–143
Intercourse variables, 133
Intermediate variables, 133–136
Internal migration:
  age, 368, 369
  defined, 365
  in less developed countries, 389, 390–394
  policies, 393, 394–396
  problems of, 371–374
  socioeconomic status, 369–370
  United States, 365ff, 375
  See also Migration; Migration differentials; Migration streams; Population mobility.
International migration:
  cultural conflict, 287, 314–316
  defined, 290, 291
  future outlook, 323
  historical, 293–295
  in the world today, 306–308, 318–320
  policies, 320–322
  See also Emigration; Immigration; Migration.
International Planned Parenthood Federation, 225
Intervening obstacles, 292
Intrauterine device (IUD), 202–203
In vitro fertilization, 178, 216

Japan, 19, 34, 137, 148, 301, 389
Jenner, Edward, 69

Job Corps, 10

KAP Studies, 192
Kenya, 44, 46, 261, 413, 414
Knowlton, Charles, 186
Koch, Robert, 69, 96
!Kung, 144

Labor force:
  concepts, 437
  differential participation, 441–444
  female participation, and fertility, 164, 165
  occupation, 440–444
  participation rate, 438
  social significance of, 437
  trends, United States, 438–440
Latin America, population growth trends, 49–52, 248
Length of life. See Life expectancy.
Leparoscopy, 204
Less developed countries. See Developing countries.
Lifeboat ethic, 122–123, 343–344, 355
Life cycle, 406
Life expectancy:
  defined, 59, 478, 502
  historical, 5, 29, 59, 61
  international differences, 59, 63
Life span, 58
Life style, and mortality, 82, 104–105, 125
Life table. See Appendix C.
Lister, Joseph, 70
Literacy, international differences, 445
Literacy test, 302
Little Comestock laws, 224
Local moves, 289
Longevity, 58

McCarran-Walter Act, 304
Malaysia, 226
Malnutrition, 5, 63, 171
Malthus, Thomas R., 186, 188, 253, 264–265
Malthusian, 219, 236, 253–254
Man-land ratio. See Density.
Marginal man, 287, 315
Marital status:
  exposure to intercourse, 137–138
  mortality, 116–118
  social significance of, 416
  trends in the U.S., 416–419
Marriage, age at, 137–138
Marriage boom, 416
Marriage rate, 139
Marriage squeeze, 140, 417, 418
Marx, Karl, 188, 219, 254–255
Massachusetts, early vital statistics, 77
Maternal mortality, 103

Medical science, death control, 71, 72
  See also Public Health; Sanitation.
Medicare, 10
Megalopolis, 345
Menarche, 131
Menopause, 131
Menstrual extraction, 202
Menstrual regulation, 190, 202
Mental illness, migration and, 372
Metropolitan community, 386
  expansion of, 386–388
Metropolitanization, 385, 387, 388
Mexico, 261, 287, 319, 362
Middle East, population growth trends, 309, 319
Migrant, U.S. definition of, 364–365
Migration:
  causes of (push-pull), 291–293, 391–392
  concepts and types, 289–291, 364–365
  consequences of, 287–288, 308–317
  definition, 286, 289
  illegal, 306, 307–308, 336
  measurement of, 488, 489–490, 491, 507
  origin and destination areas, 291–292
  population distribution, 287–288, 293, 374–388
  problems of data, 286
  refugees, 304, 306, 318
  repeated, 363
  social significance of, 287–288
  sources of data, 463–464, 489–490
  voluntary, 290
  See also Internal migration. International migration; and following specific topics.
Migration differentials, 367–371
  age, 368, 369, 410
  color, 368
  mental health, 372
  problems of, 372
  sex, 367
  socioeconomic status, 369–370
Migration streams, 292, 319–320
  black population, 288, 380
  east-to-west, 374–378
  rural-to-urban, 380–384
  to rural areas, 384–385
  to the Sunbelt, 288, 378–379
  Suburbanization, 386–388
Mini-pill, 201
Mistimed births, 179, 180–181
Mobility. See Migration.
Moral restraint, 264
Morbidity, 120–121
  measurement of, 480–482
  relative nature of, 121
Morning after pill, 202
Mortality:
  attitudes toward, 6
  crossover, 109
  definition and concepts, 58–60
  measurement of, 60, 474–480
  policies, 121–123
  population growth, 36
  See also Cause of death; and following specific topics.
Mortality decline, 6
  agricultural development, 66
  causes of, 30–31, 65ff, 99–100
  food supply, 35, 66
  industrialization, 35–40
  less developed countries, 73–76, 277
  medical science, 71, 96
  public health and sanitation control, 68–71
  Sri Lanka, 40–41
  stages of, 72
  Sweden, 40, 61–62
  United States trends, 77ff, 94–95
  See also Mortality trends.
Mortality differentials, 92ff
  age, 94–102
  color, 107–110
  divisions and states, 119
  international, 92, 95, 100–102, 103–104
  life-style, 82, 84, 104–105, 125
  marital status, 116–118
  nativity, 107
  occupation, 111, 112
  sex, 102–107, 418
  significance of, 93
  socioeconomic status, 110–115, 121
  urban-rural residence, 118–119
Mortality levels:
  in antiquity, 5, 29, 61, 63
  colonial America, 77
  fertility, 34, 136, 145
  food supply, 63
  in less developed countries, 38–39, 73
  physical environment, 64–65
  pre-industrial, 35
  United States, 76
  See also Mortality differentials; Mortality trends.
Mortality ratio, 112
Mortality trends:
  cause of death, 82–84
  future outlook, 123–125
  less developed countries, 73–76
  modern era, 65ff
  pre-1900, 77–78
  twentieth century, 78–82
  United States, 77ff, 82, 94, 104–105, 109–110
  See also Mortality decline.

National Center for Health Statistics (NCHS), 463, 465, 467

National Origins Quota System, 303–305, 320
    discriminatory basis, 303
    repeal of, 305
National Survey of Family Growth, 194, 465
Nativity, 421–423
    age, 422
    mortality, 107–108
    social significance of, 420, 423
Natural fertility, 132
Natural increase, rate of, 27, 334, 486
Natural resources, depletion of, 340–341
Neomalthusian, 254
Neonatal mortality, 97, 98, 100, 478–479
Net migration, 492–493
Net production rate, 487, 504–505
"New" immigrants, 298, 301
    discrimination against, 301–305
New International Economic Order (NIEO), 255, 343
Nixon, Richard M., 3, 217
Nonfamily household, 419, 420
Nonmetropolitan areas, growth of, 384–385
Nonmigrant, 365
Non-quota immigration, 305, 306

Obesity, and mortality, 125
Occupation:
    death rates by, 111, 112
        group differences, 443–444
        trends, 440–441
"Old" immigrants, 298, 302
One-child family, 238–240
One-parent family, 435
Open spaces, loss of, 344–345
Opportunity costs of children, 150, 159, 165
Oral contraceptives, 201–202
Organization of Petroleum Exporting Countries (OPEC), 266, 273, 310
Out-migrant (Out-migration), 291, 309, 491–492
Overseas Development Council, 249
Ovulation, 199, 200
Ozone layer, 348

Parasitic disease. See Infectious diseases.
Parity, 131
Parturition, defined, 130
Pasteur, Louis, 69, 71, 96
Per capita daily calorie intake, 266, 267
Period fertility, 482
Pesticides, 67
Physical Quality of Life Index (PQLI), 249–250
Pill, contraceptive, 201–202
Place, Francis, 186
Pollution. See Environmental pollution.
Population Bomb, 6, 26
Population censuses, 453–460
    defined, 453–454
    errors in, 469–471

    history of, 453–455
    United States, 455–459
Population composition, 19, 328, 444–445
    defined, 404
    demographic composition, 405ff
    socioeconomic composition, 423ff
    See also specific topics (e.g., Age composition).
Population Council, 468
Population data, 467–468
    See also specific sources (e.g., Vital statistics).
Population distribution, 20, 328, 374ff
    color, 380, 387–388
    metropolitan residence, 386–388
    region, 374–380, 381
    role of migration, 287–288, 374
    urban-rural, 380–384
Population dynamics, 13
Population estimates, 489–490
Population Explosion, 5, 26
    European, 31, 327
    Third World, 31–32, 38–41
Population growth:
    Africa, 42–46, 248
    annual rate of, 25
    Asia, 46–49, 248
    Caribbean, 50–51
    components of, 33, 328
    developed countries, 53–54
    doubling time, 28, 32
    economic development, 227, 250–252, 253–254, 259
    historical, 29–32, 37
    Latin America, 49–52, 248
    less developed countries, 6, 32–33, 38–41, 248, 251–258, 276–277
    Middle East, 301, 319
        outlook for the future, 257–258, 263, 275–278
    modern era, 24–25, 30–32
    neolithic, 29–30, 251
    pre-neolithic, 29
    problems of, 4, 8, 11–12, 219, 248–250, 259–263, 337ff
        environment, 347–349
        food crisis, 263ff
        implications for peace, 6, 257, 263, 272–273
        poverty, 248–250, 253–254, 257–258, 272
        qualitative problems, 344–349
        resources, 5, 259, 269, 273ff, 339–344
        threat to freedom, 349–354
    recent world trends, 4, 31–32, 33, 276
    regional patterns, 41ff
        See also specific regions (e.g., Asia).

United States trends, 7, 327ff
    See also Demographic transition.
Population mobility, 363ff
    concepts and definitions, 363–365
    differentials, 367–370
    international patterns, 388–394
    problems of, 371–374
    See also Internal migration.
Population policy, antinatalism, 223–224
    defined, 121
    Eastern Europe, 220–223
    fertility, 216ff
    India, 225, 230–232, 234
    internal migration, 394–396
    international migration, 301–308, 320–322
    mortality, 122–123
    People's Republic of China, 228, 229, 235–240
    pronatalist, 220–223
    Singapore, 226–227, 235
    United States, 217–219, 223, 301–308, 339
Population projections, 337, 338, 408, 507
Population pyramids, 261, 362, 410–412
Population Reference Bureau, 468
Population registers, 466–467
Population statics, 13
Population structure, 405, 410–415
Population trends:
    consequences of, 8–9
    determinants of, 8
    See specific topics (e.g., Fertility).
Positive checks, 264
Postneonatal mortality, 97, 98, 478–479
Poverty:
    United States, 68, 433
    world, 219
Poverty rate, 433
Preventive checks, 264
Primate cities, 392, 393
Pronatalism. See Population policy.
Prostaglandins, 202, 208
Protestant Ethic, 152
    influence on fertility, 153
Public health programs, and mortality, 68ff, 72, 74, 78, 124
    See also Medical science; Sanitation and mortality.
Purdah, 147
Push-pull theory, 291–292

Race, 108, 109
    education, 430
    income, 433–434
    labor force participation, 441–442, 443
    mobility, 368
    mortality, 107–108
    sociological variable, 420

    unemployment, 442
Real income, 431
Refugee migration, 304, 306–307
Relative income hypothesis, 165
Religion:
    birth control, 165–166, 189, 204
    family size preference, 147
    fertility, 189, 423
Repeat migration, 363
Reproduction, measurement of, 486–487
Residential mobility. See Internal migration.
Resources and population, 273–275, 339–344
    problems of depletion, 273–274, 340–341
Restrictions on emigration, 322
Restrictions on immigration, 301–305, 321–322
    agitation for, 301
    discriminatory basis, 302, 303
    See also Immigration policies.
Rhythm method, 199–200
Romania, 175, 220, 222
Rural population:
    decline, 380–384
    education, 430
    income, 434
    mortality, 118
    renewed growth, 384–385
    See also Urbanization.

Sample surveys, 464–466
Sanger, Margaret, 187, 190
Sanitation and mortality, 64–65, 70–71, 124
    See also Medical science; Public health programs.
School enrollment, 424–426
    differentials, 426
    rate of, 424
    trends, 424–425
Sequential pills, 201
Sex composition, 408–410
    elderly population, 410
    mortality, 102–107, 410, 418
    social significance of, 405
    United States, 408–410
    urban-rural differences, 409
Sex ratio:
    at birth, 410
    defined, 408
    determinants of, 408–409
Singapore, 34, 41, 47, 226, 227, 228, 235
Slavery, 380
    slave trade, 294, 421
Slum cities, 387
Small family ethos, 152
Smoking and mortality, 84, 106
Socioeconomic status, 110–115, 369–370
    mortality differences, 110–115, 121
    See also Education; Income; Occupation

South Africa, 107, 108, 320
Soviet Union, 101–102, 188, 222, 321, 322
Spermicide, 198–199
Sri Lanka, 40, 41, 47, 154, 226, 276
Standard Metropolitan Statistical Area (SMSA), 384
Stationary population, 502–504
Stem family, 138
Sterility, 131
    See also Fecundity.
Sterilization, 204–205, 230–231
Stokes, Marie, 187
Structural assimilation, 316
Suburbanization, 386–388
Sunbelt:
    defined, 378
    migration to, 378–379
Suppositories, 198
Surrogate mothers, 178
Survival rates, 490, 506
Sweden, 40–41, 61–62, 142, 148, 149, 157, 223, 261, 362, 413, 414
Symtothermal method of birth control, 200

Taboos, 142
Teenage fertility, 182–184, 218
Test tube babies, 176
Tikopia, 144
Timing of wanted births, 178, 180–181
Total fertility rate, 335, 484–485
Traffic problems, 347
Transitional growth period, 37–38
Transmigrant, 291
Triage, 123
Tubal ligation, 204
Two income families, 434
Underdeveloped countries. See Developing countries.
Underpopulation, 450
Unemployment, 439
    differentials, 443
    teenage, 442
United Nations, 6, 24, 144, 255, 268, 270, 467
United States:
    age-sex structure, 140, 405–410
    aging, 407–408, 415
    baby boom, 156–158, 332–333, 412–413
    baby bust, 158–159
    death, cause of, 82–84, 120
    distribution trends, 374–388
    educational characteristics, 423–430
    ethnic characteristics, 420–423
    fertility control, 186, 187, 190, 195–197, 206–207, 217, 223–224
    fertility differentials, 161–163
    fertility trends, 155ff, 217, 333, 334
    future growth outlook, 335–337, 338
    household composition, 142, 419–420
    immigration to, 292, 294, 295ff, 310–317, 331
    income characteristics, 431–436
    infant mortality, 97–100
    internal migration, 363ff
    labor force and employment status, 437–444
    marital status, 139–141, 416–419
    mortality differentials, 94ff, 333, 334
    mortality trends, 77ff
    occupational composition, 440–441, 443–444
    population data, sources of, 456–458, 463, 464, 465–466
    population growth, 327ff
    problems of population growth, 337ff, 371–374
    residential distribution, changing patterns of, 374ff
U.S. Agency for International Development (AID), 218
U.S. Bureau of the Census, 76, 337, 408, 462, 467, 468
Unwanted fertility, 176, 178–180, 183–184
Urban, definition, 382
Urban concentration, relation to mortality, 118, 294
Urban sprawl, 386–388
    megalopolis, 345
    problems of, 387–388, 393–394
Urbanization:
    defined, 15, 380
    economic development, 390–394
    fertility, 152, 154, 155
    historical trends, 294, 380–384, 390
    mortality, 66–67, 118
    regional variations, 390
    social significance of, 294, 390
Use effectiveness, contraception, 197
U.S.S.R. See Soviet Union.

Vaccine, antipregnancy, 208
Vaginal suppository, 198
Vasectomy, 204–205, 230
Venereal disease, 177
Vital statistics, 460–463
    United States, 77–78, 462–463
Voluntary migration, 290, 318–320

Walker, Frances, 311
Wanted births, spacing and timing of, 176
Water pollution, 348–349
Westward expansion, 374–378
Willcox, Walter, 461
Withdrawal. See Coitus interruptus.
Women, status of, in relation to fertility, 5, 6, 146, 153

Wonder drugs, 70
World Bank, 252, 268, 276, 392
World Fertility Survey, 145, 147, 179, 193, 199, 225, 465
World Health Organization, 6, 58, 201
World Population Conference, 175, 219–220, 234, 238, 255
World systems theory, 254

Youth:
    changing proportion of, 406–407, 412
    influence on society, 412–413
    in less developed societies, 259–263, 413

Zero population growth, 335, 337, 354–355
    People's Republic of China, 235

AUTHOR INDEX

Abernethy, Virginia, 250, 279
Adamchak, Donald J., 127
Adams, R. S., 325
Aird, John S., 236, 241
Anderson, John E., 179, 180, 209
Andorka, Rudolf, 163, 167
Antonovsky, Aaron, 111, 113, 127

Baldwin, Wendy H., 182, 209
Banks, J. A., 150, 167
Barnett, C. R., 180, 210
Becker, Gary S., 150, 168
Behrman, S. J., 168
Beier, George J., 397
Benjamin, Bernard, 471
Bentley, Judith, 324
Berelson, Bernard, 191, 210, 224, 241
Bernstein, Judith, 113, 127
Besant, Annie, 210
Biggar, Jeanne C., 397
Birdsall, Nancy, 252, 259, 260, 279
Blake, Judith, 133, 134, 168
Bogue, Donald J., 147, 170, 276, 280, 398
Bongaarts, John P., 206, 212
Bouvier, Leon F., 23, 56, 87, 127, 128, 212, 280, 310, 325, 326, 335, 337, 356, 357, 399, 408, 447, 448, 493, 500, 508
Breiver, Michael, 356
Brown, David, 398
Brown, Lester R., 266, 268, 270, 279, 340, 356
Bryant, L. S., 189, 210
Bumpass, Larry L., 190, 210
Bureau of Labor Statistics, 442, 444
Buttell, Frederick, 279, 357
Butz, William P., 155, 356, 447

Caldwell, John C., 154, 168
Campbell, Arthur, 210, 212, 218, 241
Cancellier, Patricia, 305, 325
Cann, H., 210
Cecelski, Elizabeth W., 268, 280, 357
Chalmers, James A., 398
Chandrasekhar, S., 136, 168, 186, 210
Chen, Pi-chao, 236, 237, 238, 242
Chiazze, Leonard, 399
Chilman, C. S., 242
Choucri, Nazli, 211
Clark, Colin, 251, 279
Clark, R., 143, 186
Close, Angela E., 56
Coale, Ansley, 149, 168
Cockcroft, James D., 279
Commission on Population Growth and the American Future, 3, 9, 22, 217, 242, 354, 356
Council on Environmental Quality, 5, 22, 274, 279, 341, 356
Crane, Barbara B., 56, 242, 256, 279
Crimmins, Eileen M., 81, 86
Curtin, Leslie B., 153, 168

Dauer, Carl C., 482, 493
David, Henry P., 207, 210, 220, 221, 222, 223, 242
Davis, Cary B., 447
Davis, Christopher, 101, 127
Davis, Kingsley, 19, 23, 25, 56, 133, 134, 140, 141, 168, 232, 233, 242
Day, Alice T., 344, 352, 356
Day, Lincoln, 344, 352, 356
DeJong, Gordon F., 398
Demeny, Paul, 147, 168

521

Demerath, Nicholas J., 230, 236, 242
Devereux, G., 144, 168
Dickinson, R. L., 189, 210
Dublin, Louis I., 61, 118, 127
Duncan, Otis Dudley, 23, 471

Easterlin, Richard A., 150, 160, 168
Eaton, Joseph, 132, 168
Eberstadt, Nick, 241
Eckholm, Erik, 5, 23, 63, 86, 268, 279
Ehrlich, Anne H., 348, 356
Ehrlich, Paul R., 348, 356
Environmental Fund, 267
Eriksen, Eugene, 210
Eriksen, Julia, 177, 210
Eversley, D. E. C., 169

Feshbach, Murray, 101, 127
Finkle, Jason L., 56, 242, 256, 279
Firth, Raymond, 144, 168
Ford, Kathleen, 170, 195, 210, 212
Fox, Greer Litton, 168
Francese, Peter K., 471
Frank, Andre G., 254, 279, 392, 398
Frank, Odile, 210
Freedman, Ronald, 134, 135, 154, 168, 177, 191, 210
Friedan, Betty, 158, 169
Fryer, Peter, 186, 210
Fuguitt, Glenn V., 386, 398

Gilbert, Alan, 398
Gilland, Bernard, 279
Glass, David V., 169
Glick, Paul C., 139, 169, 447
Goldscheider, Calvin, 234, 242
Goldstein, Sidney, 363, 398
Gordon, Linda, 184, 210
Gordon, Mitchell, 348, 357, 398
Gortmaker, Steven L., 114, 127
Gottman, Jean, 354, 357
Green, Cynthia P., 169, 211, 226
Greenwood, Michael J., 398
Groat, H. Theodore, 130, 150, 159, 165, 169, 189, 210, 211, 232, 242
Grove, Robert D., 471
Guest, Felicia, 210
Gugler, Josef, 398
Guttmacher Institute, 182, 183, 184, 210
Gwatkin, Davidson R., 76, 86

Haenszel, William, 399
Hajnal, John, 138, 169
Handlin, Oscar, 325
Hardin, Garrett, 123, 127, 343, 357
Hartley, Shirley F., 181, 210

Hatcher, Robert A., 184, 198. 201, 202, 204, 205, 210
Haub, Carl, 280, 356
Haupt, Arthur, 493
Hauser, Philip M., 23, 112, 113, 127, 471
Heaton, Tim B., 398
Heer, David M., 279
Hendershot, Gerry E., 168
Henshaw, Stanley K., 206, 210
Hetzel, Alice M., 471
Himes, Norman E., 185, 186, 210
Hodgson, Dennis, 23
Hostetler, John, 210
Humphrey, Craig, 279, 357
Huntington, Gertrude, 210

International Bank for Reconstruction and Development, 253, 266, 280, 393, 445

Jackson, J., 210
Jamison, Ellen, 147, 169
Johnson, D. Gale, 270, 280
Jones, Elise F., 162, 164, 165, 166, 169, 170
Jones, Landon, 447
Jones, Stephanie, 210
Julian, Joseph, 68, 86, 348, 357

Kammayer, Kenneth C. W., 16, 23
Kane, Thomas T., 493
Kantner, John F., 170, 212
Kaplan, Charles P., 457, 471
Keeley, Charles B., 325
Kendall, Maurice, 137, 169
Kent, Mary M., 242
Kim, Y. J., 212
Kirk, Dudley, 147, 169
Kiser, Clyde, 212
Kitagawa, Evelen M., 112, 113, 127
Knisley, Lynn G., 210
Knodel, John, 151, 154, 170
Knowlton, Charles, 186, 211
Kolata, G., 144, 169
Kols, Adrienne, 236, 237, 238, 242
Kritz, Mary, 325

Laidlaw, Karen A., 40, 56, 62, 149, 257, 280, 357, 391, 399
Langer, W. L., 66, 86
Larson, Ann, 242
Laska, Shirley B., 399
Lauersen, Niels, 185, 211
Lee, Everett S., 293, 325
Leridon, H., 199, 211
Lewis, David T., 153, 170
Li, Wen L., 242
Lichter, Daniel T., 386, 398
Lightbourne, Robert, 146, 169, 179, 193, 194, 211, 226

Linder, Forest E., 459, 471
Long, Harry H., 398
Lotka, Alfred J., 127

Madigan, Francis C., 105, 127
Malthus, Thomas Robert, 264, 280
Markides, Kyriakos, 127
Martire, G., 143, 168
Mauldin, W. Parker, 175, 211, 229, 242
Mayer, Albert, 132, 168
McFalls, Joseph A., 176, 211
McFarland, Connie, 127
McKenzie, Roderick D., 386, 398
McKeown, Thomas, 35, 56, 62, 66, 86, 149
McNamara, Robert S., 276, 280
McNeill, William H., 293, 294, 325
Mecklenburg, Marjory E., 218, 242
Metropolitan Life Insurance Company, 111
Meyers, Robert J., 86
Miller, Arthur S., 353, 357
Money, John, 211
Morrison, Peter A., 385, 398
Mosher, William D., 195, 196, 211
Munson, Martha, 179, 211
Murdock, William W., 280
Murphy, Elaine, 280, 305, 325, 356
Murphy, Francis X., 189, 211
Musaph, Herman, 211

Nagi, Mostafa H., 114, 127, 310, 325
Nam, Charles B., 109, 127
National Center for Health Statistics, 81, 86, 94, 96, 98, 102, 103, 108, 127, 156, 181, 211, 474, 497, 505
National Commission on the Causes and Prevention of Violence, 388, 398
Neal, Arthur G., 130, 150, 169, 180, 210, 211
Nelson, Verne, 108, 128
Newland, Kathleen, 127, 287, 309, 325
Newsholme, Arthur, 113, 128
Nordburg, Olivia S., 175, 191, 205, 211
Nortman, Dorothy, 204, 206, 211, 224, 225, 242
Norton, Arthur J., 139, 169, 447
Notestein, Frank W., 211

Omran, Abdel R., 41, 56, 86, 105, 128, 357
Ophuls, William, 357
O'Reilly, Kevin, 206, 210
Osborn, Frederick, 357
Osborn, Richard, 212
Ostresh, Lawrence M., 399

Packard, Vance, 363, 398
Paddock, Paul, 123, 128
Paddock, William, 123, 128
Parke, Robert, 168
Patterson, John, 212

Pendleton, Brian F., 87
Perry, Joseph B., 232, 242
Petersen, William, 188, 211, 277, 280, 291, 325
Piotrow, Phyllis T., 263, 280
Pirenne, Henri, 294, 325
Place, Francis, 186, 211
Polgar, Steven, 210
Population Reference Bureau, 26, 43, 44, 46, 56, 62, 74, 75, 115, 149, 169, 222, 227, 229, 235, 238, 239, 242, 250, 260, 261, 267, 268, 280, 287, 325, 338, 357, 398, 447
Potts, Malcolm, 142, 169
Powers, Mary G., 169
President's Commission on Immigration and Naturalization, 325
President's Commission on World Hunger, 268
Presser, Harriet B., 211
Preston, Samuel H., 128
Pryor, Robin J., 398

Rainwater, Lee, 114, 128
Record, Frank, 5, 23, 63, 86, 268, 279
Reid, John, 448
Repetto, Robert, 234, 242
Retherford, Robert D., 106, 128
Reynolds, Robert R., Jr., 399
Ridker, Ronald G., 268, 280, 357
Rindfuss, Ronald R., 161, 169
Rosen, H., 168
Rosenblatt, Roger, 178, 211
Russell, J. C., 61
Ryder, Norman B., 137, 162, 170, 189, 212

Salaff, J., 235, 242
Salkever, David, 212
Salvo, Joseph J., 169
Schearer, S. Bruce, 191, 211
Schild, Romuald, 56
Schnaiberg, Allan, 357
Schoen, Robert, 108, 128
Schwartz, David W., 210
Schwartz-Nobel, Loretta, 271, 280
Segal, Sheldon J., 175, 191, 205, 211
Select Committee on Population, 396, 398
Selman, Peter, 142, 169
Serron, Luis A., 280
Shryock, Henry S., 58, 86, 388, 398, 461, 471, 474, 488, 493, 494, 508
Siegel, Jacob S., 86, 398, 471, 493, 508
Simmons, Alan B., 399
Simon, Julian L., 251
Singh, Sushella, 169, 211, 226
Sirageldin, Ismail, 212
Smith, Richard F., 325
Soldo, Beth J., 447
Spain, Daphne, 388, 399
Spiegelman, Mortimer, 127

Stewart, Felicia, 210
Stewart, Gary, 210
Stockwell, Edward G., 40, 56, 62, 86, 106, 108, 113, 114, 127, 128, 149, 257, 280, 357, 391, 399, 471, 493, 508
Sundquist, James L., 399
Sweet, James A., 161, 169

Tabbarah, Riad B., 56
Taeuber, Conrad, 297, 325, 399
Taeuber, Irene B., 297, 325, 399
Taeuber, Karl, 363, 399
Teitelbaum, Michael, 151, 170, 211
Teitze, Christopher, 205, 206, 207, 211, 212
Thomlinson, Ralph, 325
Thompson, James G., 399
Thompson, Patricia G., 218, 242
Thompson, Warren S., 153, 170
Tien, H. Yuan, 236, 238, 239, 242, 243
Todaro, Michael P., 399
Toffler, Alvin, 363, 399
Tsui, Amy Ong, 147, 170, 276, 280

United Nations, 25, 33, 46, 56, 64, 87, 101, 104, 108, 116, 117, 128, 220, 227, 228, 229, 243, 248, 262, 270, 280, 318, 319, 321, 325, 326, 391, 394, 399, 414, 454, 460, 470, 471, 472, 474
U.S. Bureau of the Census, 4, 23, 32, 44, 56, 79, 83, 94, 98, 139, 141, 142, 155, 159, 162, 170, 205, 212, 298, 300, 329, 333, 336, 338, 357, 364, 366, 367, 368, 370, 375, 380, 381, 382, 383, 384, 385, 387, 388, 389, 399, 407, 409, 415, 417, 419, 421, 423, 425, 427, 428, 429, 431, 432, 434, 435, 438, 441, 447, 492
U.S. Office of Technical Assistance, 208, 212

van der Tak, Jean, 269, 280, 357
van der Walle, Etienne, 151, 154, 170
Van Valey, Thomas L., 457, 471
Vaughan, Barbara, 197
Verbrugge, Lois M., 128
Visaria, Leela, 138, 170, 230, 231, 243
Visaria, Pravin, 138, 170, 230, 231, 243

Waite, Linda J., 448
Wallerstein, Immanuel, 254, 280
Wardwell, John M., 398
Weatherby, Norman L., 128
Weeks, John R., 23, 56, 87, 128, 163, 170, 212, 253, 280, 326, 399, 448, 472, 474, 493, 508
Weinstein, Jay A., 399
Weller, Robert H., 23, 56, 87, 128, 165, 170, 212, 280, 326, 357, 399, 448, 493, 500, 508
Wendorf, Fred, 29, 56
Westoff, Charles F., 137, 141, 160, 162, 166, 168, 170, 189, 211, 212, 224, 243
Westoff, Leslie Aldridge, 224, 243
Wheeler, Judith P., 385, 398
Whelpton, Pascal, 177, 210, 212
Whitney, Steven, 185, 211
Wicks, Jerry W., 108, 113, 114, 128, 169, 211
Wilkinson, Kenneth, 399
Wilkinson, Richard S., 250, 280
Wong, A., 235, 242
World Bank. *See* International Bank for Reconstruction and Development
World Health Organization, 87

Yang, Shu-O W., 87
Yinger, Nancy, 185, 212

Zelnick, Melvin, 141, 170, 183, 192, 212

DATE DUE			
DEC 12 1984			
FEB 13 1985			
SEP 04 1985			
NOV 01 1989			
DEC 11 1991			
DEC 22 1994			
DEC 16 1996			

DEMCO 38-297